"These bottom-up histories, written b... ...housing-
er historians, provide a fascinating lo... ...al city
shaped a pivotal decade. From hote... ...workers to
campuses to city streets, collective livii.g to urban gardening, this book captures the sights, sounds and desires of a city in revolt. Its pages reveal the
roots of our current struggles." — Dan Berger, editor of *The Hidden 1970s:
Histories of Radicalism*

"Militant urbanist and writer, Chris Carlsson, has brought together a brilliant
collection of essays by historians and memoirists of a neglected decade that
reveal the originality and solidity of social movements which, despite tragic
failures, have guaranteed that San Francisco would maintain a utopian vision of what is possible. Each contribution is a jewel, storytelling at its best."
— Roxanne Dunbar Ortiz, author of *Outlaw Woman: A Memoir of the War
Years, 1960-1975*

"What a vivid, well-written tour through the wide range of community
struggles and movements in this most political of American cities." —
Chester Hartman, author of *City for Sale: The Transformation of San Francisco*

"*Ten Years That Shook The City* cracks open our understanding of San Francisco's cultures and communities during one of the most formative yet under
analyzed periods in recent history. It succeeds not only because it collects
an amazing range of San Francisco voices reflecting on an awesome spec-
trum of topical issues between '68 to '78, but also because those voices
speak to us in a compelling variety of forms. It's thoroughly edifying to sink
into these grassroots San Francisco stories and discover a lively mix of personal memoir, ecological field guild, political-economy, deep neighborhood
history, workers' struggles, visual study and more on issues as far reaching
as radical Third Worldism, urban farming, rock concerts, garment workers,
street posters, and comic books." — Sean Burns, author of *Archie Green:
The Making of a Working-Class Hero*

"*Ten Years That Shook the City* is a brilliant palimpsest of a time and a place:
San Francisco in a revolutionary decade that changed just about every
part of the city and everything about how we live today. This magnificent
collection brings together voices from the cutting edges of feminism, gay
liberation, Latino and Asian mobilizations, environmentalism, community
housing and more, and proves once again what an extraordinary city we
have the good fortune to inherit." — Richard Walker, Professor of Geography, University of California, and author of *The Country in the City* and
*The Conquest of Bread*

"*Ten Years that Shook the City* examines the early history of many of San Francisco's cultural treasures that provide the bedrock for today's social change efforts. Written by people who were active in building the everyday institutions we now take for granted, the collection examines the radical democratic ethos that still permeates the city's politics and cultural life. This is a vital resource, which provides the backstory for all of us who came to San Francisco because of its radical culture and politics." — Dorothy Kidd, Professor of Media Studies at the University of San Francisco

"For anyone who lived through San Francisco's greatest years, the 1960s and 1970s, this book is a treasure-house of reminders, information and perspectives on what happens when a community really AWAKENS politically, ecologically and socially. No one has ever done a better job of capturing this than Chris Carlsson in this book. For those who were not here, settle down and learn what the '60s-'70s cultural revolution in the city may teach us about how we should deal with a difficult future. This is great reading for anyone." — Jerry Mander, author of *Four Arguments for the Elimination of Television* and *In the Absence of the Sacred*

"What did happen in the years following the storied 1960s? Did political and social activism die away, move to the country, or get co-opted by the mainstream? Clearly not, as detailed in this new book of essays, edited by local community activist and historian, Chris Carlsson. Primarily first-person accounts, each chapter is chock full of stories from the front lines, written by participants who organized, agitated, and created social change in the city well into the 1970s and beyond. Currents run together from the anti-war and labor movements, gay and women's liberation, struggles against redevelopment and racism and towards the building of cooperatives, ecological awareness, and political art and culture. Gathered together, these snapshots of activism tell a powerful story, showing how the groundwork was laid for much of the progressive movement that still exists today in San Francisco. The lessons of continuity are strong, with the foundations of many of today's institutions and organizations rooted in the radical political and cultural movements from this time period." — Susan Goldstein, City Archivist, San Francisco Public Library

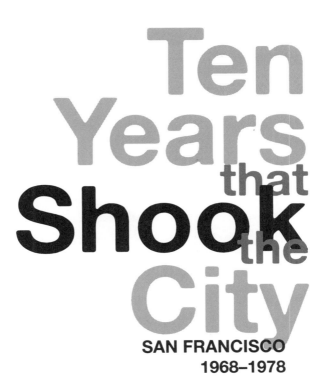

# Ten Years that Shook the City

## SAN FRANCISCO
## 1968–1978

A Reclaiming San Francisco Book

**Edited by Chris Carlsson
with Lisa Ruth Elliott**

**City Lights Foundation Books**

Front and back cover photos by Stephen Rees

 Ten Years That Shook the City: San Francisco, 1968-78 was made possible in part by a San Francisco Arts Commission Cultural Equity Grant for Individual Artists.

Library of Congress Cataloging-in-Publication Data

Ten years that shook the city : San Francisco 1968-1978 : a reclaiming San Francisco book / edited by Chris Carlsson with Lisa Ruth Elliott.
    p. cm.
 Includes index.
 ISBN 978-1-931404-12-9
1. Social movements—California—San Francisco—History—20th century. 2. San Francisco Bay Area (Calif.)—Social conditions. I. Carlsson, Chris, 1957- II. Elliott, Lisa Ruth. III. City Lights Books. IV. Title.

 HN80.S4T46 2010
 303.48'4097946109047—dc22

                                    2011005597

City Lights Books are published at the City Lights Bookstore, 261 Columbus Avenue, San Francisco, CA 94133.

Visit our website: www.citylights.com

# Acknowledgments

The many people who contributed to this book amply demonstrate the cooperative nature of a project like this. First off, thanks to my collaborator Lisa Ruth Elliott, without whom this project might never have been pursued and whose diligence and attention to detail has helped see it through. Thanks to the San Francisco Arts Commission, who believed in the project and gave financial support to help launch it. Thanks to the many writers who have contributed their time, their memories, and their great writing to this book. Thanks to the San Francisco History Center at the Main Library, an indispensable archive of publications and photographs of the City's history.

Thanks to CounterPULSE and its community of supporters, who have provided a home for *Shaping San Francisco* these past five years, where we hold public Talks three times a month and I host bicycle history tours regularly. The friends and contacts made through *Shaping San Francisco*'s public life in the City via these forums were essential to this book.

Thanks to Adriana Camarena for her love and support during this year-long marathon, and her many helpful suggestions and editorial contributions. Thanks to my parents, too, for their unflagging support all these years. Thank you to Steve Stiles for assistance in scanning the *Comix Book #1* cover appearing in Jay Kinney's history of underground comix.

Lastly, thanks to San Francisco for being such a great place to live and work these past three decades. I've had plenty of chances to go elsewhere, but I always come back. This is home, and I'm happy and proud to be part of the City's evolving history. I hope this book will fill in some of the blanks, especially for those who were born after this period of time, but even for a lot of us who lived through part or all of it. No matter how much you think you remember or know, studying history keeps showing us that what we don't know is far greater than what we do! This book is another piece of the puzzle, trying to figure out how the world came to be like *this*, rather than any of an infinite range of other possibilities.

—Chris Carlsson

*This book is dedicated to the thousands of San Franciscans who have been here for the past 40-50 years, doing the everyday things that continue to make this a lively, stimulating place to live. More than that though, their efforts kept alive a utopian spirit that that might otherwise have winked out during the dark decades we've been living through.*

*It is also dedicated to the more recent arrivals, whether by birth or immigration, who keep the contrarian spirit alive and well in San Francisco. Hopefully this book will provide a rich resource to old and new alike, as they relentlessly push for a better life for all.*

# Table of Contents

Shaken, AND Stirred ...................................................................................7
  By Chris Carlsson

On Strike! We're Gonna Shut it Down:
  The 1968-69 San Francisco State Strike ...................................... 15
  By Margaret Leahy

"With the Soul of a Human Rainbow": Los Siete, Black Panthers, and
  Third Worldism in San Francisco.................................................. 30
  by Dr. Jason M. Ferreira

"All Those Who Care About The Mission, Stand Up With Me!": Latino
  Community Formation and the Mission Coalition Organization ..48
  By Tomás F. Summers Sandoval, Jr.

Poetry and Solidarity in the Mission District ................................. 61
  By Alejandro Murguía

Lost Murals of the Seventies.............................................................. 71
  By Timothy W. Drescher

Mujeres Muralistas ............................................................................. 81
  By Patricia Rodriguez

My World Incomplete/To Complete My World ................................. 92
  By Roberto Vargas

Where Did All the Flowers Go?
  The View from a Street in Bernal Heights.................................. 95
  By Peter Booth Wiley

Up Against the Bulkhead: A Photo Essay with Text........................121
  By Stephen Rees with Peter Booth Wiley

My Teacher, My Friend .......................................................................121
  By Andrew Lam

Filipino Americans in the Decade of the International Hotel...................126
  By Estella Habal

"Hush Puppies," Communalist Politics, and Demolition Governance:
  The Rise and Fall of the Black Fillmore .......................................141
  By Rachel Brahinsky

The Fight to Stay: The Creation of the Community
    Housing Movement in San Francisco, 1968-1978 ............................154
    *By Calvin Welch*

Reflections from Occupied Ohlone Territory..................................................163
    *By Mary Jean Robertson*

Making Sexism Visible: Private Troubles Made Public................................170
    *By Deborah A. Gerson*

Sometimes You Work With The Democrats, And Sometimes You Riot .183
    *By Tommi Avicolli Mecca*

Coming Together: The Communal Option......................................................192
    *By Matthew Roth*

San Bruno Mountain ........................................................................................209
    *By David Schooley*

The Farm by the Freeway ...............................................................................219
    *By Mirjana Blankenship*

A Personal History of the San Francisco People's Food System.............232
    *By Pam Peirce*

Ecology Emerges ...............................................................................................241
    *By Chris Carlsson*

San Francisco Labor in the 1970s ................................................................258
    *By Jesse Drew*

The Rise and Fall of the Underground Comix Movement
    in San Francisco and Beyond....................................................................272
    *By Jay Kinney*

San Francisco Bay Area Posters: 1968-1978...............................................285
    *By Lincoln Cushing*

Jung Sai Garment Workers Strike of 1974 ..................................................303
    *By Harvey Dong*

When Music Mattered ......................................................................................317
    *By Mat Callahan*

Contributors........................................................................................................329

Index ....................................................................................................................332

# Shaken, AND Stirred!
## An Introduction

### by Chris Carlsson

This collection of historical essays starts in 1968, the year of the San Francisco State College Strike, and runs to 1978, when the twin traumas of Jonestown and the assassinations of Mayor Moscone and Harvey Milk punctuate a tumultuous and influential decade. These are ten years that shook and shaped the City today. Few of the essays stick to that time-frame rigorously, most having to look before 1968 or go beyond 1978 (or both) to fully make sense. The 1960s is a seminal decade in world history, and it is sometimes defined as running to 1972 or even 1974 in a "long Sixties" perspective. But this is a book more about the 1970s, when many of the initiatives described here came to climaxes, sometimes deepening and evolving from their initial impetus into lasting cultural and institutional forms. The popular explosions and experiments of the era morphed and were taken in by the larger culture, or found ways to survive in its margins. From today's organic food and community gardening movements to environmental justice, gay rights and other identitarian social movements, neighborhood anti-gentrification efforts, and much more, the 1970s are the years when transformative social values burrowed deeply into society.

New understandings of politics and history have their roots in this era, too. Previously excluded populations became vocal and insistent, reshaping urban politics and reorienting the framing of history itself. The deep distrust of government at all levels dates to this period, whether in response to the national government's venality in Vietnam and subsequent Watergate scandals, or the local government's unabashed efforts to dismantle working-class neighborhoods through redevelopment.

With a long pedigree of contrarian culture and political radicalism, San Francisco was in the mid-1960s still dominated by the large corporations headquartered in downtown, and the old and newer elites who owned them. The City's liberal reputation and tolerance for dissent and diversity have been much touted, but the underlying history of the City is one of old monied families dominating property ownership and commercial development throughout California and the Pacific Rim. By the mid-1960s Bay Area corporate planners had already restructured the Bay Area economy to "regionalize" production, an important precursor to the wider campaign to accelerate globalization from 1970 to the present.

Organized labor was squeezed in the 1970s. On one side newly aggressive and globalizing capital was determined to reduce the leverage and wealth gained by the working class since the upheavals of the Depression and post-WWII prosperity. On the other, the national economy was no longer globally pre-eminent and emerging world market competition was shrinking the room to maneuver, too. A seminal agreement by the dockers and shippers in 1960 ushered in the mechanization and modernization of the waterfront, and the containers that came in its wake inadvertently set the stage for the deindustrialization of the US. But it was not going to be a quick process.

Workers in the Bay Area, like their counterparts in the old mid-country Rust Belt, still had ideas of their own. Jesse Drew looks back at "San Francisco Labor in the 1970s," remembering the smells and sounds of a still-industrial city. He examines how new social actors, finding themselves in local factories, offices, hospitals, restaurants, and universities, sought to build on the legacies of labor radicalism once familiar to the entire City. Harvey Dong ("Jai Sung Garment Workers Strike") provides a detailed account of an early 1970s Chinatown strike involving a small group of over 100 workers, but because it was against the plant that made clothes for the up-and-coming designer label Esprit, their fight took on additional meaning. It galvanized Chinese workers and garment workers more generally, and created new connections among youth activists and an older generation. It also confronted the amnesiac San Franciscan middle classes with the dirty reality behind their new prosperity.

The organized Left, rooted in the longshoremen and other unions had led vigorous protests against the House Un-American Activities Committee that rocked City Hall in 1960. Some of the same students who were washed down City Hall steps in May of that year helped the Civil Rights Movement come to San Francisco. Students at San Francisco State were speaking freely at The Commons on campus as early as 1962 and that agitation was central to the 1963 eruption. That year Civil Rights protesters demanding racial equity in employment besieged Auto Row on Van Ness and the Palace Hotel downtown. This multi-ethnic youthful grassroots energy crossed the Bay to re-emerge in the 1964 Free Speech Movement at UC Berkeley. In September 1966, a White officer shot a young unarmed Black man running from a stolen car in Bayview-Hunter's Point. A three-day riot ensued, leading to a declaration of martial law in the two predominantly Black neighborhoods in San Francisco. 1966 was also the year when students at San Francisco State began pushing for new classes on "Black consciousness" as part of a general political awakening happening on many campuses across the country. With the assassinations of Bobby Kennedy and Martin Luther King, Jr. in 1968, and social revolts erupting from Paris to Prague, and Beijing to Mexico City, San Francisco too was a churning ground zero for political opposition and cultural experimentation.

At San Francisco State College in 1968, the discharge of an African-American lecturer led to a faculty strike, followed quickly by a mass student strike led by the Black Student Union and the Third World Liberation Front. They demanded the teacher's reinstatement, but also insisted on a new approach to education, incorporating new curricula on overlooked and underrepresented populations. Margaret Leahy, a young woman born and raised among the Irish-American Catholics of San Francisco's Sunset District, tells the story of the Strike from inside in "On Strike! We're Gonna Shut it Down!" showing how events can alter individuals and institutions. Spilling out from the brutal police repression of the State Strike, student activists became vital participants in the unfolding social struggles of the ensuing decade.

Native Americans in San Francisco, some of whom were enrolled at San Francisco State and other local universities, and inspired by the Third World strikes, occupied Alcatraz from 1969-1971. The surge of self-confidence and pride that arose from this bold move galvanized the American Indian Movement as well as the quarter-century-long effort to establish an International Treaty on the

Rights of Indigenous Peoples. Mary Jean Robertson follows the activists from the Alcatraz Occupation back to the City and various reservations, and ultimately across the country to the capital and the United Nations in "Reflections from Occupied Ohlone Territory."

Black power and Brown power movements arose, partly driven by ongoing police repression, partly driven by a new sense of self-awareness and an urgent need to establish community self-reliance and dignity. In the wake of the brutal police assaults during the State Strike, members of the Black Student Union as well as other students who were part of the Third World Liberation Front, were well prepared for the gritty urban confrontations to come.

This new shared Third World sensibility is the subject of Jason Ferreira's groundbreaking analysis in "With the Soul of a Human Rainbow: Los Siete, Black Panthers, and Third Worldism in San Francisco." Black Panthers organized and launched breakfast programs while decrying the imprisonment of their leaders and the violent harassment and murder of their members. During a protest of Huey Newton's imprisonment at San Francisco's Federal Building on May 1, 1970, across town in the Mission, a policeman was killed while investigating an alleged burglary. This led to a protracted legal battle over the fate of the seven young accused Latinos, who became known as "Los Siete de La Raza." Ferreira shows how the overlapping struggles of the City's different ethnic communities forged a new expansive identity that built solidarity among many of the era's local political movements.

The Vietnam War brought thousands of troops and tons of war materiel through SF's ports, while a steady stream of casualties and discharged soldiers returned by way of the City's Presidio. The anti-war movement gained strength across the country, and San Francisco was one of its epicenters. Radicals poured in from elsewhere and, having settled in the City, made vital contributions to the increasingly diverse and multiracial metropolis. Peter Wiley's "Where Have All the Flowers Gone? The View from the Street in Bernal Heights" recounts his community of friends, many from Madison, Wisconsin, and their efforts to launch a left-wing theoretical journal, while settling in to a quiet working-class neighborhood on the northern slopes of Bernal Heights. The relationships and projects that they started 40 years ago still resonate today, and a surprising number of individuals and institutions are still shaping the City. Along with Stephen Rees's poignant photojournalism, Wiley also contributes an account of GI anti-war organizing that more than anything else stymied Nixon's efforts to prolong the war in "Up Against the Bulkhead."

San Francisco writer Andrew Lam was a refugee from Southeast Asia in the early 1970s, fleeing the defining conflict of the era, and his poignant story "My Teacher, My Friend," reminisces about the small world of the refugee child, which happens to have been the same world the rest of these contributions address from so many angles.

Redevelopment was already changing San Francisco by the end of the 1950s. The old Italian neighborhood centered on the produce district between North Beach, the waterfront, and the Financial District, was the first to be dismantled. The old White ethnic majority (mostly Italian and Irish) that had dominated the City began leaving for the suburbs, along with the jobs that once made San Francisco an economic powerhouse. As it became more white-collar—tourism, medicine, education, and financial services—the new workforce diversified with the City's changing population. Immigration from both in and outside the US brought growing numbers of highly atomized, hyper-mobile people, perfectly suited to the new metrosexual and dress-for-success culture of business.

Aggressive urban redevelopment efforts of the City's elite sought to clear neighborhoods for these new urbanites. One of the City's largest powerbrokers and real estate tycoons was locked in an epic battle with the elderly Filipinos of the I-Hotel at the edge of downtown and North Beach. Young Asian Americans flocked to their cause, and the I-Hotel became an iconic headquarters for militants of many stripes, notably hard-Left factions from the Chinese and Filipino communities. Estella Habal was one of them and she tells the story in "Filipino Americans in the Decade of the International Hotel." They also targeted the neighborhoods where African-Americans (the Fillmore) and Latinos (the Mission) were concentrated. Over a hundred community groups formed the Mission Coalition Organization in 1968 to contest the plans to impose redevelopment on the Mission District. The MCO was rocked by internecine conflict, but out of its demise in 1970 dozens of social service nonprofits and grassroots groups continued to shape the politics of the neighborhood and the City, once again with strong involvement of activists who had been at State in 1968-69. Tomás Sandoval recounts the fascinating history of the MCO in "All Those Who Care About the Mission, Stand Up With Me!"

Rachel Brahinsky delves into individual and institutional memories of the devastating neighborhood destruction that was imposed on the Black Fillmore District in the name of redevelopment in "Hush Puppies and Demolition Governance: The Rise and Fall of the Black Fillmore." Calvin Welch, a 40-year activist in San Francisco's progressive movements, provides an overview of the Community Housing Movement in "The Fight to Stay." Nonprofit housing developers combined with rent control have been crucial to preventing San Francisco from turning itself into an exclusive enclave of the super rich. The mid-'70s electoral effort to bring about district elections and run progressive campaigns for municipal office was rooted in this same citywide coalition-building effort of the time, an oft-fractured "progressive coalition," that nevertheless still has a presence in municipal politics today.

In the early 1960s the Save the Bay movement arose to stop its destruction. In the late 1950s and early 1960s San Franciscans revolted against freeways and stopped most of the plans to crisscross the city with them. Up north in Sonoma County the beginnings of anti-nuclear activism stopped the big utility PG&E from building a nuclear plant on the San Andreas fault at Bodega Bay. Out of these nascent efforts, Bay conservation was tightened with popular support while open space movements from San Bruno Mountain to the Marin headlands carved out a legacy much treasured today. When an oil tanker spilled into the Bay in 1971, the myriad strands of the local ecology movements gained new urgency. A cluster of articles adds new chapters to our local history. David Schooley describes the decades-long effort to save "San Bruno Mountain," the ecological treasure dividing San Francisco from the rest of San Mateo County. Pam Peirce edited *Turnover*, the journal of the People's Food System in the mid-1970s, and she recounts her story of that legendary effort in "A Personal History of the People's Food System." Urban gardening, food conspiracies, people's cooperative food stores, and collective food wholesalers and producers reshaped American cuisine and shopping paradigms as well. Mirjana Blankenship digs up the history of "The Farm by the Freeway," an unlikely rural redoubt practically underneath the freeway at the edge of the Mission District. And Chris Carlsson takes a wider view of the nascent modern ecology movement in "Ecology Emerges," asserting that the anti-war movement was the crucial cauldron which turned it from its patrician roots. Political currents running from rural Northern California to San Francisco's neighborhoods and back again, moved activists to go beyond the limits of historic environmentalism to contest nuclear power, the oil industry, automobilism, and much more.

In 1966, the San Francisco Diggers staged politically sophisticated "Death of Money" and "Death of a Hippie" celebrations to shape the emerging political underground before the storied and hyped Summer of Love fed a media frenzy in 1967. During the hippie crescendo that the Diggers were trying to radicalize, San Francisco was the urban launching pad for an extensive back-to-the-land movement that brought a fresh approach to the urban/rural dichotomy. Matthew Roth examines the 1970s movement of communal living that resulted in "Coming Together: The Communal Option," tracing its roots back to early America, but showing how diverse the experiments were, too. Alarmingly, the bucolic fantasies of retreat from modern life's contradictions were often distorted and even destroyed by other kinds of madness.

Women's liberation emerged in the late 1960s as a potent rebuke to the traditional male-dominated New Left as well as the overwhelming male-oriented power structures of society. A women's self-help health movement took shape, leading to underground clinics for abortions and birth control information, but also challenging many of the paradigms shaping western medicine at the time. Deborah Gerson revisits a time when so much of what we now take for granted was new and still had to be fought for, in her "Making Sexism Visible: Private Troubles Made Public."

Though a gay-baiting politician lost the 1959 mayoral election, police repression of the growing gay population persisted as religious leaders sought tolerance, leading to a premonitory riot of queer youth at Compton's Cafeteria in 1966. Tommi Avicolla Mecca ("Sometimes You Work with Democrats, Sometimes You Riot") describes how an assimilationist homophile movement gave way to a range of more assertive homosexual rights activists, themselves divided among left-wing politicos and more flamboyant cultural radicals, who for a time were united by Harvey Milk's candidacies, as well as the rising tide of reactionary homophobia.

As mentioned, the Mission District successfully fended off redevelopment, in part thanks to the strong cultural resistance that grew in the neighborhood. One strand of that cultural resistance was provided by the poets and writers that came together in the early 1970s in a collective called Editorial Pocho-Ché. Alejandro Murguía's "Poetry and Solidarity in the Mission" not only describes their early literary efforts, but also brings us to the late 1970s when Mission District activists joined the Nicaraguan revolutionary movement by repeatedly occupying the local Nicaraguan consulate. Roberto Vargas, another Mission veteran who later became a Nicaraguan ambassador after the Sandinistas took power, regales us with a poem, "My World Centered," that takes us back to the foggy Mission District streets of the 1970s.

Nowadays the murals of the Mission are world-famous, but it was during the early 1970s that the movement began. Patricia Rodriguez was one of the "Mujeres Muralistas" who helped launch the mural movement. Tim Drescher has been documenting and writing about public murals since that era too, and he brings a number back to our memory in "Lost Murals of the 1970s." The explosion of new kinds of artistic expression was not limited to the mural movement. Political artists produced hundreds of stunning posters, a small sampling of which is presented in "San Francisco Bay Area Posters 1968-1978" by long-time collector and curator Lincoln Cushing. Another movement that got its start during this era, coincidentally also situated in the Mission District, was underground comix. One of the early participants, Jay Kinney, maps it out for us in "The Rise and Fall of the Underground Comix Movement in San Francisco and Beyond."

Another essential front in the culture wars that percolated through this era was music, at first rooted in the free parties and performances of the mid-1960s. The San Francisco Mime Troupe began performing in public parks for free in 1965, and LSD-inspired parties shattered many preconceived notions of what was possible, before the drug was made illegal at the end of 1966. Electrically amplified rock 'n' roll infused the new social milieu with liberatory energy before being channeled into the familiar album-and-concert form that we mostly remember. Mat Callahan, a San Francisco native, lived through the rise of rock 'n' roll and free music and dance festivals only to witness its rapid commercialization, and he brilliantly analyzes that process in "When Music Mattered."

Diminished and partially dispersed by the climactic 1978 assassinations of Mayor Moscone and gay Supervisor Harvey Milk, followed days later by the traumatic mass suicide of San Franciscans (many who had been left-wing activists) at Jonestown, Guyana, the alliances, programs, goals, and activities of that historic decade continue to shape San Francisco (and the US, perhaps the world) in the early 21st century. Left-wing party politics following traditional models all went into long-term decline by the end of this period, but a rebellious, anti-authoritarian sensibility was not crushed. It mutated like a smart virus, and took on a highly decentralized, superficially less political form. The cultural and political experiences of that era shaped a generation; millions of people still carry a common sense of justice and fairness, and hope for a world based on ecological sanity, without discrimination or grossly unequal division of wealth. The inheritors of this era are potentially a formidable political impediment to the authoritarian tendencies that dominate the United States. The Culture War between neoconservative right-wingers (Christian fundamentalists and Big Capital in an unstable alliance) and "the rest of us" is rooted in this same persistent shift in values, a common refusal to submit to stupid rules imposed for religious or ideological purposes. This volume provides a broad look at diverse ways these ten years shook the City, and shaped the world we're in today.

# On Strike!
## We're Gonna Shut it Down
## The 1968-69 San Francisco State Strike

### by Margaret Leahy

*What follows is not and cannot be comprehensive; rather, it is the Strike viewed from the perspective of one young San Francisco woman as she journeyed from passive observer to a political activist. Within the context of these struggles, the San Francisco State College ("State") student community was bringing the same issues to a campus where their struggles culminated in the longest student strike in the history of the United States—four and one-half months, from November 1968 to April 1969. That strike and my perceptions as to what led up to it, what happened during and after it and what lessons it might have for today are the topic of this chapter.*

As a second generation San Franciscan, I am a product of my city's history. The City I grew up in was a city of ethnic and racial neighborhoods. North Beach was primarily Italian. Chinatown, Chinese. The Fillmore/Western Addition had become primarily African-American during the migrations from the South and after the internment of Japanese Americans during World War II. The Mission and other areas "South of the Slot," had housed primarily Irish laborers and civil servants but were changing as the next generation moved to newer homes with grass in front and large back yards in the Sunset and Richmond Districts. My character and conscience were molded by my experience as a post-World War II White, Irish-American child of the Sunset District who attended parochial schools— Holy Name grammar school and Mercy High School, just across 19th Avenue from State. My neighbors and schoolmates were overwhelmingly White, although they were an odd mix for the time comprising Protestants, Catholics and Jews, gays and straights, and differing political persuasions, ranging from Democrat to Republican to (according to the House Un-American Activities Committee) communist. While neither my school nor community was racially integrated, racial slurs or acts of overt racism were not part of my experience. Although my dad died when I was in grammar school and my mom during my senior year in high school, my early family values had strong roots, which, combined with other life experiences, taught me to stand up for what was right and against what was wrong.

From the age of 15 until my early twenties, while I went to school I worked as a meat wrapper right across from Mercy and down the block from State at Stonestown Meats. My work exposed me to days filled with hours of hard, physical work and, for the first time, overt racism. When I asked why all the butchers and meat wrappers were White, I was told that no one would buy meat touched by "colored" hands. When I went home and told my mom, she said that some people had wrong ideas that differed from ours but not to say anything at work because we needed my pay now that my dad was dead.

Just as the City was changing in the post-World War II era, so was State. At its new campus on 19th Avenue and Holloway, State—along with City College—

comprised San Francisco's contribution to California's Master Plan for Higher Education that guaranteed every "qualified" high school graduate a place for post-secondary education. Community colleges provided vocational training and AA degrees that would allow transfer to state colleges or universities. State colleges were to focus on undergraduate degrees, teacher training and a limited number of MA degrees. The university system, such as UC Berkeley, provided undergraduate education but focused on graduate degrees and faculty and graduate research. State was seen as the choice for San Francisco's working- and middle-class community college and high school graduates who had proven themselves academically. Many, if not most, were the first in their family to go to college. State was close to home and affordable. When I started in fall, 1963, student fees were approximately $48 per semester. When I finished my MA, they had risen to about $95 per semester.

When I first crossed 19th Avenue to begin studying at State, the campus was already politically aware. A free speech platform was built in 1962, before Berkeley's Free Speech Movement, and allowed for speakers of various political persuasions to address the student body from a grassy part of the lawn in front of The Commons, a place where students gathered to eat and socialize. Tables sponsored by differing campus groups were a constant in front of the Commons, as well. Some were recruiting for fraternities and sororities, while others sought to get students involved in Civil Rights actions such a Freedom Summer in the South or others closer to home. These issues were yet to be vocally addressed on campus, however.

I remember in particular a table in the spring of 1964 where students, including one I remembered who had dated my cousin, were explaining the racist hiring and promotion policies at the San Francisco Palace Hotel. It reminded me of my experiences in the "Whites only" meat market. I knew the policies were wrong and could easily identify with the injustices that were occurring at the Palace Hotel. I was told of a sit-in that was to be held at the hotel to expose these practices and demand their elimination. I went to the hotel that evening, not knowing what to expect or what I would do. Upon seeing those who were sitting-in I felt conflicted. On the one hand, I agreed with their demands but on the other, I was frightened about the consequences of joining in and nervous because I didn't recognize anyone whom I could join. I left and rationalized my leaving by convincing myself that this was not my fight, nor part of the world in which I lived day-to-day. Although I left, I was ashamed at not joining because I knew not standing up against what was wrong was, itself, wrong.

## Precursors to the Strike

Unknown to me at the time, the issues of racism and exclusion were beginning to be addressed on campus. The election of a progressive slate to run the student government, Associated Students (AS), in 1962 led to a change in resource allocation and in fall, 1964, a student-sponsored tutorial program began in the Fillmore to address the inadequacies of the education given to students of color that made most "unqualified" for admission to the college. While students at UC Berkeley made headlines with the Free Speech movement on campus, students and faculty at State quietly began the AS-funded Community Involvement Program, which sought to ensure active community participation in the Tutorial Programs, and address issues impacting housing and employment.

By fall 1965, Malcolm X had been assassinated and the Watts riots gained national attention for the condition of Blacks outside the South. By this time the Tutorial Program had expanded outside the Fillmore District and operated at nearly a dozen sites with a few hundred volunteers. More students began working with community groups to alter the social and economic barriers that hampered the educational potential of poor and minority students as much as poor schools did. Connections between campus and community groups developed which would later be key in garnering community support during the Strike. As might be expected, however, such activities were perceived as unwanted intrusions and not well received by the City's educational establishment.

The spring of 1966 saw the development of two more precursors to the 1968-69 Strike: the emergence of the Black consciousness movement and the Experimental College. Black pride was not only manifest by wearing Afros and dashikis, but in Experimental College-sponsored classes on Black Nationalism and the AS-funded Gallery Lounge performances by Black performers. Students discovered a new reality, one not offered as part of the traditional White, Eurocentric curriculum. Students also inserted themselves into their education through student-run course evaluations that assessed the relevancy of course content and the effectiveness of instructors. Such a student voice was unheard of at the time, although university-mandated and -constructed evaluations are now the norm.

By the summer of 1966, the Tutorial Program was altered to reflect the ideas of racial and ethnic self-determination, changing from an interracial, though primarily White, set of students focused on community organizing to a program where people from various racial communities worked with members of their own community groups—Black with Black, Latino/a with Latino/a, and Asian with Asian. In tandem with these new perspectives was a change in the focus of the small Black student body. The Negro Students Association became the Black Student Union led by Mariana Waddy and, under the leadership of Jimmy Garrett, began to actively engage in the politics of self-determination rather than integration. By 1967, the Latin American Student Organization (LASO) was organized as a social/cultural club. With Roger Alvarado at the helm, LASO developed a political identity, as well.

Some White students also began to question the relevance of their education through exposure to new ideas presented in Experimental College classes by a few faculty members who were also questioning the "truths" of academia, and through the questions of a national and international social movement that no longer simply accepted what it was told by those in positions of authority. Making the connections between campus reality and the world at large was the focus of another new organization on campus mainly comprised of White students, Students for a Democratic Society (SDS). At State SDS was an umbrella organization composed of students with various left-of-center political positions who came together in opposition to the war in Vietnam and racism.

The Vietnam War engaged everyone. All males over the age of 18 had to sign up for the draft, which, at that time, usually meant a quick trip to the induction center. Most everyone knew someone who was going, had gone, or who wasn't coming back. While some students supported the war and others were already opposed to it, most students weren't clear as to why we were there. Male students with good academic standing were, however, exempt from the draft, which might explain why some tried not to think about it. State students of all races got involved in draft counseling off-campus and the war became a topic of discussion within a limited number of classrooms. The administration and most faculty did not see such discussion as appropriate. They believed the college should be an apolitical ivory tower, something that stood apart and observed the society from above. More and more students began to disagree with the war and, in spring, 1967, an AS resolution was passed to stop the college from providing the Selective Service with the academic standing of draft-age males. When the college administration refused to go along with the student vote, a small number of students staged a sit-in in the president's office to protest.

During this period the BSU was attempting to make the curriculum of the university more relevant to the realities of African-American students and to increase the disproportionately low number of Black students at the school compared with the percentage of African-Americans in the Bay Area. College presidents were authorized to grant admission waivers to 2% of admitted students and the BSU wanted the president to allocate these seats to Black students who had been in the Tutorial Program. The BSU also worked to create an Institute of Black Studies to house the new curriculum being proposed. Initially, then-President John Summerskill agreed to the creation of such an entity and also to the hiring of any "qualified" person nominated by the BSU to direct it. However, even thought the BSU secured foundation money to support the Institute for the fall of 1967, it did not become a reality. Rather, classes were dispersed throughout various departments, which had the final say over class content and instructor hiring and no program for admitting Black students was implemented.

Students became increasingly frustrated with the administration. These frustrations exploded in the fall of 1967 with two incidents ending in student suspensions by the president. The first suspension was that of Jeff Poland and the student-funded "alternative" newspaper *Open Process*, where he was a writer. Poland and *Open Process* were summarily suspended for writing and publishing an alleged pornographic poem about a member of the Athletic Department faculty. Soon thereafter, in response to a racist attack on Muhammed Ali in the Journalism Department's "official" newspaper *The Gator*, a physical confrontation ensued between the paper's editor, Jim Vasco, and members of the BSU. Six members of the BSU were summarily suspended, but not Vasco. In a clear case of pre-judgment and violation of the basic presumption that someone is considered innocent until proven guilty, the president suspended students prior to any judicial hearing. In addition, the BSU argued that the summary suspension of the BSU members but not Vasco was a racist prejudgment.

The BSU demanded the reinstatement of its members and SDS helped to form the Movement against Political Suspensions (MAPS), which focused on mobilizing White students around the idea of due process for students and student control of student-funded publications. When President Summerskill agreed to reinstate Poland and *Open Process* until a judicial hearing, but refused to reinstate the BSU members because, he argued, they had been violent, MAPS joined the BSU in characterizing the president's actions as racist. The president was presented with a demand to reinstate the BSU members until a judicial hearing and given a deadline for doing so.

Believing in the rightness of the demands, I took my first political act joining those who went to the president's office to present the demands. No one really knew who I was and, looking back, I'm sure that I looked a bit out of place marching to his office in my mini-skirt and heels. But I felt comfortable. I had a class with many of the other marching students and had heard them speak at MAPS meetings and in class about the situation.

When the president had not acted by the required time, we took action. At noon on December 6, 1967, students of all colors and ethnicities held a rally at the Speakers Platform and marched to the Administration Building with the purpose of taking it over with a sit-in until the students were readmitted. We found the doors chained shut. The president forgot, however, to close his office window which was only about six or seven feet from the ground. A courageous Iranian student, Kosoro Kalantari, climbed in, followed by my professor from the International Relations Department, John Gerassi. At the same time, students smashed the glass doors to the building. As I marched up the stairs towards the entrance I saw the broken glass and, waiting on the other side was Gerassi who held out his hand and asked me which side I stood on. I took hold of his hand and went through the opening. With that action I also crossed the line from being a passive, if concerned observer, to becoming a politically unsophisticated activist.

I didn't know what to expect when I entered the building so I stayed close to my professor and those students I knew. Soon I came across a number of young Black men all dressed in black leather jackets and wearing black berets. I asked someone who they were and was told, "Oh, they're the Panthers." My response was, "Who are the Panthers?" Until then I was unaware of the Black Panther Party and its position on self-defense against police brutality, its breakfast programs for children, and its community connections with students in the BSU at State. Although people remained in the building for a while, the president did not call the police. He was an avowed liberal who wanted to keep things peaceful and orderly on his campus, so he closed the campus down for the day and soon the students left. Arrest warrants were not issued until later.

On campus, neither side could claim victory but the actions that day did have repercussions. The actions at the Administration Building were successfully framed as violent and the students involved were painted with the same brush. As a result, rather than garnering greater student support, the actions of that day drove many potential student supporters away. The president's action in closing the campus rather than confronting the protesters with police solidified then-governor Ronald Reagan's and the California State College Board of Trustees' determination to maintain centralized control over the campus at any cost.

During the early spring of 1968, Chinese-American, Filipino-American, and Mexican-American student organizations solidified internally into political organizations, strengthened ties with their respective communities and joined collectively into what became the Third World Liberation Front (TWLF). President Summerskill accommodated some of the BSU demands, hiring Professor Nathan Hare to develop a Black Studies Department and offering special admission to 200 Black students. However, faculty teaching what could be termed black or ethnic studies courses were still untenured lecturers at the mercy of the departments where their courses were housed. The primary issue of contention in this regard revolved around the question of the academic validity of these classes, the quality of the faculty teaching them and, of course, who should make these determinations.

In response to the ongoing tensions on campus, the reverberation in the Black communities and on campus stemming from the assassination of Martin Luther King, Jr. and the all-too-obvious lack of students of color on campus, the Board of Trustees increased the percentage of "special admissions" from 2% to 4%. The Mexican American Student Coalition (MASC) had been actively engaged in the Mission District, tutoring and preparing high school students for admission to the college. Along with other groups within the TWLF, they organized students to come to the campus and demand the increased number of slots be filled with students from their underrepresented communities. The administration panicked at the thought of hundreds of Third World high-school students on campus and quickly claimed that they did not have the power to grant such waivers. The History Department used the "threat" posed by these students as an excuse to inform one of its lecturers who had been teaching Mexican-American history, Juan Martinez, that his contract would not be renewed, contending that he urged students to attack members of the administration.

Infuriated and frustrated with both the college and History Department administrators, the TWLF joined forces with SDS, which was similarly frustrated in its unsuccessful demand to have the Air Force ROTC (AFROTC) program removed from campus. Together, the groups made four demands to be implemented by fall 1968:

1. 400 Third World special admissions students would be enrolled;
2. Martinez would be rehired;
3. Eleven Third World faculty positions would be allocated and;
4. AFROTC would be removed from campus. Since the BSU had already secured a promise of 200 special admissions and the establishment of a Black Studies Department with Hare as its director, they did not become involved.

In order to insure these demands were met, the TWLF and SDS began a sit-in at the Administration Building on May 21, 1968. I joined the sit-in and the experiences of the next few days literally changed my life and the way I viewed the world. The demonstrators passed the time sitting in small groups discussing why the sit-in was necessary, why the college was structured as it was and whose interests the institution served. What had before been mostly intellectual understandings became concrete when one evening a Black gentleman who identified himself as living in the Ingleside District approached a group I was sitting with and handed me some bread and salami. He said he didn't have much but he wanted us to have it, as what we were doing would help his grandson to possibly accomplish what he hadn't been able to do himself. It was clear that what we were doing, and what the Tutorial and Community Involvement programs had done, had real meaning. The System was a problem that could only be changed by our standing together to make social institutions truly serve the needs of the people.

Those of us occupying the Administration Building were conscious that our actions were being observed not just by the administration, but also by the press. The community at large and our fellow students whose support we wanted and needed would assess our actions within this frame. We were careful to explain ourselves to the press in a way that made sense and was not viewed as confrontational or antagonistic. We even made sure the building was kept clean. The one thing we were criticized for was using the faculty-staff bathrooms—but we even cleaned them!

President Summerskill allowed the sit-in to continue and directed that the campus be open 24 hours a day so the occupation occurred within normal business hours. He had tendered his resignation as of the start of fall semester 1968, and most likely did not want a confrontation between students and police at the end of spring term to define his legacy. He quickly found out that the decision was not to be his, however, as the Chancellor of the Board of Trustees called for his immediate resignation and the end of the sit-in. On the evening of May 24, with soon-to-be ex-president Summerskill tearfully apologizing, police entered the building and through a bullhorn stated that the sit-in constituted an illegal assembly and that if the demonstrators did not leave the building immediately they would be subject to arrest. Most of the students left but about 25 volunteers, myself included, remained and were arrested and taken out of the building by police.

For the first time students at State saw uniformed police on their campus arresting fellow, peaceful students. And these were not ordinary police. They were members of the newly created Tactical Squad (Tac Squad) outfitted presumably to evoke fear in knee-high leather boots, face-guarded helmets, and motorcycle jackets, and who were trained to effectively wield their three-foot long Billy clubs. As I defiantly walked out with clenched fist raised I remember my arresting officer saying, "Put the fist down, bitch." Seeing the lights and hearing a large crowd, I naïvely believed he wouldn't hurt me and refused his order and was placed with others inside a paddy wagon. A few minutes later I looked out the small window to see our attorney, Terrence Hallinan, profusely bleeding from a club to his head. I realized then that neither cameras nor a crowd was a deterrent to the Tac Squad. I later read that some of the other 500 or so students gathered outside the building also had their first confrontation with police clubs that night.

The semester ended with students from the sit-in awaiting trial and sentencing and others with warrants for their arrest from the the December 6 seizure of the Administration office. Over the summer, the Board of Trustees appointed Professor Robert Smith president. The limited gains agreed to from the sit-in were eliminated and the new president found himself confronted with an increasingly angry and frustrated student body and community. With the assassination of Bobby Kennedy so soon after Dr. King's, people lost hope that peaceful solutions could be found to end the war and racism. The police riot at the 1968 Democratic convention also highlighted the power of the state towards peaceful protest.

George Murray, a student at State, member of the BSU and the Minister of Education for the Black Panther Party also traveled to Cuba that summer to address a meeting of representatives from movements for self-determination from throughout the Third World, making the connection between the Black struggle in the US and that which was occurring worldwide. The 1968 student massacre in Mexico City and the Black Power salute at the 1968 Olympics exposed systematic repression against those pressing for change and highlighted black anger in the US. Closer to home, racial tensions heated up when a Black man was seen as unjustly murdered by police in the City and the increased police presence in communities of color and in their high-schools was seen as symbolic of occupation. In response to all this, and in learning from the apparent success of the BSU in gaining a Black Studies Department, the TWLF called for its own Institute of Third World Studies.

As the fall semester began, a major controversy erupted between Professor Hare and a Political Science Department professor, John Bunzel, over academic quality. President Smith attempted to subdue the controversy by restating his commitment to the creation of a Black Studies Department with Hare as its director. Also in the fall, Murray was hired as a lecturer in the English Department with responsibilities that included working with those Black students that had gained special admission.

The Board of Trustees was not happy with the situation at State and began to assert its control over the college. First, it proposed a revision to the State Education Code that would give the Chancellor, not AS, control over student fees. This would more than likely decimate the Tutorial, Community Involvement Programs, and The Experimental College, and eliminate funding for recognized student organizations such as the BSU and TWLF. The Chancellor then called for the suspension of Murray and his removal as a faculty member in the English Department, noting his participation in the events of December 6 and his position within the Panthers (which the Chancellor considered an organization advocating violence against the government). This action by the Chancellor was seen as not only sidestepping long-standing faculty hiring and retention practices but as another attempt to block the development of a Black Studies Department.

The BSU called a student strike for November 6, 1968 and issued a set of ten non-negotiable demands. The TWLF immediately joined and presented its own list of five non-negotiable demands. After a heated discussion over whether or not to issue its own demand that AFROTC be removed from campus, SDS agreed that the Strike was against institutional racism on the campus, not the war, and joined in support of the Strike demands. SDS saw its role not in articulating demands but in educating White students to support the Strike.

## Student Demands

The Strike demands of the BSU centered around establishment of a Black Studies Department and control over its curriculum and faculty. The demands also included provisions for a major increase in Black student enrollment, a reconfiguring of control over the Office of Financial Aid, maintenance of the on- and off-campus programs that facilitated Black empowerment, and a policy of no recriminations against any strikers. Two specific personnel demands were also included: that Nathan Hare be appointed Chair of Black Studies as a full professor with salary commensurate with his qualifications and appointment level, and that George Murray remain on faculty for the Academic Year 1968-69.

The TWLF demands called for the development of a School of Ethnic Studies with faculty and curriculum determined by Third World ethnic groups, 50 faculty positions which would encompass 20 for Black Studies, an increase in Third World enrollment, and the retention of George Murray and "any other faculty person chosen by non-White students." (See Appendix f for specific demands.)

Underlying both sets of demands was the belief that communities of color, both on- and off-campus, have a say in their own education and that of their children, and that the campus had a responsibility to benefit these communities.

## The Strike

The first day of the Strike was fairly quiet, with a small picket line marching on 19th Avenue and some classes disrupted as striking students sought to have them cancelled by claiming they were "dismissed." The next day about 500 students marched to the Administration Building in support of the demands. By the end of the week, an ad-hoc faculty committee joined in the Strike. Until this time, with the exception of some very minor property damage, everything was peaceful. On Wednesday, November 13, all of that changed.

Following a noon rally at the Speakers Platform, the leadership of the BSU and TWLF held a press conference in front of their offices which were located in the huts, wooden structures housing student organizations near the front of the Commons. As the press conference was ending a unit of the Tac Squad marched in front of hundreds of students standing and sitting around The Commons. Before anyone knew what was happening, they broke ranks and charged the huts and attacked the BSU and TWLF members with clubs. The nearby students were both panicked and infuriated at the sight of club wielding police and attempted to push them away from the Commons area, all the while shouting, "Pigs off campus!" Each side charged at the other with the police, according to the next day's *San Francisco Chronicle*, "plucking students out of the crowd." At least one student even had a gun pointed at him. The faculty was holding a meeting nearby and hearing of the dangerous situation outside, marched into the crowd to put themselves between the students and police. After a few tense moments, the police marched away. But the students, led by former state assemblyman, Professor Bill Stanton, marched back to the Speakers Platform. Everyone was angry and needed to vent. I'll never forget Professor Stanton, with a full head of white hair and scholarly looking, screaming into the bullhorn, "We're going to close this motherfucker down!" At the end of the day, the police claimed 9 arrested and 11 injured and temporarily out of service, but their actions generated increased student and faculty support for the Strike.

President Smith closed the campus in response, claiming that the situation was not conducive to learning. Then-governor Reagan demanded that the campus be reopened, "by any means necessary." President Smith agreed to open the campus on Wednesday, November 20, not for regular classes, but for a campus-wide convocation on the issues. The time for discussion was over, however, and the convocation was more of a confrontation than a conversation. After a week, on November 26, the convocation ended and, under pressure from the state and realizing that there was nothing he could do to resolve the issues, Smith resigned.

Professor S. I. Hayakawa was then appointed acting-president of the college and, as his first act, ordered the campus closed for an early Thanksgiving vacation. Over the break he declared a state of emergency on campus, which gave the administration greater powers. When the campus reopened, over 1,000 demonstrators marched along 19th Avenue in front of the campus accompanied by a parked sound truck calling on people to join the Strike. Along with a few others I was standing on the bed of the truck when I noticed a man in a funny hat and glasses climbing aboard and throwing blue ribbons. I had no idea who he was as he brusquely pushed some of us away from the person holding the megaphone and yanked it away, trying to address the crowd. All the while these blue ribbons were flying about. As the others, not so gently, tried to remove him from the truck, I remember saying, "Don't hurt the old man, he's just crazy." I quickly learned that this "crazy man" was the new acting-president. After Hayakawa left, as the demonstrators moved on to campus, there were random attacks by the police throughout the morning. After the noon rally, police once again attacked the demonstrators in the central campus. But the worst brutality occurred the next day.

All those who participated in the Strike know Tuesday, December 2, as "Bloody Tuesday." Joining about 2,500 student and faculty demonstrators at a noon rally were leaders of the Black, Asian, and Latino communities, as well as religious leaders. By the end of the rally, one non-striker estimated the crowd at approximately 5,000. The rally was attacked—no other word describes what occurred—by police coming from all sides. Fighting between police and demonstrators filled the central campus. The two sides were not evenly matched. While the demonstrators outnumbered the police, the police were armed with clubs and guns. Unarmed students lost all fear and jumped on the backs of police who were beating students, only to be pulled off and clubbed to the ground themselves. The afternoon WAS bloody! Hayakawa, however characterized it as the most exciting day since his tenth birthday when he rode a roller coaster for the first time!

There were 32 arrests and not only students were arrested. Carlton Goodlett, editor of the *The Sun Reporter*, a Black newspaper, was unceremoniously taken to jail and the Reverend Gerald Pederson, the campus minister of Ecumenical House, was arrested after being pushed to the ground with a club pressed against his clerical collar. In reaction to the police riot, support for the Strike swelled. Numerous community groups and religious leaders used their platforms to condemn the police, the City, and Hayakawa, which garnered even greater support for the Strike. The campus chapter of the American Federation of Teachers (AFT) began to pressure the San Francisco Central Labor Council for strike sanction. Even The Friends of the IRA came out in support of the Strike and publicly chastised their Irish brethren in the police forces for forgetting their own history of oppression and fighting for the wrong side.

Throughout the week community participation increased and became more vocally militant. Rallies and arrests continued even as Hayakawa tried unsuccessfully to drive a wedge between striking groups by offering concessions to the BSU but nothing to the TWLF. The next week began with Mayor Alioto and some labor groups attempting to find ways of negotiating an end to the conflict. Like Hayakawa, their attempts were unsuccessful. The AFT did not wait for Labor Council approval before setting up an informational picket line along 19th Avenue. In conjunction with others they sloshed through a very rainy few days. On Thursday the rain died down just in time for a noon AFT-sponsored rally that was approved by the administration. Speakers from the AFT, student, and community groups all spoke out in favor of the 15 demands and against the administration and police brutality. Joining in was one group that was a surprise to most at the rally: Officers for Justice, an organization comprised of Black San Francisco police officers who refused assignment to State and who condemned the violence perpetrated by their fellow officers. The officers themselves were surprised when during a march to the Administration Building after the rally, they were among those attacked by the police.

By this time the Strike had developed a new dynamic. True solidarity had emerged among the various campus and community groups. Rather than being intimidated by the police violence, people learned to rely on one another for support. Solidarity came through collective struggle as the campus and the community stood side-by-side in support of the 15 demands and against the collective power of the campus administration, the Board of Trustees, the City of San Francisco, and the State of California. The following week presaged even greater community support as students from local junior and senior high schools would begin their Christmas breaks. However, on Friday, December 23, as demonstrators began a noon rally, Hayakawa's voice came over the loudspeakers atop the Administration Building and announced that the campus was being closed for Christmas vacation that day, a week early. Maybe even more startling than the early break was the president signing off his announcement by singing a few bars from, "Have Yourself a Merry Little Christmas."

The first two weeks after the break saw demonstrators strengthening the picket lines around campus. The decision by the Central Labor Council to give strike sanction to the AFT meant that other unions would not cross. Campus operations were effectively shut down. Sympathy strikes on other campuses around the state also grew as students and faculty marched out of classes not only to support the Strike at State, but to issue their own demands. At State, demonstrators continued to picket under attack from the police, as they waded into the lines to make selective arrests or serve warrants on people. At times 19th Avenue was a sea of chaos with the sound of cracking skulls and hoof beats as mounted police from all over California chased demonstrators. The violence became so dramatic that the San Francisco Human Rights Commission urged Mayor Alioto to stop police from making arrests on campus. In defiance of Hayakawa's proclamation that three or more people grouped together on campus constituted an illegal assembly and determined to take the campus back again, the BSU and TWLF called for a mass rally at noon on January 23.

Everyone knew that confrontation and arrests would ensue that day. I knew that, too, but was consciously absent on the 23rd. Throughout the semester, in addition to picketing, chanting, running from, and fighting the police, I found myself spending most late afternoons and evenings across the street from the jail at Barrish Bail Bonds attempting to secure bail reductions and release for those arrested that day. My second job came about unexpectedly and most likely because I had a car to get from campus to the bail office and was trusted to deal with the money we collected almost daily. Over time I learned how to push the right buttons to get demonstrators out of jail, via bail reductions, family guarantees, and how to quickly arrange bail for those who might face deportation and possible death if not released before an immigration hold kept them incarcerated until deportation. Knowing the potential for a large number of arrests, the owner of the bail office threatened not to bail people out if I were to go to the rally and be arrested that day. Not really believing him but not being sure, I stayed away. I was embarrassed and uncomfortable with my decision but I now believe I was probably right to do what I did.

Although demonstrators marched towards the Speakers Platform fully aware that Hayakawa would respond, the noon rally on the 23rd was massive. As the rally was underway and without any audible warning, the police appeared and quickly moved in pincher formation from all sides to surround the demonstrators. Some at the rally were able to run and get away. Others fought their way through police lines. In the end, 435 people were corralled in what became known as the Mass Bust.

When word arrived at the bail office, everything went into high gear. People had learned to yell out their name when arrested to let others know who they were and had memorized the bail office phone number—I still remember it—to use when making their call from jail. Those arrested at the Mass Bust kept chanting the phone number that was heard on television around the state and, from the response generated, I would guess thoughout the nation. Cash, checks, and phone calls poured in. Faculty, friends, and families came in to co-sign bail forms. Attorneys let us know they were willing to do whatever they could.

Getting everyone out of jail took three days and we worked around the clock. Every eight hours a doctor came by and gave me something to stay awake. Restaurants, especially Magnolia Thunderpussy in the Haight, made sure we had something to eat and that there was always food for those released from jail.

The jail was hectic, too. One woman had been placed in solitary confinement and the other women kept screaming for her release. The response of the jailers was to turn the fire hoses on the women. Once everyone was released, they had to be arraigned before a judge within a few days. There was a mass arraignment for all those arrested in the Mass Bust held in an auditorium at the Hall of "In"justice, just above the jail cells. As was the case at the sit-in arraignment, Hallinan was once again the students' attorney. Just imagine 435 defendants, their friends and families in one large room. Few of the defendants or their families had much respect left for the System. This was also the time when *Laugh-In* was one of the most popular shows on television. As the Judge walked on to the stage, without prompting but in unison, the Laugh-In chant went up: "Here comes da Judge. Here comes da judge. Order in the courtroom, here comes da judge." Only after three pleas by Halllinan did people finally quiet down and let the arraignment proceed.

As spring term began in mid-February, striking students enrolled in classes to be taught by striking teachers to ensure that both groups retained their right to be on campus. Over the previous semester the administration learned that police violence, rather than serving to break the Strike, only forged stronger collective campus resistance and generated greater community support. Working hand-in-hand, the campus administration, the Board of Trustees and the courts focused their efforts on a less visible but highly effective judicial offensive.

By now hundreds of students had to focus attention on lengthy legal battles. In the end, a small number of those arrested in the Mass Bust were acquitted but most were convicted in group trials where they were sentenced to pay a fine, given a suspended sentence and placed on probation, one of the conditions being that they not engage in "illegal" political activity on campus. Those considered leaders of the Strike were all convicted of various misdemeanors and felonies and subsequently sentenced to jail, some for a year or more. On campus, Kangaroo Court disciplinary hearings suspended or expelled students, which made their presence on campus illegal. The Board of Trustees put the AS into receivership, eliminating funds for undesirable student groups and activities, namely the BSU and TWLF. Additionally, student newspapers that supported the Strike were left without funding for publication. Hayakawa himself suspended the activities of the Educational Opportunity Program that served low income and non-White students. The AFT strike lost Labor Council sanction when specific work-related grievances were negotiated. Not only did this force reluctant faculty to return to the classroom but also required other unions that had been supporting the Strike to resume their work.

The 15 non-negotiable demands became negotiable. Hayakawa appointed a Select Committee to meet with the BSU and TWLF Central Committees and, together, they negotiated an end to the Strike. As with all negotiated settlements, neither side could claim complete victory but, on March 21, nearly four and one-half months after the Strike began, a settlement was announced.

The agreement provided for the establishment of a College of Ethnic Studies that would include a Black Studies Department along with departments representing the other ethnic groups involved in the Strike. The Administration committed to fulfilling the "special admissions" quota for underrepresented students and to seek legislative approval for an increase in the percentage of students who would be admitted through such provisions. No agreement was made to maintain all student-run on- and off-campus programs, nor to reconfigure the Office of Financial Aid. No strikers were given amnesty from the university and neither George Murray nor Nathan Hare was given the faculty positions originally demanded. Perhaps most importantly, control over curriculum and hiring and community involvement in the College was not included.

## Strike Legacy and Lessons

In the short term, two figures who vigorously opposed the Strike rose to political prominence: S. I. Hayakawa and Ronald Reagan. Hayakawa was elected to the US Senate where his service was mediocre, at best. He was primarily known for his naps on the Senate floor. His one quotable moment came in debate over return of the Panama Canal to Panama during which he claimed that the US had "stolen it fair and square," and it should remain ours. Governor Reagan became the darling of the conservatives and rode his popularity all the way to the White House. With regard to his tenure as president, (I can only say that to the extent that the Strike propelled him into that position, I apologize to the tens of millions of people in the US and the world who suffered.)

On the other side, my side, the consequences are both concrete as well as less obvious. Forty years after the Strike, San Francisco State (now) University (SFSU) has a College of Ethnic Studies comprised of departments of Africana Studies, Asian American Studies, Native American Studies and Raza Studies, and is still growing. The College has the same status as all other Colleges on campus, which is both positive and negative. The reality of the College of Ethnic Studies is important as previously unexamined experiences are now solidly incorporated into the academic framework not only at SFSU, but on campuses throughout the country. This would have not been possible without the Strike. In order to achieve such legitimacy, however, much of the connection to the community that was a primary focus of the Strike and a major factor leading to its success, has been lost. While a small number of faculty in the College still focus on college–community connections, the structure of the academy has forced the College to adhere to traditional academic benchmarks to maintain its existence: curriculum must be approved by university committees and academically accepted scholarship and publications must drive all hiring, retention, and tenure decisions.

The student community at SFSU is now much more racially diverse, although outside Ethnic Studies most faculty are still White. The student diversity has not necessarily come from Bay Area communities, however, as greater numbers of students are from around the state or are from out-of-state and from other countries. Such students do not always have a connection to the community in which they live and are therefore less likely to make the connection between college and community.

Today, you see more women students and professors. In my own field of study, International Relations, there were few women students in the 1960s and early '70s. Today, women are a majority of the students and are well represented on the faculty. And, unlike their earlier counterparts, female students are a vocal presence in the classroom. I am an example of one unintended consequence of the Strike, that of women finding their voice through struggle and, in supporting self-determination for others, embarking on their own road to self-determination.

As I write this chapter, SFSU and all public higher education in California is under attack. The Master Plan for Higher Education has been smashed. No longer does California promise an affordable, quality higher education to all who are academically eligible. State budget cuts have led to large increases in student fees, elimination of classes and faculty and pay cuts for all but those in charge of the system. Students can no longer afford a college education and, even if they can bundle together loans and grants, can't find the classes they need to graduate. Qualified students are even being turned away as there is no more room. Standing in front of an overflow class I ask myself why there is so little outrage now, why everyone grumbles but accepts what is happening. The best answer I can come up with is that times are different.

In the 1960s, the academy as well as the governing system, were exposed as instruments built to serve the controlling interests. Within the US and throughout the world people were collectively organizing and challenging these systems. Nothing was sacred and everything was possible. Looking back, we truly believed that positive change was possible and that we could be the agents of such change. Today no such movements are actively seen as portending possible, positive change. That belief in the possibility of change for the better must be infused into a new generation by actions large and small and with a leadership that can assist students to move in politically participatory directions.

In order to do this, students must learn to act collectively, with those of similar minds off-campus, to challenge a system that is injurious to all. The politics of self-determination must move from the small "we" to the collective "WE." What gave the Strike its strength was its multiracial character which, under the leadership of the BSU and TWLF, had deep connections to a politically engaged community off-campus. When we stood in solidarity, we had the power to confront the college administration and the state, along with its police and its courts. Together, we won a small battle in what, I hope, is a greater and ultimately successful war. After forty years I still believe that THE PEOPLE UNITED WILL NEVER BE DEFEATED!

# APPENDIX
## Strike Demands

## Black Student Union

1. That all Black Studies courses being taught through various other departments be immediately part of the Black Studies Department and that all the instructors in this department receive full-time pay.
2. That Dr. Nathan Hare, Chair of the Black Studies Department, receive a full professorship and a comparable salary according to his qualifications.
3. That there be a department of Black Studies which will grant a Bachelor's degree in Black Studies; that the Black Studies Department, chairman, faculty and staff have the sole power to hire faculty and control and determine the destiny of its department.
4. That all unused slots for Black students from Fall 1968 under the Special Admissions program be filled in Spring 1969.
5. That all Black students wishing so, be admitted in Fall 1969.
6. That twenty (20) full-time teaching positions be allocated to the department of Black Studies.
7. That Dr. Helen Bedesem be replaced from the position of Financial Aid Officer and that a Black person be hired to direct it, that Third World people have the power to determine how it will be administered.
8. That no disciplinary action will be administered in any way to any students, workers, teachers, or administrators during or after the strike as a consequence of their participation in the strike.
9. That the California State College Trustees not be allowed to dissolve any Black programs on or off San Francisco State College campus.
10. That George Murray maintain his teaching position on campus for 1968–1969 academic year.

## Third World Liberation Front

1. That a School of Ethnic Studies for the ethnic groups involved in the Third World [Liberation Front] be set up with the student in each particular organization having the authority and control of the hiring and retention of any faculty member, director and administrator, as well as the curriculum in a specific area of study.
2. That 50 faculty positions be appropriated to the School of Ethnic Studies, 20 of which would be for the Black Studies program.
3. That in the Spring semester, the College fulfill its commitment to the non-white students in admitting those who apply.
4. That in the Fall of 1969, all applications of non-White students be accepted.
5. That George Murray and any other faculty person chosen by non-White people as their teacher be retained in their position.

# "With the Soul of a Human Rainbow"
## Los Siete, Black Panthers, and Third Worldism in San Francisco

### by Dr. Jason M. Ferreira

O n May 1,1969, over seven thousand individuals converged on the steps of the federal building in downtown San Francisco to demonstrate their support for Huey P. Newton, Minister of Defense for the Black Panther Party. Representatives from diverse organizations chanted and marched for over four hours, declaring solidarity with the Black Panther Party and its jailed leader, but also—in the spirit of May Day—with the notion that systemic change was necessary in the United States. Revolution was in the air. On hundreds of signs and banners, a large red star, invoking the international symbol of revolutionary struggle, silhouetted a defiant image of Newton. Bobby Seale, Chairman of the Black Panthers, described to those gathered how the politics of revolution sweeping the Third World—from Mozambique and Guinea-Bissau to Cuba and, most significantly, Vietnam—was now taking firm root within the "belly of the beast." "Hold your Red Books up and tell [them] where we getting some new ideology from, " Seale declared:

> I want you to repeat after me: I am a revolutionary! They have never liked the Black Panther Party standing up and saying we are revolutionary and practicing revolutionary action. They have never liked the Black Panther Party proving through social practice that we are not racists but proving that they, in fact, are the real racists. They have never liked the Black Panther Party saying that we want some socialistic programs implemented in the Black community so that we can survive and be free.[1]

Some might have interpreted this as nothing more than the heated rhetoric of angry youth, but even well established, middle-class leaders from within the local African-American community echoed these views. "I must now confess," explained Dr. Carleton Goodlett, editor of the popular *Sun Reporter*, "my generation has failed. We have been on a treadmill for 25 years negotiating with an establishment that is totally insensitive to nonviolent petition." And then, indicating just how far-reaching this radicalism had become, he counseled the massive crowd, "I now say that if we are called upon to die for freedom, let us die for freedom in our Black ghettos. It is better to die at home than to be buried in an unmarked grave in Vietnam."[2]

While multi-generational, the rally was also multiracial. Representing the Third World Liberation Front (TWLF) at San Francisco State College, Tony Miranda coupled the politically charged imprisonment of Newton to the ongoing incarceration of TWLF leaders George Murray (who, at the time, also served as

Minister of Education for the Black Panther Party) and Roger Alvarado. Alvarado, a well-regarded spokesman for the TWLF, had been scheduled to speak at the widely anticipated "Free Huey" rally, but in a preemptive move, a San Francisco judge ordered him held in the County Jail without bail. Speaking in his place, Miranda linked the developing Third World struggles of the Bay Area to those occurring within the wider Third World, while stressing the rising wave of political repression faced by those struggling for a radical transformation in society. Alex Hing, leader of the recently established Red Guard Party in San Francisco's Chinatown, informed the crowd that communities of color would no longer be complacent, nor fall victim to 'divide and conquer' strategies: "We now feel that an attack on one Third World group is an attack on all of us."[3]

Many narratives of the Sixties trace the now familiar transition of a domestic agenda of civil rights, guided by a philosophy of nonviolence and liberal interracialism, into a more radical politics rooted in human rights, racial liberation, and militant demands for deep structural change. The events of May 1, 1969, readily demonstrate these dynamics. Yet, individual moments or historic flashpoints, such as this particular public gathering, equally reveal other important processes underway. New forms of community were being established and expressed. Much has been written, for instance, of how as Black nationalism gained greater currency within "the Movement," challenging the tenets of liberal interracialism, Black and White activists reexamined and renegotiated the terms of their working relationship. Yet, remaining largely overlooked in this moment, and thereby lost to our collective memory, are the profound political and personal ties that existed *between activists of color*. The recognition of this unique relationship has been obscured by the tendency to discuss racial matters (and movements) in strictly White-non-White terms. Yet, the boundaries separating these different struggles were extremely porous and a profound cross-fertilization of both ideas and people occurred which has not been fully recognized. Instead, many scholars (even on the Left) continue to paint these movements as narrowly nationalist. For sure, there were those that articulated a parochial "identity politics," contributing to what Elizabeth "Betita" Martinez humorously calls the "Oppression Olympics." Yet, not every political project exhibited this narrowness—least of all in the Bay Area. Instead, as Hing's comments indicate, many articulated an identity and a set of politics that were rooted *within* a particular community, yet simultaneously *opened outwards* to embrace the struggles of others.

Thus, the "Free Huey" rally on May Day 1969 reveals a convergence of diverse, overlapping spheres of insurgency that collectively constituted a wider polycentric social movement. Rooted in the racialized, lived experiences faced by urban working-class communities of color in San Francisco, this "community of resistance" took shape around a pre-existing web of social and political relations found amongst diverse activists of color and was animated by, and articulated itself through, Third Worldist concepts (self-determination, anti-imperialism, and Third World unity). The Black Panther Party, the Red Guard Party, the Third World Liberation Front (TWLF), and United Native Americans emerged as a few organizational expressions of this larger polycentric movement.[4]

The events of May Day 1969 are significant, however, for one final reason. Listening to the numerous speeches in the back of the audience were two TWLF activists from San Francisco State, Yolanda Lopez, a now well-known Chicana artist, and Donna Amador. Amador recalls: "I was standing in the back of the crowd near a police motorcycle when I heard from the crackling radio that a police officer had just been shot in San Francisco's Mission District (my home). An all-points bulletin went out for a number of Latin men, and, coincidentally, one of the suspects [Ralph Ruiz] was standing right beside me! My priorities changed instantly. Education was important for the brothers and sisters, but the fight for freedom from the oppression and injustice of the real world suddenly took me away from San Francisco State."[5] Authorities arrested six young Latinos, a mix of Salvadoreños, Hondureños, and Nicaragüense. Later, seven individuals were put on trial and became collectively known as Los Siete de La Raza.[6]

Within a few days of their arrest, Amador, Lopez, Alvarado (after being released from jail), Roberto Vargas (a Nicaraguan poet/activist in the neighborhood), Ralph Ruiz and a number of other Latinas/os from the Mission District joined together to form El Comité Para Defender Los Siete de La Raza. Very quickly, this defense committee transformed itself into a full-blown community-based organization, also known as Los Siete, which focused on the political, economic, and cultural empowerment (or self-determination) of Latinas/os in San Francisco. In building the organization, individuals drew materially and ideologically from the interconnected network of Third World activists within the local area. Thus, while grounded in a specific social-cultural space (the Mission), Los Siete represented the distinctly Latina/o component of this wider Third Worldist movement sweeping the Bay Area.[7]

The exact events that took place on May 1 at 433 Alvarado Street (located in Noe Valley, a quiet residential neighborhood bordering the Mission District) might never be fully known. What *is* undisputed, however, is that Joseph Brodnick and Paul McGoran, two White undercover police officers known as *Mission 11*, stopped a group of young Latinos (claiming they looked "suspicious") who were moving a television set from a parked car into the home of Jose Rios. After a number of insults were exchanged, in which McGoran referred to the youth as "wetbacks," a fight broke out that resulted in a dead cop. In the ensuing struggle, Brodnick had been shot with his partner's .41 Magnum. Fearing for their lives, "the brothers," as they came to be called, fled the scene. In the immediate aftermath, with one of "their own" down, the San Francisco Police Department responded with brute force, virtually declaring martial law in the Mission District. After roughly a week on the run, the six men were apprehended outside of Santa Cruz. Yet, who *actually* shot Brodnick outside the Rios home remained entirely unclear and became a vital point of contention in the legal trial of Los Siete one year later. The defense argued that McGoran, noted for having the volatile mix of a loose temper, a racist disdain for youth of color, a proclivity to pull out his gun to intimidate "suspects," and a serious drinking problem (they demonstrated, in fact, that he had been drinking earlier that morning), accidentally shot his own partner during the scuffle. On the other hand, despite evidence indicating two of the young men (Nelson Rodriguez and Tony Martinez) were at the College of San Mateo, and that two others (Jose Rios and "Gio" Lopez) were in an upstairs bedroom when Brodnick was actually shot, the prosecution still pushed to convict all seven men and send them to the gas chamber. Authorities reasoned, "if they were innocent, why run?" The answer to that question, however, turned on an appreciation of police-community (of color) relations in San Francisco. Understanding this larger context allows us to not only comprehend the specific situation confronted by "the brothers" on May 1 (i.e. why the conflict occurred and why they fled) but also provides insight into the initial agenda of Los Siete.

★★★

As with the Black Panthers, the Red Guard Party, and other Third Worldist organizations, the issue of the criminal justice system, from police and prejudicial courts to prisons, played a formative role in Los Siete's political development. Growing up in the Mission District during the 1950s, Alvarado recalls what life was like for Latina/o youth in the rapidly changing neighborhood:

> It was like, man, you didn't have a chance. You're just nothing, nothing! You [were] just used, abused…and you didn't have any so-called status.… A homeless guy once said that people tell me to go away.… He says, 'Now, they don't mean just go away, they mean go away, they mean disappear, they mean fall off the face of the earth and die. That's what they mean by 'go away.' 'That's what it was like in the Mission.

Oscar Rios, the older brother of Jose Rios and another founder of Los Siete, attests to Alvarado's memories, "It was very rough in the Mission. If you were hanging around, riding around, [the police] would stop you. Whatever they felt like doing to you, they would do it."[8] Paul Harris, a community-based lawyer who worked as "in-house" legal counsel for Los Siete de La Raza in later years, describes the San Francisco Police Department in a similar fashion:

> The Panthers called it an occupation army (that's the way they described it in Oakland) and that's what it was; it was all White. And there was no understanding of what it meant to be living in the community.… People would get beat up in the Mission Station, in the basement, on a regular basis. The level of harassment was such that a policeman would stop a client of ours on the street, on Mission Street, just walk up to them and say 'take off your shoes I want to see if you got any pot on you.' Or, then there were these incredible police riots, where the police would just come in to peoples' houses. They wanted you to know that they had the power. They had the power to do whatever they wanted.

Some of this conflict clearly arose out of racist disapproval of the demographic changes occurring in San Francisco. By 1970, Whites only accounted for 57.2% of the City's population, down from nearly 82% just a decade prior. More significant: the City's youth population had become overwhelmingly "Third World." With the increase of Latino, Black, Native American, and Asian-American families into the City—mostly poor and nearly all expecting their lives to improve—came a subsequent need and demand for jobs, housing, education, health care, recreational facilities, and greater political and cultural representation. San Francisco's political economy, however, was undergoing a radical transformation itself, as a shrinking manufacturing and tax base directly impacted the provision of such necessary social services.[9] Thus, aside from personal prejudice, these racial tensions between the police and members of the community reflected a deeper, more fundamental struggle over political, economic, and cultural power in an increasingly young, non-White city. Besides the public school system, the police formed the front-line of the City's established institutions in dealing with these new realities and social pressures. Both failed miserably at containing these contradictions, as Third World student strikes shut down local educational institutions and police responded with ever-increasing levels of repression to preserve "law and order" and—in their eyes—to "keep the jungle at bay."[10]

McGoran and Brodnick were infamous in the Mission District, particularly among youth. Brodnick, though considered the less-brutal of the two partners, typically carried around a two-foot rubber hose to intimidate uncooperative "suspects." McGoran, for his part, had a long record of abuse that extended as far back as his rookie year in the mid-1950s. Both men had grown up in the neighborhood and resented both the cultural and political changes taking place. Colleen Crosby, Brodnick's own niece, later testified to the prevalent feelings within the Mission District station:

> Once I tried to ask my uncle about racism in the police department. He said it was a long discussion and he didn't want to get into it....So I asked my cousin [Brodnick's daughter] about it. She said there was a strong feeling among the San Francisco cops about the brown people in the Mission—that the whole purpose of their lives was to cause trouble. My cousin said they related to Latinos in the street as dirty. They said they were going to bring peace to the Mission where the dirty Latinos are.[11]

Therefore, contrary to mainstream media coverage following May 1, which characterized the Los Siete de La Raza incident as a random encounter between two groups of strangers, "the brothers" (portrayed by the press as a "gang" of "latin hippie types") and the McGoran/Brodnick team ("police heroes" that were the City's "most respected law enforcement team") were already quite familiar with one another.[12] By the spring of 1969, widespread police brutality threatened to tear the City apart, as incident after incident occurred between the predominately White San Francisco Police Department and residents within diverse communities of color. As a result, these experiences, rooted in both individual and structural racism, greatly contributed to the formation of new organizations like the Black Panther Party, the Red Guard Party, and Los Siete.

★★★

With the founding of Los Siete in the Mission District, Amador and Oscar Rios traveled throughout the Southwest soliciting support (and funds) from different Chicano Movement organizations in order to mount a solid defense. Amador was especially instrumental in this regard as she had met Chicana/o activists from throughout the Southwest when she and Hing traveled to the Poor People's March in early 1968.

"We stayed in DC for probably four or five months. We camped out there. And so I had a chance to really get to know people from a lot of different places and build alliances. And that was very valuable later. I mean, I did not know what 'networking' or anything like that was, but when we came to form Los Siete a lot of those alliances were very, very valuable."

Unfortunately, outside of the Crusade for Justice in Denver and "Betita" Martinez and her *El Grito del Norte* staff in New Mexico, Los Siete members were unable to secure much help beyond symbolic words of support.[13] That Los Siete developed a special relationship with these two groups, reporting on each other's activities and providing political refuge for one another, reflects the fact that the Crusade for Justice and *El Grito* came to represent the Left pole of the Chicano Movement, as they increasingly linked the situation of Chicanas/os to international struggles throughout the Third World. For Amador and others, however, it would be regional political networks that proved more fruitful, as well as more influential to the political direction of their fledgling organization.

Returning to the Bay Area, Los Siete connected with comrades in the Black Panther Party who lent assistance without any hesitation. Oscar Rios remembers, "Right away Bobby [Seale] came out and said, 'Okay, this is what we can give you: we'll give you one side of our paper...we'll give you space at rallies, anything you want...'." [He] had an interview on Channel 9, and he immediately mentioned... 'los saytay.' In addition, the Panthers offered the services of their attorney, Charles Garry, despite the fact that he already had his hands full representing both Newton and Seale. Finally, the Black Panther Party committed $25,000 to their legal defense. The issue of accepting support from the Panthers, however, became a defining matter for the newly formed group.[14]

In the immediate fall-out of the incident on Alvarado Street, the response to the arrest of "the brothers" varied within the Mission District. On the one hand, there were many within the community who succumbed to the propaganda of the mainstream media; whether it was "crime," "hoodlums," "hippies," or "militants," efforts by the police and the media to generate fear within the city were partially successful. Meanwhile, others saw their case as emblematic of racial injustice within the community but did not want to overly politicize the affair. Mission Rebels, a federally funded group working with Mission District youth, offered $50,000 to the defense committee as long as "politics" and "ideology" would be kept out of the campaign. They counseled, instead, a more traditional legal defense. The issue of whether or not to accept support from the Panthers directly raised the political question as to what type of organization Los Siete would become. Yolanda Lopez recalls one early, pivotal meeting:

> [There] was Jimmy Queen, Roger Alvarado, Al Martinet, Donna James [Amador], and a few other people. It was a small group... many of us out of State College. And what happened was, there came [a time] to make a decision about whether to accept the support of the Panthers. And the argument was that if we get support from the Panthers, the community of the Mission won't support us. Because, you gotta remember, this is when the Panthers were being killed and there was just horrible publicity going on and tremendous misinformation in the newspapers. So there was a big discussion and what happened at that general meeting was that the group split in two. Jimmy Queen, who developed RAP [Real Alternative Programs], said not to go with the Panthers, that it would be too alienating. Roger Alvarado, who was a speaker at the

Third World Strike, said 'Well, we're going to go do it [anyway]. Whoever wants to come with me can follow me.' I ended up going with Roger. And we were the group that became Los Siete. The group that stayed with Jimmy Queen ended up developing RAP. So from the beginning there was a real difference.[15]

In his recollection of events, Alvarado agreed:

I couldn't see how you could do it without the Panthers. Certainly with their experience and with their background, as well as with getting Garry and the rest of the attorneys involved... So, no, to me, they were critical. What were you gonna do with a traditional case, cop a plea? Cop a plea, point to one of the brothers and let everybody else live the rest of their life while they hang or something? Nah...there was no traditional defense in their case. They were 'the brothers'...what happened to them is what was happening throughout the area, throughout the city. It was what you knew, what you knew was going on.

Indeed, the only difference, this time around, was that a cop and not a nameless person of color ended up on the wrong end of a police officer's gun.

The argument over an alliance with the Panthers masked a deeper debate that revolved around one political question: revolution versus reform. Frustrated by earlier experiences within liberal War on Poverty organizations, those that formed Los Siete sought to develop a radical alternative to all the reformist organizations operating in the Mission District (such as Mission Rebels and the Mission Coalition Organization). Amador recalled, "It was a huge rejection. A lot of us had been in those other organizations, or were close to people in those organizations.... Many of us had been in these different organizations and wanting to make a change.... We wanted to make a *real* change." Speaking to the antagonism that developed, Yolanda Lopez remembers:

Yes, the loyalties were *very, very strong*, and, I think, in part, because there was also pressure from the FBI, as far as [fomenting] a sense of distrust.   Ultimately, however, it was not so much, I think, about the Panthers, but rather an association with the government and an association with liberalism, about being a liberal or being a revolutionary. What would work best for social change and political change?

Therefore, by early June 1969, Los Siete transformed itself from a defense committee concerned with freeing seven individuals into a revolutionary organization committed to defending and bringing self-determination *to an entire community*. The organization advocated a revolutionary transformation of society, linking racial oppression to anti-imperialist and anti-capitalist politics.

★★★

From the beginning, Los Siete worked closely with the Black Panther Party. Besides connecting the organization with Charles Garry to represent "the brothers" in court, the Panthers and Los Siete engaged in political education classes together, mobilized in support of each others activities, and—most notably—labored together on the newspaper. Until Los Siete could become a self-sustaining organization, the Black Panther Party freely donated one side of their newspaper to the editorial staff of *Basta Ya!*—Los Siete's official newspaper. Two times a month, beginning with the second issue in June and continuing until late 1969, *Basta Ya!* was published as part of *The Black Panther*. "I remember one of the most exciting things that I ever did with Donna," Yolanda Lopez recalls, "was when we went over to the Panther headquarters and met Emory Douglas. He showed me how the Panther newspaper was laid out and how to cut-up from a newspaper.... I learned a lot from him [and] to me, it was very exciting." Finding her artistic voice, Lopez ultimately came to play the same role within Los Siete that Douglas did within the Black Panther Party, becoming the principal artist who not only developed the official masthead and provided illustrations for the newspaper but also designed buttons, silkscreen posters, and placards for use at marches and rallies. Amador, meanwhile, served as the editor, compiling articles and making sure deadlines were met. Drawing upon the organizational structure of the Panthers, Yolanda and Donna, two Latinas, formed the core of Los Siete's Ministry of Information.[16] The relationship with the Panthers, therefore, was more than symbolic or rhetorical. Lopez notes, "The thing is, at the time, you can't tell what is socializing and what is business. There was just a lot of crossover [and] mutual support.... It was intimate on an organizational, social, and ideological level." Though many Los Siete members knew individual Panthers from earlier struggles, political and personal bonds of solidarity were only reinforced and deepened as individuals labored together to put out their respective publications, serve as security at each others rallies, or engage in political education.

The Black Panther Party, with its national presence, was able to provide crucial connections for the new Mission District-based organization. Through public speaking engagements, articles in *The Black Panther* and other Movement publications (in particular, *The National Guardian*) the Panthers informed activists from throughout the country about not only the legal case of Los Siete de La Raza and the activities of Los Siete, but also educated them to conditions in the *barrio*. Los Siete was put in touch with other radical organizations across the country, such as the poor White Young Patriots Organization and the Young Lords Party of New York City. The social impact of solidarity between Los Siete and the Panthers transcended Movement circles. A new appreciation of Black-Brown relations emerged even among everyday working people. Los Siete worked hard to counter the mainstream media's campaign to demonize the Panthers. Through *Basta Ya!* Los Siete reported on Panther programs, always drawing parallels between the two communities. They also struggled against the internal racism of the Latina/o community, calling attention to and celebrating the African heritage of *Raza*. At the same time, Panther support for Los Siete de La Raza made significant inroads into changing the perception of Latinas/os in the Black community. A letter sent from a working-class African-American to the Los Siete office offers a glimpse of what impact Panther solidarity was having. He writes:

> This contribution of $5.00 is awfully meager! However, as a relatively poor Black American, this amount was all I could send at this time [but] I wanted to write to express support for you and the Brown community. I know that there have been and still

are many ill-feelings and hatreds between the Black and Brown communities. From experience, I know many Chicanos/Latinos view Blacks in the same manner as do Whites; Blacks too express their dislike of Brown Americans for stereotypic reasons. I can only hope that basic understanding, mutual respect, and then true friendship and love will develop between Brown and Black people in the US. Buena Suerte [and] ¡Viva La Raza![17]

When "the brothers" were acquitted and released from jail in November 1970, one of the first things they did was to convey their appreciation to the Black Panthers, noting the significance of their solidarity in developing a new consciousness between Latinas/os and Blacks. Tony Martinez wrote, "By the help that we have received from the Black Panther Party, we—both Black and Brown people—have reached a higher level of camaraderie and brotherhood…. It is the responsibility of the Third World to make their position known [regarding] the true solution to the needs of oppressed peoples—Revolution. In celebrating our victory, our hearts are filled with much more happiness at knowing that Black and Brown people are now truly united in the vanguard. ¡POWER TO THE PEOPLE! ¡QUE VIVA LA RAZA![18]

This solidarity, it should be noted, between Los Siete and the Panthers, between radical Latinas/os and African-Americans, did not arise out of mere tactical considerations or a sense of charity (a hierarchical concept) but instead—as Martinez indicates—out of a profound commitment to Revolution, to the *real* notion of developing "All Power to the People." What bound different radicals of color together, therefore, was **not** the politics of identity, but rather an identity forged out of a politics, a politics of Third World revolution and the mutual struggle for self-determination. As groups organized within their respective communities, it was the issues—the various aspects of racial oppression (police violence, education, health care, housing, and preservation of one's history and cultural life)—not racial identities in themselves that formed the basis for such solidarity. Therefore, rather than envisioning themselves as part of a liberal, multicultural coalition, joining together as discrete interest groups to gain greater leverage in the acquisition of resources, Third Worldists in San Francisco related to one another largely as comrades in a wider, racialized class struggle to remake society itself. They built this radical movement in a way that could unify different peoples without sacrificing their diversity and uniqueness. Specific racial, class, and cultural realities within the community were appreciated rather than minimized, thereby enriching rather than fragmenting Third Worldism in San Francisco.

★★★

As a distinct product of the Mission District, Los Siete came together as a pan-Latino organization, encompassing Chicanas/os, Central Americans, Puerto Ricans, Cubans, and South Americans. They envisioned themselves as part of what 19th century Cuban anti-imperialist Jose Martí called *Nuestra América*— or, perhaps, more precisely, within the revolutionary current of Ernesto "Che" Guevara's explicitly Marxist Pan-Latin Americanism. Yet, as has been discussed, Los Siete simultaneously articulated themselves to be part of a larger Third World community. Los Siete did have non-Latinas/os within the group, such as Tom

Yoneda, son of Japanese-American Communist Party legend Karl Yoneda; Terry Collins, a Black veteran of the TWLF at San Francisco State; and Judy Drummond, a Cahuilla Native American activist from East Los Angeles. Their participation alone, however, is not what made Los Siete a Third World organization, but rather it was the Third Worldist orientation that allowed them to feel comfortable within the group, that ultimately enabled them to see that the struggle for, say, Brown Power was/is inextricably linked to Black, Red, or Yellow Power. Los Siete, in short, was infused with the same radical Third World precepts—self-determination, anti-imperialism, and anti-capitalism—that were circulating among other Third Worldist organizations. In its second issue of *Basta Ya!*, Los Siete provided a working definition of the Third World for its readers:

## THIRD WORLD

is: African warriors and Spanish peasants, Indian fisherman, and Chinese laborers;

is: a common history of oppression and slavery and centuries of our blood shed in a continuous struggle for our rights as free men;

is: our mother tongue of Spanish and the thousand and one languages and dialects which have made our people;

is: the history of Mexico and Peru, El Salvador and Puerto Rico, Spanish Harlem and the Mission;

is: a hungry child whose future is doubtful and whose stomach is often empty;

is: to be taught in your schools that your people are stupid, your native language alien and your history non-existent;

is: a people who have become aware of the source of their misery and are arising to change conditions which they had been taught were hopeless;

is: a recognition that the word 'ghetto' which is meant for blacks and the word 'barrio' which is meant for Latinos are in actuality one and the same;

is: a recognition that the enemy is not our brother whatever his shade of skin but a system which attempts to divide and destroy us by pitting brother against brother in a vicious cycle of self hatred;

....

is: a recognition of our common humanity in the face of the brutal inhumanity which has oppressed us;

is: a passionate sense of our dignity as a people and the courage which unity provides us.[19]

The Third World was, in other words, a shared vision of an alternative future in which Black, Asian, Native, and Latina/o communities could fully develop and express their humanity free of a historically-constructed, global system of oppression. Importantly, like the term Chicana/o, which connoted a sense of history and an activist orientation towards the future—it indicated you marched in support of the United Farm Workers, campaigned for La Raza Unida Party, etc.— to identify as Third World was also more than *descriptive*—such as the contemporary notion of "people of color"—it was *prescriptive*, reflecting a certain racial and class politics that were rooted in a specific social praxis. The idea of a Third World consciousness, a Third World identity, has been largely forgotten, trivialized, or dismissed as baseless. Writing within a slightly different context, but speaking of a similar dynamic, Chris Iijima from the famed Asian-American musical group *Grain of Sand* states:

> Asian-American identity was meant to be a means to an end rather than an end in itself. It was created as an organizing tool to mobilize Asians to participate in the progressive movements of the times. It was as much a mechanism to identify with one another as to identify with the struggles of others, whether it is African-Americans or Asians overseas, and [significantly] it was less a marker of what one was and more a marker of what one believed. That it has now become synonymous with "pride in one's ethnic heritage" is a complete evisceration of what it was originally, and what it was meant *to be*.[20]

★★★

In San Francisco, the notion of revolutionary Third Worldism was profoundly facilitated by the sheer fact that many individuals within these Bay Area organizations had known each other for years. As already mentioned, Alvarado worked closely with members of the Black Student Union and Black Panther Party; Amador, as a student at City College of San Francisco, organized on campus with—and was actually dating Hing, years before either of them ever founded Los Siete or the Red Guard Party. LaNada Means, a spokeswoman for Indians of All Tribes during the 19-month occupation of Alcatraz, not only joined and helped lead the Third World Liberation Front at Berkeley, but also—upon arriving on Relocation—lived in the Mission District and worked with eventual members of Los Siete in local War on Poverty organizations. Richard Oakes, another leader on Alcatraz, studied at San Francisco State and socialized with other campus activists, like Alvarado and Amador. Nicaraguan poet Vargas was friends with other poets of color, such as Janice Mirikitani and Al Robles, a now-famous Pilipino poet, who—at the time—was organizing to defend elderly *manong* from eviction at the International Hotel. In short, the polycentric Third World movement in San Francisco that existed was as much a social network as it was an imagined political community.

It would be a mistake, therefore, to claim that the idea of the Third World, as articulated by Los Siete and others in the Bay Area, was only an imitation of a more *real* political process underway in Africa, Asia, and Latin America. Or, that activists of color carelessly imported ideas from the global arena into the local, simplistically drawing inspiration and imposing conclusions from classic revolutionary texts of the era, such as Frantz Fanon's *Wretched of the Earth*, Albert Memmi's *The Colonizer and the Colonized*, or Mao Tse-tung's *Red Book*. Instead, as Karl Marx once observed, "it is not the consciousness of people which determines their existence, but on the contrary, it is their social existence which determines their consciousness."[21] The political analyses of different international revolutionaries were indeed influential, providing young radicals with a specific language and theoretical framework to interpret their realities, but the origins of the Third World consciousness in San Francisco—which activists creatively drew upon—was rooted deeper in the material conditions (and structural contradictions) that communities of color confronted in their post-war San Francisco neighborhoods.

The same social existence that facilitated the notion of being *Raza*, or Latina/o, in the Mission District extended to include other communities of color. Amador describes:

> In the Bay Area, or at least in San Francisco, people lived right next door to each other. Its not like LA where: "Here is West LA, here is Compton, then Watts, and then here is East LA way over here…." I mean, they didn't mix in the same way; they don't go to school together; they don't live together; they don't shop for groceries together…. In San Francisco, even if somebody lived in the Fillmore and somebody lived in the Mission, in terms of high schools, there just weren't that many, so people tended to know each other casually. It wasn't like barriers existed. A lot of folks just knew each other, and when you know somebody, it's really easy to say 'Hey, I'm gonna go do this, come on, let's go do it together. It's not like we're strangers. And I think in the Bay Area, there was just a lot more of that going on.[22]

The physical and social geography of the city played a special role in the construction of a Third World identity; San Francisco, after all, is less than forty-nine square miles. Alvarado puts an even finer point on it, stating,

> Take transportation in the city, like the 22 [Muni bus line], if you went from Hunter's Point to Chinatown, you went through everybody's district, right, and you were exposed to all of that. So you had a lot of mixing between people and connections being made.[23]

This "mixing between people," however, produced more than personal friendships and notions of cultural tolerance. Instead, it contributed to an acute appreciation of the common oppression shared by working-class communities of color. Alvarado adds:

> You know, somebody would talk about something in their neighborhood and everybody knew that that's *exactly* what their neighborhood was like as well. You know, you weren't just talking about one neighborhood; you were talking about a lot of neighborhoods. You were talking about a lot of the same experiences. I mean anybody who had gone to school, certainly a school in the Fillmore, the Mission, Hunter's Point, or Chinatown, they knew what you were talking about. Because everybody had had the shared experience.[24]

Perhaps of all the neighborhoods in the City, due to its unique mixture of Latinas/os, Native Americans, Samoans, Blacks, and Pilipinos, the Mission District *barrio* served as a sort of epicenter for this fresh consciousness. In describing his childhood, Vargas gives a poetic sense of the vibrant cultural and political world, known simply as *La Misión*, when he writes in "Managua to Mission":

> Towards the end of the '50s there was one dominant class in the

Mission, the workers. Every being trying to escape the assimilation of other cultures, but inevitably blending into this concrete and wooden barrio called the Mission. With the dominance of the English language and values threatening to absorb our Cultura, we adopted, organically, a bit of each other's cultures so that it would be still more difficult to be swallowed up in this red, white & blue melting pot called America…. The Mission is now an expression of real culture, a many-faceted being…with the soul of a human rainbow…. [It] is now an implosion/explosion of human color…aware of itself as a body of many people, all tribes aware of themselves….a collective feeling of compassion for each other Nicas Blacks Chicanos Chileños oppressed Indios. The sense of collective survival, histories full of Somozas Wounded Knees written on the walls: Muera Somoza Free Angela…. It's about my pueblo and yours learning how to struggle and survive again together making the necessary connections to our tribes, to our roots/past, creating one big NOW…. together here we will work to free Indios and African brothers and sisters in mind jails and avenues of oppression…. [25]

By the late Sixties, by acknowledging the Third World within—in particular the Native American and African heritage of *La Raza*—a greater commitment to, and solidarity with, other Third World communities deepened—which, in a dialectical fashion, ended up working the other way too. In the process, the notion of "Aztlan," rather than being discarded by *activistas* in the Bay Area, was reinterpreted and reworked in such a way as to open outwards and to embrace the struggles of all oppressed peoples.[26]

Ironically, the radical conception of culture and community circulating within *La Misión* and the Bay Area remains marginalized in historical re-constructions of the Chicano Movement at the exact same time as it provides many of the images and sounds associated with that defining era. First, take the world of music: the Mission District produced Malo, whose song "Suavecito" has since become somewhat of a Chicano standard. Most notable, however, is that of Santana, another "Latin Rock" group (or, at least, that is what the record labels attempted to classify them as) who drew upon the diverse musical traditions of John Lee Hooker and Buddy Guy, Armando PeRaza and Chano Pozo, Tito Puente and Ray Barretto, Miles Davis and John Coltrane, and Ravi Shankar. Santana, furthermore, consistently connected his artistic expression to political struggles for freedom and liberation, reflected in such song titles as "Incident at Neshabur" and "Toussant L'Overture" (two songs inspired by the successful Haitian slave revolt of the early 19th century), "Free Angela," and—in the 1980s—"Free All the People (South Africa)." In the month prior to his arrest, Tony Martinez, as a student activist at the College of San Mateo, brought Carlos Santana to play in the college gymnasium to support campus recruitment efforts and an early Ethnic Studies curriculum for students of color.[27]

Northern California, likewise, had a dynamic artistic community. The artwork of Rupert García, Malaquias Montoya, and Yolanda Lopez, considered "heavies" of the Chicana/o Arts Movement, are considered central to the Chicano Movement, yet typically without any appreciation for the specific historical and political crucible in which they developed their artistic voice. Rupert García created his first silkscreen, an image of Marxist revolutionary Che Guevara entitled *Right On!*, in support of the TWLF-led strike at San Francisco State. Likewise, upon entering Berkeley in 1968, Montoya began producing silkscreens for that campus's TWLF. Shaped by the Third World consciousness prevalent in the area, Chicana/o artists resisted narrow nationalist conceptions of *El Movimiento* (or of Aztlán) and instead infused a Third Worldist aesthetic into their work. Both Garcia and Montoya have developed a body of work that has demonstrated consistent support for Third World struggles, as evidenced by Garcia's self-explanatory *¡Fuera de Indochina!* (1970) and *Benefit for the New People's Army* (1978), a poster done for the revolutionary KDP (Union of Democratic Pilipinos) based out of San Francisco. The internationalism of Montoya can equally be witnessed in such titles as *Viet Nam Aztlán* (1972), *STOP! Wells Fargo Bank Loans to Chile* (1979*), Recognize the People's Republic of Angola!* (1976), *Angola Lives!* (1979), and *A Free Palestine* (1989). Out of *La Misión* emerged artistic institutions to support and nurture this form of cultural activism, such as Galería de La Raza and La Raza Silkscreen Center/La Raza Graphics.[28]

Though the theme of Third World solidarity within the Chicana/o Arts Movement is lauded by scholars and activists, less attention has been paid to the related Third Worldist political organizations, such as Los Siete, which actively practiced in local communities what musicians and artists sought to represent and promote in their art. Yet, long before becoming internationally renowned artists, Montoya, Garcia, and Yolanda Lopez cut their political teeth either working with, or within, campus TWLFs. Yolanda Lopez, for instance, continued her political activism as a member of Los Siete, discovering her artistic voice in an organization that was shaped by the Mission District but guided by the same radical precepts animating Third Worldist organizations in other communities of color.

***

In this way I'd like to highlight the *improvisational* nature of culture itself. Rather than something which is handed down—vertically—from generation to generation, fixed and unchanging, subject to the dualistic forces of assimilation or cultural preservation, the oppositional Third World consciousness—and culture— in *La Misión*, and the broader City, reveals how working-class, racially-oppressed peoples—drawing horizontally—have constructed something entirely new out of the crucible of their lived experiences. Further, this must be understood as more than a mechanistic response to a negative set of circumstances. Though forged out of the harsh material conditions of the inner-city, this new consciousness is, first and foremost, an expression of the human impulse to not only survive, but to create, commune, celebrate, and maintain a sense of human dignity and spirit. "For us" Yolanda Lopez remembers, "it wasn't just the politics, it was the *culture*.... It just filled the air, and that colored Los Siete tremendously...that kind of convergence."

Thus, radicals of color sought out and developed a political and cultural framework that made sense to them; it reflected something they knew, namely that Black and Brown and Yellow and Red San Franciscans were connected, by buses, by schools, by neighborhoods, by cultures, and ultimately by histories. So Third Worldism was not a desperate, last ditch, attempt to link with people thousands of miles away for the purposes of making liberals or White people feel bad. Nor was it a mere tactical choice to ally with other groups in order to leverage position with the dominant society. Rather, it reflected an evolving and considered response to peoples' changing conditions *born out of their own life experiences*. The oppositional consciousness represented in the Third World coexisted, intersected with, and built upon other dynamic identities. The occupation of Alcatraz, for instance, concretized a process by which different indigenous peoples/nations, such as the Dine, Lakota Sioux, Mohawk, and Klamath peoples, identified in pan-Indian terms. Shaped by 500 years of colonialism, people from diverse backgrounds, speaking different languages and inheriting distinct cultural traditions, promoted a new identity while *still* maintaining their previous sense of self. Likewise, in Chinatown/Manilatown, the struggle to defend the International Hotel reflected and contributed to the development of an Asian-American identity and culture. And, as mentioned earlier, Los Siete clearly promoted a pan-Latino identity—*Raza*—as they developed their social praxis in the working-class Mission District community.

To conclude then, the political and cultural radicalism embodied in Los Siete reveals that—in San Francisco during the late 1960s and early '70s—a radical crossing of borders—even a blurring of borders—took place between both communities and movements. It reflects a process by which activists of color dialectically formed an expanded sense of identity through both political struggle and the articulation of a new set of transformative politics. As a result, a new "community" was formed, a new identity was envisioned as activists re-oriented themselves not only to one another in their respective neighborhoods, but also in relation to the country and the rest of the world.

I would like to briefly highlight two important implications of this "community of resistance." First, contrary to scholars who predict an inevitable rise in conflict between communities of color, I submit we need not be afraid of the dramatic demographic changes that are re-shaping California and the nation.[29] There is nothing "natural" or "inevitable" about interracial conflict. In fact, there have been other moments in history—such as the period of I've been describing—when, within a political economy marked by deindustrialization and strained public resources, communities of color converged and constructed social and political relationships on the basis of cooperation and solidarity, instead of competition and conflict.[30] One essential ingredient, however, will be education; an education—such as that offered within Ethnic Studies—which is both critical and comparative. Mason Wong, from the TWLF at San Francisco State, put it this way in an interview after the Third World Strike of 1968-69, "The main idea of Third World Studies is to get Third World people to begin to work with each other…to stop fighting among each other and to get together…Every student will be required to take courses outside his own department."[31] This is as important today as forty years ago. The second implication of remembering Los Siete lies in the realization that unity is only developed within the context of struggle. Unity (either within communities of color or between them) is not something we can patiently await to arrive someday; instead, it is something that can *only develop in struggle*. Los Siete and the Black Panther Party—though they valued and placed a high priority on the concept of Third World unity—only made that idea a material force by *working together*. Struggle builds trust and understanding between groups. Multiracial unity, therefore, is more than a goal, it is a process to commit to and engage with. In a poem entitled "Canto de Liberacion Pa' [Los Siete],"Vargas writes:

*Extend your arm*  
*To the multitude of humanity*  
*In the name of love and mutual defense*  
*Plant the seeds of consciousness*

*Extiende tus brazos*  
*a las multitudes humanas*  
*en nombre de amor y defensa mutual*  
*planta las cemillas del conscientimiento*

*And raise the spear of liberation*  
*Because with open eyes/hands*  
*The chains (loosen)*  
*¡ y el tiempoesya!*  
*¡y el tiempoesya!*

*y levanta la espada de liberacion*  
*que con ojos/ manosdispiertas*  
*lascadenas (aflojan)*  
*¡y el tiempoesya!*  
*¡y el tiempoesya!*[32]

## Notes

Oral history interviews were conducted by the author with Roger Alvarado (July 29, 2002), Donna Amador (July 25, 2002), Paul Harris (July 24, 2002), Yolanda Lopez (June 24, 2002), Maria Elena Ramirez (May 31 and June 14, 2002), and Al Robles (May 5, 2002). Where quotes in the article are uncited, they are derived from these interviews.

1.  *May Day*, videocassette, produced and directed by Newsreel, (1969); "Chairman Bobby Speaks at May Day Rally to Free Huey," *Black Panther*, May 11, 1969, 11.

2.  "2000 March at Newton Hearing," *San Francisco Examiner*, May 1, 1969, 5; "No Decision on Newton—Big Rally," *San Francisco Chronicle*, May 2, 1969, 1, 26; "SF Huey Day big rally, no bail—yet," *The Guardian*, May 10, 1969, 3.

3.  Making the absurd claim that Roger Alvarado was a "flight risk" the judge ordered him held without bail, thereby forcing Alvarado to spend nearly a month in jail. Of course, the unofficial objective for his detention had been accomplished: the neutralization of Movement leadership. For public evidence of this repressive legal strategy, see "The Mulford Gap," *San Francisco Chronicle*, February 6, 1969, in which "law and order" Assemblyman Don Mulford from Oakland warned California judges (especially from the Bay Area) that they would face "heavily financed opposition" come re-election time if they failed to punish demonstrators to the fullest extent of the law; "SF Huey Day big rally, no bail—yet," *The Guardian*, May 10, 1969, 3.

4.  Of course White radicals played a part in the fight against racism and imperialism, but communities of color, based upon their common experiences growing up on the receiving end of racial (and cultural) oppression, approached the Third World movement from a fundamentally different position; put another way, their relation to an "imagined" community of the Third World differed in basic ways. These distinctions played themselves out publicly when White radicals confronted the question, beyond providing assistance to Third World groups struggling for "self-determination" and "liberation": What should the role of White revolutionaries be in relation to organizing White communities? One early expression, of course, was the Young Patriots, a radical White organization composed of Appalachian youth that joined together with the BPP and Puerto Rican Young Lords Organization in Chicago to form the first so-called Rainbow Coalition. See Ron Jacobs, *The Way the Wind Blew: A History of the Weather Underground* (New York: Verso Press, 1997), and for the attempt to build a multiracial communist movement, see the excellent book by Max Elbaum, *Revolution in the Air: Sixties Radicals Turn to Lenin, Mao, and Che* (London: Verso Press, 2002).

5.  Donna Amador. "The Third World Liberation Movement and the Rise of Latino Power," in *The Whole World's Watching: Peace and Social Justice Movements of the 1960s & 1970s,* ed. Berkeley Art Center Association (Berkeley: Berkeley Art Center Association, 2001) 84–85.

6.  These seven young men were Jose Rios, Gary "Pinky" Lescallet, Danilo "Bebe" Melendez, Nelson Rodriguez, and real-life brothers Tony and Mario Martinez. George "Gio" Lopez, the seventh, was never apprehended but was tried in abstentia. For the story of the trial, see Marjorie Heins, *Strictly Ghetto Property: The Story of Los Siete de La Raza* (Berkeley: Ramparts Press, 1972).

7.  Ralph Ruiz and others, for instance, drew upon their personal contacts from the Third World student struggle at the College of San Mateo (such as Japanese-American activist Warren Furutani), while Alvarado and Amador utilized their close relations with members of the Black Panther Party, Pilipino activists beginning to organize around the International Hotel, and Native American students, such as Richard Oakes, from San Francisco State College.

8.  Emily Gurnon, "Enduring Legacy of 'Los Siete,'" *San Francisco Examiner*, April 30, 1999.

9.  Further complicating the City's fiscal situation were the deep cuts in state spending (health care, education, welfare, housing assistance) by then-Governor Ronald Reagan. For a revealing analysis of California's

pivotal role in the rise of the New Right, see Mike Davis, "The New Right's Road to Power," in *Prisoners of the American Dream: Politics and Economy in the History of the US Working Class* (London: Verso Press, 1986), 157-180; Census data quoted in Brian J. Godfrey, *Neighborhoods in Transition: The Making of San Francisco's Ethnic and Nonconformist Communities* (Berkeley: University of California Press, 1988), 97.

10. A close relationship, in fact, existed between the City's school system and hostilities with the police in that students of color, mostly living in poverty-stricken neighborhoods with under-funded and culturally incompetent schools, experienced a high drop-out (more appropriately, push-out) rate, and therefore, without any recreational facilities or meaningful employment to absorb them, many turned to hanging-out in "the streets," which set them squarely in the sights of racist police officers on patrol; for reference to keeping the "jungle at bay," see Gurnon, "Enduring Legacy,'" *San Francisco Examiner,* April 30, 1999.

11. Heins, *Strictly Ghetto Property,* 73.

12. For details related to Paul McGoran's record of abuse see File-Investigation (McGoran), carton 11, Legal Files, Charles Garry Collection, Bancroft Library, University of California at Berkeley. As the lead attorney for Los Siete de La Raza, Garry did research into the history of McGoran and found he was quite cognizant of his notorious reputation amongst communities of color. In a paranoid letter to his ex-wife dated October 31, 1968 (six months before Brodnick's fatal day), McGoran asked if she could promptly return his personal gun, stating, "I know I am going to be a target. I had a dandy run-in with the Reverend Jesse James of the Mission Rebels. He came back with four of his nigger friends looking for me....So if you still have the rifle I may have some use for it in the line of self-preservation." Then, indicating something of his personal relationship, he added, "Maybe it's too much to ask. You wanted to put a bullet in me yourself, now maybe someone else will do it for you." As well, these two officers had experiences patrolling local college campuses during the wave of student strikes led by the TWLF.

13. For their part, the Crusade for Justice and *El Grito* proved to be of assistance in other important ways. "Gio" Lopez, the only member of Los Siete de La Raza never to be apprehended by police, went underground after May 1st. Eventually, after evading police in Northern California in September of 1969, he turned up in Denver where he briefly worked with the Crusade for Justice under the pseudonym 'Juan Gomez.' Thereafter, he lived in a rural New Mexico collective, before finally hijacking a DC-8 plane on July 1st, 1970 from Las Vegas to Cuba, the epicenter of revolutionary Third World politics in the Western hemisphere. "Brodnick Case Suspect Held, Freed in Error," *San Francisco Chronicle,* October 5, 1969; on his experiences with the Crusade for Justice, see Ernesto B. Vigil, *The Crusade for Justice: Chicano Militancy and the Government's War on Dissent,* (Madison: University of Wisconsin Press, 1999) 100-103; on the hijacking, see *National Advisory Committee on Criminal Justice Standards and Goals. Task Force on Disorder and Terrorism, Disorders and Terrorism: Report of the Task Force on Disorders and Terrorism* (Washington, DC, 1976); According to Amador, upon his arrival in Cuba, "Gio" Lopez shed his "street person, crazy boy attitude," got an education and eventually became a university professor in Cuba. He still resides and teaches there today.

14. Heins, *Strictly Ghetto Property,* 161; Charles Garry and Art Goldberg, *Streetfighter in the Courtroom: The People's Advocate* (New York: E.P. Dutton, 1977), esp. chaps. 5 and 7. With Garry as lead attorney, Los Siete de La Raza were acquitted in November 1970. Unfortunately, in an otherwise fascinating autobiography, Garry neglects to recount his courtroom experience in the Los Siete de La Raza trial. For the most detailed account of the trial, based on court transcripts and interviews, see Heins, *Strictly Ghetto Property.*

15. While Los Siete no longer exists, Real Alternatives Project (RAP) continues to work with working-class youth of color in the Mission District.

16. "Los Siete de La Raza," (internal document, Los Siete, November 1969), Yolanda Lopez Collection, 4.

17. Dwight Scott to "Brothers," file—Contributions to Defense and Expense, carton 11, (n.d.) Garry Collection.

18. Rodolfo Martinez to "Our Black Brothers and Sisters," file-Press and Publicity, carton 11 (mimeo, n.d.) Garry Collection,

19. "Third World," *Basta Ya!,* 1, no. 2 (July 1969)

20. Steve Louie and Glenn Omatsu, *Asian Americans: The Movement and the Moment* (Los Angeles: UCLA Asian American Studies Center Press, 2001), 7.

21. Karl Marx, "Preface to A Contribution to the Critique of Political Economy," in *The Marx-Engels Reader,* ed. Robert C. Tucker (New York: Norton, 1978; 2nd edition), 4.

22. To varying degrees, these types of interactions did occur in other areas (even Los Angeles), but Amador is correct in recognizing the uniqueness of San Francisco.

23. Indeed, a ride on San Francisco's 22 MUNI Line, from one end to the other, takes a passenger from Bayview/Hunter's Point through Potrero Hill into the Mission District, along 16th Street (which, at the time, was known as the "Little Rez," the heart of the City's Native American community), down through the Fillmore/Western Addition, and ends up winding through Chinatown.

24. Describing a similar process underway in Oakland, BPP Chief of Staff David Hilliard explains, "the internationalism [of the Black Panther Party] is emphasized by the fact that Oakland, like Mobile, is an

integrated community. You don't simply find whites and blacks, but yellows, browns, Native Americans too. New York is famous for its many ethnic communities. But I'm surprised at how groups don't mix: the city is multiracial, not intraracial....[W]hen the young people of Oakland crowd the park...the array of skin shades is beautiful and impressive." Though racial segregation did/does exist in Oakland, his overall observation is right on point. David Hilliard, *This Side of Glory: The Autobiography of Daivd Hilliard and the Story of the Black Panther Party* (Boston: Little, Brown and Company, 1993), 68.

25.   Roberto Vargas, *Nicaragua, Yo Te Canto Besos, Balas, y Sueños de Libertad: Poems* (San Francisco: Editorial Pocho-Che, 1980), 18-23.

26.   Maria Elena's earlier observation that "we're so mixed already anyway" affirms recent scholarship by Robin D.G. Kelley and Vijay Prashad regarding the polycultural—not multicultural—world we live in. Prashad explains the distinction: "a polyculturalist sees the world constituted by the interchange of cultural forms, while multiculturalism (in most incarnations) sees the world as already constituted by different (and discrete) cultures that we can place into categories and study with respect." Vijay Prashad, *Everybody Was Kung Fu Fighting: Afro-Asian Connections and the Myth of Cultural Purity* (Boston: Beacon Press, 2001), 66-67. Therefore, in relation to Black cultural politics, Kelley concludes, "All of us, and I mean ALL of us, are the inheritors of European, African, Native American, and even Asian pasts, even if we can't exactly trace our blood lines to all of these continents. While this may seem obvious, for some people it's a dangerous concept....To acknowledge our polycultural heritage and cultural dynamism is not to give up our black identity or our love and concern for black people. It does mean expanding our definition of blackness, taking our history more seriously, and looking at the rich diversity within us with new eyes." Robin D.G. Kelley, "People in Me," *Color Lines* 1, no. 3 (Winter 1999), 5-7. Likewise, in considering her recent trip to Spain, scholar-activist Elizabeth Martinez writes of the complicated polyrhythms (though she doesn't explicitly use this term) comprising *Raza*, "When Raza speak of being a mix of indigenous people, invading Spaniards, and enslaved Africans—which is certainly true—we rarely remember that Spain itself was a very mixed nation. We rarely remember our Arab roots or think about what they mean. We don't even know that the very word Raza comes from the Arab ras, meaning head of, or beginning of, a lineage.... Filled with contradictions, my visit [to Spain] ended in an exciting certainty about the need to stretch our minds beyond what's assumed." Elizabeth "Betita" Martinez, "A Chicana in Spain: Remembering our Arab Roots," *Color Lines* (Spring 2001), 34-36.

27.   Significantly, the other major band laying the soundtrack for the urban Chicano experience of the late 1960s and 1970s was the Los Angeles-based group War, a predominantly African-American jazz-funk (Danish-born Lee Oskar was the exception) group hailing from Long Beach, California. With songs like "Lowrider," "The Cisco Kid," "Cinco de Mayo," "The World is A Ghetto," and "Slippin' into Darkness," the sounds of War reflected both the cultural and political currents of the era. Chicano comedian George Lopez uses "Lowrider" as the theme song for his show, invoking its lasting sonic force in the celebration of Chicano identity. Historian Daniel Widenor at UC San Diego is currently working on a project which, in part, explores the complex cultural interactions between Chicana/o and Black artistic communities of Los Angeles in the 1960s. My thanks to him for his insight on this subject.

28.   Carol A. Wells, "La Lucha Sigüe: From East Los Angeles to the Middle East," in ¿*Just Another Poster? Chicano Graphic Arts in California*, ed. Chon A. Noriega (Santa Barbara: University Art Museum, 2001) 171-201. Wells' article is an excellent survey of internationalist posters arising out of the Chicano Arts Movement, correcting the faulty perception that Chicana/o artists were only engaged in cultural nationalist iconography and politics; yet, she fails (and admittedly it is an overview) to historically contextualize the artistic production under review, thereby overlooking the glaring fact that a majority of the pieces she discusses originated in Northern California. Third World Communications, ed., *Third World Women* (San Francisco: Third World Communications, 1972) and Editorial Pocho-Ché, ed., *Time to Greez! Incantations from the Third World*, (San Francisco: Glide Publications and Third World Communications, 1975).

29.   A flurry of print has appeared in newspapers and magazines over the years describing Black-Brown tensions. This cynical perspective is best outlined in Nick Vaca's *The Presumed Alliance: The Unspoken Conflict Between Latinos and Blacks and What It Means for America* (New York: Rayo, 2004).

30.   My argument is not that tensions do not exist between communities of color, but rather that their existence is perpetuated by the inadequate framework or political lens with which we interpret and deal with them. In other words, it is as much a critique of contemporary leadership within communities of color as anything else. Recent organizing, however, while not reported on with same fascination in the mainstream press, demonstrates that grassroots activists in both communities are increasingly making those connections and building key relationships. David Bacon, "Black and Brown Together," *The American Prospect*, March 2008. http://www.prospect.org/cs/articles?article=black_and_brown_together

31.   "Strike Over But Struggle Goes On," *The Movement*, May 1969, 14-15.

32.   Roberto Vargas. "Canto de Liberacion," in *Primeros Cantos* (San Francisco: Ediciones Pocho-Ché, 1971), 16-17.

# "All Those Who Care About The Mission, Stand Up With Me!"
## Latino Community Formation and the MCO

### by Tomás F. Summers Sandoval, Jr.

"We are mainly a Latin American community which is proud of its heritage," proclaimed Ben Martinez at the second annual convention of the Mission Coalition Organization (MCO). Standing before more than 800 community leaders—collectively representing 81 local civil rights, labor, church, and community organizations—Martinez publicly recognized the new dominant racial/ethnic group in the Mission as the foundation of coalition-building. "But this is also a mixed community," he continued, "and I know that the Samoan, the Black, the Italian, the Irish, the Filipino, the American Indian, the Anglo, and every other group in this community is proud of its heritage." Speaking as president of the MCO in October 1969, Martinez had already overseen a growth in membership, programs, and public reputation for the fledgling organization. Now, hoping for more success, he addressed a looming limitation to the collective and grassroots effort of this poor, diverse neighborhood. "It is in our interest to recognize the identity each of us has, and then to go from that point to developing a working program that will meet all of our interests."[1]

Beginning in 1967, the largely working-class, heavily immigrant, and decidedly multiracial neighborhood of the Mission District underwent a profound transformation. Incited by the specter of urban redevelopment, and set against the backdrop of local movements for racial justice, this multigenerational population of both the politically-active and previously uninvolved came together under the common cause of community as embodied in the MCO. Called the "largest urban popular mobilization in San Francisco's recent history," they united for jobs, housing, education reform, and the power to implement their collective vision.[2] In the process, they asserted a powerful sense of *cultural citizenship*, "of claiming what is their own, of defending it, and of drawing sustenance and strength from that defense."[3] By 1973, when the formal organization declined, the Mission remained a far more cohesive community than it was before, reshaping their sense of collective identity in fundamental ways.

Designed as a grassroots, multi-issue coalition composed of scores of local organizations, the MCO actively involved 12,000 residents who sought democratic control over their neighborhood on behalf of the more than 70,000 people who lived there. At its height, the MCO became an institutional force, both the recognized voice of the district in political circles and the local group controlling funds from the Model Cities Program—a 1966 community development effort by the federal government mandating citizen participation. Through an assortment of programs and campaigns, they made lasting and meaningful changes to the infrastructure of everyday life for both contemporary and succeeding generations of local residents. The legacy of the MCO—balanced on a multiracial and working-class population successfully claiming rights and ownership over their neighborhood—

extends beyond the programmatic. In the ways it envisioned its collective effort, and integrated and deployed the racial/ethnic diversity of the Mission, the MCO nurtured a collective community identity within the population largely of Latin American descent. As a result, they recreated the historic community identity of the Mission District, substantively rooting a hybrid and shifting form of class-based *latinidad* in the neighborhood, an identity which continues to shape its present in myriad ways.

In the spring of 1966, the cause of urban renewal served as the catalyst for this transformation. On the surface, the Mission seemed an ideal candidate for renewal, or publicly-funded development to cure urban blight. By mid-decade, however, the promise of federal dollars for local redevelopment created a backlash within poor and working-class communities in the City. An urban renewal project in the Western Addition, rather than improving life for the primarily Black, working-class residents, resulted in massive dislocation, leaving the area's core surrounded with vacant lots, public housing units, and a growing crime rate. Widely studied as an example of failed urban planning, and popularly understood as urban *removal*, by the 1960s the bureaucratic buzzwords of "urban redevelopment" incited fear among the City's communities of color. Not surprisingly, when rumors of a proposed study by the San Francisco Redevelopment Agency (SFRA) circulated through the Mission, constituencies as seemingly disparate as landlord and tenant found a common ground of opposition.

In 1966 the SFRA secured funds for a study of the "Mission Street Corridor," the core of the district where BART construction would be located. Almost immediately, local property and business groups organized their opposition. Led by realtor Mary Hall and self-described "right-wing populist" Jack Bartalini, the conservative group included longtime homeowners' associations like the Potrero Hill Boosters, East Mission Improvement Association, and Noe Valley Improvement Club, in addition to local merchants. Each feared the proposed clearance of deteriorating properties and the forced relocation of businesses, labeling the downtown-led redevelopment "creeping socialism."[4]

Bartalini and Hall spoke for constituencies with political clout but a diminishing presence in the Mission. These mostly White, propertied residents with long roots in the district had been joined in the previous decade by a multiracial mix of migrants, most with roots in Latin America. Local officials and the press noticed the growth of the Spanish-speaking population at roughly the same time as the growing exodus of White ethnics and declining conditions in the Mission, leading some to suggest the two were connected. One local resident expressed the views of many when he described the Mission as "running down something awful. Twenty years ago, my wife and I used to stroll around the block after supper, but the streets aren't safe at night anymore." To others, the newcomers represented the future potential of the neighborhood, informing formal efforts to assure "they'll want to stay."[5] Indeed, in the eyes of many informal leaders of the neighborhood, the multiracial population embodied the strength that had always marked the Mission's past. As one local priest put it, "whether they were Spanish-speaking, English-speaking, or they came from Nicaragua or Guatemala—whatever part of the world—they were neighbors."[6]

Though few noticed, the "new" Mission had already begun addressing the issues of working-class renters in a neighborhood in structural decline. These Latin

American organizational efforts also helped constitute the collective voice of the new majority in the struggle against redevelopment. For their constituencies, the prospect of urban renewal was mixed—it meant the possibility of new jobs in both construction and subsequent business and commercial development, but at a potentially fatal cost. Even the SFRA estimated the "improvement activities" would result in the displacement of "1,900 families and 1,300 single individuals."[7] When coupled with the known outcome of earlier development plans, leaders of Latin American descent knew that any future their constituencies had in the City depended on their ability to organize an effective opposition. Just such a coalition began to emerge when organizations—all in some way committed to empowerment of the Latin American community—began to craft a unified voice for the Spanish-speaking.

The Latino wing of the opposition included groups like the local chapter of the Community Service Organization (CSO), a statewide, grassroots Mexican-American group with a presence in the City since the 1950s. One of their local leaders, Herman Gallegos, was perhaps the most respected Latino voice in the City at the time. While still a part of the CSO, Gallegos helped establish OBECA/ Arriba Juntos, a pro-integration effort "to prepare Hispano Americans to enter the job market." Based out of Catholic Charities, the group's other leader— Leandro Soto—had begun helping Latinos connect their needs to federal efforts as part of the War on Poverty. Their interests were further served by groups like: the Mexican American Political Association (MAPA) and the League of Latin American Citizens (LULAC), both decidedly political organizations; the Catholic Council for the Spanish Speaking, an institutional effort holding some influence in this decidedly Catholic town; and the Mexican American Unity Council, Puerto Rican Club of San Francisco, and others dedicated to cultural, educational, and civic endeavors. As established and respected organizations, each added credibility to the anti-redevelopment movement, as did leaders like Gallegos, perhaps *the* informal representative for the Spanish-speaking in local politics.

Other groups also lent support, further suggesting the depth of local opposition. Local labor—who theoretically had much to gain from redevelopment—added another base of anti-redevelopment support. The Mission's most prominent union was the Building and Construction Workers Union, Local 261; their support came most visibly via Abel Gonzalez, head of the union caucus Centro Social Obrero. Focusing on service issues for the Spanish-speaking population in the union, the Obreros had made a name for themselves through their popular English-language classes and citizenship programs. The Catholic Church remained a force in both neighborhood and citywide politics. Many of the City's priests, committed to a philosophy of social change, viewed support for the poor as synonymous to their religious ideal of service. Protestant churches, overcome by a progressive mission mentality, were already involved in local race politics, seeking to improve the material conditions of life in the City's ghettos and barrios. Reverend William R. Grace, director of the Department of Urban Work in the Presbyterian Church, sought social change by implementing the grassroots model for change designed by Saul Alinsky. Grace's assistant, Reverend David Knotts, already worked as a minister in the Mission.

Serving as a counterbalance to the conservative alliance represented by Bartalini and Hall, the Mission's radical Left—consistently dedicated to fighting for the rights of the local poor—added another oppositional voice to the diverse mix. Skeptical of government-sponsored community development and proponents of mobilizing communities for their own control, the Progressive Labor (PL) Party worked to create a meaningful movement for change among the district's poor. Led by John Ross, and finding organizational and representational focus in the Mission Tenants' Union (MTU), their neighborhood influence flowered as they became widely-known as a credible voice for the rights of poor renters. As evidence of their success, despite their espoused dedication to a Marxist ideal, even politically-moderate church leaders sent their parishioners to the MTU when experiencing problems with their landlords.

Individually, each organization represented a slice of the Mission District. Joined together under the threat of redevelopment, they left few recognizable constituencies unrepresented. This unlikely merging of the neighborhood's political and demographic diversity began in earnest when Bartalini called Ross. Revs. Grace and Knotts also saw the issue as a potential catalyst for a broad-based community movement. These varied efforts culminated in 1966 with the creation of the Mission Council on Redevelopment (MCOR). Though Bartalini and Hall demanded MCOR stand unequivocally opposed to the SFRA plans, the organizational base was more interested in creating an authentic representational body whose voice City Hall could not ignore. Only in that way could residents control their neighborhood's future. To preserve that possibility, they did not oppose urban renewal, but instead sought the power of the veto over its local manifestation. Recognizing that goal could only be met if they legitimately represented their neighborhood, MCOR recruited the Catholic network, the Obreros, block clubs and tenants' associations, Protestant churches, and various Latino organizations.

MCOR represented the authentic diversity of the Mission, inclusive of poor and middle class, propertied and renter, Catholic and Protestant, and the multiracial population who called it home. The Mission Renewal Commission—comprised of large, local merchants—represented the lone, local voice supporting urban renewal. Consistently asking, "Where am I in this picture?" as plans progressed, MCOR demanded everyday people be considered as redevelopment came before the Mission and, later, the Board of Supervisors. Though the homeowners left MCOR in opposition to their willingness to negotiate, and the Obreros and other labor groups provided only minimal support, MCOR emerged successful in the early winter. When Mayor Shelley could not accede to an MCOR veto, the group sought to scuttle any redevelopment efforts. In December 1966, faced with the overwhelming opposition of most of the community, the Board of Supervisors squashed renewal.[8]

Once they won the Board's vote, MCOR—organized as a single-issue coalition—ceased activity in early 1967. The Mission, however, still confronted the fundamental issues inciting the city's redevelopment crusade. In one square mile tract, representing the heart of the district, more than 2,000 units out of 15,000 were classified as deteriorating. Two hundred and sixty-two homes were listed as dilapidated. Local groups estimated that by the mid-1960s only 20% of the residents owned their own home. Additionally, residents confronted an inadequate education system, a lack of jobs and job training, and no effective political voice. Local grassroots organizers, in particular those focused on Latinos, sought to sustain the level of activism beyond MCOR. Single-issue and diffuse campaigns garnered some attention and success, notably revealing an emerging, new leadership. A young Latina named Elba Tuttle rose up in the Mission Area Community Action Board (MACABI). Martinez achieved prominence within the OBECA group. Reflective of the growth of Latino labor, Gonzalez and the Obreros helped secure the electoral victory of Mayor Joseph Alioto. As the War on Poverty began to provide funds for varied community efforts, community members also nurtured their political and organizational development. The lack of a cohesive effort, however, as well as growing conflicts over federal funds, revealed the deep fissures which remained due to the divisions of race, nationality, and generations. Mission activists were learning that "overcoming poverty is not simply a matter of political will; it is and has become even more one of political structure."[9]

The potential for structure seen in MCOR's organizing strategies presented itself again in February 1968 at the Spanish-Speaking Issues Conference sponsored by MACABI. Mayor Alioto, speaking before the group, suggested he would seek Model Cities funds if a "broad-based group representative of the Mission" so desired.[10] The Model Cities Program—part of the Demonstration Cities and Metropolitan Development Act of 1966—provided funds for community improvements ranging from structural development to issues like housing, education, employment, and health. Realizing the potential for a more sustained grassroots coalition, Rev. Knotts, Tuttle, Martinez, and others took the lead. By June 1968, a coalition of about 25 groups formed, calling themselves Temporary Mission Coalition Organization (TMCO).*

Several key principles guided the MCO. First, it strove to be a multi-issue organization. Another was the principle of democracy, suggested by several structural elements such as a steering committee, which met weekly; a monthly council meeting; and an annual convention of member organizations. They remained dedicated to nonviolence, hoping to utilize the full tactical range of the Civil Rights Movement. Finally, they believed they could only succeed if they were representative. The commitment to a broad-based movement meant any and all identifiable constituencies in the Mission must be allowed to join. That meant making room for organizations with varied membership bases, as well as clear constituencies without active organizational outlets. They needed to represent the diversity of the Mission, a neighborhood composed of Central Americans (Nicaraguans and Salvadorans being the largest two groups, followed by ethnic Mexicans), Puerto Ricans, and South Americans, as well as Irish, Italian, German, Russian, Filipino, Native American/Indian, Samoan, and African-American constituencies. Organizers began their work of mobilizing support for the MCO's inaugural convention, carefully strategizing to unify a cosmopolitan neighborhood.

As the first mass meeting of the MCO, the convention would foster their democratic ideal by providing for the selection of officials, committees, and bylaws. But it could only work if a representative group showed up. As the organizing group's leader, Martinez sought to harness the support of labor, who had only been lukewarm participants in MCOR. Exploiting his close ties to Gonzalez, he recruited the Obreros, and Local 261 also provided financial support. Tuttle and John McReynolds focused on organizing the grassroots constituencies for the convention. Mike Miller—with connections to Saul Alinsky and experience in SNCC—was hired as the full-time community organizer. The United Presbyterian Church donated money and staff support, in the assignment of Rev. Knotts. The Roman Catholic Archdiocese of the city was also on board. Though diverse, like MCOR, the MCO relied on a broad Latino organizational base.

At the first convention, in October 1968, over sixty organizations participated, representing an attendance of between six and seven hundred. Almost immediately, the gathering exposed the tensions within the district. Seemingly a debate on political tactics, the tensions also exposed a generational divide. Established and fairly mainstream organizations sought control over Model Cities funds, a status only assured if the city recognized the MCO as the legitimate representative in the district. To a varied youth contingent empowered by local, radical politics, this suggested a kind of reformism out of step with meaningful change. Groups like the Mission Rebels in Action, for example—an active youth-serving agency— embodied a militant posture. Seeing convention leaders as "sell-outs," the Rebels took to the stage during the proceedings, seized the microphone, and called the gathering a "farce." As the *San Francisco Chronicle* reported, the Rebels then tried to nominate their own platform of leaders.[11] While their tactics upset most in the audience—especially those who knew the group was partially funded by the Equal Oppportunity Commission and, hence, part of the aid bureaucracy in the Mission—the group did manage to stall the agenda.

The convention might have ended in disarray if not for the fortuitous scheduling of keynote speaker Cesar Chavez. Too ill to attend the meeting in person and confined to a hospital bed, Chavez spoke by telephone to the crowd. Quieting the room, Chavez addressed the need for collaboration, inadvertently diffusing the confrontation. Promoting a hybrid ethnic/racial identity infused with class sensibilities, Chavez cautioned against the disabling effects of in-fighting and inaction:

> The poor have much in common, common dreams and desires
> of social justice. The question of goals should not be a problem.
> The question that kills coalitions is the inability to take that first
> step in the most common causes, and that is, to determine who is
> an adversary...La Raza to me was the whole human race.[12]

His plea did not move everyone, as Mission Rebels leader Jesse James took to the microphone once again and proclaimed, "You're being used again and you don't even know it." Accusing MCO leadership of being an inauthentic voice he said, "You're speaking about community and you don't even live here."

Sensing a favorable response to Chavez's words, Gallegos, moderator of the convention, challenged James to work in the spirit of cooperation. According to local reports, he then chastised the Rebels, saying, "a lot of people out here want a better place to live and you're not letting them." In a simple yet moving articulation of common cause and interrelation, he shouted, "All those who care about the Mission, stand up with me!" The convention majority took to their feet, effectively neutralizing the Rebels. They agreed to a compromise, allowing last-minute nominations from the floor. The convention proceeded, electing officers, committees, and bylaws. The organizational platform was tabled to a later meeting.

Unwilling to support the organization, the Mission Rebels remained in small company. Composed primarily of Black youth, with some Latinos, whites, and Samoans, the Rebels could not envision cooperation beyond their own organizational interests. Other constituency groups also disagreed with the MCO vision but stayed and participated. Members of the PL Party, for example, whose Mission Tenants' Union took decidedly radical stances, objected to the use of conciliatory language in the MCO platform, but worked for compromise. Others who disagreed with the MCO never attended, such as the various homeowners' associations represented by Bartalini and Hall.

The second half of the convention concluded in November 1968. There, the MCO solidified an organizational structure and established a platform, all while the heated debate reached a provisional consensus. The PL Party continued to voice concern over some of platform resolutions, wanting a more forcefully militant language along with a list of direct issues to focus the MCO's work. The compromise came with the agreed use of moderate language while adopting the platform of advocating tenants' rights, reducing unemployment, improving police-community relations, and attending to various education issues. Another disagreement arose over the stance on Model Cities, with the conference leadership advocating a desired participatory stance. Embodying the majority's agreement, the convention approved a thirteen point platform outlining future Model Cities involvement. The platform included the demand for absolute veto power within the Model Cities program and the right to name two-thirds of the Model Cities Neighborhood Corporation—a 21 member representative body charged with making decisions as demanded by the federal requirement for community participation. Veto power meant the MCO could stop any redevelopment effort it thought adversely affected the community. The demand for two-thirds control meant the ability of the MCO to exert absolute community control over federal funds. As the staff organizer Mike Miller remarked, "The lesson of words vs. real power was yet to be observed."

Even considering the non-participation of certain Mission District interests, the foundational convention of the MCO emboldened the hundreds of participants. With 24 year-old president Martinez at the helm, the Coalition began the work of organizing the community into a mass movement as they sought to meaningfully address community issues and secure local control of Model Cities funds. As Martinez framed it, "We don't want the money unless we in the Mission have a major voice in how it will be spent."[13] This commitment to self-determination— described by Martinez as "the opposite of colonialism, which is a system in which someone else says he knows what is best for you and in which he has the power to make you do what he thinks is best for you. We want to decide what is best for us"—came with the participation of now more than 80 local organizations and nearly a thousand residents by its second convention. In less than a year, the MCO would become one of the most effective community coalitions in US history as they got to work addressing neighborhood needs while mobilizing for a head-to-head battle with the Board of Supervisors.

Already the generationally-infused political rift between moderate and radical had dominated the first convention. Illustrative of the local assortment of student, antiwar, and racial movements embodying a high degree of coherence between radical ideologies and their practices, youth increasingly professed a politics only minimally finding purchase within the older generation. Additionally, a far more widespread and long-standing tension was comprised of the rivalries between nationalities, in particular the resentment between an ethnic Mexican population (with longer roots in the city) and a more recently arrived Central American population.

Despite representing roughly forty percent of the Latino population in the City, ethnic Mexicans most often occupied positions of greater visibility and power in local politics, much as they did within the Spanish-speaking cultural milieu of the city. Their dominance helped nurture the integration of new migrants from Latin America, whether they came from Mexico or Nicaragua, El Salvador, Guatemala, or Puerto Rico. The high rates of intermarriage within Spanish-speaking populations is testament to the manner in which a more established Spanish-speaking population could "pull everybody together." Indeed, as one resident saw it, when members of her family came to the city in the early twentieth century, they came to a "Mexican America."[14]

By the late 1960s, however, Mexican predominance seemed anachronistic in a Mission District where Salvadoreños and Nicaraguenses combined to form the majority. Prior to the MCO, "it was a fact that Mexican Americans tended to head most of the funded organizations of the Mission."[15] Accordingly, to remain true to its vision, and to strengthen its coalition by addressing potential weaknesses, the MCO would have to create space in its structure for constituencies whose voice might not be best served by an already recognized organ of the community. The solution came via the MCO Steering Committee—composed of the President, seven Executive Vice Presidents, and the various committee chairs—which met weekly as it took responsibility for implementing the action plan of the Convention. Toward the goals of inclusivity and accountability, the delegates created a Vice Presidential position for each racial/ethnic constituency in the Mission, adding an assortment of VPs to the leadership. Always in the service of coalition, the MCO recognized the value of its diversity, reflected in each of the following positions: Mexican, Nicaraguan, Salvadoran, business, national, youth, senior citizens, block clubs, Mexican-American, Central American, South American, Afro-American, Anglo-American, and Filipino-American.

To outsiders, the identified constituency groups might have seemed redundant. From the perspective of an MCO organizer, the community had a tacit understanding of how it worked:

> The understanding was that neither the Nicaraguans nor the Salvadorans would go for the Central American position. Either a Guatemalan or a Honduran would get that. But we couldn't, we didn't want to have a Honduran Vice President, or a Guatemalan Vice President because they were small enough in number that the Salvadorans and Nicaraguans said well if you're going to have a Guatemalan Vice President then we want three…and then… you were going to have a body of sixty or seventy people.[16]

Most significantly, by recognizing the diversity of the Mission, *as understood by the residents of the district,* the MCO positioned their endeavor to be more than symbolically collective. A blanket assertion of "Latin American-ness" (or *latinidad*) would ring hollow in a district where the needs of bilingual Mexican Americans differed between those of Central American immigrants, African-American youth, and Filipino families. Though the MCO certainly embodied a kind of *latinidad*, it did not rely on a limiting definition of who belonged. Unlike a traditional barrio identity, rooted in formal and informal segregation, the MCO's *latinidad* relied on the integration of multiple voices, needs, and identities, coalescing in a collective expression of common cause. At their height, a VP position existed to be filled by Puerto Ricans, Pacific Islanders, Cubans, Europeans, Americans, American Indians,

Irish Americans, Italian Americans, Colombians, and labor. Even clergy had their own Vice President.

Once a representative structure was solidified, the MCO refocused their energies toward that common cause. Indeed, without tangible results, its representative structure would be meaningless. The MCO committees took on the work, functioning like issue-specific, grassroots campaigns. The committees reflected the collective concerns of the MCO, focused on issues like housing, the police, youth, employment, health, and community maintenance. Comprised, as it was, by an assortment of active and effective community organizations—many of which had experience with these issues—an initial wave of success for the MCO was not surprising. Of course, each concrete victory also fostered increased community support, making MCO membership a source of community pride.

Early MCO campaigns sought to create new playgrounds, ban pawn shops on Mission, and convert an adult theater in the neighborhood into a family theater. In each instance, they sought both cosmetic and systemic change, finding creative ways to make their district more responsive to the needs of its family residents. For example, earlier redevelopment in South of Market area pushed some businesses southward to the Mission. One of those businesses was an adult theater whose presence in the neighborhood would have been unheard of in an earlier generation. After unsuccessful negotiations with the owner, the MCO targeted theater patrons, picketing the theater entrance. They handed out fliers declaring their intention to notify the patrons' neighborhoods of their patronage. To add a serious tone to their tactic, members followed theatergoers and took down their license numbers. They even had a nun take photos as customers entered, though her camera had no film.

The Housing Committee focused on absentee landlordism and the local stock of deteriorating housing. Involving respected members of the District—like Father Jim Casey, Elba Tuttle, and Luisa Ezquerro—as well as radical groups like the Progressive Labor Party, the Housing Committee sought meaningful mechanisms for tenants to secure and protect their own rights. The committee began organizing residents to negotiate with landlords, peacefully and respectfully informing property owners of the problems tenants faced as well as suggesting solutions. Meeting every Saturday morning, the committee invited landlords by mimicking the process by which a tenant might be evicted—issuing a first, second, and, if needed, third notice—with each succeeding notice communicating a harsher tone:

> So you'd get your first notice…very polite, "We would like to meet with you, please call us." If we don't hear from you within a week, second notice, "Please call us within three days." If you don't call us within three days, third notice, "If we don't hear from you within forty-eight hours, we will take further appropriate action." It didn't say what the further appropriate action was.[17]

When a landlord appeared, the committee tried to negotiate a solution. If the landlord ignored them, or failed to appear at an agreed time, the MCO traveled to the landlord's home or business and picketed. Seeing the utility of social coercion, they distributed fliers in these neighborhoods informing locals that an abusive, absentee landlord lived among them. The combined tactics produced results; in their second year, the MCO served as the official dispute agent for 23 district buildings, each with their own grievance procedures and maintenance agreements. Sometimes they even helped landlords deal with irresponsible tenants.

The Employment Committee was widely regarded as the MCO's most successful, in particular when measured by the membership growth they incited. In their second year, they developed a youth employment campaign. They secured a meeting with Wonder Bread and Hostess Bakery, intending to secure summer jobs. When the meeting was cancelled, a dozen members of the committee staged a sit-in at the office of the manager they had been scheduled to meet, forcing a new meeting. When negotiations were completed the MCO secured about a dozen positions—each for a third of the summer—and the power to place local youth in the positions. But who would get the jobs? Internal committee deliberations stalled until a young woman, silent up to that point, asked, "Why don't we give the jobs to the people who worked to get them?" The result was the MCO Point System, where members earned points through their support of the MCO. Points could be earned by attending meetings, participating in actions, or other forms of support. Then, as jobs came in, they were awarded to the people with the most points, who could take it or pass it along. Within weeks, youth participation rose to more than one hundred. By fall, with full-time jobs the goal, regular weekly participation grew ballooned to 300.

Success propelled growth in membership, adding to the perceived legitimacy of MCO within the City and framing a stronger position for negotiating a Model Cities agreement. Knowing whoever controlled the Model Cities Neighborhood Corporation, controlled the future of the Mission, Martinez sought to convince City Hall that the MCO was the only representative body who could speak for the diverse community. This would compel their involvement, since the legislation mandated "maximum feasible participation" with the goal of assuring "broad-based community support." After six months of negotiations with the mayor, the parties reached an agreement in May 1969 giving functional control of the Corporation to the MCO on its own terms. While the MCO sacrificed their demand for veto power, the compromise required the mayor to appoint 14 of the 21 board members from a list provided by the MCO. Additionally, the MCO could create a committee to review proposals for funds, evaluate the work of the corporation, and recall board members they originally nominated.[18]

The agreement now required the support of the Board of Supervisors. There, the MCO faced opponents seeking to portray them as a non-representative body. The first step was the Board's Planning and Development Committee, which met on September 16—Mexican Independence Day. The MCO mobilized more than five hundred community members to attend, using the public testimony session to present 75, two-minute speeches in support of the agreement with City Hall. The local press described the MCO and their "orderly, disciplined show of strength" in contrast to the unorganized opposition of no more than 150, people who called the agreement an "unholy alliance" and accused one Supervisor of being a "political prostitute."[19] The most organized opposition group called themselves the San Francisco Fairness League, led by Mary Hall. To express their united front, they presented the committee with a petition signed by more than 100 locals, most self-identified as homeowners. The MCO did the same, but with a stack of more than 2,500 signatures of propertied and non-propertied alike.[20] The Planning and Development Committee voted to approve the agreement, forwarding the issue to the full Board.

Maintaining their visible community support through multiple mass actions in the fall, the MCO worked toward assuring formal approval at the full Board of Supervisors meeting on December 1, 1969. At that meeting, the Board had to vote on both the proposed bylaws for the Model Cities Corporation as well as a request for federal funds to "plan and develop a comprehensive City Demonstration Program in the Mission area." Citing "doubts as to whether or not the Mission Coalition represents the people of the Mission District," some supervisors sided with the opposition. The majority sided with the MCO, with one supervisor calling it "a significant step forward for putting the decision-making power in the hands of the people of the neighborhoods." The twin resolutions passed by a vote of 7 to 4.[21]

The Model Cities struggle continued when the Department of Housing and Urban Development (HUD) vetoed the approved bylaws as giving too much power to the MCO. Beyond calling the agreement a "conspiracy between Mayor Alioto, the local Offices of Economic Opportunity and labor," the San Francisco Fairness League missed their opportunity to exploit the federal decision.[22] Mayor Alioto himself sought to undermine the MCO's position, assigning a staff member to encourage some of his local allies to pull out of the MCO, but City Hall's political networks were no match for the MCO's service record. At St. Peter's Catholic Church, Father Jim Casey refused to cooperate, expressing his support for the MCO's housing goals. Enjoying the improved commercial climate as a result of the MCO's efforts to close pawnshops and the Crown Theater, the Mission Merchants' Association also refused.

As the MCO and Alioto negotiated a new deal in the spring of 1970, the Coalition sought to fortify their representational status. Martinez invited the mayor to take a walking tour of the district to view their efforts firsthand. Suggestive of their ability to work within the parameters of traditional politics, the MCO also invited the Board of Supervisors, State Assemblymen, and a representative from Governor Reagan's office. When Alioto cancelled, the MCO conducted the tour for the other dignitaries, to favorable press coverage. The mayor's absence stood in contrast to the attendance of key Democratic and Republican leaders, including an aide from the head of the State's Model Cities Liaison Group, who declared, "The governor has heard of radical elements in the coalition, but the people you see aren't that at all."[23] Soon thereafter, Alioto reached an agreement with the MCO, which the Supervisors ratified, 6 to 5.

The second MCO convention came in the midst of their Model Cities campaign. The celebratory mood reflected their continuing success, leading Martinez to reflect on the passage of only one year. "I can remember when I first chaired MCO meetings that all the faces were familiar," he wrote in a memo, "This has changed a lot." Among the changes was a growing consensus on the political divisions of the previous convention. As Martinez noted, the PL Party and other radicals pulled out as "the valid issues that they had monopolized in the past are now being worked on by MCO without the Mao Tse-tung rhetoric."[24]

In the ensuing years, the MCO struggled under the bureaucratic weight of its new responsibilities regarding the federal funds of Model Cities. Internal political disputes—reflected in Martinez' successful attempt to amending bylaws allowing for a third term as president—incited further withdrawals from the Coalition. By 1973, the MCO maintained control over the Corporation but engaged in fewer actions as a coalition, focusing attention on the distribution of federal funds. As one activist put it, "the MCO [lost] opportunities to develop a broad-based CDC [Community Development Corporation] because of community politics including a fight for power which did not exist, and the co-optation of activists by City Hall by putting them on the Model Cities payroll."[25] Often derided as "poverty pimps," playing the role of bureaucratic agent held less appeal than community organizer.

But the MCO was hardly a failure. At its height, it successfully involved more than twelve thousand Mission District residents in the bettering of their own community and the planning of the district's future. Transforming a fractious community divided by class, generational, and ethnic conflicts, the MCO made major inroads in creating an environment where all its members could begin to understand their common interests as well as realize the power of their common efforts. For the Latin American, Spanish-speaking majority of the Inner Mission, the MCO orchestrated their emergence as a visible constituency, the group most associated with the post-war Mission. Buttressed by their demographic predominance in the district, their recognition as a collective entity emerged simultaneously with their organizational work nurturing this common identity. This collective identity coalesced within their movement, balanced on the vision of a common past while respectful of its location in a crucible of diversity. This is notable, for in an era when Mexican Americans throughout the Southwest came together in multiple forms of political action, usually under a Mexican-American based form of cultural nationalism known as *chicanismo*, the MCO exemplified a population predominantly of Latin American descent uniting under the umbrella of a multiracial and multiethnic coalition. Such efforts relied upon their ability to express shared identities based upon class, race, generation, and national origin, but they also required the recognition of difference. In the case of the MCO, this found organized expression in a hybrid form *latinidad*, most often under the term *Raza*, a collective identity encompassing difference while suggesting similitude.

While it suffered as a bureaucracy, the MCO achieved lasting victories as a coalition movement. The political culture of self-determination and collaboration remain in the district today, as does the dignity that comes with a meaningful, grassroots movement. After all, as the MCO lead organizer described it, their greatest success was the dignity gained:

> When we came out of the phone company meeting—we got an agreement for, I think on an annual basis it was in the hundreds of jobs—and the guy who was the chairman of that negotiating committee was Segundo Lopez...So we're walking out of the front door, I turn and say "Segundo wasn't that fantastic?" And I'm talking about the jobs. He looks at me and says "Yeah, Mike, you know that vice president called me Mister Lopez."[26]

Segundo Lopez was not alone in his newfound sense of pride. In countless other situations, thousands of residents encountered the same transformations within themselves. As they looked toward their future within the City, with increased expectations of the role they could play in shaping of their destinies, succeeding generations of Latino residents of San Francisco would also benefit from the work of the MCO.

# Notes

Thanks to Mike Miller for giving this essay a close read and making many helpful corrections and suggestions. For a much longer and more in-depth insider's view of the MCO history, check out his book *A Community Organizer's Tale* (Heyday Books, Berkeley, CA: 2009).

1. Ben Martinez, "The State of the Community" (address, Second Annual Convention of the MCO, October 18, 1969).

2. Manuel Castells, *The City and the Grassroots: A Cross-Cultural Theory of Urban Social Movements* (University of California Press, 1983), 106.

3. William V. Flores and Rina Benmayor, eds., *Latino Cultural Citizenship: Claiming Identity, Space, and Rights* (Beacon Press, 1997), 13.

4. Mike Miller, "An Organizer's Tale" (unpublished, 1974), 11.

5. David Braaten, "A Place of Many Voices." May 1, 1962; "Signs of a Renaissance." May 4, 1962; and "Slow Decay—and the Problem of Indifference." May 5, 1962. All *San Francisco Chronicle*.

6. Fr. James Hagan, interview by Jeffery Burns, July 5, 1989, Archives of the Archdiocese of San Francisco.

7. San Francisco Department of Planning, San Francisco Redevelopment Agency, *A Survey and Planning Application for the Mission Street Survey Area* (May 1966), File 148-66-3, Archives of the San Francisco Board of Supervisors, San Bruno, CA.

8. San Francisco Board of Supervisors, *Journal of Proceedings* (December 19, 1966), 61:53, 951.

9. Thomas F. Jackson, "The State, the Movement, and the Urban Poor: The War on Poverty and Political Mobilization in the 1960s," in *The "Underclass" Debate: Views From History, ed.* Michael B. Katz (Princeton, NJ: Princeton University Press, 1993), 412.

10. Miller, "Organizer's Tale," 25.

11. "Mission Coalition's Fighting Mad Start," *San Francisco Chronicle*, October 5, 1968.

12. "Cesar Chavez habla: his speech to the Coalition Convention," *La Nueva Mision* 2, no.10 (November 1968): 7.

13. "Mission Group's Tough Demands," *San Francisco Chronicle*, November 4, 1968.

14. Helen Lara Cea, interview with author, October 4, 2001.

15. Miller, "Organizer's Tale," 37.

16. Mike Miller, interview with author, October 4, 2000.

17. Ibid.

18. Scott Blakey, "Mission Plan Clears One Hurdle," *San Francisco Chronicle*, May 10, 1969.

19. Russ Cone, "Stormy Hearing on Mission Model Cities," *San Francisco Examiner*, September 17, 1969.

20. Petitions of the San Francisco Fairness League and the Mission Coalition Organization, File 401-69-1, Archives of the San Francisco Board of Supervisors, San Bruno, CA.

21. San Francisco Board of Supervisors, Res. 838-69 and Res. 377-68, *Journal of Proceedings*, (December 1, 1969), 64:48, 974.

22. "Opposition to Mission Coalition," *San Francisco Chronicle*, November 27, 1969.

23. Joel Tlumak, "MCO Impresses Top Reagan Aide," *San Francisco Examiner*, July 19, 1970.

24. Memo from Ben Martinez to Lou White, November 24, 1969, located in MMA.

25. Leandro P. Soto, "Community Economic Development: More Than Hope for the Poor" (San Francisco, 1979), 8-9.

26. Miller, interview.

# Poetry and Solidarity in the Mission District

## By Alejandro Murguía

There are two kinds of fog in San Francisco but most people are unaware of this, thinking only of fog, as if all fog is the same. There's the summer fog that comes in from the ocean and is a good fog that cools down the City—and then there's the tule fog that comes from inland, clinging low, seeming to rise from the very ground, and this is the worst kind of fog. The tule fog comes in the fall and winter, and can cut visibility to nearly zero, and it is deadly in that way for anyone on the road.

The fog that I was looking at on that day in 1976 had come in from Ocean Beach, skirted Twin Peaks, then stopped, and though it wouldn't reach where I lived it would cool down the Mission District.

It was usually sunny in the Mission in spite of the rest of the City being fogged in. There were no cafés in the *barrio* then. If you wanted to have that sort of drink you went to North Beach. The only taqueria was on 20th and Folsom and it was the first place that served burritos in our part of the world. On 24th Street Guadalajara de Noche Restaurant had the only neon sign and a block east was La Victoria Panadería. Next to the panadería, on the side of it, was a restaurant, a sort of extension of La Victoria. At least everyone called it a restaurant. At lunchtime everyone who was anyone in the barrio gathered around the small plastic-covered tables that practically abutted each other. Politicos and would-be power brokers. Poverty pimps and locals. I would go there for the lunch special, chile colorado with rice and beans for $1.50, and pick up an earful of *bochinche* to go with it.

I lived then at 2758 22nd Street in a bottom flat. Before this I had lived at 2962 22nd Street, so I had lived most of my time in San Francisco within a few blocks. This afternoon I had walked from my place to Folsom Street, turned left, and crossed 24th Street, and kept going another three blocks to what was then called Army Street. Crossing Army Street, but still on Folsom, the street turns uphill, and goes past a small park called Precita, on the corner of which stood a bar where I had once worked. The Ribeltad Vorden had been a hangout for anarchists and crazy poets, but now it was closed. It was too bad that it had closed because it had been a good place to conspire. This was Bernal Heights, a working class neighborhood of Italians, Irish, "Flips," Samoans, and Latinos. A few more blocks past the closed-down bar I came to the end of the houses and the beginning of the hill known as Bernal Heights named after the old man, José Bernal, who held the original land.

I walked up the hill to test myself, my stamina. Once I reached the road that circles the hilltop, I rested for a minute, then climbed a trail to the very top of the hill. A giant telephone disk antenna, like Mickey Mouse ears, had been set up there, but other than that, it was pretty rustic on the hilltop. You also had an incredible view of the Mission District and beyond that the skyline of San Francisco. It had been warm when I started walking from 22nd Street but now a tsunami of fog had formed off the port side of the City. *Los Pechos de la India*, as we called Twin Peaks, were the only things holding back the advection fog. It would cool the City down in another ten, fifteen minutes.

I stayed up on the hill a little longer. I was winded, my legs sore, and sweat had beaded on my forehead. I wondered what it was like to be some place like Nicaragua, someplace on a mountainside, with no shelter, scant food, bad water, monkeys howling day and night, while the National Guard wants to splatter your brains the first chance they get. I also knew that elsewhere there was a third kind of fog: mountain fog, cold and damp as a wet overcoat which made San Francisco fog more like a kitten playing. Mountain fog could rot not only your clothes and boots but also your skin and fingertips, a condition known as mountain leprosy, so rare that there was little knowledge on how to cure it, or prevent it.

The news those days from Nicaragua told of a small group of guerrillas that were up in the mountains, a ridiculously small group of 27, maybe 28 of them. But they were armed with whatever weapons could be scrounged—shotguns and .22s, a few M-1s—and they carried on, month after month, issuing communiqués that urged the overthrow of the dictator. The dreaded, murderous *Guardia Nacional*, with all their firepower and armament and planes and US advisers, had not been able to destroy this armed nucleus deep in the mountains.

After a few more minutes I walked back to where I lived, hoping to beat the fog if it poured around *Los Pechos de la India*. Bernal Heights was nothing like those mountains. This was just Bernal Heights. But, Nicaragua and the Mission District were linked. The Mission District, because of its population and history, was linked to all the Central American countries, and by extension to all Latin America. It was so obvious to me—and yet exciting —an interesting discovery I told myself. And the walk back wasn't as tiring, nor did I become winded.

By the time I reached 22nd Street near Bryant the fog had pulled back and like a giant wave was returning to the ocean. Once in the flat I sat in the little living room catching the last of the light, that nice end of daylight that I like so much. When the woman I was now living with came in from work later, I opened two beers for us, and we sat for a while in the kitchen, not saying anything, just enjoying the day's dying light.

## Publishing Collective

It was in the flat on 22nd Street that I first thought up the idea of publishing a magazine. Initially we formed our own publishing house, Editorial Pocho-Ché,[1] when the entire body of Chicano literature consisted of three or four books. Editorial Pocho-Ché was a collective of poets intent on breaking the literary blockade that publishing houses had imposed, more through their own ignorance than anything else, on Chicano-/Latino writers. We also came together with other San Francisco writers and artists and created Third World Communications (TWC), publishers of the first women of color anthology, *Third World Women*. [2] Later the collective edited the anthology published by Glide Publications, *Time to Greez! Incantations from the Third World*.[3] The collective was a loosely organized collaboration, though sometimes we held formal meetings.

We saw ourselves as cultural workers, not just strictly poets, and and so we organized readings, lots of readings. We put one together at the short-lived City Lights Theater on Mason Street with Fernando Alegría and Victor Hernández

Cruz in May 1972 where the Mexican writer José Revueltas showed up. Another memorable reading was one for Neruda and Chile to protest the 1973 military coup that overthrew Salvador Allende. This was typical of the times—the CIA overthrowing democratically elected governments and assassinating Third World leaders. Rupert García did the poster, a dual portrait of Allende and Neruda, and Roberto Vargas and I posted it overnight on Mission Street. Glide Memorial Church was packed with angry people that night, October 4th, 1973, for the reading. This event was a watershed of poetry and perspectives, from Ishmael Reed to Janice Mirikitani to Michael McClure to Jack Hirschman. Dr. Fernando Alegría, who had been the Chilean cultural attaché in Washington and had escaped Chile dressed as a priest, brought the house down with his poem "Viva Chile M."

The most way-out reading occurred at the storefront that TWC had at 1018 Valencia Street near 21st. Pedro Pietri from New York came into town and David Henderson, who published a Latin issue of his African-American literary magazine *Umbra*, brought him to *La Misión*. A reading was organized and everyone was invited to read a poem, including Jessica Hagedorn, Ntozake Shange, and Hernández Cruz. This is probably the only time when all these poets read on the same bill. It was beautiful. There must have been a hundred and fifty people jammed into the storefront, wine flowed, and the energy was intense. Pedro closed the show with his Rent-a-Coffin routine delivered deadpan style in his mortician's outfit, his black briefcase, and his Rent-a-Coffin sign. The place just cracked up. One of the poems he read that night was "Puerto Rican Obituary," the great epic of the Neoricans.

In 1974, the Pocho-Ché collective finally published its own magazine, *Tin-Tan: Revista Cósmica*. In terms of the international perspective of the editorial staff, we were pushing the boundaries. The premier issue featured two world-class artists. Michael Rios created a full color, tropicalized Mission, with swaying palm trees for the outside covers; the inside covers were powerful collages of South America and South Africa by Rupert García. The following issues of *Tin-Tan* featured covers by the best artists in the Mission: Graciela Carrillo, Juan Fuentes, and García again for issue Number Three, who created a beautiful dual portrait of Ché, in life and in death. The writers were a constellation not just of Aztlán but of all Latin America, which was the connection we wanted. *Tin-Tan* covered everything, from the FBI attack on the Oglala people on the Pine Ridge Reservation to the guerrilla war in Nicaragua, from Enrique Buenaventura and El Teatro Experimental de Calí to the death of Roque Dalton and the history of Salvadoran poetry. One of the founding editors of *Tin-Tan*, Daniel del Solar, recovered the lost text and photo of Frida Kahlo's painting "The Birth of Moses," which was later cited by Hayden Herrera in her definitive biography of the artist. We published Roberto Márquez, Victor Manuel Valle, translations of Mayakovsky by Hirschman, and interviews with the Latino musicians Ray Barretto and Willie Colon. Also included were political analyses of Peru, El Salvador, and Nicaragua, as well as short fiction by Harry Gamboa, Jr. and poetry by Lorna Dee Cervantes, among many, many others.

During this period the writers and artists of the Mission were greatly influenced by the Latin American writers of the generation known as the "Boom." Writers such as Juan Rulfo, Gabriel García Márquez, Julio Cortázar, and Guillermo Cabrera Infante taught us not only about Latin America but also to think of ourselves as Latin Americans. Because of these writers, and many others, we realized that the Mission was a typical Latin American pueblo, since all the characters and situations of these novels could all be found on 24th Street, from the poets, locos, and exiled revolutionaries, to palm trees and even parrots—like the parrots of *100 Years of Solitude* that announce the coming of the gypsies. Then, as now, the palm trees of Dolores Street were home to flocks of parrots, especially those known as chocoyos which are native to Central America. The parrots of Dolores Street were a metaphor of the different pueblos that now populated the Mission.

It was certainly a fecund literary period for *La Misión*. We had our own modest "Boom" in a way. In between running workshops for the San Francisco Arts Commission's Neighborhood Arts Program, and the incipient *Tin-Tan*, I found time to write my first short stories. One of them was inspired by seeing a young junkie on the corner of 22nd and Folsom waiting for his connection. I would launch not only *Tin-Tan* from the flat on 22nd Street, but also a new series of Pocho-Ché books that included the prison-barrio poetry of Raúl R. Salinas, a new volume of poetry by Roberto Vargas, and the poems of Nina Serrano.

## Poetic Politics

The most influential, both artistically and politically, of this wave of Central American poets, was the Nicaraguan-born Roberto Vargas.[4] He grew up among the new generation of Nicaraguans coming to the Bay Area during and after World War II. As a young man, he traveled to the Far East as a merchant seaman, worked in a mattress factory, and for the American Can Company in the Mission, which would later morph into Project Artaud. He was one of the few Latinos to participate in both the Beat era/North Beach scene and the Haight-Ashbury scene. With the rise of the anti-Vietnam War movement and the Civil Rights movement of the 1960s, Vargas became active in the Chicano movement and the Third World Liberation movement.

Without Roberto, *La Misión* would not be what it is now. He deserves a book about his life, or at least a plaque somewhere on 24th Street. He arrived in San Francisco from Nicaragua at the age of five. By 1971, he'd already lived 25 years in *La Misión* and knew everyone in the barrio. He graduated from Mission High School. Like everyone else he had been radicalized by the '60s, organized for the Farmworkers movement led by César Chávez, formed a Brown Berets chapter in *La Misión*, fought the Tac Squad at the San Francisco State Strike, and organized around Los Siete de La Raza—seven young Latinos from *La Misión* who'd been charged with killing a cop on Alvarado Street.[5] In other words, he was very high energy.

Roberto wore an earring, hippie beads, Indian bracelets, and a "*Viva La Raza*" button. When he didn't wear his brown beret, his hair puffed out in an Afro-do. He sometimes drove a sports car, at other times a converted mail truck. He once totaled a 1954 Jaguar 120 XK roadster on the Bay Bridge and survived to tell about it. He boxed at Newman's Gym, had been in the Marine Corps, sailed to Vietnam with the Merchant Marines, and was the best poet I'd ever heard. He was the first in the Mission to combine poetry with music, reading in his bebop Latin jazz style, accompanied by conga drums and sometimes timbaleros. His work was not just poetic, it was political, and excellent theater. He was such a standout, Jane Fonda picked him to go on tour with her and Donald Sutherland in their anti-war troupe called the FTA (Fuck or Free the Army) Tour. He also had the courage to turn down a publishing contract with Dell Books, considering publishing in New York to be selling out. Instead he published with our own community-based press. The political activity of the Brown Berets and Los Siete de La Raza inspired some of Roberto's best poetry of that era: "Canto al Tercer Marcha de Delano," "They Blamed It On Reds," and "Elegy Pa' Gringolandia."[6]

Roberto's first book of poems, *Primeros Cantos*, defines his style—rhythmic and imagistic. The poems are meant to be performed, which the poet often did accompanied by congeros. The images are clear and precise, and flowing, often without connecting phrases, just the pure image carrying the poem.

Vargas captures the breath of his experience in a prose-poem titled "Then There Was...," an extended jazz-like riff recounting the poet's early years in this country, from his arrival through high school years in the Mission District, his stint in the Marine Corps concluding with the death of his first wife. The influence of US music, rhythm and blues, oldies, mixed with boleros, mixed with nostalgia for his homeland and his emerging political consciousness, mark this prose-poem as one of the most innovative of his work. It was first published by Warren Hinckle in *City Magazine* in 1975.

In 1972, Roberto had shown me a little chapbook by a Nicaraguan poet living on a small archipelago on Lake Nicaragua. The poet was Ernesto Cardenal, who was a priest, and according to Roberto, also a revolutionary. The book was *Gethsemany, Ky.* It was a series of small poems about Cardenal's stay in a monastery, under the tutelage of Thomas Merton, a catholic writer-philospher whom I had read in high school. This book was my introduction to the poetry of Cardenal and the history of Nicaragua.

Later that year, during the winter when it rained for months, a seminal event occurred in Nicaragua, although at that time no one was aware of the impact it would have on the history of our continent. On December 23, 1972, an earthquake destroyed Managua, leveling three fourths of the capital and killing 10,000 people. Roberto, being Nicaraguan, rushed to an emergency ad hoc aid committee in San Francisco. But soon the word circulated among the exiled Nicaraguan community that Anastasio Somoza and his National Guard were stealing the aid, everything from money to canned goods. Somoza already owned everything in Nicaragua, from the biggest ranch to the Mercedes-Benz dealership, but his greed in the aftermath of the earthquake helped politicize the 50,000 Nicaraguans then living in *La Misión*.

We were usually doing three or four things at the same time, so it wasn't unusual for influences, committees, events even to overlap.

At this critical moment, after the destruction of Managua and the subsequent pilfering of the aid by Somoza, Vargas set out an ambitious plan to bring the Sandinista National Liberation Front (FSLN or Frente) and the plight of Nicaragua to the attention of United States literary and political figures. Besides being a key organizer of *La Gaceta Sandinista*, the official organ for the FSLN, he organized poetry readings throughout the United States in support of the Sandinista cause. He also organized Cardenal's historic first visit to the San Francisco Bay Area and the United States, serving as host, guide and translator in 1976.

The support of North Americans was now critical and several important poets and writers took the lead, including Miguel Algarín, Daniel Berrigan, Robert Cohen, Pietri, Allen Ginsberg, Muriel Rukeyser, and Ntozake Shange, who read at a poetry reading Roberto organized as a benefit for the Frente in New York. Other poets, such as Lawrence Ferlinghetti, Ginsberg, Diane di Prima, and Hirschman read at benefits for Nicaragua, and later, after the Sandinista triumph in 1979, many of the above poets visited the homeland of Rubén Darío. Being Chicano, with Mexica roots, I am connected to Central America through culture. In Mesoamerica, the Nahuatl culture spread as far south as Nicaragua, whose indigenous Nahuatl name, Nicarahuac, means, "Hasta aquí llego el Nahua," or "The Nahuas came this far." So culturally I'm connected to Nicaragua, and politically it goes without saying. Historically, California and Nicaragua have been linked since 1849 when New Englanders headed for the riches of the gold fields would dock at Greytown on the Atlantic Coast of Nicaragua, sail up the Río San Juan to Rivas, then cross the fifteen mile strip of land before boarding another ship on the Pacific to take them the rest of the way. One other point connects me historically to Nicaragua: when the Tennessee filibuster, William Walker, set out to invade Nicaragua in 1855, he sailed from San Francisco. During the years 1977-79, when many of us flew out of San Francisco to help free Nicaragua, we would remember what Walker had done, especially his burning of Granada, on the ruins of which he left this graffiti, so chillingly prophetic of North American involvement, "HERE WAS GRANADA."

So for me it was natural to support Nicaragua.

Early one morning in 1974 just before New Year's Eve, Roberto came to my house. "We have to meet," he said. He had urgent news from Nicaragua. An FSLN commando had taken over the house of Chema Castillo in Managua and had captured a slew of Somoza's lackeys. They wanted to exchange them for Frente prisoners, five million dollars, and passage out of the country. The Frente had issued a communiqué in Managua; our task was to translate it, print it, and distribute it here in San Francisco. I went to work immediately on the translation, while Roberto organized a march. That Saturday morning, with a thousand copies of the communiqué printed under the banner of *La Gaceta Sandinista*, we met with several dozen people at the 24th Street BART Station. Casimiro Sotelo and Roberto spoke at the rally, then we all marched down Mission Street. There were maybe 30 of us at that march. We carried these beautiful black and red posters of Sandino silkscreened by La Raza Graphics, and we waved them at passing traffic, and stood outside El Tico-Nica bar exchanging insults with Somoza sympathizers. This was the first rally ever held for Nicaragua in the Mission District or the United States.

Although it was a small start, word soon spread through the Nicaraguan community. The Frente sympathizers were organized around El Comite Civico Latinoamericano Pro Nicaragua en los Estados Unidos (El Comite Civico, for short), which published *La Gaceta Sandinista*, a newspaper that brought stories, reports, photographs, and Frente communiqués to an information-starved community of Nicaraguan exiles. The meetings of *La Gaceta* took place at a storefront on 22nd and Bartlett, and the first members were Walter Ferretti, Raúl Venerio, Lygia S., Haroldo Solano, and Bérman Zúniga. All of them would later play an important role in the overthrow of Somoza.

While we kept on organizing cultural events and printing the newspaper, on the sly we bought a couple of shotguns at a pawnshop on Mission Street. Later, the key contact of the Frente, who always stayed in the background, Herty Levitez, known by his pseudonym "Mauricio," was arrested crossing the border into Mexico with a car full of weapons. Our shotguns were part of his stash. He did six months in a federal penitentiary for that one.

But other work was more successful. A solidarity committee popped up in LA, another one in Washington DC. Roberto created a Non-Intervention in Nicaragua Committee (NIN) made up of North Americans to pressure Congress to stop military aid to the Somoza regime. Eventually NIN scored a two day hearing on human rights in Nicaragua, Guatemala, and El Salvador before the Subcommittee on International Organizations of the House of Representatives in Washington DC. Several documents were submitted to the committee including sworn statements by Pedro Joaquín Chamorro, regarding human rights violations he observed while being held a prisoner in Somoza's jails, and a letter from Monsignor Miguel Obando Bravo, Archbishop of Nicaragua, regarding restrictions on religious expression. Father Fernando Cardenal, brother of Ernesto Cardenal and also a priest, testified at the hearings about the imprisonment, torture, and disappearance of campesinos in Nicaragua. The hearings also raised the contradictions in State Department policy with regard to Central America, in particular Nicaragua, since the United States was providing training to National Guard members in counterinsurgency, irregular warfare, jungle warfare, and advance police and investigation tactics that were being used against workers, students, intellectuals, and other political opponents of the Somoza dictatorship. This support of the dictator was in direct violation of the Rio Pact, a mutual assistance document dating back to 1947 and signed by the US which states, "the obligation of mutual assistance and common defense of the American Republics is essentially related to their democratic ideals."

By 1977 with the Nicaraguan resistance growing stronger, *La Gaceta Sandinista's* print run of 5,000 copies (all of which were given away free) went like hot tortillas to the Nicaraguan community. The solidarity committees were attracting more recruits. But as the resistance grew internally and solidarity expanded internationally, Somoza and his *Guardia Nacional* intensified the repression.

Those of us in San Francisco knew that we also had to develop new strategies and tactics to harass the dictatorship even from a distance. Eventually we decided on the most daring of all acts of solidarity in the exterior—one that would not only send a message to the dictatorship, but also awaken the consciousness of the North American people and slap awake the US media that didn't yet know of the life or death struggle going on in Nicaragua.

## Taking the Consulate

The idea to take over the consulate in San Francisco had come from Roberto—but also from down below, as we used to refer to those in the Frente. We already knew the basic layout of the consulate, where it was located on 760 Market Street, the employees, and even the Consul General himself. So we started scoping out the place, checking on the comings and goings of the staff. We waited for the right moment—and stayed occupied with other work, rallies, candlelight vigils on 24th and Mission Streets, petitions, even telegrams in the case of important political prisoners held by the Somoza regime. We were also organizing several groups at once, including the Comite Civico Pro-Liberación de Nicaragua and NIN.

Parallel with the continued literary and cultural activities we were involved in, our preparations for the takeover of the consulate went into high gear. Our intent was to bring attention to the atrocities that were being committed in Nicaragua, and to disrupt business as usual at the consulate office. It was not meant to be a violent action but a symbolic action, and within the parameters of what we were doing, a peaceful one as well, more agit-prop than anything else. It would be part of an international strategy to isolate and disrupt the Somoza regime wherever it found itself attempting to conduct business as usual. Soon the operation was ready to be launched.

By this time in 1976, the most militant and dedicated of our cadres were already in Nicaragua involved in the armed struggle. Nonetheless, the cadres that remained in San Francisco were also of the highest quality and commitment. I will name only those who were actually involved in the takeover of the consulate office.

Without a doubt, the key figure and instigator of this action was Roberto Vargas, who was the catalyst for the whole group. Diana Diaz-Vargas, a Chicana with Native American roots was a key support person for *La Gaceta Sandinista*, was the wife of Roberto, as well as my comadre. Anuar Murrar, one of our youngest and brightest cadres, and his companion at the time, Dolly Beliso. Magaly Fernández, being half Nicaraguan, was deeply involved too. I and others rounded out the group.

The action would not be without risk. Although we had carefully thought out the plan, and everyone would be unarmed and nonviolent as I mentioned, there was no way to predict what the reaction of the police would be. After all, the SFPD had had an antagonistic relationship with our community for years. The case of Los Siete de La Raza was just one example. And this would be the first time anything like this had ever gone down, a takeover at the consular level. What would be the reaction of the Consul General or his staff? Regardless of the consequences, we were firm in our resolve that we would take the Nicaraguan Consulate on Market Street, the largest of all of Somoza's consular office, and we would not leave without getting our message in the media.

Three cadres were chosen to occupy the consulate office while the rest of us were assigned support work such as having lawyers ready, handing out our communiqué to the media, and organizing a rally outside the consulate to express our solidarity with the takeover as well as with the Nicaraguan struggle.

Early one September morning, tense but confident, we departed the Mission District. Once downtown each of us took our positions, each with clearly delineated tasks. Our plan went off better than any of us had expected. Once our cadre was in the consulate "Kike," "Armando," and "Arlen," wearing red-and-black bandannas covering half their faces, shooed out the staff, all of whom left eagerly, as if they were in sympathy with our action. The doors were quickly barricaded from the inside, and then the rest of us went into action. My particular job was to call all the newspapers and televisions to let them know that the Nicaraguan Consulate had just been occupied and that a statement would soon be released. I had a list with me of all the telephone numbers and I walked across the street and used a pay phone to make the calls, making each call to the media sound as urgent and exciting as possible. Another cadre called the police station to let them know that it was a peaceful takeover and that those inside were unarmed and all we wanted was to get our message out. The fire department was also called and told what was happening so that there would be no need to knock down doors or anything. While this was going on, other members had organized a picket line in front of 760 Market Street and were shouting slogans and handing out leaflets and our communiqué.

Within minutes, sirens were converging on the Flood Building and TV reporters were out there with their cameras and microphones, even a helicopter flew overhead, adding to the drama. The news media wanted to know why we were doing this and we explained the situation in Nicaragua and how the US government had been supporting this dictatorship for over forty years, and had in fact created this dictatorship. I don't think that a single one of these reporters had ever heard of Nicaragua, and certainly most of them couldn't find it on a map even if it bit them in the ass.

The police lined up in front of the consulate but were hesitant about storming inside, since they apparently knew that all consulate and diplomatic offices are sovereign territory and cannot be entered by the host countries law enforcement units. Late in the day, after we had presented our communiqués to the media, tense negotiations continued outside the consulate between our three cadres and the police department. Finally after nightfall an agreement was reached: our cadre would leave the consulate and no arrests or prosecutions would be made. We figured we had made our point with the media, and at the same time had sent a message to the dictator Somoza that he would be harassed and disrupted wherever his lackeys might appear.

At the agreed upon time, those of us outside the consulate formed a corridor in the hallway to usher our cadres out. Suddenly the door of the consulate swung open and "Kike," "Arlen," and "Armando" emerged, shouting slogans in support of the Frente, while we all joined in with them. Then the whole group of us, maybe twenty in all, stormed out of the Flood Building and made our getaway, untouched by the police. Our operation had been an outstanding success; we had hurt the dictatorship without suffering losses ourselves. The most important part was that finally we had the media's attention as to what was happening in Nicaragua.

The takeover of the consulate sent shock waves throughout the Nicaraguan community. Somoza must have received the news in his bunker in Managua. What that fat old dictator thought of this is not recorded, but he must have figured he would swat us away like bothersome mosquitoes. But it was so successful that we would do it on several more occasions, assigning different cadres different roles, disrupting their work, distributing our communiqués, and rallying the morale of the people.

In April 1978 when the Salvadorean compañeros asked us for support in taking over the Salvadoran consulate we were in complete solidarity, we knew it was the same struggle for justice and human dignity.[7] In the meantime, the situation in Nicaragua had reached the level of insurrection. The October 1977 attacks on the *Guardia Nacional* barracks across the country had been the initial round in the insurrection. Somoza had won the first round but the Frente had shown he could be bloodied. We intensified our own training—learning to break down an M-1, practicing at the firing range in Sharp Park, and running counterclockwise laps around the hilltop of Bernal Heights.

That night of the first takeover of the Nicaraguan Consulate we all gathered in Roberto's house on Bernal Heights afterwards to analyze the action and critique ourselves, but also to celebrate. Our daring move had turned out perfectly. It was exhilarating that we could pull off something of this magnitude, and yet it was humbling, knowing that regardless of the joy and pride we felt, we all knew it was just a grain of sand on the beach. We were all painfully conscious that in Nicaragua the struggle was brutal and bloody and the Guardia gave no quarter, and that there was going to be much hurt and sacrifice still to come. We didn't know it then—who could have known—the overthrow of Somoza was still two long hard years away.

# Notes

1.    Editorial Pocho-Ché was an offshot of the magazine *El Pocho Ché*. It was basically a collective of poets from the Mission who published a series of poetry books and one magazine.

2.    Third World Communications (TWC) was a collective of collectives, formed by the poets around Editorial Pocho-Ché and Asian-American, Native American, and African-American writers. *Third World Women*, published in 1973, was one of two anthologies produced and edited by TWC.

3.    Editorial Pocho-Ché, ed., *Time to Greez! Incantations from the Third World*, with an introduction by Maya Angelou (San Francisco: Glide Publications and Third World Communications, 1975). This was TWC's second anthology.

4.    The other important Nicaraguan poet of that decade is Pancho Aguila, who became a cause célèbre for many writers in the Bay Area. Pancho Aguila is the poet's *nom de guerre*, adopted when he was first jailed in the early 1970s. Aguila spent most of the decade of the '70s, and part of the '80s, incarcerated at Folsom Prison, where he was a key organizer of the Folsom Prison Writer's Workshop. In his life and his work, Aguila always considered himself a political prisoner, and the act for which he was jailed, bank robbery, a political crime. As could be expected, his work exhibits a strong political stance in favor of the oppressed and all political prisoners. The poems published by Second Coming Press in 1977 under the title *Dark Smoke*, are typically angry, but within the anger, there is an unmistakable gleam of hope and sincere humanity. One other Nicaraguan poet published a book during this decade. Although Denis Corrales Martínez's book (a chapbook titled *Pinceladas Nicaragüenses*) did not have the impact or power of Vargas or Aguila, it is important to note that his book was all in Spanish, whereas the other poets were writing in English. Corrales Martínez's work is also characterized by a more simplistic form—he uses the traditional verso of Hispanic literature—and also by his poetic concerns. Being a recent newcomer to San Francisco when he published this book (recent in comparison to Vargas and Aguila, who spent decades here), the poems are more traditionally Nicaraguan. The themes are of the Nicaraguan workers, especially campesinos, and their oppression; the poems also emphasize the poet's concern for the environment and ecology.

5.    See Jason M. Ferreira's essay "With the Soul of Human Rainbow" in this volume for more information on the events surrounding Los Siete de La Raza.

6.    His influence is such that his work appears in all the major Chicano anthologies of that period, including Luis Valdez and Stan Steiner, eds., *Aztlán: An Anthology of Mexican American Literature* (New York: Knopf, 1972), and Alurista, ed., *Festival de Flor y Canto: An Anthology of Chicano Literature* (Los Angeles: University of Southern California Press, 1976).

7.    On the morning of April 6, 1978, three members of the Salvadoran solidarity group El Pulgarcito used the same tactics we had perfected. But this time it didn't turn out so good. The FBI appeared unexpectedly, and ignoring the protocol of sovereignty, used a battering ram to smash the glass doors. Then they stormed in and arrested the three who were inside. Two of them were men, and one was a woman, "La Dominica." The FBI, being the FBI, once the men were handcuffed, kicked them in the balls, and manhandled "La Dominica." It was just a small sample of what was going on in Central America, now transferred to San Francisco. Our attorney Paul Albert went into action and they soon made bail. But for us it was clear that the tactic of taking the consulates would no longer work. The struggle would have to go to another level.

# Lost Murals of the Seventies

## by Timothy W. Drescher

Riding through San Francisco neighborhoods (by bike, bus, or car) in the twenty-first century, one sees refurbished, modernized storefronts, in buildings often of stucco instead of old painted redwood, and few vacant lots, as properties have mostly been developed or are in the process of being developed/redeveloped/gentrified. There are fewer murals than before, at least fewer of those that put San Francisco on the community mural movement map. The new residents and businesses are more oriented toward commerce than community issues; not as mural-friendly. Many seminal seventies murals have been destroyed, now existing only in nostalgia-tinged photos, absent markers of a time when political engagement found its way onto San Francisco's neighborhood walls. A glance at these photos tells us something about what has been lost with their passing. One doesn't know whether to scream in anger or weep at the loss.

In the 1970s San Francisco's diverse and activist artists became national leaders in murals. Collective mural-painting groups formed here as well as in Santa Fe, New York, Chicago, and Los Angeles. The most influential was San Francisco's *Mujeres Muralistas* because this group showed that women could paint monumental outdoor projects without the help of men. They inspired countless women artists across the country. Local muralists also developed the idea of the mural cluster—several thematically-related murals painted in a single location. The 1973 murals painted upstairs at the Jamestown Catholic Youth Organization (CYO) at 23rd Street and Fair Oaks inspired painting of the Mini Park mural cluster on 24th Street near Bryant Street in 1975, and the further muralizing of Balmy Alley in the next decade, and triggered New York's *La Lucha Continua* mural project.

Murals painted in the seventies in San Francisco neighborhoods often represented important issues such as housing, the Vietnam War, and the ravages of industrialization. From 1975 to 1980, however, SF murals were often funded by the federal Comprehensive Education and Training Act (CETA) program and most activist murals stopped being produced, but not all. Led by 1970s veterans, some muralists carried on in the same spirit of rebellion and criticism, but most turned toward spiritual or simply institutional funder-based imagery (styles, to be fair, which had been present if not significant since the beginning of the movement). The end of the seventies was signaled, of course, by the election of Ronald Reagan as president.

In both murals and political graphics, there was a direct line of influence from the New Deal thirties to the seventies. This was personified by Emmy Lou Packard, among others, who had worked with Diego Rivera, and also advised Chuy Campusano on his 1974 *Homage to Siqueiros* mural, still in existence today at the Bank of America branch at 23rd and Mission Streets. However, some New Deal works were also threatened in the seventies, such as Anton Refregier's marvelous *History of San Francisco* at Rincon Annex, which was saved only after a prolonged struggle. Such battles are not over yet. In 2010, Ruben Kadish's exquisite and anomalous 1937 *Dissertation on Alchemy* at the University of California Berkeley Extension Laguna Street annex is threatened by commercial redevelopment.

Mural destruction has sometimes provoked varied audience responses, including being glad the mural is gone and liking its replacement. The 1976 *Our History Is No Mystery* suffered repeated racist attacks over a decade until it was replaced by its original artists, the Haight Ashbury Muralists. Their new version, *Educate to Liberate*, has not suffered those attacks. Domingo Rivera's two murals in the Mission District were never much appreciated by local residents, users of both the Mini Park near 24th and Bryant Streets, and Garfield Park a few blocks away. *Psychocybernetics*, in the Mini Park, was replaced by Michael Rios's beloved *ABC Mural*. The Garfield Park wall remains blank. Though their destruction represents the dominance of different ideologies today, it does not signify the end of the issues.

Other important 1970s murals have been destroyed over the years (more than a dozen at Fort Mason, Fran Valesco's *Puerto Rico Social Club*, Dewey Crumpler's *Education Is Truth*, several at the American Indian Center on Valencia Street…the list goes on), but Precita Eyes Muralists, founded in the mid-1970s, continues to carry the torch of sharing San Francisco's mural history and creating new works, and remains one of the most important mural groups in the country.

ALL PHOTOS BY TIMOTHY W. DRESCHER

# Some Lost Murals of the Seventies — San Francisco

*Above and on facing page bottom: I-Hotel Mural* (1975). 868 Kearny Street. Painted by James Dong and the Kearny Street Workshop on the side of the International Hotel, the mural combined traditional and contemporary Chinese figures. It was designed to show diners, who had just feasted on inexpensive meals in Chinatown, where their food had come from. The two window spaces being held by the man were originally supposed to contain large mirrors so passersby could see themselves as reliant on peasant agricultural labor, but the artists could not afford the mirrors. Incorporating the exhaust vent into the design as a three-dimensional basket was a brilliant use of an extremely difficult architectural characteristic, and was the last part of the I-Hotel destroyed at its demolition in 1979, leaving an anguished worker holding an empty basket. After the mural was destroyed along with the I-Hotel, the site remained an empty hole in the ground for over a decade until the new Manilatown Hotel was built there.

*The Fire Next Time I* (1977). Located at the Joseph Lee Recreation Center, 3rd and Mandell Streets in Hunter's Point/Bayview. One of Dewey Crumpler's major murals, it cast the neighborhood's Black nationalist leanings into a complex cultural framework instead of an activist-political one. In depicting three aspects of local residents' lives (education, religion, culture) against a background of Orozco-inspired flames, the mural showed traditional practices of burning after crops are harvested, the flames of biblical apocalypse, and the fires of a local riot in 1969. The mural's title, of course, refers to James Baldwin's famous essay, and asks which of the flames will arrive next. The building it was painted on was destroyed in 2008 and replaced by a new community center.

*Latinoamérica* (1974). 2922 Mission at 25th Street. Painted by the *Mujeres Muralistas*, the mural captures the variety of origins of the Mission District's residents—Bolivia, Guatemala, Peru, Mexico, Venezuela. The Mission District is not a Chicano neighborhood. Residents with Mexican origins made up only the fourth-largest group when the mural was painted, which accounts for, among other things, the wider variety of restaurants there than in most United States *barrios*. On the right hand side, contrasting with the lush scenes across the rest of the mural, the contemporary Mission District is presented in stark black and white. This was the first major mural painted by the *Mujeres Muralistas*, the first (anywhere) painted by women, and passersby said, "It's about time." (see page 85)

*WAPAC Mural* (1977). 1956 Sutter Street, near Fillmore. Painted by David Bradford. San Francisco housing issues did not begin in the Mission, where the current focus of that struggle is located. In the Fillmore and Western Addition they arose after the 1906 earthquake and fire when owners of apartments not built to code began renting to people of color as temporary residents moved into other parts of the city. In 1942, when American citizens of Japanese descent were forced from their homes and businesses into the dreadful "internment" camps, recently arrived workers from the South began to occupy their homes. In the 1960s, an urban renewal plan for the area was so blatantly racist it became known as "Negro Removal." Bradford contributed this mural on the Western Addition Project Area Committee (WAPAC) building to raise awareness of housing issues in the neighborhood, depicting Black Americans in their strength and creative glory, including a list of inspiring figures such as King, Malcolm, Jackson, among others. The mural at last succumbed to the forces it opposed.

*Holly Courts Murals* (1976, 1980). Appleton, Highland, and Patton Streets near Holly Park on Bernal Heights. Fran Valesco, in 1976, and Mike Mosher and Claire Josephson, in 1980, painted murals in this public housing project. One of Mosher's, *Unified Diversity* (shown), is an iconic portrayal of the multi-racial, multi-ethnic makeup of San Francisco's population, reflecting the tenants' pride in the ethnically mixed nature of their housing, and that everyone got along well. Asserting his power, a housing administrator had the murals painted out in 1980, claiming that residents preferred plain white to colorful murals, but resident graffiti taggers soon proved him wrong. This destruction prompted local muralists to demand written protections for their works in city contracts.

*MCO* (1972). 23rd and Folsom Streets. Michael Rios painted this mural on the side of the Mission Coalition Organization, near the also-destroyed Horizons Unlimited mural painted by Spain, Ruben Guzmán, and Chuy Campusano. Rios painted local residents as dogs, because that's how they are treated by authorities; and as moles, because the real life in the Mission District is underground. When he also painted police as pigs, he was arrested on an outstanding parking ticket and beaten by the cops. Showing courage and integrity, if not a high degree of self-preservation, Rios returned and finished the mural as planned. It was painted over during routine maintenance.

*Mission Rebels* (1973). 18th Street and South Van Ness. Painted by a group of local artists— Ruben Guzmán, R. Crumb (yes, that R. Crumb, his only known mural), Bob Cuff, Chuy Campusano, Gerald Conchca. Like WAPAC, the Mission Rebels was a grassroots neighborhood organization typical of the sort that sprouted in poor neighborhoods across the country during the sixties (c. 1960-1974) to provide advice and other forms of support to residents struggling against such threats as urban renewal, absentee landlords, etc. The atypical thing about the Mission Rebels was their muralized building on Mission Street.

*Jamestown* (1973). 180 Fair Oaks St. This interior mural at the Jamestown CYO Community Center was perhaps the most influential early mural in San Francisco because it was painted by Patricia Rodriguez, Chuy Campusano, Ruben Guzmán, Consuelo Mendez, Jerome Pasias, Elizabeth Raz, and Tom Rios, each of whom worked on their own portion of the wall, but within a shared framework that tied the images together. This project was the inspiration for Michael Rios's subsequent Mini Park murals (below).

*Sistersongs of Liberation* (1974). Painted by Jane Norling for the a women's law collective office in Berkeley, the mural made brilliant use of a very difficult space so that from within the hallway, the walls were painted with landscape, but seen though the office door, a multi-national group of women charged toward the viewer. A detail of this section was made into an International Women's Day poster, and in that format traveled around the world, becoming the basis for a nationalist mural in Belfast, Northern Ireland, where an IRA woman soldier was substituted for the central Black woman. The mural, painted on canvas, was removed and remounted at the San Francisco Housing Authority office in 1975, from which it disappeared.

*Para el Mercado (Paco's Tacos)* (1974). Near 24th Street and South Van Ness. Discussed by all the *Mujeres Muralistas*, but painted on the planks of a wooden fence by two of them, Consuelo Mendez on the left, Graciela Cabrillo on the right (for consistency the mural's palette was designed by Susan Kelk Cervantes, founder of the Precita Eyes Mural Arts Center). The mural was funded by the owner of the Paco's Tacos stand when he learned a McDonald's was planned for just a block away. Some years later, in preparation for a new building on the site, the mural was removed and half of it taken to the Precita Eyes workshop. The remaining half was stolen.

*Hot Air Balloons Over Bryce Canyon* (1975). 14th and Mission Streets. This mural represents a cluster of murals at Valencia Gardens housing project. An example of Housing Authority efforts to brighten up (or cover up) its properties, Jack Frost, who became a professional billboard artist, took advantage of the verticality of the apartment buildings by creating a view from the bottom of Bryce Canyon with ascending hot air balloons carrying the United Farm Workers logo (a popular rallying focus of local Chicano residents, nearly all of whom had toiled in the fields of agribusiness), and the Mexican national flag. In other parts of the housing project, George Mead, Shoshana Dubiner, R. D. James, and Guillermo Pulido painted other murals. As a mark of the respect these artworks engendered, they were not defaced. All these artworks were destroyed when Valencia Gardens was demolished in 2004 in preparation for new housing now on the site.

*Whale* (1977). 1152 Oak Street, originally Truck 6, Engine 27 of the San Francisco Fire Department, but used for storage in the seventies. Mike McClosky, after years of slogging through various impenetrable City bureaucracies, including the building-owner SFFD, finally went out with a ladder and painted the beloved cetacean over a long President's Day weekend. It remained until obscured by an immediately adjacent new building in what had been a bank parking lot.

*LULAC* (1975). Folsom and 26th Streets. Designed by Mexican artist Gilberto Ramirez for an industrial location in Gary, Indiana, which is why it seems out of place in San Francisco. When he found himself in San Francisco with the wall offered to him, he put this mural up in an astonishingly short period of time as local muralists watched and marveled at his technique. The palette and design (especially use of flames and expressionist painting style) are heavily influenced by José Clemente Orozco. The mural was lost when the building was demolished in preparation for new housing on the site.

*Vietnamese* (1975). Bryant and 24th Street. One of the few anti-Vietnam War murals nationally, and perhaps the only one painted in San Francisco. It reminds viewers that the war's effects, and our country's conduct in it, remain with us—infuriatingly true nearly four decades after the mural was painted. A new building now stands up against the mural's wall, covering it completely.

# Mujeres Muralistas

## by Patricia Rodriguez

*Our interest as artists is to put art close to where it needs to be. Close to the children; close to the old people; close to everyone who has to walk or ride the buses to get places. We want our art either out in the streets or in places where a lot of people go each day, the hospitals, health centers, clinics, restaurants, and other public places.... We offer you color we make.*

—Mujeres Muralistas, 1974[1]

The *Mujeres Muralistas* was a group of Chicana/Latina artists in the Mission District that pioneered large-scale, woman-painted outdoor murals. The work of the varying number of women in the group was part of the flourishing of public murals in the Mission District, throughout the Bay Area, in California, and even nationally in the 1970s. A glimpse at our motivations, at our training, at our relation to other muralists and politics of the time, and at the murals we painted reveals a rich history of the *Mujeres Muralistas*.

One big motivation for us was recognizing that there had been no successful women muralists in the Mexican mural movement. We wanted to show that women could also paint large outdoor murals.[2] Another factor was the lack of support from the men painting murals in the Mission District who were also critical of the subjects we wanted to paint. We knew that because we were not harassed by police like the men were, and because we had not suffered by having fought in Vietnam, we had a different visual story to tell. We had the freedom to paint whatever we wanted, and we chose the beauty of women and their Mexican and Latino cultures. As *Muralista* Irene Perez put it, "We brought fine art to the streets and added the beauty of women in our culture."

Our first effort was an experimental mural project on a garage door across the alley from the building I shared with Graciela Carrillo at 54 Balmy Alley in 1972. We asked the neighbor for permission and our experiment was to see if we could collaborate as muralists and draw large-scale designs. At this time there were no fancy mural paints, so we used outdoor house paint we got from neighbors. For the bright colors and to complete our palette we bartered paint from various artists. In the beginning, men teased us and harassed us, and so did women who poked fun saying, "Anyone can paint and do what you're doing!" Some even started their own mural, also in Balmy Alley near 25th Street, to prove their point, but it was never finished. Ralph Maradiaga, co-director of the nearby Galería de La Raza, was our only constant source of support, and he documented the mural-painting process, sharing his slides with us. He was also the one who suggested our name. Obviously, it stuck. Although few people thought we could complete the project, we did, and we discovered we liked it and wanted to continue painting in collaboration with others.

## Beginnings

The advent of the *Mujeres Muralistas*, and of much of the art in the Mission District of the time, was the result of a fortunate confluence of 1960s political activism and students at the San Francisco Art Institute (SFAI). Through the Civil Rights, Women's Liberation, and anti-Vietnam War movements, Sixties activism affected everyone, and Chicanos were most influenced by *El Movimiento*, which focused its struggle for universal civil rights on Chicanos in particular. In joining this movement, the *Mujeres Muralistas* were inspired by such activists as Bert Corona, Cesar Chavez, "Corky" Gonzalez in Denver, and Reis Lopez Tijerina in New Mexico, and we began applying to universities in order to get an education and eventually get better jobs than had been available to us in the *barrios*. We understood that fighting for *La Raza* also meant fighting for ourselves, and that it could open up access to our dreams of becoming artists.

At SFAI, admitted under the minority students tuition waiver plan, I met other activists and students: Rene Yañez, Graciela Carrillo, Michael Rios, Consuelo Mendez, Irene Perez, Jerry Concha, and many students from other ethnic groups. We grew very frustrated. I was in the painting major and I was being asked to be a minimalist, and I didn't want to be a minimalist. I wasn't interested. But I was very persistent and did something very colorful. My professor asked me if I thought I was Diego Rivera but I didn't know who Diego Rivera was. I was 19, 20 coming from the barrio and didn't know. We didn't discover that we had culture, that we had roots, that the Mayans discovered the zero, that there were Aztecs. We didn't know any of that until we got to college in the '60s. This is the first time that Chicanos were being let into the university, we didn't know anything about ourselves. We didn't have that background.

In 1970, inspired by studying art with other like-minded students from similar backgrounds, Graciela and I thought of having a women's art exhibit at the recently-founded Galería de La Raza in the Mission District.[3] Luckily, Graciela was co-founder's Rene Yañez's girlfriend, and she persuaded him to agree with our plan for the exhibition, which we called "Exposición de Mujeres" ("The Women's Exhibition"). In those days publicity was by word of mouth and through flyers passed around to artists in the community. To our amazement Chicanas and Latinas from all over the Bay Area heard about the show and wanted to participate.

The April 1970 show had lots of color, crocheted and macramé wall hangings, installations, paintings, and political posters discussing current community issues. The mostly male Galería members were impressed, discovering there were women artists doing work in the community that needed to be heard and seen. This exhibition established a presence for Chicana/Latina artists in the Bay Area. Today some of those women artists (e.g. Yolanda Lopez, and myself) are still active and have become well-known.

Another Mission institution that influenced the *Mujeres Muralistas* was the La Raza Silkscreen Center. As early as 1970, its organizers and artists designed and printed posters in a makeshift studio in the back of La Raza Information Center, which was one of many nonprofit organizations that dotted 24th Street. The Los Siete de La Raza Defense Committee was housed in an adjacent storefront; both were near 24th Street and South Van Ness.[4] The La Raza Information Center ran many programs, including Centro de Salud, a free breakfast program, and a community newspaper, but the Defense Committee was its main program. I started teaching screen-printing there as a volunteer, working with Pete Gallegos, Oscar Melara, and others. Many artists from other places passed through La Raza Silkscreen Center, including a special group from Mexico that wanted to help with what they thought was an imminent revolution. They were students from "La Esmeralda" and Bellas Artes, both art schools located in Mexico City. They were all excellent graphic artists and produced vibrant posters documenting community issues of the time, such as Los Siete de La Raza. I taught them how to camp in Yosemite, and they schooled me on printing, Mexican graphics, and history.

## Jamestown—the first large-scale collaborative mural

In 1972, I asked Consuelo and Graciela to help me design a mural at the Jamestown Community Center, where the Catholic Youth Organization was located. They were so happy, they were eager to do something outside in the community that was away from SFAI and the minimalist stuff that they were trying to teach us. Our design created large trees that ran on both sides of the hallway and connected at the top and which left equal spaces between the trees for the creation of different Mission District scenes. Our time was limited since we had to finish our semesters, all our school assignments, and work part time jobs, so we needed help. We invited fellow artists Michael Rios, his brother Tom Rios, Ruben Guzmán, Chuy Campusano, Jerome Pasias, and a few others to assist. Some of the men had just returned home from Vietnam and their imagery tended toward that experience, and Chicano political statements coming directly from the struggles of *El Movimiento* and the Chicano muralists in Los Angeles and the Southwest. They painted those and the story of drugs and police brutality in our community. We painted positive things like children of different nationalities playing together. As a group we painted our Latino heritage, and it was a great collaboration with the male muralists on this particular mural. This project inspired a lot of the artists to continue to look for other walls on which to create murals, but at the same time the men saw us women as competition, and they did not invite us to collaborate with them until much later.

Around this time we were contacted to paint a mural in the Childcare Consortium on Shotwell Street, which was funded by the Model Cities Program.[5] It was located in a large warehouse remodeled for a new community childcare center. The directors wanted traditional images of the ABCs and numbers. Graciela and I convinced them to let us use a design featuring animals on a large pink tree with fun things like flying fish between the branches, each in groups of different numbers (i.e. two bears, three birds, four monkeys, etc.). We also made sure our design worked well with the layout of the windows.

## *Latinoamérica,* 1974

The *Mujeres Muralistas* made its formal public appearance in 1974 with a large mural painted for the Mission Model Cities organization, located at Mission and 25th Streets. Consuelo was approached by a friend who worked at Mission Model Cities and asked if we could design and paint a mural representing Latinos in the Mission District. The organization gave us $1,000 for the whole project. Consuelo, Graciela, Irene, and I got together and decided to accept the invitation. The four of us met at our home in Balmy Alley and brainstormed a design. Our house became the central headquarters of the *Mujeres Muralistas*. Each of the women had a key to the house and could come by at any time of the day. There was a large table in the laundry room ready with all the drawing tools necessary to work on the design.

We worked as a collaborative group, sharing information, research, and discussing what kind of mural we wanted.

This mural, *Latinoamérica,* was our introduction to the broader community as muralists. Everyone was watching us and interviewing us for newspapers, television, and radio. We represented a new generation of muralists depicting our own reality at that present moment of time, exploring new ideas and new styles, and speaking about the Latinas who lived in the Mission District. As a result, more women wanted to join the group and some just wanted to help out in whatever way they could. Miriam Olivo from Venezuela and Ruth Rodriguez from Puerto Rico were invited to join us by Consuelo. Ester Hernandez and Xochil Nevel were introduced to us by Irene. They came by and helped us paint.

In our decision-making and research we discovered each other's talents and assigned ourselves the particular tasks that best utilized our skills. Irene was very good at hard edge images due to her experience as a graphic artist and she volunteered to do all the vegetation. Graciela was good with figures, traditional clothing, and fantasy. Consuelo was good with figures and had strong concepts. I was good at dividing and placement, and solving problems. The mural still had to look like one person designed it, and thanks to our similar backgrounds and sensitivity to our cultural history and colors, it worked out beautifully as we understood each other very well. We designed on a scale of one inch to a foot, on white paper with black ink drawings of the images we were planning. We decided that the color for the mural would be dealt with once we got to the wall.

Latinoamérica, detail.

The small Model Cities budget was spent on paint and scaffolding to reach all of the twenty-foot wall. Whatever was left over we split up to buy groceries. There was never enough money for rent and food so we managed to survive with part-time work and lots of bartering. We had the scaffolding delivered but not assembled. We figured out how to put it together ourselves, and secured it to the wall for safety. The drawing on the wall took almost three weeks because we underestimated the size and drew a two-foot grid on the wall instead of one foot to an inch. Once we started again with one-foot squares, we could draw the mural images on the wall with a simple cartoon line

Latinoamérica

of each of the images. We typically worked from 7 a.m. until 3 p.m. By that time it was either too hot, or the winds would dry our paints too quickly, or everything flew off the scaffolding. When men watching us discovered we were women, they would not leave us alone, and especially if they were drunk they wanted to touch us. In general the Latino community was our primary audience and they let us know they were grateful. They brought us gifts of beer, tamales, and flowers for honoring them and their culture. They also brought their children to introduce them to their Latino heritage so they would not forget where they came from. The mural seemed to heal some of the community's wounds.

The mural had elements connected to our culture but we didn't want to produce another copy of the Mexican pyramids or paint a homage to the style of the *los tres grandes*. Instead, we used a pyramid made of corn stalks to emphasize the importance of the corn that fed the indigenous people of the Americas as well as the whole world. The mural also spoke to who we were and where we came from. As Latina artists raised and educated in the US we had the best of both worlds, connecting art school influences with our cultural roots.

Even though our painting instructors at SFAI knew about *los tres grandes* muralists in Mexico and the Diego Rivera mural located on the SFAI campus, our mural work as female students did not relate to anything they had ever known. Even though we told them what we were doing, it still did not register; they could not understand why a painting on a wall was so important. They discounted it as graffiti, so they ignored our request to value anything we did outside the classroom. But when one of my instructors read about the *Mujeres Muralistas* in *The New Republic* he said, "I have been an artist all my life and never got a write-up in such a prestigious magazine."[6] They were impressed that we got such publicity, and then paid attention to what we were doing. I insisted that they come to see our mural, squeezed them into my VW Bug, and drove them to the Mission to see *Latinoamérica*. They had no idea we were painting such large-scale murals. The story ends well when we passed our painting classes and graduated from SFAI.

We were constantly challenged by our male artist friends and questioned about the lack of political imagery in our work. Our intimate relationships suffered because we didn't consult the male artists, who were our colleagues and boyfriends. We were our own bosses and worked hard to achieve what we wanted to say on the wall. The *Mujeres Muralistas* introduced working as a collective group unlike Rivera or Siqueiros who were the sole directors and designers of their murals and used assistants to help them complete their murals. The male Mission District artists worked this way. We, on the other hand, worked as a team and shared information and tasks. Painting this mural gave us the opportunity to celebrate our *cultura*. Our mural was the voice of modern women, depicting the various tasks and hardships women endure, from bearing children, to cooking, to educating the young, and creating beauty all at the same time. Not too long ago, women were allowed to paint only flowers and dogs. We learned we were the first Chicana/Latina mural collective in the history of the United States and that *Latinoamérica* was one of the first Latino murals to use modern influences from art school and ideas from the popular artists of the times, such as Robert Crumb and Roy Lichtenstein, as well as our own Mexican/Latino influences.

Within a short time the whole community knew we were available to paint and many invitations came our way. This was also the beginning of the Women's Liberation Movement, when women were pursuing non-traditional jobs and pushing to be accepted. Some of the jobs included climbing poles for PG&E, working on building roads, driving large equipment trucks, and doing construction. We filled the bill as liberated women who could paint murals and erect scaffolding and basically work as hard as men. Women from feminist magazines began to include us as part

*Para el Mercado* at Pacos Tacos.

of the second wave of feminists in the arts. We were surprised, and rejected being categorized as feminist at the time. The feminists we knew did not include us in their groups. We often felt left out and did not agree with all their politics.[7]

*Latinoamérica* opened many doors for women muralists. We were now an official mural group that could do monumental public art and all the community agencies wanted a mural by the women artists. Many educators and historians also became interested in the group, and so did scholars from France, Japan, Mexico, and Spain. In 2010 European students still interview us and study how we work as artists in our communities. Many European countries are experiencing a new influx of immigrants from neighboring countries, and they want to study how we do things in our ethnically mixed community.

1974 was a year of opportunities for us women muralists. For example, I got an artist-in-residence from the California Arts Council, to work in the schools with Ruth Asawa creating murals with children. It was difficult because we found the teachers working in the schools then to be very conservative and without much knowledge about art, much less about murals. The murals were a rich experience for the children and the schools. We taught the teachers to allow the children to express who they were instead of just following narrow guidelines.

By this time there were many requests for more murals in the community, so we started to spread out in smaller groups to meet the requests. As the *Mujeres Muralistas* grew we had to assign people to different mural projects, and each project required different demands and schedules. We were all going in different directions. The new women helped paint whenever they could, but the group was large and we found it difficult to meet and agree on many things.

## After *Latinoamérica*—Paco's Tacos

A telling mural request then came from the owner of Paco's Tacos, a hot dog and taco stand, who wanted to keep his small business open and not be wiped out by the redevelopment happening in the Mission at the time. As in other *barrios* across the country, many small businesses were being crushed by big junk food franchises moving in, like McDonald's, scheduled to open on the corner of Mission and 24th Streets, a block away from Paco's Tacos. The owner succeeded in preserving his business for a while as people came to eat and also enjoy the mural they knew was painted by local artists.

The mural, *Para el Mercado,* was designed by Graciela and Consuelo. We did not realize that Consuelo and Graciela did not get along well. They worked in their own styles on separate sides of the mural, which looked divided but at the same time found consistency in its colors because Graciela invited Susan Kelk Cervantes to help paint with the group and design the color scheme for the mural. Consuelo's memory is that the experience of painting *Para el Mercado* was a bit mixed, but ultimately successful. She recalls:

> There might have been differences between Graciela and myself. I have a feeling now that it was not important. What is true about the experience is that it points out the difficulty of collective work and that we were able to work it out in an unusual way by separating because the format of the wall gave us that chance. Graciela and I worked on our own spaces but

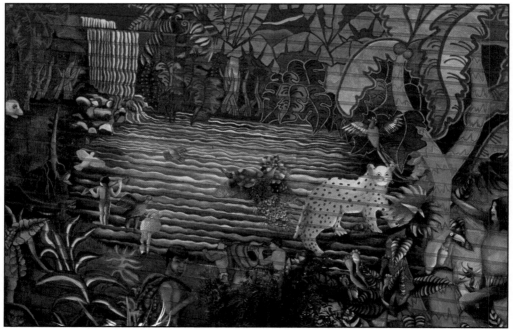

Fantasy World for Children, 24th Street Mini Park, detail.

respectfully towards each other. At the center of the wall we met
and the two worlds came together only in that place.
I also remember the neighbors and the nice people who worked
around the neighborhood of Paco's Tacos. In that sense the mural
was a warm experience. We worked hard every day and finished
on time. The Paco's Tacos mural included images of our food and
market culture that were dear to us as Latina artists in the US.[8]

Our last project together as a whole group was painted for the San Francisco
Arts Festival in 1974 when we were awarded the Award of Merit for our murals
and were invited to create a project for the San Francisco Arts Commission in
front of City Hall. We had to create a design where people could walk around
it and see our work. I came up with a three-dimensional parallelogram, which
basically was a large box with slanted sides, supported on its axis. Ester, Miriam,
and Ruth joined us for this project. We painted on 10' x 10' square panels, but it
was difficult to unite everyone, so some of the women worked together on one
panel or assisted the main artists with their designs. In the end it was interesting
but not as fully developed or well integrated as our previous murals. By this time
the group was too big to work as cohesively as we had in the past.

In 1975, some of the *Mujeres Muralistas* continued at the 24th Street Mini Park
on the mural *Fantasy World for Children*, which is also when CETA support money
began to find its way into the Mission District.[9] Graciela, Irene, and I designed
and painted the Mini Park mural, which is the only original work that still exists
there today (the others have been refurbished). The Mini Park was supposed to be
used by children and the families who lived near it, but it was blighted for many
years—full of wine bottles and dog droppings—and the local families were not

using it. Michael Rios went to the City to propose a mural project there in order to improve the park and make it usable again. He was given the money, and he invited us to paint there as well. We were surprised but also knew we finally had been accepted as muralists by the male artists. We were excited by the possibilities and of course accepted the invitation.

We went to work on our design, thinking of our audiences: children with their parents or grandparents enjoying a warm sunny day in the park adorned with colorful murals depicting fantasy and beauty. This vision was a stark contrast to the Vietnam War mural the men painted before they changed it to a large image of Quetzalcoatl with kids climbing all over it.

In 1975 and 1976 Graciela, myself, Susan, Michael, Sekio Fuapopo, and Fran Valesco worked with Bernal Dwellings housing projects tenants on a group of murals, although this was not an official project of the *Mujeres Muralistas*. We designed the first one to reflect the music the tenants liked and used colors that represented the different cultural groups living in the neighborhood.

In 1976, we spread further out. Graciela and I went to Potrero Hill on Wisconsin Street to paint a mural of Black political leaders—Martin Luther King, Jr., Angela Davis, and Marcus Garvey. At this time Fran joined the *Mujeres Muralistas*. The Potrero terrain was a bit away from our own community and attracted men who watched us daily. By three o'clock we needed to pack up and leave, because by then the men became very drunk and aggressive. In Fran's memory:

> It was street theater, as we interacted with people who came by, especially the folks that hung out at the small market there. One time, John [Langley] Howard, one of the Coit Tower muralists, introduced himself and invited us to his house nearby. That was so special—it connected us with a great historical movement of murals and social subject matter and a great flowering of the mural art form in the 1930s. We were given respect and inclusion as fellow professional muralists.[10]

Winter rains made painting more difficult. The mural was on a steep hill, and it wasn't long before a car crashed into the mural wall and tore it up. The owner took too long to repair it and the people in that community began to steal the painted panels. In the end the owner of the property decided to not do the mural after all, and put up a metal fence instead. We lost that mural altogether.

## Individual work post-*Mujeres Muralistas*

The Mission District community was changing rapidly and inner city monies that funded our murals were beginning to dry up so there were fewer mural projects. Requests for murals from the *Mujeres Muralistas* group were disappearing too. We all began to do other things, and this pulled us further apart because we no longer agreed on politics or painting strategies. We were too large to function effectively as a collective, although each of us continued to paint murals in different places.

Graciela and I went to Sacramento State University to study for our Master's degrees. Shortly after that I was invited to teach at UC Berkeley in the Chicano Studies Department where I taught for five years. Graciela was engaged to be married, and left the Bay Area for a while. Consuelo was planning a family and she and her husband went back home to Caracas, Venezuela. She and I have remained productive artists, as has Irene, who moved back to Oakland. Fran went on to paint other murals in other San Francisco neighborhoods, and to teach printmaking at City College and San Francisco State College. Susan founded Precita Eyes Muralists and the Precita Eyes Mural Center, which have been responsible for painting hundreds of San Francisco murals. Graciela became ill and moved away. Ester works primarily as a graphic artist and lives in the Mission District.

The *Mujeres Muralistas* created a significant body of mural work on the streets of San Francisco and left an influential legacy showing what a group of young Latinas can accomplish when they decide to work together and challenge the establishment, the college, and the community with their artwork. As Fran remembers:

> "It was pioneering work which was the foundation for much of the art outreach that is done in contemporary art, with its use of vernacular materials and broader audiences beyond a small world of galleries and museums. At the time, community art didn't have much respect, but we were truly professional...It taught me how beloved art can be for a neighborhood and how art can change people's lives."[11]

The time was right and we were at the right place to create monumental murals with very few resources. We could not do this the same way today. Times have changed and the resources that were available then have dried up.

I always say that we were like a rock and roll band. We created our art and put it out to the public. Our work is archived in art journals, and in interviews with university students for their dissertations and master degrees. We live on in books and research papers.

## Notes

1.    Victoria Quintero, "A Mural Is a Painting on a Wall Done by Human Hands," *El Tecolote* 5, no.1 (September 13, 1974): 5, 7, 12.

2.    A view of the relationships between *los tres grandes*—Diego Rivera, José Orozco, and David Siqueiros—and potential women muralists can be found in Elena Poniatowska, *Las Siete Cabritas* (Mexico, D.F.: Ediciones Era, S.A. de C.V., 2000), 79-100.

3.    The origin of the Galería de La Raza can be traced to a spring 1969 exhibition in Oakland, "New Symbols for La Nueva Raza," sponsored by the Mexican American Liberation Art Front (MALAF). Aimed at "integrating art into the Chicano social revolution sweeping the country," MALAF brought together Chicano/Latino artists Esteban Villa, Manuel Hernandez, Malaquias Montoya, and René Yañez. In 1970 they formed the Galería de La Raza collective on 14th Street and Guerrero Street in San Francisco. Like many other such *centros*, it was a product of the Chicano civil rights movement which called for artistic emphasis on everyday lives and on community activities of the Chicano/Latino people. These principles guided the Galería and set it apart from mainstream art organizations.  Founding members included Rupert García, Peter Rodríguez, Francisco X. Camplis, Graciela Carrillo, Jerry Concha, Gustavo Ramos Rivera, Carlos Loarca, Manuel Villamor, Robert González, Luis Cervantes, Chuy Campusano, Rolando Castellón, Ralph Maradiaga, and Yañez. Maradiaga became administrative director and Yañez the artistic director.  In 1972 the Galería moved to its present location at 24th Street and Bryant Street. Officially, it is a nonprofit community arts organization that promotes Chicano and Latino art and culture in the San Francisco Bay area and beyond. Throughout its history the Galería has striven not only to make art accessible to the community, especially in the largely Latino Mission District of San Francisco, but also to involve the public in the very creation of artworks.

4.    The Los Siete de La Raza Defense Committee was established to support seven Mission District youth who were falsely accused of shooting a San Francisco policeman in 1969. See Jason M. Ferreira's essay "With the Soul of a Human Rainbow" in this volume for more information on Los Siete.

5.  The Model Cities Program of 1966 provided funds for community improvements ranging from structural development to issues like housing, education, employment, and health. In 1973, President Richard Nixon cut federal funding of the Model Cities Program. See T.F. Summers Sandoval, Jr.'s essay "All Those Who Care About the Mission, Stand up with Me!" in this volume for extensive information on the Mission Coalition Organization, its acquisition and use of Model Cities funds, and the redevelopment proposals for the Mission District. In the late 1960s the San Francisco Redevelopment Agency proposed high-density towers to be built at 16th and 24th Streets as adjuncts to the new BART stations being built at those locations. These projects would have razed many blocks and displaced hundreds of people living in apartments there. Fearing a repeat of the notorious Western Addition Renewal Project, which displaced over 4,000 families, the Mission community mobilized a popular front which included everyone from the Brown Berets to the remaining White homeowners in the neighborhood. From this victory, local activists went on to form the Mission Coalition Organization in order to qualify for federal Model Cities Program funding. MCO eventually included over one hundred organizations, including churches, unions, and nonprofits. Many of the murals painted in the Mission District in the early 1970s were funded through the MCO. Michael Rios painted a mural on its building. The MCO supported a network of social service agencies that is still around today: Mission Housing, Mission Hiring Hall, and the Mission Neighborhood Health Center. From one of its splits, La Raza en Acción Local was formed in 1970, which, unlike the MCO, tried to combine Latino culture with community organizing and service programs. They went on to create other Raza organizations in the Mission, including Centro de Información de La Raza, La Raza Centro Legal, and the La Raza Silkscreen Center.

    The divisions within the MCO were too big to overcome. In its first convention, the more radical groups, including the Mission Tenants Union, the Mission Rebels, and the La Raza Party, walked out. and the MCO later disintegrated in infighting.

6.  Peter Barnes, "Bringing Back the WPA," *The New Republic*, March 15, 1975.

7.  See, for example, Eva Cockcroft, "Women in the Community Mural Movement," *Heresies Magazine: A Feminist Publication on Art and Politics* 1 (January, 1977): 14–22.

8.  Consuelo Mendez, private correspondence with author, October 2009.

9.  The Comprehensive Employment and Training Act (CETA) was a US federal law enacted in 1973. It stated that jobs must be for public service, which was defined as including, but not being limited to, work in such fields as environmental quality, health care education, public neighborhood improvements, rural development and conservation, beautification, and community improvement. The funds were given to cities that assigned them to local public agencies. In San Francisco, the Art Commission hired muralists through its Neighborhood Arts Program (NAP). In 1975 CETA money began to reach community organizations including the artists in the Mission who were already painting public murals. The first people from our community to receive this funding were Michael Rios and his team, then the Samoan artists, then the *Mujeres Muralistas*. (I was actually the first Latina artist in the City to receive CETA wages.) We had to attend meetings and talk about what we were doing in the community and present problems and give solutions. Here we met Roberto Vargas and Alejandro Murguía who were involved in creating the Mission Cultural Center. We also met Peter Coyote (who came to NAP meetings dressed in leather moccasins with deer skin Indian bags), the art critic Alfred Frankenstein, and many other interesting characters.

10. Fran Velasco, private correspondence with author, January 2010.

11. Ibid.

# MY WORLD INCOMPLETE/ TO COMPLETE MY WORLD

## by Roberto Vargas

### I

The years were piling up behind me/ in my tracks
circling from Nicaragua to San Francisco,
(y regreso) from tears to struggle, to home again.
In 1965 I Revisited Nicaragua
guided by my Nica neighbor on Bernal Heights.
Bérman Zuniga/ pilot/ leather salesman
former Guardia Nacional/ Air Force Cadet
who formed part of an attempted air assault/ coup against Somoza
was betrayed then flew his small plane to refuge en Cuba.
Bérman became my mentor/ introduced me to combatientes urbanos from the FSLN.
En Managua I rediscovered mi papa Silvestre/ myself/ poetry.
10 years later Bérman and I delivered our *GACETA SANDINISTA* newspapers
in bookstores/ tiendas on 24th St./ in Los Angeles/ in his old Mercedes
hot off our press.

### II

In 68 Che was resurrected in 3 continents,
in the coffee rich hills of Matagalpa, Nicaragua/ 1968
birthplace of Carlos Fonseca Amador, as Sandino/ patriarca of the FSLN
30 years before him.
Che's Bolivian crucifixion engendered the politico-cachorros
of Sandino's diáspora en el mero barrio de La Misión/ de Dolores/ de Post-Partum
where we fought for human rights, voting and union rights/ womens', gay,
and national liberation struggles with one hand on the Bible and the other on my gun/
organizing poetry and prayer of resistance at St Peter's Church
where I met Casimiro Sotelo in '74
after he handed me a WANTED poster of Somoza
"Dead or Alive."
Casimiro's brother Casimiro was a founder of The FSLN,
Killed in combat in a Managua barrio against Somoza's tanques.
I embraced Casimiro with Bernal Heights behind us
posing as momotombo LIGHT in that San Francisco Autumn.
*La Gaceta Sandinista* bore its first leaves/ first soldados.

# III

I met Raúl Venerio pumping gas at 21ˢᵗ & South Van Ness
Mismo barrio de San Francisco.
With the skill of a pilot and the passion of Picasso,
Raúl became first editor of *La Gaceta Sandinista*/ arquitecto del CyberPuente
guided by compadre Gato/ first jefe at the Centro Cultural de La Misión.
Alejandro, loyal keeper of the Pocho-Ché Press/ *Gaceta Sandinista*/ keeper of the fire,
where we created word webs to other barrios where Nicas lived worked struggled.
Gato taught the technical trucos of how to lay out the fonts/ lead articles/ distribution
Gato transforming/ became compañero Ulises en el Frente Sur,
Comandante Venerio and Bérman teaching us how to fly over Pacific Coastal beaches
in mock raids over simulated somocista targets in 1974 Pacifica rent-a-plane,
dripping of the confidence radiated by moral authority/ of innocence/
umoved by the size of the risk posed by a Ronald Reagan military recon's ability to detect
4 Sandinista Mouse-That Roared rebeldes in frenetic flight to a July 1979 rendezvous.

# IV

Then came Anuar/ Palestino-Nica/ student at UC Berkeley /on motorcycle
Nimble, quickfooted, still in his teens, balancing academia with his martial arts
demonstrating love and courage between grenades
with the humility of his heroism, el Flaco Armando.
followed by mi cuñado Ray Solis, Campion Nacional Black Belt Karate-Do
who led us in Wing Chun ritual/ commitment
as we watched the faint steam of CHI rise from his shoulders
fingers upstretched to the sky in appeal/ reverence/ meditation
in our village within a village mi pueblo adoptado
the BART station on 24ᵗʰ and Mission morphed to Sandino Plaza
1/2 a block away in '77, Poeta padre/ Ernesto Cardenal
Exorcizes with word alchemy/los somosauros from the
MissionCentro Cultural/ Yin-Yan temple/
baptizes children/ parents/ mi hijo Ariel
Liberation theology of the heart/ of chololandia en praxis
engendered Comandantes Chombo Ferretti/ Raúl/ Venerio/ Tono/ Anuar
poeta combatiente Gato Murguía/ ConsulGenerales/ Casimiro/ Bérman
Compañeros that lived and died for/ and still live and fight for/ paz justicia y libertad.

# V

I met Walter Ferretti at the Hyatt Regency joven cocinero
with his poet soul and pure of smile, of a comandante.
that later was flashed in 1978 *Time* magazine foto.
Comandante Chombo combat coordinator of the Asalto al Palacio Nacional.
Chombo trained the grupo de asalto comprised of young indios from Monimbo/Masaya

using Ray's Wing Chun training/ messages/ tense-relax-at will
KATAs thick as incense in Chombo's prepping for combate
August 22 1978: Commandates. Cero/ Dora María/ Chombo, y los 30 monimbosenos
began to rewind the historical clock/ time's up
liberated Somoza's National Palace/ La Chanchera Congreso/
Commandate Raúl in support.
Days later Anuar- Roberto- y Tono Gringo took their longest walk
into our sacred mountains with Pomares/ with Joaquín Cuadra/ el Zorro
to contribute our share of bullets, sacrifice and love for our pueblo.
Memories surfacing of childhood joys/ sorrows of nuestro barrio/
Nina, Diana, Magaly/ our loved ones training with us around Bernal Heights
El Gato Ulises trained and deployed cholomandos from Fresno into and
beyond the 19th of July for a Patria Libre O Morir!
por Nicaragua from any Rincón of this planeta/ Americana
from Homeboy Heroics to/ our homeland security/ to historical memory.

# VI

Today we remain unmoved this side of the 19th of JULY
jaded by the size of the 9/11 mandate to muzzle and maim dissent
by the US 4th fleet subtle seabound message to Daniel, Evo, to Chávez from Cheney
carved on Roose-Bush's's big stick policy/ no lap top carrots from Plan Colombia
policies that engender new men new women, no fear no pain just armed love.
Engendered Bolivian Indigenous liberation 40 years after Che's crucified there/
ignited my first poems/ novitiate prologue to my newfound identity
still resisting TODAY!! In the barrios of the Bronx/ San Antos/ La Misión
defending our familias EN NUESTRA AMERICA.
El pan nuestro de cada día/ our very water/ in Venezuela Nicaragua
with the gift of survival ingrained by los abuelos/ en Bolivia Ecuador
gift of love for our selves/ our pueblos en Brazil Chile en Asia Africa.
40 years later in Iraq, Afghanistan, Syria still so much loyalty to bogus principles
false premises false promises patriotic index down 40 years
as global mortgage melt-down tips the iceberg for impending food phenomenas/ famine
oil-drilling in forbidden territories/ Gallon of heating oil costs nearly 8 bucks in Alaska
The global economy is in Las Vegas, Wall Street rolls the dice!

# VII

40 years came & went/ time to cover the walls again with our colors of anger and pain
art of survival, murals of militant love options/ of Miranda, Mike Rios
TIME TO cover the streets with transparent voices/ real commitment
show the way
on this 40th anniversary of ARTE DEL PUEBLO
en San Francisco
UNIDOS in love and struggle VENCEREMOS
PATRIA LIBRE Y VIVIR.

# Where Did All The Flowers Go?
## THE VIEW FROM A STREET IN BERNAL HEIGHTS

### by Peter Booth Wiley

*I arrived in San Francisco from Madison, Wisconsin, on January 28, 1968, married, with a seven-month old daughter and a master's in US history, with both agitation and academia on my mind.¹ I was still pulled—after seven years of activism in the anti-war movement, as a community organizer in the coalfields of eastern Kentucky, and an organizer of teaching assistants at the University of Wisconsin—between two choices: continue down the path of activism or become an academic historian. Plan A: start a radical magazine to replace the defunct* Studies on the Left, *which was founded by graduate students at the University of Wisconsin. Plan B: study Italian, apply for a grant, and ship out to Italy to research my Ph.D. about the Allied occupation of Italy during and after World War II.*

In Madison a friend had warned, "Don't live in the Haight." As soon as we were settled temporarily at a friend's house in Berkeley, my wife Carole Deutch and I dropped by the Rental Library on Lombard Street where for $15 we were granted access to shoeboxes filled with dirty, tattered 3X5 cards, each with a rental address on it. We settled on Mullen Avenue in Bernal Heights.

Mullen was perfect, a quiet street hedged by modest single-storied houses, two chicken houses converted to residences, a shotgun shack, and a couple of two-unit flats. Our house was a roomy, drafty dump with a yard for our dog and space for our daughter to play when she got up on her feet. For many years before we moved there, the house was owned by the Ochoa family. Mr. Ochoa was a longshoreman. The family, his children told us, lost the house due to their father's drinking. Indeed, when I was digging out the basement where some of the kids had slept in a room with a plank floor laid on dirt, I found an enormous stash of wine bottles behind a rotting wall. Our rent was $150/month.

I bought some paint, and while Carole stayed with our daughter Celia in Berkeley, I painted the two bedrooms, living room, and kitchen-dining room. At the end of the day, waiting for Carole to pick me up, I sat at the top of the stairs that led up from the street sipping from a bottle of my brother's homemade wine watching the kids play in the street. A group of pre-teen girls dressed in parochial school uniforms—blouse, sweater and skirts with hemlines hiked to the highest level permitted by the sisters—played some kind of ballgame that involved a lot of screaming. Kids playing in the street, a street that was like a giant play yard, this was our new home.

Bernal at the time was largely a working class neighborhood with an odd, but small, assortment of professionals, students, post-grads, a few gay couples (mostly closeted), an occasional beatnik, and a hippie or two including Chet Helms, the rock impresario from Texas who brought Janis Joplin to San Francisco and opened the Avalon Ballroom, and then the Family Dog on the Great Highway after Bill Graham took over the Avalon. One resident who arrived in the late 1950s recalled that someone had said to her, "If you can't afford to be a starving artist on Potrero Hill, move to Bernal." The ethnic and racial mix was complex and a definite foreshadowing of the city San Francisco was becoming: White with an emphasis on Irish and Italian heritage, Black, Native American, Latino, Chinese, Filipino, and Hawaiian with numerous admixtures. Clearly, this was nothing I had ever seen in a small-town New Jersey suburb, an elite New England men's college, or the mighty University of Wisconsin. Nor was it like the poverty-stricken hollows of Eastern Kentucky.

In and around Mullen lived longshoremen, sailors, barkeeps, hotel workers, phone company employees, a waiter, a house painter, a doctor, a gay couple (one of whom was the house husband, the other sold records), a retired bootlegger from Oklahoma, and Killer Diller, an alcoholic retired longshoreman. When you greeted Killer, he responded to his dogs, but his dogs didn't pass it on. Our first mailman was a lovely, long-legged lady in a miniskirt. You could find her at the Ribeltad Vorden at the west end of Precita Park with the rest of the locals after work. Later she was replaced by Vern, a Native American, who was also an actor. His biggest fans were the neighborhood dogs. When he walked the streets—there were no leash laws in those days—a troop of dogs followed in his path. When he drove his pickup from one part of the hill to another, the dogs rode in the back.

We seemed to be surrounded by musicians, including for a time Carlos Santana and three members of his band, who lived down the street. For Santana, nearby Precita Park was ground zero, "where it all started," as he wrote years later in the introduction to *Voices of Latin Rock: The People and Events that Created This Sound.*[2] Music came from all directions provided by a host of lesser-known bands and musicians who favored rock and roll, but also offered up a blend of classical and jazz.

I wrote my first book in our attic listening to jazz drummer George Marsh jamming with Kwaku Daddy, the renowned Ghanaian drummer and folklorist. Among our housemates and neighbors were members of the San Francisco Mime Troupe, including co-directors Dan Chumley and Joan Holden and musicians from the Mime Troupe's Marching Band. Muralist and underground comix artist Spain Rodriguez lived down the street, and from time to time I would see Robert Crumb, another comix artist, strolling from Spain's house to Terry Zwigoff's.[3] Zwigoff would capture Crumb in his documentary of the same name.

Many neighbors owned their homes. At least two, one a house painter, the other a longshoreman, owned multiple dwellings. Until the passage of the Rumford Fair Housing Law in 1963, the deeds to the homes in the City's better neighborhoods contained covenants restricting their sale to Whites only. Not so in Bernal where people of color could buy and a small handful of closeted gays also felt comfortable buying.

Living was easy. Rents were low, particularly as people began to gather into formal and informal communal living arrangements. For those of us who considered agitation our core commitment, post office, cab driving, and teaching jobs were readily available as were food stamps for those who needed them or could justify the scam. Food was cheap thanks to food banks operating out of people's garages, which offered basic staples like fruit, vegetables, potatoes, cheese, and grains. And gas was 27 cents a gallon when we arrived. Weed, mostly from Mexico and Panama, none that I knew of from California yet, was also cheap and abundant as were acid (blotter, sunshine, you name it—Stanley Owsley was still the acid king of the Haight), mescaline (real and synthetic), psilocybin mushrooms, and peyote. While some musicians were succumbing to heroin, politicos eschewed "bad" drugs, and cocaine was yet to show its ugly face.

My family's presence was part of a migratory gathering of people from Madison, Wisconsin. Plans for *Leviathan,* our radical magazine, began to jell, giving focus to our political efforts. Academia was gone forever. The core *Leviathan* group, which included Carole and my brother Brad, were hardened politicos, multi-year veterans of The Movement, the all-inclusive descriptor that reflected our often overblown sense of self-importance. More often than not my compatriots were the children of what was known as the Old Left. Carole had been active in the Civil Rights support and anti-war movements in Madison. My brother was an army vet, and active in Students for a Democratic Society at Johns Hopkins and the anti-war movement.

Danny Beagle and his wife and son were the first to arrive from Madison. Danny, the son of teachers who were unionist activists and staunch Norman Thomas socialists, cut his teeth in student politics at Columbia, then went to Prince Edward County, Virginia, in 1963 to teach in a Freedom School. Before Madison he spent Freedom Summer (1964) working in the West Tennessee Voter Registration project as did his wife. In 1965, Danny left Madison for a year and went back to Tennessee before returning to get a master's degree in history.

Bob Gabriner, *Leviathan's* business manager, arrived soon after we did. Both his parents, while fellow travelers rather than Party members, were doggedly pro-Soviet. At Cornell, Bob fell in with a leftist crowd that included faculty members Hans Bethe, Philip Morrison, Douglas Dowd, and Walter LeFebvre.[4] Bob edited the student newspaper, moved from Ban the Bomb activities to rent striking organizing in Harlem, and then to the West Tennessee Project, which was conceived as the Cornell community's contribution to the Civil Rights Movement.

By 1968 the underground or alternative press was a well-established factor in the growing radicalization of students and other young people, the so-called Youth Revolt. Among the Bay Area publications were the *San Francisco Bay Guardian,* the *Berkeley Barb,* which offered a blend of politics, counterculture, and naked female breasts, *The Black Panther,* the Black Panther Party paper, *Steps,* a short-lived UC Berkeley publication, *The Mid-Peninsula Observer,* founded by current and ex-Stanford Students, the *San Francisco Express Times,* founded by Marvin Garson, a former UC Berkeley student radical, and *The Movement,* a national radical publication that began as the newsletter of the Bay Area friends of the Student Nonviolent Coordinating Committee (SNCC).[5] The number of Bay Area publications, which would grow in the years ahead, was a testament alone to the depth and range of the Movement.

In the summer of 1967, looking to replace Madison's *Studies on the Left,* which had just folded, my brother and I, still in Madison, put together a proposal for a new publication. Participation in the Movement, inspired by Civil Rights activities in the South, community organizing in poor Black and White communities, and growing opposition to the war in Vietnam, had reached a new quantum level. Tens of thousands, hundreds of thousands of people were on the move. In April, 1967, more than a half a million people participated in anti-war marches in San Francisco (est. 100,00) and Washington D.C. (est. 500,000). In the fall some protesters turned to militant, direct action. Simultaneously in October, thousands of Bay Area students and young people marched on the Oakland Army Induction Center during the nationwide Stop the Draft Week engaging police in running street battles. In

Washington D.C. 100,000 protestors marched on the Pentagon where skirmishes broke out, and during an all-night encampment hundreds burned their draft cards. In Madison, attempts to prevent representatives from Dow Chemical, the manufacturer of napalm, from recruiting on campus led to bloody clashes with the local police.

In our proposal we positioned the magazine as an analytical review that would look at the underlying social forces that were driving or preventing radicalization and the resulting political and cultural movements. We picked San Francisco for our office because it was one of the principal centers of radicalization with an abundant potential readership made up of students and post-grads. Our aspirations, however, were to reach a national audience. In September my brother traveled to Ann Arbor, Michigan, where he met with editors from New York-based *Viet Report*, a New York-based magazine founded in 1965, and people from the New England Free Press, which had published *The Paper Tiger*, a Boston area underground paper. Founded in 1965 as "An Emergency News Bulletin on Southeast Asian Affairs," *Viet Report* began by offering in-depth coverage of the Vietnam War, publishing, for example, the 1954 Geneva Accords and first-hand accounts written by the editors and others about conditions inside of North and South Vietnam.[6] *Viet Report* had been moving systemically beyond reporting on Southeast Asia to coverage of other countries and regions touched by American imperialism and to an analysis of domestic issues, such as the state of our inner cities. The *Viet Report* people decided to merge with our effort, and we launched *Leviathan* with an editorial office in New York and an editorial and administrative office in San Francisco. On the masthead of the first issue in March 1969, the New York group listed three editors (Carol Brightman, Beverly Leman—now Gologorsky, and Kathy McAfee) and seven staff members. The San Francisco group, which described itself as a collective, included five core members (two Wileys, Carole Deutch, Danny Beagle, and Bob Gabriner) plus Al Haber, one of the founders of SDS; Bruce Nelson, a seminarian turned anti-war activist; and David Wellman, a Berkeley post-grad working at the Institute for Industrial Relations and a founder of *The Movement* newspaper.

It was easy to pull together a national network inclusive of radicals and wannabe radicals.[7] This was a testament to the openness, enthusiasm and good feelings that still characterized important parts of the Movement in 1969 despite the vicious ideological battles, replete with mind-numbing rhetoric, borrowed from the worst of the Old Left during which various elected and self-selected leaders of Students for a Democratic Society would wreck the largest student organization in the history of American politics.

In San Francisco we were ready to sign a lease with the owner of an empty jewelry factory at 20th and Mission Streets when we were offered space for $25 a month at 330 Grove Street, the site now occupied by the Performing Arts Garage. An abandoned photo processing factory, the building was on the edge of the Western Addition, which was suffering through the ethnic cleansing of its Black, Japanese, and Jewish residents at the hands of the City's Redevelopment Agency. Bulldozers, following eviction notices, were in the process of leveling thousands of grand, if decaying, Victorian apartment buildings and residences. The neighborhood looked like it had been carpet-bombed. Black and Japanese-American resistance to the real estate developer-inspired destruction of their neighborhood was one of the City's pivotal political struggles in the 1960s.

Jamie Jamerson, a Bernal neighbor who grew up in the Western Addition, had somehow prevailed upon the Redevelopment Agency to turn 330 Grove over to him for a cultural center. Jamie had plans for a Black cultural center, but wanted some White groups to leaven the mixture. A crew of volunteers quickly gutted the building stripping out, among other things, the endless miles of rubber tubing that ran from sink to sink and floor to floor in this former photo processing building. Furniture was secured from the few remaining secondhand stores run by some of the few remaining Jewish residents of the Western Addition. We raided the burned-out ruins of the pre-1906 earthquake opera house, that once stood at the corner of Grove and Laguna, for shelf lumber, finding trunks full of rotting costumes and a spectacular supply of rock posters designed by artists like Alton Kelly and Stanley Mouse. The Black Writers Workshop moved into a mezzanine office. Other space was occupied by Zack Thompson's Black Light Explosion Company and underground comix printer Don Donohue, Liberation News Service, and *Dock of the Bay*, yet another underground newspaper. *Leviathan* moved to the second floor where we were soon joined by *The Movement,* Liberation News Service, and *Dock of the Bay*.[8] The top floor was used for karate lessons and creating light shows for rock concerts.

The building teetered on the brink of chaos and disaster. During the winter of 1968-69, we suffered through days and days of torrential downpours. The roof leaked, rain puddled on the floor, and the furnace worked episodically. One morning, a man who had come to the building with a group of light show artists was found dead from an overdose on the top floor. The building's occupants fled, leaving Jamie and me to deal with the police, who promptly named us suspects. Zack flipped out, chasing some of our White brothers around the building with a hammer. That was enough for us. In 1970 we moved to a new office at 968 Valencia Street.

For the *Leviathan* group the future was about possibilities that even five years earlier, no one in his right mind would have imagined. We were among thousands, veterans and supporters of the Civil Right and anti-war movements, who believed that we needed to radically remake both the political and economic system. With the Democratic Party deeply involved in the marginalization of Black voters in the South and an unapologetic supporter of the continuing decimation of Vietnam, we were convinced that there were no prospects for reform in that direction. Introducing our first issue we wrote that "*Leviathan* will serve the Movement as it builds a mass revolutionary force and a new society." We described how, having grown up with the Movement, we had changed from activists "who sought to persuade those in power to reform the most obvious aberrations in the social order" to radicals who had "learned that a social system constructed on the principles of private ownership of resources and increasing centralization of control could not create an orderly, rational, and humane society even in terms of its own distorted values." We had learned valuable lessons from struggles "in the factory, in the community, and in the army as well as on the campus and in the ghetto." Rather than seeing the successful struggle for civil rights legislation, for example, as a be-all and end-all, we now understood we were at the beginning of "a struggle for power itself, the power to control and build new institutions with the resources presently produced by all and monopolized by a few."

Our vision for the future was now clearer, and it included the broadest outlines of a new society:

> "As a prerequisite for a new social order we must have redistribution of wealth on the basis of need, production for use, and democratic control of the economic process.

"At the same time the socialization of the economy must allow us to create a
decentralized political environment in which we can develop autonomous
communities on the basis of cultural diversity.

"Social liberation has to extend and complement personal liberation; individual
aspirations and collective needs must coincide by mutual agreement."

We acknowledged that in the past confrontation had been our principal
teacher, but that these confrontations had revealed "tremendous inadequacies. Too
often we became obsessed with confrontation in its narrowest tactical sense. We
ritualized our struggle, disregarded the political consequences, and stridently and
self-righteously decreed our own isolation."

New people were joining the Movement. We thought we were at the beginning
of a new era in which the Movement had the potential to grow beyond "a militant
minority" to "a political force drawing its strength from a variety of social groups."
*Leviathan*, we hoped, would contribute to an "intense and sustained debate about the
Movement and the system."

Why, by 1969, had so many young people of all colors, perhaps tens of
thousands of them living in the Bay Area, given up on ideas of reform and
committed themselves to a radical reordering of society? The answer is simple: it
was because of the way in which "the System"—the established political parties, the
corporate economy, the political machines that ran the largest cities and dominated
politics, and the military—had responded negatively to well-intentioned efforts to
introduce incremental change.

For a newly-arrived San Franciscan, it felt like we were moving into a time
of boundless opportunities. This was the California of utopian experimentation,
political, sexual, and spiritual, with its own unique radical history including the City's
1934 General Strike and Upton Sinclair's unsuccessful gubernatorial campaign in
the same year. (He called upon the state government to end unemployment by
seizing idle fields and factories and turning them into cooperatives). In New York
and Chicago you risked getting your ass kicked by blue collar workers when
you demonstrated against the war. In the Bay Area, the ILWU voted to oppose
the war in Vietnam. Students from San Francisco State Strike were welcomed on
picket lines in Richmond when the Oil, Chemical, and Atomic Workers struck
the Union Oil refinery, and a faction within the Bay Area Teamsters opposed
not only Jimmy Hoffa's leadership, but the union's support for California grape
growers' attempts to break the United Farm Workers Union.

We were young, mostly in our middle twenties, supercharged with physical,
intellectual, and sexual energy. The city was a kind of hedonist Mecca with pristine
beaches and Irish green, then golden hills and mountains rolling away from the
ocean and the bay, vistas that we would explore in psychedelic ecstasy. Our tribal
gatherings, whether for music or politics, brought together the beautiful, the
damned, and the stoned, draped in colorful new apparel, even the naked and fully-
tanned. Here was a place where you didn't have to wait until summer to make love
in the great outdoors.

For a time *Leviathan* followed its editorial plan producing writing, some of
it groundbreaking. We published articles about community organizing in New
Haven and the limits of community organizing in San Francisco, about a mutiny at
the San Francisco Presidio's military stockade, the new feminism, local community-
controlled (read Black-controlled) school boards in New York City vs. the United

Federation of Teachers, corporate plans to garner public funds spent in the ghetto and expand their influence in the Pacific Basin, popular music, radio broadcasting, the new comix, and much more.

In June 1969, the two factions that were vying for control of SDS split the organization with each faction proclaiming their revolutionary purity and their singular devotion to Marxism-Leninism, which had about as much relevance to an American form of democratic socialism as the writings of Krishnamurti. The next year the faction known as Weathermen went underground, descending into a phantasmal world in which they imagined that they were the American Viet Cong. Larger and larger segments of the most radical members of the Movement were morphing into sects and tribelets. Cult-like behavior was on the rise.

So what did *Leviathan* do? In December 1969, we published Shin'ya Ono's essay, "You Do Need a Weatherman to Know Which Way the Wind Blows," detailing his conversion to the Weatherman line. Ono presented three reasons for his conversion: (1) "the primacy of confronting national chauvinism and racism among working class whites"; (2) "the urgency of preparing for militant, armed struggle now"; (3) "the necessity of building revolutionary collectives that demand total, wholehearted commitment of the individual to struggle against everything that interferes with the revolutionary struggle and to struggle to transform oneself into a revolutionary and a communist."

As I recall discussions about the article, probably not entirely accurately, we agreed that the Weathermen represented a legitimate faction within the Left and that, since we were committed to an open discussion of all points of view, we should let them speak through *Leviathan*. An examination of *Leviathan's* content before the magazine went out of business in 1971 shows that we ourselves were being seduced—how much depended on the individual—by the hyper-revolutionary posturing of the Weather faction and their fellow travelers. We continued to publish thoughtful reportage and analysis about the economy, student organizing, Latin American politics, the League of Revolutionary Black Worker's activities in the automobile industry, the politics of the anti-war movement, and an entire issue devoted to the women's movement. We also published interviews with Carlos Marighella, Brazil's apostle of urban guerrilla warfare, and Leila Khaled, a Palestinian woman and member of the Popular Front for the Liberation of Palestine, who took part in the simultaneous hijacking of four airplanes in 1969. But, then, we neither solicited nor were sent writing that offered a much-needed critique of the politics of violent confrontation. Clearly we ignored our original critique of the Movement's tendency to be "obsessed with confrontation in its narrowest tactical sense" and to "stridently and self-righteously decree[d] our own isolation."

In parallel many of us were increasingly drawn to the introspective and most often destructive internal conversations, which took the form of Maoist-inspired criticism-self-criticism or struggle sessions, but could sound like a combination of Oprah confessionalism and Rikki Lake trash-talking. Describing Weatherman's criticism and self-criticism sessions, Bill Ayers had this to say: ". . . before long a purifying ceremony involving confession, sacrifice, rebirth, and gratitude took hold of us. . . . We began to speak in proverbs from Che or Ho [Chi Minh]. Soon all we heard in the collectives was an echo."[9]

As sexual experimentation increased, men and women, women and women, and men and men spent long hours talking about smashing monogamy and the admitted shortcomings of male behavior and the need for women's leadership. People moved in and out of relationships, swapped partners, and practiced group sex. The language was arcane, the practices exotic, but ultimately not entirely destructive. Many men acknowledged their own shortcomings, and many men and women were able to acknowledge for the first time that they were gay, triggering another social movement that persists today. The anti-war movement continued to grow both among civilians and inside the military, while student militancy on campuses was still on the rise. We saw a great potential for deeper radicalization. Ironically, important elements of the Movement's leadership, while blasting "White working class youth" with rhetoric about fighting their own racism and chauvinism and the need for revolutionary violence, were making fewer and fewer connections with those they aspired to organize.

In the end *Leviathan* fell victim to its own lack of staying power. Factionalism, lack of interpersonal cohesiveness, the inability to build a strong organization and reshape our editorial direction to fit the changing politics of the Movement, and the desire of many in the core group to move on to other forms of political action took their toll. We shuttered the magazine in 1971, after three years of work that seemed more like ten. Many of us at *Leviathan* always felt drawn in different directions. We were media workers and propagandists, but some of us found it more and more difficult to ignore the spectacle of death and destruction in Vietnam and the rapid growth of the anti-war movement and its apparent potential for radicalization. Others were drawn to building collectives and "organizing the working class." All of us continued to participate in the anti-war movement. I moved on to organizing military servicemen and working on *The Bulkhead*, an anti-war newspaper that was distributed to GIs. As the civilian anti-war movement faltered and diminished after 1970, resistance in the military grew at a striking pace.[10]

By 1973, as the drawdown of American troops in Vietnam continued and the air war lessened in intensity, many of us experienced a kind of directionless malaise. Having dedicated most of our working hours to radical politics, we had to consider what came next in the way of work. We were caught between the intensity of our Movement lives and the "real" world. People wandered off in different directions. Others stayed put and tried to figure out what to do next. I had no idea how to adapt my radical publishing and writing experience to a job in the straight press. I assumed, perhaps incorrectly, that I was unemployable at any of the local newspapers. When I applied for a community organizing job in Hunter's Point, the interviewers took one look at me and my resume, where I didn't say much about my organizing experience, and asked if I was lost. In a sense I was. The days of the interracial movement of the poor, a concept that guided our organizing work in Kentucky, were history. In what was left of the Movement, Black, Latino, Asian, and White activists barely spoke to each other. To clear my head for whatever was to come next, I took a job driving for Yellow Cab.

## Bernal Heights 1970s

In retrospect, we can see the Movement as one aspect of that strange and magnificent flowering of creativity that led many to consider alternatives to the established order. Young people, including many of our Bernal neighbors, hived off from urban youth ghettoes like the Haight to set up communes in the countryside.[11] Others set up cooperative food banks where one could buy fruit, vegetables, and staples at wholesale prices.[12] The Mullen Avenue crew, with more Madison exiles among us, pulled four households together into an eating co-op. Those of us with children organized the Baby Farm, a childcare co-op on Capp Street. At first we provided daycare for half a dozen children. Within a year, we had enough children and parents to hire a teacher and move the Baby Farm to the Precita Neighborhood Center, expanding it to 25 children.

Bernal was where Carole and I continued to engage with a community in need (myself much less than Carole). On our street we made friends quickly. Some of our neighbors, particularly the kids, were openly curious about their new neighbors. But as our hair grew longer and our clothes more colorful, some adult neighbors remained indifferent or even hostile. In what was a fairly conventional working class neighborhood with its fair share of dilapidated houses, unpaved streets (that's right!), vacant lots, and people on public assistance, we were the exotics, an alien element in the neighborhood.

The neighborhood did have its own hidden roots in oppositional movements. Across the street, there was an abandoned house occupied variously by rats and raccoons. The kids told us that it had belonged to someone called "Scratchy Man." One of the teens, after quietly entering the house while Scratchy Man slept on the couch, lifted his wallet only to find that Scratchy Man wasn't asleep; he was dead. The wallet was returned post haste. When Carole explored the house, she found a hank of hair hanging in a closet and a William Z. Foster for President button. Foster ran as the candidate of the Communist Party in 1924, 1928, and 1932. Many Bernal residents were active union members. With the radical influences at play in local unions like the ILWU, Scratchy Man's Foster button wasn't a surprise.[13] With an eye on the Western Addition, many of our neighbors were keenly aware of the damage that the Redevelopment Agency could do to the neighborhood. Organizing to keep Bernal Heights out of the grasp of the Agency began in the late 1950s and met with success in 1967 when the Agency scrapped its plans to works its magic in Bernal and the Mission District. A neighborhood had saved itself from surefire destruction![14]

We learned fairly quickly that the teen males in particular were a curious lot: they wanted to know what kind of purloinable goodies we kept in our cars and houses. My shotgun, hung carefully inside a closet so that it couldn't be seen without walking all the way into the closet, was our first and last valuable asset to disappear at the hands of a local teenager. These young men were especially unpopular in the neighborhood, seen as larcenous punks—an attitude not easily dismissed since many of them had impressive police records, usually for theft and truancy. For the most damaged, certain aspects of their lives were a litany of horrors, a striking contrast to their physical beauty and the sophistication and warmth with which some of them, when treated with respect, interacted with adults.

Li'l Phil, identified as such by the jailhouse tattoo on his chest, was a handsome, skinny twelve year old when we met him. His first run-in with the police came when he was seven years old. He broke into a store and stole $500 worth of candy, a lot in the middle Sixties. After a night at the Youth Guidance Center, he was released by a judge who wanted to know, "What's this baby doing in my court?" In his next encounter with the police while burglarizing a house, he was shot in the arm though still a runty kid who weighed less than a hundred pounds. Philip lived with his mother, but also slept in abandoned cars on the streets. He was particularly fond of "borrowing" VW bugs for a joy ride or to take a date to the drive-in next to the Cow Palace. When finished, he would abandon the car. Once, when locked up in the Youth Guidance Center, he escaped by removing some of the glass blocks that served as a wall in the showers and ran in his underwear all the way to Richard and Della's house. He was sent up the river to the Youth Guidance Center in Stockton after that escapade. In the years ahead, Philip gave up the street life, went to work as a sandblaster on the Golden Gate Bridge, became a Jehovah's Witness for a time, married, and raised a family.

David was the son of a very supportive mother who lived just over the hill. Of mixed race (African-American and White) and with no father, he could switch from polite and mature to wildly antagonistic at the drop of a Seconal (the street drug of choice) chased by a few Mickey Big Mouths. David was a brawler and ultimately, long after he had been kicked out of Grambling College and went to work on the oil rigs in the Gulf of Mexico, he would kill one of his friends in a drunken fight. I worked with his mother to get him paroled from a Texas prison many years later, but he went back to jail quickly. When he got out the second time, he and his prison guard girlfriend ran a shoplifting operation that supplied their clothing store. David made it to about forty, then died of cancer as did his mother. And so it went, on and on: parental violence and alcoholism, horrendous instances of child abuse, abandonment, lack of direction and support, poor schools, lack of recreational facilities, and saddest of all a very high mortality rate among young males from alcohol, drugs, AIDS, and violence.

In 1969 Richard and Della Hall moved in two doors down. Richard was a graduate student at San Francisco State contributing to his family's support as a parking attendant at the Park Merced garage.[15] Della was a teacher at a Potrero Hill grade school. Warm, friendly people with the parental instincts of good social workers, they were drawn to the kids in the neighborhood. Only a decade to a decade and a half older, with our own tendencies toward outlaw behavior, we recognized that our young neighbors were looking for a place in the world (often with little help or outright hostility at home and on the streets). This situation was compounded, the kids explained, because there was nothing to do and nowhere to go. Both of our households opened the door to our young neighbors. Richard and Della went a step further, turning their garage over to the kids for a clubhouse. They installed two couches, painted the walls black, and hung rock posters. They kept things neat and tidy and tried to lock up with their own keys at a reasonable hour and maintain order on the street. To the door they nailed "B5," the number of the admitting room at the Youth Guidance Center where many of them had spent far too much time. One of them suggested that the first child conceived in the garage should be named B5.

In 1968 we hung a bed sheet with Mullen Avenue Liberation Front painted on it from the front of our house and convened the first neighborhood block party. For years our block parties were a regular event attracting people from around Precita Valley and the south Mission District. The street was our living room and recreational space where we danced and partied, played touch football, and hung a rope across the street between utility poles as a volley ball net. A Mullen team regularly challenged residents of the Bernal Dwellings to tackle football games without pads in Precita Park. The young people became a part of our network of relationships which was spreading beyond Mullen Ave. Or perhaps it is better to say that we became a part of their local network as we shared meals together and partied while hiring some of the young women to babysit our two children.

Soon Richard and Della found that B5 was attracting more people than a windowless, one car garage could accommodate. The Precita Neighborhood Center at the foot of the hill looked like the logical replacement, but that was easier said than done. The Center lacked funding for a full day of programming, particularly in the afternoon and evenings when young people would want to use the place. The board and its advisory committee were generally hostile to the neighborhood's young male population. We finally persuaded the board to allow us to set up a film program with the Mullen crew at the Center. One of our neighbors, a Brooklyn street kid, former jailbird (Riker's Island, New York), and member of the San Francisco Mime Troupe, had introduced the B5 crew to San Francisco Newsreel, the radical collective that made and distributed films. Working with the kids, one of whom introduced the program, they showed "The Battle of Algiers," and "May Day," a Black Panther film, to 150 people at the Center. That was the last film showing at Precita Center.

After six months, Richard and Della shut B5 down. The next step, they decided, was to move to a more organized approach to help the kids work on their own behalf. Our housemates Minnie Tuck and Dennis, and Carole and I helped when we could. Minnie, Dennis, and my time was limited by our involvement with the GI movement. For the Mullen people, we helped organize larger and more elaborate field trips, including camping trips to the middle fork of the Yuba River and the Santa Lucia Mountains. So that the kids could help defray the costs of the trip through events like bake sales in Precita Park, we organized the Brothers and Sisters of Mullen Avenue. Della and Carole talked with the young women about birth control and introduced them to Planned Parenthood. When the Neighborhood Youth Corps was funded by the federal Comprehensive Employment and Training Act in 1972, we helped the kids find jobs. Until 1975 when they split up and sold the house, Richard and Della, working with Carole and the Brothers and Sisters, continued to contribute to the development of youth programs in Bernal Heights. In 1975 Carole, after we also split up, became the new director at the Precita Center. She went on to be one of the founders of Carnaval, which began in 1979 as a modest affair in Precita Park.

Home prices on Mullen began to increase in the middle 1970s. Little did we know that middle-class radicalism and assorted bohemianisms were the harbingers of gentrification. Many, but not all of the neighboring blue-collar families, moved out. The kids, with a handful of exceptions, dispersed as well. Some made it in the "real world" working, for example, in city jobs, the trades, and low level white-collar jobs. The days of waterfront jobs were long gone. No one, with the exception of David and his sister, went on to college. Over the next two decades, all too many of the kids, then in their thirties, forties, and fifties died.

As for our political struggles, we won and we lost. The Civil Rights Movement changed race relations forever. The US withdrew from Vietnam, and two old social movements, feminism and environmentalism, were reinvigorated. At least one new one, the struggle for gay, lesbian and transgender rights, came out in the open. As for our larger radical agenda, that, of course, was never realized.

From my studies and my organizing experience, I wove together thought strands about dual power as spelled out by Trotsky and Andre Gorz, utopian communalism as described by Engels and writers like Charles Nordhoff, and anarcho-syndicalism as practiced by the Industrial Workers of the World and elements of the European working class before these ideas were crushed between state power and Marxism-Leninism. I understood dual power to mean that in the societal womb it was possible to nurture a more humane alternative to the existing order that, as the existing order crumbled or was swept away, would flourish. European and American utopians and even the apolitical communards of the Sixties seemed to be fumbling through experiments with new social possibilities while the anarcho-syndicalists offered direct democracy, real people's power. In the Sixties this was what democratic socialism meant to me. Given that no one was able to spell out a humane socialist agenda and build a truly democratic socialist organization, today it is clear that those of us who shared these beliefs or similar ones were naïve and utopian.

It is important to note that many of us went on to work in the most important of our public institutions—schools, libraries, hospitals—while others helped to extend old and build new nonprofit organizations, which today are the most encouraging and intriguing of our parallel institutions.

As with religion, when it comes to a belief in socialism, I have become an agnostic. The word seems terminally corrupted. I do know that down deep what all of us wanted—and what I believe every human being wants today—was a purposeful community. Presuming to speak for my friends and lovers, I think we wanted a community that would allow us to share with others a way to confront the issues that we faced in the Bay Area and beyond—racism, sexism, poverty, environmental degradation, and militarism. These were the ugly spawn of corporate capital which we wanted to confront so that the next generation would not have to return to the barricades. If anything, from a global perspective these problems have become more dangerous, ultimately threatening our very existence on the planet. And the opportunities offered to young people like our beloved brothers and sisters of Mullen Avenue are all too often worse rather than better.

I wouldn't suggest that there is a progression from the self-destructive, cultish behavior of the Weathermen to the absolutely off-the-wall fantasies of the so-called Symbionese Liberation Army to the horrors of Jonestown (which after all was another form of utopian socialism), but there are underlying causes that need to be explored to understand why so many of us wandered into the darkness. Meanwhile the gap between the dire threats to our existence, especially environmental degradation, and our ability to counter these threats appears to be growing. For our future's sake that must end.

As you age, you learn that what seemed to be so vital and so permanent never is. Life is flux, never-ending change, but from each fleeting experience we hope to pass along the flickering candle of knowledge to help others illuminate life's dark passageways and, dare we hope again, to find a way into the light.

## Notes

1.    For me and my friends, Madison was a profoundly formative experience, a generally joyful exercise in living history. The intellectual atmosphere, with its emphasis on understanding the great historical social movements and engaging in their contemporary counterparts, was shaped by professors like historians William Appleman Williams, Harvey Goldberg, and George Mosse, and sociologists Han Gerth and C. Wright Mills. Williams was one of the principal reasons that I decided to go to Wisconsin. With our

connections to the pivotal movements of our era, we read, wrote, studied, agitated, and organized with a deep commitment to using our education to contribute to a more just and humane society.

2. Jim McCarthy with Ron Sansoe, *Voices of Latin Rock: The People and Events that Created This Sound* (Milwaukee, WI: Hal Leonard, 2004).

3. See Jay Kinney's essay "The Rise and Fall of the Underground Comix Movement in San Francisco and Beyond" in this volume.

4. Hans Bethe was a Nobel laureate physicist. He and Philip Morrison, also a physicist and briefly a member of the Communist Party at UC Berkeley, had worked on the Manhattan Project and were both opposed to nuclear testing in the atmosphere. Walter LeFebvre was a history professor and a student of Wisconsin Professor Williams, the New Left historian of American thought. Douglas Dowd was a Marxist-influenced economist.

5. Founded in 1960 the Student Nonviolent Coordinating Committee (SNCC) was conceived as an antidote to the moderation and passivity of established civil rights organizations, such as the National Association for the Advancement of Colored People, the Congress of Racial Equality, and Martin Luther King, Jr.'s Southern Christian Leadership Conference. SNCC called for nonviolent direct action and sent hundreds of organizers into the most racist areas of the Deep South.

6. *Viet Report*, with contributors like Bernard Fall, John Gerassi, Michael Klare, Jean Lacouture, and Staughton Lynd, offered the kind of information that was essential to understanding the US's growing intervention in Vietnam and to shaping an argument for why the US should exit that country immediately. An understanding of the Geneva Accords helped illuminate the ways in which the United States had done everything in its power to turn the temporary division of Vietnam, after the French had surrendered to Ho Chi Minh, into a permanent bifurcation of the country. The Eisenhower administration's avowed intent was to prevent Ho, the hands down favorite according to Ike himself, from being elected president of the newly-independent country.

7. *Leviathan* also had contributing editors in Boston, Chicago, Detroit, Los Angeles, Madison, Philadelphia, and Washington.

8. Zack Thompson began his career in North Beach, choreographed for television, performed with Dinah Washington and Aretha Franklin, was the lead dancer at the Lido Night Club in Paris, performed with San Francisco's Civic Light Opera, and assisted Maya Angelou on her first PBS special titled *Black, Blues, Black*. He founded Black Light Explosion in 1969, taught at Polytechnic High School, lived in Amsterdam in the 1970s and 1980s, and was affiliated with Alonzo King's Lines Ballet until he died of AIDS-related causes in 1996. Don Donahue was printing the second run of *Zap Comix #1*, conceived and drawn by Robert Crumb, on a press originally acquired by Allen Ginsberg. *Dock of the Bay* was a short-lived underground newspaper. Liberation News Service, founded in New York in 1967, served as a source of articles and photographs for the extensive network of underground newspapers.

9. Bill Ayers, *Fugitive Days, A Memoir* (Boston: Beacon Press, 2001) 156.

10. See a photo essay by Stephen Rees and myself "Up Against the Bulkhead" also in this volume for more information on GI anti-war activities.

11. See Matthew Roth's essay "Coming Together: The Communal Option" also in this volume for more information on the back-to-the-land movement of this decade.

12. See Pam Peirce's essay "A Personal History of the People's Food System" also in this volume for more on food conspiracies and the new food economy.

13. When I made my pitch on behalf of unemployed miners in Eastern Kentucky to ILWU Local 10's Executive Committee in 1965, I was struck by the number of members reading copies of the *People's World*, the local CP newspaper.

14. See Tomas Sandoval's essay "'All Those Who Care About The Mission, Stand Up With Me!'" also in this volume for more information on organizing in the Mission.

15. Besides my recollections, I drew on Richard Wayne Hall, "Mullen Avenue: A Study in Community Human Relations" (master's thesis, San Francisco State University, 1993), a copy of which is is the San Francisco Public Library.

# Up Against the Bulkhead
## A Photo Essay with Text
### By Steve Rees with Peter Booth Wiley

**Steve Rees:** *I got my political start at my temple Sunday school in the Palo Alto area, where I was recruited in 1964 to be a junior member of Friends of the Student Nonviolent Coordinating Committee. From there I went to the University of California Santa Cruz in 1966, where I became active in Students for a Democratic Society (SDS) and the anti-war movement. As early as 1966, I began to read about GI resistance to the war.* Ramparts, *a national magazine of the nondenominational radical sort, covered the court-martial of Captain Howard Levy, an army doctor who refused to teach Green Beret medics because of the atrocities American troops were committing. Levy was convicted and did time in the military stockade at Fort Leavenworth. The same year I read ex-Green Beret and Vietnam veteran Donald Duncan's essay, "The Whole Thing's a Lie" in Ramparts and then his book,* The New Legions. *The War Resisters League and the American Friends Service Committee, both venerable pacificist organizations, touched me through their people and their publications*

*The breakthrough for me came with the Presidio 27 trial. I was a university student at UC Santa Cruz when in October 1968, twenty-seven GIs, who had been imprisoned in the Presidio stockade, sat down during morning formation inside the stockade and sang "We Shall Overcome." They were protesting the shooting of Richard Bunch, a mentally-disturbed fellow prisoner, who was walking away from a work detail. Bunch had instructed the young MPs guarding him to make sure that they shot to kill if he ran. When the court-martial opened at Fort Ord in Monterey, a group of us drove down from Santa Cruz. The closed nature of the pre-trial hearings, the mutiny charges themselves, and the courage of the 27 men who were my age but did not enjoy my freedom, all moved me. I felt their taking a moral stand at great risk was a challenge to me personally. This encounter contributed to my decision to leave the university in July 1969, and work against the war by supporting soldiers who dared defy their command.*

*In 1969 I began to work with a group of active-duty GIs, veterans, and civilians. Their storefront in Berkeley, right across the street from Berkeley High, was local headquarters for the Movement for a Democratic Military, little brother to SDS. They located the storefront so that it was accessible to many Bay Area military bases including the Alameda Naval Air Station, Oak Knoll Naval Hospital, the Oakland Induction Center, the Oakland Army Terminal, 12th Naval District Headquarters on Treasure Island, and 6th Army Headquarters at the Presidio in San Francisco. Getting legal assistance for GIs was the above ground part of our work. The below ground part was helping people who wanted to hit the trail for Canada, getting them false papers, getting them legal counseling, or getting them into sanctuary at Bay Area churches if that's what they wanted to do. Starting in May 1970, we also published* Up Against the Bulkhead *(later* The Bulkhead*), initially for sailors at Alameda and Treasure Island.*

**Peter Wiley:** *While we worked on* Leviathan, *all of us participated in the ever-growing anti-war demonstrations. (See previous chapter.) But, with the US government raining death*

# UP AGAINST THE BULKHEAD

968 Valencia, San Francisco 94110     Vol 2 / Number 1 / Issue 6     January, 1971

# JOIN THE REVOLT!

January 1971 *Up Against the Bulkhead* front cover.

*and destruction on the people of Vietnam while destroying the lives of tens thousands of young*
*Americans, taking to the streets didn't seem to be bringing us any closer to the end of the war.*
*Many of us felt compelled to look for new ways to undermine the US war effort. The GI*
*movement proved to be the perfect answer. In 1970 I met Steve Rees, a photographer, activist,*
*and journalist who was working with a group of servicemen and civilians on* Up Against the
Bulkhead, *an anti-war newspaper aimed at GIs in the Bay Area. I joined up.*

The Bay Area, with its numerous military installations, was the cattle chute
through which ten of thousands of GIs were herded on their way to Vietnam.
Inevitably it became a center of GI resistance. The area was crawling with
anti-war activists while both Berkeley and particularly the Haight-Ashbury were
magnets for the young, the adventurous, and the disaffected. The inmates of the
Presidio Stockade called the Stockade "the trapdoor to Leavenworth." The Haight
was where numerous stockade escapees and AWOL GIs ran to, and the Haight was
where many of them were arrested and sent back to the Stockade before being
shipped on to Vietnam or Leavenworth.

In 1967 Bay Area activists Fred Gardner and Donna Mickelson opened the
first GI coffee house near Fort Jackson in Columbia, South Carolina, the base
where Howard Levy had refused to train Green Beret medics. The coffee houses
provided space for enlisted men and an occasional officer to hang out beyond the
confines of military discipline, read anti-war literature, watch anti-war films, receive
legal counseling including information about how to become a conscientious
objector, and organize. Dozens of coffee houses and related organizing projects

After the Presidio Mutiny in 1968, Sixth Army Headquarters became a focus of anti-war
activities. This showdown in September 1971, took place at the main gate. Anti-war activists
challenged the Army's research into gene-specific diseases at Letterman Hospital. Activists
suspected that the Army's interest in sickle cell anemia was intended to advance biological
weapons, rather than aid in the cure of the disease.

sprang up over the next five years, some as far away as Australia, Germany, Hong Kong, Japan, and the Philippines.

Organized resistance surfaced dramatically in San Francisco in 1968. In April forty active duty servicemen and women led an anti-war march down Market Street. In July nine servicemen refusing to go to Vietnam took sanctuary in a church in the Haight. After a bomb threat, the Nine for Peace moved to a sanctuary in a Marin City church where they remained chained together for three days until the police hauled them away. An October march was led by an even larger contingent of GIs— two hundred of whom were active duty plus one hundred reservists. In the fall came the GI and Veterans March for Peace during which servicemen and women led the parade down Market Street. Two days later, the so-called Presidio Mutiny drew unprecedented media attention to anti-war GIs.

This sailor at the October, 1971 anti-war march, which was led by a contingent of active duty serviceman, wore a jacket with patches from the destinations on his Western Pacific (WESPAC) deployments. These cruises included the deployment of American aircraft carriers off the coast to carry out the massive bombardment of Vietnam, Laos, and Cambodia. At the top of his jacket, he taped the phrase, "Keep it home."

## The Coral Sea

In 1971 a handful of sailors from the *USS Coral Sea*, an aircraft carrier based at the Alameda Naval Air Station, showed up at the *Leviathan* office at 968 Valencia Street, which also served as a maildrop for *The Bulkhead*. The Navy's carrier strike force, including ships that sailed from San Diego and Alameda to their duty station in the South China Sea, was subjecting tiny Vietnam to an aerial bombardment more intense than the bombing of Europe during World War II. Ultimately, a million citizens, many of them the victims of aerial bombardment, would die in Vietnam and neighboring Cambodia and Laos. The sailors had read *The Bulkhead*, specifically stories about about anti-war organizing on aircraft carriers. They were ready for action and were particularly interested in meeting David Harris, the Stanford draft resister who was working with civilians and anti-war sailors on the carrier *Constellation,* which was homeported in San Diego.[3]

We were pleased, but not surprised that these sailors had tracked us down. On any given night, people from *The Bulkhead* collective and the Pacific Counseling Service (PCS) could be found at the San Francisco Airport or on Market Street where GIs drifted between the seedy bars in the Tenderloin, including one called The Coral Sea, and the United Service Organization's drop-in center nearby on

Market St. We were handing out *Bulkheads* and information about the legal support offered by the PCS to GIs. Invariably the GIs were friendly and receptive. The *Coral Sea* sailors were a colorful lot, veritable hippies in uniform. (As a concession to growing dissension among sailors, Admiral Elmo Zumwalt, who became Chief of Naval Operations in 1970, issued his famous "Z grams," permitting sailors to wear beards, mustaches, sideburns, and longish hair as long as they were well-groomed.) The *Coral Sea* brothers considered themselves freaks and were more than eager not only to investigate ways to oppose the war, but also ways to sample the offerings of countercultural hedonism. In time some of them would join the network of interlocking political households that was spreading beyond Bernal Heights.

We helped our new comrades rent a house on Fairmount Street near Chenery. Amazingly our friends took us on a tour of the *Coral Sea* on family day. (What was the Navy thinking about when it came to security?) We visited their sleeping quarters where one sailor had decorated the gray steel ceiling, walls, and pipes with psychedelic paintings—in time he would do the same to the Fairmount house. We also visited the fantail where our friends spent hours talking and tripping on whatever drugs were available (mainly a form of speed known as crosstops supplied by shipboard nurses). When we walked past the fighter jets stored on the hangar deck and the nearby bombs racks, we wondered whether there were nuclear weapons nearby.

In September 1971, the *Coral Sea* sailors with our support decided to organize an SOS campaign aboard the *Coral Sea*. Support Our Sailors, or Stop Our Ship, which started in San Diego, had spread to the Bay Area. Our intention was to do the near impossible: prevent the *Coral Sea* from departing for the South China Sea when it was scheduled to sail in November. It was our hope that enough sailors would go AWOL to keep the *Coral Sea* from sailing. To build civilian support, the *Coral Sea* sailors led the huge anti-war demonstration that streamed up Market Street on November 6. There were two more demonstrations at the main gate at Alameda before the carrier finally sailed on November 12. Somewhere in naval records is the list of sailors who did not sail. Our shipboard comrades estimated that they numbered in the hundreds, but not enough to prevent their ship's departure.

As the *Coral Sea* sailed westward, the protests continued. In Hawaii the sailors were treated to a special performance of the FTA (Free/Fuck the Army) show, an anti-war theatrical revue created by Jane Fonda and Donald Sutherland. The FTA show provided an alternative to the pro-war USO shows staged in Vietnam with Bob Hope and John Wayne. In Hawaii fifty-three sailors deserted. Aboard ship anti-war sailors launched *We Are Everywhere*, their own underground publication. When Secretary of the Navy John Chaffee came aboard for an inspection tour, he was handed an anti-war petition signed by thirty-six crewmen.[4] When the *Coral Sea* returned to the Bay Area in the spring, we hung a "Welcome Home" banner off the Golden Gate Bridge, which was quickly confiscated by the Highway Patrol. Below on the flight deck, invisible in the fog, our comrades spelled out SOS in formation.

At the time we had no idea what impact the GI movement was having on military thinking. We did some of our research for *The Bulkhead* at the Presidio Base Library, no questions asked (not even a stare). In the summer of 1971, we came across an article by former Marine Colonel Robert Heinl in the *Armed Forces Journal*. "The morale, discipline and battle-worthiness of the US armed forces," Heinl wrote, "are, with a few salient exceptions, lower and worse than at any time in the history of the United States."[5] Up until then it seemed that no matter how large and militant anti-war demonstrations became, no matter how many campus buildings were seized and draft boards were attacked or burned, the war machine rolled on like some demon Moloch up to its armpits in blood and body parts. With GIs, apparently, we were getting results.

Encouraged, we pushed on. We put together a sophisticated distribution system for *The Bulkhead* that reached as far as Vietnam via packages mailed to GIs who used Armed Forces Post Office addresses in San Francisco. We also received help from stewardesses who worked the chartered commercial aircraft that flew troops out of Travis Air Force base in Vacaville to Tan Son Hut near Saigon. We supplemented copies of *The Bulkhead* with packets of articles about Vietnam and Southeast Asia gleaned from the straight press. We pulled the articles from the files of the Bay Area Research Project, which was organized by Berkeley Professor Franz Schurmann and journalist Orville Schell when they founded Pacific News Service in 1969. From the Vietnamese we received black buttons depicting an Armalite rifle with its bayonet stuck in the ground. Inscribed on it in Vietnamese were words that were a signal to Vietnamese soldiers not to shoot at the US troops wearing the buttons. We sent them along to our contacts in Vietnam.

It was only after the war ended in 1975, that we began to understand the truly vast nature of the GI movement and the impact this militancy would have on whether to remain in Vietnam or not. The immediate impact in the Bay Area was dramatic: in the first three months of 1970 during which *The Bulkhead* and PCS began an extensive schedule of leafleting, 1,200 soldiers scheduled to ship out through local facilities delayed their departure by seeking conscientious objector status. The Pentagon quickly retaliated, instructing West Coast base commanders to stop accepting applications for CO status. Still, the GI movement rolled on. In 1971 Heinl estimated that there were 144 underground newspapers published on or near US military bases. These papers, which ranged from broadsheets on newsprint to mimeographed newsletters on standard 8x11 paper, provided *The Bulkhead* with news from around the movement while we, acting as a kind of news service along with the GI News Service, provided them with content. In 1972 the Department of Defense estimated that there were 245 GI newspapers. In his carefully researched book, David Cortright lists 259 publications. The Department of the Army reported that the number of "acts of insubordination, mutiny and willful disobedience" increased from 252 in 1968 to 382 in 1970 and then to 450 in 1971, according to the *New York Times*. Before the war ended there were ten reported "major incidents" of mutiny within Vietnam itself.[6]

With the onset of Vietnamization and the drawing down of ground forces in Vietnam, we could see that resistance was shifting to the Navy and the Air Force, exactly those branches of the military that were providing cover for Nixon's plan to increase the bombing of Vietnam, Cambodia, and Laos while abandoning the South Vietnamese Army (ARVN) to fight alone. Knowing their enemy's shortcomings, the North Vietnamese Army and their South Vietnamese allies responded in 1972 with an offensive that sent the ARVN into retreat. Nixon, frothing at the mouth about how "the bastards have never been bombed like they're going to be bombed this time," initiated a dramatic escalation of aerial attacks on North Vietnam.

Sailors and airmen responded. From its beginnings on the *Constellation* and the *Coral Sea*, the carrier movement spread to the East Coast and the South China

Sea. In November 1972, the *Constellation*, steaming toward the South China Sea, was the site of what the *New York Times* described as "the first mass mutiny in the history of the US Navy." When a group calling itself the Black Fraction began to protest discriminatory promotion policies and the unequal application of military justice to African-Americans, the ship's command responded by handing out dishonorable discharges to 15 men identified as the Black Faction's leaders while another 250 sailors were administratively discharged. The sailors, Black and White, countered with a sit-in on the flight deck and later, when the *Constellation* returned to San Diego to disembark the discharged sailors, with a dockside strike. In the same year, two carriers, the *Forrestal* based in Norfolk, Virginia, and the *Ranger* based in Alameda were stopped from sailing by acts of sabotage. The House Armed Services Committee, reporting on the "alarming frequency of successful acts of sabotage and apparent sabotage on a wide variety of ships and stations," acknowledged that rebellious sailors were jeopardizing the carrier fleet's contribution to Nixon's bombing campaign. [7]

The rebellion was spreading to the Air Force as well, revealing the international dimensions of the GI anti-war movement. According to Cortright, the first mass organizing among airmen and women took place in England inspired by film star Vanessa Redgrave and other British activists. Led by American airmen and women, PEACE (People Emerging Against Corrupt Establishments) quickly reached out to all eight US Air Force bases in England. Similar groups, staffed in part by Pacific Counseling Service activists, set up shop at Yokota Airforce Base in Japan, Kadena in Okinawa, and Clark in the Philippines. In Okinawa, Zengunro, the Okinawan base workers union, organized a violent strike against the US military, protesting working conditions on the local bases, the seizure of more and more land for military purposes, and the US occupation of Okinawa, which began when the Americans seized the island from the Japanese in 1945. [8]

In May, 1971, rioting swept Travis Air Force Base in Solano County. What began as a brawl between Black airmen and women and military police escalated into a three-day battle during which a group of White airmen joined their Black brothers and sisters in an attempt to free African-American personnel confined to their barracks. On the domestic front the movement spread rapidly. By 1972 ten underground papers directed at Air Force personnel became thirty, and the number of organizing projects at airbases surpassed those at Army and Marine bases. In Thailand, there were two known instances of pilots, one piloting a B-52, the other an F-4, refusing to fly combat missions. In May 1973, the Air Force, citing cost, announced that it was reducing its bombing missions over Cambodia by 40 percent. The *Washington Post* reported that the Defense Department was actually concerned about "an increasing morale problem among B-52 crews."[9]

In 1975, a series of rolling offensives by the Vietnamese People's Army routed the Army of the Republic of Vietnam with an ease that surprised the VPA generals. Aboard waves of helicopters the Americans fled Saigon, and the war was finally over.

The GI movement was the result of an interesting wave effect. As the force field generated by the civilian movement expanded outward, it started a sympathetic wave that continued to grow after 1971 even as the civilian movement declined in size and militancy. Despite the decline in civilian militancy, Nixon and his cronies still made decisions about the timing and intensity of their bombing campaigns in Indochina based on their fear of mass protests. In the end, the GI movement, added

Emotion ruled the day as the *USS Coral Sea* returned from another long assignment to Vietnam in October 1974. Tension is in the air, as these women wonder what conditions their husbands are in. Will they be the same men who set sail months before? Will the strain of the long work hours under poor conditions have taken a toll?

to the civilians' protest, played a major—perhaps even the largest role—in Nixon's decision to sign the Paris Peace Accords in 1974 and Gerald Ford's decision to abandon Vietnam the next year.

## Notes

1.   This essay does not pretend to be an exhaustive study of the GI anti-war movement in the Bay Area. The full extent of what happened during the Vietnam War will probably never be known. This is an account of what happened to the authors and their friends.

2.   For a description of the Presidio 27 "mutiny" and court-martial, see Fred Gardner, *The Unlawful Concert: An Account of the Presidio Mutiny Case* (New York: The Viking Press, 1970). Gardner was a founder of the GI coffee house movement.

3.   David Cortright, *Soldiers in Revolt: GI Resistance During the Vietnam War.* (Chicago: Haymarket Books, 2005), 111-112. First published in 1974, this is the fullest account to date of GI resistance to the war in Vietnam. Drafted into the army, Cortright became an anti-war activist.

4.   Ibid., 112-113.

5.   Colonel Robert D. Heinl, "The Collapse of the Armed Forces," *Armed Forces Journal* (June 7, 1971).

6.   Cortright, *Soldiers in Revolt*, 17, 23, 35, 55, 124.

7.   Ibid., 121.

8.   Ibid., 127-129.

9.   Ibid., 131-137.

(above) Tony (left), a Marine based at Camp Pendleton in Southern California, sought sanctuary in a Los Angeles church in 1969 after receiving orders for Vietnam. Headed for Canada as a deserter, he settled in San Francisco where he helped organize GIs against the war. In 1972 Tony decided to turn himself in and face the consequences. He and civilian supporters, David Weinstein (above right) and Steve Rees, headed south along Highway 1 on Tony's last road trip "in the world."

(right) Back at Camp Pendleton, Tony, with a Marine haircut and in uniform, feared he faced years in a military prison. Instead he was assigned to a work detail, which included being sent to the motor pool where he and his friends played cards all day. After four weeks, he was discharged "for the good of the service."

ABOVE: Bobby (left—an Army deserter), Evan (center—a sailor), and Tony (right—a Marine deserter). Bobby and Tony helped organize GIs out of the MDM office in Berkeley. All three became active members of the Bay Area anti-war movement. Evan, a Seminole from Oklahoma, also participated in the Native American occupation of Alcatraz in 1969.

RIGHT: Tom Csekey, a sailor discharged from Treasure Island Naval Base, was one of the founders of the Movement for a Democratic Military in the Bay Area. Originating in southern California, MDM, an anti-war organization for GIs inspired by SDS, spread rapidly to other parts of the country and overseas. From the MDM office in Berkeley, a group of civilians, veterans and active-duty GIs leafleted on the streets, in the airports, and at military installations. Plans to open a coffee house in Oakland fell through, but the MDM group did start *Up Against the Bulkhead*, which became the third anti-war newspaper for servicemen and women in the nation.

These four sailors were among the more active in the SOS organizing drive. Their energy and joy is palpable as one of them leads a chant. Their contingent includes well over a hundred active duty sailors, whose long hair helped them blend into the civilians who surrounded them. The Navy's policy at the time was tolerant of both beards and long hair.

Active duty servicemen lead a march of recently-discharged veterans and their civilian supporters along Market Street. *Coral Sea* sailors Larry Harris (left) and Bobby Musa (right), who were leaders of SOS and the attempt to prevent the *Coral Sea* from sailing for the South China Sea, carry a mock-up of the aircraft carrier on their shoulders.

Civilian anti-nuclear activists blend easily with the sailors in this crowd. Opposition to nuclear testing was not a big leap for many sailors, some of whom came to oppose war itself in the course of their personal paths to sign the petition to Congress to oppose deployment.

At a demonstration near the *USS Coral Sea* at Alameda Naval Air Station in December 1974, Rose Hills, a sailor's wife, refused to turn over her banner to base security. She had held it up for the crew to read only a moment before. It read, "Good luck on your captain's suicide mission." She was one of the leaders of Save American Vessels, a campaign to keep the Coral Sea in port until it was seaworthy.

On the Alameda Naval Air Station pier next to the *USS Coral Sea,* Vicki Kelly, co-leader of the second campaign to prevent the carrier from deploying to the Western Pacific in December 1974, tells a television reporter about the wives' concern for their husbands' safety. She complained of maggots in the food, lice in the bedding, and leaks in the hull. Due to repeated deployment for the aerial war against Vietnam, Cambodia, and Laos, living and working conditions and the condition of the ships themselves were deteriorating. On the *Coral Sea's* Dependents' Day cruise outside the Golden Gate in November 1974, a fire broke out in an engine room, and the Navy's guests had to wait in line for hours for lunch. Inspired by the 1971 SOS campaign, these women  petitioned Congress to keep the carrier home until it was seaworthy.

Vicki Kelly and Rose Hills display their banner in front of the *USS Coral Sea*, 1974.

# My Teacher, My Friend

## by Andrew Lam

San Francisco—The man who stood at the entrance to my new world passed away recently, and though I hadn't seen him in more than three decades, the news of his demise left me unexpectedly bereft. I remember a warm voice, expressive eyes, and bushy eyebrows that wiggled comically at a pun or a joke. I remember someone who treated me with care, made me feel special when I—a stranger on a new shore—was terribly lost and bewildered.

Ernie Kaeselau was my first teacher in America. Having fled Saigon in spring of 1975 during finals in sixth grade, I landed in San Francisco a couple months later and attended summer school in Colma Junior High in Daly City, preparing myself for seventh grade. Never mind that I didn't speak English, only Vietnamese and passable French, and that two days after my mother, grandmother, sister, and I left in a cargo plane, communist tanks came crashing through the Independence Palace in Saigon, and the war ignominiously ended. Never mind that in between those few months I subsisted in two refugee camps and spent most of my nights in a tent praying for the safety of my father and other relatives and friends who remained behind.

I never knew what Mr. K's politics were—liberal is my guess—and if I had any then, ours would have surely clashed when it came to the politics of Vietnam. But when it came to me—the first Vietnamese refugee in his classroom—his policy was plenary kindness.

Mr. K's first question was my name and his second was how to properly pronounce it in Vietnamese. He would ask me to repeat this several times until, to my surprise, he got the complicated intonation almost right. A day or two later, he'd ask again and practice it until it was perfect, and soon thereafter, the Vietnamese refugee boy became the American teacher's pet. It was my task to go get his lunch, erase the blackboard, and collect and distribute homework assignments. When I missed the bus, which was often, and sometimes deliberately, he'd drive me home, a privilege that was the envy of the other kids.

America was full of rowdy, undisciplined children. In Vietnam, we all dressed in uniforms—blue shorts, white shirts—and bowed to the teachers, but American kids wore colorful clothes, smoked in the bathroom and swore at each other, and sometimes, even at their teachers—something unheard of in Vietnamese tradition.

At first, I was terrified, fearful of the big, rowdy kids of all races who got into bloody fights in the schoolyard. But Mr. K's classroom was a haven. Lunchtime and the "good kids" made a beeline for it. Away from the schoolyard bullies, we ate our lunch, played games, and did our homework. I remember plenty of laughter, arguments, gossips and, yes, even budding flirtations, and Mr. K reigned over the chaos with ease, sitting behind his desk, reading a newspaper or helping one of us with our assignments.

For a while, I was his echo. "Sailboat," he would say while holding a card up in front of me with an image of a sailboat on it, and "sailboat" I would repeat after him, copying his inflection and facial gestures. "Hospital," he would say, with another card held up. And "hospital," I would yell back, a little parrot. I listened to his diction. I listened to the way he enunciated certain words when he read passages from a book. If he could say my Vietnamese name, surely I could bend my tongue to make myself sound more American.

That first summer, he gave me As that didn't count. He took our little group bowling, formed a team, taught us how to keep score, and bought us soft drinks. Then, he took us on a baseball field trip, my first. He took his time to explain to me the intricacy of the game. It was followed by a trip to Sonoma to see wineries and cheese factories. I remember crossing the Golden Gate Bridge for the first time, with Mr. K's voice narrating its history, how it was built, and I remember asking him afterward, in broken English, if it was made of real gold, and the entire bus erupted in laughter.

Most memorable, however, were the books that came in a carton box. Along with a bowling team, Mr. K formed a little book club. And for a few dollars, we— children of the working class and immigrants—became owners of a handful of books. The box came one morning in the middle of class, and it felt a bit like Christmas in July. We jostled each other to be up front at his desk as Mr. K read the title of each book out loud, then matched the book with the name of its owner. My first book in America was *The Wind in the Willows*, by Kenneth Grahame, and I remember poring over its pristine pages in wonder. Perhaps it was then that the smell of fresh ink, paper, and glue indelibly became for me the smell of yearning and imagination. I did not yet know how to read in English—But oh, how impatient I was to learn!

That summer, I bought my first typewriter from a cantankerous junkman whose inventory was down the street and who my family was fond of calling "Old Angry Junkman." It cost $1.25 and some keys didn't work very well and the ribbon had long faded. Nevertheless, I typed out Grahame's famous tale about Mole, who left his underground home and went up for air and ended sailing down the river toward adventures. I read many sentences from it out loud as I typed. Precocious, perhaps, but by the time I joined seventh grade in the fall, I was something of a typist and a reader of the English-language novel.

If I pushed myself so hard to move forward I had plenty good reasons: In Vietnam, I was a child of an upper-class family, insulated in a world of villas, lycee, servants, walled gardens, and sports clubs. In America, I was the son of impoverished refugees who subsisted with another refugee family in a ramshackle apartment near the end of Mission Street, where the promises of San Francisco ended and the working-class world of Daly City began. My homeland abruptly evaporated, my family and clan were torn apart, and my sheltered life was gone. Thrust upon an alien world, I understood intuitively that I had best run far and fast if I were to leave all my losses behind.

Thus, this way my world split into two: night and I wept myself to sleep, longing for my lost world, for my father, dreaming a recurring dream of a Saigon in smoke and myself abandoned in an old villa as the Vietcong ransacked the city; but daytime—in school, at lunch, in English and art classes—I became a rowdy, giggly boy, chatting up a storm. I remember talking, a lot, and when my vocabulary failed me, resorted to using French words or drawing in my notebook or on the blackboard to convey my ideas and thoughts.

Within a few months, I began to speak English freely, though haltingly, and outgrew Mr. K's cards. I began to banter and joke with my new friends. I acquired a new personality, a sunny, sharp-tongued kid, and often Mr. Kaesleau would shake his head and marvel at the transformation. I remember his astonished face when I argued against the class clown and won; my tongue was being sharpened even if my sentences remained fragmented.

I made friends—Samoans, Whites, Blacks, Filipinos, Chinese, Mexicans. I wrote valentine cards to giggly girls. I joined the school newspaper, became something of a cartoonist. By my second year in, I was getting straight As, no fake As needed anymore, thank you. I joined the honors club. I found my bearings; I embraced my new world. I was becoming, as my mother complained to my father, who escaped Vietnam on a naval ship and joined us a few months later, "an American brat."

★★★

When I graduated from junior high, I came to say goodbye to Mr. Kaesleau and he gave me the old cards to take home as mementos, knowing full well that I didn't need them anymore. That day, a short day, I remember taking a shortcut over a hill and on the way down, I tripped and fell. The cards flew out of my hand to scatter like a flock of playful butterflies on the verdant slope. Though I skinned my knee, I laughed. Then, as I scampered to retrieve the cards, I found myself yelling out ecstatically the name of each image on each one of them—"school," "cloud," "bridge," "house," "dog," "car"—as if for the first time.

It was then that I looked up and saw, far in the distance, San Francisco's downtown, its glittering high rises resembling a fairy-tale castle made of diamonds, with the shimmering sea dotted with sailboats as backdrop.

"City," I said, "my beautiful city." And the words rang true; they slipped into my bloodstream and suddenly I was overwhelmed by an intense hunger. I wanted to swallow the breathtaking landscape before me.

And that was that, as they say. And I sailed on.

It turned out I didn't go to Jefferson where many of my closest friends ended up. I went to Serramonte High, an awful, unchallenging school known for its smoking pit and frequent robberies in bathrooms. But thanks to a relative whose address was in a coveted ZIP code, I transferred to Lowell High School—a prestigious public school in San Francisco. Superior to any schools around, Lowell provided high achievement standards and advanced-placement courses. I made new friends and ended up at UC Berkeley. That is to say, I left the working-class world where Mission Street ended, and worked myself toward where Mission Street began—toward the city's golden promises—and in one of those shiny towers by the water is where I live now.

I didn't bother to look back, didn't bother to keep my mentor and friend abreast of my progress. Several decades later, a seasoned journalist and essayist who had traveled the world a few times, I decided to write an article about learning English, and Mr. K was featured prominently.

Did I know that Mr. K read and treasured that article? Did I know that he, in retirement, kept coming back to it, to my writing—to me?

No. Not until his best friend, another teacher, sent me this note to inform me of his passing:

> Most of us know what pleasure Ernie got from your article. While he was proud he was also a modest man. ... He sent copies to many relatives back East. I'm sure he couched it in pride for what

you have accomplished, but he was deeply honored. What no one knows is he was a bit unhappy that there was no retirement recognition. He told me many times he didn't want any big deal, but as the years passed, he would speak somewhat wistfully of the lack of acknowledgement. You gave him acknowledgement.

To be honest, it never occurred to me to see the story from Mr. K's angle. When I tried to see the classroom from behind his desk as the years streamed by—students after students, generation after generation—I could not see myself standing out. I might have been the first Vietnamese refugee to turn up in his classroom, but I was not the last. My cousins came, so did others, and surely, later on, other needy, traumatized refugee children from other bloody conflicts. I might have been precocious, but how could I have possibly stood out to a man who taught for decade after decade?

I had grieved for my lost homeland, for many other things. I had traveled to exotic countries, to war zones, and even back to Vietnam to say my proper goodbyes to my interrupted childhood, but I didn't go back to where Mission Street ended, to where that little junior high stood at the foot of the mountains amid cemeteries often veiled in the morning fog. Living so near, I had felt, unreasonably, that were I to drive down Mission Street and peek through the window of my mentor's classroom, he would still be there—that Mr. K would always be there, making other needy kids feel special, and that there would always be little bowling teams and little book clubs in the summer and rowdy speed tournaments at lunchtime. And in dreams and reveries, haven't I revisited him countless times?

But that's the trouble with childhood, isn't it, especially happy ones? Happy children don't question their contentment any more than fish wonder about the river's current; they swim on. My childhood, interrupted by war, was rekindled by kindness, and instead of cynicism and bitterness, my curiosity and imagination took hold and kept growing in the New World. And because I felt blessed and happy, I went on blessedly with my business of growing up. Mr. K opened America's gate and ushered me in, and I, so hungry for all its possibilities, rushed through.

"I think your leading off would be very appropriate unless it makes you uncomfortable," wrote Mr. K's friend. "Lord knows I heard him talk about you several times. He kept mentioning it near the end."

★★★

The retired teachers sat on their pews to somber organ music. Wizened, gray-haired, they rose, one by one, moving slowly, some in arthritic pains, to speak with affection and humor of a man who was known as much for his aesthetic sensibilities and practical jokes and friendship as he was for his devotion to the art of teaching and to his students. Shared memories echoed inside the gilded columbarium like some ode to beauty itself ...

> *He was a talented organist ... loved driving cross-country ... Spanish architecture and colonial history of California ... this thing where he mimicked people while walking behind them ... created beautiful stained glass objects ... collected antique silver and botanical prints ...*

> *He was especially fond of orchids ...*

To all this I would say yet that his greatest talent is empathy: He intuited how one felt and, like a bodhisattva, performed his magic to assuage grief.

But if there's a sad statement to the American scholastic experience it is that the passing of a beloved teacher is often not mourned by his or her students, but by, if he or she were any good, mostly peers. Father's Day and Mother's Day are remembered, but a good teacher, alas, rarely receives a card by his former students on Teacher's Day. Drinking coffee and eating finger sandwiches afterward, I kept asking anyone younger than me if he or she had been a student of Mr. K. And the answer was always no.

The refugee boy not only led, as it turned out, he was the only former student of Ernie Kaeselau's to cry at his memorial.

★★★

*suddenly he stood by the edge of a full-fed river. ... All was a-shake and a-shiver—glints and gleams and sparkles, rustle and swirl, chatter and bubble. The Mole was bewitched, entranced, fascinated. By the side of the river he trotted as one trots, when very small, by the side of a man who holds one spell-bound by exciting stories.*

I did not fully appreciate the beauty of Grahame's words. Yet even then, not sure of what I read and typed, I knew that it had something to do with me—who, like Mole, albeit against my will, also left my insulated world and sailed toward the unknown. I also knew by the end of that first summer that I too, for having set out unflinching, would be awarded with friendship and new ways of seeing things.

A charmed life is one that goes down a river not knowing what's behind the bend, but confident nevertheless that gracious strangers will be there in one form or another to aid and abet and be a guide through turbulent waters. Charmed was how I felt when I first came here and more than three decades later, charmed is how I feel today—and much of that, I will acknowledge, has to do with Mr. K.

And so—the river glimmers and sparkles and I sail on. Because I could not go back, I will send ahead to the further stretch where I will not go, to where the storyteller's flesh crumbles to dust but his stories, when told from the heart, may live on yet. For this, tendered by enchanted memories, tinged with regrets, is one of requited love.

# Filipino Americans in the Decade of the International Hotel[1]

## by Estella Habal

In November 1968, a group of elderly, first-generation Filipino immigrants held picket signs and demonstrated in front of the International Hotel. They were protesting imminent eviction by a landlord who wanted the choice location at 848 Kearny Street to demolish the building and open a parking lot. On the corner of Jackson and Kearny, the International Hotel loomed for years in the eyes of developers and city officials itching for "urban renewal." The I-Hotel, re-built in 1907 after the earthquake, was the last remnant of the 10-block Manilatown neighborhood that stretched along Kearny Street between San Francisco's Chinatown and the Financial District. Bit by bit, the old neighborhood of single room occupancy hotels, barber shops, restaurants, and pool halls familiar to the men since early in the century had been demolished. The aging Filipinos were mostly bachelors or without their families, living alone as a result of anti-miscegenation laws or because it was too difficult to bring families to San Francisco during the harsh early days of immigration. They had worked for years in the agricultural fields of California and the Northwest, in the homes of the wealthy as domestic workers, in canneries up the coast to Alaska, and on merchant ships; many were veterans of both World Wars. Now they were being displaced, dispersed, and discarded. The presence and even the memory of these humble, yet strong and dignified, men and of the hotel they called home would soon be erased.[2]

Flash forward to the very early morning hours of August 4, 1977. Chanting "We Won't Move!" thousands of Filipinos, Chinese, and all types of people from San Francisco and throughout the Bay Area linked arms in front of the International Hotel. Police on horseback repeatedly charged into the "human barricade" of nonviolent demonstrators and clubbed their way to the front door. Once inside, sheriff's deputies dragged off other supporters who had linked arms in the halls, broke down the doors of the tenants' rooms with sledgehammers, rousted the elderly Filipino and Chinese tenants, and led them out the door with only the clothes on their backs. Each frail tenant was accompanied by a young activist who was there to assist but also to help prevent police abuse. One by one, the tenants stepped through the I-Hotel's front door and out to the street where they were met with a roaring and weeping crowd of supporters that was kept back by police lines.[3]

The anti-eviction movement had quickly grown from the core of first-generation immigrants in 1968. The people of San Francisco sympathized with the elderly tenants the more they learned about them. By the time the eviction took place, a wide range of constituencies beyond Asian-American communities had become active in the anti-eviction movement: Civil Rights activists, labor leaders, and rank-and-file members, religious spokesmen and their congregations, anti-war and anti-imperialist activists, advocates for gay rights, and organizers for district elections. The International Hotel was also part of a resistance to urban policies aimed at transforming San Francisco according to the master plans of commercial and financial interests. Many people in San Francisco strongly favored the need for available, affordable housing in contrast to the demands for corporate expansion. Homelessness was not yet a massive phenomenon, but many residents of the City feared that costs would be so high that they could be denied housing altogether, which gave the International Hotel a broad appeal.

At certain times, particularly between 1975 and 1979, the fate of the International Hotel became a major issue in the electoral arena, and the anti-eviction movement helped to shape a center-left coalition that successfully challenged the status quo in city politics. Saving the I-Hotel also won considerable support from Mayor George Moscone, city supervisors, and other major politicians. Even the sheriff went to jail rather than carry out the eviction—until he acquiesced to the courts.

In 1968, "Manhattanization," or the high-rise expansion of the financial district in downtown San Francisco, had been well underway for more than a decade. The downtown area was the focus of the business elite, and city planners expected to expand downtown upward with numerous high-rise office buildings (such as the Transamerica Pyramid, just two blocks from the I-Hotel) and to move outward into adjacent neighborhoods. Manilatown, spread out along 10 blocks of Kearny Street, north from Market Street to Columbus Avenue and right on the eastern edge of Chinatown, was just one block west of the financial district. At such a prime location, the neighborhood stood in the way of "progress," or "higher use" as many of the advocates of redevelopment called their development plans.[4]

Much was at stake in the I-Hotel battle: It was a fight for housing rights versus private property rights, for a neighborhood to exist versus extinction and dispersal, and for democratic rights to be extended to the poor and working class. San Franciscans defended the hotel because it was also a stand for the City to be affordable, livable, and diverse. But for the Filipino community the I-Hotel also became the place where a self-conscious identity as Filipinos in America was forged through a struggle for survival and dignity.

Radicalized Filipinos and other Asian-American youth were drawn to the plight of the I-Hotel tenants. Students aroused by the San Francisco State Strike, and the Third World Strike at UC Berkeley that had also erupted in 1968, were moved by the call to serve the community. When the first generation of Filipinos in San Francisco's Manilatown resisted eviction from their home and the last remnant of their community, Filipino college students and other young people were inspired to become activists themselves.

I, too, was drawn to the I-Hotel. I first visited the International Hotel in 1970 as part of a field trip of the Filipino youth organization I helped to found in Los Angeles, and when I moved to San Francisco a couple of years later, I gravitated to the hotel because that's the place where young Filipinos and the *manongs* (respected elders) converged. I ended up playing a key role in the anti-eviction movement, working closely with the tenants as part of a team from the leading Filipino radical organization at that time, the Katipunan ng mga Demokratikong Pilipino (KDP) or the Union of Democratic Filipinos. In this essay, I regard the story of the International Hotel—and the Filipino community in San Francisco—from that perspective.

As we worked together to fight the eviction, young and old Filipinos created a bond to preserve the legacy of the early days for a community that was undergoing rapid change. The elderly tenants were the heart of the movement, and they were backed by mass action of people of all backgrounds and neighborhoods of San

Francisco and around the Bay Area. Thousands of people were ready to defend the hotel from eviction with a call from the telephone tree, busloads of demonstrators from all kinds of groups would come to rallies, and politicians felt insistent pressure from voters to help the tenants.

## Peace With a Lease

Soon after the tenants received their eviction order in 1968, they formed the United Filipino Association (UFA) to represent tenants and the storefront businesses. The landlord, Walter Shorenstein, was president of Milton Meyer and Company, and a wealthy and influential donor to the Democratic Party. Assemblyman John Burton worked out a deal with Shorenstein to suspend the eviction. In 1969, a suspicious fire killed three International Hotel tenants and gutted the third floor. But the UFA worked out a lease agreement—"Peace with a Lease"—to last three years. Student activists joined the manongs to restore and refurbish the building, organizing work crews.[6]

During this period, the basement and storefronts housed businesses and community organizations, such as the Chinatown Cooperative Garment Factory, Tino's Barber Shop, and the Mabuhay Restaurant on the one hand, and on the other, the Manilatown Information Center, Asian Legal Services, Everybody's Bookstore, the radical Chinese-American groups Wei Min She and I Wor Kuen, and the radical Filipino group Kalayaan International. Eventually, the Asian Community Center and the Chinese Progressive Association, organizations led by Chinese radicals, also made their home in the basement offices. As the lease became due, the International Hotel Tenants Association (IHTA) was founded, and the tenants demanded a new lease agreement. In the midst of this, the Four Seas Investment Corporation, run by a shady businessman from Thailand, bought the International Hotel. Shorenstein was probably relieved to unload the property that damaged his liberal standing. In 1974, once again, the tenants faced eviction. A series of court cases ensued, as the tenants fought eviction and demolition orders.[7]

In 1976 Mayor George Moscone proposed a plan whereby the City would buy the building under eminent domain and after a few years have the tenants buy the hotel back. The tenants were divided about the "buy-back plan," with some supporting it as a way to at least forestall eviction and others objecting that it was a trick, since the tenants would never be able to afford the building. No matter what, despite demonstrations and broad support for the I-Hotel, the courts rejected the use of eminent domain, and the threat of eviction increased. Sheriff Richard Hongisto and Undersheriff Denman refused to carry out the eviction and were charged with contempt of court, and in April 1977, the sheriff served 5 days for contempt of court in San Francisco County jail. In July, the State Supreme Court lifted all legal barriers to immediate eviction of tenants, even though appeal on eminent domain had yet to be reviewed in the State Court of Appeal. Meanwhile, conservative politicians attempted to stop the victory of district elections by presenting voters with two propositions, one seeking the end of district elections and another recalling the mayor and all elected officials. Both propositions lost in an election on August 2, 1977. Although the mayor had soundly beaten the right-wing attack, he decided that the I-Hotel had become a political liability and authorized the eviction on the night and early morning of August 3rd and 4th.[8]

## Finding Our Roots

One of the major characteristics of the I-Hotel struggle for Filipinos was the way bonds were formed between generations, between the elderly manongs and the radicalized youth who were looking for their "roots." These bonds were cultivated because both the old and the young saw themselves as part of a progressive, working-class, anti-colonial, anti-imperialist Left. Many of the elders had been active in trade-union struggles, fought in the military against fascism, and had experience with left-wing politics. Many were educated intellectuals with deep, organic ties as thinkers and leaders to other early immigrants. The youth, undergoing an awakening, discovered that both the old and the young shared internationalist perspectives and common experiences, and both generations sought to rediscover the Philippines. The manongs fought against racial discrimination and economic exploitation, and they felt they were part of a greater "proletarian solidarity." At the same time, the youth came to understand the social, economic, political, and historical processes in the Philippines that prompted immigration to the United States.[9]

"Find Our Roots," we cried out, and the youth set out to form our own Filipino identity movement. Like other people of color, we were inspired by the Black Panthers' call for Black Power and self-determination. "Find Our Roots" linked us to our immigrant parents who struggled for a better life for their children. Filipinos and other minorities who began to identify themselves as integral to the Third World created their own ethnic-based identity movements which had a "Third World" quality, linking the United States-based movements for racial equality with current struggles in their respective countries.

As Filipino students joined the strikes at San Francisco State and UC Berkeley, they looked to the Philippines, as other Third World activists looked to their own homelands, for cultural meanings, icons, symbols, and values to highlight their Filipino culture and identity. Many of the young identified with a mythical past which belonged only to the indigenous and un-colonized native, and Filipinos joined that trend. There was great excitement as we self-consciously rejected old ways of thinking that we considered to be colonized, submissive mindsets learned from Spain and America. We were searching for the "authentic" Filipino, and we romanticized the pre-colonial *Indio* (the Spanish name given to the indigenous peoples of the Philippines, as well as those of the Americas).

We considered ourselves to be held back by our "colonized mentalities," and our goal was the de-colonization of the mind as well as the land. Filipino-American students felt the struggle in the Philippines against neocolonial, imperialist domination was part of a worldwide anti-colonial upsurge of historic proportions, and we were proud that we held a place in the pantheon of Third World liberation movements. The Filipino community in America was very small at that time (less than 1%), but we felt a sense of importance and purpose because we were participating in a world historical process.[10]

The United Farm Workers union (UFW) had galvanized the labor and Civil Rights Movements, and we learned firsthand from Filipino farm workers that they had been instrumental in organizing the 1965 Grape Strike and the boycott. We were proud of our Filipino leaders, such as Larry Itliong, Assistant Director to Cesar Chavez; Philip Vera Cruz, second Vice President of the UFW; and Pete Velasco, third Vice President of the UFW, who were the first to organize the Delano grape strike. In the San Francisco Bay Area, young activists worked with Pablo Valdez and Mario Hermoso, who had been labor organizers in the 1930s. We heard the stories directly from the manongs of how the first Filipino immigrants worked for low pay and hard conditions and were racially oppressed in a system that got rich from their labor and then abandoned them, to be forgotten in Manilatowns.

For the manongs, there was no previous Filipino generation to rely on, no sizable number of lawyers and other professionals who could contribute to their causes economically or give them credibility outside of their class.[11] With no Filipino community to help them, the manong generation relied on themselves or sought support from those outside the Filipino community to rally to their causes. At that time, the Communist Party and its affiliated organizations, along with some unions and other leftist organizations, were among the few "American" groups to help the manongs fight their economic and political battles. Soon after 1968, the Filipino-American youth and students championed issues that affected the early, first-generation Filipinos—the lack of decent health care, inadequate housing, and the need for workers' rights, as demonstrated in the grape strike in Delano.

Cross-generational relationships developed between elderly and youth activists because of the unique combination of factors: the confluence of campus and youth activism in the community, the plans of city officials to employ "redevelopment" to raze "blighted communities," particularly minority communities, the need for youth to assert their identity, and the elderly generation's search for supporters among fellow Filipinos. As a result of this bonding between young and old, the Filipino youth identity movement developed working-class values at its core. Traditional Filipino cultural values, such as respect for elders, combined with an American working-class ethic that included a respect for labor. During this time, the term of endearment 'manong' was popularized, honoring a Filipino elder generation's political struggle for economic and racial justice.

Some of the student activists were children of the few manongs who were able to marry Mexican, Native American women or, in some states where it was legal, even White women. More were, like me, children of immigrants who came after WWII. Many of our parents were roughly the same age as the manongs, but their experience of immigration, while hard, was not as difficult as the manongs. Many had been in the Philippine Scouts, the American colonial force, or in the US military. After the war, nurses and other professionals were also able to make it through the restrictions in immigration. Once here, the immigrants brought over their families, escaping the isolation of the working men who came before. Family members who followed were not necessarily professionals themselves, and they began working in agricultural and service jobs. Many of these immigrants felt beholden to the United States; the military men, in particular, were grateful to General MacArthur and the United States for liberating the Philippines from Japan. While the youth opposed the war in Vietnam, many of their parents supported the war or deferred to whatever the military decided. We felt that Filipinos from the post-WWII stream of immigration tended to be unduly subservient, and the youth were often alienated from our own parents. We extended our families to include the manongs.

While some of the elderly Filipino tenants at the I-Hotel had been political and social leaders in their youth, others developed as leaders as the need to stop the eviction demanded that they step forward. Outsiders to the I-Hotel would sometimes not understand the relationship between the old and the young, suspecting that the elderly had been misled or manipulated by young radical students.[12] These old men had worked all their lives, had experienced social and emotional pain as a result of the gender imbalance in the population, and were ostracized by White society. To make matters worse, many Filipino immigrants who arrived after the war or after the immigration reform of 1965 would regard them with shame: the manongs suffered dire poverty, lacked formal education, and displayed embarrassingly too-Filipino ways, such as thick accents, ethnic foods, and traditional music.

Wahat Tompao was one of the manongs who stepped forward to lead. He served in the US Navy from 1928 to 1949, and he first stayed at the International Hotel in 1929, making it his permanent home in 1963. Manong Wahat was from one of the tribal peoples in the Philippines; he was proud of his heritage; and he refused to be embarrassed because of his accent.

Felix Ayson was another extraordinary character. Born in 1894, he graduated high school and joined the US Armed Forces during World War I, returning to fight again in WWII. Manong Felix was a schoolteacher before the war, and he came to America to further his education, but he ran out of money and was forced to work in the fields and canneries. He became a union organizer, staying at the I-Hotel periodically since 1926. After the war, he went to school to become an electrical engineer under the GI Bill, and he married a Creole woman from New Orleans. But he couldn't make a living because of discrimination and ended up working as an elevator operator. His wife died in a car accident a few years before he moved into the hotel permanently in 1969.

Frankie Alarcon had been a sailor and had traveled all over the world. He was a veteran of both World Wars. Manong Frankie had a strong sense that he was entitled to equal rights, and, like Manongs Wahat and Felix, he believed in America. He loved to dance with the young girls who would come to support the tenants, and during the Sunday social events we would organize, showing off his tango, fox-trot, and two-step. But he was always a gentleman.[13]

Despite the suspicions of outsiders, the tenants of the I-Hotel constantly astonished the youth and the various supporters who had come to know them. Tenant leaders—Ayson, Claudio Domingo, Tompao, and others—educated the other tenants and helped to organize and mobilize meetings and demonstrations. Many outsiders were fooled by their advanced age, their frailty, their heavy accents, their lowly status, and their brown skin into thinking they would be easily bulldozed by those in power or they would become tools of the students who supported them. These leaders were educated in the world and in struggle, whether as military veterans or self-taught intellectuals or union organizers. They were shrewd and able to navigate the twists and turns of court cases and politicians' promises, and they were able to mesh with the youth who came to their aid. And they were willing to fight.

## Political Priorities

Before 1965, the few Filipino families in San Francisco lived in the Western Addition and parts of the Richmond District. But when immigration laws were reformed in 1965, Filipinos arrived at a rapidly increasing rate. Middle-class professionals, college students, and political elites made America their choice destination because of the legacy of American colonial presence in the Philippines—most immigrants already spoke some English—and the desire for economic opportunities. Filipinos, along with African-Americans, were increasingly pushed out of the Western Addition by urban renewal, and the recent immigrants concentrated in new neighborhoods. Many of the less wealthy settled in the side streets of the South of Market area, while the better off moved to Daly City, just south of San Francisco, turning it into one of the largest enclaves of Filipinos outside of the islands. As the Ferdinand Marcos regime grew more and more dictatorial in the 1970s, many Filipinos also came fleeing repression.

Because of the political situation, a new group began coming to Kearny Street, young revolutionaries radicalized in the Philippines. They too gravitated to the I-Hotel to seek out their counterparts among progressive Filipino Americans. In June 1971, a dozen Filipino-American activists and recent arrivals from the Philippines met at the back of one of the I-Hotel storefronts to form Kalayaan (Freedom) International, an anti-imperialist organization and newspaper collective. The name came from the official organ of the revolutionary league founded by Andres Bonifacio, the peasant leader of the 1896 struggle against Spain. This new incarnation spoke out against racism in the US and imperialist domination, advocating community support for the Philippine "national democratic" revolutionary movement. In its first issue, the editors of the *Kalayaan International* stated that its goal was to make the Filipino in America "aware of the multi-faceted problems of its people, both here and back home. Like its predecessors, it hopes to serve as the vanguard of truth and dissent, where truth is shielded by ignorance and dissent intimidated into silent discontent."[14]

The radical exiles arrived with intense experience in the nationalist and student movements opposed to the Marcos dictatorship, particularly the resurgence of the communist movement. The Maoist influenced radicals declared the need to "rectify and reestablish" the old, pro-Soviet and moribund party, and in 1968 they founded the new Communist Party of the Philippines (CPP). The new party launched armed struggle with the formation of the New People's Army (NPA).

The new immigrants coming to the I-Hotel called themselves "Philippine nationals" or "foreign nationals," which underscored that they were sojourners, never expecting to fully assimilate culturally in the United States. But, as time went on and the Marcos dictatorship dug in for years, even the term "exile community" outgrew its usefulness, and it became clear that the new arrivals were also settlers in the United States. The Left called these expatriate radicals "revolutionary nationalists," emphasizing their anti-imperialist or anti-colonial nationalism. Their political relationships remained strong, even as the new immigrants became permanent residents or US citizens.[15]

In September 1972, Ferdinand Marcos declared martial law, and the opposition against repression and dictatorship became an even broader front. In July 1973, KDP was founded, modeled after Kabataang Makabayan (Nationalist Youth) in the Philippines as a nationwide revolutionary mass organization, led by Cynthia Maglaya, Melinda Paras, Bruce Occena, and others. KDP based itself on the same combination of exiles and Fil Ams as Kalayaan International, and the organization projected a dual US-Philippines program: to support democratic rights and, eventually, socialism in the United States and to oppose the Marcos dictatorship and fight for the national democratic revolution in the Philippines.

Filipino Americans                                                                 133

Kalayaan, and the KDP, fused the Philippine student movement—characterized by advanced political theory, organizational sophistication, radical action, and direct experience of violent repression and resistance—with the radical politics of Filipino Americans challenging racism and class society in the United States. The Philippine-born radicals affected the Fil Am youth profoundly, adding to the radicalization already underway.

The Fil Ams, as compared to the transplanted radicals, usually had weaker ties to the Philippines, and they knew almost nothing of their history and culture. As children, many participated in Filipino customs, practices, and community events, but as they grew older they let whatever Filipino cultural practices they knew fall aside. There were no language classes in the community among the American-born, as in Chinese and Japanese communities where cultural ties were maintained in after-school programs or cultural courses. In fact, American colonial education in the Philippines made English its mother tongue and Filipino parents followed this dictate. And in the context of US hierarchical race relations, assimilation for their children meant no longer speaking any of the Filipino languages. Their parents' political views tended to be conservative and entirely too beholden to US policies and interests. The way their parents assimilated no longer worked for the young Filipino Americans. Their parents rejected the Filipino culture, custom, and history in favor of the "all American" way. In fact, Fil Ams began to regard themselves as "overseas Filipinos," as part of the Filipino Diaspora, although they did not intend to return permanently (and demanded equality in America). There were other ways to return to the homeland, by means of the cultural renaissance underway through memory, written and visual texts, visits, monetary contributions, demonstrations, or a combination of all of these. Filipino Americans began to identify themselves as part of the Philippine nation, despite their American birth and citizenship. They became "Pilipino," as transnational politics permeated the Filipino-American community.[17]

However, much of the community was frightened and quiet in response to martial law, with some conservatives, such as Alex Esclamado, editor of *Philippine News,* anchoring what we called the "elite opposition" to Marcos. Liberal Catholic clergy, particularly those who were influenced by liberation theology, held masses for political prisoners and in other ways expressed opposition. Filipinos would demonstrate every September at the anniversary of the declaration of martial law, rallying at the Philippine Consulate on Sutter Street. KDP joined with others to form coalitions and alliances, educating the growing Filipino community about the dictatorship.[18] The KDP sold its newspaper at major gatherings, churches, and neighborhoods with front page news coverage on the situation in the Philippines. Soon, because of the relative vacuum in the opposition to Marcos and the unity of the Filipino left, the KDP became the leading organization in the Filipino community to champion the Philippine cause.

Except for its radical character, the KDP was similar to other ethnic-based community organizations that expanded their transnational character during that time period. Professionals and semi-professionals began forming such groups as the Filipino Nurses Association, Filipino Postal Employees Association, and Filipino Medical Technicians, alongside traditional regional or town organizations such as the Bicol Club or Pangasinan Club. Within the context of ethnic organizing, Kalayaan and the KDP were not unique formations but rather logical extensions of these broader social dynamics between the Philippines and the United States.

Within this flow of transnational and ethnic politics, the radicalized Filipino student exiles brought with them a sense of nationhood and national pride that was counter-posed to the histories of both Spanish and American colonial domination. This identity became a base for them to oppose racial subordination and White domination in the United States. Nationalist ethnic organizing was a response to their integration within the Filipino-American community. However, only the revolutionary elements sought out a base among Filipino-American youth searching for their identity. Newly formed immigrant groups usually do not organize among the American-born, because of economic, political, and/or cultural differences. Kalayaan and the KDP were unique in this regard. Because they were conscious about racism, imperialism, and colonialism as aspects of the same oppressive system, this sector of new immigrants could ally more easily with American-born Filipinos. Nationalist pride and the painful effects of racism helped to bond the two groups.

While the KDP reflected the political needs of the anti-Marcos movement in the Philippines, its dual program included support for socialism and extension of democracy in the US. Concretely, that meant the organization targeted social and economic justice for the Filipino minority in the US. For example, the KDP supported striking workers in a local struggle at Blue Shield in San Francisco where many Filipinos worked. It embarked on a national campaign in defense of two Filipino nurses, Filipina Narciso and Leonora Perez, who were wrongfully accused of killing patients in a Chicago hospital.[19] This case, which displayed much racial bias, ended in acquittal for the nurses. The I-Hotel organizing team in the KDP fought for low-income housing for the elderly with Filipinos at the struggle's core, knowing that it would take a broad effort, not just Filipinos, to win the battle.

As contacts with Philippine activists deepened, Filipino-American political and ethnic identity grew away from its pan-Asian American political origins. While maintaining ties with other Asian-American groups, Fil Am activists transformed their political and ethnic identity from what was a romantic cultural connection, even quaint and nostalgic, to be a self-aware, anti-imperialist political consciousness. The revival of pre-colonial values was part of the decolonization efforts to liberate themselves from a colonial mentality. Histories of the Philippines produced by Filipino nationalists highlighted resistance to foreign domination and oppression. Filipino-American history situated the Filipino immigrant experiences with those of other immigrant peoples who also face exploitation, racism, and national oppression. When Filipino farm workers of the 1920s and 1930s were elevated to heroic status, Filipino-American activists had found a way to combine an anti-colonial past in the Philippines with traditions of class resistance in the United States. The KDP, like the other radicals, advocated what has been described as Third World Marxism, but the organization consciously stepped back from regarding itself as having the goal of renewing the left for all Americans.[20]

In the course of the '70s, the KDP began to mature, and it gained a reputation for effective organizing and honest dealings among the traditional and established groups. Nevertheless, vociferous conservatives in the Filipino community grew more and more opposed to KDP's politics, making it increasingly difficult for the activists on Kearny Street to gain new supporters for the I-Hotel. The fact that KDP advocated Leftist politics in a forthright fashion made it a target within the community.

With its dual program and dual social base, there were often conflicting political priorities, in addition to dealing with the anti-communist reactions in the Filipino community. Nonetheless, the KDP played a decisive role in the International Hotel struggle, exercising leadership even though its social base and its program pulled in two directions. At the same time, KDP gained increasing credibility because the organization was disciplined, serious, and capable of working within broad alliances and with elected officials. Despite all the contradictions inherent in these "dual" dynamics, KDP activists did manage to help the manongs to lead the struggle, while the elderly tenants—shrewd, determined, and militant—kept the young activists from getting confused, falling to despair, and losing our bearings.

## Organizing Against Eviction

While many KDP activists had ties to the I-Hotel, it was only in 1975 that the organization formed a team to anchor the work there. It was a three-person team, consisting of Emil De Guzman, Jeanette Lazam, and me. We sought to work closely with the IHTA, watching out for the tenants' well-being, and helping them strategize. As the swirl of political maneuvers, court cases, mass demonstrations, and internal security concerns heightened, we would meet every day, assessing the situation, and then go off to our different responsibilities. We patiently explained to the manongs the various legal issues and the actions of city officials, always deferring to the wishes of the tenants. One of our most important tasks was making sure that the tenants' voices would be heard and not get overwhelmed by the often loud and chaotic coalition of supporters. The KDP was supposed to assign other members to join in the mobilizations and to assist us, as well as to provide close political guidance. Many KDP members did come to the demonstrations or sign up for security (to prevent an arson fire or other sabotage and to be on the lookout for eviction attempts), but there was little organizational support. Right after the I-Hotel team was established a team was formed to support us, but it fell apart. Drawn in too many directions, and with many of the exile radicals more focused on the anti-Marcos movement, the KDP leadership lagged in giving us guidance, and the I-Hotel team had to operate on our own for most of the time.

The last year of the struggle grew increasingly tense, as we blocked one eviction attempt after another, while dealing with conflicts within the IHTA. Emil, Jeanette, and I were overwhelmed by the daily crises and political maneuvers. Joe Diones, the manager of the hotel and president of the IHTA, began to act erratically and to impose his will with violence. Eventually, the tenants voted him out of office and swiftly voted for Emil to replace him as president. The different coalitions of supporters disagreed about the Moscone plan, and this threatened to split the tenants and the support groups.

I was stretched beyond my limit. Unlike most of the *kasama* (comrades), I was a single mother with three children, and although KDP organized childcare for them—someone was always at the apartment with them—I constantly felt anxious that I was away. I was forcing my children to make sacrifices that I had chosen for myself, and I felt guilty. But we were committed to being cadres, and we were devoted to the elders. Revolution was personal for me, as well, not an abstraction. I came from a poor background, and women's liberation had freed me from the barrio, literally. I had divorced my first husband because he was obsessively jealous and domineering, not even allowing me to attend school, and the ideas of women controlling their own lives gave me the ability to escape. Women were encouraged to lead in the KDP, and there were many women in the top leadership positions. For me and for many others, the I-Hotel provided a sense of family that was missing in other parts of our lives. The elderly men and the few women who lived in the hotel were the uncles and aunts that I never had while growing up because mine had remained in the Philippines until immigration laws were eased in 1965.

When the eviction finally came with all of its violence, I was devastated, as were many others. After winning the support of the mayor, the Board of Supervisors, even the sheriff, the forces of private property, particularly the courts, overwhelmed us. The tenants were traumatized. Right after the eviction, the tenants and their supporters gathered in a small park in Chinatown. Manong Wahat laid face down on the pavement, weeping uncontrollably. Jeanette Lazam, who had accompanied him out the front door, kneeled alongside him to comfort him. Years later, she described her bitterness and despair:

> For the first time ever, since I started living and organizing in the Hotel, I couldn't offer the tenants encouragement. I couldn't offer them hope that our Hotel would be saved. I felt so totally helpless. By five o'clock in the morning, it was all over. I walked out of the Hotel arm in arm with Wahat Tompao, leader of the IHTA. We walked out the front door, he turned to look at the Hotel and fell on his knees sobbing like a child. Wahat had been one of the strongest people I knew in this struggle. He was relentless and tireless in trying to stave off the eviction. He collapsed again in St. Mary's Square. Wahat was a warrior, and now this warrior, this fierce noble tribesman, wept in my arms.[21]

Eighty-year-old Felix Ayson embodied the spirit of resistance, and his words that day resonated with all of the tenants:

> I am crippled. I am deaf. I am very old. I'm alone here and they put me out on the street. I will feel solitary and afraid on the street. I want freedom, the principle of American democracy, the richest country in the world. Do you think our mayor has a place for me? No. No, because I was happy here.[22]

Manong Felix died a year later. Getting evicted and losing a home is so traumatic that it can have a terrible effect on anyone, and the shock could threaten the lives of the elderly. In the course of the next couple of years, several of the other tenants got sick or died. I, too, was traumatized, collapsing about a month after the eviction. The pressure of being a single parent during times of extreme activism had taken its toll.

## Filling the Hole

Eventually, most of the tenants went to live in the Stanford Hotel, which was located further down Kearny Street, far from Chinatown. Some supervisors put a proposition on the ballot, a non-binding policy statement asking if the City should buy the I-Hotel, bring it up to code and turn it over to the Housing Authority for low-rent housing. But Proposition U lost in the November 1977 election. Voters were confused by the new district election system and the many candidates running for the Board of Supervisors. Moderates to conservatives in city politics had mobilized against the new system and brought voters to the polls in large numbers, fearing that district elections would produce an "ultra-liberal" new Board of Supervisors.[23] The turnout was unexpectedly low, favoring the Right. Not only did the incumbents win, but also moderate to conservative newcomers. In the new Board of Supervisors, only Harvey Milk actually fully supported the new system. Proposition U lost by a two to one margin, a decisive defeat.[24] The IHTA and supporters fought to save the building, but it was fully demolished in 1979.

Famed *San Francisco Chronicle* columnist Herb Caen employed his typical wit to comment right before the election. He sarcastically described "old San Francisco" as a "repository of freedom, tolerance and understanding." He found a guidebook for the City published in 1882, the same year that the Chinese Exclusion Act was passed in Congress. He discovered an ad for an earlier incarnation of the International Hotel. According to the ad, the International Hotel was "The Best Hotel in San Francisco," and lauded the amenities offered by the hotel. Caen ended the quotation with "the ultimate inducement to the sophisticated traveler: 'No Chinese Employed In Or About the Hotel.'"[25]

But this was not the end of the story. Soon after the assassination of Mayor George Moscone and Supervisor Harvey Milk, Mayor Diane Feinstein ordered the creation of the International Hotel Block Development Citizens Advisory Committee (CAC) to monitor any new projects to be built on the site and the entire block. Feinstein appointed to the CAC tenant representatives from the IHTA, along with Chinese community leaders. Even though the Four Seas Investment Corporation was able to demolish the building in 1979, it was prevented from constructing a garage or any other commercial building on the site. The City had taken the steps to put the use of eminent domain back on the table, and Four Seas was forced to negotiate for mixed-use development. Four Seas could no longer dispose of the property without oversight, and no project could be built until the company made a deal that involved low-income housing at the site. Nothing was built at the hole in the ground at Jackson and Kearny for 25 years, until a coalition came together to build a new International Hotel composed of the Chinatown Community Development Center, the Kearny Street Housing Corporation, the Catholic Archdiocese, St. Mary's Catholic Center, the Mayor's Office, the Housing and Urban Development office of the federal government, and the Manilatown Heritage Foundation.[26]

In August 2005, a new International Hotel was opened on Kearny Street. It is a 15-story building with 104 studio and one-bedroom apartments for low-income seniors, mostly from Chinatown. On the ground floor opened the International Hotel Manilatown Center, an exhibition, performance, and educational space that pays tribute to those evicted from the original I-Hotel and to all the early Filipino immigrants, as well as the contemporary Filipino community. The Center was sponsored by the Manilatown Heritage Foundation, a group initiated by poet Al Robles. He had made a lifelong commitment to the manongs and to keeping the memory of Manilatown alive, and he felt it was crucial for there to be a Filipino presence in the new project. He was joined by housing and labor activist Bill Sorro, Emil De Guzman, myself, and others. After so many years, this was a victory of sorts, although almost none of the tenants who were evicted lived long enough to savor it.

"People ask, 'Do you feel vindicated now that they are filling that hole up?' No, we don't," Sorro explained to a reporter at the opening celebration. "We don't feel vindicated because justice don't work like that. Justice isn't something simple, so that if you fill the hole up with this much justice then you're equal. The lives of the people who died as a result of the eviction and the trauma of being displaced, these elderly people—is it now OK because we are going to fill it up with 104 units? Is it OK that a community was destroyed and there is no remnant of a Filipino community that thrived there? It is not OK."[27]

The International Hotel struggle moved an extraordinarily large number of people who came to defend the elderly victims of the country's history of colonial and racial injustice. Supporters came to defend the remnants of a community, to defend "home" and human values rather than "market" values, to advocate a broader understanding of civil rights to include the right of affordable housing and of the elderly to live in dignity and not impoverished humiliation. It was also a fight to allow the poor, the working class, even the middle class to remain in San Francisco as Manhattanization gave way to gentrification.

Radicals, particularly Asian radicals, were at the core of the mass movement to defend the hotel, and they cultivated the grassroots, dynamic character of the struggle. The International Hotel was where much of the Asian-American movement developed, where students moved from campus activism to working with the community, where they grew to oppose war and racism and to identify with Third World liberation movements and to fully develop Marxist politics.

Thousands of people came to the support of the tenants during the anti-eviction battle, working on media and legal committees, doing stints on nighttime security to protect the tenants, forming medical teams, organizing countless demonstrations. Finally, thousands joined the human barricade around the building to be beaten by police and dragged away. The International Hotel became a major experience in the lives of thousands, just as the 1934 San Francisco General Strike was for an earlier generation.

For the Filipino community, specifically, the I-Hotel was especially important because we formed a unique sense of identity based on the embrace of generations. Without the Manilatown Center, many Filipino Americans would have believed that the community's history started in 1965, and the contributions of the first generation of immigrants would be forgotten, as well as the role of the students who came to their aid. The Manilatown Center does not program events only about that past, however, since the community is always being shaped by new experiences and new arrivals. The Center displays exhibitions by contemporary artists, holds lectures on the political situation in the Philippines, sponsors hip hop concerts, and in other ways encourages all aspects of Filipino-American experience today. Young people are once again involved, defending the rights of aging Filipino WWII veterans or exploring their role in American society. Yet another generation has joined the family of Filipinos in America, and the International Hotel remains as a reminder of our past and a commitment to our future.

# Notes

1.  For a more complete history and more detailed documentation of the International Hotel conflict, see Estella Habal, *San Francisco's International Hotel: Mobilizing the Filipino American Community in the Anti-Eviction Movement* (Philadelphia: Temple University Press, 2007). In that book and here I rely on countless hours of interviews and conversations with Emil de Guzman, Jeanette Lazam, Al Robles, Bill Sorro, and others, and I am grateful for their contribution. It helps to have a live-in editor, and I thank my husband Hilton Obenzinger who assisted me in editing this article.

2.  George Murphy, "Filipinos March for Their Home," *San Francisco Chronicle*, November 28, 1968; for more on the early days of the struggle, see Carol Deena Levine, "The City's Response to Conflicting Pressures—A Case Study: The International Hotel" (master's thesis, San Francisco State University, 1970), 2.

3.  News coverage of the eviction was exceptional by all the mainstream media, as well as the progressive and radical press: George Snyder and Birney Jarvis, "The Explosive Clash Between Cops, Protestors," *San Francisco Chronicle*, August 5, 1977; Katy Butler, "Final Hours Inside," *San Francisco Chronicle*, August 5, 1977; Katy Butler, "How They Took the Hotel," *San Francisco Chronicle*, August 5, 1977; "How Cops Routed Tenants: Combined City Force Routs 1,000 International Defenders," *San Francisco Examiner*, August 4, 1977; Robert Levering, "The I-Hotel Evictions: A Report from the Scene—And a Call for Action," *San Francisco Bay Guardian*, August 11, 1977; Barry Alterman, "Police Attack I-Hotel, Evict Tenants," *San Francisco Bay Guardian*, August 17, 1977; Chester Hartman, "San Francisco's International Hotel: Case Study of a Turf Struggle," *Radical America* 12, no.3 (May-June 1978): 47-58.

4.  Chester W. Hartman and Sarah Carnochan, *City for Sale: The Transformation of San Francisco* (Berkeley: University of California Press, 2002).

5.  "Filipinos Win a New Lease on Life at International Hotel," *San Francisco Examiner*, July 23, 1969; "Appeal for Help to Restore Hotel," *San Francisco Chronicle*, September 12, 1969; David Prowler, "International Hotel Study" (unpublished manuscript, San Francisco, c. 1981), Manilatown Heritage Foundation Archives, San Francisco, CA.

6.  David Johnston, W.A. Van Winkle, William Ristow, Bruce B. Brugmann, David Hatcher, "The Godfather of the International Hotel," *San Francisco Bay Guardian*, May 19, 1977; Teri Lee, "International Hotel: One Community's Fight for Survival" (masters thesis, University of California, Berkeley, 1976).

7.  "City Hall Picketed in Eviction Fight," *San Francisco Chronicle*, July 28, 1976; Marshall Kilduff, "Moscone Tells Plan to Save Hotel," *San Francisco Chronicle*, July 30, 1976; "State High Court Rejects Appeal in Hotel Evictions," *San Francisco Chronicle*, September 4, 1976; "New Order to Evict Hotel Tenants," *San Francisco Chronicle*, December 4, 1976; "Judge Refuses to Stay Hotel Evictions," *San Francisco Chronicle*, December 15, 1976; Harry Jupiter, "Hotel Eviction Case: Hongisto on Trial for Contempt," *San Francisco Chronicle*, December 21, 1976; Jupiter, "Testimony in Hongisto Case Ends," *San Francisco Chronicle*, December 31, 1976; Jupiter, "Contempt Case: 5 days in Jail For Hongisto," *San Francisco Chronicle*, January 11, 1977; "International Hotel: Stage is Set for Eviction," *San Francisco Sunday Examiner and Chronicle*, January 16, 1977; see also Vivian Tsen, "The International Hotel: Anatomy of a Housing Issue" (master's thesis, University of California, Berkeley, 1977).

8.  Roberto V. Vallangca, *Pinoy: The First Wave (1898-1941)* (San Francisco: Strawberry Hill Press, 1977).

9.  Jovina Navarro, "Toward a Relevant Pilipino Education," in Navarro, ed., *Lahing Pilipino: Pilipino American Anthology* (Davis, CA: Mga Kapatid, 1977); Karen Umemoto, "On Strike: San Francisco State College Strike, 1968-1969: The Role of the Asian American Students," *Amerasia Journal* 15, no.1 (1989): 15-19; Third World Liberation Front, "Scope and Structure of Ethnic Studies Examined in Final TWLF Proposals" (leaflet, UC Berkeley, 1969); Steve Louie and Glenn K. Omatsu, *Asian Americans: the Movement and the Moment* (Los Angeles: UCLA Asian American Studies Center Press, 2001).

10. For a breakdown of occupations and professionals, see Royal F. Morales, *Makibaka: the Pilipino American Struggle* (Los Angeles: Mountainview Publishers, Inc, 1974); for more on the early immigrants, see Fred Cordova, *Filipinos: Forgotten Asian Americans* (USA: Demonstration Project for Asian Americans, 1983), and UCLA Asian American Studies, *Letters in Exile: An Introductory Reader on the History of Pilipinos in America* (Los Angeles: Regents of California, ULCA Asian American Studies Center, 1976).

11. When Felix Ayson was asked by a reporter about student radicals influencing him, he retorted, "No way, I'm influencing them!"

12. Habal, 102; 96-97; 62-63.

13. Editorial, "An Emerging Alternative," *Kalayaan International*, June 1971.

14. Rene Cruz, "The KDP Story: The First Ten Years," *Ang Katipunan* IX, no. 8 (September 1983). For the situation in the Philippines, see Jose F. Lacaba, *Days of Disquiet, Nights of Rage* (Quezon City: Rapid Lithographics, 1982).

15. For a critical review of changes in Filipino American attitudes, see Oscar Campananes, "Filipinos in the United States and their Literature of Exile," in *Discrepant Histories: Translocal Essays on Filipino Cultures*, ed. Vincent Rafael (Philadelphia: Temple University Press, 1995), 159-192. Also, Luis H. Francia, "Inventing the Earth: The Notion of 'Home' in Asian American Literature," in *Across the Pacific: Asian Americans and Globalization*, ed. Evelyn Hu-De Hart (Philadelphia: Temple University Press, 1999).

16. The first organization was the National Committee for the Restoration for Civil Liberties in the Philippines (NCRCLP). Later, it became the Anti-Martial Law Coalition (AMLC). Outside of the Filipino community were other organizations like Friends of the Filipino People (FFP).

17. Catherine Ceniza Choy, *Empire of Care: Nursing and Migration of Filipino American History* (Durham, NC: Duke University Press, 2003), 139-165. Choy sums up the defense campaign led by KDP activists.

18. For a history of Third World Marxist movements in the United States, see Max Elbaum, *Revolution in the Air: Sixties Radicals Turn to Lenin, Mao, and Che* (New York: Verso, 2002), 41-162.

19. Jeanette Lazam, interviews with author, tape recordings, San Francisco, CA, May 25, 1990 and October 10, 1990. We were both inside the building during the eviction. I witnessed this episode and she recounted it for me during these interviews.

20. Quoted in Ed Diokno, "Hotel Spirit Still Lingers," *Philippine News*, August 13-19, 1977.

21. Jerry Burns, "New S.F. District Supervisors—Six Incumbents are Elected," *San Francisco Chronicle*, November 9, 1977.

22. Jerry Carroll, "Billboard Ban, Hotel Lose—Bonds Okd," *San Francisco Chronicle*, November 9, 1977.

23. Herb Caen, "My Kind of Thing," *San Francisco Chronicle*, November 7, 1977.

24. Lloyd Watson, "Big I-Hotel Project Set to Roll—Again," *San Francisco Chronicle*, January 29, 1990; Linda Sherry, "126 Units of Senior Housing for International Hotel Site," *Asian Week*, December 6, 1991; Gerald D. Adams, "Project Set for I Hotel Crater," *San Francisco Examiner*, December 7, 1991; Chinatown Community Development Center, "20-20 Vision: 20 Years of Vision and Action," San Francisco: Twenty year anniversary brochure, December 1998, MHF Archive; Chinatown Community Development Center, "International Hotel Senior Housing Update," memo, February 2002, MHF Archive; Hartman and Carnochan, *City for Sale*, 338-339.

25. Quoted in Neela Banerjee, "Resurrection of the I-Hotel," *Asian Week*, June 13, 2001.

# "Hush Puppies," Communalist Politics, and Demolition Governance

## The Rise and Fall of the Black Fillmore

### By Rachel Brahinsky

The Western Addition in the 1970s was still a hotbed for Black radicalism, a center for the Black Panther Party, the welfare rights movement, and emergent civil rights groups. Activists had their hands in many pots, and were deeply connected to important organizations, movements, and religious institutions throughout the City and nationally. At the same time, and not coincidentally, it was a community in crisis, reeling from decades of fighting with the San Francisco Redevelopment Agency (SFRA) over the fate of the community's housing stock and its once-thriving business district.

The neighborhood struggle was set off against a backdrop of rising downtown skylines, symbolic of the influx of corporate-backed development capital flooding into the City, which was angling to flow rapidly into the village-like neighborhoods. Simply put, the Western Addition/Fillmore District community was locked in a battle for the right to exist in San Francisco.

Although significant aspects of the City's redevelopment scheme for the area were already completed or well underway before the mid-'60s, the decade of the '70s was a time when community members amplified their struggle for permanence, drawing on the larger narratives of ethnic solidarity and sustainability that were ascending in San Francisco and nationally.

Looking back from 2010, as an outsider, it's difficult to call much about the redevelopment plan a success. A walk down the drab beige, cement-heavy, lower Fillmore—a study in contrasts between a few remaining low-rent businesses and high-end restaurants that pay homage to the decimated 1940s Jazz district—reveals a muffled sense of place. The community would feel entirely different had the Victorians that once lined these streets remained, as they do just a few blocks to the north, south, and west. Of course, it's not just the buildings that would be different—the population, had the City done more to fund rehabilitation than demolition, may be quite different as well.

On the other hand, without the multiple complexes of affordable housing that now fill out the community, most Black families—and nearly all of the low-income families that still live there outside of federal public housing—would probably be long gone from the Fillmore. These were mostly built through the Redevelopment Agency in the middle years of the long period of redevelopment that stretched from 1948 all the way to 2009. Much of this housing was a concession from the agency in response to intense community pressure. Residents had revolted quite dramatically in the 1960s, laying bodies in front of bulldozers and clogging the SFRA's top-down demolition program with lawsuits. Through the '70s, residents worked to embed humane values in the bureaucracy, with some positive results. These facts are just some of many contradictions that make up the socio-geographic landscape of the Fillmore District.

Conversations with activists, pastors, and residents who have remained since the '70s uncover something of a community-scale existential crisis that is intimately connected to a larger demographic shift underway in San Francisco today. As the numbers of African-Americans in the City decline year by year (since the peak in 1970), the City's Black cultural and economic base has eroded tremendously. Many Black San Franciscans who remain despair of any deep or lasting connection to a place that has nevertheless been theirs for decades.

In the 2000s a mayoral task force convened to look at the "Black exodus" problem, which largely stems from the nexus of rising housing costs with the continued erosion of the Black community's economic stability. It's a story that has played out in many northern cities, where Black families have moved to the more affordable suburban fringes, but the speed of San Francisco's African-American dispersal has been unmatched nationally—and it essentially began the moment the first bulldozers hit the Fillmore in 1953.

Most accounts of urban renewal blame a walled-in imperial Redevelopment Agency, which is an appropriate and easy target—since most of the key players are gone from the spotlight or have died. But the agency was not the only player, and a look at the '70s uncovers a time of both dynamic opposition and determined cooperation in the Black community as it struggled to both be a "community" and to reform and challenge the top-down politics that characterized urban planning in the 1950s and '60s.

## Human Removal

Many San Franciscans have seen the 1999 KQED documentary on the neighborhood known as the Fillmore, or Western Addition (depending who you ask), which lays out the history of redevelopment's failures. Not as many may have come across a much earlier film, a 1974 black and white documentary dubbed *Redevelopment: A Marxist Perspective*. Opening with a bouncy warble of horns and voices, the film follows the San Francisco skyline as it rises from the 1940s onward—until a band of voices chants in movement-style folk rhythm, "Stop! We don't want what you have to offer!" With that, the singers announce the presence of political resistance, and the camera begins to pan through the empty lots and crumbled bricks of the mid-1970s Western Addition—an apocalyptic, disintegrating landscape.

Later in the film, the camera settles on the face of a young Black man named Arnold Townsend, who offers a sharp critique of San Francisco's plans for his neighborhood. "The problems of urban decay that face the Fillmore… were manufactured," he insists, noting that the first public step in the crusade to tear down the Fillmore was a newspaper campaign highlighting isolated examples of deterioration and extreme overcrowding. Images of boarded-up businesses and vacant lots shared space on the pages of the *San Francisco Chronicle* with 1940s and '50s headlines reading "San Francisco Slum Areas Breed Disease," "More Blighted Housing Found in SF," and "City Planners to move 10,000 out of Slum Area."

Those headlines presaged the initiation of a complete re-scaping of the neighborhood, a concept that was first hatched back in the 1940s when business leaders formed an alliance focused on revamping a few key neighborhoods. It was one prominent variation of a nationwide effort to restore land values in US central cities following the Great Depression and World War II. The racial and political overtones of the choices made (in terms of which neighborhoods would be targeted for change) set off decades of community response. What had been pitched nationally as "urban renewal" was re-christened, using the racial parlance of the times, as "Negro removal."

Indeed, many redevelopment zones selected in San Francisco were working-class areas, often home to people of color, including the old produce market near the Embarcadero (now developed as the Golden Gateway), South of Market (which was home to working-class single room occupancy hotel dwellers and gay leather bars), and two massive portions of the Western Addition, which by then was largely (but not entirely) African-American and Japanese-American.[1]

City planners and mayors legally justified their claims to these spaces by naming them "blighted," and called for an urban reclaiming in the name of the public good. The public that would benefit the most from these new land claims was a specific group, narrowly defined. As best described in Chester Hartman's epic *City for Sale: The Transformation of San Francisco*, a downtown-government coalition emerged to promote a very specifically targeted urban makeover. The rise of business-class leaders as de facto urban planners was solidified through the formation of the Blyth-Zellerbach Committee and the San Francisco Planning and Urban Renewal Association (SPUR), which promoted targeted neighborhood revivals that emphasized demolition rather than preservation. Redevelopment czar M. Justin Herman, by all accounts a brilliant and autocratic official, was the agency's most infamous figurehead.

City officials—organized after passage of the federal 1949 Housing Act through the new Redevelopment Agency—first identified what would be named Western Addition A-1 by the mid-'50s, basically in tandem with the City's plan to widen Geary Street into a four-lane boulevard at the intersection of Fillmore Street. The 44-block area of A-1 included a small chunk of lower Fillmore Street, spanning from Japantown out to St. Mary's Cathedral at the corner of Geary and Gough (the Japantown mall, many nearby hotels, and the massive cathedral were all products of the A-1 plan).

It was just one piece of what had become the City's primary majority African-American neighborhood, during the population boom that came with the World War II labor surge—and with the forced removal of Japanese-American families to internment camps during the war.[2] Black property owners in the district, once the area was named blighted and targeted for demolition, stopped or slowed repairs in anticipation of the neighborhood overhaul. While SFRA policies called for the purchase of structures and payment to families to leave rentals, displaced families and businesses reported dealing with intimidation tactics and years-long struggles to get loans or other support to keep their structures whole, struggles that typically ended with their displacement. Many were not technically evicted, but they argue that by virtue of facing a system that refused to help them invest and develop, their properties crumbled and were then easily devalued as slum structures by the SFRA.

By the mid-60s, most of the A-1 demolition was complete, with 4,000 people displaced—and Geary Street had become a "Mason-Dixon Line" dividing a poor, Black lower Fillmore from the largely White and increasingly wealthy Pacific Heights. By then a larger zone, A-2, was also underway. The new project increased the SFRA zone by an additional 60 square blocks, from Van Ness Avenue on the east side to St. Joseph's Street to the west (near Masonic), and north to south from Bush to Grove Streets.

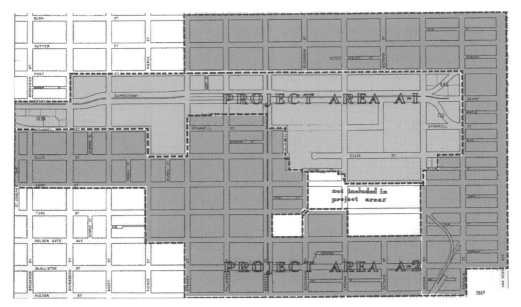

*The two Redevelopment Agency "Project Areas" A-1 and A-2.*

The A-2 program did not move forward with the same pace and vigor as A-1, largely because the A-1 experience politicized the community—and because an A-1-related lawsuit forced the SFRA to promise replacement homes for the displaced. The trick of holding the SFRA (or any agency) to that goal is still a problem today, but the 1968 lawsuit was one of many legal efforts nationally that gave displacees a legal promise of relocation assistance.

The fight against A-1 had offered a template for resistance in the next round. The fight over A-2 would be materially different, with more community participation and more affordable housing built. Still the SFRA would demolish hundreds of structures by 1970, displacing 10,000–13,000 people.[3]

## Making of the Black Fillmore

Prior to the war, White San Francisco already had a terrible track record in its treatment of racial and ethnic minorities. Violently enforced labor discrimination and housing and businesses-district segregation against the Chinese and Japanese has been well documented.[4] When it comes to Blacks, the often-repeated story is that African-Americans were well-treated until World War II. The idea is that because their population was relatively tiny, Blacks weren't viewed as threatening to the larger society and were therefore either generally accepted or ignored.

In fact, the number of racist incidents that took place was small, but the rate—the number in relation to the population—was not particularly small. Albert Broussard's finely detailed text *Black San Francisco* shows that the tiny Black community wrestled with a long march of cases of discrimination in housing, work, and education. Yet these events didn't seem to significantly mar the City's liberal/progressive reputation, which was built largely on its history as a maverick political center and its position at the forefront of labor and environmental struggles, not racial ones.

When the US Navy, Kaiser, and other massive shipyard managers recruited

Blacks from the South to build World War II fighting ships and bombs, anti-Black discrimination was suddenly much more visible. The Black population leapt from around 4,800 in 1940 to more than 43,000 ten years later. Around 12,000 Black newcomers settled in the Fillmore, which was one of the few places that would accept African-American tenants, partly because of the newly available homes made vacant by Japanese-American families sent off to internment camps.

The Fillmore community had been multi-ethnic—the City's "little United Nations"—since the 1906 quake pushed many communities together there. The Black in-migration turned the community into a central space of cultural production for the City at large. It wasn't a utopia—but it was a time and a place that supported Black-owned businesses, with a thriving nightlife, and with that delicate creature that we call a sense of community beginning to take root.

That sense was just budding—Blacks had come from Texas, Oklahoma, Tennessee, Alabama, and more, settling with cousins and others from their hometowns. The same social networks that helped people get to the City (and find housing and jobs) were nurtured by the close quarters of the neighborhood. In interviews residents recall a small-town feeling in the middle of the City. In that sense it was no different from many other San Francisco neighborhoods.

Also, like many City neighborhoods (with Chinatown and Japantown as the most visible remaining examples) the Fillmore took shape because of exclusion. Blacks generally couldn't live in most of the City, often because landlords wouldn't rent or sell to them (most famously, even Willie Mays faced racially exclusive covenants when he tried to buy a house below Mt. Davidson). The Western Addition was one of a handful of places without such covenants—so the newcomers crowded into Victorian flats, often squeezing many families into one home, sleeping and cooking in shifts to share the space. [5]

It was the kind of experience that brought people together—and which simultaneously engendered stereotypical racialized thinking on the part of the White majority. Thus, because Blacks were forced to crowd together, the racist notion that Black people like or tend to live that way was one of many racially-inscribed memes that later provided support for redevelopment.

The Jazz District was lively and world-renowned, luring Billie Holiday, Duke Ellington, Miles Davis, Dinah Washington, and others to play in its clubs. In local memory it was a place that attracted and welcomed people of all backgrounds, but it was one of the few places with a wealth of businesses welcoming to African-American customers. The unwritten rule was that Blacks stayed west of Van Ness to socialize, and it was a center for Blacks in other small pockets of the City. Those living all the way out at Hunter's Point, next to the naval shipyards, generally weren't welcome in the Third Street business district adjacent to their homes. So they traveled across town to visit Fillmore theaters and bars, too.

When the SFRA was "finished" with the Fillmore, 883 businesses had closed, 4,729 households had been forced out, and 2,500 Victorian homes had been demolished.[6] The map of segregation began to shift. With the fall of Fillmore Street, African-Americans turned to Divisadero Street, which was already a central economic zone in the Black community. But Divisadero never grew to be the thriving social center that Fillmore had been. This period also saw the rise of the Third Street Black business community, as the Hunter's Point Black community swelled with Western Addition refugees.

## Politics and Networks

The double blows to Civil Rights politics represented in the slayings of Martin Luther King, Jr. and Bobby Kennedy in 1968 was felt in the Fillmore. Residents had become increasingly radicalized through the formation of the Western Addition Community Organization (WACO) a few years earlier, in a political milieu that was heavily inflected with the national and international movements of the times. There were cooperative houses where residents tried carving out alternative lifestyles. James Farmer's Congress of Racial Equality had an active local chapter, and many residents were embroiled in the San Francisco State College fight for ethnic studies that erupted that same year.[7] The Black Panther Party had an office on Fillmore Street, near the intersection of Eddy Street (where Yoshi's jazz club now stands), alongside neighbors who had played a key role in electing a young and relatively radical African-American, Willie Brown, to the very White California State Assembly back in 1964.

In the context of the federal War on Poverty, which created funding streams for social programs, many of the keystone ideas of the affordable housing movement emerged during this time, and the Western Addition housing battles—which influenced policymakers like Brown and US Congressman Phil Burton—played a key role. This included policies like inclusionary zoning (which requires a portion of new housing developments contribute to a city's affordable housing stock), local hiring requirements (so that development projects employ local residents), and the mandate that governments provide replacement housing for redevelopment evictees.

The Black community in the Fillmore was largely made of three wings, as activist Wade "Speedy" Woods remembers it.[8] The ministers and few remaining business owners made up one flank; the Afro-centric cultural nationalists (following Kwanzaa creator Maulana Karenga) formed another; Woods was part of a third, politicized wing, made up of the Panthers and many others who were focused on class struggle. The three were not necessarily at odds with each other; it was a time during which African-American politics was consciously expanding and evolving. All three camps were connected to the greater Bay Area Black political scene, where Blacks were challenging the White power structures of the East Bay (gaining some institutional success through the election of Black—and self-proclaimed socialist—Ron Dellums to the US Congress in 1970).

Terry Collins, who migrated from Indiana via Los Angeles in 1967, remembers study groups where people read Marx's *Capital*, and where political consciousness was crafted through a collective process. Collins was sucked into the redevelopment fight immediately, and became an active member of WACO. "We watched Victorians on Gough Street ripped to the ground. I actually cried," he remembers now.

A group steeped in Saul Alinsky's organizing model, and inspired by the anti-bulldozer writings of Jane Jacobs, WACO was the central organization for radical anti-SFRA activism. (Herman opposed WACO, calling it a "passing flurry of proletarianism.") Collins had linked up with WACO as a member of the Black Students Union (BSU), based at San Francisco State. The SF State branch was a largely working-class group, part of a national web of BSUs, devoted to tying student members to local community struggles. (The BSU mission had been sealed at the 1967 Black Youth Conference in Los Angeles—the same event that spawned the boycott threat against the 1968 Olympics.) Graduates from this time were among the founders of KPOO radio (89.5 FM), the first Black-owned independent station in the west.

For some BSU students co-op housing in the Western Addition was home. One such place was called the Big House, at 560 Page; another was called the Black House. Recalls Collins, "We lived collectively, had meetings there, we did political education. We'd have fundraising parties. We thought internationally and globally." Global conflicts and national liberation efforts in South Africa, Nicaragua, El Salvador, and Cuba, felt connected to the fight with the SFRA.

WACO, originally founded by White activist ministers, but later taken over by Blacks, had grown increasingly militant at the end of the decade. Its organizing efforts spawned a key lawsuit. The suit took the SFRA to task for failing to consider replacement housing during the first round of demolitions; when the plaintiffs won, federal funds were halted for the Western Addition until the SFRA developed a substitute-housing plan.

The attorneys managing the case came from the legal backbone of the movement, the San Francisco Neighborhood Legal Assistance Foundation (SNFLAF, known colloquially as Sniff-Laff). "SNFLAF had about 60 attorneys, five neighborhood offices and a law reform unit downtown. They were kind of a wild bunch, as you can imagine, a very aggressive group of people who really wanted to do stuff," says Sid Wolinsky, SNFLAF's first director of litigation. "We did an in-depth study of what was most needed for the poverty community in San Francisco and it didn't take long for it to emerge that housing was the number one problem."

SNFLAF also brought lawsuits on jobs, sweatshops, police brutality, gender discrimination, and other things. But, Wolinsky says:

> there was no question, housing was it. And we saw this huge agency, the Redevelopment Agency, gobbling up what was left of affordable housing. We took on representation of the WACO suit, but frankly we were too late. We did what we could there, but almost immediately turned to Yerba Buena, which was in a much earlier phase, and we were able to be much more successful.

One of the key figures in the WACO suit and in the community-at-large was Mary Rogers, a neighborhood icon self-schooled in redevelopment legalese. Rogers was one of many residents who risked their lives in front of the City's bulldozers, and she remained an outspoken advocate until her death in 2006.

"Mary was the one," remembers Collins. "She knew more about this stuff than anybody. She saved so many houses. A lot of the 236 [federally funded affordable] housing was because of her. She was involved in education, housing, welfare rights, everything." Rogers stood out, but she was only one of a political cohort that included many female leaders. "There were a lot of women who were really something in those days, really strong women who'd get out and fight against any injustice: Inez Andres, Lily Ransom, so many others. These people are all gone now."

## Negotiating Participation

On the heels of the WACO lawsuit, SFRA chief Herman and Mayor Joe Alioto—who had once headed the SFRA commission—decided to try a new tactic to deal with the active and angry community. Thus was born the PAC-system of community participation in the SFRA. The Western Addition Project Area Committee (WAPAC) created an institutionally accepted—and funded— venue for community involvement. Bit by bit the key players in WACO were lured onto the PAC. Its board had more than 70 members at the beginning, including Hannibal Williams, who had been a central WACO leader.

WAPAC soon became the primary venue for local development politics, signaling a potential end of widespread radical anti-redevelopment activism in the community. By creating an official venue through which community members could participate, the SFRA co-opted community power, offering radicals an insider seat. When first "Speedy" Woods and then Rev. Arnold Townsend (the young man from the Marxist documentary later became a church leader) tried to win a seat on the city Board of Supervisors, they partly based their citywide pitch on their experience with WAPAC.

Rev. Townsend remembers WAPAC's formation as the death knell for WACO, "The way that it was set up was so brilliant. You create WAPAC and you put the money in WAPAC—so everybody went there and WACO kind of died out. Before any development can go forward, the rule was you have to go through the PAC, and if the PAC can't make a decision in 45 days then the Agency can do what it wants." Herman's brilliance (if indeed it was Herman's idea) was in making WAPAC so huge, which made achieving consensus a near impossibility. Even a simple majority might be hard to come by, as each project bidder lobbied board members under the 45-day rule. Says Rev. Townsend, "By the time I became chair [in the early '70s] there were 54 people. With that number you still have a tough time getting a quorum."

By its very structure, the PAC both allowed people to have a say, and diluted their participation. During Rev. Townsend's tenure as chair, he oversaw a reduction in the board's size to 25, and then 15 later on, which he thought was more manageable.

Though the rage of the '60s was perhaps tempered by WAPAC, and by the new protections that appeared to be coming for the second redevelopment zone, Western Addition politics were not always civil and ordered. Former Black Panther Bennie Stewart remembers:

> there was one occasion where Justin Herman was attacked at a public meeting. There was this guy named Christopher Lewis (in those days he was a "jammer"). He was about 6'2", weighing about 225 lbs., not a small guy. There was one occasion where Chris leaped over a lectern and collared Justin Herman and threatened to slap the shit out of him. Some people say Justin never really fully recovered from that threat.[9]

Herman died from a heart attack not long afterwards in 1971. Townsend remembers being at meetings, when he was chair of WAPAC years later, where he believes he was the only person in the room without a gun. "As far as we were concerned, it was a life-and-death struggle."

## 'Hush Puppies'

Of course, it wasn't just the radicals who were pulled in to work within the SFRA. The Fillmore community had many more centrist political leaders—who often were best known for their Sunday-morning work behind the pulpit. Rev. Wilbur Hamilton eventually was promoted to Agency head. Hamilton was just one of many pastors that tried to work from the inside; many more engaged in development deals that shaped the housing and economic stimulus plans of the SFRA.

With religious leaders' importance in the Black community, the eventual involvement of nearly all Black Western Addition pastors in the SFRA web— either as employees, leaders, or as development bidders later on—was probably inevitable. It also seemed to suck the life out of any potential opposition leadership as the last of the major bulldozing tore a multi-block gash that was to remain through the 1990s in the center of the district.

Some versions of the Western Addition story blame the preachers for linking up with the SFRA by sponsoring housing developments—alongside unions— and getting a piece of redevelopment's housing-subsidy largesse. Townsend sees it differently. "Preachers were integral in the community. They were misunderstood. In a lot of ways they were cheated. They were inexperienced. But the housing that they built is what kept some people here." There were multiple dimensions to the process: it was in the preachers' financial interest to sponsor initiatives to keep congregation members in town—and their efforts also helped people stay who could never have otherwise afforded San Francisco housing in the '80s and '90s.

The churches were important community spaces for many reasons, including survival in a racist society, particularly for those not interested in experimenting with the Hippie variation of collectivist living. Reverend Amos Brown, who arrived in San Francisco late in the decade, puts it this way, "Blacks were not accepted anywhere. The only place where Blacks could be somebody was in church on Sunday morning."

Rev. Brown tried his hand at redevelopment, and found that even the title of Reverend didn't entirely smooth the road to accessing investment funds, leaving him with a bitter story of racial redlining. His focus was the vacant six acres between Turk, Steiner, Eddy, and Fillmore Streets that now includes Safeway and the massive Fillmore Center. "When I got here we had exclusive negotiating rights, but lenders wouldn't support our efforts there. It was vacant for years. There were [impromptu community] gardens down there when I got here. But then Don Tishman shows up wanting to do that area."

Essentially, Rev. Brown felt that the SFRA pushed his development group together with Tishman, who is White. "We were over a barrel, so we reluctantly became partners with him. We insisted that there be one Black-owned building in that complex—and there is one," although even Tishman, he says, couldn't finance the project entirely through local banks. Part of the problem was that federal housing dollars were shrinking from the mid-'70s onward. Redlining by public and private institutions exacerbated the problem. Townsend and Woods also blame lending discrimination on the racial makeup of the developers and the community they were trying to serve.

Although he was involved himself, Rev. Brown—who later used his pulpit to launch a brief political career on the Board of Supervisors—also sees the role of church leaders critically. For him, involving pastors in development was the SFRA's not-so-subtle attempt to silence opposition to the City's plans and muffle anger about racism in lending. "Involving the churches was part of a 'hush puppy program,'" a loaded term that has etymological roots in slavery, as Rev. Brown tells it:

> When they had fish fries in the South, when they had cornmeal left around, they'd roll it in the grease and throw it out to the dogs who were yapping and barking outside, and say 'hush puppies.' And the slaves that were out there that couldn't get enough to eat would snatch up the food for themselves. That's where it came from, 'hush puppies' were supposed to shut them up.
>
> And so we did throw some hush puppies out to Black ministers, to shut up the masses to keep them docile. ... You look at these churches that were gotten under redevelopment, and you look at some of this housing. What was not done [alongside those projects] was what was necessary to give Blacks the economic security that was needed, through jobs, through loans, so that businesses could develop. They didn't give that to us.

Indeed, the continual degradation of African-American economic stability has challenged efforts at community uplift. "Black people couldn't get loans," for housing rehabilitation, for business expansion—for much of anything, says Collins, who was once embroiled in his own multi-year struggle to buy his Webster Street home. Once the well-paying jobs of the war years had disappeared, for those interested in experiments in community there were a few options. Collins participated in a Food Conspiracy[10] on Downey Street in the Haight-Ashbury and took advantage of the free clinic movement for health care.

But those '60s innovations weren't accessed by everyone. Many just gave up on San Francisco, moving to the East Bay and beyond. Some, like Townsend and Woods, stuck around, trying to direct redevelopment in any way that they could. "It was a time of resistance in the community. But because we knew it was a *fait accompli*, we were trying to make it work for us," Townsend says.

And they were working with a changing agency. After Herman's death in 1971, the SFRA was never quite the demolition-happy entity it had been, and there was some space for reformers, although it was uneven. John Elberling today runs TODCO, the nonprofit housing corporation in SOMA that was created out of its own epic SFRA fight. As he puts it, "A-1 was clearly racist; then, times change. And with A-2 the city powers-that-be had two things in mind. Yes, slum removal—but maybe also the ability to build a better African-American neighborhood."

The interplay between a morphing liberal agency—which nevertheless had the protection of urban land values as a core concern—and a desperately struggling community happened against the backdrop of deepening economic insecurity. In that climate Woods says Blacks in the Fillmore both used, and were used by, minority contracting programs:

> You'd have Blacks that wanted to become developers and get in on the development boom and you'd see them go to the agency and the guy would say, "this is my 30% minority partner." Then when they'd go back to the agency after the project was approved and everything, and they'd say that because of the financial markets, things like that, he only owns 1% now. You had

a lot of people just going out for themselves instead of looking out for the community.

And then lot of people died during the '80s—but in the '70s it was an exciting time, you'd get a lot of groundbreaking ideas. The big thing that didn't happen that everybody had hoped for was the commercial opportunities. You walk down Fillmore St. now and, all the businesses that were replaced, you can count them on one hand. The economic opportunities that people hoped for never materialized—or they didn't go far enough. That happened across the country, you'd see communities that went through urban renewal, but they never got going economically."

## Rise and Fall

Outside of the micro-politics of the Western Addition, a bifurcated political scene was evolving. The '60s had ended with a liberal-progressive turn in national housing policy that favored rebuilding over razing. But the election of Richard Nixon in 1968 signaled the eventual slow starvation of poverty-program funding. Progressive redevelopment ideas, community health programs and legal services like SNFLAF, creations of the War on Poverty, struggled to survive.

Locally the City was shifting slightly leftward. The 1975 citywide Community Congress pulled together groups from all across town. One of the core goals that emerged from that event was a commitment to transform elections to the Board of Supervisors to a district-based system. The district elections fight became a central plank in Western Addition politics. By the mid-'70s residents had decided that electoral reform was necessary to bring real change to the SFRA (in a shift that mirrored radical Black politics nationally). Concurrently blue-collar jobs moved out as San Francisco was remade as an office- and service-based economy.[11]

Nevertheless, redevelopment fights garnered attention on the national level, with the passage of the Uniform Relocation Act (URA) in 1970. The law insisted that displacees from federal development zones be guaranteed housing replacement. It was a tremendous milestone in the legal battle to protect urban communities. Enforcement of the URA still plagues San Francisco, however. An early attempt by SNFLAF was only partially successful in forcing the City to honor the "certificates of preference" for new Western Addition housing that were issued to A-2 displacees. Arnold Ellis, a Black Western Addition-born SNFLAF attorney, cut his legal teeth on the URA case in the late '70s. "We had a client named Mary Rogers who had been displaced," Ellis recalls. "Our goal was to force the SFRA to allow people to return, and it became a class-action suit. Some of our named plaintiffs were able to move in [but] we didn't get anything near what we wanted. Many people had moved to the South, or lost their certificates."

Success in the Fillmore, then, is perhaps best measured in doses—small projects pushed forward, small victories for individual families or businesses who managed to survive. Woods takes pride in having convinced the SFRA to preserve a few particularly well-kept Victorians which were moved to a mid-Fillmore spot. Dubbed Victorian Square, for a time the group of buildings was mostly Black-owned, including the site where Marcus Books—the West Coast's oldest Black-owned bookstore—still remains in 2010. But each success like this comes laced with stories of Black-led development partnerships that were denied contracts or delayed for so long that they could never get off the ground.

Woods and Townsend didn't win their citywide bids for Supervisor, but the pitch for district elections was successful, ushering in Ella Hill Hutch and Harvey Milk to the Board of Supervisors in 1977, after the election of George Moscone as mayor in 1975. Yet as the decade wore on, the visible symbol of redevelopment's failures glared out from empty development sites like Rev. Brown's. The ghost town feel those vacant lots created would haunt political leaders. In an interview with KQED in the 1990s then-mayor Willie Brown conceded that one of the worst mistakes he and others made in the Fillmore (while he was the leader of the State Assembly) was allowing the bulldozing to happen without precise clarity on how quickly new projects would move forward.

The progressive impulse in the Western Addition was also stymied by one of the stranger plot twists of 1970s history. Jim Jones and his People's Temple—located in the center of the Fillmore District—captured the political and social imagination of many African-American Western Addition residents. Lured by Jones's promise of an antiracist, egalitarian society—and deeply frustrated with the decimation of the Fillmore—many radicals, according to longtime housing activist Calvin Welch, were among those who died in Jones's 1978 mass suicide. [12]

Eventually, a decent amount of affordable housing was developed although it never matched the housing that was destroyed. And it was not restricted to low-income families who had been directly displaced by the Redevelopment Agency. A 1996 SFRA assessment counted 2,794 affordable units in A-2 and 2,009 in A-1, alongside 2,727 new and refurbished market rate apartments. [13]

In light of this, one longtime observer and political insider insists that it is wrong to label the Fillmore story as a failure, noting that the number of African-Americans in that area remained high for many years. It's true that the Black Fillmore didn't shrink as quickly as the Black population elsewhere in the City. From 14,000 in 1960, the number of Blacks living in the Western Addition dropped to about 10,926 in 1970, but stayed steady for the next decade as the citywide population dropped. These numbers were calculated for John Mollenkopf's book *The Contested City*. A later assessment of block-by-block data would likely show significant change, however; the total citywide African-American population had dropped to 46,779 in 2005 (down from 88,000 in 1970) including a large number of Blacks living in Bayview-Hunter's Point.

Although a period of racial stability in the 1970s and '80s can be read through census figures, those numbers don't tell the whole story. By the time replacement housing was available, many evicted families were either uninterested or unable to return, or were unaware of the new housing opportunities. Longtime residents say that the Black community that remained through the 1980s and '90s included many new families and individuals. They happened to be African-Americans, but they weren't old timers. That very particular sense of community that had been forged in the pre-bulldozer years—as cousins moved in together, and small town Southern friends reunited—was never recovered.

And although some community members returned, the Black business community was never resuscitated. Today's Fillmore and Divisadero business districts have just a handful of Black-owned enterprises, and quite a few of those are inaccessible to the low-income families (of any ethnic background) living nearby.

It's been a half century since the first bulldozers ripped apart the redwood structures lining Geary, Post, and Sutter Streets—a demolition governance program born out of liberal "urban revival" planning. The contradictory framework that sought to renew generalized (read: White) public spaces by eliminating the public and private spaces of a particular community inspired Fillmore residents to fight back. A key piece of the Fillmore legacy, then, is political and legislative success that rippled out through the city and nation. Still, though it galvanized a generation of activists, urban renewal bled the heart of the Black Fillmore, and the impact of that history still colors redevelopment's legacy today.

## Notes

1. Other neighborhoods affected by redevelopment include North Beach, Chinatown, and the Mission. See Estella Habal's essay "Filipino Americans in the Decade of the International Hotel" in this volume.

2. Though they shared community boundaries with Japanese Americans, and shared a common battle against the SFRA's program of community removal, the story for Black and Japanese-American Western Addition residents has been different. The Japantown scheme, laid after Japanese-American citizens returned from WWII internment camps, was designed to draw in Japanese capital. The mall complex built there did not revive much of the pre-war residential community, but international capital made a difference in creating something quickly that African-Americans, just a few blocks away in the same neighborhood, could not replicate. Another essay is needed to do justice to the Nihonmachi story.

3. Pinning down the exact number of displaced people in the Western Addition is difficult. Various sources offer different numbers, but this range is probably very close.

4. On the Chinese, see Alexander Saxton, *The Indispensable Enemy: A Study of the Anti-Chinese Movements in California* (University of California Press, 1971).

5. For more on Fillmore covenants, see Lynn Horiuchi's "Object Lessons in Home Building: Racialized Real Estate Marketing in San Francisco," in *Landscape Journal* 26, no. 1, (March 2007).

6. Leslie Fulbright, "Sad chapter in Western Addition history ending," *SFGate*, July 21, 2008, http://www.sfgate.com/cgi-bin/article.cgi?f=/c/a/2008/07/21/BA6511Q4G0.DTL (accessed February 23, 2010).

7. See Margaret Leahy's essay "On Strike! We're Gonna Shut it Down!" in this volume for a deeper look at the SF State Strike.

8. Thanks to the many people who generously shared their time and insights in interviews for this essay, including: Terry Collins, Rev. Amos Brown, Wade "Speedy" Woods, Rev. Arnold Townsend, Arnold Ellis, John Elberling, London Breed, Calvin Welch, and several SFRA staffers.

9. Bennie Stewart (lecture, New College of California, 1994). Cited online at www.foundsf.org/index.php?title=WACO_Attacks_Redevelopment (accessed February 23, 2010).

10. See Pam Peirce's essay "A Personal History of the People's Food System" in this volume for the reach of the Food Conspiracy movement.

11. See Jesse Drew's essay "San Francisco Labor in the 1970s" in this volume for an in-depth analysis of labor during this decade.

12. See Matthew Roth's essay "Coming Together: The Communal Option" in this volume for a more indepth look at People's Temple.

13. *San Francisco Redevelopment Program Fact Book 1995-1996—Summary of Project Data and Key Elements.*

## Further Reading

Broussard, Albert S. 1993. *Black San Francisco: the Struggle for Racial Equality in the West, 1900-1954*. Lawrence, KS.: University Press of Kansas.

Hartman, Chester. 2002. *City For Sale: the Transformation of San Francisco*. Berkeley: UC Press.

Jacobs, Allan B. 1978. *Making City Planning Work*. Chicago: American Society of Planning Officials.

Mollenkopf, John. 1983. *The Contested City*. Princeton: Princeton University Press.

# The Fight to Stay
## The Creation of the Community Housing Movement in San Francisco, 1968-1978

### by Calvin Welch

*"…it is not that the solution of the housing question simultaneously solves the social question, but that only by the solution of the social question, that is, by the abolition of the capitalist mode of production, is the solution of the housing question made possible."*
—Frederich Engels, "The Housing Question," 1872

*"…something is happening here, but you don't know what it is…"*
—Bob Dylan, "Ballad of a Thin Man," 1965

Before 1968 there simply wasn't much of a community-based "housing movement" in San Francisco. There was little organized effort in various San Francisco neighborhoods aimed at shaping City policy as it affected housing availability, preservation, cost, and its future development. The principal exception to this rule was the post-WWII efforts by some civic and professional organizations to combat discrimination against African-Americans, whose numbers increased ten-fold during the war. The arrival of this substantial population sparked strong anti-Black sentiment in White San Francisco, often manifested by a refusal to rent or sell homes to African-Americans. (A similar racist resistance confronted Japanese Americans returning from the WWII internment camps, challenging their attempts to regain the homes they lived in before 1942.)

One would be hard pressed to find a mayoral election before 1975 in which housing and land-use issues were central to the campaign. The current dominant role played by these issues in San Francisco politics came to the fore as they garnered identifiable supporters and opponents and citywide importance in that crucial decade between 1968 and 1978. George Moscone's election in 1975 was the first that included them, which is not to say that developers and the growth coalition (big business and big labor) did not have great political influence. Before Moscone adopted a "balanced growth" public campaign, calling for limits on both urban renewal and high-rise office development, pro-growth politics completely dominated San Francisco mayoral politics, with all candidates toeing the same line. The fight over housing and land-use issues later drove one mayor from office (Art Agnos in 1991), fueled the first write-in candidacy for mayor in the City's history (Tom Ammiano in 1999), and elected a second (Gavin Newsom in 2003). Rent control, tenancy in common conversions, "gentrification," out of scale residential development, live-work lofts, displacement of light industry by market-rate housing, the development of "affordable housing," homelessness—these are the issues that came to dominate municipal politics then, and continue to shape the

City's political alignments to this day.

Housing and land-use issues cannot be understood by merely looking at the narrow technical issues directly involved with the development of housing. It's not sufficient to understand (or to fine-tune) the building code, the planning code, conditional use permits, annual condo conversion limits, or any other technical specifics of the development process to understand the important political role they play in San Francisco. In short, as Engels argued 130 years ago, the politics of urban housing can only be fully understood in its full social context. Who works in a city determines who lives in a city. This simple fact is made all the more significant in San Francisco when combined with two other facts which dominate housing reality in the City. First, it is an extremely compact place, some 46 square miles, perched on the tip of a peninsula with no ability to expand through Bay fill or annexation. Second, it is "physically mature" with all its available land developed. Most new land uses, including new housing, usually displace an existing use. Development politics in such a compact and already fully developed area means that there are real losers and winners in the outcome. Winners get to live and work here, losers don't. It is this "zero-sum" aspect of housing and land-use battles in San Francisco that fuels such conflicts with characteristic passion and longevity.

## The Context: Urban Renewal and the Economic Transformation of San Francisco

San Francisco between the years of 1968 and 1978 underwent the most significant transformation of its economic base, arguably, since it became an Anglo city when it was seized by the US Navy in 1846. The decade saw the rise of a dizzying array of historic changes in San Francisco's economy and built environment:

- the rise of a truly economically integrated "Bay Area" made manifest by the creation of the Bay Area Rapid Transit system (Transbay tube completed in 1969 with the first train running in 1972);
- the displacement from San Francisco to Oakland of most shipping after the Mechanization and Modernization contracts signed by the Pacific Maritime Association and the International Longshore and Warehouse Union from 1960 to 1966, which allowed for containers to replace hand loading and unloading of ships. This made large areas of San Francisco's southern bay shore economically redundant and eliminated crucial employment opportunities historically filled by the City's African-American population;
- the designation of eleven separate urban renewal areas and the massive demolition of low-income affordable housing in the Western Addition and South of Market neighborhoods by the San Francisco Redevelopment Agency (SFRA);
- the explosion of commercial office buildings as the driving force of the City's economy, in an attempt to transform San Francisco into the "corporate headquarters" of the Pacific Rim.

While a detailed accounting of each of these changes is beyond this essay, the rise of the economic power of the Bay Area was critically facilitated by the development of BART and the shift of the maritime economy to the East Bay.

Along with these two changes, the parallel rise of Silicon Valley in the South Bay reduced San Francisco's regional importance by the end of the 20th century to that of a high end "bedroom" for the workforce of the more economically dynamic Bay Area. During the 1968-78 decade, though, San Francisco was at the economic heart of the regional economy.

A combination of these four economic changes led thousands of San Franciscans to consider leaving the city of St. Francis. There was an active and well orchestrated effort to "renew" the City, coordinated initially by Mayor George Christopher (1956-1964) and then consolidated and aggressively implemented by the Joe Alioto administration (1968-1976). The urban renewal bulldozers especially confronted residents in central and eastern San Francisco: Chinatown/Manilatown, South of Market, Western Addition, Haight-Ashbury, and the Mission where project areas were either established or being proposed.

Fear of urban renewal was not simply the paranoid fantasies of uninformed community residents. In 1966 the San Francisco Planning and Urban Renewal Association (SPUR) published a paper which boldly stated:

> If San Francisco decides to compete effectively with other cities for new 'clean' industries and new corporate power, its population will move closer to 'standard White Anglo-Saxon Protestant' characteristics...Economically and socially, the population will tend to range from the lower middle class through the lower upper class...Selection of a population's composition may be undemocratic... [i]nfluence on it, however, is legal and desirable for the health of the city.[1]

These grand plans revolved around Mayor Joseph Lawrence Alioto, who was an enthusiastic and early supporter of urban renewal. Appointed to the Agency Commission by Mayor Christopher in 1956, Alioto presided over the City's approval of redevelopment plans for Western Addition A-1 and Golden Gateway and the Agency's designation of new surveys for Chinatown, Western Addition A-2, and the South of Market's Yerba Buena Center (YBC). As Mayor he oversaw the Agency's approval of redevelopment plans for Hunter's Point and the India Basin Industrial Park as well as the implementation of the YBC plan that started when he led the Commission. Obituaries written at his death in 1998 in both national and local papers were unanimous in identifying his impact on the City as being these massive projects. None mentioned the impact these plans had on the people of San Francisco, nor the political reaction to them that shaped modern San Francisco politics.

The plans of the Alioto years eventually resulted in the demolition of some 12,500 homes and single room occupancy hotel rooms in the Western Addition and South of Market by public action, with another 1,800 hotel rooms demolished by private action in the downtown area. These over 14,000 lower income affordable homes were eventually replaced by a total of 5,000 Redevelopment Agency units by the year 2000.[2] Other than administrative jobs created in the Agency itself, and the temporary jobs in construction, Alioto's large-scale urban renewal projects created few permanent jobs, especially for lower income San Franciscans who lived in these neighborhoods. The combined demolition of affordable housing and the resultant displacement of its residents, and the lack of permanent jobs created by urban renewal led to a widely held conviction that in San Francisco it did in fact mean "the selection of a population's composition" as urged by SPUR. In more common language, urban renewal was understood as "Negro removal."

It is hard to imagine today the colossus that was the Alioto-era Redevelopment Agency. Directly funded by a total of some $700 million (in 2008 dollars) in federal urban renewal money and governed by a commission that was totally appointed by Alioto, the SFRA had its own police department, planning department, legal department, and provided its own health and social services. Subject to no meaningful operational nor budget oversight by the Board of Supervisors, it was a government all its own, one based solely on the power of one man, the Mayor. For the people of neighborhoods subject to redevelopment, this second government, one in which they had no voice or vote, ruled their lives more totally than the "real" government ruled the rest of the City. Of course there was a strong and passionate community reaction to this extraordinary situation. The community politics that grew under this second government developed a style and practice all its own, isolated from the politics of the rest of the City, but which tended to reinforce the social and economic isolation that made them vulnerable to urban renewal in the first place.

## Fighting for "Community Control"

The first stirrings of community reaction happened in the Western Addition,[3] then quickly followed in the South of Market. Both community responses were shaped by the Redevelopment Agency actions and both used the courts as the method of attack.

In late 1967, White progressive ministers in the Western Addition formed the Western Addition Community Organization (WACO) to organize low-income Black tenants against the A-2 redevelopment program. Inspired by their success as part of a large multi-neighborhood coalition that fought and stopped the Panhandle Freeway the year before, the hope of the organizers was to stop the displacement of residents in the A-2 portion of the project area south of Geary Street that had occurred in the earlier redeveloped A-1 portion, north of Geary Street. Black tenants quickly assumed leadership positions in WACO and, with the assistance of the San Francisco Neighborhood Legal Assistance Foundation (SFNLAF), a federally funded legal services agency created in 1966, sued the SFRA over its failure to provide a relocation plan for area tenants. By December 1968 WACO won the lawsuit and HUD was enjoined from giving the SFRA any additional money until a relocation plan was prepared.

In 1969 tenants and small business owners in the central South of Market formally joined together to create Tenants and Owners Opposed to Redevelopment (TOOR). Assisted by student interns from San Francisco State College (itself undergoing a major transformation with the four-month student strike in 1968-69[4]) the "old Left" labor organizers of TOOR brought a level of political/ organizational sophistication not yet seen in San Francisco's anti-urban renewal fight. Taking a page out of the old 1930s anti-fascist handbook, TOOR linked residential tenants with small, commercial business owners (whose customers were being displaced by public actions) into a single community organization creating what had been referred to as "a united front from below" back then. Learning from WACO, TOOR approached SFNLAF and filed a lawsuit against the SFRA for its failed relocation plan for residents and small businesses. Like the WACO suit, TOOR won an injunction stopping the Agency's South of Market activities.

The SFRA reacted to the two suits in totally different ways. First, it sought to outmaneuver WACO by creating a new Project Area Committee (WAPAC) with some of WACO's members but recruiting more local residents in favor of redevelopment. They also appointed a Western Addition-born trade unionist, Wilbur Hamilton, to be the Project Director of A-2. Within a year WAPAC had replaced WACO as the "voice" of the community on all matters of redevelopment in A-2. The SFRA's stance towards TOOR was the exact opposite: it sought to ignore TOOR and defeat it in court. No attempt was made to create an alternate South of Market community advisory committee; no offers of employment were made to long-time residents of the area. Instead the SFRA attorneys, directed by Mayor Alioto (himself a very successful lawyer), sought to have the case transferred from local federal judges. The legal maneuvering went on for three years until a settlement was reached in 1973 that gave TOOR and its community-based development arm, Tenants and Owners Development Corporation (TODCO), four SFRA sites to develop replacement senior housing.

The creation of TODCO was the second community-based housing development corporation created as a result of rejected urban renewal policies of the Alioto administration. The first, formed in 1971, was in the Mission after successful community opposition to the creation of a redevelopment program for the area in 1967. As a result of the failure, Alioto proposed that the Mission become a "Model Cities" area. The Mission Coalition Organization was formed in 1968 and it in turn created the first community-based and -controlled nonprofit housing development entity in San Francisco, the Mission Housing Development Corporation (MHDC).[5]

The threat of urban renewal in Chinatown also stimulated a community response aimed at housing issues. By 1968 funding for the initial (in fact, as it turned out, only) Chinatown development project at Portsmouth Square was flowing, and the Alioto administration pressed for its expansion to include all of Chinatown. Community resistance stopped this proposal and led to the creation of the Chinatown Coalition for Better Housing in 1972 to look for alternatives to urban renewal.

In 1973 two other community-based organizations were formed to resist specific aspects of urban renewal: Citizens Against Nihonmachi Eviction (CANE) was formed to fight for the remaining Japanese-American residential and small business community in the A-2 area north of Geary between Gough and Steiner. The Goodman Group also formed in 1973 to fight for artist live-work space in the Goodman Building on Geary just east of Franklin, on the eastern edge of the A-2 development area.

But the battle for community control over housing was not limited to SFRA project areas alone. Private sector developers and large hospitals were also very active during the Alioto administration. The most famous battle with private developers was the International Hotel, a residential hotel housing some 100 senior Chinese and Filipino seniors in the heart of the fast fading Manilatown at the eastern edge of Chinatown on Kearny Street.[6]

Tentatively planned to be the A-3 project area of the Western Addition redevelopment area, by 1968 the Haight-Ashbury was saved from redevelopment by the hippie invasion. The huge influx into the neighborhood of young people not only changed the City's plans for the area but also dramatically changed the social and political dynamics within the neighborhood. By 1969 hard drugs were replacing psychedelics and working class runaways replaced the first wave of hippie middle class "searchers." The neighborhood underwent a classic real estate blockbusting wave as real estate speculators used the relocation of Black property owners from A-2 to drive down prices from scared White property owners, and then flip the property at inflated prices to new buyers. Additionally, the neighborhood's four hospitals were each planning massive expansion requiring the demolition of hundreds of residential buildings. The two largest, St. Mary's and UCSF, actually had eminent domain powers just like the SFRA. In the late 1950s and early 1960s the two hospitals had condemned and acquired well over 1,000 housing units in the neighborhood. Indeed, UCSF had been a major supporter of the Panhandle Freeway as a way to link it with the Berkeley campus.

The Haight-Ashbury's central location made it a transitional neighborhood between the then mainly White homeowner neighborhoods of western San Francisco and the heavily minority and immigrant tenant neighborhoods of eastern San Francisco. The issue of hospital expansion affected several middle-income neighborhoods—the Inner Sunset, Eureka Valley, the Richmond, and Pacific Heights. All had hot resident/hospital fights—and provided fruitful grounds for coalition efforts. Learning from the Panhandle Freeway fight, Haight-Ashbury activists learned the value of coalitions and the importance of planning and land-use issues in creating durable political organizations.

In 1970 Mayor Alioto announced the creation of the Mayor's Committee to Restore the Haight-Ashbury, dominated by property owners and real estate agents, and chaired by the Chancellor of UCSF. Community response was immediate and hostile as it was viewed by both youth and long-time residents as an attempt by Alioto to redevelop the neighborhood.

Alioto's Mayor's Committee started a series of discussions between veterans of the Freeway Revolt and other local political struggles—mainly Sue Bierman, a principal organizer of the multi-neighborhood anti-freeway movement, and her ally Ed Dunn, a native San Franciscan, retired President of the Fire Fighters Union. Also invited were young Haight-Ashbury activists from the anti-war, student, and counterculture movements residing in the neighborhood. These meetings were formalized as the "Saturday Meetings," taking place every week at 409 House, an Episcopalian Church-funded community organizing and youth service center at 409 Clayton. Soon these meetings involved folks from other neighborhoods as well as the Haight-Ashbury, including the Western Addition, Inner Sunset, and Eureka Valley. The meetings addressed first the issues raised by Alioto's Committee for the Haight-Ashbury but soon were enlarged to address more general land-use issues, including redevelopment and the growing concern about downtown high-rise growth. Participants included Sue Hestor (later an influential community land-use attorney), John Bardis (District Supervisor elected from the Inner Sunset in 1979), and Mary Rogers (active in WACO). Folks in the Haight-Ashbury began to understand that they were not simply a self-invented "High Hippie" enclave, totally self-contained, but instead an urban neighborhood facing problems not unique, but shared with other urban neighborhoods. There was an entire world outside the Haight-Ashbury that had things to teach and presented opportunities for joint action on joint problems.

The immediate response to the lessons learned from the Saturday Meetings at 409 House was the first neighborhood-initiated rezoning of a residential neighborhood in City history (in 1971). In 1973, a "community development corporation" was founded in part to purchase and rehabilitate housing for existing residents, and to augment the efforts of the Tenant Action Group (TAG, founded in 1970, from which the San Francisco Tenants Union grew). By 1975 Haight-Ashbury activists had formed a coalition with Inner Sunset groups and created a "Mt. Sutro Community Master Plan" calling for the limitation of UCSF growth and the return to community use of all housing taken by UCSF. Both goals were eventually realized.

The successful rezoning of the Haight-Ashbury created interest in the Mission and after a series of community meetings a coalition of Mission groups led by the La Raza Information Center (a group which also included middle class homeowners) rezoned some 4,000 properties in the Mission in 1975, reducing speculative pressure on them from the private market.

## From the Particular to the General: Building a Citywide Housing Movement

Between 1968 and 1975 housing and land-use issues had gone from the back burner of a local community agenda to front and center. Throughout eastern San Francisco, inside and outside of urban renewal, community-based organizations were formed. From South of Market to Chinatown, from the Haight-Ashbury to the Mission, "community controlled" organizations and entities were formed and a cadre of self-taught community development activists were in place. Yet, many of these organizations were so focused on a particular building or community that there was resistance, for a variety of reasons, to learning from their respective battles and applying those lessons to a more general, much more radical, citywide movement for community control over development.

The first attempt to create a citywide organization based upon these various battles occurred in late 1974 with the formation of the Peoples Action Coalition (PAC). Oddly the motivating event for the organizing effort had nothing to do with housing or land-use, but rather it was catalyzed by the kidnapping of Patty Hearst by the Symbionese Liberation Army (SLA). In late February the SLA released a pre-recorded tape demanding that the Western Addition Project Area Committee be the central coordinating body in organizing a $6 million food give-away demanded by the SLA as part of the ransom for the release of Hearst. WAPAC asked for help from other community-based groups it knew from its land-use battles, some of whom responded. It was that joint experience of working together in the high stakes Hearst food distribution that cemented trust between these organizations and raised the prospect of staying together at a citywide level around land use and housing issues.

Representatives of SFNLAF, TOOR, IHTA, CANE, Goodman Group, public housing tenants, TAG, 409 House, St. Francis Hospital expansion opponents, and opponents of the demolition of the City of Paris met to discuss the creation of a multi-issue land-use citywide coalition. Some five meetings took place in which the history and needs of each group/struggle were presented. A set of "general principles" was debated. CANE and the International Hotel Tenants Association (IHTA) were insistent that the PAC remain solely focused on housing and "mutual support, respecting the autonomy of each group." 409 House urged the group to take notice of the newly passed federal legislation ending HUD funding of urban renewal, creating the Community Development Block Grant Program. It urged that the PAC become the advocate for community use of these funds for housing and community development initiatives. Finally, in January 1975 a majority of the groups voted to remain focused only on housing and mutual support. This apparently sapped the will of groups and individuals to continue meeting in a citywide form, because within a few months PAC ceased meeting.

In May 1975, the effort to create a citywide housing movement then shifted to the Community Congress planning process. A community housing convention was held at which some 30 positions were taken including a call for rent control, the development of "special needs housing," and ending discrimination in housing against people of color, families, and seniors. The convention declared the basic housing policy of the City should be to "preserve and expand housing opportunities for people who presently live in the City" and the Convention called for an end of the City's actual policy of "housing for profit." These 30 positions, along with two dozen more, were adopted at the citywide convention in June along with several score more specific economic polices aimed at putting neighborhood development in the hands of the community.

In 1977 a new citywide coalition attempt was launched by the San Francisco Housing Coalition (SFHC), made up of some 50 neighborhood and community organizations. Three significant developments had occurred since the failed attempt at joint citywide organizing in 1974 that made the 1977 SFHC possible: the June 1975 Community Congress, the November 1975 election of George Moscone as Mayor, and the successful election of a district-elected Board of Supervisors in November 1977 (district elections were adopted in 1976). These three events meant that not only was there an agreed-upon tactical program for action rising out of the Community Congress but that there was an ally, not an opponent, in the Mayor's office. There was now a clear and direct route to bring about citywide housing and land-use change: getting six votes on the newly elected district board of Supervisors and the certain assumption of a Mayor's signature on the reform legislation.

In late 1977 the SFHC developed an anti-speculation ordinance. The ordinance would establish a graduated increase in the City's existing transfer tax that would tax 80% of the profit of a resale made in less than one year, down to no increase in a resale of a property held for ten or more years. The ordinance was aimed at addressing the first wave of what would come to be called gentrification. City living had risen in popularity, speeded by the combined effects of the 1974 OPEC oil boycott (which drove gasoline prices to more than $1 a gallon (!) and dramatically increased the cost of commuting to downtown) and the explosion of commercial office development in San Francisco. Incoming residents put pressure on property values in the central City and housing costs took their first huge leap. This set off a wild round of real estate speculation in the Haight-Ashbury, Hayes Valley, Mission, and Eureka Valley by the mid-1970s.

The draft anti-speculation ordinance was introduced in mid-1978 by the newly elected District 5 Supervisor, Harvey Milk, whose district included three of the four rapidly gentrifying neighborhoods. It was supported by Mayor Moscone, then eager for a new City revenue source with the June passage of Proposition 13 which cut tens of millions from the City's budget. Strong opposition on the Board led by Supervisor Feinstein and her loyal ally Dan White held up adoption of the ordinance until after the yearly budget in September. The matter got through committee and was pending before the Board for a vote in late November 1978. The vote never happened. On November 27th Moscone and Milk were assassinated and new Mayor Feinstein later prevailed upon the Board to table the legislation.

## Community Development of Permanently Affordable Housing

A new citywide housing movement had been launched. By 1979 housing and/or community development corporations had been or would soon be formed in the Haight-Ashbury, Chinatown, Tenderloin, Bernal Heights, Bayview/Hunter's Point, and the Western Addition joining the first two originally formed in South of Market and the Mission. They would, by 2008, develop nearly 26,000 permanently affordable housing units, mainly for families and seniors earning less than 50% of the median income of the City.

The existence of the community housing movement by 1977 would so influence the district-elected Board of Supervisors that in 1979 they passed San Francisco's Rent Stabilization and Arbitration ordinance, which by 2008 covered some 170,000 rental units. By 2008 an additional nearly 2,000 units of inclusionary housing (permanently affordable units) have been developed, also as a result of the advocacy of the community-based housing movement.

These 198,000 units of price-controlled housing constitute some 54% of San Francisco's entire housing stock. No such permanently "price-protected" housing existed in 1968 outside of the relative handful of public housing units which made up less than 1% of the housing stock. Over half of the City's housing remains within reach for most of its residents solely because of the struggles, events, victories, and setbacks of the decade of community organizing between 1968 and 1978.

## Notes

1.   SPUR, "Prologue for Action," 1966 as quoted in Chester Hartman et al, *Yerba Buena: Land Grab and Community Resilience in San Francisco.* (San Francisco: Glide Publications, 1974).

2.   San Francisco Redevelopment Agency. "AB2113 Talking Points," May 2, 2000; and DCP. "Housing Inventory," various years.

3.   See Rachel Brahinsky's essay "'Hush Puppies,' Communalist Politics, and Demolition Governance: The Rise and Fall of the Black Fillmore" in this volume for a more thorough treatment of the Western Addition Redevelopment struggle.

4.   See Margaret Leahy's essay "On Strike We're Gonna Shut it Down: The 1968-69 SF State Strike" also in this volume for more information on the SF State Strike and its effects.

5.   See Tomás Sandoval's essay "'All Those Who Care About The Mission, Stand Up With Me!'—Latino Community Formation and the Mission Coalition Organization" in this volume.

6.   See Estella Habal's essay "Filipino Americans in the Decade of the International Hotel" in this volume for more on the International Hotel.

# Reflections from Occupied Ohlone Territory

## by Mary Jean Robertson

S acred sites were being destroyed. Nations were terminated. Drug and alcohol addiction was rampant on the reservations. Something had to change. The people told a story, had a vision, sang a ghost dance song. The young people gathered on the western edge of Turtle Island and the smoke of the tobacco, cedar, and sage carried their prayers to the creator. The spirit of the people would start in the West and return to the East to bring a new consciousness of sovereignty and self-determination to the Native Nations.

All over the world Nations were gaining independence from their colonizers. Young men were fighting, dying, and returning from Vietnam. Women were changing roles and status. In the city that birthed the United Nations, an invisible minority took a step into the spotlight of history.

> *"Alcatraz, Alcatraz, none has seen your beauty like the Indian has."*
> —Redbone[1]

The two decades leading to the occupation of Alcatraz in 1969 were the most difficult for individuals to deal with. Life for Indian peoples was like a pressure cooker. Generations of children were taken from their families to suffer in government- and church-sponsored boarding schools.[2] The families lost their traditional ways of passing information through stories and example. The religions and languages were attenuated to the point of disappearance. The children of the boarding schools were suffering from the first forms of Post-Traumatic Stress Disorder and Stockholm syndrome. They were encouraged to identify with their captors and learned the lessons of punishment. Traditionally in Native societies children were cherished, corporal punishment was unheard of, and the cutting of hair was a sign of mourning the death of a close family member. The bewildered children brought to the schools thought that they had lost their family forever when the staff cut their hair to make them conform to the White culture's sense of civilization.

World War II brought the warriors to the forefront where the traditions of defending the lands of the people translated into serving in all branches of the Armed Forces.[3] After the war the knowledge of how people were treated outside of the reservation led to anger, depression, and despair. It was at this point that the Government, wanting to solve the "Indian Problem," came up with a three-pronged approach. The tribal government-to-government status promised by treaties would be terminated (a unilateral abolition of Indian sovereignty). The American Indian Civil Rights Act promised individual Indians the right to the same rights and responsibilities of any other citizen without any of the group rights guaranteed by the treaties. The federal Indian Relocation Act of 1956 promised jobs and housing assistance if families would move off the reservations into the cities.[4] San Francisco was a terminus point for the relocation program on the West Coast. The plan was to terminate the Government's treaty responsibilities to the Indian Nations because all their citizens would have become assimilated Americans. There was a policy in the Bureau of Indian Affairs (BIA) and the Indian Health Service (IHS) to consider all Native Americans who had left their reservations as non-Indians and therefore not eligible for housing, healthcare, or any other federal programs for Native Americans. The next generation of children was supposed to lose their identity as tribal members and become ordinary working-class Americans, just like all the other ethnic minorities were melting into the dominant culture.

The social workers, the Mormon Church, and the IHS worked together to remove Indian children from their families so that they could be adopted into White families where they would not have to suffer the poverty and hunger that existed on the reservations. The Indian Health Service practiced their own form of eugenics, sterilizing most young women who gave birth in the IHS hospitals.[5]

In Vietnam, American Indians once again served in the US armed forces in a much higher per capita rate than any other group. The young men, trained to fight for democracy, freedom, and justice came home and found their homelands invaded, their people in poverty and despair. They used the GI bill to go to school to learn how to bring back hope to their people. John Trudell had served in the Navy, Richard Oakes was using the GI bill to attend San Francisco State College.

The San Francisco American Indian Center burned to the ground in October 1969 and there was no longer a meeting, gathering place for all the displaced Indians. No place to have memorial services, no place to have potluck dinners, no place to get a little help with the social service agencies, a job search, the cops. No one to help with a little money to get back home or to translate English so that an ID for work was obtainable.

The American Indian Movement was patrolling the streets of Minneapolis to protect Indian people from the police. San Francisco State College was on strike. Students and teachers were meeting outside the classrooms and demanding relevant courses. The demands of the Civil Rights Movement resonated with the Indian peoples. The Reies Lopez Tijerina Courthouse raid in New Mexico[6] demanded a more activist approach to challenge government policies. It was into this perfect storm of possibilities that the determination to occupy Alcatraz Island was born. The San Francisco movers and shakers came up with a plan to exploit Alcatraz Island to make money for the wealthy elites. Mr. Lamar Hunt of a Texas oil money family tried to buy Alcatraz Island for $2 million and turn it into a $4 million tourist park, landscaped with a shopping area that resembled San Francisco in the 1890s. That was the last straw.

Just as when a pot of water is put on the stove to boil, and a few air bubbles form on the bottom and crawl up the sides of the pot, the Alcatraz Occupation had a few early attempts. In 1964 a group of young people landed on the Island and claimed it by right of the Sioux treaty of 1868. This claim was taken to Federal Court. Judges are very conservative, they could have determined that the Ohlone people were the original inhabitants of San Francisco and returned the land to them. Instead the court determined that the treaty only applied to the Sioux and other signatories of that treaty and did not apply to the West Coast at all. Again on November 9, 1969, Adam Fortunate Eagle, Richard Oakes, and others took a symbolic cruise around the Island on the *Monte Cristo*. Halfway around the Island Richard took off his shirt and dove into the water to swim to Alcatraz; he was followed by several others. Joe Bill, an Alaska Native familiar with the sea jumped when the boat was a little further along so that the tide would carry him to the Island. His was the only successful landing of that cruise. Later that night 14 activists spent the night on the island only to be returned to the mainland by the Coast Guard on the following morning. The 18-month occupation really started on November 20, 1969, at about 2:00 a.m., when almost eighty American Indians from more than 20 tribes landed on Alcatraz. Some stayed for the full 18 months of the occupation, some only for a day or two, but in the end over 5,600 Indians of All Tribes claimed "the Rock."

Alcatraz changed everything. The event resulted in major benefits for American Indians. In his memoirs, Brad Patterson, a top aide to President Richard Nixon, cited at least ten major policy and law shifts.[7] They include passage of the Indian Self-Determination and Education Assistance Act in 1975, a revision of the Johnson O'Malley Act to better educate Indians, passage of the Indian Financing Act of 1974, passage of the Indian Health Care Improvement Act in 1976, and the creation of an Assistant Interior Secretary post for Indian Affairs. Mount Adams was returned to the Yakima Nation in Washington State, and 48,000 acres of the Sacred Blue Lake lands were returned to Taos Pueblo in New Mexico. This was the very first return of land to the Indian Nations. During the Island's Occupation second Christmas, Nixon signed papers rescinding Termination stating, "This marks the end of Termination and the start of Self-determination."

Almost a month into the occupation, KPFA—and the other Pacifica Stations, KPFK in Los Angeles and WBAI in New York—broadcast the show Radio Free Alcatraz for 15 minutes a night to about 100,000 listeners. John Trudell was the voice from Alcatraz, covering Indian issues, interviewing residents, arranging talks on culture, fishing rights, the taking of Indian lands, and allowing the elders to tell the stories that had been passed down from generation to generation. This began a tradition of community radio that linked the Bay Area with the ongoing struggles across the country.

The Native college students would leave the island to attend their classes and to participate in founding the Ethnic Studies program in Berkeley and San Francisco State. They would return to Alcatraz on the weekends bringing the support of other students and community members. The negotiations dragged on into 1971 with the Government shutting off all electricity and removing the water barge which had provided fresh water to the occupiers. Three days later a fire broke out on the island. Several historic buildings were destroyed. The government blamed the Indians; the Indians blamed undercover government infiltrators trying to turn non-Indian support against them. Finally on June 10, 1971, armed federal marshals, FBI agents, and Special Forces police swarmed the island and removed five women, four children, and six unarmed Indian men. The occupation was over.

San Francisco was the City of Love, the third eye of the world, the place of prophecy. Rolling Thunder came to speak to the spiritual communities and they said he could speak if a Native woman would vouch for him. Patricia Clarke was the founder of an intentional community called the California Dreamers. As a Nez Perce woman she interviewed Rolling Thunder and found him to be a Medicine Person with sacred powers. He was then asked to speak at many gatherings of holy people in the City. The White Roots of Peace came to San Francisco and Mad Bear Anderson of the Mohawk Nation inspired Richard Oakes with his knowledge of the sacred wisdom of the Iroquois Confederacy. The Hopi Messengers, David

Monongye and Thomas Banyaquaya, told the San Francisco Native Community about the time of Great Purification. Leman Brightman, founder of United Native Americans founded the first Native Studies Department in Berkeley. Richard Oakes inspired the beginning of the Native American Ethnic Studies Department at San Francisco State College. Many Alcatraz supporters would go on to teach in these new programs and others would join them. Don Patterson would teach Music, Dr. Bernard Hoehner would head the Native American Department from 1970 to the early 1990s. Vernon and Millie Katcheshawno were well known educators and activists. San Francisco State's Student Kouncil of Indian Nations, or SKINS, was founded soon after the Alcatraz Occupation ended. Randy Burns and Barbara Cameron would found the very first Native American Gay organization, Gay American Indians (GAI).

While on Alcatraz and soon afterward many people were talking about the Ghost Dance Vision of the return of the Indian Spirit from the West Coast back to the East. The Navajos and the Cherokee talked about the "Long Walk" and the "Trail of Tears." Many would overhear the words, "We should reverse the walks and take back our rights, our courage, and our lands." This series of conversations led to the Trail of Broken Treaties Caravan from San Francisco to Washington DC. Gathering tribal people all along the way they joined together to demand recognition and empowerment from the US Government, the Department of the Interior, and the BIA.

One of the radio stations covering the Trail of Broken Treaties was a small community radio station in San Francisco. A member of the KRAB nebula radio community founded by Lorenzo Milam, KPOO was located on Natoma Street near 7th and Mission near the former Greyhound Bus Station where so many relocated Indians took their first steps on the streets of San Francisco. Chicken, Charlie Steele, and Tiger started a Native radio program that was called *Red Voices*. When Joe Rudolph and others from San Francisco State's student Strike took over the station and made it the first Black-owned community radio station on the West Coast, they made a commitment to the Native Community: there will always be a show produced by Native People on KPOO. *Red Voices* covered the armed takeover of the Village of Wounded Knee, interviewing the warriors, asking for food and supplies, and announcing the benefits to raise money for the travel costs to get the supplies to South Dakota.

The years between 1973 and 1976 were some of the most violent in the history of the modern Indian struggle. 271 deaths occurred on the Pine Ridge Indian reservation, mostly of the traditional people who were trying to maintain their own religion and life ways.[8] Many of the American Indian Movement members were arrested, in jail, on the run, or being extradited. The Bay Area was the center for legal activities. The Wounded Knee Legal Defense Offence Committee (WKLDOC) raised monies, came up with defense strategies, and developed a network of pro bono lawyers to defend the young warriors who had been arrested. The Native American Solidarity Committee was a group of young people committed to support the rights of Indian peoples to their lands and their own governments. There were a lot of interesting conversations about the difference between solidarity and support going on with many of the young people outside the Native community to find out about their own backgrounds and the struggles of their own peoples. The Sami organization got a couple of supporters who found that the tribe they came from was indigenous to Scandinavia. A young woman of Irish descent took a trip to Ireland and became active in the Irish community.

The American Indian community was empowering itself by turning to the past, to the traditions and religions of their own Nations. Leonard Crowdog came to speak about re-establishing the practice of the forbidden Sundance in the Lakota Nation. Ruben Snake spoke of the ability of the Native American Church to cure alcoholism and drug addiction by returning to the old traditions. These and many other conversations resulted in the passage of the American Indian Religious Freedom Act in 1978 to protect the participants. In the land of religious freedom it took an act of Congress to protect the Indians who wished to practice their own religion.

In the summer of 1974 the Movement activists left the Bay Area to join the Lakota Sioux in order to form the International Indian Treaty Council. The founding conference was on the Standing Rock Reservation. The founding document of the International Indian Treaty Council raised the conflict to the international level, calling upon the world's peoples to join in recognizing the sovereignty of the Native Nations. The Treaty Council opened and maintained an information office in San Francisco to produce the *Treaty Council News* and to have ongoing interviews with the local Native Radio programs. *Red Voices* interviewed Oran Lyons, Phillip Deer, and Mad Bear Anderson on their way to the United Nations gatherings in New York and Geneva. The Hopi talked on the radio about fulfilling their prophecy by knocking on the door of the "House of Mica" (the UN in New York).

The annual Thanksgiving Holiday became a day for ceremony, fasting, and prayer beginning with a sunrise ceremony on Alcatraz Island. The American Indian Center was relocated to Duboce and Valencia. It became a safe place to gather to plan benefits, to raise money for the lawyers, to have a meal together, and laugh and forget for a while the hardships of the people. In a little house around a kitchen table in San Francisco, a group of women gathered and talked about an organization to support the men and strengthen the women's ability to survive. That organization was called Women of all Red Nations (WARN) which refused to be relegated to the end of the agendas and the back of the rooms in the women's conferences and gatherings. "We cannot support the agenda that once again takes our children away from us to be raised by government child care centers. We have a different experience and a different history that also needs to be honored and respected."

Bill Wahpepah founded and maintained the AIM for Freedom Survival School to teach our youngsters their own history without being told that they were extinct or of no value. Weavings were being rewoven to bring many peoples together. Vernon Katchshawno went to Mexico and found and met with the Mexican Kickapoo. He returned to Oklahoma and reintroduced his Mexican cousins to his family back in Oklahoma. The American Indian Movement sent representatives to stand in front of the International Hotel to prevent the evictions of the Pilipino elders. Teveia Clarke and her son were near the corner of the I-Hotel when a Sheriff on horseback tried to ride into the protesters. Teveia was a Nez Perce woman; her people developed the Appaloosa horses and bred them for color and stamina. She blew into the horse's nose and chanted. The horse backed away, reared, and when the sheriff fell off, the horse stepped on his foot. "You shouldn't mess with a Nez Perce woman if you are on a horse," she said.[9]

Teveia's son would stand on Haight and Ashbury selling *Akwesasne Notes* alongside others selling papers like the *Oracle* and the *Berkeley Barb*. The San Francisco Arts Commission was dragging their feet about supporting the Neighborhood Arts Program's demands for cultural centers and culturally relevant arts for all people not just the elite supporters of the Symphony, Opera, and the Ballet. The American Indian Arts Workshop helped to found both the Mission Cultural Center in the old Shaft Furniture Store and Brannan Street Cultural Center (now SOMArts Cultural Center). There was a wonderful program called Comprehensive Employment and Training Act enacted in 1973 that paid a living wage to people who had not been able to be paid for their work before. Bill and Alberta Snyder taught music and beadwork. Ed and Madelyn Payett taught archery and the most beautiful ribbon work. Teveia Clarke and I were oral historians, talking story and developing programs for students after school and on the radio. Barbara Cameron and Sherol Graves were silkscreen artists and photographers. Jean McLean was the director who wrote the grants and ran the organization.

One of the demands from the Occupation of Alcatraz was the protection of sacred sites. In 1976 the California State Government passed AB 4239, establishing the Native American Heritage Commission (NAHC) as the primary government agency responsible for identifying and cataloging Native American cultural resources. One of NAHC's primary duties is to prevent irreparable damage to designated sacred sites as well as to prevent interference with the expression of Native American religion in California. This commission was charged with protecting Native sites without adequate funding to do so. It has always been an honor and a privilege for Native women and men to volunteer their time and money to this organization. This has not prevented museums and universities from retaining human remains and grave goods in their collections. However the laws passed first in California helped to push forward the passage of the American Indian Graves Protection and Repatriation Act in 1990.

The Longest Walk began February 11, 1978, on Alcatraz Island. The Longest Walk was a brilliant organizing tool. Walking across the country kept everyone informed of all the issues across Indian country and connected the coasts with everyone in between. It hit all the high points: Pit River, Washoe territory, Western Shoshone, Big Mountain, Leonard Peltier's incarceration. The walkers were the marginalized, the homeless, the abused, and the alcoholics who found that the prayers and the staffs of eagle feathers healed them and empowered them. Only 20 people have affidavits that they walked all the way and of those only 10 have survived. *Red Voices* radio carried reports from the Walk on every show. San Francisco heard where the walkers were and where they were going to be. Shoes and socks were sent on ahead of the walkers. The stories of the 11 bills in Congress to terminate all treaties with Indian Nations, and the stories of the young women sterilized by IHS programs without their knowledge or consent, were on the air in San Francisco. The People's Temple had a benefit to raise money for the Longest Walk.[10] The churches and neighborhood centers raised the awareness of the community around the issues. The bills were all defeated and the Indian Health Service programs were investigated.

As a result of the Longest Walk Congress passed the Indian Child Welfare Act (ICWA) later in 1978. American Indian children had been removed from their culture and fostered or adopted into non-Native families at a rate greater than any other group. The passage of the ICWA stemmed the tide of the removal of the children. The American Indian agencies in the San Francisco Bay Area were in the forefront of advocating for and passing the Act. In the Courts of San Francisco the reasonableness of ICWA became the standard of how to treat all children in the foster care system. All children are placed in homes that are aware of the cultural traditions of the children and if possible within families of the same ethnic background.

The decade inspired positive change in the Native American community. However the struggle continues. The Winumum Wintu are fighting to regain their federal recognition so that they can protect their last remaining sacred sites from the rising waters of Shasta Dam. The Ohlone are returning to San Francisco to take their rightful place as the caretakers of the lands and waters of the area. The United Nations passed the Rights of the Indigenous Peoples and of the four nations who voted against the passage New Zealand, Canada, and the United States remain opposed. We look forward to a time where the generational trauma can be healed by acknowledging what happened to the Native People here and requesting their wisdom in caring for the waters, the lands, the plants, the animals, and the people.

## Notes

1.  Formed in 1969 in Los Angeles, California, by brothers Patrick Vasquez (bass and vocals) and Lolly Vasquez (guitar and vocals), the name Redbone itself is a joking reference to a Cajun term for a mixed-race person ("half-breed"), the band's members being of mixed blood ancestry. In 1973 Redbone released the politically oriented "We Were All Wounded at Wounded Knee," recalling the massacre of Lakota Sioux Indians by the Seventh Cavalry in 1890. The song ends with the subtly altered sentence "We were all wounded 'by' Wounded Knee."

2.  Julie Davis, "American Indian Boarding School Experiences: Recent Studies from Native Perspectives," *OAH Magazine of History* 15 (Winter 2001).

3.  Alison R. Bernstein, *American Indians and World War II: Toward a New Era in Indian Affairs* (University of Oklahoma Press: 1999).

4.  "The Relocation Act of 1956, resulted in more than half of the 1.6 million Indians in the U.S.A. to relocate to urban centers, signing agreements to not return to their respective nations/reservations in the future." *Redhawk's Lodge*. http://siouxme.com/lodge/land.html (accessed July 23, 2010).

5.  "Sterilization of Native American Women." http://www.ratical.org/ratville/sterilize.html (accessed July 23, 2010).

6.  "Reies López Tijerina and the Tierra Amarilla Courthouse Raid," *Southwest Crossroads Spotlight*, http://southwestcrossroads.org/record.php?num=739 (accessed July 23, 2010).

7.  Bradley H. Patterson, Jr. *The White House Staff: Inside the West Wing and Beyond* (Brookings Institution Press; Rev Upd edition, May 2000).

8.  There are many sources to understand what happened during that time. Two good ones are Peter Matthiesson, *In the spirit of Crazy Horse* (New York: Viking Press, 1983), and Stephen Bain Bicknell Hendricks, *The unquiet grave: the FBI and the struggle for the soul of Indian country* (New York: Thunder's Mouth Press, 2006).

9.  See Estella Habal's essay "Filipino Americans in the Decade of the International Hotel" in this volume for more information on the struggle to save the International Hotel.

10. See Matthew Roth's essay "Coming Together: The Communal Option" in this volume for more on the People's Temple role in activism.

# Making Sexism Visible
## Private Troubles Made Public

### by Deborah A. Gerson

*...[W]e did do some demonstrating out in the street, right, but I'm not sure that was the biggest deal...it was a much bigger deal that fifty of us met every week in Glide Church basement and talked...twelve women met in somebody's home and told the truth about our lives...we were taking ourselves seriously, setting aside time...and came together to talk about what we were doing and what we wanted. The air was electric.*
—Cathy Cade[1]

How did I join the women's liberation movement? In August 1968, after a speech by Naomi Weisstein at the Socialist Scholars Conference in New York City, I joined with women who met together for many hours. In the space of one day I became a feminist—though I did not yet use that word—and a member of the women's liberation movement. I was invited to join a women's group. We had no leader, no agenda, and no formalized affiliation with any other body, although we felt ourselves to be part of a great ferment.

Beginning in the late 1960s, small groups of women in the US began meeting together and talking about their own lives. While the first groups began as a response to the sexism of the New Left, by the early 1970s thousands of autonomous groups were meeting around the United States. Within these consciousness-raising groups women talked about sexuality, body image, housework, marriage, work, and their minds. Consciousness-raising enabled women collectively to name sexism as the source of women's subordination; as individuals it helped women to extricate themselves from oppressive situations.

Nyla Gladden, a single mother on welfare, recalled a Students for a Democratic Society (SDS) meeting at San Francisco State College dominated by men, fighting over the production of a leaflet. "I went home to try and find my welfare check...and I remember the anger I came home with and I realized I needed something for me. That SDS was not for me and it didn't have a place for women." Chude Allen (Pam Parker) was a veteran of Mississippi Summer, living in New York and then moving to San Francisco, sidelined from earlier involvements by the exclusion of Whites from the Civil Rights Movement after 1964. Allen described her mobilization into women's liberation not as a step on her previous political trajectory, but rather as a response to her situation as woman, wife, and former Civil Rights activist:

> .... [M]y own entry into [women's liberation] happened as an individual being married and working in a low level position in a social work agency and feeling totally outside the movement at that time, totally lost, totally alienated, very confused... I was desperate...two years of being married and being out of a movement.[2]

While pre-existing networks enabled women to find each other and form new groups, the intensity of the connections generated were new to the moment. Estelle Jelinek read "an article by Pam Allen...it was like a 100% turnaround, there was like no way I could go but on from there...It was the end of the past and the beginning of the future." Forest (Gretchen) Milne "remember[ed] the feeling of excitement, that it was something extremely new, and everything was yet to be."

An unhappy history with male-dominated movement politics often motivated a search for women's liberation. Judy Brady (then Syfers) highlights the San Francisco State Strike of 1968-69 as the moment she searched for a connection to women's liberation:

> ...my husband was part of the union...this house became known as the Strike annex. I had two small kids, I was a housewife. But I was running the Strike annex out of this house...[one] room was a mailing room [with] a series of typewriters and filing cabinets and I had crews of people working 10-14 hours typing letters before the days of computers...It was all done manually...after the San Francisco State Strike ended...there was a last meeting of the union where they thanked people for all the work they had done. They thanked my husband for raising $40,000 out of this house.

This became the incident which prompted her to attend her first women's meeting. Early in the movement, seeking out women's meetings did not guarantee success in finding a functioning political space. Groups from both the Old and New Left, from the Spartacists to the Weather Underground, critiqued and undermined the nascent and fragile consciousness.

Establishing their own political "free space" became the first hurdle of the emerging movement. Cade recalled a meeting in New Orleans of former Civil Rights and New Left women who were

> very nervous about whether this was politically correct....we were mostly White—there was one Black woman there—and came from different class backgrounds. But obviously, compared to the Black people of Mississippi, we had more social advantages...We were really wondering whether this was the right thing to do and whether there was really a need, because obviously, we were all strong women.

Women found it difficult to organize around women's oppression until a clear explanatory ideology emerged to legitimate that organizing. At the same time, until a space was cleared for women to meet and talk, the possibility for the development of such an ideology was constrained. The development of autonomous small groups in which "women [support] each other" went hand-in-hand with development of analysis that identified women's oppression as a legitimate subject of political struggle.

Women joined women's liberation small groups as a path out of isolation, invisibility, and alienation. Judy Knoop, divorced with three young children, recalled, "I was like a stone...completely silent, I didn't speak. And there was a part of me that was not there, not alive, that was dead. ...Our marriage broke up at just the time that this women's movement was beginning, and I knew I needed to be there." Sandy Boucher summed up her emotional state prior to joining the movement as, "Sometimes I'd wake up and think, should I make a cheese sandwich or should I kill myself?" Judy Brady described women's liberation as "The first time I was going to be taken seriously, that was really new. I was what? An academic's big toe and incidentally mother of some kids... and that is what was at the basis of the depression: it was being a non-person."

The earliest assertions of women's liberation consciousness emphasized the necessity for the transformation and reconstitution of individual women, damaged and compromised by life in a male-dominated society. The Sudsofloppen paper, *Free Space*, written by members of the first San Francisco group, asserted that small groups must "cope first with [women's] deep personal struggle over feelings of inadequacy and inferiority."[3] An early group named itself the Gallstones, a double entendre engendered by a member's gallstone surgery, "We were supportive to her, that was the concept," as well as the space cleared for members' intense and angry feelings. These small consciousness-raising groups had a pull for women, meeting needs and feelings unmet by prior involvements. Jean Crosby, a staff member at Glide Church who was involved in the National Organization of Women (NOW) commented, "My heart was really in...women's liberation; I eventually dropped out of NOW. [Consciousness-raising] ...was really life changing for me...I began to understand in-depth just how sexism works."

Women joined women's liberation by joining small consciousness-raising groups. Groups were formed through word-of-mouth invitations and later through announcements in women's liberation newspapers. *CHANGE*, a women's liberation newspaper, announced, "Come to a meeting and find out just how many of your 'personal problems' are really the social problems of a sexist society."[4] The telling of one's own story, collectively shared, became the genesis of a developing ideology, of an analysis of women's oppression.

The explosion of consciousness that was accomplished by small groups was aided and abetted by the explosion of print: new writing by, for, and about women. By early 1971, the Bay Area had three functioning women's newspapers (*CHANGE, It Ain't Me Babe,* and *Mother Lode*), numerous newsletters, and access to magazines and newspapers published in other cities. Like the underground newspapers of the Sixties and similar to the 'zines that developed in the Seventies, women's liberation papers were impolite, sassy, and creative. Cartoons, historic photographs, hand-written headlines, a mixture of typefaces, and an absence of what would commonly be understood as news characterized these newspapers.

First-person narratives dominate this press. The banner issue of *Mother Lode* contains the widely reprinted piece, "Why I Want a Wife," as well as three other pieces and one poem, all in the first person. Syfers begins, "I belong to that classification of people known as wives. I am a Wife. And, not altogether incidentally, I am a mother." She begins each sentence with, "I want a wife who," and continues with an ironic listing of wifely duties, "I want a wife who will take care of my physical needs... who will keep my house clean...who is sensitive to my sexual needs...who will not demand sexual attention when I am not in the mood..." She ends with the rhetorical question, "My God, who *wouldn't* want a wife?"[5]

For other women, release from the work of being a wife was not primary. Pat Smith—a lesbian before women's liberation—remembered engineering school. "There was a department of 1500 people and there were five women, four in Architecture, and me...in Engineering." Smith moved to San Francisco

and found a group of slightly older (meaning in their thirties) southern, lesbian academics. Jackie W. described her embrace of women's liberation as "not a political move at the time. It really had to do with being attracted to women and that was very scary for me." When Jackie moved to San Francisco she joined a women's communal household, and got involved in the collective putting out *CHANGE*. (Indeed, for years I identified her as "Jackie from *CHANGE*.") Her new household exposed Jackie to the volatile stew of young lesbians becoming feminists, feminists coming out as lesbians, and older lesbians, designated "old gay," telling their stories about lives lived outside of the constraints of heterosexual marriage.

Alta, Pat Parker, Susan Griffin and Judy Grahn were four poets who "led a renaissance in women's poetry" in the early 1970s.[6] Alta and Griffin wrote of motherhood and children, Parker and Grahn were out lesbians, but these were never ideological or political divisions. All described in detail the oppression, struggle, and resistance of women. Grahn's *Common Woman Poems* contained portraits of seven women, one described as loving women, and others in the voices of a working woman, neighborhood women, a waitress, a mother. The poems, first written and spoken at Bay Area women's liberation events became anthems of the movement. "All by themselves they went around the country…they were reprinted hundreds of thousands of times, were put to music, danced, used to name various women's projects, quoted and then misquoted …for use on posters and T-shirts."[7]

In "I Like to Think of Harriet Tubman" Susan Griffin begins with reference to a then-current program, *"The legal answer / to the problem of feeding children / is ten free lunches every month, / being equal, in the child's real life, / to eating lunch every other day."* The poem becomes a battle cry for resistance, as well as testimony to a historic legacy of struggle, *"I want them / to take women seriously. / I want them to think about Harriet Tubman, / and remember, / that she was beat by a white man / and she lived / and she lived to redress her grievances."*[8]

This "enthusiasm of women hungry for realistic pictures" of themselves, of their lives, likewise inspired the photography of Cade. "Women's work was invisible; women were not supposed to work. And so there were no images of women working… I started taking pictures of all kinds of women's work." Her photographs had an eager audience: exhibits at Glide Church, the working women's newspaper *CHANGE*, and later, the *Union WAGE* (Women's Alliance to Gain Equality) newspaper. Cade emerged as a documentarian of lesbians, bringing a working women's consciousness to her photos. "...[T]he lesbian mothering pictures, I called them 'mothering' not just 'lesbian mothers' because nobody talked about mothering and what a job [it] was, and that it had skills. Part of what I wanted to do in those pictures was to articulate, 'What do mothers do?' Not just what do lesbian mothers do but, 'What is the job of mothering?'"

Through print, story, song, photos, and poems, the women's liberation movement constructed shared public representations of the experiences, insights, and visions revealed by consciousness-raising. By 1971, major news weeklies (*Time, Newsweek*) had run features on women's liberation and demonstrations were covered in daily newspapers. Able to circulate their new visions; to challenge received knowledge; and develop new ways of speaking, thinking, seeing, and understanding women's lives, the nascent women's movement challenged the consciousness of a whole culture.

## Speculums and Bodies

The first photograph on the first page in the very first movement-published issue of *Our Bodies Ourselves* shows women sitting on the floor in a circle, in a consciousness-raising group.[9] Sitting and talking to each other women told the secrets of their bodies: How we felt about our flesh, our sex, our faces, our muscles, our minds; how we were too short, too tall, too fat, too loud, too desiring, too cold—our secrets were exposed. What seemed shameful, weird, pathological, ugly, or unacceptable was examined, reframed, and transformed.

As women met and talked in consciousness-raising groups, much of what we changed was our embodied selves. Women had sex differently, with different partners: we began to dress differently rejecting dresses and pantyhose. Women looked at their vulvas and cervix, examined their breasts. Others took up sports and recreational activities on their own. How women lived in their bodies, as much as how we thought about and felt about our bodies, radically changed.

Were women's liberationists bra burners? The historical record reveals that the women demonstrating against the Miss America pageant in 1968 did not actually burn bras, but they did throw them into a trash can. While many women would continue to wear bras, what was burned was not the literal bra but the social bra, the political bra, the brassiere as symbol and practice of the exploited breast, the controlled breast, the subordinated, domesticated, playboy breast, the imperfect if not perfect breast, the man's breast.

In 1969, New England Free Press published "The Myth of the Vaginal Orgasm" on orange paper (four pages, 5 cents a copy); $1.00 got you twenty copies. Passed hand-to-hand, it became a quick organizing tool.[10] In December 1970, the same press printed 5,000 copies of *Our Bodies Ourselves*; by the end of 1971, another 60,000 copies were in circulation. But San Francisco women did not, indeed could not, depend on the Boston Women's Health Book Collective for direction or organization.

Knoop was already a member of the Gallstones when she and Geri Robertson traveled to Los Angeles and returned with a bag full of plastic speculums. She recalled her excitement, "They were doing this thing called 'self-exam'...We spent three or four days down there and our minds were just blown by it. It was another way to empower ourselves, that you could know your own body in that way." Knoop organized a group of women to learn self-health, and eventually form a walk-in storefront women's health collective. The 24th Street Health Collective became a repository of education and information but rejected the idea of attempting to provide direct service. Young women learned about methods and problems with birth control, about pelvic exams and infections. Pregnant women learned about bodily changes, what they should know, look for, and ask for from medical providers. Older women, who became involved through viewing the film *Self Health* by Allie Light, were incorporated into the work of the collective. Beverly Rutzick recalled, "I was fifty, thirty years older than them...Verna [Pedrin] was already in the health center...and the two of us got together and decided there had to be some kind of program for older women [on] menopause." Rutzick and Pedrin organized women, listened to women in workshops, and "developed a program. We gave workshops from menopause to midlife. We were kind of local experts for a while."

Dress, clothing, body stance, decorum, what sociologists call "the presentation of self," were contested in multiple spheres. Nursing students (at that time still overwhelmingly female) began rejecting the nursing cap, the white clothes. Knoop addressed her nursing school instructors "I will not wear white...I won't wear a hat...are the two men in our group wearing hats? You know these are signs of subservience...and really, a nurse's uniform is a maid's uniform."

For then-law student (now attorney) Zona Sage, a confrontation at Hastings Law School occurred when she refused to take off her hat at the request of a law professor. Sandy Blair remembers an escalating scenario as the professor ordered Sage to remove her hat, and "stormed up to the Dean's office, and he said, 'it's her or me.' This hit the front page of the *Chronicle*...They tried to throw her out of school and they had this trial...Her lawyer was Jenny Rhine, now a Municipal Court judge." Prior to this "trial" Sage was offered, and refused, a variety of compromises if she'd exit the class. She ultimately left Hastings and completed law school at Boalt Hall School of Law at UC Berkeley.

Laurie Cahn recalled that her women's group started as a self-help group where women learned to do self-exam and educate themselves about their own bodies, but moved on to consciousness-raising, mutual support and political action. "After six months (of self-exam)...we were really sick of this. Then we told each other our sexual histories, and from there...we met for the next six years." For Cahn, now a martial arts teacher, the changed sensibility about her body, combined with her anti-war politics led her to pursue a martial arts class. Seeing pictures of "Vietnamese women carrying guns" and hearing about a Gung Fu class led her to Project Artaud. "There were two women in the class doing push-ups on their fingers. People were punching and kicking...I just thought WOW, that's like the coolest thing I have ever seen. I want to do it; I want to be good at it. And I signed right up and here I am, 24 years later, still doing it."

But entry into these classes, like entry into other male-dominated contexts, did not assure either acceptance or success. To resist male put-downs, "Some of the women in class, we'd get together and encourage each other...or say to the person [man] 'hey, y'know, FUCK YOU, y'know, SHUT UP!' ...and you learn how to handle that stuff...that's what it was like: you had to work harder being a woman doing it." Getting better at Gung Fu, becoming stronger, had implications beyond the class. Cahn explained, "One of the things you get out of martial arts is getting in touch with either the potential or actual power that resides inside of you…People, women [feel], 'oh, alright, maybe I'm not as much of a wuss as I thought I was, maybe I could take care of myself, maybe I could speak up, maybe I'm stronger than I thought…maybe weight and height and muscle mass doesn't matter as much as technique and leverage and having a strategy for how to deal with situations'…You practice hard, you get better at it." For women, this sense of power and control enlarged their scope of participation in many movement activities. In 1977 when the struggle over the International Hotel culminated in a violent eviction, Cahn remembered, "a lot people who ended up at the I-Hotel were in that [martial arts] class."[11]

These bodies were not masculinized or androgynous bodies, denying their female parts. The body practices of women's liberation claimed clitoris, vulva, vagina, breasts, childbirth, orgasm, biceps,and triceps, but also punches and kicks, hiking boots, running shoes, hats, and helmets. Women's bodies were under re/construction by a movement. The political body of the women's liberation movement remade and re-envisioned women's bodies. Embodied women, together, were making a movement.

## A Movement Not an Organization

Bluntly stated, San Francisco women's liberation—like in much of the United States—was a movement, not an organization. No pre-existing organizations became key players in women's liberation and the organizational structures that emerged in the early period did not survive. Early women's groups were suspicious of attempts to *organize* women, distrustful of Left agendas that had subsumed a variety of constituencies (Blacks, Latinos, women, gays) into their broader agenda. In the first edition of *Free Space*, Allen wrote, "although justice and equality were the goals (of the pre-existing movement), the everyday reality for women was that of manipulation, insensitivity and exploitation."[12] In contrast to the Civil Rights Movement, the student movement, and the anti-war movement, the local structure of women's liberation was totally independent of any state or national structure, and the local projects and organizations which emerged were—for the most part—independent of each other and not accountable to any coordinating, leadership, or supporting body.

Discussion and analysis in small groups also engendered awareness of how women's lives were constrained: domineering husbands, unequal division of labor in the home, limited job opportunities, the very structure of childrearing. But changed consciousness did not lead seamlessly to transformed lives. Insight, support, and solidarity could lead to individual empowerment and a newfound sense of freedom, but they did not alter the conditions of daily life. Women wanted to, indeed began to, try and organize to change the world around them. But how to do this remained a quandary for the nascent movement.

In 1970, Gerlach and Hine described movements, in contrast to institutions, as (1) *Decentralized and polycephalous* (many headed); (2) *Segmented*, that is having many parts which can combine or divide; and (3) *Reticulate*, "resembling a network—tied together…through intersecting sets of personal relationships and other intergroup linkages."[13] In this early period, San Francisco's women's liberation fit their description of a movement. Women's liberation spawned multiple projects, newspapers, cultural events, health collectives, demonstrations, actions, collective households, and several women's centers. But no organization, institution, council, or collectivity directed these activities.

By 1970, SFWL was publishing a mimeographed newsletter, which attempted to cover, and tentatively coordinate, the range of activities generated by women's liberation. An "Announcements" list contained items including "looking for a small group," a meeting called to plan "revenge on the *Chronicle*," and a meeting to plan and organize for a women's center. Other announcements ranged from the explicitly political: "International Peace Rally: Downtown Peace Coalition holds meetings every Sunday…do we want to participate?" to those announcing a "free dog," a reasonable babysitter, the Mission Food Conspiracy, poetry readings, gay women's dances, requests for recipes for a "People's cookbook," and a "new alternative school for kids 8-12."[14]

The SFWL *Newsletter #3* included the item "Action Group Reports" which asked, "Action groups, do you seek new members? Want help on specific actions?…Consider preparing a brief summary of past and planned activities…to use as part of a presentation to talk to the semi-monthly meetings (we'd all like to talk about it.)" But the newsletter and the semi-monthly meeting were not the most efficacious source of action. The intense relationships formed in small groups, living collectives, and friendship circles were the genesis of activist projects.

Tanis Walters recalls Breakaway, a women's school offering classes, discussion, and small groups, as emerging from discussions after a demonstration when "a group of us who were just friends went off to a café." Breakaway began by organizing a series of salons, where women shared poetry, music, slide shows, and photography. Later the planning went on to initiate a series of three forums: on the family, on ecology, and on the economy. Walters described the planning for the forum on the family as the impetus for Brady Syfers to write "Why I Want a Wife." For women not in consciousness-raising groups, or those who wanted discussion, action, and connection that went beyond the life issues of the small group's members, Breakaway become a resource. Allen taught a class on racism in the women's suffrage movement which argued for the importance of making anti-racism central to the new women's movement and Syfers and Linda Daucher taught an "Introduction to Women's Liberation" class, allowing women to connect with the movement without joining a small group.

Glide Church was the site of often fractious, exhilarating, and frustrating citywide meetings. The SFWL *Newsletter #3* details a set of questions for future meetings: "Are we political? Do we need politics?…Are we anti-capitalist? Are we anti-male?"[15] While the meetings were the site of wildly unfocused and extraordinarily broad discussion, the very fact of their happening attests to the shared hope that women could find a unifying terrain of thought and action—if they talked long enough. Issues of structure, content, ideology, strategy, tactics, emotion, and analysis reeled back and forth in a dizzying manner.

For Cade, the internecine squabbles that emerged in the Glide Church meetings paled in import next to the fact that these meetings made women's liberation visible and accessible. "You knew where the women's movement was: it was at Glide Church at 7:30." But even more important was the visibility of lesbians. "Eight to twelve lesbians from the East Bay would all come in together and sit down. They were always together, always had this energy…and that spirit was what I wanted." For Cade and many other women, encountering out lesbians in a context of female solidarity and an explicit critique of male domination, helped them come out and participate in the construction of lesbian community.

Presentations by lesbians about their lives shaped the politics of the emerging movement. Women came to understand lesbian-baiting as a way of attacking and dividing women. "It was almost immediately that we were called lesbians, and we said, 'Hey, this is the way they curtail women from making any complaints.'" Homophobia was revealed as an oppressive force, even within historically women-centered institutions. Ann Farrar recalled her sister's history at Wellesley College where "a whole batch of them got kicked out—this is in 1960, 59-60."

Women's collective households often became exclusively lesbian as discomfort or outright disapproval of heterosexual relationships increased. Similarly, project groups and workgroups had difficulty reconciling the needs of lesbian and heterosexual women. Allen recalled, "Tanis felt that Cathy and I would never be able to be in the same room together…Forest and I didn't speak for years…this after we organized Breakaway." Allen named the disjuncture as a conflict between personal or cultural priorities, which might include art, relationships, or living collectives, and those who saw the need for outreach and organization. While the notion that "the personal is political" gave credence to the perspective that individual life choices and relationships had political import, it also served to justify and legitimate a withdrawal from the hard work of organizing. At that time, in sharp contrast to current struggles about gay marriage and gays in the military, lesbian politics were almost totally a cultural or lifestyle politics, with little attention towards state structures.

Meetings at Glide Church went on for over a year, and ended in 1972 without any organizational structure to replace them. Crosby explained the ending in logistical terms, "I had the keys…when I stopped working at Glide there was no one to open the building for women's liberation." The end of the mass meetings at Glide Church—for a multitude of reasons—meant the decline (if not the fall) of the hopes for a grand plan for the end of sexism, the fall of male domination. No singular institution, organization, ideology, or strategy was able to mobilize and direct the many women whose consciousness and life trajectories were transformed by consciousness-raising.

## Moments of Faltering: After Consciousness-Raising…?

As early as 1971 critique had emerged about the limits of consciousness-raising. In *Notes from the Second Year*, Carol Payne wrote an article entitled "Consciousness Raising: A Dead End?"[16] Jo Freeman validated the intimacy, support, and transformation developed by consciousness-raising, while warning that, "It is virtually impossible to coordinate a national action, or even a local one—assuming there could be any agreement on issues around which to coordinate one."[17] Her article "The Tyranny of Structurelessness" began circulating nationwide, arguing that a mode of organizing built on consciousness-raising groups "is politically inefficacious, exclusive and discriminatory against those who are not or cannot be tied into the friendship networks."[18]

By 1972-73 women's liberation faced a set of internal tensions and began a process of splintering and sectoralization. Though the mass meetings ended, women who'd been mobilized and politicized through consciousness-raising groups poured energy into a variety of grassroots projects: women's health collectives, anti-rape groups, women's centers, bookstores, lesbian collectives, childcare collectives, and continued meetings about forming a women's organization.

*Ms. Magazine* began publishing in 1972; NOW continued functioning in most major cities, even while eclipsed in fervor and militancy by the newer, younger women's liberationists. But in San Francisco and the greater Bay Area, these ideological divisions were not so clear and some of the fervor of what Echols calls "radical feminism" was maintained. Women who had been mobilized into women's liberation while maintaining ideological and political ties to anti-racist, anti-capitalist, and the ongoing anti-war movements met together in the hopes of forming socialist-feminist organizations. The Berkeley Oakland Women's Union (BOWU) was organized in 1973, and the San Francisco Women's Union in 1974, with the hope of creating a practice that would address the impact of class and race as well as gender on women's lives. These organizations were short-lived—by 1976 both organizations had ended, victim to internal debates and the inability to develop structures that could enable activism without overwhelming participants.[19]

A small group of women with focus and savvy, incorporated as Women's Centers Inc., succeeded in renting and staffing a small office. The tiny space on Sanchez and 16th Street belied the giant step in organizing it represented. Indeed, that office, and the one that followed in 1971 on Brady Street, called San Francisco Women's Centers, became core components of organizing and fundraising, and served as a hub for communication, resources, and the development of new projects. It also became the structure that led to the purchase and development of the San Francisco Women's Building in 1979.

Most accounts of the transformative impact of women's liberation focus on the disruptions in love, sex, and family relations. Women's liberation, like most other parts of what was known as "the Movement," was mostly comprised of young people—under 30—at a time when identity and sexual relationships are often in formation and in flux. Within the women's movement, women who had not attended college were a minority, real wages were rising, housing costs had not escalated, and social spending was increasing. Young, white, middle-class, and childless women could rightfully believe that personal transformation would garner them a better life. Younger, childless lesbians would put their energy into community building, and commit to a politics of separatism. But other women, constrained by traditional marriages, childrearing, poverty, or dead end low paying jobs, could not easily remake their lives.

Women's liberation fueled a re-ordering of women's relationship to paid work and to the labor market. While the movement was dominated by college-educated women, they were, for the most part, ill-prepared for good wage earning, having been schooled in a gender regime in which men were the main wage earners and women's secondary status assumed. Most of my interviewees altered their relationship to the labor market during the period of early women's liberation. Women's enrollment in professional schools—law, medicine, the humanities, and social sciences—rose from about 10% in the mid 1960s to close to 50% by the mid-1970s. Women challenged the sexism in psychology and psychiatry, returned to school, formed feminist therapy practices, and professionalized the work that had been done through small groups.

Women already in the labor force, as well as those who entered the labor force and understood work as desired and/or necessary to their lives, expanded the new gender analysis to look at work and class relations and developed organizations to challenge women's second class status at work. In March 1971, Union WAGE was founded at a conference at UC Berkeley with the express purpose to achieve "equal rights, equal pay, and equal opportunity" for working women.[20] ERA (Equal Rights Advocates) formed in 1974 with a similar mission but a very different mode of action. ERA was an organization of lawyers committed to litigation, while Union WAGE published a newspaper and attempted to organize through lobbying, testifying at various hearings, and organizing women workers. The Coalition of Labor Union Women (CLUW), a national organization, also formed in 1974 with a program that brought some of the issues highlighted by WAGE and ERA to the national stage. Women attempted entry into the better paid, unionized blue collar trades like carpentry, electricity, and printing. At the same time, they formed support groups, and organizations to assist them with the difficult task of challenging entrenched sexism.

Despite their short life, the socialist-feminist women's unions in the Bay Area and around the US were the voice of a politics that sought to combine an understanding of race, class, and gender. The notion that either radical feminism or cultural feminism was the dominant tendency of the emerging women's movement can only be sustained by ignoring women of color and working class and union women who were all actively organizing. Indeed, the complexity of analysis, the emphasis on race and class as well as gender, was absolutely central to women of color feminism as it emerged in the Third World Women's Alliance (TWWA) which formed its West Coast chapter in 1971. The TWWA lasted until 1980, outliving the socialist-feminist women's unions by several years.[21] The constituency and analysis that fueled the TWWA led a decade later to the formation of the Women of Color Resource Center in 1990. The organization still flourishes, lending logistical and political support to a wide variety of organizing projects.

Competing factions within women's liberation engaged in difficult and divisive conflicts. Lesbian and straight women often developed differing circles of friends and networks of activity. Nevertheless, new projects and organizations emerged to challenge institutional power in ways that consciousness-raising groups could not. The trajectory of women's health politics in San Francisco through the 1970s illustrates this movement from alternative, prefigurative institutions, to working within the public sector, encompassing both a radical critique of the medical establishment and attempts at reform. A critique of sexist medical practices gained traction as women organized to change the attitudes and practices dominant within gynecology and obstetrics at the same time that women gained and sought admission to medical school in increasing numbers. In the mid-1970s women from the 24th Street Women's Health Collective got funding to bring the ideas of self-health—of women knowing about their own bodies, and having autonomy and decision making—into San Francisco General Hospital. Penn Garvin recalled that they taught the nursing staff, worked with the medical residents, developed a lot of material in Spanish and English (both written and audiovisual), and did a lot of counseling. They taught prevention and emphasized that women have the right to know their own bodies. Knoop remained a presence at SF General for over 20 years, moving from doing classes on contraception and birth to educating about menopause.

In May 19, 1975, as a representative of the Haight Ashbury Women's Health Collective, I testified at a hearing to amend the regulations governing consent to sterilization procedures. Prior to the passage of the new regulations, patients were being asked for consent during active labor. Inordinate numbers of Puerto Rican, Black, and other minority women were coerced into sterilization. The testimony emphasized the disparities of race, class, and sex between patients and surgeons and asserted, "We hope that the [proposed] regulations will be accepted as a first and small step toward giving patients adequate protection of the law and preventing coercive, sexist and racist sterilization abuses."[22]

The 1970s also saw the birth of Women's Studies in Bay Area higher education institutions. Early classes with a focus on women began at San Francisco State College in 1973 under the auspices of what was deemed "New School," an offering of theme-based and experimental courses. The classes followed a Women's Studies Conference at UC Santa Cruz in 1971, and the initiation of Women's Studies courses at Sonoma State College and Santa Rosa Junior College. After this one-semester experiment, San Francisco State began the process of forming a Women's Studies Department, which has flourished since that time, with six full-time faculty, and a robust program offering over twenty classes a semester.

As Cade quipped in 1970, one found the women's movement at Glide Church on Friday nights. Today, we find the women's movement in San Francisco at the Women's Building on 18th Street between Valencia and Guerrero. But before entering, one should walk around the building, and even cross the street, to see the four story *MaestraPeace* mural which covers two sides of the building, and "celebrates and honors both famous and unsung women, political activists, artists, scientists and healers..." Inside the Women's Building are a variety of activities and programs, including a range of bilingual (Spanish) services, a food pantry, legal assistance, and a computer lab. The eleven organizations housed in the building operate independently, but all support and promote the mission of the building, which includes increasing economic security, building community through art and culture and "promoting Social Change to increase women's status and power..."[23]

Sara Evans argues against an analysis of the women's movement that would divide liberal from radical from socialist feminism, or neatly separate the activities of consciousness-raising from the organizational, advocacy, or legislative activity of subsequent groups. The range of activities engendered by women's liberation in its forty plus years in San Francisco supports Evans' contention that, "as a social movement [the women's movement] defies most of the dichotomies that social movement historians and activists alike have tried to impose."[24]

Consciousness-raising and the movement it birthed, women's liberation, did not change the world for women. But by giving voice to the experiences of women of all classes and colors, women grew in voice and power, and began to challenge the multiple ways that our lives are constrained. Transforming possibility and probability for ourselves, for our sisters and daughters, our mothers and friends, for women here and around the world, remaking and revisioning the world for women—that is our legacy.

# Notes

1.   Thanks to the many people who generously shared their time and insights in interviews conducted between 1992 and 1995 for my original research, and who are quoted throughout this essay: Cathy Cade, Nyla Gladden, Chude (Pamela Parker) Allen, Estelle Jelinek, Forest (formerly Gretchen) Milne, Judy Brady (formerly Syfers), Judith Knoop, Sandy Boucher, Jean Crosby, Pat Smith, Jackie Weiss, Beverly Rutzick, Sandy Blair, Laurie Cahn, Tanis Walters, Ann Farrar, and Penn Garvin.

2.   Chude (Pamela Parker) Allen, interviews with author June 16, 1993 and June 30, 1993. (Allen active in the Civil Rights Movement as Pamela Parker married Robert Allen. She later took a new first name and is known as Chude Allen.)

3.   Pamela Allen, *Free Space, a perspective on the small group in women's liberation* (New York, Times Change Press, 1970).

4.   *CHANGE: a Working Women's Newspaper*, (March 1971): 7. Microfilm, Women's Herstory Collection, Doe Library, UC Berkeley.

5.   *Mother Lode*, no. 1, (January 1971). Microfilm, Women's Herstory Collection, Doe Library, UC Berkeley.

6.   Judy Grahn, "Introduction, Alta: Saying Stuff," in *The Shameless Hussy* by Alta (Trumansburg, New York: The Crossing Press, 1980) vii.

7.   Judy Grahn, *The Work of a Common Woman, The Collected Poems of Judy Grahn 1964-1970* (Trumansburg New York: The Crossing Press, 1978) 60.

8.   Susan Griffin, *Made From This Earth, An Anthology of Writings* (New York: Harper & Row, 1982) 253-265.

9.   Boston Women's Health Book Collective, ed., *Our Bodies, Ourselves* (Boston: New England Free Press, 1970).

10.  Ann Koedt, *The Myth of the Vaginal Orgasm* (Boston: New England Free Press, 1969).

11.  Laurie Cahn, interview with author, 1995; See Estella Habal's essay "Filipino Americans in the Decade of the International Hotel" in this volume for more information on the struggle.

12.  Sudosfloppen in Allen, *Free Space*, 4.

13.  Luther P. Gerlach and Virginia Hine, *People, power, change; movements of social transformation* (Indianapolis, Bobbs-Merril, 1970) 55.

14.  San Francisco Women's Liberation Internal Newsletter. Microfilm, Women's Herstory Collection, Doe Library, UC Berkeley.

15.  Ibid.

16.  Carol Payne, "Consciousness Raising: A Dead End?" in *Notes from the Second Year: Women's Liberation, Major Writing of the Radical Feminists*, ed. Shulamith Firestone (New York: Radical Feminism, 1970).

17.  Jo Freeman, "The Origins of the Women's Liberation Movement," *American Journal of Sociology* 78 (January 1973): 809.

18.  Joreen (Jo Freeman), *"The Tyranny of Structurelessness,"* in *Radical Feminism*, eds. Ann Koedt, Ellen Levine and Anita Rapone (New York: Quadrangle/The New York Times Book Co., 1972).

19.  Karen V. Hansen, "Women's Unions and the Search for Political Identity," in *Women, Class, and the Feminist Imagination*, eds. Hansen and Ilene J. Phillipson (Philadelphia: Temple University Press, 1990) 215.

20.  Union Women's Alliance To Gain Equality Records, 1986, file 22, Electronic Inventory, History, Labor Archives & Research Center, San Francisco State University.

21.  Kimberly Springer, *Living for the Revolution, Black Feminist Organizations, 1968-1980* (Durham and London: Duke University Press, 2005) 66.

22.  Deborah Gerson (Testimony, Hearing on Sterilization Regulations, May 1975). Original in possession of author.

23.  The Women's Building, *A Room of Our Own*. (brochure, San Francisco, n.d.), or www.womensbuilding.org.

24.  Sara M. Evans, "Beyond Declension, Feminist Radicalism in the 1970s and 1980s," in *The World the Sixties Made*, eds. Van Gosse and Richard Moser (Philadelphia: Temple University Press, 2003) 53.

# Sometimes You Work with the Democrats, and Sometimes You Riot

## by Tommi Avicolli Mecca

By 1968, San Francisco's LGBT community was experiencing the same generation gap as the rest of the country. The reason was simple: the old homophile activists who had managed to forge a gay civil rights movement amid the extreme sexual repression (not to mention anti-Communist hysteria) of the 1950s and early 1960s found themselves out of touch with young queers who were among those clashing in the streets with police over the Vietnam War, and taking over the offices of college campus administrators to demand more freedom of speech and assembly. Revolution was in the air. Those young people got high, dropped acid, listened to rock music and rejected most social norms. They walked around in jeans, t-shirts, and with long hair. They lived in communes. They experimented with sex.

For homophiles, there was no room for "doing your own thing." At its annual July 4 Reminder Day Demonstrations outside Philadelphia's Independence Hall, homophile activists walked the picket line properly dressed: men in suits and ties, women in dresses and heels. No one was permitted to participate in jeans or t-shirts—or in drag! Movement leaders all over the country thought that by putting their best foot forward they could achieve success. By reinforcing the idea that not all gay men were effeminate and all lesbians butch, homosexuals would be accepted as "just like everyone else," except of course for what they did in bed.

## Rioting in the Cafeteria

In San Francisco, the gap wasn't only along lines of political ideology. It was also manifested in the militancy of transgenders who were on the cutting edge of social change. They weren't sitting around waiting for homophiles to invite them to the table.

In 1961, José Sarria, a Latino drag performer at the Black Cat Café in North Beach, who often led patrons in a rousing chorus of "God Save Us Nelly Queens" (to the tune of "God Save The Queen"), declared himself a candidate for a seat on the San Francisco Board of Supervisors. He did it to protest police harassment and shakedown (as in payoffs) of gay bars. Though he didn't win, he managed to get 5,600 votes citywide, quite a feat for an open drag queen.

Sarria was as unapologetic about being queer ("There is nothing wrong with being gay, the crime is getting caught," he used to say) as one could possibly be. He started working at the Black Cat in the 1940s. Before long, he was singing opera at the club, changing the lyrics of the arias to warn patrons of possible police entrapment at gay hangouts. After closing with "God Save Us Nelly Queens," he sometimes led patrons on impromptu marches to the nearby jail to sing to the gay prisoners, men arrested in those raids. "United we stand, divided they will pick us off one by one," he always said. Though police tried in 1949 to close the bar, owners sued and the California Supreme Court ruled that it could not be closed simply because its patrons were gay.

In August, 1966, a riot at Compton's Cafeteria in the Tenderloin, a poor area of town, exploded after cops tried to escort a rowdy queen out of the eatery and other transgenders came to her defense. Compton's was popular with queens, hustlers, and others that society (and even the gay and lesbian community) considered marginal at best. Queens were generally not permitted in the gay bars. During the melee that night, the diner's front windows were shattered. Police had to call for help to calm the crowd. The following night, transgenders picketed the establishment and again, the windows ended up in pieces on the ground.

In the aftermath of that incident, transgenders started working with neighborhood police liaison Elliot Blackstone, and with an activist doctor at the Department of Public Health who headed up what was then called the Center for Special Problems. They also formed a group, Conversion Our Goal, at the local Glide Memorial Church, a progressive Christian denomination which would soon become a center for social change under the leadership of the Rev. Cecil Williams.

## "Society for Idle Rap"

Change was happening on other fronts as well. Society for Individual Rights (SIR), which started out in 1964 as an assimilationist group ("Responsible action by responsible people in responsible ways" was its motto), turned more radical under Leo Laurence, who was hired in 1969 as its magazine editor. SIR published *Vector*, a nationally distributed publication that could be purchased on newsstands in San Francisco. SIR had already been branded the "Society for Idle Rap" after the group refused to come out against the Vietnam War because it might make queers look bad. The group preferred gays *in* the military, rather than *out* on the streets protesting the war.

Laurence was at odds with that stance. He had been radicalized in 1968 while working as a reporter during the tumultuous Democratic Convention in Chicago at which protesters were beaten and tear-gassed by an out-of-control police force under orders from Mayor Richard Daley. Within no time at all, Laurence offended the sensibilities of what he termed SIR's "middle-class, uptight, bitchy old queens," by calling for queers to form alliances with radical groups such as the Black Panthers. He also advocated for a gay revolution and an abandonment of the reformist politics SIR and other homophile groups engaged in.

The final straw for the "old queens" came after a photo of Laurence and his boyfriend Gale Whittington appeared on the cover of the underground newspaper *Berkeley Barb*. The *Barb* obtained the photo from a photographer who had shot pictures of the two men for a *Vector* article on gay men's fashion trends. It was taken from among the more informal shots he did. The paper used it to illustrate an interview with Laurence about the new gay militancy.

Laurence was fired from his position as editor. His lover, too, lost his job after his employer at the States Line Steamship saw the picture. Laurence and Whittington didn't take any of it sitting down. They formed the Committee for Homosexual Freedom, which was more in your face than SIR ever was. They also organized pickets at Whittington's old job, which didn't succeed in getting Whittington's job back, but added a more militant flavor to the movement in those days just before Stonewall.

## Here a Ghetto, There a Ghetto

The gay ghetto area of San Francisco was in flux, too. While in the early 1960s it had been centered in the Polk/Tenderloin, by the end of the decade, refugees from the Haight-Ashbury Summer of Love and from all over the country were pouring into a place known as Eureka Valley. The residents of the heavily Irish (and to a lesser degree Italian and Latino) neighborhood were moving on to their piece of the American Dream and renting out their rundown, old Victorians for low rent.

The hippie and countercultural gays began setting up collective households and shaping what would become the world's most famous gay ghetto. Other arrivals, who were less politically inclined, forged the infamous "Castro clone" look: short hair, jeans, plaid shirts, boots. They hung out in the bars and out on the streets. The division between them and the activists wasn't always that clear cut.

As Mark Freeman relates in "Coming Out as a Reluctant Activist in a Gay Maoist Cell who Mostly Just Wanted to Get Laid" in *Smash the Church, Smash the State: the early years of gay liberation*, "As gay activists, we leafletted the bars, and gay libbers typically chanted "Out of the bars and into the streets!" as we marched by. I was more than a little interested in getting myself into the bars and between the sheets."[1]

Within no time at all, businesses from the Polk started relocating to the new hood.

Neither the Castro nor the Polk was the first gay neighborhood in San Francisco. That distinction goes to North Beach, which was home to the City's Italian/Sicilian immigrants. Bars such as the Black Cat Café, Finocchio's, and Mona's featured drag entertainment before the Beat poets found their way to that part of town. Poet Lawrence Ferlinghetti set up a bookstore and publishing house called City Lights that would bring Beat poetry worldwide attention.

Ferlinghetti and his bookstore would face their first legal challenge when *Howl*, a collection of verse from a queer Beat named Allen Ginsberg, was banned as "obscene" because of its queer content (lines such as "who let themselves be fucked in the ass by saintly motorcyclists"). Fortunately, Ferlinghetti was acquitted in 1957 and went on to publish many more wonderfully "obscene" poems. Ginsberg became a central figure in the youth movement, and in fact, one of its first out queer voices.

In the early '60s, after police started cracking down on the North Beach bars, the Polk and Tenderloin areas, which adjoin each other, became the central gay hood. By 1966, there were scores of gay bars, bathhouses, sex shops, and hotels. The areas became a refuge for poor, working-class, and street working gay men and transgenders. Many queer organizations set up office space there, including the Mattachine Society, Daughters of Bilitis, the first community center operated by SIR, and the National Transsexual Counseling Unit.

## Friday of the Purple Hand

In summer 1969, a new activism suddenly spread across the country from the East Coast after a routine police raid on the Stonewall bar in New York in June 1969 turned into a riot. The Gay Liberation Front (GLF), which took its name from the National Liberation Front, the Vietnamese group fighting US occupation of its country, formed within days of that incident and established a new consciousness that saw the fight against gay oppression as part of other liberation struggles. GLF made coalitions with feminists, anti-war groups, the Young Lords (a Puerto Rican organization), and the Black Panthers.

Post-Stonewall activism in San Francisco would mirror what was happening elsewhere. As a local 1970 pamphlet described it, "The Gay Liberation Front is a nation-wide coalition of revolutionary homosexual organizations creating a radical counterculture within the homosexual lifestyles." More militant queer organizations formed and LGBT folks visibly joined the ranks of anti-war marches and be-ins in Golden Gate Park, not to mention challenged the Left to deal with its homophobia.

It wasn't always a bed of roses. Leftist males used "faggot" as a putdown of enemies, such as Richard Nixon and his Secretary of State Henry Kissinger. They didn't always understand that the word was offensive to gays. In *Smash the Church*, former New York GLFer John Lauritsen relates how at a Youth Against War and Fascism conference in support of the Black Panthers (who were being murdered and arrested by the government), gay liberationists raised a fuss about a speaker who kept using the word "faggot." "The YAWF organizers were taken aback momentarily," Lauritsen writes, "but then did the right thing: They explained to him that the word faggot could not be used in their forum. He finished the talk, still angry, without using the word again. For the three of us, this episode was a milestone in our journey to self-respect: no more silently listening to antigay insults, no more crap!"

No more crap indeed. On Halloween night 1969, members of GLF and SIR gathered outside the *San Francisco Examiner* building to protest anti-gay articles that had been running in the daily. Like other periodicals around the country, the paper had a policy of printing the names and addresses of men arrested in gay bar raids or even in tearooms, bathrooms where gay men sometimes had sex. When employees on the roof spilled purple printer's ink down onto the demonstrators, the queer radicals used it to scrawl "Gay Power" and other slogans on the wall. They also left imprints of their hands on the surrounding buildings, thus giving rise to what became known as "Friday of the Purple Hand."

Larry LittleJohn, who was then SIR president, relates what happened next:

> At that point, the tactical squad arrived—not to get the employees who dumped the ink, but to arrest the demonstrators who were the victims. The police could have surrounded the *Examiner* building...but no, they went after the gays...Somebody could have been hurt if that ink had gotten into their eyes, but the police came racing in with their clubs swinging, knocking people to the ground. It was unbelievable.[2]

The media wasn't the only target. The American Psychiatric Association (APA) classified homosexuality as a mental illness. Homophile groups had been lobbying the APA for years to change that designation. San Francisco GLF disrupted a 1970 gathering of shrinks at a convention center downtown. That same year, GLFers in Los Angeles took over a similar meeting of the APA and conducted a consciousness-raising session with the befuddled doctors. The APA eventually succumbed to the pressure and in 1973 dropped homosexuality from its list of diseases.

## What Was on Everyone's Minds

Politics wasn't the only arena in which the new radical queer consciousness took root. The Cockettes, a radical gay male hippie drag troupe that mocked both traditional gender roles and social norms in general, became the City's most popular alternative entertainment, packing in crowds at every performance.

The name Cockettes came from group member, Ralph. As Rumi Missabu remembers, "He named us Cockettes after the Rockettes because it was always on our minds anyway." Success swelled the ranks of those who called themselves Cockettes. "Originally we were a company of 13 that included 10 men, three women and an infant," Missabu said. "Within six months and after a lot of publicity, there were 65 people onstage for the first Halloween show. Now, as archivist, I count 168 people who were in one show or another."[3] Among those Cockette alumni was Sylvester, an African-American gay man who knocked them dead with his rendition, in his own voice, of old Bessie Smith songs. Sylvester would emerge a decade later as one of the country's hottest disco singers.

In finest Sixties tradition, all one had to do to be a Cockette was to show up for a rehearsal. Though the troupe considered itself nonpolitical, its antics made a political statement nonetheless. A good example was its video spoof of Tricia (daughter of then-president Richard Nixon) Nixon's wedding that included a drag Eartha Kitt spiking the punch bowl with acid. The ensuing sexual orgy between the Nixons and the guests at the wedding made it an overnight underground success and a fitting mockery of the country's then-ruling class.

## Like the Jewish Bread

Berkeley's GLF came together in the summer of 1970. It gave birth to *Gay Sunshine*, a local queer newspaper with a heavy blend of gay and leftist politics. In its premiere issue, August 1970, collective member Nick Benton, who now publishes the leftist *Falls Church News-Press* just outside Washington, DC, wrote that the publication would be for "those who understand themselves as oppressed—politically oppressed by an oppressor that not only is down on homosexuality, but equally down on all things that are not white, straight, middle class, pro-establishment." GLF member Winston Leyland eventually took the publication to San Francisco where he published it for over a decade, elevating it to national prominence. In its heyday, it featured interviews with such gay luminaries of the mainstream arts world as playwright Tennessee Williams, author Gore Vidal, writer Christopher Isherwood, and French existentialist writer/playwright Jean Genet.

In 1974, Bay Area Gay Liberation (BAGL), pronounced like the Jewish bread, continued the work of earlier liberation groups. Like its counterparts, it, too, saw the connection among all oppressed groups and blended socialism and gay liberation.

Tom Ammiano, now a California State Assemblymember, was a member of BAGL. He writes in *Smash the Church* that BAGL "only lasted for one year—too many sectarians spoil the stew—but what a year it was! We took to the streets. We picketed. It was exhilarating and effective."[4] Ammiano, an out gay teacher at the time, took on the San Francisco School Board because sexual orientation was not included in the district's nondiscrimination policy. In June, 1975, Ammiano and his supporters were victorious and the Board passed a policy protecting queer teachers. Ammiano would eventually become president of the School Board. And afterwards, a longtime member of the Board of Supervisors.

The year 1975 also saw the repeal of California's sodomy laws. Introduced every year since 1969 by Assemblymember Willie Brown (who would serve two terms as mayor of San Francisco in the 1990s), the legislation to grant consenting adults the right to non-missionary position sex acts finally passed after Democratic State Senate Majority Leader George Moscone (who would be elected mayor in 1977) forced legislators to remain behind locked doors until a deadlock was broken.

## Strangers in a Strange Land

While many of the post-Stonewall groups had lesbian participation, they tended to be male-dominated. Many lesbians preferred to work with other women, either queer or straight.

Lesbians thrived not so much in the Polk or the Castro, but instead along the Valencia corridor of the Mission District where rents were cheaper. They set up bookstores and separatist households. They worked with their feminist sisters on projects such as the San Francisco Women's Centers which opened in 1971, and is still going strong as the Women's Building.[5] They sponsored cultural events at which out lesbian poets, such as Pat Parker and Judy Grahn, read, and musicians sang about the pride and power of the emerging lesbian community. By 1977, the National Center for Lesbian Rights had been established and Joani Blank, a sex therapist, opened up Good Vibrations, a sex shop for women that was an alternative to the dark, dingy places men inhabited.

Queers of color, too, found themselves strangers in a strange land. They didn't always feel welcome in the Castro or in White-dominated organizations. In 1964, a bar owned by and operated for African-American gays opened in the Fillmore area, a predominantly Black section of the City that would later be targeted for "urban renewal" by the Redevelopment Agency in a project out gay author James Baldwin termed "Negro Removal." Thousands of Blacks were displaced when bulldozers smashed their houses. [6]

Unfortunately, White queers were sometimes among the gentrifiers, which caused problems with communities of color. As Grahn relates:

> Then around 1978 the Haight-Ashbury began to revert to its gay ghetto origins, this time with a new coat of paint, as it was 'gentrified' by single white men with money to invest in the beautiful old Victorian houses and to open small, attractive businesses. These investors were continually pointed out as Gay. Many poor people, especially Black, who had moved to the Haight to take advantage of the lower rents or who had been there all along, were pushed out and forced to move, accelerating the anti-Gay feeling in the Black areas.[7]

In the 1970s, people of color organizations formed within the LGBT community, including Gay American Indians (founded by Randy Burns and Barbara Cameron in 1975), Gay Latino Alliance (in 1975), and Gay Asian Information Network (founded by Randy Kikuchi in 1977).

# The Orange Juice Queen Cometh

Perhaps the greatest test for the new queer movement came in 1977 when orange juice spokesperson and former Miss America runner up Anita Bryant waged a successful campaign in her hometown of Dade County, Florida to repeal its newly enacted gay rights bill. Her conservative Christian movement spread throughout the country, toppling other gay rights bills in its wake and leading the way for the emergence of the so-called Moral Majority, led by evangelical preacher Jerry Falwell. Immediately after the Dade County bill went down in flames, San Francisco Assemblyman Art Agnos (who would go on to become mayor in 1988) withdrew his proposed statewide gay rights bill.

Conservative California State Senator John Briggs, having been with Bryant on election night to witness her tremendous success, led the charge on the West Coast with Proposition 6, also known as the Briggs Initiative, an attempt to ban out queer teachers in the schools. With rhetoric such as, "Defend your children from homosexual teachers," Briggs' California Defend Our Children (CDOC) swung into action to try and make the state the first to officially ban gay educators.

San Francisco activists played a huge part in its defeat. Out gay Supervisor Harvey Milk, along with activists Sally Gearhart, Gwen Craig, and others, took a direct approach to the fight, confronting Briggs and his supporters on their homophobia. Milk even debated Briggs, despite the fact that more moderate activists such as David Goodstein, publisher of the gay weekly, *the Advocate*, wanted a professional advertising agency to handle the campaign.

What many think tipped the scales in favor of the queer community was a statement from Ronald Reagan, who had stopped being governor only two years before, "Prop. 6 is not needed to protect our children. We have that legal protection now. It could be very costly to implement and has the potential for causing undue harm to people." The gay community had flexed its muscle like never before.

# Real Estate Predators

A new threat loomed. In the late 1970s, the Castro neighborhood was targeted by real estate speculators and without rent control and just cause eviction protections, many gay tenants were displaced. Harvey Milk lost his camera store and apartment on Castro Street when his rent was tripled. All the work that gays had done in fixing up the Victorians would pay off—for the real estate predators out for a quick buck.

The Housing Rights Group, an anti-gentrification mobilization, published a newspaper about the encroaching gentrification. In it appeared the names of the speculators and others responsible for "the steady increase of rents and property values; renovated buildings; for-sale signs; and exodus of black and other Third World people, especially families out of the neighborhoods." The paper also said:

> In areas like Castro/Eureka Valley, rents have risen so fast that gay people who do not have a lot of money are now finding it difficult to rent in that area...Recently this played in the hands of real-estate profiteers who are 'referring' gay people in need of housing to low-income minority neighborhoods. With the shortage of housing in San Francisco, gay people find themselves

in competition with other people, especially Third-World families who seek decent, reasonably-priced housing. This situation is often the underlying cause of tension and hostility between gay people and their neighbors.

Even a non-political magazine such as *After Dark*, a now defunct, slick arts magazine with heavy gay overtones, noted the change in everybody's favorite new gay hangout.

Unfortunately, things would get even grimmer. In November 1978, Milk was shot, along with Mayor George Moscone, by Supervisor Dan White. The former cop got off easy on a junk-food defense (known as the "Twinkie Defense," for the popular snack of the decade). He was sentenced to only five years in prison. Queers rioted on the day of the sentencing, setting police cars on fire and smashing the glass doors of City Hall. It was a fitting ending to a tumultuous decade that saw us go from homophiles and rebellious queens to militants who understood that sometimes you worked with the Democrats and sometimes you tore up City Hall.

## Aftermath

Today, the Castro is much quieter than it has been in the past 40 years. Gentrification has taken its toll. Gone are the weekly protests that used to fill the corner of Castro and Market, Harvey Milk Plaza, as it is called, with angry activists demanding government action on AIDS; an end to antigay discrimination in housing, employment and public accommodations; the defeat of anti-immigrant or anti-affirmative action initiatives; and the legalization of medical marijuana.

When the dot-com boom hit the City, thousands of long-term tenants were evicted, pushed out by greedy landlords anxious to re-rent their apartments for more money. Those landlords found ways to get around the City's rent control protections. In the Castro, horror stories abounded: a man with AIDS on a respirator, who didn't have long to live, was given an eviction notice. In another case, several men with AIDS, including a nationally syndicated gay cartoonist for the *Advocate*, were thrown out of their apartments that they had lived in since the early 1970s.

Young queers, still fleeing to the Castro as they had for three decades, suddenly found that, even with jobs, they could not afford the rents. Many ended up living on the streets, which caused merchants and land owners in the neighborhood to freak out. Battlelines were quickly drawn. Some of us reacted with compassion, setting up services for the newly homeless—specifically a food program, a place to shower, and three winter emergency shelters.

By the end of the 1990s, the neighborhood would erupt with a political campaign like no other, an effort to elect the City's first gay progressive mayor. The candidate: Tom Ammiano. Though the effort ultimately failed, what the Ammiano campaign managed to do, in addition to mobilizing the Left in San Francisco as it had probably not been for a long time, was to win six seats on the Board of Supervisors the following year for neighborhood activists of a progressive bent. But after the campaign posters came down, the neighborhood further gentrified.

A similar fate awaits the Polk/Tenderloin, the last refuge for poor queers. As the *San Francisco Bay Guardian* reported just two years ago, former gay male and transgender bars in the neighborhood are now hangouts for twenty-something straight yuppies.[8] Even trendy restaurants have moved in. One of the new businesspeople wants to rename the area "Polk Village" to make it more appealing to the folks he wishes to draw in. The neighborhood associations want to permanently evict the working-class and poor residents, most of them queer. They have enlisted the help of the police and even the District Attorney. It looks as if it's a matter of time before what once was a haven for sexual outlaws and poor transgenders will become what San Francisco doesn't need more of: another high-rent district.

As Mattilda Bernstein Sycamore, a Polk resident and editor of several queer anthologies, told the *Guardian*:

> Polk Street has been the last remaining place where marginalized queers can come to figure out how to cope, meet one another, and form social networks. That sort of outsider culture has been so dependent on having a public space to figure out ways to survive. That is the dream of San Francisco — that you can get away from where you came from and cope, and create something dangerous and desperate and explosive.[9]

These days, that dream is looking more and more like something from out of the past.

## Endnotes

1. Mark Freeman "Coming Out as a Reluctant Activist in a Gay Maoist Cell Who Mostly Just Wanted to Get Laid," in *Smash the Church, Smash the State: The Early Years of Gay Liberation*, ed. Tommi Avicolli Mecca (San Francisco: City Lights Books, 2009).

2. en.wikipedia.org/wiki/LGBT_symbols (accessed February 21, 2010).

3. Mecca, *Smash the State*.

4. Ibid.

5. See Deborah Gerson's essay "Making Sexism Visible: Women's Liberation Emerges in the Turbulent Decade" in this volume for more on intersections between the lesbian and the women's movement.

6. See Rachel Brahinsky's essay "'Hush Puppies,' Communalist Politics, and Demolition Governance: The Rise and Fall of the Black Fillmore" in this volume for issues of urban renewal and redevelopment.

7. Judith Grahn, *Another Mother Tongue: Gay Words, Gay Worlds* (Boston: Beacon Press, 1984).

8. *San Francisco Bay Guardian* 48 (August 29, 2007).

9. Ibid.

# Coming Together
## The Communal Option

### By Matthew Roth

Communal living, labor collectives, and cooperative economies have a storied history in the United States, from several of the first Pilgrim settlements, to frontier communities pushing west into the wilderness, the Owenite Socialists in the 1820s, Mormons shortly after, Abolitionist colonies prior to the Civil War, the Knights of Labor and collective organizing during the Long Depression after the Civil War, and the barter economies among great masses of the unemployed living in Hoovervilles during the Great Depression. In times of political, social, and economic difficulty, Americans have consistently turned to each other for help, cooperating rather than competing, helping each other create better conditions for life and social associations.[1]

At no point, however, did more people seek out community than in the mid-to-late 1960s. At the height one of the most prosperous moments in American economic history, hundreds of thousands of young people turned away from the money and material comfort their capitalistic nuclear families provided in search of a more authentic expression of connectedness to the people around them, creating the largest swelling of communalism in US history. These predominantly young, White Americans chose to cooperate and share, disavowing the wider economic, social, and political norms, to posit themselves in a radical stance just outside the boundaries of normative, "straight" society.

Though many communards didn't consider themselves political radicals, most could be dubbed, as historian Laurence Veysey argues, cultural radicals. In Veysey's analysis, political radicalism "engages directly in the immediate struggle for power, relegating all other consideration to a distinctly secondary role." On the other hand, the "self-directed living of life rather than the contest for power is the primary aim of cultural radicals."[2] Another useful label for the communal experiments was "contraculture," coined by the sociologist J. Milton Yinger in 1960, a word meant to indicate a movement in opposition to the dominant culture and intended to reform the mores and ethos of that dominance. By the time Theodore Roszack's *The Making of the Counter Culture* appeared in 1968, "counterculture" had become the nominal term used for hippie communards and the cultural radicalism they embodied.[3]

My parents were two of those cultural radicals. They joined a spiritual commune in Santa Barbara, California, my father in 1969 and mother in 1972, and lived communally until 1987. Although the setting of their commune was several hundred miles south of San Francisco, their experiences mirrored those of many of San Francisco's communards.

My father, like so many his age, lived a comfortable life in a tranquil town 30 miles south of San Francisco. His family wanted for nothing, but he couldn't shake a growing feeling of discomfort with the lifestyle his parents led. The television transmitted images of Black marchers on the business end of fire hoses and German Shepherds, and a Vietnam War growing daily less defensible or winnable. He became distrustful of his government and the narrative that it preached: America did only right by the world.

While attending Stanford University, he tried LSD for the first time, which sharpened his alienation from his family and his straight friends. He went out to La Honda and tripped with Ken Kesey and the Merry Pranksters; he saw the Diggers in San Francisco's Panhandle, giving away food for free. He spent time with the Jesus People and witnessed the Hare Krishnas chanting and singing through the Haight, before he finally landed in Santa Barbara with a group led by Norman Paulsen, a disciple of the Hindu mystic Paramahansa Yogananda, whose *Autobiography of a Yogi* was one of the more accessible texts for hippies trying to understand eastern religious teachings (another disciple of Yogananda's, Donald Walters or Sri Kryananda, founded the Ananda Institute in Nevada City, California, a three-hour drive from San Francisco).[4]

As the meditation circle in Santa Barbara morphed into an urban commune, the members raised the money to buy land outside of town, where they planted orchards and vegetable crops. They built homes and a retreat, sold food and wares in stores they founded, and took the name Sunburst (alternately Brotherhood of the Sun). By the time my mother joined the commune in 1972, there were over a hundred members, on the way to a high census of 350, and their businesses brought in enough revenue to support the membership's basic needs.

My mother, who grew up in New Jersey, had been inspired to live communally when she was in Marin County for an internship. She read Edgar Cayce and Gestalt therapy founder Fritz Perls, started meditating, and longed to find a spiritual teacher and commune. After traveling to communities in Colorado, Oregon, and California with a girlfriend, they settled at Sunburst. A few years later, I was born into the hands of a midwife in a small farmhouse that the community built from the foundation up.

Our commune never turned violent, though Paulsen put his inner circle through numerous loyalty tests, some of which involved automatic rifles and delusions of shoot-outs with local law enforcement. My parents finally left the commune after nearly two decades when they couldn't stomach the hypocrisy of living with a leader who commanded total obedience and discipline from them, and who turned around and debauched when he assumed they were not looking.

What's still difficult for me to understand is that my parents remained within Paulsen's orbit years after they learned of his alcohol and substance abuse, the rumors (later confirmed) of sexual abuse of minors, and the financial tax and funding schemes that brought the commune to its knees on several occasions, forcing migrations to northeastern Nevada, to Utah, and eventually back to California (where Sunburst continues).

My parents were devoted to, perhaps blinded by, the ideal of community, despite the dream they saw crumbling around them over the course of a decade. Their commitment might give an inclination into why so many other communards stayed too long with the unstable and dangerous leaders like Jim Jones of People's Temple, who led more than 900 of his flock to death in Jonestown, Guyana. Fortunately for my family, Paulsen was not Jim Jones and we were able to walk away without physical harm.

## Communalism in San Francisco

Although communes sprouted up all over the country in the late 1960s, few regions saw more people living communally than Northern California, with San

Francisco as its epicenter.[5] Estimates of exactly how many people lived communally in this era are varied, particularly given the strong desire among many communards to eschew media and academic attention. Most scholars on the topic, however, generally agree that upwards of 5,000 communes flowered nationally during the late 1960s and 1970s, with hundreds of thousands, if not a million, people living in them.

The roots of cultural radicalism in California go back to the 1940s when poets and writers began to settle on the Big Sur coast and shuttle back and forth between there and the Bay Area. Beat writers and musicians found sanctuary and community with each other in San Francisco in the 1950s and early 1960s, particularly in the North Beach neighborhood. Allen Ginsberg, in a speech he delivered in London in July 1967 to the Congress on the Dialectics of Liberation,[6] elaborated a basic mantra of self-improvement-as-political-engagement that was central to many communes, both secular and religious:

> Political activity linking up with social-construction activity—…
> Pound constantly quotes from, I guess, Confucius: 'To straighten out the
> nation, straighten the provinces; to straighten the province, straighten
> the city; to straighten the city, straighten households; straighten your
> household, straighten your family, straighten yourself.'

If great numbers of people embark on this path, feeling unified in this kind of effort, maybe this would be the beginning of "a friendly communism, or communion, or community, or friendly extension of self outward; if they have glimpsed that and if they are willing to trust that."[7]

By the early 1960s, Ken Kesey's Palo Alto home had become one of the urban proto-communes that led to the wider growth of communal living. In 1959, Kesey had volunteered to be a subject of controlled experiments with psychoactive drugs such as LSD, which he and his visitors used repeatedly for several years. His home became a regular hangout for beat poets, musicians like Jerry Garcia of the Grateful Dead, and all manner of experimental trippers who wanted to explore the effects of the drug, which was legal until 1966. With the proceeds from the sale of *One Flew Over the Cuckoo's Nest,* in 1963 Kesey purchased a larger rural property in La Honda.[8] The La Honda encampment was dotted with people living in claptrap dwellings or vehicles that had been altered to accommodate sleeping facilities. Though Kesey eventually grew tired of the scene he had fostered—what he began calling "The Communal Lie"—his La Honda experiment presaged an explosion of back-to-the land communal experiments that grew up around San Francisco and in many other parts of the country by the late 1960s and early 1970s.

## The Diggers

While some members of the San Francisco communes were overtly political or had experienced political activism and organizing from the Civil Rights, Free Speech, and anti-Vietnam War movements, many more had moved to San Francisco during the Summer of Love in 1967, or shortly thereafter, to be a part of a burgeoning movement. Many read about the Haight-Ashbury hippies in coverage in the mainstream press, which by 1968 was routine. By July 18th, 1969, when *Life Magazine* published a photo essay and article of a rural commune under the title, "The Commune Comes to America," the idea of living communally had gone mainstream.

Anticipating the flood of people coming to San Francisco to be a part of the scene, a catalyzing collective of guerrilla theater actors and anarchists calling themselves the San Francisco Diggers became the standard-bearers of urban communal liberty. Living primarily in the Haight-Ashbury, the Diggers spun off of the San Francisco Mime Troupe, where they had been performing avant-garde productions in playhouses and in public parks. Embracing the old English Digger maxim of free access to the commons, the San Francisco Diggers articulated a vision of community self-sufficiency amid the bountiful surplus of post-war capitalist San Francisco. They printed broadsheets, either anonymously or under the name of The Communications Company, which they pasted around town to promote their doctrine of "Free," a utopian vision for society liberated from money, hierarchy, and property distinctions. Starting in October 1966, The Diggers went on rounds through the Haight and nearby neighborhoods each morning, what they called "garbage yoga," to collect surplus food from markets and restaurants, which they prepared and gave away for free to anyone with an appetite each afternoon at 4 p.m. in the Golden Gate Park Panhandle at Ashbury Street.

On December 3rd, 1966, the Diggers opened a "Free Store" on Page Street where they gave away donated goods and wares.[9] They dubbed it the Free Frame of Reference, derived from a tall yellow picture frame that visitors stepped through upon entering the shop, another echo of the Ginsbergian-Confucian maxim that the ability to change the world comes first from a willingness to change one's own point of view. Doctors who empathized with the Digger Free ethos began providing free medical care at the Free Store, which eventually spawned the Haight-Ashbury Free Medical Clinic.[10]

By 1968, almost as quickly as they came on to the scene, the Diggers disbanded. The actor and Digger Peter Coyote explained in his memoir that after the Summer of Love in 1967, the Haight-Ashbury was no longer the draw it had been:

> We needed land bases from which to integrate ourselves into new communities, to expand our resources and our reach. Since we had no money, we substituted cooperation and energy and helped one another establish a series of camps that we hoped would evolve eventually into networks of support.... By the time this chain of camps was established, we had begun to refer to ourselves as 'the Free Family' as often as 'the Diggers.' Our diaspora spread north out of San Francisco, and Highway 101 resembled the thread of a beaded necklace that connected us to family sites along its length.[11]

Though they inspired activists as far-flung as Abbie Hoffman and Jerry Rubin in New York City (Hoffman initially called himself a Digger until the San Francisco Diggers demanded he stop),[12] the community they inspired was on the streets and in the free stores and clinics of the Haight. Their impact on the San Francisco counterculture was as profound as any other group, with their unique appropriation of theater to politicize a new way of living in the city.[13]

## Rural Communes: Morningstar Ranch and Black Bear Ranch

Some in the Digger diaspora had already moved to the country even as the Diggers were ascendant in the city, where they settled properties and lived under the symbolic (and sometimes literal) banner, "Free Land for Free People." One of the earliest and arguably most well-known of the rural communes in California was Morningstar Ranch, a 32-acre plot of land near Sebastopol, owned initially by Lou Gottleib, the bass player for folk-music trio The Limeliters, before he deeded the property to God (in an effort to avoid having the property condemned by Sonoma County bureaucrats who disapproved of the communards living there).[14]

Gottlieb purchased the land in 1963, but didn't consider opening it up to those who sought to live communally until 1966, when he met Stewart Brand, the publisher of the *Whole Earth Catalog* and eventual co-founder of *Wired Magazine*, and Ramon Sender, a Digger whose first wife was the great-granddaughter of John Humphrey Noyes, founder of the nineteenth century utopian Oneida Community in New York State.[15] Brand piqued Gottlieb's interest in the concept of a rural commune and Sender asked Gottlieb's permission to move up to live on the land post haste. Sender was the first of many to move from San Francisco and camp out on the property, building dwellings, and tending to the apple orchard, whose bounty the Diggers spread around San Francisco.[16]

Morningstar had relatively few rules and encouraged the self-expression of those who came for a visit or to live, especially when it was artistic and sexual.[17] Not all were searching for spirituality, but Sender was, and he introduced Gottlieb to various spiritual teachers, some of whom made a great impression. Visitors included Swami A.C. Bhaktivedanta, founder of Hare Krishna, who converted a few denizens of Morningstar when he visited in 1967, and Ciranjiva Roy, a hedonistic, illicit-substance-loving former beggar from India who founded Siva Kalpa and had in tow eight "goddesses," who sired 22 of his children. Gottlieb took to Roy and considered himself a disciple, even after Roy had moved on.

As the population of Morningstar grew, scrutiny from county officials and law enforcement followed suit. Police raided in search of drugs and Sonoma County officials condemned the property for building code and sanitation violations. Gottlieb tried to outflank county officials by deeding the property to a higher authority, but the presiding judge was unmoved and the county bulldozed the buildings. In 1973, after several attempts at re-populating the land, followed by further raids, the residents of Morningstar gave up and moved away.

Further north, another rural community formed in 1967 at Black Bear Ranch, the site of a former gold mine at the end of a long dirt road in the Trinity-Siskiyou Wilderness near Mt. Shasta. Many of the residents of the commune were Diggers who had hustled the money to buy the ranch from friends with means and a few celebrities who admired the Digger style, including the Doors, Frank Zappa, Steve McQueen, Peter Tork of the Monkees, and designer Charles Eames.[18] Some of the early Black Bear settlers were drawn to the rough environs with visions of learning survival skills should revolution break out. As Peter Coyote explained it:

> We thought the government was going to be overthrown in two years and there was going to be a new culture rising from the ashes. We wanted to have an alternative, a non-mercantile alternative that offered citizens options for being something other than a consumer or an employee…. A lot of people were choosing to fight the government politically, but we saw the problem as culture. We tried to create living possibilities of an alternative culture that we hoped, when push came to shove, people would defend.[19]

Richard Marley, who put the down payment on the ranch with his wife Elsa, considered the location ripe for militant training. "Some of us thought it was a good idea to start a place out in the mountains where our city warriors [could] rest up, learn skills, [and] from which we would make forays down into the city. After all, Castro had done it just a few years before. I wanted blood brothers who would cover my back the way I would theirs when the shit hit the fan, as it was going to."[20]

Most of the early denizens of Black Bear had been raised in cities and the learning curve for survival in the remote wilderness was steep, particularly given the heavy snowfall the first winter. Though they nearly ran out of supplies, the group survived and news of the remote commune became legendary in the counterculture.[21] Waves of subsequent visitors brought with them less confrontational aspirations, softening the edges of Marley and the other early arrivals.

Cedar Seeger described his feeling for Black Bear thus, "I was really scared and lonely. The draft was breathing down my neck. When I came to Black Bear, I found that acceptance and that love. I felt like I had come home. I was like a warm puppy."

In 1987, nearly 200 former Black Bear inhabitants signed a document turning the ranch into a land trust in perpetuity, so future generations will be able to continue to bear the "Free Land for Free People" mantle.[22]

## Kaliflower

Not everyone in the Free Family left the city for rural confines. Hundreds of communes sprung up in San Francisco, Oakland and Berkeley, often composed of 10-20 people living in old Victorians, usually adopting their physical street address as their communal name. One of the more significant of these was originally situated at 1873 Sutter Street in San Francisco, and later, after they had to move because of the machinations of the Redevelopment Agency, 1209 Scott Street.

The Sutter/Scott Street commune was founded by Irving Rosenthal, a native San Franciscan who studied at the University of Chicago through much of the 1950s.[23] As editor of the *Chicago Review* in 1958 and 1959, Rosenthal published Beat writers like Allen Ginsberg, Jack Kerouac, Edward Dahlburg, Phillip Whalen, and Gregory Corso. After publishing the first parts of William Burroughs' *Naked Lunch* in the Spring and Summer 1958 issues of the *Review*, Rosenthal provoked the ire of the University, which suppressed the Winter 1959 edition. Rosenthal quit his position, moved to New York City, and raised money to publish the censored writing in a literary review he founded and called *Big Table*, which eventually led to the United States Post Office seizing the magazine and embroiling him in a protracted court battle over obscenity charges. Rosenthal prevailed in the obscenity case, moved to Tangier to live with Burroughs for two years, then returned to New York City, where he continued to edit and publish Beat writers and finished a novel of his own, *Sheepers*.[24]

In late 1967, Rosenthal moved to San Francisco, explaining in a letter to Ginsberg dated November 24th that he intended to:

> [S]et up a publishing commune bit by bit, from my part now more of a desire to give the children something better to do than shoot A…, and the first thing we need is hdqs., like a Victorian house

that might cost 30 grand and require a 10% down payment....
We think we want a house in the city or just outside it, for
convenience of shipping & printing supplies, though we might
eventually want an agricultural branch in the country. The goal
is for the commune to be completely self-supporting.[25]

The Sutter/Scott Street commune published a weekly inter-communal
newsletter titled *Kaliflower*, which by 1971 was being distributed to more than
300 communes in the Bay Area, at least 50 of them East Bay.[26] The newsletter was
printed on a Chief 15 offset press in the in the commune's basement, what became
known as the Free Print Shop. Because of the popularity and ubiquity of the
publication, the commune eventually became known to most of the outside world
as Kaliflower. The newsletter was published weekly by the commune from April
1969 to December 1971, and intermittently thereafter. Initially *Kaliflower* served
as an inter-communal bulletin board, listing items needed by one commune, items
offered by another, with light editorial content, and occasional poems and missives.
The newsletter also contained how-to articles and skills sharing. In a *Kaliflower*
from November 26, 1970, an article provided instructions for building cold boxes
to grow food, as well as a recipe for squash soup. The *Kaliflower* from December
10th, 1970, offered instruction for "Yoga Nazal Cleaning" and herbal hair care.

Gradually the editorial content of *Kaliflower* became more involved, offering
historical context for modern communalism among a long lineage of American
utopian experiments. In the cover article "Communal Archaeology," from May 6,
1971, the first issue of Volume Three with a larger format, the authors acknowledge
the debt the communal movement of the 1960s and 1970s owed to the Revivalist
explosion of communes in the 1820s and 1840s, notably the Oneida Commune
of John Humphrey Noyes:

> [Noyes] also relates the Socialist movements which formed so
> many of the communes to the Revivalist movements which
> turned on the nation during the same period—these waves
> seem like the spiritual and social revolutions of nowadays, and
> the Secrets of Success seem to spring, then and now, from
> the commingling of the juices of these two aspects. There are
> differences, of course, between our communes and those of the
> last century—we inhabit the magical margins of the Surplus
> Society, while they were made up of Common People, who
> had to work hard for economic survival, though their toil was
> lessened by communal living.[27]

Those who lived in Kaliflower often cut ties to non-communalist friends and
relatives, taking their communal brothers and sisters as their adopted new families.
Chandler Downs, a former member of Kaliflower, said that attachment to a single
sexual partner was frowned upon and most communards were polyamorous, sleeping
in a group bed and regularly rotating sexual partners in what was loosely considered
group marriage. When new members joined, they gave up their savings to the group
and were encouraged not to take outside jobs, but to grow food in the communal
garden or work in the Free Print Shop and help deliver the newsletter.[28]

Decisions about the direction of the commune tended to be made by an inner circle of Kaliflower residents that had been there longest, though unresolved differences deferred to Rosenthal's authority. A group encounter session called "The Criticism" was used to vent concerns and anger with other community members. One person was called in front of a committee of others and anything could be said about them, though they couldn't respond until three days later, and only then in writing. While sessions could be embarrassing or highly critical, according to Downs, they also made one stronger. "The psychology of being secretive was not cool. It broke apart your centers."[29]

Like the Diggers, Kaliflower acknowledged the role the great bounty of the post-war society had on their undertaking and embraced the ethos of Free. Rosenthal wrote in a long essay titled "Deep Tried Frees" in Volume V of *Kaliflower*:

> [I]n the midst of a drastic social and religious upheaval, free was put forward as an ideal whose time had come—a way of feeding and caring for a swelling number of hungry and jobless people.... Among the Kaliflower communes, free was not absolutely necessary for survival (though it made life a lot easier). For us it grew into a way of expressing closeness. Nuclear family members don't usually buy and sell to each other, are in fact communistic, and we wanted nuclear family intimacy among the communes. We wanted a society of communes so unestranged that everyone felt like each other's brother or sister. This became the *raison d'être* of intercommunal free, and free became the communes' hallmark. So free was carried from 1969 forward, not strictly from hunger. It showed itself to be an ideal with more strings to play than one.[30]

Kaliflower helped organize the Free Food Conspiracy in 1968 (later the Free Food Family), where participating communes pooled member food stamps and bought large volumes of food to distribute to each commune based on need.[31] By 1973, 150 member communes participated in San Francisco.[32] Rosenthal considered the Food Conspiracy an important test of cooperation between communes, which he hoped would lead to further pooling of resources to buy property and land for the Free Family.

The various food conspiracies in the Bay Area and across the country (national estimates: 5,000 to 10,000) caught the attention of those in Washington DC. Congress amended the Food Stamp Act in 1971, including a provision meant to directly target communes by limiting welfare to houses where the inhabitants were related. Though the US Supreme Court in *USDA v. Moreno* in 1973 would strike down the commune clause under the equal protection provision of the 5th Amendment, Congress clearly considered the communal embrace of welfare abusive and the communes knew they were being targeted.[33]

By then, the San Francisco Food Conspiracy had reached its upper limit and many communes stopped pooling. Rosenthal bemoaned this failure. "Simply put, most participating communes actually liked where they were at and felt no need to commit themselves more deeply. The Free Food Family actually was a kind of watershed, in that it brought us to the absolute outside limit of intercommunal cooperation."[34]

## From a Monday Night Class to The Farm

One of the seminal communitarians bridging the urban with the rural, the cultural radical with the spiritual, was Steven Gaskin, a faculty member at San Francisco State. Gaskin wasn't particularly interested in hippie culture until his students convinced him to watch The Beatles' *A Hard Day's Night*, after which he "fell in love with John Lennon." He started using LSD and exploring the hippie scene, which suited him very well. In 1967, he convinced the college to let him use its Gallery Lounge so he could discuss his acid trips with other people who had been experimenting. From this modest beginning, Gaskin began attracting larger crowds, until he drew upwards of 1,500 participants to his Monday Night Class at the Family Dog Ballroom on the Great Highway, a concert hall most other nights of the week.

"It was easy to tell when we were onto something hot," he related in his memoir, *Monday Night Class*. "I could see the expressions move across those thousand faces like the wind across a wheat field. It was like being inside a computer with a thousand parallel processors."[35]

Gaskin led classes on a range of topics, from the effects of various drugs and trips on consciousness, to the many religious traditions that he studied and practiced. The printed transcripts of those classes demonstrate a cursory knowledge of a range of topics, just enough expertise to keep the room interested and to draw connections between religious traditions and practices. When the question was "How do you plug up the holes in your bucket?" or "What is Energy?" Gaskin waxes at length about the topic.

When he is challenged, however, by an angry person in the audience to explain how his sermons can mitigate government violence, like the shooting of Black Panthers and the students at Kent State, he is stumped:

> Audience member asks, "How do you walk away from a bullet? How fast do you run?"
> Gaskin: "Dig this? Politics, man. Bad vibes."

And Gaskin later in the class, "What you do about it is you get your head together. What the country is dying of is a lack of good vibes, man. I hate to say that. Somebody has got to hang on and do that if we're ever going to get this country back off and out of this morbid zombie state it's wandering around in."

Perhaps the most powerful idea to come out of Monday Night Class was the decision to leave San Francisco in 1970 on a speaking tour and take a caravan of followers with him, eventually constituting one of the largest communities in motion at the time. When the caravan finally settled in southern Tennessee, they started The Farm, arguably the largest of all the communal experiments from the era.

## Hare Krishna

The International Society of Krishna Consciousness (ISKCON), familiarly known as Hare Krishna, was a communal, monastic endeavor based around the spiritual teachings of A.C. Baktivedanta, an elderly Indian expatriate believed by his followers to be a conduit to the Indian deity Krishna. Founded in 1966 in New York City, Baktivedanta relocated to San Francisco in 1967 with a group of about fifteen acolytes, where he opened a temple in the Haight-Ashbury. The move was a tremendous success for ISKCON, as some 150–200 new members joined by 1968. Using San Francisco as its base, ISKCON developed a large international movement, so that by 1974 there were 54 temples throughout the world. Jainanda, a temple leader from San Francisco explained, "The temple here is like a seed bed for Krishna. We plant the seeds and the devotees come up like flowers for Krishna all over the world."[36]

Likewise, ISKCON leadership were keenly aware of the pool of recruits from which they drew. One early recruitment poster read:

> *Stay high forever.* No more coming down…. *Turn on* through music, dance, philosophy, science, religion, and prasadam (spiritual food). Tune in. Awaken your Transcendental Nature! Rejoice in the Ocean of Bliss…! *Drop out* of movements employing artificially induced states of self-realization and expanded consciousness…. *End all bring-downs,* flip out and stay for eternity.

ISKCON devotees were often countercultural radicals, similar to those in other communes, but their discipline and behavior was controlled more absolutely. Devotees were expected to live as monks, renouncing worldly pleasures and distractions and taking vows of poverty. Sexual activity was regulated and personal affectations were minimized, so that the commitment to the group trumped individuality. Devotees could form partnership bonds with the opposite sex, but they were expected to refrain from sex for pleasure, only for procreation. Devotees cut off their hair, wore identical clothes, and spent a large part of the day chanting and meditating to Krishna, a complete erasure of individuality in service of the group.

## est and the Human Potential Movement

Many people who weren't committed to giving up their jobs or their private homes to live collectively, but still wanted to be a part of the transformation that was happening in California, paid to attend weekend sessions with teachers and self-help gurus. As one writer on the Human Potential Movement put it, paraphrasing Ginsberg's earlier maxim, they thought it impossible to change the political and cultural paradigms without first throwing off the shackles of their inner selves. "They see that, if society is to realize its potential, they must first realize theirs."[37]

While the geographic center of the Human Potential Movement was Esalen, a hot springs and retreat near Big Sur that catered to those who could afford to take classes from the likes of Gestalt therapy founder Fritz Perls, Aldous Huxley, or Joseph Campbell, the person who most thoroughly benefitted from the Human Potential Movement was Werner Erhard, whose Erhard Seminars Training, or est, promised to free participants "from the self that limited them," for a tidy fee, of course.[38] Erhard, who changed his name from Jack Rosenberg when he abandoned his first wife and four kids in Pennsylvania in 1960, had been a used-car and door-to-door encyclopedia salesman before reinventing himself as the prototypical self-help guru.[39]

Erhard's teachings were often expressed in platitudes and tautologies, many of them maddening:

> Being centered is being able to tell the difference between your ass and a hole in the ground. That's all. It ain't no big deal. You're an

asshole, because you can't tell the difference between your ass and a hole in the ground....

People got a chance to turn around so fast that they actually saw themselves as other people see them. The first shot you get of that is, you don't like what you see, but people who come really to see themselves deeply are moved to tears by who they are. You can only get to that place where you can see yourself if you're willing to take a look at that first glance, which is really a tough one.[40]

This consistent gazing at one's spiritual navel among Human Potential Movement adherents led Tom Wolfe to dub the 1970s the "Me Decade," where human potential teachers sold the "old alchemical dream [of] changing base metals into gold." Wolfe argued that the luxury of being able to dote on oneself was a product of the same post-war society of plenty that the Diggers and communards tried to subvert:

This had always been an aristocratic luxury... since only the very wealthiest classes had the free time and the surplus income to dwell upon this sweetest and vainest of pastimes.... Much of the satisfaction well-born people got from what is known historically as the 'chivalric tradition' was precisely that: dwelling upon *Me* and every delicious nuance of my conduct and personality. [italics original][41]

The first est class was taught in late 1971 at the Jack Tar Hotel in San Francisco. 250 people paid $250 each to sit in straight-backed chairs for eighteen hours a day over two days, listening to Erhard's admonitions about sphincters and self-discovery.[42] The classes were a great success and between 1971 and 1984, 700,000 people took est seminars, making Erhard a millionaire many times over.[43] After a number of very negative stories in the media, including a *60 Minutes* piece where one of Erhard's daughters accused him of incest (later recanted)[44] and another daughter accused him of raping her,[45] Erhard sold his intellectual property in est to his brother and left the country in self-imposed exile. Erhard's legacy is in the business and personal self-help classes offered to this day at the Landmark Forum, a direct descendent of his teaching style.

## Synanon

With so many of the communes seeking to isolate themselves from the dominant cultural and political norms in San Francisco, both Synanon and People's Temple stood out for the degree to which they were involved in social programs and local politics.

Charles "Chuck" Dederich started Synanon in 1958 in Santa Monica as a treatment center for narcotics addicts, before relocating in 1965 to a large property in Tomales Bay, just north of San Francisco, and transforming the center into an intentional community, where squares were as welcome as addicts.

Synanon's communal re-organization was not just a trend of the time, but an aspect of addict rehabilitation that Dederich considered essential. When addicts kicked their habit cold turkey, as Dederich demanded, they needed a great deal of support and needed to make a greater social and ideological commitment to the group around them. The sociologist Richard Ofshe, who participated in Synanon group exercises in the 1970s, pointed out that Dederich's authority over other individuals was written into the structure of the organization, just as individuals agreed to give their autonomy to him upon becoming a member. "The experience itself of living in Synanon, under its military-like atmosphere of concern, must be recognized as part of Synanon's therapeutic program."[46]

The Synanon Game attracted a lot of people to the organization and it helped to keep many of them there. The Game was an intense encounter group format where eight to fifteen Game players would listen as one or two of the group talked about themselves, their lives, their strengths, and weaknesses. Those being "Gamed" often were harangued by the group for their perceived "hang-ups" and inadequacies. Many Game players however, felt a sense of empathy and truthfulness that they couldn't get anywhere in their lives. [47] As Ofshe said, "participation in Synanon's game club meant participation in Synanon life."

Dederich used his influence while Synanon maintained its reputation as a successful rehabilitation to create social programs and public events that were very popular in San Francisco. The group was known around the Bay Area for its street fairs, the largest of which drew 60,000 people in June, 1968. As part of its economic enterprise, Synanites "hustled" goods and products, which they sold to help the organization or gave away to other groups in the Bay Area, including the Black Panthers and the United Farm Workers (UFW). Cesar Chavez and many members of the UFW played the Synanon Game, as well as Black Panther founder Bobby Seale, and former California Governor Jerry Brown. Dederich even compared Synanon's hustling to the Digger Free Stores.

For years Dederich and Synanon retaliated against their critics, starting with a number of libel lawsuits against the media, like the *San Francisco Examiner* and *Time Magazine*, intimidation and eventual physical violence against "splittees" who left the group, and a bizarre attack on a Los Angeles attorney just a month before the Jonestown massacre. The attorney, Paul Morantz, who had won several child-custody lawsuits and a wrongful imprisonment and kidnapping case against Synanon, was bitten by a rattlesnake that had been stuffed in his mailbox after having its rattle removed. Morantz survived, but Synanon reeled from the negative national publicity the event generated. This was compounded only months later when the publishers of the *Point Reyes Light*, who had spent more than a year chronicling Dederich and his followers in a damning series of investigative articles, won the Pulitzer Prize together with Ofshe for meritorious public service.

## People's Temple

The most famous of the communes in San Francisco was also the most tragic. The mass suicide of more than 900 members of People's Temple in Jonestown Guyana on November 18th, 1978, was the largest in recorded history, radically transforming the perception of communes and their leaders, casting a dark shadow in the eyes of the general public on any communal undertaking. Until the dramatic departure of more than 1,000 people from San Francisco to Guyana practically overnight in 1977, however, People's Temple had been a model of communal living, an amalgam of cultural radicalism, political activism, and spiritual discipline.

People's Temple leader Jim Jones was a very adept political strategist who engaged the San Francisco political establishment and earned its support until the very end, despite unfavorable press and persistent rumors that he abused Temple members. Jones's early church from the 1950s in Indiana was a model, integrated organization and his political leanings became socialist, verging on radical, which was well-suited to the San Francisco of the 1960s and 1970s.

Because Jones demanded complete obedience from his followers and because they were so well organized in the various Temple housing facilities, he could activate his flock in an instant and have them present at a political rally or in front of the cameras.

Willie Brown, a State Assemblyman at the time who would later rise to be the leader of the Assembly and eventual Mayor of San Francisco, said when Jones and his people showed up, multicultural and of all ages, "you had an instant crowd... They were part of the staging." He remembers:

> People's Temple was the number one politically-involved religious institution. All of the politicians of every stripe, national, state and local, paraded through People's Temple for an opportunity to talk to the people, and a leader who was preaching God's will, who was implementing God's will here on earth and politicians love that. And particularly when it didn't appear to cost us anything.[48]

Roxanne Dunbar-Ortiz also recalls:

> When I was a member of the Bay Area American Indian Movement (AIM) Council in the mid-1970s, the People's Temple, led by Reverend Jim Jones, was at the height of its local political influence. The AIM Council organized constant demonstrations at the San Francisco Federal Building and in public parks in response to the endless severe repression against AIM members around the country. Very few people would show up to hear our pleas and speeches, but inevitably a People's Temple bus would show up and out would come the ready-made demonstrators, mostly older African-American women. I found it awkward since they didn't seem to know what the cause was, but it didn't curb their enthusiasm in shouting "power to the people" and singing "We Shall Overcome." The roving People's Temple demonstrators appeared at most demonstrations, many of them at City Hall.[49]

The Temple mobilized to help elect George Moscone as Mayor of San Francisco in 1975, a very close election won by less than 4,000 votes. Jones made sure to highlight his role, albeit exaggerated, in delivering votes.[50] A year later, when Walter Mondale came through San Francisco during the presidential election cycle, Jones met with him. Around the same time, Jones managed to secure a meeting with Rosalynn Carter, wife of future President Jimmy Carter. Though the meeting was only ten minutes long, Jones felt like he had the president's ear, a connection he tried several times unsuccessfully to manipulate later.[51]

All of this was very exciting to Temple members, many of whom were poor and working class, with little or no previous exposure to figureheads and power outside of church dealings. In the San Francisco period, recruitment to the church was largely from the Black community, until 70-80 percent of the Temple's membership was African-American.[52] Much of the draw of the temple was found in the community bonds and freedom from debt and financial strain.

A smaller minority, usually White and better-educated, were drawn to the utopian socialist rhetoric of creating a classless society. Laura Kohl, who moved to San Francisco in 1970 and joined the Temple shortly after, had gone to school in Bridgeport, Connecticut and boarded several Black Panthers in the lead-up to the Alex Rackley murder trials that radicalized so many White students in and around New Haven. Whereas relations with the Panthers as a White student in Connecticut were challenging, said Kohl, People's Temple was realizing a dream of interracial cooperation she hadn't found anywhere else. According to Kohl, Jones would routinely say, "'You know what, the ministers want us to think that it's okay to have heaven. You know, we're going to live a hard life, and there's going to be racism around us and we're going to endure all this and then we're going to have heaven when we finish our life.' And he would say, 'Why would we have heaven after we've lived a hard life? Why not make heaven on earth?'"[53]

Behind the veil of good works and a transcendent, happy congregation, Jones became increasingly paranoid as central Temple members were defecting and rumors of physical abuse and custody battles became public scuttlebutt. For several years, Jones had been secretly planning an exodus to a large plot of land he purchased in Guyana, and with the glare of an increasingly interested media, he expedited those plans. When *San Francisco Chronicle* reporter Marshal Kilduff started investigating Jones and the abuse rumors in 1976, Jones began ordering Temple members to get passports and visas. Only weeks before Kilduff's devastating exposé with interviews of former members appeared in *New West Magazine* on August 1st, 1977, more than 1,000 members had relocated to Guyana, including their spiritual leader. What followed over the next year is an all-too-well-known tragedy.

## Conclusion

Because of the Jim Joneses and Charles Mansons and Chuck Dederichs and Werner Erhards, we have a wiser appreciation of cults and megalomaniacs, but we shouldn't discard communes on principle because of the example set by those individuals. The emptiness of life that motivated the communal enterprises from the 1960s and 1970s in San Francisco is only more pronounced today, and the misrepresentation of the hopeful and largely benign communes narrows options for people who might seek collectivism.

Stephen Gaskin's Farm continues to this day in Tennessee, the Hare Krishna are still active around the country, and Esalen is a thriving retreat and meditation center visited by thousands yearly. Despite Erhard's scandals, The Landmark Forum is a thriving entity that trains individuals and corporations (for a tidy fee, of course). Modeled after business and personal leadership training like Steven Covey's Seven Habits of Highly Effective People (where, ironically, my father worked ten years after leaving Sunburst), the Forum pitches itself largely to a corporate audience. Synanon didn't fare well after the Morantz rattlesnake media storm, though people lived communally on the property until 1989, when the IRS revoked its tax-exempt status and members formally disbanded. Charles Dederich died in 1997.

The roots of Free that grounded the Diggers, Kaliflower, and numerous other communes sees its fruit in Food Not Bombs, the Really Really Free Markets, cooperative food systems, bicycle repair and tinkerer workshops, community gardens, and farmers' markets. Also encouraging are the smaller communal exercises like Kaliflower and Black Bear, which both continue to operate despite the time that has passed, and have evolved to fit the needs of the changing cooperative landscape.

Despite the horror of the Jonestown massacre, Kohl related to me that there has been nothing in her life that compared to the feeling of working cooperatively with her Temple peers. Like other former members, Kohl said she continues to seek community, whether through reunions with People's Temple members or through the Quakers, with whom she is very active in San Diego. She continues to humanize the experience of Temple members and tries to counter the stereotype of "crazy cultists" they have been branded with by the media and deprogrammers. San Diego State University hosts the website, "Alternative Considerations of Jonestown & People's Temple," which is a definitive archive. And former members like Kohl have clung to the dream of living communally, despite the tragedy that still brought her to tears in an interview 31 years later. "You know you can't just forget about them. They gave up the ultimate price; you have to respect that they worked so hard for a better world."[54]

While we may not see a surge of communalism as vertiginous as that which occurred in the late 1960s and continued through the 1970s, recent economic and political times may lead large portions of the population to pursue another way of life. A great majority of the country is disillusioned by the travesty of the country's housing bubble and banking scandals that have led many to question the boom and bust economic violence inculcated by the American economic machine. In fact, over 120 million Americans, roughly 40 percent of the population, are involved in 48,000 cooperatives, such as housing, farming, telephones, electricity production, purchasing, credit unions, and bicycle repair, and living as squatters and communards (*Communities Directory* lists nearly 1,000 intentional communities, with more added all the time).[55] There are many other less formally organized groups that function as reinforcement of cooperation and community in spite of the dominant cultural paradigm. What lessons contemporary communards learn from their forbearers is unknown, but their lineage from San Francisco during the turbulent decade from 1968-1978 will be indisputable.

## Notes

1.  For a remarkable history of collectivism and communalism in the US, see John Curl, *For All the People: Uncovering the Hidden History of Cooperation, Cooperative Movements, and Communalism in America.* (Oakland: PM Press, 2009).

2.  Lawrence Veysey, *The Communal Experience: Anarchist and Mystical Communities in Twentieth-Century America.* (Chicago: University of Chicago Press, 1978) 52. An excellent analysis of The Diggers amid the milieus of cultural and political radicalism can be found in Michael William Doyle, "The Haight Ashbury Diggers and the Cultural Politics of Utopia, 1965-1968" (dissertation, n.d.) chap. 1. San Francisco History Center, San Francisco Public Library, chap. 1.

3.  Peter Braunstein and Michael William Doyle, ed., *Imagine Nation: The American Counter Culture of the 1960s and '70s* (New York: Routledge, 2002) 7.

4.  Timothy Miller, *The 60s Communes: Hippies and Beyond* (Syracuse: Syracuse University Press, 1999) 105.

5.  Ibid., xix.

6.  Doyle, "Haight Ashbury Diggers," 12-13.

7.  Allen Ginsberg, "The Dialectics of Liberation; A Speech," in *The Digger Papers*, published in *The Realist* no. 81 (n.d.) 4-7. San Francisco History Center, San Francisco Public Library.

8.  Miller, *60s Communes*, 18.

9.  Dominick J. Cavallo, "'It's Free Because It's Yours': The Diggers and the San Francisco Scene, 1964-1968," in *A Fiction of the Past: The Sixties in American History* (New York: Palgrave. 1999) 101; Date of Free Store opening from Doyle "Haight Ashbury Diggers," 147; "Garbage Yoga" in Digger broadsides, The Hippies Collection, the San Francisco History Center, San Francisco Public Library.

10. Miller, *60s Communes,* 44.

11. Peter Coyote, *Sleeping Where I Fall: A Chronicle* (Berkeley: Counterpoint. 1998) 130.

12. Michael William Doyle, "Staging the Revolution: Guerrilla Theater as Countercultural Practice, 1965-1968," 89.

13. Doyle, "Haight Ashbury Diggers," chap. 3.

14. Miller, *60s Communes,* 46; For a detailed account of Morning Star Ranch, read Ramon Sender, *Home Free Home: A History of Two Open-Door California Communes.* www.diggers.com/homefree.

15. Miller, *60s Communes,* 12.

16. Sender, *Home Free Home,* chap 3.

17. Miller, *60s Communes,* 48-51. This account of Morningstar is largely based on Miller's book.

18. Coyote, *Sleeping.* 149. Also from the documentary film, *Commune* (Five Points Media, 2005).

19. Ibid.

20. Ibid.

21. Coyote, *Sleeping,* 151-153.

22. *Commune.*

23. The Irving Rosenthal Papers, Green Library Department of Special Collections, Stanford University include early family records, journals, resumes, bankbooks, travel documents, correspondence, and professional writings.

24. Ibid.

25. Box 9, Folder 9, ibid.

26. Both the San Francisco History Center, San Francisco Public Library, and the California Historical Society have excellent catalogs of original Kaliflower newsletters; For distribution totals www.diggers.org/kaliflower/kf.htm; for Berkeley specifics *Kaliflower* 2, no. 20 (September 10, 1970).

27. *Kaliflower* 3, no. 1 (May 6, 1971).

28. Chandler Downs, interview with author.

29. Ibid.

30. *Kaliflower,* n.s. 3, April 30, 1973. www.diggers.org/kaliflower/dtf.htm.

31. See Pam Peirce's essay "A Personal History of the People's Food System" in this volume for more information on the food conspiracies in San Francisco.

32. Curl, *For All the People,* 213.

33. Shep Melnick, *Between The Lines: Interpreting Welfare Rights* (The Brookings Institution, 1994) 323. Justice Brennan delivered the majority: "The District Court held that the "unrelated person" provision of 3 (e) creates an irrational classification in violation of the equal protection component of the Due Process Clause of the Fifth Amendment.... In practical effect, 3 (e) creates two classes of persons for food stamp purposes: one class is composed of those individuals who live in households all of whose members are related to one another, and the other class consists of those individuals who live in households containing one or more members who are unrelated to the rest. The latter class of persons is denied federal food assistance. A three-judge District Court for the District of Columbia held this classification invalid as violative of the Due Process Clause of the Fifth Amendment. 345 F. Supp. 310 (1972). We noted probable jurisdiction. *409 U.S. 1036* (1972). We affirm." http://laws.findlaw.com/us/413/528.html.

34. *Kaliflower,* n.s. 3, April 30, 1978.

35. Stephen Gaskin, *Monday Night Class* (Summertown, TN: Book Publishing Company, 2005) 7-9.

36. Gregory Johnson, "The Hare Krishna in San Francisco," in *New Religious Consciousness*, eds. Charles Y. Glock and Robert Bellah (Berkeley: University of California Press, 1976) 32-47.

37. Donald Stone, "The Human Potential Movement," in Glock and Bellah, *New Religious Consciousness.* 93.

38. Interview from the documentary film, *Transformation: The Life and Legacy of Werner Erhard,* (Symon Productions, 2006).

39. Steven Pressman, *Outrageous Betrayal: The Dark Journey of Werner Erhard from est to Exile* (New York: St. Martin's Press. 1993) 1-9.

40.   *Transformation.*

41.   Tom Wolfe, "The 'Me' Decade and the Third Great Awakening," *New York Magazine*, August 23, 1976, 26-40.

42.   Pressman, Steven. *Outrageous Betrayal.* 67.

43.   Snider, Suzanne. "est, Werner Erhard, and the Corporatization of Self-Help." *The Believer.* Vol 1. No. 2. 2003.

44.   ibid.

45.   Pressman, *Outrageous Betrayal*, 142-144.

46.   Richard Ofshe, "Synanon: The People Business," in *New Religious Consciousness*, Glock and Bellah, 121.

47.   Rod Janzen, *The Rise and Fall of Synanon: A California Utopia* (Baltimore: The Johns Hopkins University Press, 2001) 13-16, 236-237.

48.   Willie Brown, interview with author, July 30, 2009.

49.   Roxanne Dunbar-Ortiz, email communication with author, November 10, 2009.

50.   Tim Reiterman, *Raven: The Untold Story of the Reverend Jim Jones and His People* (New York: Dutton, 1982) 267.

51.   Ibid., 302-305.

52.   Ibid., 156.

53.   Laura Kohl, interview with author, August 10th, 2009.

54.   Kohl, interview.

55.   Curl, *For All the People,* 1-2

# San Bruno Mountain

## By David Schooley

*It should be said the Mountain wrote these words on me whenever quiet, the Place in its own defining/informing energies, the buckling of an ancient seabed, prehistoric summer fogs, their records written minute in helical couplings of bearberry, great migration of roots and seeds before advancing northern ice, its leavings, a boreal huckleberry* (Mianthemum kamchaticum)*, a newborn hawk, millions of tiny deaths and hatchings, creeks fed into the bay, and man. Man to focus and name these energies, join them again with origin, investing the Mountain with sacredness or use, heeding its articulations (and where, heedless, liable to scrape its slopes and canyons bare, diminishing also himself).*

*For the Ohlone native people who lived in its valleys, the Mountain was sacred as well as sustenance.*

*For the Spaniards who logged the oaks and souls for the church, grazed their livestock on the slopes, it was sustenance and obstacle.*

*To industrial man its articulations are merely obstacle, easy to remove.*

*The miracle is that San Bruno Mountain has survived so long. The tide of San Francisco suburbs parted at its base and moved on to leave the Mountain the last island of true Franciscan country left on earth, its plant and animal communities little altered, its Ohlone village sites surprisingly undisturbed by the bay, rare and endangered species visibly intact.*

What first struck me about San Bruno Mountain was, "Why is it still here?" Surrounded on every side by cities and industries of the North Peninsula, it was one last holdout of wild Franciscan land.

Early in the summer of 1969, from the window of a Greyhound bus traveling south on the Old Bayshore highway, I suddenly glimpsed a shimmering oak forest and chaparral ridge just before reaching the town of Brisbane. I couldn't believe how, after the Cow Palace and Visitacion Valley, and the odd flat terrain beyond the Old Railroad Round House, the road suddenly opened onto wild lands rising above an "industrial park."

I walked straight into what is now called Buckeye Canyon; silent, delicate scrub, graceful ridges covered with farewell to spring, a bubbling creek, and mountain fold after fold of coast live oak up to Islais ravines. Then, a little higher, distant ridges—an impossible landscape, hidden in plain sight beside the slaughtered Bay lands of Highway 101 and San Francisco Airport.

I rented an apartment in the little "country town" and began exploring. I found a shellmound village site between two creeks in Buckeye Canyon, and went to UC Berkeley to confirm. There was no reference to it in any reports or even in the N. C. Nelson shellmound maps from the early 1900s.

The next weekend, I did a pre-dawn to full moon midnight circumambulation of the Mountain, following civilization's edges; into pristine ravines above Brisbane industry, discovering another shellmound (larger than the one in Buckeye Canyon and on record), perennial creeks, a badger (!), a young Great Horned Owl disturbed from a buckeye tree, many-colored dragonflies, abandoned cars, hermits' huts—acre on acre without trails, impenetrable.

I continued my research, first at the California Academy of Sciences, where I found *A Flora of the San Bruno Mountains* by Elizabeth McClintock, published in 1968. Then I researched at UC Berkeley, Stanford University, the cities of Brisbane, South San Francisco, Colma, Daly City, and, more importantly, by talking to people who lived around the Mountain and knew its secrets.

I learned that from 1920 to 1960, the City of San Francisco inadvertently saved the Mountain. The marshes, lagoons, and creeks at the base of San Bruno Mountain slowly filled with the shining City's garbage, acre after acre of up-to-date stench floating beside its ridges and canyons. Black communities took root there, as well as a poor 'Okie' village in unincorporated Brisbane. "Ticky-tacky houses" on the Daly City hillside, Colma cemeteries, and the no-man's land of South San Francisco—'The Industrial City'—spread around the Mountain's flanks. Impressive negatives protected its secret presence of wilderness. People stayed away. It was not until 1960, when the great effort to save the Bay took place that the stench quietly receded and a new curiosity and greed arose, hoping to profit from this strangely unknown, surviving land. And then, to confront the greed, a careful war began which continues today, part of a wider, intricate earth world war. Out of that, the watchers and workers arise.

San Bruno Mountain felt like a vital open secret, hidden just below visibility in our cultural focus. No Yosemite, no looming Tamalpais. No redwoods. Not even a Bishop pine. It was mercifully the neglected stone, *Lapis Exilis*. I thought of it as the stone cast away by the builders, which, in Jesus's parable, it is said we must find and make our cornerstone as altogether different kind of builders. If we could learn to see and involve ourselves carefully with its quiet life, there might be more than hope for the planet and ourselves on it. But mine has not been the only vision of San Bruno Mountain's destiny.

Early in botanical investigation of California, the Franciscan plant zone

*David Schooley with school kids on San Bruno Mountain, mid-1980s..*
PHOTO: SAN BRUNO MOUNTAIN WATCH

was considered to include the entire face of the Bay Region, from Sonoma to Monterey. A more attentive look in recent years has disclosed a much smaller "Type Area" covering the southern edges of Marin, the hills of San Francisco and ending at the southern limb of San Bruno Mountain and the northern ridges of Sweeney's Ridge.

It was James Roof, creator of Tilden Botanical Garden in Berkeley, a man born at the coastal base of San Bruno Mountain, Lake Merced, who told me more about the north peninsula's geography, about its native plant life as an ancient island of San Francisco, and about San Bruno Mountain, whose manzanitas and butterflies are unique within the Bay Area.

The inner region, so long overlooked by us, was the biotic range lived in by Native Americans whose tribal, hunting, and gathering territory precisely coincided with the set of conditions that form the inner Franciscan zone. Village names around the Mountain were Urebure/Siplichiquin to the south, Amuctac/ Tubsinte to the north, and around San Francisco, of the Yelamu communities.

As warm valley air rises, cold wet Pacific air is drawn inland through the Golden Gate at the northern end and the Lake Merced/Colma Gap to the south. The full yearlong force of this weather against the arc of San Francisco/San Bruno hills in between has given rise to an apparently treeless landscape where Ice Age plants have been able to survive and other coastal scrub plants have evolved varieties not to be found anywhere else: a dwarf burn-sprouting manzanita no more than ankle high; sandy, west-facing lessingia; a buckeye with tough-ribbed salt-weathering leaves; fog shadow canyons with nothing but hummingbird sage. At the same time, in sheltered ravines, the abundance of Pacific moisture nurtures intricate oak, Islais (wild cherry), and wax myrtle forests. The scale is vast, wild exposure with an intimate texture of abundance.

Village sites of both Urebure and Amuctac/Tubsinte tribelets of the Ohlone remain intact in the lower valleys of the Mountain surrounded by the plant life used for food, fiber, and medicine by their inhabitants. Mountain creek-bay entrances are gentle compared with the rough San Francisco ocean-bay entrance. San Bruno Mountain villages were larger than the northern peninsula sites because of more fresh water and calmer lagoons, where reed boat routes to and from the east bay were easier to use. Local inhabitants traded ocean abundance for inland necessities for thousands of years (Oakland Sibley lava rock was used as mortars and pestles in Brisbane, South San Francisco, and Buckeye Canyon). Beside a remnant estuary and salt marsh, once rich in shellfish and water fowl, the village sites and surrounding plant communities provide glimpses of the ghost of a direct economy.

On the other hand, efforts to use land for upscale residential and commercial development continue on land around San Bruno Mountain. Many of the people who now live around the Mountain recognize development proposals as a death threat to what little they have left of community and to San Bruno Mountain itself, which is by now a symbol of what we are fast losing to a blueprint vision of place as real estate, and community as something to be grid-planned and mass produced.

Except for San Bruno Mountain, there is no wild land left on the northern San Francisco peninsula. Professor E.O. Wilson of Harvard University calls San Bruno Mountain "a global treasure," one of "eighteen global biodiversity 'hot spots' in need of immediate protection," but adds, "as in the case of so many other global treasures, this great fortune is not being handled with adequate care."

Some planners and local officials recognized this in the 1970s and moved to acquire and preserve the Mountain as parkland. Though welcomed by local activists, the suggested scope of preservation seemed incomplete and inadequate since it left out the upper headwater valleys and softly undulating terrain most suited to a park.

Late one evening in 1969, Mike Kiser and Helen Sullivan, citizens of the Brisbane mountain, took me up to the wild town "acres" with a jug of wine and city records detailing Brisbane's horrifying plans for the Mountain. At the Brisbane Library, Midtown Market, at city meetings, and from locals Byron and Milton Jensen and Tony Attard, I gathered more disconcerting information. Richard Burr and Paul Goercke told me about a plan to shave off the Mountain top. Luman Drake told me about how local citizens resisted the city of Brisbane's once willing cooperation with San Francisco's massive garbage dumping in the Mountain's Bay waters, for which Brisbane received financial benefits. These revelations, along with my increasing exposure to the Mountain's ancient secrets, quietly drew me in.

Concern mounted and public pressure was to follow, in an uprising which miraculously took the first crucial steps toward stopping the machinery of development and demanding that a new look be taken at San Bruno Mountain and its meaning to the Bay Region.

One day in 1973, while walking through South San Francisco's Paradise Valley neighborhood on the Mountain's southern slope, I saw a sign in a front yard—"Save The Mountain." I knocked and Bette Higgins opened the door. That meeting led to the formation of "The Committee to Save San Bruno Mountain." Bette, Mimi Whitney, and I formed a grassroots, nonviolent, wild Mountain army. We took hundreds of people up on the Mountain in protest, celebration, and wild theatrics. Hundreds of people came to County and City Park and Recreation meetings. At one critical San Mateo County Park and Recreation Supervisor's meeting, along with concerned Native Americans, a mountain climber, and a goat, we protested the small size of a "proposed park" on ridiculously steep, unbuildable land, and after our demonstration, the whole group marched out. The decision was postponed.

Before a number of County Supervisors meetings, the essential question was: would there be more Mountain people in attendance or building trades' allies, who supported development? Far more Mountain supporters almost always showed up.

During this period we distributed leaflets, bulletins, press releases, and Mountain calendars and T-shirts to the neighborhoods, schools, stores, and libraries at the Mountain's fringes. When the Mountain's owners, Visitacion Associates (Crocker, McKesson, Amfac, Great America, Brookfield, Southwest Diversified, Inc.) distributed their building plans to public officials and agencies in a slick, glossy text, we were able to qualify for Legal Aid Society assistance to help us develop a document exposing the real significance of these plans, and how their project would irreparably damage local communities as well as the Mountain. Dated May 23, 1975, our citizens' document was released well before Environmental Impact statements were required and was far more honest, scientific, and historically factual. It outlined predictable results of proposed construction, including the benching of hills, destruction of wildlife, new roads to service planned subdivisions, and expansion of infrastructure in surrounding communities, from sewers to schools. This document helped to educate the decision makers in San Mateo County and the State and to shift them toward our side.

During this period we also started to work for pro-Mountain candidates in local elections and began to get direct political representation. At one County Supervisor's meeting in Redwood City, Bette and Mimi expressed their vision in the form of a huge, beautiful cake baked in the shape of a mountain, its most sensitive places marked with little candles. Presenting it to the supervisors, they said, "We, the local community for San Bruno Mountain have brought you our future park…" and offered the cake, inviting them to, "Eat it."

After ten long years, a critical part of the Mountain was saved when development of the "Saddle," the owners' most keenly sought-after project, was halted. After much political resistance, a state bond purchase finally became available. State and County sections were designated, and the result was the creation of the San Bruno Mountain State and County Park in 1978. While it preserved some land from development, it did not fulfill the vision of many for what this park might properly be, and still left much of the Mountain under threat.

The history of the last thousand years has been one of increasing legal recognition of inalienable rights, from the Magna Carta in 1215, to the Declaration of Independence, the Emancipation Proclamation, women's suffrage, the Civil Rights Movement's full-scale nonviolent assault on racial segregation in the 1960s, and the new protection this country offered to threatened plant and animal populations through the passage of the visionary 1966 Endangered Species Preservation Act (amended in 1969, and repealed and replaced in 1973 by the current Endangered Species Act). Unfortunately, though, events on San Bruno Mountain have quietly changed the course of wildlife and environmental protection in this country for the worse.

In the early 1980s, there were still plans to build on large swaths of the Mountain above Brisbane, South San Francisco, and Daly City. A second wave of concern and protest rose to save these areas. An amazing serendipity, one decade in the making, then occurred. Since the early 1970s Dick Arnold from the University of California in Berkeley, along with Larry Orsak, had been scientifically observing and researching the rare Mission Blue Butterfly found on the grassy southern slopes of the Mountain. In the early 1980s Arnold published his results. His paper identified the Mission Blue as among America's very first "rare and endangered species" to fit the criteria of the Rare and Endangered Species Act. Builders suddenly found themselves faced with a formidable legal roadblock, and the bulldozers stopped dead in their tracks.

By this time, some members of our group were serving on local town councils. Even some long-time political incumbents had become closer to us, respecting our "victories." Some of us thought America was finally changing for the better, beginning to bring honesty and justice to its treatment of wild lands and creatures.

Trouble, though, began within the Save the Mountain community. It soon would become clear how power can divide even a grassroots group which has maintained unity during long and meaningful struggle. At first, perhaps, most of us thought that the Endangered Species Act would work to help us preserve the Mountain. Gradually, though, more and more Mountain board members began to lean toward "compromise" of the Act's essential provisions. They'd been told that the law's current language was too rigid and restrictive and that without compromise the powerful private landowners' lobby would prevail in Congress, and the entire Endangered Species Act might be repealed.

A number of meetings took place with senior government officials, legal groups, and even faraway property owners from San Diego and Los Angeles, as well as with builders and with Thomas Reid & Associates, a company hired by San Mateo County to perform "environmental oversight."

Something decisive was happening with great speed, but most of us had no idea what it was. A proposed Habitat Conservation Plan (HCP) turned out to be a manipulation of critical protection criteria, cleverly gutting the Endangered Species Act by redefining the Act's Section 10(a). This section states that an agent can kill a butterfly, for example, or any creature, if the destruction occurs in the context of studying the species in an attempt to help it survive. The HCP transforms this provision to allow scientists (hired by developers) and developers (in the name of science) to destroy whatever lies in the path of their plans, including entire habitats, as long as some other habitat that approximates the original can be made available. Section 10(a), which had originally tolerated the loss of individual creatures if their loss helped the species as a whole, was replaced by a developer-friendly scheme with no track record that assumed a species can be transplanted to a different habitat like interchangeable parts of a machine. These changes were enacted by Congress in Washington DC, but were to have immediate and grave implications on the Northeast Ridge of San Bruno Mountain.

The HCP's compromise was the first of its kind. Many of us saw it as an obvious end-run around the spirit of the Endangered Species Act for the convenience and profit of developers. In the face of this new legal reality members of the Committee to Save San Bruno Mountain felt they had to take sides, and their divisions became unbearable. The Committee broke apart.

Fred Smith, Tom Adams (who had been the Committee's lawyer), and Ellie Larson were willing to accept the need to kill endangered species on private property. The majority of us (myself, Mark Huntington, Alice Howard, Ellen Mark, Gregory Bergman, Brian Gaffney, Robin Crabill, and Anne Kroll) rose in protest against the "compromise."

Those willing to compromise took the original name of the group and incorporated. At their meetings, where vital issues were being discussed, I was turned away at the door. They joined with local and national politicians, ignoring the protests of many scientists and environmentalists, and quietly hammered out for San Bruno Mountain a compromise to the critical Endangered Species Act, which had been offering strong protection and prospects of renewal to threatened plant and animal populations.

The plan looked good on paper, but with respect to San Bruno Mountain endangered species, there was no careful long-term scientific study of the proposed habitat switch. It is clear now that the viability of creating "new habitats", which was permitted for the first time by the HCP, should have been tested for at least ten or twenty years before destruction of any portion of the original habitat.

The Mountain's Saddle area was deemed an ideal place to "re-create" Mission Blue and Silverspot Butterfly habitat, which development of the Northeast Ridge would destroy. The theory was that non-native gorse (*Ilex europaeus*) would eventually spread from the Saddle to the Northeast Ridge, choking grassland and destroying the butterflies' habitat anyway, so why not allow the building of houses on the Ridge, thereby stopping the gorse's advance, and eradicate gorse on the Saddle so that butterfly habitat would be created there? No proof was required of this untested theory, and responsibility for carrying out the necessary environmental study and management was turned over to unsupervised, for-profit contractors.

As the details of the HCP became known, however, and as lepidopterists from around the world increased our understanding of the fragility of the San Bruno Mountain habitat, more conflict arose. Many members of our first organization, now a protesting group, felt that rather than dividing or attempting to "create" habitat in another place, more space surrounding the endangered habitat should be preserved and this led to the emergence of a new, still grassroots group— San Bruno Mountain Watch—which is an incorporated 501(c)3 nonprofit and remains vigorous today. (In 2009, as part of a long-term plan to acquire portions of the mountain from its private owners, San Bruno Mountain Watch became San Bruno Mountain Watch Conservancy. Our goal is to ensure that creeks and wildlife corridors which radiate from the Mountain into neighboring terrain are also preserved as part of an interdependent biosystem.)

As news of the HCP began to circulate, San Bruno Mountain Watch received letters from scientists around the world in disagreement with it. We joined with concerned university and legal groups in publishing articles critiquing the HCP. These appeared in the California Academy of Sciences' *Pacific Discovery*, as well as in KQED's *Focus Magazine*, the *San Francisco Chronicle*, and in other publications. Powerful proponents of the HCP in Washington, though, helped to convince influential "environmental" groups such as the Sierra Club and the Environmental Defense Fund of the HCP's necessity, and these organizations turned away from us and toward a compromise with corporate power.

Together with Friends of Endangered Species, we went to court with our lawyer, Michael Freund. Our defense of the Endangered Species Act reached the California State Appellate Court. However, although no scientific evidence was presented to support the HCP's weakening of the Act's protection of endangered wildlife, we lost the case.

Bulldozers began running on critical land and the legal destruction of endangered species, now permitted through the HCP process, began not only on San Bruno Mountain, but across the United States, its authorization now hidden in an arm of the noble environmental Endangered Species Act. During this period, local politicians, the Committee to Save San Bruno Mountain, and the press turned against us. I was accused of rabid protest, of being worse than Earth First! But long-time allies of the Mountain on the Peninsula and members of the university community re-turned the tide for us with letters, public statements, and published articles. San Bruno Mountain Watch grew while the old Committee to Save San Bruno Mountain fizzled out and disappeared.

Over the next twelve years, carefully documented sequential time photographs made it clear that, because of weather patterns, gorse will not move onto the Ridge, and the Saddle will not support the grassland which the butterflies need. The microclimate on the Northeast Ridge is often sunnier, creating hotter and drier grassland terrain suitable for butterfly host plants, while fog flows over the Saddle, making it cooler and wetter, thus more suitable for coastal scrub. Even if the non-native gorse were removed from the Saddle, and native plants returned, which in any case, was not done, this area would not become significant Mission Blue and Silverspot habitat. This fundamental discovery means that the HCP is now demonstrably unworkable, yet precious butterfly habitat on the Northeast

Ridge is gone forever, displaced by houses. It is not surprising, but a bitter irony that across the valley on the Northeast Ridge, where rare and endangered habitat on the Mountain has been destroyed, streets within the new subdivisions carved out of the Mountain's flanks now bear names like "Mission Blue Drive" and "Silverspot Lane."

The San Bruno Mountain HCP became precedent across the nation for hundreds of other similarly flawed "habitat conservation plans," which have allowed mining, logging, quarrying, and other development of sensitive habitats.

## Epilogue

Fortunately, as a result of dedicated work by San Bruno Mountain Watch and its allies the State Bond Act was passed in 1989, and Buckeye and Owl Canyons were added to the State and County Park system. There are 20 rare plant and animal species remaining on the Mountain, and the threat to their habitat continues.

Another fragile battle, resolved in 1999, was a many year "coyote dance" to protect the largest, unruined indigenous village site between Brisbane and South San Francisco, a sheltered mountain valley by the Bay. San Bruno Mountain Watch's legal suit (through our lawyer, Brian Gaffney) concerning endangered species, damaged wetlands, and other issues related to the Urebure/Siplichiquin shellmound halted all construction, including high-rises in the valley from Indian Ridge to the Sierra Point boundary. Also, along with the Trust for Public Land, Jack Myers, Inc., and Patrick Orozco of the Pajaro Valley Ohlone Indian Council, we finally purchased this land, which was then deeded to the State and County Park of San Bruno Mountain in 2004.

Attempting to understand the shellmound and sacred site, we are also returning native plants, culling non-native growth, and, most importantly, honoring it by leaving it alone with the hope that it will suffer no further alteration or disturbance.

Aggressive, delicate dreams move forward. We continue our ongoing restoration work, reparation of creeks flowing from the Mountain to the Bay, and expansion of wildlife corridors beyond the current park. Our Conservancy's vision of routes connecting San Bruno Mountain to McLaren Park and Sweeney Ridge, protection of the Lake Merced dunes, these are part of the historical descent of San Bruno Mountain into the ocean. We seek to heal the Bay landfill and the watershed of San Bruno Mountain, while planting and returning rare species to the lower Brisbane Acres, and building a native plant nursery and greenhouse in 2009 to replenish the Mountain.

While some battles were lost and others won, a different kind of potency has always been in the background, a vision of San Bruno Mountain as a native place rather than issue or image. Perhaps, some thought, the concept of Park or Preserve can be turned inside out here on San Bruno Mountain—no longer an enclosure under siege, a senescent remnant under glass, but a seed ground; not a place to get away from it all, but a place to get into; not a place to look at, but a place to see from.

Perhaps we can put forward the vision of a new kind of dedicated land, beginning with: What kind of park might be made on the Mountain without the Park and Recreation Department that presently manages it and is subject to political manipulation? Beyond "nature interpretive centers," there do exist many real and untried models. Some see the need for a reinhabitory vision which might become a working reality.

All over the planet are sacred mountains, groves, and water courses of traditional cultures—Mt. Kailas in Tibet, Prescilly Top in England, Wu Tai Shan in China. These were recognitions of innate potency of Place, and so became places to enter into the learning of origin. Australian Aborigines held that particular places were of the Dream Time and a young man might make his Walkabout there as rite of passage, learning his ground. There were routes of pilgrimage, sacred ways and precincts where use and habit might fall away, learning to be found in earth's own feature. And there were the guides, shamans, hermits and tricksters, the Old Woman of the Forest, the Old Man of the Mountain, who knew their ground, might show you the edible roots, the place where a hawk drinks and bathes in the summer, or precisely the way to get lost. Modern science can look superficial and invasive alongside ancient learning born of generations of attention to a single place.

Such guides in their native landscapes might point us to a vision of a preserve conceived and guided to nurture Presence and discovery of an "actual earth of value" (Charles Olson). It need be no Olympus or Fujiyama, no Sinai or Gethsemane. The closer and longer we have to look, the more clarity, and a backyard mountain like San Bruno Mountain offers itself easily to the need—the more so since already it bears the wounds of our inattention. Its very lowness on the horizon of our significance becomes the mystery and the learning.

One model for this vision has been a couple dwelling on the Mountain for the past 14 years. Besh and his wife Thelma made their home in the wild crevices of the Mountain, at the base of a three-hundred year old oak tree. Unknown to local officials, they lived lightly on the landscape, drawing fresh water from a nearby spring, going to town for groceries, and carefully tending their environment, not only to keep from harming it, but to fight invasive non-native plants in their area. For many years, they welcomed school classes and hiking groups, showing them the simplicity with which life can be lived in a natural environment, while quietly offering presence within their fragile landscape.

There are still those who turn their backs on the ever-expanding urban grid and its "comforts" which surrounds the Mountain's formidable wilderness. Characterized by some as "homeless" and "troubled", they have, in fact, been extraordinarily sensitive to the Mountain's inner life, and found ways to live in harmony with it. Besh and Thelma are just two of the many who have quietly entered the poison oak forests of San Bruno Mountain over the years. An unwritten borderline of steep secret scrub oak hills deters most urban dwellers. Not even police venture there. Shimmering canyons are hardly seen even from Brisbane or Daly City. But there are hardy ones who have slipped into the hidden chaparral.

In 1969, I discovered a moldering collapsed cabin in the willows of upper Daly City, with a homemade table, chair, and wooden bed. In 2008, after an interim of 80 long years, fire swept through Buckeye and Owl Canyons and exposed an even older rock cabin, concealed for perhaps 200 years. Occasionally, we stumble upon hidden settlements deep in the Mountain—where people knew how to find water, were able to handle fire secretly, and to use the natural camouflage of air, wind, fog, and rain, to carefully disguise the paths to their dwellings; to survive without a store nearby.

Among the hermits there have been hostile and troubled people, as well as friendly souls. One long-time hermit died on the Mountain. Each of them, in their way, have sought space and healing in the shelter of wild land, leaving behind the often unforgiving judgements and pressures of the world we have made. In this way their journeys honor the earth and their experiences are a source of learning for us.

Since parts of the Mountain became State and County Park after 1980, its hermits have experienced many ups and downs at the hands of local authorities. San Mateo County and the City of Brisbane were ruthless in their eviction of Besh and Thelma even though some rangers expressed gratitude for their careful management of the land.

When local officials chose to alter a tacit policy of "leaving them be," Besh and Thelma's quiet, ingenious homestead was demolished and they were forced to move on. Yet those who witnessed the impact of their presence on literally thousands of schoolchildren continue to hope for a nature preserve which would welcome the presence of such hardy, knowledgeable, and dedicated souls, who have chosen to live out the values of simplicity and ecological consciousness, and who are teachers of the timeless ways of being with the natural world.

In this way, San Bruno Mountain might become not just a place we need to save, but a place that may save us.

*Wooded Buckeye and Oak Canyons seen from the Northeast ridge, quarry at right.*

PHOTO BY CHRIS CARLSSON

# The Farm by the Freeway

## by Mirjana Blankenship

> *Liberation of nature is the recovery of the life-enhancing forces in nature, the sensuous aesthetic qualities which are foreign to a life wasted in unending competitive performances: they suggest the new qualities of freedom.*
>
> —Herbert Marcuse, *Nature and Revolution* (1970)[1]

> *I think of The Farm as a place where acrobats, actors, activists, artists, dancers, poets, kids, clowns, rabbits, rosebushes, flowers, vegetables, chickens, cats, dogs, old people, young people, middle-aged people, workers, loafers, builders, readers, researchers, writers, students, philosophers, ecologists, cooks, gardeners, dreamers & doers, all hang out and somehow hang together—creating a lively and wonderful environment in the two warehouses and some land by the side of a freeway.*
>
> —Molly Rannells, "What is the Farm to you?" (1976)[2]

The present day Cesar Chavez Street freeway interchange in San Francisco is a tangle of asphalt and vacant lots, where cars, skateboarders, and the homeless co-exist in liminal urbanity. This transitory space was once a place of productivity where life grew and roots deepened. From 1974 to 1987, the derelict spaces underneath and beside the freeway sprouted corn stalks, vegetable gardens, fruit orchards, goats, children, and circuses—all under the umbrella of art and ecology. Crossroads Community (The Farm) was one of San Francisco's early community cultural spaces that sought to connect people, animals, plants, and resources, heralding a new form of ecological thinking in an increasingly industrial and gentrified city. While post-millennial San Francisco is a city where Victory Gardens grow by City Hall and urban farming thrives, in the 1970s the concept of a farm by the freeway was not an ordinary sight, but the inception of a revolution.

In 1974, Bonnie Ora Sherk and co-founder Jack Wickert helped create Crossroads Community (The Farm), affectionately known as The Farm. On an accumulated seven acres located partially underneath and adjacent to the then Army Street freeway interchange in San Francisco, they—with the help of the community and collaborators—turned two warehouses, concrete, and open space into a site-specific sculpture, farm, community center, school without walls, and human and animal theater. The San Francisco Mime Troupe, Make-a-Circus, and The Jones Family all took up residence there, as did artists, poets, dancers, punks, kids, gardeners, animals, and members of the community.

The Farm sought to create a radical ecological model that facilitated non-hierarchical interactions. Everyone who entered The Farm or lived there—plant, human or animal—was seen as an integral part in the ecosystem. For Sherk, it reflected her concept of the "life frame," meaning a practice that becomes a microcosm for living life. The Farm evolved out of her earlier performances and installations that

*The Farm was built in the bottom of the V of freeways adjacent to the big cement lot. The lot was turned into La Raza Park. This photo c. 1970.*

delved into the relationship between humans, animals, and the natural environment as well as the visions of her collaborators. In 1981, Lucy R. Lippard hailed The Farm as "the most ambitious and successful work of ecological art in this country," yet it still remains relatively unknown today even in the Bay Area.[3]

In 1970, Sherk inserted herself into locations around the city as part of the *Sitting Still* series. In *Sitting Still I* (1970), she dressed in a formal gown and sat in a found armchair in a shallow pond of collected water and trash off the side of the James Lick Freeway, where the new freeway interchange was in the midst of being built.[4] As she sat still amidst the urban landscape facing her "audience"—the cars that sailed by on the freeway—a series of warehouses and open spaces were visible in the distance, the future site of The Farm. Sherk's practice in the early 1970s, characterized by her merging of theater and ecology, and her interventions into—and reflections on—urban and natural environments, culminated in her vision for The Farm.

It was in fact during one of her performances that she met Wickert, a musician, taxi driver, and member of the Mime Troupe. In order to earn a weekly wage, study "cultural costumes" and perform "life theater," Sherk worked the graveyard shift as a cook and waitress at Andy's Donuts, a twenty-four hour diner on Castro Street. Late one night during the ongoing performances entitled *Short Order Cook* and *The Waitress* (1973–1974), Sherk started talking to a customer named Jack about her desire to start an urban public art and agriculture project and, in turn, his need for a performance space.[5]

At the time, Sherk lived across the street from Borden's Dairy near the almost completed Army Street freeway interchange; partially underneath and adjacent to this structure were several pieces of land covered with concrete and several warehouses that collectively encompassed seven acres.[6] After repeatedly passing by this dormant space, she had a vision to transform the barren land into a working farm, performance space and community center. Wickert had grown up in the projects on Potrero Hill and spent his childhood nights playing in the buildings scattered amidst the industrial wasteland. After meeting that night, they took a walk to the monolithic Army Street freeway interchange and while exploring the land underneath they shared ideas about its possible transformation. Together they posed the question: what can we do with this field of concrete and warehouses? They answered with a most unlikely idea: create a farm.

Architect and theorist Yona Friedman wrote in 1972, "Utopian proposals are provoked by dissatisfactions within a society that has not found remedies for them."[7] When The Farm was founded in 1974, there was still a war in Vietnam, misogyny was commonplace, and the ethos of the San Francisco Diggers was still in the air. A myriad of revolutionary projects exploded onto San Francisco in the early 1970s that sought to challenge and amend the concepts of community, equality and art. Joan Holden, a member of the Mime Troupe and an active participant in The Farm, said that in this atmosphere "Everything seemed possible, it seemed possible to recreate society."[8]

The Diggers and the Artists' Liberation Front, both offshoots of the Mime Troupe, brought happenings to the streets of San Francisco in the mid-1960s.[9] The Diggers turned life into a performance of political theater taken into the streets to help aid and heighten the lives of others. They were the zeitgeist of Haight-Ashbury in the 1960s with their utopian proposal for Free Cities.[10] The spirit of the 1960s—the Civil Rights Movement, anti-war protests, feminism, and hippie sensibilities—became internalized on a much more intimate, domestic scale in San Francisco. Activism was alive in the theaters, the streets, the hangouts, and eventually at The Farm.

Like Sherk's concept of the "life frame," the Diggers asked people to step through "The Free Frame of Reference," a giant yellow picture frame that encouraged people to shift their perceptions on life. While Sherk's earlier performances were temporary works of theater and ecological sculpture, she recognized the need to create a more enduring form. The Farm sought to create a more sustained model in hopes of investigating and cultivating individuals' relationships with community, plants, animals, and natural processes under the umbrella of art and ecological transformation:

> Our original mandate was to create a unique multi-cultural, agricultural art and environmental learning and gathering Center in the midst of an urban setting, where people of all ages could

experience plants, animals, and each other in an enriched series
of environments within a context of art.[11]

The microcosm of The Farm reflected the potential for social change that
Marcuse saw in ecological action:

> What is happening is the discovery (or rather the rediscovery) of
> nature as an ally in the struggle against the exploitative societies
> in which the violation of nature aggravates the violation of man.
> The discovery of the liberating forces of nature and their vital
> role in the construction of a free society becomes a new force
> in social change.[12]

The Farm did not reject technology or capitalism, but instead worked within
the extant framework to make life better. Lippard describes how the project "…
nonchalantly incorporates the incredible technical monolith called the 'Freeway,'
like a garden beside a cathedral."[13] It was not just a physical manifestation, but also
a conceptual premise for reevaluation. Sherk explained her goals for the project,
"I'm trying to expand the notion of what art is…Take the rabbit, burrowing
tunnels. She's an incredible architect."[14] In the "life frame," each element, from
grass, to chicken, to child, became part of the sculpture.[15]

The Farm was not a commune—there was only one bedroom there that
rotated use throughout its tenure—though it embodied many of the same tenets
as communes. A contemporary communal living experiment that set an important
precedent was the Integral Urban House, an ecological demonstration house started
in Berkeley by the Farallones Institute in 1972. Bill and Helga Olkowski, members
of the Farallones Institute, bought a Victorian home in Berkeley in 1972, which
was converted into a model of urban sustainability complete with gardens, animals,
composting, recycling, and solar-heated hot water. The Integral Urban House was
a communal living space, but also an ecological demonstration home; the structure
and its residents embodied a set of principles of sustainable living that they were
eager to share with the public.[16] Like Sherk, the founders of the Integral Urban
House considered their project to be "a mini-ecosystem in which rabbits, chickens,
fish, honeybees, plants, microbes, and people interact in a flourishing example of
interrelated self-reliance."[17] While both The Integral Urban House and The Farm
were urban homesteads, they differed in their trajectories. The Integral Urban House
was a revolutionary ecological commune as well as a living how-to manual for the
public, while The Farm was framed as a piece of "life theater," an alternative to
alternative arts space and an agricultural and multicultural community center.

What these projects share is a radical rethinking of the role of ecology and
the role of humans within it. "Man is in the world and his ecology is the nature
of that *inness*," wrote Paul Shepard. By creating productive ecosystems outside
that were mirrored through non-hierarchal interactions inside, the Integral Urban
House and The Farm, sought to challenge the role of humans as oppressor, battle
intolerance, and empower people to enact positive change.[18]

This utopic vision was about progress as an ongoing struggle redefined by each
successive generation. By facing and fighting against accepted realities—including
sexism, racism, ageism, ignorance, and abuse of animals and the earth—The Farm
sought to create an alternative social structure. It was a model, but it was also a

work in progress. Sherk, who acted as Founding Director until 1980, said "It's a play, a sculpture and a sociological model. There are also elements of plumbing."[19] Diversity of people, species, and ideas were one of the strengths of the project, while diversity of intention was part of its undoing. The Farm meant many things to many people; it was a farm, a school, a collective, a community center, a theater, an art gallery, a club, and a place to break bread and smoke dope. While Sherk and Wickert embarked on creating The Farm together, their altering visions for the project soon created a rift between them.

The creation of an urban farm was no easy task. It involved dedication, vision, persuasion, and compromise. The reclamation of the land and buildings that became The Farm was an act that Wickert described as "hammering, sawing, digging, picking, carrying, lugging, toting, hauling, sweeping, mowing." Sherk and Wickert leased the 1.5-acre concrete lot with several dilapidated buildings, while Sherk contacted Huey Johnson at the Trust for Public Land to consult with the City about acquiring the adjacent lot. Between 1974 and 1975, she collected thousands of neighbor's signatures, and in 1976 the City agreed to purchase the 5.5-acre lot under the stipulation that it would be developed into a park.

Carol Blumenfeld (now Sachal), a Board Member at The Farm, described "the Mission at the time as a forgotten child," which transformed in the mid-1970s due to Galería de La Raza, mural projects, and the rise of community cultural centers.[20] In 1978 Galería de La Raza curated an exhibition called *Slow Arte*, which featured locally made lowrider cars. Lowrider cars were becoming an integral part of Chicano culture all across California and the Southwest. In San Francisco, the empty lot adjacent to The Farm became the gathering place for this movement. The Low Riders appropriately called it The Lot and it became a place where they would gather before cruising through the Mission in their lowrider cars. The Low Riders looked to the People's Park in Berkeley for a model in hopes to create a place where the culture and politics of the surrounding Mission area could have their forum. While it was through efforts by The Farm to collect the requisite number of signatures and weather negotiations with the City that led to the purchase of the lot in 1976, the Low Riders were definitely instrumental in the shaping and naming of La Raza Park in 1980. There was cross-pollination between the neighboring groups and with the help of Board Member René Yañez, a group of kids came to The Farm and painted a mural about their lifestyle. The Farm and The Lot became a locus of activity, where people from the neighborhood came to gather.

As a nonprofit organization, Crossroads Community (The Farm) applied for and received grants and funding from public and private sources including the National Endowment for the Arts, (NEA) The Comprehensive Employment and Training Act (CETA), and the California Arts Council (CAC). Wickert describes the natural delegation of roles, "Bonnie was more into the agricultural aspect than I was, but I ended up driving the dump truck that hauled all the compost in the City."[21] The "Garden on State Land" was developed with the help of volunteers and donated materials. Vegetables, flowers, and orchards were designed and planted by Sherk, Wickert, gardeners Vicki Pollack and Jeff Brown, and adults and children from the neighborhood and nearby Buena Vista Elementary School. With the help of CETA funding and an "Alternative to Education" CAC grant, The Farm was able to hire art teachers, gardeners, and educators. They formed a managing board that brought together artists, dancers, actors, and community members from adjacent

*Kids on the Farm, c. 1976.*                                    PHOTO: VICKI POLLACK

neighborhoods and interested members of the corporate world in an attempt to create a diverse cross-section of society.

The Farm was a flourishing hive of activity composed of an ongoing collaboration of people, animals, plants, and ideas that is difficult to encapsulate. On November 15, 1977 from 10:45 a.m. to 12:45 p.m., Pollack made a series of 32 photographs called *2 Hours at The Farm*. The series documents the range of overlapping activities that took place within a short time span. In one image, adults gather around the kitchen table strewn with papers, in another children dig in the garden against the backdrop of the freeway, and performers stretch on mats in the lofty theater space. From this collection of images we can gain a sense of the continuous motion and momentum at The Farm.

One of the warehouses was converted into a farmhouse, and the other into a theater. In the theater, people tumbled through space, swung from the trapeze, and donned costumes on stage while below animals put on their own performances. The building was transformed into two theater spaces—a human theater on the first floor—where groups such as The Jones Family, Tumbleweed, Pickle Family Circus, and Make-a-Circus rehearsed and performed—with an animal theater below.

The nearby Buena Vista School was the first alternative elementary school in San Francisco. It was originally located in a junkyard where kids held court amidst the ruins. Tom Ammiano (now a San Francisco Democratic Assembly member) taught at the school and Pollack—a former Digger—was hired with CETA funds to be a school gardener. Pollack brought her classes to The Farm and eventually became one of the head teachers at The Raw Egg Animal Theatre (T.R.E.A.T). T.R.E.A.T. was an indoor and outdoor environment envisioned by Sherk, which was composed of bales of straw, trees, a stage, mirrors, wooden fences, small houses, and domestic animals, including cats, pigs, goats, rabbits, sheep, ducks, geese, and chickens. It was envisioned as a classroom following her "life frame" where children, adults, and farm animals were all students and performers, interacting with each other in an open setting in an effort to close the distance between them.

Pollack describes how she tried to "give children real experiences and expose them to as many things as possible."[22] The whole farm became a classroom where artists, musicians, dancers and ecologists acted as instructors. Children performed acts of their own creation on the theater stage for an adult audience and could learn about biology firsthand through witnessing the life cycles of plants and animals. Interspersed with the miracles of birth and growth were harsh lessons about animal savagery, exemplified by a litter of baby bunnies that were killed by city rats. Sarah Davis—whose father Jack Davis was a board member—describes growing up playing with animals in T.R.E.A.T. and then frequenting The Farm again for punk shows during her teenage years. Radical performance artist Stanya Kahn describes The Farm as the "magical place we went to from school." Growing up going to The Farm was a formative experience for hundreds of children and the exposure and freedom afforded them a unique type of independence.

On the second floor of the Farmhouse, The Reinhabitory Theatre—composed of founders of the Diggers including Peter Berg, Judy Goldhaft, and Peter Coyote—mimicked the animals next door as part of their act. The troupe took up residence at The Farm, where they practiced, studied animal behavior in T.R.E.A.T. and translated these observations into their own actions. Coyote writes about the group's daily practice of inventing a new piece:

> Our organizing principle was to use "stories" from our bioregion, both ancient and new. Our perspective would be "multispecies"—telling the tales from the points of view of all local species, not just humans.[23]

Through their study of animal behavior, the Reinhabitory Theatre developed humorous performances based on collaborative narrative in an effort to understand other species in a more sensitive and conscious way, echoing Sherk's intentions for The Farm.

The second floor also housed an "International Parlor," an exhibition and performance space with adjacent darkrooms.[24] Starting in 1978, The Farm received grants from the NEA to be "an alternative to alternative arts spaces"—a combination community, agricultural, ecological, performance, and exhibition center—with an artist-in-residence program. In San Francisco in the early 1970s, there were several alternative arts galleries with an emphasis on experimental art, performance, poetry, and literature, including Intersection for the Arts (founded in 1965), and New Langton Arts and La Mamelle (both established in 1975). At The Farm, artists such as Chip Lord, Richard Mock, and Douglas Hollis created indoor and outdoor exhibitions responding to the spirit of the place. Hollis describes his site-specific installation on the The Farm land as "rural architecture," a mix of skeletal structures made of wire rods, baled hay and mounds of dirt, which responded to the hybrid landscape.[25]

The first floor was converted into a domestic space with a farm kitchen, living room area, and an open space for workshops and community gatherings. The kitchen was the hearth of The Farm, where people would come to break bread and hatch plans. There was no insulation in the warehouse, so one of Wickert's friends built a wood-burning stove to stave off the cold. Sarah Davis remembers Jack manning the coffee pot throughout the day to keep refreshing visitor's cups. The first floor of the farmhouse was a gathering place, an office and a celebratory spot, where members of the community of all ages could come together to relax, feast, and share resources.

In the basement a state preschool was founded that utilized T.R.E.A.T. as part of its curriculum. In addition to the preschool, over a hundred children per week from over 75 different schools in San Francisco and the Bay Area shared this "school without walls" with the animals, where they also made art, planted vegetables, and maintained the gardens. Throughout The Farm's tenure, a variety of nonprofit research groups would utilize rooms in the farmhouse for their operations, including a center run by the group Earthworks to research and distribute information on agribusiness and nutrition.[26] At night, poetry readings, and musical and theatrical performances took place at T.R.E.A.T., the "Barn Theater," and the farmhouse.

Outside, the land was developed into a working farm with a greenhouse. Yet, the grounds were not initially suitable for gardening as the soil was contaminated with lead and other toxins. With the application of compost and new soil, the trees, fruit, and an assortment of vegetables flourished, creating a surreal tableau that included a field of corn growing by the freeway. Children and neighbors partook in gardening the land and making scarecrows; festivals punctuated the harvest and spring. In the city-owned lot adjacent to the warehouse, concrete was removed and beds planted, kids drew on the remaining pavement assigned to envision future iterations of the space, and Low Riders congregated there and together cruised through the Mission.

The March-April 1979 issue of the bi-monthly *Farm Calendar* advertised a "Care and Feeding of Edible Landscapes" class, which was free and open to San Francisco residents. Programs included: an artist-in-residence program, artists' presentations, festivals, pageants, workshops, lectures, exhibitions, dancing, acting, Native American pow-wows, music rehearsals and performances, the on-site pre-school, and eight classes from three different elementary schools visiting during weekdays. The calendar was marked with neighborhood days and hoe-downs and anyone who wanted to teach a class was welcome to share their knowledge. Much of The Farm's funding came from renting the space for weddings, community events, practice space, and parties. Plans to purchase the 1.5-acre lot of land with warehouses and to secure funding for additions such as a tearoom, senior center, and a multicultural nutrition center were outlined. Sherk and many of those involved with the project saw The Farm as an ongoing way to cultivate both the earth and the community.[27]

Rhodessa Jones characterized The Farm as "one of the early industrial multipurpose, multidisciplinary, multicultural spaces in San Francisco."[28] In the mid-1970s through the 1990s came a rising wave of alternative art spaces and neighborhood cultural centers including Intersection for the Arts, 848 Community Space (now CounterPULSE), and Galería de La Raza. In 1979, SOMArts Cultural Center was established through the Neighborhood Arts Movement, an activist effort to provide government support for art and community spaces.

In addition to its utopic vision, The Farm was a nonprofit that depended on securing outside funding to sustain its average $10,000 monthly expenses for

*Looking north from The Farm's roof, c. 1976.*                    Photo: Vicki Pollack

operating costs, rent and salaries.[29] Compounding these demands was the San Francisco Parks Department's decision to turn the adjacent city-owned lot into a self-enclosed neighborhood park. Sherk's plan had been to sculpt the park out of natural resources and recycled materials, creating sloping hills, meadows, community gardens, windmills, and a pond fed by the waters below while integrating this maintained landscape with The Farm next door. The Parks Department did not accept or understand this vision and opted to create a more traditional urban park with an artificial pond separated from its neighbor by a fence.[30] The *San Francisco Chronicle* on October 9th, 1980, announced a "Growing Threat to S.F. Farm" caused by the Parks Department's decision to run drainage pipes for the new city park through The Farm. In the article Sherk expressed her regret, "We will be wiped out….We've been told we'll have to move out while they bulldoze 30-foot swaths through our growing areas."[31] Five days later, Sherk submitted her letter of resignation to the board.

Yañez, who was on the Board of Directors, saw The Farm as a gathering space unique for the "spiritual outreach that it carried to San Francisco."[32] The Farm straddled an urban/rural divide; it was a public space and a pastoral landscape that welcomed a cross-pollination of people, animals, and perspectives. Blumenfeld described a "fractionalization" that was felt markedly at The Farm in the late 1970s, yet the project endured on a tenuous path until 1987.[33] Wickert was still involved as well as a steady succession of directors who each imprinted the project with their mark and struggled to keep it afloat. The CETA program ended in 1980 disabling much of the staff funds. Trouble with the landlords began in 1981 leading to a temporary restraining order by The Farm to ensure the protection of the gardens. While the children still visited during the day, at night The Farm was a notorious venue for punk shows by seminal punk bands like Minor Threat, Black Flag,

Polkacide, The Lookouts, and The Descendents. Brown, a gardener at *The Farm*, said about the changing atmosphere of the space:

> It was a hard transition for me to come down there and to see that maybe the greenhouse hadn't been watered or that the barn was getting really rank and that nobody was really interested in the vegetable garden and would rather shoot pool during the day.[34]

While The Farm was still a farm it also became a club and a haven for roadies and runaways. Anything and everything could happen at The Farm and it was for this reason that it ended.

"They had to step on it because it existed and flourished outside all official channels, it was out of control . . . The same reason we loved it and it represented life to us, they had to kill it . . . because it represented disorder, misrule, anarchy."[35] For those involved, The Farm represented freedom, but to many on the outside it was a dangerous proposition. In the 1980s, issues with the landlords over The Farm activities became heightened to the point that they were evicted on November 5, 1987. The landlord claimed that they would be willing to rent the space to any nonprofit at "fair market value," except to the residents of The Farm. Sixty animals were dispersed to nearby farms and a space that nurtured many forms of life and aspects of community for 13 years became empty again.

For some The Farm was a beacon against the perceived onslaught of the greed and aggressive capitalist exploitation of American society; for the children and animals who ran and grazed in the hay and pasture it was a place of freedom; and for the local government and property landlords it was a baffling utopian demonstration. To Sherk, The Farm was "an environmental performance sculpture," a "Performance of Being," and a series of "life frames," while to Wickert it represented "a collective consciousness coming together with a sense of community."[36] It was an attempt to actualize a utopian dream, something that was ultimately "an impossible illusion to fulfill."[37]

## Postscript

> I saw the total integration as a new art form—a triptych (human/plant/animal) within the context of a counter-pointed diptych (farm/freeway) (technological/non-mechanized), etc.  —Sherk, 1980[38]

> Whenever I pass The Farm I think, "They did it," and this inspires me also to attempt the impossible. Whenever I look down the hill and see it sprawling there in the middle of a concrete wasteland, wrapped up in a roaring freeway, I think that, despite the mindless and relentless expansion of money, technology, and power that there still is a human spirit and it still has a chance to prevail.                                    —Holden, 1976[39]

The field of corn by the freeway, the elaborate scarecrows, the children's pageants, and punk shows all juxtaposed against the cacophonous freeways seems a surreal tableau caught in time. On Channel Road in San Francisco, the funky homemade houseboat community still continues to float against a backdrop of gleaming newly minted highrises. In the parking lot adjacent to The Farm (now La Raza Park), the community garden (Potrero del Sol) thrives. The dynamic tension between homogenization and industrialization versus new ecological thinking and alternative culture is still tangible, leading to new generations of grassroots activism and an ever-expanding litany of projects.

When The Farm disbanded, many of those involved hoped that it would become revived in a different location. While this never happened, the momentum and ideas that were explored at The Farm were reinvested back into the community to help create and develop other local organizations. Jack Davis helped found the Neighborhood Arts Movement and SOMArts and was the Director there for 20 years. Yañez started Galería de La Raza and the San Francisco Arts Commission Gallery. Pollack co-founded The Children's Book Project. Wickert continued to perform with the San Francisco Mime Troupe and is on the board of SOMArts and several other local art nonprofits. In the 1980s, Sherk began to work on *A Living Library (A.L.L.)*, her ongoing plans for transferable educational and ecological community centers framed by art and affiliated with schools that she describes as the creation of "an international network of interactive life frames."[40] Currently there are three *A Living Library & Think Parks* in San Francisco, one in New York City, and interest to open more national and international branches.[41] While the stage has shifted, Sherk's current practice poses the same question she asked over thirty years ago at The Farm: "If we are to continue on this planet and grow as conscious beings we must attain a more spiritual and ecological balance within ourselves and among larger groups and nations. How can we do this?"[42]

The Farm was an amalgam of elements and an anomaly at the time that attempted to provide an alternative vision of what art could achieve, what an art space could be, and how living systems could be integrated into the urban sphere. It was a product of its moment—rooted in ideas of utopianism and the expanded practice that pervaded the counterculture. Sherk wanted The Farm to transcend art and become an environmental and social process: "We relate to ourselves and each other, with those in the surrounding communities, and with different life forms, in the hopes of experiencing a richer humanity and a possible, positive survival."[43] Will Bradley wrote that The Farm vacillated "between an institutionally accepted ethic of art and the practical ethics of the wider state machinery." The City of San Francisco's residents and its bureaucracies were not accepting of the project's radical gesture.[44] Despite the impossibility of its long-term survival, The Farm was a groundbreaking project that prepared city soil for similar projects, setting a seminal historical precedent for the lively profusion of urban agricultural and environmental artistic projects that are steadily being adopted into the landscape of San Francisco and other cities.[45]

Sherk wrote, "Art is Culture is Nature;" perhaps these staid boundaries collapsed temporarily for many who entered The Farm by the side of the freeway. Novelist Ernest Callenbach wrote in 1976, "The Farm is a little piece of Ecotopia here among us now—a sort of 'center that can hold'—a place for things to happen freely but with biological purpose and coherence."[46] While the utopia was a surreal vision with a center that could not ultimately hold, The Farm created a legacy for practices that continue to help shift social and ecological paradigms in the Bay Area and beyond.

# Notes

1.   Herbert Marcuse, "Nature and Revolution," in *The Continental Aesthetics Reader*, ed. Clive Cazeaux (1970; repr. New York: Routledge, 2000), 258.

2.   Molly Rannells's response was to Bonnie Ora Sherk's question in 1976, "What is the Farm to you?" The answers were included on Sherk's "An Alternative to Alternative Art Spaces" poster from 1979.

3.   Lucy R. Lippard, "Gardens: Some Metaphors for a Public Art," *Art in America* 69 (November 1981): 146.

4.   The water that collected was from the below ground Islais Creek, the same source that fed *The Farm* and Sherk's current project, *A Living Library*.

5.   Sherk had since 1973 been thinking about starting a public café environment:

     "I was looking for a space where different kinds of artists and also nonartists could come together and break down some of the mythologies and prejudices between different genres, styles and cultural forms. All of this had to be connected with other species—plants and animals." —Linda Frye Burnham, "Between the Diaspora and the Crinoline: An Interview with Bonnie Sherk," *High Performance* (Fall 1981): 61.

6.   The warehouses had previously been a dairy processing center belonging to Borden's Dairy and the seven acres were owned by six different entities, both public and private.

7.   Yona Friedman, "On Models of Utopias and Social Ecology," *Leonardo* 5, no. 1 (Winter,1972): 37.

8.   *The Farm*, DVD, directed by Kathy Katz and Mike Kavanagh, (San Francisco: Jack Wickert, 1990).

9.   The Diggers sought to develop the first Free City in San Francisco, through the distribution of surplus goods and labor at Free Facilities throught the city, including bread baked at the Free Bakery and the creation of the first free medical clinic, Free Medical Thing. They adopted their name and many of their philosophies from the English Diggers, a group of agrarian activists in 17th century Britain, who sought to create common land for all. See The San Francisco Diggers, "The Post-Competitive, Comparative Game of a Free City"(August 1968), in *Art and Social Change: A Critical Reader*, eds. Will Bradley and Charles Esche (London: Tate Publishing, 2007), 152.

10.  The San Francisco Mime Troupe, a countercultural political theatre group that had been founded by writer R.G. Davis in 1959, still exists today. In San Francisco, through street theater, activism, art happenings, performance, and ethos, the Diggers were performers who sought to change society through dedicated labor.

11.  Bonnie Sherk, "The Farm" (San Francisco, 1980) 2.

12.  Marcuse, "Nature and Revolution," 257.

13.  Lucy Lippard, *Overlay: contemporary art and the art of prehistory* (New York: Pantheon Books, 1983) 234.

14.  Katy Butler, "A Farm Flourishes Beside the S.F. Freeway," *San Francisco Chronicle* (March 18, 1977).

15.  The Kentish Town Farm, originally called Fun Art Farm or City Farm 1 was the first urban farm and art space of its kind founded in London in 1972. This farm was, and still is, a community that allows people to partake in gardening, animal husbandry, horseback riding, and educational and creative activities for free, harkening back to the practice of both the English and San Francisco Diggers.

16.  The Farallones Institute was founded by Sim van der Wyn in Sonoma County in 1969 and was disbanded in 1990. It was a research organization that focused on sustainable gardening, water conservation, and green building. The house was open to the public for tours on Saturdays and a book on the project, *The Integral Urban House*, which functions as a do-it-yourself instruction manual, was published in 1979.

17.  Julie Reynolds, "The Integral Urban House," *Mother Earth News* (November/December, 1976): 1.

18.  Paul Shepard, "Introduction: Ecology and Man—a Viewpoint," in *The Subversive Science*, eds. Daniel McKinley and Paul Shepard (Boston: Houghton Mifflin Company, 1969) 1.

19.  Sherk, "An Alternative to Alternative Arts Spaces," poster, 1979.

20.  Carol Sachal, interview with author, September 12, 2009, Petaluma, CA.

21.  Chris Carlsson, interview with Jack Wickert, March 31, 2008, San Francisco, CA.

22.  *The Farm*, DVD.

23.  Peter Coyote, *Sleeping Where I Fall* (Berkeley: Counterpoint Press, 1998) 328.

24.  Sherk also called it the "Tea Room To Be" as she hoped it would also become an elegant tea room.

25.  Thomas Albright, "'Rural Architecture' Near Army Street," *San Francisco Chronicle*, December 4, 1979.

26.  Caroline Drewes, "The Farm," *The San Francisco Examiner*, August 6, 1980.

27.  One year after *The Farm* broke concrete in San Francisco to make way for gardens, the Living Theatre, a radical theater collective from New York City, created their first "Garden Play" called *Turning the Earth: A Ceremony for Spring Planting in Five Ritual Acts* (1975). The play was part of an ongoing program called the *Legacy of Cain*, which began in the mid-1960s and consisted of free renegade performances in unconventional venues like the prisons of Brazil and Pittsburgh steel mills. On March 21—the vernal equinox—The Living Theatre ritually planted a vegetable garden with the participation of residents, in a small lot in front of 500 West North Avenue, a communal home the troupe was living in at the time in the North Side area of Pittsburgh. They wrote about *Turning the Earth*:

> "The play deals in its practical aspect with property, that is, with land, and its reclamation by the people of a community to be used for growing vegetables. The intention of the play is to stimulate a fresh relationship in the community towards the earth, towards land, towards the question of property." —The Living Theatre, "Turning the Earth: A Ceremony for Spring Planting in Five Ritual Acts," *The Drama Review: TDR* 19, no. 3 (September 1975): 94.

28.  *The Farm*, DVD.

29.  Maitland Zane, "Growing Threat to S.F. Farm," *San Francisco Chronicle*, October 9, 1980.

30.  The park did incorporate Sherk's plan for community gardens.

31.  Zane, "Growing Threat."

32.  *The Farm*, DVD.

33.  Carol Sachal, interview with author, September 12, 2009, Petaluma, CA.

34.  *The Farm*, DVD.

35.  Holden, ibid.

36.  Wickert, ibid.

37.  Bonnie Ora Sherk, "Statement—1979," (San Francisco, 1979) 1.

38.  Linda Frye Burnham, "Between the Diaspora and the Crinoline: Bonnie Sherk interviewed by Linda Frye Burnham," *High Performance* (Fall 1981): 62.

39.  Joan Holden, included in Sherk "Alternative to Alternative Arts Spaces".

40.  Sherk, "The Creation of A Living Library: An International Network of Life Frames," *Leonardo* 24, no. 2 (1991): 223.

41.  San Francisco Board of Education member Jill Wynns used to take her children to *The Farm*, which she describes as a model of the spirit of freedom and optimism of the 1970s, and how that vision eventually transitioned into a more grounded and institutionalized model; "*A Living Library* was the perfect evolutionary step for *The Farm* and San Francisco the perfect evolutionary environment." Jill Wynns, phone conversation with author, March 26, 2009.

42.  Sherk, "Position Paper," (presentation, Center for Critical Inquiry 1st International Symposium, San Francisco Art Institute, November 1977).

43.  Sherk, Invitation to *The Farm: An Environmental and Social Process*, San Francisco Art Institute Atholl McBean Gallery, November 1976. In December of 1976, Sherk curated this exhibition, a combination of installations, performances, lectures and reflections that raised awareness about *The Farm*.

44.  Will Bradley, "Let it Grow," *Frieze* 94 (October 2005). http://www.frieze.com/issue/article/let_it_grow (accessed October 18, 2008).

45.  Some of the ongoing ecological projects framed within an artistic context that are taking place in San Francisco are Rebar's annual *PARK(ing) Day*, Amy Francheschini's *Victory Gardens 2007 and 2008*, Robyn Waxman's *FARM*, and Amber Hasselbring's Mission Greenbelt Project.

46.  This was Callenbach's answer to Sherk's question in 1976, "What is the Farm to you?" His quote was included on "An Alternative to Alternative Art Spaces".

# A Personal History of the
## San Francisco People's Food System
### by Pam Peirce

These days, food is often in the news. The food habits of many Americans, encouraged by corporate food marketing, are leading to high rates of obesity and diabetes. Food travels an average of 1,300 miles to our tables, using a vast amount of fossil fuel in the process. Food gardening is in fashion, as a way to spare transport energy and to provide ourselves with fresh, whole foods. All of these topics have antecedents in movements that have been underway for several decades, and this is a story of one of those movements.

The story began with people looking for something good to eat. What began as a countercultural search for good food, became a multimillion dollar network of collectively run businesses: the San Francisco People's Food System. I will tell you about my involvement in this network, its significant accomplishments, and the sinister forces that brought about its collapse.

## Food Conspiracies

In a time before Whole Foods, Rainbow Grocery, Trader Joe's, and organic produce in supermarkets, one had to shop rather widely in San Francisco to assemble a grocery list of whole foods and organic fruits and vegetables. In the early 1970s, for bulk dry goods there was Oh's Fine Foods, a narrow storefront on Mission Street with a wooden floor and open burlap bags that felt as if it had been there for a century (and may have for all I know). For organic produce, there was the Alemany Farmer's Market. For cheeses there were various Italian delicatessens. You might travel to a store only because it carried a particular item, such as peanut butter without hydrogenated fats or cream cheese without additives.

In that time of experimentation and alternative institutions, there arose groups that called themselves Food Conspiracies. Perhaps the first was the Free Food Conspiracy, which was formed by a number of communes—that is, communal living groups. They pooled their food stamps, bought food in bulk, and distributed it to members according to need. The Free Food Conspiracy only lasted about a year as participants balked against having to give up "imported cheeses and health food extravagances"[1] for the common diet it provided. But others took up the idea and created food conspiracies that used cash to buy just what each household, communal or not, wanted to eat. Conspiracies saved shopping time and provided high quality food, often at lower prices below what was otherwise available.

The idea was popular, so conspiracies multiplied. Members rotated through tasks such as collecting orders and money, shopping, and dividing the food. Using this system, one could purchase bulk dry goods, fresh in-season produce, honey, peanut butter, dairy, cheeses, ravioli, chicken, and tofu. My conspiracy was called Ongoing Picnic. My household had the task of going to the Alemany Farmer's Market at 5:30 a.m. on Saturdays. We loaded up a Volkswagen bug with produce—trunk, back seat, floor, passengers' laps. As much as possible, we purchased produce that was certified organic. We would drop off the food at the distribution garage, then go home to eat breakfast. When we returned to the garage, other volunteers would have done their work. Orders for each household would be neatly arranged in boxes on the floor around the edge of the garage, with the order lists attached.

Ongoing Picnic worked pretty well, though there were occasional glitches. On one memorable Saturday morning, the people who were supposed to divide the food overslept, so when we arrived to pick up our food, it was undivided. The cheese was still in big blocks, the flour and rice in big bags. It wasn't any fun to divide it when we were all crowded into the space and in a hurry to get on with our days. It seems a minor thing now, but we cited it to each other and to new members thereafter as an object lesson—a parable for the chaos that results when someone neglects civic commitments.

We were early adopters of the idea of buying locally, at least in the case of produce, since the vendors at the Alemany Farmer's Market are nearby farmers, and if they didn't have it, we didn't get it. Most of the time, members did very well with the concept, but I remember that one household insisted on ordering apples in late spring and early summer and then complained when apples were repeatedly missing from their box. We'd tell them not to order apples, but they couldn't seem to learn from experience.

Conspiracies had on the order of 10-20 member households. Rather than growing larger, existing conspiracies encouraged formation of new ones. Thus they were small enough that most members knew each other. We sometimes had potlucks or dinners provided by individual households, notably a sushi party led by a Japanese-American member and a chow fun party led by a Chinese-American member.

## Beginnings of the People's Food System

As the number of food conspiracies grew, people saw opportunities to organize wholesale buying operations. Some formed a dry goods warehouse, and one person was supplying dairy and chickens. So when three people who had just arrived in San Francisco from Iowa came up with the idea of opening a food store, some of the suppliers for that store were already in place. In about 1974, they founded Seeds of Life food store at 3021 24th Street. At first it was run by volunteers, including food conspiracy members, who would work for a couple of hours and then shop for items the conspiracy didn't offer. Soon the store was hiring staff and organizing as a collective. In a collective, decisions were to be made by consensus, with each member having an equal say.

The second store to open was the Noe Valley Community Store and then, in 1975, Rainbow Grocery (founded by members of an ashram) joined the system. At its peak, the People's Food System included 11 retail stores, the dry goods warehouse, a dairy distributor, a cheese distributor, two bakeries (one in San Francisco and one in the East Bay), a produce distributor, a refrigerator repair company, a magazine, and, briefly, a day care center.

The People's Food System founders sought primarily to provide better food at lower cost. A statement on the current Veritable Vegetable website concerning its early history says the Food System was founded "to provide a large-scale collective alternative to the corporate food system. We wanted fresh, healthy food free of chemical poisons, [with] farm worker protections, and profits kept within our rural and urban communities. "[2] Food system goals included wider access to organically grown food and better education about food and nutrition.

From the beginning, participants struggled with organizational issues and the intersection with larger issues such as sexism and racism. People talked and wrote about how to make collective decisions, including how those who did all the talking should "refrain from speaking and doing as a way of relinquishing power to others"[3] who were less able to speak up. Those who did too much of the talking were more likely to be men. In *The Storefront Extension*, the food system newsletter, women from the Red Star Cheese collective posted a handwritten note: "Where Are All The Women These Days?" They then wrote that some women were busy with children and others didn't want to "expend all the energy to get men to listen and work *with* them."

Some women preferred to work only with other women. Red Star Cheese employed mostly women, and the Amazon Yogurt collective was all lesbian. The yogurt factory never opened, however, because the collective insisted on using a female plumber to plumb the yogurt-making equipment, and was never able to find one. People's Refrigeration consisted of one woman who had trained to repair refrigerators. The collectives were delighted to use her services to maintain their usually second-hand and often malfunctioning refrigeration equipment.

Early in the Food System's history, members wanted a diverse workforce, so when the collectives began to hire paid staff, people of various ethnicities were included. Among the first paid workers at Seeds of Life were women who were recent Central American immigrants.

Issues of class were dealt with less directly. Early Food System participants were mostly college educated, which often meant middle class childhoods, but it was a time when access to college had expanded to include many who grew up with less privilege. We did recruit employees who were working class, and thought about the differences between working conditions in a hierarchical system vs. in a collective. Racism, sexism, and increasingly, gay rights, were clearer issues, and were discussed by more people more often than class. This emphasis is not surprising in America, since Americans often feel "we are all middle class here." The emphasis on race and gender also reflected the times, when these issues were being debated in the US as a whole and in the Left as never before.

Some much-discussed issues were whether to carry various foods. There were questions of cash price, real price, ecological effect, conditions of the workers who produced a food, nutrition, and the question of whether to carry foods commonly eaten by people who lived in the surrounding neighborhoods. The Warehouse chose not to carry white sugar, and stores debated whether to carry items such as canned foods, white rice, white flour, as well as white sugar. Such decisions were being made within individual collectives, and if there was disagreement among collective members about what to carry, they sought consensus, rather than just shutting up the minority.

## *Turnover* Magazine

In 1975, a friend began to help with *The Storefront Extension* newsletter, which was serving mainly as intra-Food System communications. He showed me an issue and invited me to write for it, with the idea of expanding it to speak to customers about the Food System, nutrition, and the economics of food. A member of the warehouse collective had been working on a long essay about the imperialist history of sugar production. The first article I wrote was on sugar and nutrition, to complement the history article. Together they became the first issue I worked on.

We soon changed the name of the newsletter to *Turnover: The Newsletter of the People's Food System*. *Turnover* was intended as "quadruple entendre." It referred to the turnover of goods in a store, to the filled pastry, to turning the soil to plant crops, and also to the Chinese word *Fanshen*, which meant turnover in the sense of a revolution. Later, we changed the new magazine's name to *Turnover: Magazine of Politics and Food*. We continued to carry news and information about the Food System, but also articles about specific foods, food history, food economics, and food politics. We also ran information about political issues such as a strike at canneries in the Central Valley and the struggle to save low-income

ORIGINAL COVER ART BY RICH TOKESHI

housing in the International Hotel in San Francisco. There were, all told, 19 issues of *Turnover*.[4] The sugar issue sold so well that we reformatted it to become a "Special Issue on Sugar" and continued to sell it throughout our existence.

The *Turnover* collective consisted of 3-5 regulars and several volunteers per issue, but in fact, unlike members of other Food System collectives, we were all volunteers. We paid for each issue out of sales of the last one, with nothing left for wages. (In later issues we were able to pay a nominal fee to a translator, so some of our articles, including the entire "Special Issue on Sugar", could appear in Spanish as well as English.) The magazine was printed on legal-sized paper folded over and stapled in the middle, with a colored paper cover, typed on an IBM Selectric typewriter, pasted up with rubber cement, and run off by collective members and volunteers on a small printing press. We had plenty of line drawings, charts, maps, and black and white photos, and often included cartoons, poems, and recipes. The People's Warehouse truck delivered *Turnover* to the Food System stores, as well as some non-Food System bookstores, and brought back the proceeds.

In *Turnover* we covered many food issues that have continued to be pertinent, such as cash crop exploitation of Third World nations, water shortages in California, conventional agriculture's lack of sustainability, and the push of large food processors to get us to eat their cheap, nutritionally inferior foods. We wrote about poor food in school lunches, fad diets, and the way that special interests influenced national dietary guidelines. In one article on margarine, I wrote about trans-fats and the suspicion that these never-before-existing substances could well be nutritionally harmful.[5] We also continued to report Food System news, as well as information on outside political issues that Food System members felt strongly about.

## The Food System Changes and Develops

For several years, Food System workers were opening stores, buying food, making bread, cutting and wrapping cheese, buying cash registers, preventing the refrigerators from leaking water onto the floors, keeping the books, making runs to Clover Dairy in a seriously dilapidated truck, and getting good food to a lot of people. People tried new endeavors, not all of which lasted. For a short time, the Food System included a collective that was providing eggs from an egg ranch in Morgan Hill called Left Wing Poultry. In mid-1976 they had 3,000 hens. (A *Turnover* article written by a Left Wing Poultry collective member included this gem: "Why did the chicken start to cross the freeway and stop right in the middle? Because she wanted to lay it on the line. And that's exactly what we intend to do."[6]) Despite excellent intentions, they went out of business in under two years. Another enterprise that didn't last was flour milling. A used flour mill was purchased, but never went into production because we didn't have people with the skills needed to maintain and run it.

Members also took part in demonstrations as a Food System contingent, posted political material in the stores, and participated in movements such as the fight to save the International Hotel, a residence for mainly elderly Filipino and Chinese people. Many individual members took part in the 24-hour vigil set up to defend against eviction. We bought coffee at the nearby Clown Alley restaurant and sat in parked cars through the wee hours of the night watching for any activity that would suggest an eviction was about to occur. We were on the phone tree to be notified when the eviction came, and when it did on August 3, 1977, many of us got up in the middle of the night to take part in the nonviolent human blockade to prevent the sheriff's department from dragging the tenants out of the building. Baton-swinging police peeled off demonstrators and prevented them from returning to the blockade. While we didn't stop the evictions of the elderly Asian-American tenants that night, we were proud that we helped in the blockade that changed public opinion.[7]

The collectives remained largely independent of each other. Each kept its own books and made many of its own operating decisions. The supply collectives Merry Milk, Red Star Cheese, Veritable Vegetable, People's Bakery, People's Refrigeration, and *Turnover*, were housed in the same warehouse at 20th and Alabama, while the People's Common Operating Warehouse was at another address. Earthworks, a library and institute for the study of land and agriculture, was at Army and Potrero.[8] Uprisings Bakery was in the East Bay. Most of the stores were in San Francisco, but two were in Berkeley, one in Oakland. We spoke to members of other collectives, though I never visited the People's Warehouse or any of the East Bay sites. (I was

*The early days of the San Francisco Cooperative Warehouse, c. 1975.*          PHOTOGRAPHER UNKNOWN

busy getting *Turnover* out and earning a living by other means.)

There was always tension between political activism and the fact that the collective members were dependent for their livelihood on their small businesses (except in the case of *Turnover*). The members of some collectives were more interested in politics, while in others, politics were not considered important. Some stores, for example, refused to support the boycotts called by the United Farm Workers. Other collectives felt that food was only an organizing tool to help people understand the exploitive nature of capitalism and the damaging effects of American imperialism. Alexis de Tocqueville, who wrote *Democracy in America* in 1840, said that revolutionary consciousness was the opposite of commercial consciousness, and this may be why the Food System's efforts to combine them were indeed doomed.

Because of disagreements, there were occasionally hard feelings among collectives. There was also tension between an exacting idealism and a disappointing pettiness. The pettiness was couched in ideological terms, but the differences sometimes seemed overblown. At a potluck Thanksgiving dinner for all collective members, I was told by a member of my collective not to speak to a member of another collective, since they were "not radical enough." That night, I was mainly interested in time off from a grueling schedule, and thought the order was just silly. Because of the various inter-collective tensions going on, it was also at this dinner that I thought, "We have passed the point, in size and compatibility, at which we can still have a potluck together."

Some of the more political of the collectives proposed a representative group to be called a Central Body to which all of the collectives would send members. They would create a system-wide "Basis of Unity" political statement and make system-wide decisions about which political issues to take on. Toward the end of 1976, the collectives began to pay 2% of sales into an Economic Central Fund to be spent by the representatives. In addition to Central Body meetings there were also a few all-day system-wide retreats to discuss policy. I was part of the committee that planned anti-racism workshops, too.

Some collectives didn't like the idea of a superstructure. Some still resisted being asked to take part in political movements, while others found just running the businesses to be demanding enough, without more responsibilities. In 1976, Rainbow Grocery left the Food System over such issues.

The Central Body employed democratic centralism: representatives were elected and recallable, but the body they formed could make binding decisions for the group. These decisions were meant to be based on bottom-up opinion, with the option to remove a representative who drifted into top-down decisions. While it was true that decision-making by consensus in collectives was sometimes ponderous, many people were leery of a body that could make binding decisions without a popular vote.

## Violence Strikes the Food System

In spite of these complexities and conflicts, we would probably have gone on selling food and working on political issues for some time longer, had we not become the location of a violent confrontation between people who were members of prison gangs. Because of this, the Food System has been remembered as a violent organization, a reputation that did not reflect the practice or the philosophy of the majority of its worker members. There was nothing violent about the day-to-day work we did to supply food and inform the public about our food supply and the power relationships that affect it.

Throughout its existence, the Food System made special efforts to be ethnically and racially diverse. This meant a wide variety of reference points and life philosophies, people working together and working to understand each other. These varied backgrounds and experiences played a part in the difficulties we had in seeing eye-to-eye within or between collectives. And the differences made it difficult for us to deal as a group with conflicts that in retrospect were dire threats.

Middle class people brought with them the innocence of the suburbs. Working class people brought a harder view of life. Immigrants brought views from other lands, often from the bottom economic strata of those places; veterans of the war in Vietnam brought an understanding of war and the hardships of life in a Third World economy. Some members were "red diaper babies" with a political seriousness influenced by parents who were members of the Old Left; others were followers of New Age religions.

Some collective members were active in the prison movement, trying to improve justice and conditions for prisoners, and their involvement with this movement led them to propose ex-prisoners as Food System workers. These new employees added their own viewpoints to the mix. Some were good workers who wanted to make life better for people, often with particular reference to the communities in which they grew up. Others brought criminal instincts as well as dangerous gang loyalties.

At one of the all-day retreats, a White former convict, and member of the prison gang Tribal Thumb, saw a middle class man who came from South America taking photographs, yanked the camera away from him and broke it. People were shocked, and the Representative Body asked the former convict's collective to put him on paid leave until we could discuss this matter with him. The collective refused, saying he was a good worker (perhaps they were also reluctant to pay someone who wasn't working).

A struggle ensued between those who thought events were rolling toward a dangerous cliff and those who thought we could sit down and work it out in an amicable manner. Many people felt that there wasn't really any danger, an expression of trusting middle class backgrounds that couldn't imagine the life experiences that led to becoming a prison gang member. Others knew the dangers of a prison-gang mentality gaining a foothold in the system. They feared that these individuals would carry out further violent acts.

After a week or more of arguing and debating, a system-wide evening meeting was called on April 26, 1977, to discuss the problem of a worker breaking the camera of another worker. I was not in town at the time, so my account is derived from friends who were there and published reports. It seems that Earl Satcher, the reputed leader of Tribal Thumb, a partly, or perhaps predominantly, African-American prison gang, showed up with some other gang members, and, by one account, with a couple of Dobermans. They didn't enter the hall where the Food System workers were meeting, but were just outside of it. A gunfight occurred, in which Satcher was killed. Another former convict, Willie Tate, who was not a Tribal Thumb member (and had been doing fine as a Food System worker), was badly wounded. At the time, we felt unsafe discussing what had happened, which left the public making wild guesses.

Before these events, some Food System workers had heard the name Tribal Thumb, and collectives who had hired them may have known some workers were members, but most of us knew neither. Had we been reading *Time Magazine*, which I doubt anyone was, we might have learned that another Tribal Thumb member, when arrested for parole violations, had been found with "quantities of revolutionary tracts." This Tribal Thumb member "asserted that the organization sought money from radicals, but actually is chiefly interested in non-revolutionary crime."[9]

In San Francisco Tribal Thumb was associated with a restaurant called Wellsprings Communion. I remember that South of Market restaurant (more recently it was Julie's Supper Club on Langton Alley and Howard). It served vegetarian Indian food at low prices, and asked that patrons neither talk nor read while eating. Not much fun, but the food was cheap and good. The proprietor was a White man with a gray ponytail, whose two children were sometimes in the restaurant. Then he disappeared and the place was taken over by African-American men. What happened? It was rumored that these men took over the restaurant and kicked out the founder. If I had known that Food System collectives might be hiring people from Tribal Thumb, I certainly would have objected.

## The Crash of the Food System

A recent account of the Food System history says that, "Although the shock of the gunfight soon wore off, the Food System began to succumb to larger changes," such as overwork for low pay and the rise of other stores that carried the same kinds of food.[10] I beg to differ. The pall of violence hung over the system for some time and contributed to the demise of several stores, and the eventual end of the Food System as a multi-collective institution.

It is true that working for little, or, in our case, for nothing, while supporting ourselves in other ways, was getting tiresome. But the violent events dramatically damaged the Food System's economic stability. Customers, unclear about what had happened, chose to stay away, damaging store sales, and thus sales of the wholesalers that supplied them.

In the case of *Turnover*, we had just printed our first issue on a web press, which cost less per issue, allowing a much bigger press run and a much more handsome, finished appearance. The theme was water, an important topic given California was suffering a several-year-long drought at the time. We mapped the dams and canals that served the state, gave a history of water politics, and wrote about how to conserve water. We had just "put it to bed" before I went on a trip. In addition, I had just taken a class on writing business proposals at the New School for Democratic Management where I developed a plan to incorporate *Turnover* as a nonprofit and seek grants. After the shootout—as it became known—sales of *Turnover*, rather than climbing dramatically as we expected, dropped precipitously. Because of this, I couldn't muster much enthusiasm from other collective members for my business plan. We went back to the handmade 8½ x 14 inch paper product, printed on the tiny press. While we continued to put out good issues after that, I left the collective in mid-1978, and *Turnover* ceased publication soon after.

Did the rise of other sources of good food help lead to the demise of the Food System? I don't think so. The small businesses that survived the collapse of the Food System have thrived in a favorable market which expanded dramatically. Many more people are now looking for the kinds of foods we were searching for when we began the first food conspiracies, as well as for foods we hadn't thought of then. For example, now people shop for fair trade coffee, chocolate, and bananas, grass-fed meat, fish species that aren't being over-harvested, and (science having decided trans-fats are indeed harmful) trans-fat-free products. What the Food Conspiracies began, and the People's Food System continued, is still growing.

## Today

The Food System ceased to exist in 1978, losing an avenue to advance any educational or political goals members once hoped to foster. Most of the individual businesses that made up the Food System are also gone. The only remaining former Food System stores are two that left before the Food System collapsed. Rainbow, which, as mentioned earlier, left the Food System in 1976, is now at 1745 Folsom in San Francisco. Other Avenues, now at 3930 Judah, doesn't appear on the list of Food System stores after 1977. These stores don't call themselves collectives now, but "worker-owned cooperatives." Rainbow was incorporated as a cooperative in 1995. (There was, their website reports, "no corporate statute for worker cooperatives when Rainbow was founded in 1975.") They say that it "could be said that Rainbow is a cooperative made up of collectives (our individual departments). Unlike 'Consumer' Co-ops we are not owned by our shoppers, but by our workers. Many people ask us, 'How can I join your co-op?' The only way to join is to become a worker/owner."[11]

Veritable Vegetable still sells wholesale produce (99% of which is certified organic) in San Francisco, at 1100 Cesar Chavez Street, with a hundred-strong workforce over 75% female. It is a corporation, with four co-owners and is dedicated to the concepts of shared equity and employee ownership.[12] In a recent conversation, Bu Nygrens, who has worked at Veritable Vegetable since Food System days, shared my wonder and delight in the growing interest in improving food justice, food production, distribution, nutrition—the whole "food system." Former members of the People's Food System are certainly all watching with great interest as a new generation builds on our efforts, both in food issues and in political organizing.

## Notes

1.  The Diggers Archive, "Deep Tried Frees," *Kaliflower*, n.s. 3, April 30, 1978. www.diggers.org/kaliflower/dtf.htm

2.  History page, www.veritablevegetable.com

3.  *The Storefront Extension*, April 14, 1975.

4.  The first *Turnover* was issue #9 in January/February 1976, as a continuation of the numbering of *The Storefront Extension* issues and the last was #26, in August/September 1978.

5.  Pam Peirce, "Margarine," *Turnover* 22 (November/December 1977): 23-24.

6.  Terry at Left Wing Poultry, "Left Wing Talks About Egg Monopolies," in "Politics of Food Issue," *Turnover* 13 (July/August 1976): 37.

7.  See Estella Habal's essay "Filipino Americans in the Decade of the International Hotel" in this volume.

8.  Earthworks was an unusual cultural, ecological, and political experiment, See Mirjana Blankenship's essay "The Farm by the Freeway" in this volume.

9.  "California's Underground," *Time Magazine*, October 6, 1975. www.time.com/time/magazine/article/0,9171,913516-4,00.html

10. http://foundsf.org/index.php?tittle=People's_Food_System

11. www.rainbowgrocery.org (accessed 2009).

12. Bu Nygrens, purchasing manager & co-owner of Veritable Vegetable, communication with author, August 26, 2009.

# Ecology Emerges

## by Chris Carlsson

*"There's no such thing as environmental victories, there are only holding actions."*
—David Brower

Just a half century ago, ecology as we know it was relatively unknown to the general population. An incredible range of activities and issues is encompassed by today's ecological movement, from toxic waste remediation, clean water, renewable energy and sustainable transport, habitat restoration and species preservation, to the burgeoning healthy, organic food movement, and much more. The recent arc of human engagement with the environment can be traced from early-to-mid 20th century conservationists focused on wilderness and preservation efforts through 1970s mainstream environmentalists who tried to reform the worst practices of polluters and nature exploiters, to radical ecologists who began to question progress and developed an uncompromising biocentric philosophy, all the way to today's biological diversity and environmental justice proponents.

The ecology movement emerged from a strange soup of 20th century antecedents and a concentration of specific historical events from 1968-78. By no means was it new in the late 1960s to be concerned about nature and the environment, though it was still unusual to use the expression "environmentalist," and even less likely to call someone an "ecologist." Before the word "ecology" gained prominence in the 1970s, defenders of non-human species and wild lands were generally known as conservationists, and they saw their work as essentially apolitical. Such folks were often from wealthier backgrounds, often able to contact politicians and decision-makers and have their opinions listened to. The class background of 20th century conservationists kept it a largely white, patrician movement during most of the century.[1]

The class orientation began to shift after the Save the Bay campaign of the early 1960s, which was led by three women, Esther Gullick, Sylvia McLaughlin, and Kay Kerr, who at the outset, reinforced the upper class origins of environmental campaigns (all had husbands who were University of California men—the president, the head of the Regents, and a professor). Starting as a conservation campaign to stop filling the bay in Berkeley, it became a region-wide effort that ultimately succeeded in getting a new state agency to take control over development on bay shores. The Save the Bay movement remains a monumental turning point in Bay Area history and the environmental movement, but it wasn't an isolated phenomenon, coming as it did in the wake of a contentious battle over siting a nuclear power plant on the Sonoma County coast in Bodega Bay, and a widespread citizen revolt against new freeways in San Francisco, both in the late 1950s and early 1960s. All of these efforts tapped a broad population to pressure elected officials against blindly going forward with palpably bad development projects.

A ubiquitous ecological activist since the 1980s, San Francisco's Ruth Gravanis emphasizes the important role Save the Bay played in debunking the notion that strict regulation of shorelines and bay fill would wreck the regional economy. Many people who would later be part of the emergent ecology movement met each other at Save the Bay meetings. Save the Bay also demonstrated a new way to do environmental politics. "Save the Bay and the Bay Conservation and Development Commission [BCDC] were the models of advocacy organization and institution," explains Larry Orman,[2] longtime director of the Greenbelt Alliance, which started as a conservation organization in 1958 under the name Citizens for Regional Recreation and Parks (meeting at Dorothy Erskine's home on Telegraph Hill) and in 1969 renamed People for Open Space.

Environmental groups started springing up like mushrooms after a rain, but it was a rain of bad news. Historian Warren J. Belasco captures the time, "The environmental crises peaked in 1969, when an oil spill off Santa Barbara fouled beaches and killed birds, a smog alert paralyzed Los Angeles, and Cleveland's Cuyahoga River caught fire. On top of this came a rash of news stories on DDT, cyclamates, soil erosion, world hunger, and warnings of impending earthquakes and tidal waves."[3] By the late 1960s, ecological politics started to move beyond earlier concerns for open space and parks to address urban issues from garbage, pollution, and toxic waste, to questions of food safety, energy production, and transportation, all deeply affecting a quality of life profoundly dependent on air, water, and food. Former San Francisco Digger Judy Goldhaft says, "We were into living in a more harmonious way with the planet right from the mid-'60s. There was natural medicine, natural childbirth, organic foods, sustainable living."

## Democracy Evolving

At decade's end there was also a widespread sense of imminent social revolution. As illustrated in other articles in this volume, upheavals were taking place in every area of life, from domestic roles and sexual behavior to the anti-Vietnam War movement, civil rights and urban insurrection, to university strikes and factory wildcats. Insurgencies were breaking out everywhere, and it was only logical that the revolt against "The Man" at work, at school, and in the streets, also would begin to express itself in a rejection of the toxified environment on which modern life depended.

Bill Evers, who had been a founder of the mainstream California Planning & Conservation League in the mid-1960s, and became a longtime board member of the Greenbelt Alliance, found himself surprised at the new kind of politics that had erupted in the streets: "I did not ever envision [protesting in public]. I thought it could even be counterproductive, offend people. They'd say 'that's not how democracy works. If you gotta gripe, vote another guy into office.' But I think the demonstrators have proven the value of it, in at least getting people to focus on the problem. It's crude democracy, but it is democracy."[4]

In the fall of 1968, the *Whole Earth Catalogue* was published, featuring on its cover the first widely disseminated view of Earth from space. It had a galvanizing effect on many people, and gave a major boost to seeing the interconnectedness of life on Earth. Barbara Korr writes in the *San Francisco Good Times* underground newspaper of October 2, 1969, "We look around and see everywhere the plastic encroachment of the unreal on the natural. In the ecological view man is a member of a community which includes plants and animals—all the forms of life—and when the delicate strands of our mutual interdependence are destroyed or tampered with the result is a ravaged land and a ravaged people." She was reporting on a Civic Center exhibit put on by Ecology Action, a group that was the ecology caucus within the Peace & Freedom Party, but which also started as an independent group. In 1969 they sponsored many events, including a "Smog-free Locomotion Day" on September 28 (a big bike ride through downtown Berkeley that looks a lot like a contemporary Critical Mass ride), an event that repeated itself in following years. [see photos of 1971 ride below]

The first Earth Day was held in spring 1970. Given the brutal war being escalated at the time in Southeast Asia, and the urban and campus revolts that were still underway (or at least very recent experiences), the government needed to channel this public clamor into a process. The emergent concern for the environment gave the US government an arena to proactively address a rising public demand for action. In his recent book *The Rebirth of Environmentalism*, Douglas Bevington handily summarizes the flurry of activity:

> Following the first Earth Day in 1970, there was a burst of federal legislation on environmental protection. Twenty-three major environmental laws were enacted during the decade of the 1970s, including the National Environmental Protection Act, the Marine Mammal Protection Act, the Endangered Species Act, and the National Forest Management Act. ... This environmental legislation is often presented as one of the foremost accomplishments of the national environmental organizations and as a reflection of their political clout following Earth Day. However, closer examination of the legislative history reveals that the dominant national environmental organizations played relatively minor (and at times even counterproductive) roles in the passage of these laws. [5]

The National Environmental Protection Act, passed prior to Earth Day after little debate in Congress by huge majorities in both houses, was signed by President Nixon in January 1970. It created the President's Council on Environmental Quality and required for the first time an Environmental Impact Statement for every major federal project. Bevington reports that it provided "substantially increased opportunities for public participation in agency policy making, both by

March 1, 1971, "Smog-free Locomotion Day" in Berkeley, CA.

creating a detailed public record of environmental impacts and also by providing for increased public input and oversight."[6]

Only a decade earlier, Doris Sloan (who in 1975 took the helm of the fledgling UC Department of Environmental Sciences) had attended Sonoma County Board of Supervisors meetings as an activated housewife, only to find the officials sitting with their backs to the unexpected audience. As deliberations took place over PG&E's proposed nuclear power plant in Bodega on the Sonoma County coast, there was no expectation of citizen participation, and the physical layout of government meetings reinforced the closed nature of the process. In 1970 the democratic surge outside of official channels would be given a seat at the table, at least with pre-arranged limits that reinforced who the real power holders were.

Grassroots activism flourished and provided the public foundation for a challenge to scientific expertise, given impetus by the failure of establishment science to question the uses to which it was put. "Experts" pushed chemicals and chemical warfare, nuclear power, more freeways, increasingly industrialized agricultural systems, and so on. Opposition to the juggernaut of ecological destruction could only come from an emboldened citizenry, one that had learned to think and speak for itself. Karen Pickett was working at the Ecology Center in Berkeley in the mid-1970s, and she remembers "people feeling that even if they weren't a scientist or an attorney they could go and testify at a BCDC hearing. Even if they didn't have all the answers they could produce and distribute a factsheet or a booklet on something that people needed to know."

An influential figure that is not often credited with shaping the modern environmental movement is Saul Alinsky, the author of the 1971 *Rules for Radicals: A Pragmatic Primer for Realistic Radicals*.[7] He inspired Ralph Nader and Cesar Chavez, to name but two of the many important figures who learned about community organizing from Alinsky. Nader of course went on to establish a wide variety of public interest organizations, often addressing consumer safety and health issues, an early type of pre-environmental organizing. But Chavez would use the door-to-door and house meeting techniques he learned as a member of the Community Services Organization, a group affiliated with Alinsky's Industrial Areas Foundation, to found the United Farm Workers Union.

Chavez put together an unprecedented alliance with environmental groups and consumers. The national grape boycott went on for several years before California growers gave in and signed union contracts in 1970-71. What is less remembered from that period was the agitation going on in supermarket parking lots on behalf of the grape boycott that educated middle- and working-class shoppers about the severe problem of pesticides on food. The farm workers were being contaminated by DDT and similar poisons (made infamous by Rachel Carson's 1962 *Silent Spring*). Historian Robert Gordon summarizes Chavez's new awareness:

> Recognizing the potential appeal of a fight to protect workers, consumers, and the environment, Chavez stated that 'the issue of the health and safety of farm workers in California and throughout the US is the single most important issue facing the United Farm Workers Union…We have come to realize… that the issue of pesticide poisoning is more important today than even wages.'

With boycotts and a lawsuit filed in collaboration with the early Environmental

Defense Fund and California Rural Legal Assistance, the UFW was instrumental in getting DDT banned nationally. Growers began replacing those chemicals with organophosphates (many agricultural pests were developing immunity to DDT by then) but the new pesticides were even more toxic to the workers, albeit quicker to break down in the environment. Because of this, some mainstream environmentalist organizations kept the UFW at arm's length. But the UFW/ EDF alliance, though short-lived, was one example of a broad alliance between environmentalists and labor at the start of the 1970s. Emerging out of the battles to pass the Coal Mine Safety and Health Act (1969), the Occupational Safety and Health Act (1970), and the National Environmental Protection Act (1970), rank-and-file workers along with progressive union and environmental activists, realized that hazardous working conditions, workplace pollution, and the deterioration of the natural environment were closely related.

It's telling that the United Autoworkers, United Steelworkers, United Mineworkers, Oil Chemical and Atomic Workers, and the International Association of Machinists, worked closely with the Sierra Club, Friends of the Earth, Environmental Action, and others to pass many new laws during the early 1970s. Little wonder that there was so little opposition expressed in Congress given the broad alliance pushing these changes. Perhaps it is also not surprising that the successful alliance of the time was soon torn asunder by the divergent politics that followed the oil price shock and the severe recession of the mid-1970s.[9]

## War is Ecocide

Massive anti-war demonstrations from 1967-1972 were the cauldron in which the modern environmental movement was forged. The devastation inflicted on Vietnam and Southeast Asia through massive bombardment and an unprecedented use of chemical warfare against nature itself in the region, inspired much direct opposition, but also shaped a new awareness of ecology. Here are excerpts from an open letter by Friends of the Earth in support of a telegram sent to President Nixon by dozens of environmental leaders in 1970:

### Ecology & War

*This advertisement is being placed by Friends of the Earth, a conservation group, but it concerns the war in Southeast Asia, and also wars in general.*

*Until recently conservationists have been thought of as content to fight the tragedy of a dam, the outrage of pollution, the spread of ugliness and environmental degradation, and also the economic and political solutions to that sort of mindless destruction.*

*Wars have been someone else's problem.*

*It has been as though war is not as destructive as dams. Or that an air pollution hazard in Los Angeles is a more significant danger to life than bombs landing upon non-combatants in a war, or the laterizing (turning to rock) of thousands of square miles of formerly living soil by widespread use of napalm. It is as though DDT in our vital tissues is worse than wartime chemical defoliants in the tissues of pregnant women.*

*It is not true. They are all of equal order, deriving as they do from a mentality which places all life and its vital sources in a position secondary to politics or power or profit.*

*Ecology teaches us that everything, everything is irrevocably connected. Whatever affects life in one place—any form of life, including people—affects other life elsewhere.*

*DDT on American farms, finds its way to Antarctic penguins.*

*Pollution in a trout stream eventually pollutes the ocean.*

*Smog over London blows over to Sweden.*

*An A-bomb explosion spreads radiation everywhere.*

*The movement of a dislodged, hungry, war torn population affects conditions and life wherever they go.*

*It is all connected. The doing of an act against life in one place is the doing of it everywhere. Thinking of things in any other way is like assuming it is possible to tear one stitch in a blanket without unraveling the blanket.*

*Friends of the Earth, therefore, its Board of Directors and staff, wishes to go on record in unanimous support of the recent telegram to Mr. Nixon, signed by the leaders of the nation's conservation organizations.*

The ecology-war connection goes back to the original A-bombs dropped on Japan, of course, and the 1950s campaign to end atmospheric nuclear testing. Anti-nuclear campaigning in that era was largely led by pacifists and religious organizations, especially the American Friends Service Committee of the Quakers. The spread of radioactive fallout around the planet, overwhelmingly produced by US nuclear testing, inflamed world opinion and led to the Partial Nuclear Test Ban Treaty, signed by President Kennedy in 1963 (it banned nuclear testing in the atmosphere, underwater or in space), though it was never signed by France or China.

Few remember now that Greenpeace was founded in 1970 in Vancouver, Canada to protest the US government's testing of nuclear weapons in the Aleutian Islands off Alaska. For the organization's first five years, its activities focused entirely on combating nuclear testing. Saul Bloom, a San Francisco social justice activist, founder of ARC/Ecology, and long-time ecologist joined Greenpeace in 1977 and worked for the organization for six years. He remembers, "The folks who founded Greenpeace understood the connections between environment, war and peace, and the media—that was fascinating stuff at the time."

Greenpeace, like a number of other groups in the mid-1970s, embarked on an ambitious program of door-to-door canvassing,[10] which Bloom managed during 1977-78 before eventually becoming a Regional Director.[11] Bloom moved on from Greenpeace in 1983, in part because of differences over organizing philosophies and in part because of disputes over the relative toxicity and damage caused by nuclear vs. conventional weapons systems. Still, the overarching focus was on the military's role in ecological damage, maintaining the important relationship between eco-activism and anti-militarism that was given such impetus during the anti-Vietnam War movement.

Another slightly later example of the abiding connections between environmental activism and anti-war campaigning emerged in the wake of the Sandinista revolution in Nicaragua in 1979.[12] When Reagan launched his illegal Contra War against the Nicaraguan government, a group was formed called Environmentalists for Nicaragua, sponsored by the fledgling Earth Island Institute in 1982. Later and better-known as EPOCA, the Environmental Project on Central America, co-founder Dave Henson describes their mission, "We were talking about an effort to connect poverty, war, and the environment in a Sandinista-led Central American country."

## Atomic Power and Chemicals: Energy and Food

Atomic power and chemicals were two overarching symbols of progress in the post–World War II modern world. The "peaceful atom" was heavily marketed to justify the US's enthusiastic embrace of the nuclear genie for war, while the chemical industry was promoting itself as a cornerstone of improved lifestyles ("better living through chemistry" was one marketing slogan of the time). Both of these state-of-the-art technologies underwent recasting during the late 1960s. The peaceful atom came under sharp attack from many quarters, while the public relations campaign of the chemical industry to tout its "green revolution" in agriculture began to erode under the pressure of counter narratives produced by anti-war activists on one hand, and health food proponents and farm worker organizers on the other. The unquestioned March of Progress had run firmly into a wall by 1970.

*Silent Spring* had started many people on a path away from agribusiness-dominated food supplies. The search for the natural was on. Belasco provides an excellent overview:

> Venturing into a health food store in late 1968, *San Francisco Express Times* food advisor Barbara Garson assumed the manager would be another one of those 'proverbial little old ladies in tennis shoes.' Yet in explaining why Garson should not eat sugar, the manager recounted the sordid role of US refineries in Cuba since the turn of the century. Previously wary of health food 'cults,' Garson was pleased—and surprised—that honey, whole wheat, soy noodles, organic raw milk, unusual herbs, and other health food staples could have a progressive context. Other freak explorers of the health food underground reported similar discoveries: dusty copies of hard-to-find works by critics Adelle Davis, Beatrice Trum Hunter, and Rachel Carson—all dismissed as crackpots and cranks by mainstream authorities; and assorted pamphlets with utopian, spiritual, and dietary guidance. Writers of such advice commonly dismissed technocratic experts, worshiped nature, and tended to think in whole systems, not parts. In short, the health food stores offered holistic information that might be called protoecological.[13]

Orman built on this new food consciousness in the following decade. During the mid-1970s, he devised a public campaign to preserve agricultural lands around the Bay Area, arguing for them on food security grounds as well as open space/eco-habitat grounds. He realized that in trying to sharpen the boundaries between urban, suburban, and rural, farmlands were a vital and vulnerable component. His organization People for Open Space, produced a Farmland and Conservation Study of the whole Bay Area. He explains, "Food, food shed, that was my thing and I pushed that along. I don't care if it's organic or commercial. It's important for people to be connected to their local agriculture."[14]

Goldhaft joined with other Digger women in San Francisco to find a new relationship to food. "For me ecological consciousness is involved also with food production. I went to the wholesale produce markets and learned where all the vegetables came from. We became friendly with a number of the people there. We got a lot of produce that was going to be discarded which was essentially extremely ripe produce that was ready to eat, but wouldn't hold on the shelves. At about the same time we were also invited to glean fields around Half Moon Bay. We also were given so many donations that I learned how to do canning and preserving of various kinds, because we had to. Either we had to give the food away, or find some way to preserve it."

Local agriculture was the antithesis of what was happening in the food business. In the 1970s, major grocery chains were consolidating their hold on the national food market. Local grocers and small chains were being gobbled up by Safeway, A&P, Krogers, and Lucky.[15] The march of homogenization was flattening diversity, making food tasteless, and saturating consumers with chemical-laden food. Thousands of people were dropping out and heading to the country in pursuit of a more "natural" life. Goldhaft went to a remote California commune near the Oregon border. "When people left the city and began settling outside, the 'hippies,' the back-to-the-land people, were very involved in sustainability and healthy eating, not eating food that was pesticided, preferring organic growing." This pursuit of self-reliance didn't always work out as planned, but in general a lot of folks established a new relationship with food, and usually with technology more broadly.[16] A return to artisanship was also fueled by the new embrace of "natural."

Ecological campaigns were seeded in that first wave migration to the country. Those who retained a political approach turned themselves toward combating nuclear power, one of the most overwrought and self-defeating technologies ever invented. In later years many of these same activists, now much older, would be involved in the timber wars, river restoration campaigns, toxic waste and environmental justice struggles, and more. Barbara Epstein wrote an excellent history of the "nonviolent direct action anti-nuclear and peace movements" and nicely reconnects the anti-war movement's back-to-the-land exodus with the next wave of ecological activism:

> By the early seventies, the focus of the left counterculture had shifted to the countryside. Many of the people who had made up the countercultural wing of the antiwar movement were moving to rural areas in northern New England, Northern California, and elsewhere to construct communities where they hoped to live their values and perhaps begin to build a movement expressive of them... The counterculture's use of guerrilla theater and other forms of creative expression, its lack of interest in the conventional political arena, its emphasis on the creation of alternative communities, all suggested that revolution had more to do with thinking and living differently, and convincing others to make similar changes, than with seizing power.[17]

In California the anti-nuclear movement had been growing for many years. Doris Sloan was one of the residents of the small apple-farming town of Sebastopol in Sonoma County who joined the effort to stop PG&E from building a nuclear power plant on the Pacific coast at Bodega Head (the struggle lasted from 1958-

1963). Her proto-ecological opposition was informed by her sympathetic support for the anti-atmospheric testing movement, which had begun to demonstrate the health hazards of radioactive fallout. She recalls that she and her fellow Sonoma County citizens trying to stop the PG&E nuclear power plant did not identify themselves as conservationists or by any particular label. "We just saw ourselves as a small group of people battling for safety and aesthetic reasons. We were just a bunch of people battling PG&E because we didn't think there should be a nuclear plant on the San Andreas Fault, y'know?!" PG&E was eventually stopped, but not before digging a big hole at Bodega Head, which at present day is an oceanside lagoon.

The Diablo Canyon controversy started in 1963 when PG&E gave up trying to build the Bodega reactor. Rather than face similar public opposition at Diablo Canyon, PG&E approached the Sierra Club's president and cut a deal with certain board members where Diablo would be chosen rather than the Nipomo Dunes area, which PG&E had originally chosen. The Sierra Club president forbade any chapter from opposing Diablo Canyon, so the San Luis Obispo Chapter formed the Shoreline Preservation Conference to oppose the construction on the grounds that the area had been proposed as a state park, was a sacred Chumash Indian site, had some of the largest oak trees on the West Coast, was located on the second to last coastal wilderness area in California, and was very likely sitting on the fault that destroyed Santa Barbara in a 1927 earthquake.[18]

After the oil shock of 1974, nuclear development in California was getting new support. In 1974-1975 Alvin Duskin, who played an important role in San Francisco and California environmental politics (he had funded a successful public relations campaign against the first Peripheral Canal plans in 1970, and organized hundreds of San Franciscan voters into a grassroots campaign against high-rises, popularly known as the effort to stop the Manhattanization of San Francisco),[19] was involved in funding and organizing a statewide ballot proposition to ban nuclear power plant construction. The vote was slated for November 1975, and this author and many other young college students spent weeks handing out literature in shopping center parking lots and campaigning on campuses and in neighborhoods. PG&E was pressing ahead with plans to build Diablo Canyon, while Southern California Edison was promoting Sundesert, and an additional reactor at San Onofre. Duskin explains his role in this forgotten saga:

> I worked with Another Mother for Peace in getting this thing [Prop 15] on the ballot, the people in San Luis Obispo, fighting Diablo Canyon and all that. We stopped Sundesert. We stopped it. They'd spent money on it, Southern California Edison, they spent on San Onofre. We stopped that. We led to the decommissioning of the plant up in Eureka [in 1983]. [Proposition 15] said you can't zone land in California for a nuclear power plant until you can solve the problem of waste. And for existing plants after a year or two, if the problem of waste isn't solved, the plant has to be de-rated by 5% each year. That would mean that Diablo Canyon and San Onofre would be eventually decommissioned. If they just keep losing 5% a year, it would make them uneconomic to operate.

Duskin was contacted by Sacramento legislators and agreed to help them write a law that would do everything his initiative was going to do, except the derating of existing plants. They sold it as the rational alternative to "Alvin Duskin's radical, communistic, anarchistic, free-love initiative."[20] When the legislature passed the bill a few weeks before the statewide vote, it successfully killed the anti-nuclear campaign and the initiative was defeated that November. Duskin remembers, "People were consoling me on the streets, saying 'Alvin, I'm sorry that lost,' and I said, 'No, we've actually won! They're not going to build any new nuclear power plants in California!' "

Diablo Canyon became the object of a six-year campaign of nonviolent action and full-court-press legal opposition from 1977-1983. Another Mother for Peace, along with dozens of new affinity groups and local organizations around California under the rubric of the Abalone Alliance,[21] campaigned against Diablo Canyon. The name Abalone Alliance referred to the tens of thousands of wild California Red Abalone that were killed in 1974 in Diablo Cove when the nuclear unit's plumbing had its first hot flush. They carried out an escalating campaign of direct action in the attempt to stop the plant from opening. In August 1977, 1,500 people encircled the gates while 47 were arrested. A year later, 5,000 people came and almost 500 were arrested. When the Three Mile Island nuclear plant had a partial meltdown near Harrisburg, Pennsylvania, an April 1979 rally drew 25,000 people to an anti-nuclear rally in San Francisco, followed by 40,000 demonstrators converging on San Luis Obispo for the largest anti-nuclear rally held at that point in US history. Their biggest effort came in autumn 1981 when 20,000 people rallied in support of a two-week blockade that led to 1,900 arrests. (Unfortunately the plant opened and having reached its predicted lifespan of 25 years, PG&E is now seeking an extension for its operating license.)

## Recycling and NIMBY

On October 29, 1969, a computer lab at UCLA connected to computers at the Stanford Research Institute, and then continued to spread out and connect with computers across the planet, which was the beginning of the Internet. On a much smaller scale on the same day, a dozen activists had an appointment on Montgomery Street in downtown San Francisco with Horace Blinn, boss of the Pacific Division of the Continental Can Company, and also the head of the California Anti-Litter League. The demonstrators were from the Canyon League, Ecology Action, and the Free University of Berkeley's Street Theatre Group. As they waited on the street, a crowd began to grow around them, and six barrels of empty cans appeared. After one man was arrested for littering when he refused to move the barrels, Jeremia Cahill of Canyon went in the door with a barrel to keep the appointment with Continental Can. The police pursued and forced him back out, whereupon he began a press conference. While everyone's attention was captured, another small group of demonstrators made their way to the seventh floor only to find the entire Continental Can office closed for a funeral. Their simple questions went unanswered by the one guy present, "Why do you make a product that can only be used once and then has to be thrown away? Why don't you make something that can be used over and over again, and stop stripping the world of its precious resources?"[22]

The hypocrisy of the can company executive also being the head of the anti-litter campaign was not lost on the new ecology protesters. It wouldn't be too long before recycling efforts began in earnest on both sides of the Bay. In Berkeley the Ecology

Center was founded in 1970, and a major recycling center was opened that sparked a wholesale effort by thousands of local citizens to begin sorting and recycling their garbage.[23] A similar effort was undertaken in San Francisco: between 1970, when Richmond Environmental Action (REA) was founded, and 1979, when there had grown up a dozen or more individual recycling operations ranging from REA with a yard, equipment, and staff, to monthly paper drives by churches and scout troops. Haight-Ashbury Neighborhood Council (HANC) Recycling was founded in 1974 and Bernal Recycling in 1977. Together these centers and programs attempted to apply neighborhood solutions to solid waste management.[24]

Pickett was an early staffer working as a recycler for the Berkeley Ecology Center. She remembers:

> We went from working for a long time to get people to see the value in touching their garbage, and separating things. The whole idea was that if they participated in that process, then things would be reused in the highest and best use way. We separated *colors* of glass, never mind the glass from cans. [It's] ironic that [since] it's been institutionalized and it's so acceptable that everybody is recycling, everything is thrown into the same bin.

Nowadays we have curbside recycling in San Francisco but few realize how that came to be. Sunset Scavenger likes to take the credit for it, but Ruth Gravanis was one of the activists who fought off a plan to build a trash incinerator just south of the city in Brisbane in the late 1980s. Had it been built, there would not be curbside recycling in San Francisco in 2010, "because we would be obliged by our contract to *produce* as much garbage as possible to burn as much as possible to generate electricity to sell to PG&E to pay for the trash burner!" It passed SF's Board of Supervisors, Brisbane's Planning Commission, and Brisbane's City Council. "Thanks to the good citizens of Brisbane, who put a proposition on the ballot that stopped it, we didn't get an incinerator. What a lot of people don't know who talk about San Francisco's zero waste, was that it was the NIMBYs of Brisbane who made it possible for us to have a curbside recycling program!"

The NIMBY (Not In My Back Yard) phenomenon has coursed through environmental activism and fights over all kinds of development. The Brisbane refusal to host a garbage incinerator is a good example, but what NIMBY highlights is that some populations have the political clout to get their way when they refuse a development proposal, and others do not. Evers is enthusiastic (if class unconscious) about it: "You had a great ally in NIMBY. NIMBY was the greatest friend the Greenbelt ever had. The big transition in the Bay Area was when population increased to the point that people could see they had a problem. That's when the urban boundaries were adopted by a vote in the communities," arresting the pell-mell pace of urban sprawl, at least in the Bay Area.

## The Roots of Biocentrism, Environmental Justice, Open Space

In the decades since the early 1970s, environmental activism has expanded, deepened, and subdivided into hundreds of efforts. As Orman notes, "the organizational ecology in the Bay Area is totally filled out." In the early 1970s, "before the proliferation of environmental groups, the Ecology Center was where people were meeting each other," recalls Pickett:

A lot of people got their start being turned on to other people, resources and ideas at the Ecology Center, and went on to do other things. The Ecology Center never 'owned' much of anything in terms of campaigns and issues, but was a resource and a springboard. A lot of the people that worked on styrofoam or plastics issues, or started community recycling centers, or brought projects into the schools, or started community garden groups, or creek restoration groups, wouldn't necessarily credit the Ecology Center, because there was this general sharing of ideas without ownership, but if those seeds hadn't been planted back then, I don't think we'd be where we are now.

One of the galvanizing moments for the Ecology Center was the organizing done after the January 18, 1971 oil spill. The event itself "was so dramatic and horrifying that it just totally threw in people's faces in a very big way what was happening," says Pickett. Chevron's *Arizona Standard* and the *Oregon Standard* collided beneath the Golden Gate Bridge, dumping over 800,000 gallons of crude oil into the Bay. Thousands of birds and other aquatic life were soaked in crude oil and volunteers mobilized immediately. Volunteer centers were set up in Richmond and at the San Francisco Zoo, where for two months hundreds of volunteers taught themselves how to clean oil from aquatic wildlife. "There was no place for the volunteers to come. People were horrified, people wanted to do something, people *could* do something, but there was nobody to coordinate that huge volunteer force. There would be today," notes Pickett. Coming two years after the massive oil spill along the Santa Barbara coast in southern California, the ecological consequences of the car/oil economy were suddenly starkly apparent.

An important achievement of 1970s environmental activism in San Francisco, rarely remembered but one that many of us enjoy every day, is our open spaces and parks. Billed innocuously in the 1974 local election as a "Parks Measure," San Francisco voters passed Proposition J on November 5 that year by 116,654 to 64,527. It added to the local property tax assessment, raising over $2.5 million per year to fund park improvement, but most crucially, acquisition of open space. The monies raised from this initiative since that time have gone a long way to preserving most of San Francisco's hilltops as open space, opening new parks, saving remnant habitats, and providing public land for community gardens. It's difficult to imagine how densely built out the urban environment would be had this initiative not passed at the peak of the first wave of environmental awareness and activism.[25]

Planet Drum co-founder and former San Francisco Digger Peter Berg has a different view of the environmental movement than most:

> I think the environment movement as an interesting, engaging thing ended with Earth Day [in 1970] and the founding of the EPA. Mainstream environmentalists were stuffed shirts, careerists, anthropocentric. There was a lot of careerism, a lot of middle-class values. There was a whole other approach: to harmonize with natural systems, rather than protect or defend or whatever.

Planet Drum is a small San Francisco organization that grew out of a series of cross-country trips he and his partner Judy Goldhaft made, seeking out radical communities that had gone back to the land. Everywhere they traveled in 1970-71 they encountered groups living adjacent to environmental disasters, whether clear-cutting of forests, toxic waste-spewing factories, or plans to construct nuclear power plants. Traveling with a video camera, Berg made "video postcards" from each commune, ultimately sharing his work at the 1972 United Nations Conference on the Environment in Stockholm, Sweden. On their return to the Bay Area, Berg began working with conservationist Ray Dasmann,[26] who modeled an inquisitive and observational approach to nature that Berg took to heart. Dasmann and Berg spent many weeks driving around California together, visiting unique habitats and remote sites, giving Berg a crash course in California ecology. Later Berg adapted the concept of "bioregionalism" to reorient human politics on a biocentric basis, and Planet Drum began convening "continental bioregional gatherings."

By 1978, Planet Drum had started a local gathering called the Frisco Bay Mussel Group that held regular meetings at The Farm,[27] bringing in various ecologists and activists to teach each other as much as they could about the local environment and the politics that shaped it. The Peripheral Canal was once again raising its head, with California politicians arguing over how to augment fresh water supplies for the southern part of the state by diverting it from the Sacramento River system and delta. It threatened to destroy the health of the San Francisco Bay.[28] The Frisco Bay Mussels gave Planet Drum impetus to borrow a commonly used tactic of the Sierra Club and Friends of the Earth by taking out a full page ad in the *San Francisco Chronicle*, but this time, turning their successful technique *against* the mainstream ecology groups. The full-page ad denounced the canal plans, but also had coupons that readers could clip and send to the Sierra Club—urging them to reverse their support for the canal—and Friends of the Earth, urging them to take a firm stand against the canal instead of their then-neutral position. Both organizations were deluged with coupons and came out against the canal. Later Planet Drum founded a Green City effort in San Francisco, to promote bioregional thinking in the urban context. This led to the publication of a book full of practical transformational ideas for a more ecological urban life, many of which have since been implemented.[29]

David Brower was by all accounts one of the most important people in Bay Area ecological history. He led the Sierra Club for 17 years in which he led many high profile campaigns against dams and to save wilderness before arguments over politics, publishing, and priorities pushed him out. In 1969 he was ousted from the Sierra Club, and with core collaborators like Tom Turner and Jerry Mander, founded Friends of the Earth that September. Friends of the Earth immediately became a vital voice for all things ecological. Mander worked on the original ad campaigns in the mid-1960s against building dams in the Grand Canyon. He got to know Brower during that time, and went on to collaborate with him for many years. Moreover, Brower deeply influenced his thinking:

> We're embedded in the natural world, it all comes from that, all the resources, all wealth, all health, and if we're not cognizant of that, it will die and we will die. It's absurd to think of it any other way. Brower was my opening to this way of thinking. I didn't hear 'biocentric' in those days. I heard 'ecology' from him, back

in the early '60s. He was already talking 'no growth' as a crucial element, that growth was the enemy of nature. That if we're not aware of growth as the central issue we're not going to succeed at saving the environment or saving the world.

Brower influenced everyone who came in contact with him, and anchored countless initiatives from the 1950s until his death in 2000. His own trajectory prefigures a larger transformation of the environmental movement, as he began as a mountain climber and outdoorsman, and when he became the first Executive Director of the Sierra Club in 1952, he focused his efforts on preserving wild lands slated for damming and industrial development. By the time he started Friends of the Earth, his prodigious talents were focused on specific issues like the Alaska oil pipeline, highway construction and private autos, the Supersonic Transport plan (SST, a competitor to Europe's Concorde), nuclear power, forest clear-cutting, endangered species, and more. He was good at making alliances and effectively lobbied government at all levels. But as John Knox, director of the Earth Island Institute and long-time collaborator with Brower emphasizes, "[Brower] was kind of wild. Young people would bring him an idea, and he would become the public champion of the idea. He became a machine for listening carefully and getting excited about things that needed attention." Underneath his enthusiasm and passion, a deeply critical thinker was always at work.

The reframing of urban ecological activism under the aegis of "environmental justice" since the early 1990s can be traced to an early 1970s turning point. When Brower left the Sierra Club and started Friends of the Earth, he and his colleagues could publish more radical writing than they'd been able to under the suspicious apolitical eyes of the Sierra Club Board of Directors.[30] Their new publication *Not Man Apart* sought to become a regular environmental news source, hoping to become a weekly or even a daily paper. On a shoestring budget, they did an incredible job of bringing to light themes that remain important today. In September 1971 they published an article called "Why Must We Choose Between the Environment and the Cities?" by Marion Edey, who was the Chairman of the League of Conservation Voters (which started out as a Friends of the Earth project but quickly moved out of the nonprofit umbrella to its own life as a directly political organization):

> …The rats in the ghetto, the lead paint peeling from tenement walls, the overcrowding, air pollution and inadequate transportation that plague the inner city—all these are environmental problems, and are receiving increasing attention from environmental groups. Environmental pollution is highly discriminatory. The black man in the ghetto and the working man in the factory suffer more acutely for the simple reason that they cannot escape…What is a more general, long-term problem for the rich is an immediate threat to life and health for the poor. Anyone tempted to view ecology as a purely middle-class issue should take a hard look at the following facts.

The rest of the article lays out studies and reports on pesticides, "A comprehensive study by Dr. Emil Mrak for the Dept. of HEW found that black people had almost twice as much DDT in their fat tissues as did white people." It also highlighted lead poisoning, occupational health hazards, mass transit, solid waste, water pollution, overpopulation, and air pollution, "One out of four patients in the Harlem hospital now suffer from asthma, compared with 5% in 1952." Edey concludes:

> In the past, conservationists have not paid nearly enough attention to these urban environmental problems, but there has been a dramatic change in the last few years. New environmental groups are concerned and active in all the above issues... Do not ask us to make a false choice between a livable city and a livable environment. These are not different problems, but part of the same problem.

Anchoring an environmental critique in poverty and unequal distribution of ecological consequences directly leads to the environmental justice movement emerging a decade later. Contributing even more to the foundation of this movement were the murderous affects of countless acts of industrial disposal that could no longer be hidden as the 1970s unfolded. In 1978, the residents of Love Canal in Niagara Falls, NY, were discovered to be living over a 1940s-era chemical dump. Investigations showed that one-third of the residents had suffered chromosomal damage, and after similar toxic waste disasters emerged elsewhere, the US Congress enacted the Comprehensive Environmental Response, Compensation, and Liability Act of 1980 (CERCLA), better known as the "Superfund," which is the law that requires polluters to clean up their own pollution. Love Canal residents, and soon after those of Times Beach, Missouri, argued that their working-class communities were living on toxic waste dumps precisely because they lacked the political and economic power to stop it.

Toxic waste sites were soon discovered all over the country, including San Francisco, where radiological and toxic waste still dominates the former Naval Shipyard at Hunter's Point. Several dozen other sites have been added to the California Superfund list too, many in the predominantly African-American neighborhood in the southeastern part of the City. Just beyond the southern border of San Francisco lie at least five federal Superfund sites in the neighboring jurisdictions of Daly City and Brisbane.[31]

A decade into the 21st century we are still far from having altered the underlying logic of our culture. There are successes to be sure, and countless millions of people have a more profound understanding of our interdependent existence on Earth than those alive in the mid-20th century did. Modern ecological thinking is characterized by an integrative and broadly systemic way of framing planetary life, stretching from the global awareness of climate change down to the local focuses of countless community-based organizations and an abiding awareness of both biological and social interdependence. That's all to the good. But the hundreds of ecology initiatives and organizations, with their tens of thousands of activists and volunteers, are still fighting a Sisyphean struggle, taking small steps only to be overrun by naked economic power unchecked by ecological sanity again and again. As quoted at the outset of this essay, Brower warned a half century ago that environmental victories are always temporary, and that hasn't changed much. The evolution of the ecology movement is only starting to come into focus, and this article is at best a tiny contribution to a larger history that we have to learn. A half century hasn't yet gotten us to the tipping point towards a radically redesigned way of life. But the efforts forged in the heat of the anti-war and anti-nuclear movements back then remain an indispensable foundation for our contemporary efforts to harmonize human life with Earth's natural systems.

## Notes

1. In the 1930s, a group of women organized the Marin Garden Club and raised enough money to hire the first county planner in the state because the Golden Gate Bridge was being built and "we don't want to be like Los Angeles!" Bill Evers, founder Planning & Conservation League, interview with author, November 2009.

2. BCDC was created by the 1965 McAteer-Petris Act and strengthened after a few years by the state legislature. Author interviews conducted for this article between October 2009 and January 2010 with Sylvia McLaughlin, Doris Sloan, Jerry Mander, Alvin Duskin, Larry Orman, Sam Schuchat, Ruth Gravanis, Peter Berg, Judy Goldhaft, Monica Moore, Tom Turner, Saul Bloom, Karen Pickett, John Knox, Bill Evers, Harold Gilliam, Carole Schemmerling, Julia May, Miya Yoshitani, Juliet Ellis, Jason Mark, Antonio Roman-Alcala, and Kirsten Schwind.

3. Warren J. Belasco, *Appetite for Change: How the Counterculture Took on the Food Industry 1966-1988* (New York: Pantheon Books, 1989) 23.

4. Evers, interview.

5. Douglas Bevington, *The Rebirth of Environmentalism: Grassroots Activism from the Spotted Owl to the Polar Bear* (Island Press: 2009).

6. Ibid., 241.

7. Saul Alinsky's influence goes back to his original *Reveille for Radicals,* 1946.

8. Robert Gordon, "Poisons in the Fields: The United Farm Workers, Pesticides, and Environmental Politics," *The Pacific Historical Review* 68, no. 1 (February 1999): 51, 59. http://www.jstor.org/stable/3641869?origin=JSTOR-pdf (accessed February 2, 2010).

9. By 1999 in Seattle for the WTO protests, it could be treated as remarkable and unprecedented to have an alliance of "Teamsters and Turtles," but a closer reading of history shows that just such an alliance helped produce a good deal of the legal foundation for environmental protection and workplace safety in the early 1970s.

10. I moved to San Francisco on January 1, 1978 to work for Citizens for a Better Environment (CBE, now Communities for a Better Environment). We were hired to canvas for the new California office, CBE having just migrated from Chicago and Milwaukee where they'd established themselves as a grassroots environmentalist group focused on air and water pollution around Lake Michigan. I spent the first six months of 1978 knocking on doors in every neighborhood around the greater Bay Area, getting a crash course in the issues of the day (toxic pesticides and herbicides, acid rain, sewage and waste management, and much more). It was a bit difficult to "sell" the organization door-to-door as no one had ever heard of them and during those first months they had not yet managed to file any lawsuits or achieve any policy changes through their interventions. Nevertheless, we entered the fray, crossing paths with canvassers from Greenpeace and Citizens Action League, hoping to be the first to hit a given neighborhood before they were saturated with earnest requests for money.

11. Bloom had previously canvassed for the Citizens Action League, another organization firmly rooted in the community organizing philosophy of radical reformer Alinsky.

12. See Alejandro Murguia's essay "Poetry and Solidarity in the Mission" in this volume for more on the San Francisco–Sandinista connection.

13. Belasco, *Appetite for Change*, 16.

14. In the 1980s, Orman helped bring Alice Waters, Baywolf, Green's, and local producers together, in what soon exploded into the many strands of a broad new food movement with much of its initial creative impetus emerging in the Bay Area.

15. See Pam Peirce's essay "A Personal History of the People's Food System" in this volume for a completely different story about food stores in the 1970s.

16. See Matthew Roth's essay "Coming Together: The Communal Option" in this volume.

17. Barbara Epstein, *Political Protest & Cultural Revolution: Nonviolent Direct Action in the 1970s and 1980s* (University of California: 1991) 51.

18. The Sierra Club's internal dispute over Diablo Canyon was one reason for the ouster of David Brower.

19.  Duskin was a successful women's fashion designer with his own factory in San Francisco at 3rd and Bryant in the mid-1960s when he got involved with Jerry Mander and became the public figure who undid the sale of Alcatraz to Texas oilman Lamar Hunt. Duskin credits Alinsky's influence for some of his success in those early organizing campaigns. They were neighbors in 1961.

20.  Alvin Duskin, interview with author, January 12, 2010, San Francisco, CA.

21.  The Clamshell Alliance united hundreds of affinity groups around New England in a campaign of nonviolent direct action to stop the building of the Seabrook nuclear power plant on coastal New Hampshire. Their April 1977 attempt to occupy the construction site led to 1,414 arrests, and a movie, *The Last Resort* that was shown around the country to spread the model. I was involved in screening the film in late 1977 in Santa Rosa, California, as a benefit for a fledgling group we started called Sonoma County Citizens for Understanding Energy. It raised about $82 which we banked, and within the following year, I'd moved to San Francisco and someone else had taken that money and started a chapter of the Abalone Alliance called SonomorAtomics—a much better name!

22.  *San Francisco Good Times* 2, no. 43 (October 30, 1969): 6-7.

23.  In 1967, Cliff Humphrey, a former archaeology student at University of California, Berkeley founded Ecology Action and set up the country's first drop-off recycling center.

24.  The City Office of Recycling had been formed in 1979 to plan, coordinate and expand the various activities attempting to reduce the City's waste stream. Activists from the nonprofit recyclers were involved in the effort to create this new city program. San Francisco Community Recyclers was founded in 1980 in response to two important points in the city's recycling development. First was the growth and maturation of the non-profit community based recycling centers. The second was the emergence of the city recycling program.

25.  A renewed and expanded Open Space Fund was passed by a 3-to-1 margin in March 2000, proving again how much San Franciscans appreciate their open space and parklands.

26.  Ray Dasmann was the author of *The Destruction of California* (New York: MacMillan, 1965), an important early environmental analysis of statewide ecological destruction.

27.  See Jana Blankenship's essay "The Farm by the Freeway" in this volume.

28.  As it still does today in 2010, when like Frankenstein, it is being proposed AGAIN.

29.  Peter Berg, Beryl Magilvy, and Seth Zuckerman, *A Green City Program for San Francisco Bay Area Cities & Towns* (Planet Drum Books: 1989).

30.  A decade later, Friends of the Earth split too, with Brower pushing for a more decentralized organization against those who favored an "inside the Beltway" (DC-focused) lobbying approach. Brower and others then put their energies into the Earth Island Institute, an umbrella organization that provides incubator space and a home to dozens of local, grassroots organizations.

31.  Locally, ARC/Ecology, GreenAction, Literacy for Environmental Justice, and Communities for a Better Environment all campaign against the toxic environment of southeast San Francisco. In Richmond near the massive Chevron refinery, the West County Toxics Coalition organizes political opposition to the multinational's continuing poisoning of the local air, water, and soil, along with the Asia/Pacific Environmental Network's work with the Laotian refugee community there, and Communities for a Better Environment. Parallel efforts exist in Silicon Valley in the South Bay.

# San Francisco Labor in the 1970s

## By Jesse Drew

San Francisco is a labor town. That was an acknowledged truth for many decades in the City. By the 1960s and 1970s however, there were not many people who still understood why. As wave after wave of social reformers, activists, and visionaries swept the Bay it was easier to see that the Bay Area was a cauldron of activist youth. Beatniks, Diggers, Hippies, Black Panthers, Native, Black, Chicano and Asian-American liberation movements, the anti-war movement, the rising tide of gay liberation and feminism—all were more emblematic of the City than its blue-collar union members. In the upheavals and polarization of the 1960s, US workers were often perceived by young activists as either hostile to social change, or at least too comfortable in their wages and benefits to risk any discomfort. This perception initially came more from youthful ignorance than any sober investigation, but it was greatly accentuated by the mass media and a political establishment that wanted to convince workers they were apolitical, conservative and part of a great "silent majority." Images of construction workers attacking anti-war protesters were a regular feature on television, wedged in between gross caricatures of working-class life as depicted in *All in the Family* (Archie Bunker) episodes or *Hee Haw* skits.

Towards the end of the 1960s and beginning of the 1970s the anti-war and anti-racist movements began to take a deeper look at the nature of US imperialism abroad and its connection to the exploitation of its own people at home. It was at this time that the progressive legacy of the US workers' movements came more into focus. Young people began to understand that there was a time when the leading force for social change was the organized working class. There was a long history of workers that toiled in the mills, factories, and fields battling police and troops for economic equality and social justice. Working-class personalities began to be uncovered and reinstated into the pantheon of American heroes. Posters of Mother Jones, Joe Hill, Eugene Debs, and Emma Goldman began to take their place alongside those of Che Guevara and Huey P. Newton. Events long forgotten were pulled out of the collective unconscious of US history where they had been unceremoniously buried: the 1937 Flint, Michigan sit-down strikes of the automobile workers, the 1930s miners strikes of Bloody Harlan County in Appalachia, the 1886 Haymarket martyrs of Chicago. The film *Salt of the Earth* was recovered from the archive and projected extensively, showing activists the heroic strikers of the Mine, Mill and Smelter workers in 1950s New Mexico. But one of the proudest moments in that forgotten past had happened right in San Francisco—the 1934 strike of longshoremen and seamen that shut down the City and sent a wave of fear through the American ruling class that would last for decades.

As the youthful movements opposing the war in Southeast Asia and racism at home developed, they found important allies in a small but progressive remnant of a labor movement with a rich history of struggle. Students, minorities, and labor grew closer and young activists found valuable support from an older generation who knew quite a bit about picket lines and the police baton. In 1963, ILWU president Harry Bridges addressed 30,000 people at a San Francisco rally called in solidarity with Civil Rights marchers who were attacked in Birmingham, Alabama. The Congress on Racial Equality (CORE) relied upon organized labor to assist in their fight against the discrimination in hiring practiced by many downtown businesses. It was a united protest against the Palace Hotel in downtown San Francisco that directly led to the upsurge in student activism and the Free Speech Movement at UC Berkeley in 1964. The ILWU and a few other progressive unions in the Bay Area became some of the first unions to formally oppose the war in Vietnam.

The United Farm Workers Union (UFW) in the Central Valley (led by Cesar Chavez) energized many supporters in the Bay Area. The UFW's fusion of civil rights with union organizing greatly enhanced young activists' understanding of the critical importance of an organized multinational working class. Thousands flocked to the union to help build local solidarity with the striking farm workers, among the most oppressed and abused workers in North America. Full-time houses of UFW organizers were established in San Francisco, Oakland, Hayward, and other cities. (In San Francisco, the UFW organizers lived in the nunnery of St. Paul's Church in Noe Valley, the same church pictured in the movie *Sister Act* with Bay Area actress Whoopie Goldberg.) Activists were trained in UFW labor and community organizing techniques, and many of them later went on to work in the local labor movement. As Randy Shaw comments in his study of the influence of the UFW on the contemporary labor and social justice movements, "when UFW alumni with this remarkable training moved on to future jobs, they took the skills and strategies that brought unprecedented success to the farm workers in the 1960s and 1970s with them. From 1965 to 1979, the United Farm Workers of America was the nation's leading organizer training school."[1]

In the 1970s many now-older activists found themselves joining the workforce, along with millions of other baby-boomers. The relative economic affluence of the 1960s that workers had come to take for granted began to wane. It was harder to live on the economic margins of abundance that decades of American hegemony had generated. In 1974, a recessionary shock and the first oil crisis reminded many activists that they were as much a part of the working class as anyone else. It became clear that two wage earners per household were required to maintain the standard of living American families had become accustomed to. This economic imperative coupled with a growing feminist consciousness brought many women into the workforce. Veterans of the anti-war movement, Third World liberation struggles, and other progressive movements entered the workforce en masse, and many brought their idealism and organizing skills with them. With the Southeast Asian wars grinding to a halt, and the draft ended, many activists were excited to infuse their energy into the American working class, and looked forward to ending the charges of "un-American" and "traitor" thrown at them for not supporting the genocide in Vietnam. Throughout the 1960s, many of the struggles championed by youth called for attention to what was happening elsewhere: the rural South, the fields of rural California, Vietnam. Organizing closer to home in the centers of production and commerce and in one's own community was an exciting development for those wishing to make change in the very "heart of the beast."

In the early 1970s, San Francisco was a strong financial center with banking, insurance, engineering, and healthcare at its core. These office-based industries had generated thousands of new jobs for primarily female workers, jamming them together in office cubicles at Bank of America, Blue Shield, AT&T, Standard Oil

(Chevron), and Bechtel. As the core city in the fourth largest metropolitan area in the US, San Francisco also employed many workers in the service sector who toiled in hospitals, hotels, department stores, restaurants, and other businesses, with many jobs held by women and immigrant workers from Latin America, Central America, and Asia. San Francisco in 1970 still had a strong traditional blue-collar working class based in construction, transport, warehousing, food production, and manufacturing. It is hard to imagine today, but the Bay Area as a whole was still very much an industrial center, bustling with automobile and truck manufacturing, oil refining, canning, brewing, baking, ship repair, steel and smelting, and more. Large heavy industrial plants included American Can, Peterbilt Truck, Mack Truck, Caterpillar Tractor, International Harvester, Brockway Glass, Owens-Illinois, General Motors, Ford Motors, AAA Shipyards, and assorted iron and steel works.

Many sights, sounds, and smells of San Francisco from that decade no longer linger. In the 1970s freight trains still rolled stealthily through the streets of the Mission under cover of darkness, moving finished goods out and raw materials in. One could smell the cloying sweet smell of white bread, as union workers moved tens of thousands of loaves of Kilpatricks Bread from dough to ovens to market on 16th and South Van Ness. On foggy mornings, a thick corrosive mist of vinegar would descend over the vicinity of Best Foods on Florida Street, as union workers bottled mayonnaise and other condiments. Malt and hops steam from the beer breweries made one's nose flare, as would the acrid, burnt smell of coffee roasting in the MJB and Hills Bros coffee factories in the South of Market. In the early morning, shiny tanker trucks would block sidewalks with their hoses pumping syrup and chocolate into the side of the brick Hostess plant on Bryant, producing Twinkies and HoHos for the West Coast. Hundreds of workers clocked into the Schlage lock factory in Visitation Valley. Levi's Jeans still had sewing operations in San Francisco. The bright lights of welding torches from the AAA Shipyards would flicker across from Mission Bay piers, where fisherman and happy-hour blue-collar workers would pry open Rainier Ale and Mickey's wide mouths. Itinerant workers and bohemians could still try their luck in the ILWU hiring hall, vying to unload ships that tied up on the San Francisco docks. As the 1970s began, San Francisco offered a diversified job market, in one of the most dynamic economies in the US.

Concentrations of workers in offices, services, and industry were seen as ripe targets for agitation and activism by activists who found themselves employed in these areas. These different occupational sectors raised important strategic questions. In the 1970s, most of the traditional blue-collar workplaces were already organized by unions that young activists perceived as ineffective and tired, if not actually corrupt. Newer industries like banking and insurance were not unionized and employed mostly women, posing the question as to where white-collar office workers fit within the traditional labor movement. Service workers were not exploited by corporations but provided public services for municipalities or nonprofits. Thousands of San Franciscans punched data downtown in office buildings, or made beds in enormous hotels. Were they fundamentally different from those who worked on assembly lines and conveyor belts? How could so-called white-collar and "pink-collar" workers, who were generating profits for multinational corporations for very low wages, be empowered by the labor movement? This was a central point of discussion among young labor activists throughout the 1970s.

An example of the growing synthesis between the organized labor movement and the newly emergent activist youth movements can be found in the 1969 strike of the Oil, Chemical and Atomic Workers (OCAW) at the Richmond, California oil refinery of Standard Oil. Standard Oil was a frequent target of anti-war protesters and seen as one of the worst corporate polluters on the planet. The oil workers walked out of the refinery complex and promptly found themselves with a restraining order limiting their ability to picket and keep strikebreakers out. Strikers were harassed and beaten by police in a display of brutality previously unknown to the workers. A private goon squad was hired to assist strikebreakers entering the plant. Striking worker Dick Jones was run over by a scab truck as a policeman looked on, and later died of his injuries. The union needed help and took the unusual action of appealing to radical student activists to help them win their strike. The call was answered by thousands of San Francisco and Bay Area youth, in particular from San Francisco State College, where there had recently been a powerful student strike. In the early morning air, squads of politicized students energized the picket lines of striking workers, blocking trucks, chanting, waving signs, and facing down riot police. One striking worker commented that he used to think demonstrating Berkeley students on TV were "a bunch of radical troublemakers out looking for publicity. Now I have changed my mind."[2] It also prompted a striking oil worker to say, "When I came out here (to the picket line) before daylight, I felt very good to see those students, the more the better. The goons don't come out when they are here, and the cops are too busy chasing them around to bother us."[3] In the Standard Oil struggle, oil workers picketed with students at San Francisco State and other campuses, and students walked the picket lines in Richmond, prompting the local OCAW union president to say that the alliance was "the dawning of a new era."

There were many other examples of the new alliance as well. In March of 1970 a national "wildcat" strike of postal workers broke out in NYC and quickly spread to other major cities, including San Francisco, and young activists took a great interest in supporting the efforts of the strikers.[4] San Francisco Postal Workers, both letter carriers and bulk mail center employees, already had a core of activists. In a 1969 newsletter of postal employees, they complained that jobs promised to unemployed Black workers in the wake of the 1966 Hunters Point riots were not being fulfilled.[5] As early as 1970, Bay Area postal workers published a newsletter called *The Pony Express*, advertising itself as a "rank-and-file radical newspaper about the movement inside the bowels of the Post Office." In 1971, a national telephone workers' strike broke out as well, and San Francisco activists could be seen walking the picket lines.

The Bay Area had a particularly militant department store employees union, Local 1100, and they led a series of strikes affecting San Francisco in the early 1970s, particularly at the large downtown Emporium store, and at Sears, which only had two of its hundreds of stores unionized—San Francisco and Detroit. Sears was located in two working-class areas, at the top of Geary by Kaiser Hospital and in the Mission District at Mission and Army (now Cesar Chavez). The Sears workers, many of whom were middle-aged women, received quite a lot of sympathy and solidarity from the public and their story was highlighted in the underground press in San Francisco. Local 1100 workers were eventually hit hard by the decline in downtown department stores due to non-union big box stores and the closing of the Emporium chain. The local was eventually absorbed by the United Food and Commercial Workers Union.

The wave of strikes and labor unrest in the Bay Area and across the US in the 1970s indicated a breakdown of the established order between workers and management, but also a split between younger workers, women, and people of color on one side, and the old labor establishment on the other. As labor writer George Morris remarked in 1971, "The unions are becoming younger in average age level. Young people streaming into shops and unions bring some of the rebellious spirit of the college campuses. Black and Spanish-speaking workers, the youth especially, bring the militancy of the liberation movement."[6] In the early seventies the wildcat strike became a common occurrence. The Lordstown wildcat strike of young Black autoworkers against General Motors and the White old-guard leadership of the United Automobile Workers became symbolic of this enormous divide. The growth of Black workers groups like the Dodge Revolutionary Union Movement, the League of Revolutionary Black Workers, and the United Black Brothers played a large role in encouraging the militancy of young African-American workers, among Black Muni drivers, for example, in the Transportation Workers Union.

The newer generation's influence began to surface in the mid-1970s across all sectors of the Bay Area workforce. Labor unions became regular participants in San Francisco political movements, regularly lending their organizational infrastructure to progressive causes. In return San Francisco progressive movements could be counted on to support workers' struggles and respect picket lines and labor boycotts. A case in point is the Coors Beer boycott that was started by Chicano activists against the discriminatory hiring practice of Coors. In the spring of 1977, the AFL-CIO Brewery Workers struck against Coors and also called for a boycott against the beer.[7] The boycott gained traction in San Francisco thanks to strike support by Beer Drivers Local 888 in conjunction with Chicano activists and the gay rights movement. It was due to gay-rights activists like Harvey Milk, who built on progressive sentiment in the gay community, that Coors beer was banned from the City's many gay bars. Support from these sectors surprised and enlightened the traditional blue-collar workers who worked for Coors, who were forced to re-evaluate their antipathy towards the gay community.

## Local 2 and the Alliance for the Rank and File

The tourist industry has been one of the largest employers in San Francisco, thanks to the City's rolling streets, scenic views, vibrant neighborhoods, and Barbary Coast mystique. Since the organizing drives of the 1930s, the waitresses, bartenders, maids, busboys, and hotel clerks at the large and swanky downtown hotels have had a tradition of class-consciousness and union membership. Historically, the hospitality service sector was divided up into many different union locals, grouping workers by craft as opposed to the hotel and restaurant industry as a whole. While the membership was increasingly female and Latina or Filipina, the leaders were more in the vein of the stereotypical union boss, older White men, who enjoyed a good chew on a cigar. With shrinking membership and an increasingly organized anti-union Hotel Employers Association, these locals united into one large union. Local 2 emerged from a merger of six separate locals in 1974 and became one of the largest and most militant unions in San Francisco.

Even before they merged, the rank and file was active. A 1974 copy of *The Rank and Filer*, published by workers of the Dining Room Employees Local 9, has the story of a waitress locked out of her job at the North Beach nightclub El Cid, and how the union ignored her pleas for help. Another issue argued for an elected shop steward at the Hyatt House Union Square. When Local 2 was created, it combined all the employees in the industry, and broke down many of the racial and sexual divisions that had been evident in some of the locals. It also brought together a critical mass of activists and labor reformers within its 17,000 members. A caucus emerged calling itself the Alliance of the Rank and File (ARF), with the tagline "Watchdogs not Fatcats." They contested the first election held by the new local and built an effective, grassroots campaign against the old guard led by union president Joe Belardi. The year before the election, Belardi had tried to increase dues $2.00/month. When it was learned that this money was to go to a special officer's pension fund, the rank and file revolted. James Russell reported, "Belardi was chased down the street by a group of angry maids."[8]

On April 11, 1978, David McDonald, ARF candidate, won the presidency, Charles Lamb, ARF candidate, won the executive vice presidency, and Winston Ching, ARF candidate, won one of three vice presidencies. This victory energized the union to organize the unorganized. The local began to integrate greater numbers of women and people of color into their leadership, put more resources into organizing and led a strike by workers at Zim's, a local coffeeshop chain. Unfortunately, the International Union conspired with the old guard to put the local into trusteeship, and was able to roll back the ARF victory through another court-ordered election. Well into the 1980s Local 2 was in a constant state of tumult, as rank-and-filers fought for a greater voice and for better industry working conditions.

The struggle in the Hotel and Restaurant Workers Local 2 highlights that public service workers have an additional dimension to consider. Unlike manufacturing workers, who are clear that the products they build are commodities to sell for profits, service workers heal the sick, take care of children or service the public infrastructure. Thus their strategy challenges the employer to improve working conditions while building bridges with the communities and the public they serve.

## San Francisco's Medical-Industrial Complex

San Francisco is a major medical research center and houses numerous hospitals, research facilities and clinics. Their campuses are among the most imposing structures in the City, including UCSF Medical Center in the Haight-Ashbury, Kaiser Permanente on Geary in the Western Addition, and San Francisco General Hospital in the Mission. The medical industry employs thousands of workers who care for patients, turn the beds, cook the food, clean the floors, administer tests, screen patients, and other tasks. Many of these jobs have traditionally been very low-paid, strenuous, and stressful jobs, usually going to minority and female workers. Like their counterparts in the tourist industries, the union was out of touch and not responsive to the needs and well-being of the workers. Most of the workers in San Francisco hospitals have been represented by the Service and Employees International Union (SEIU) Local 250; a fairly minor player in the labor movement as the 1970s began.

In the early 1970s, activists in the giant Kaiser system began meeting to determine how they could bring change to their union and integrate central social issues. As one activist recalls, "Many new employees were coming out of the

Civil Rights Movement, the anti-war movement, or the United Farm Workers movement. We began raising hell at union meetings, demanding the union take a stand on Vietnam or arguing for elected shop stewards. Tim Twomey, the union head, would call for the Sergeant at Arms to forcibly remove us."[9]

The activists in Local 250 put together a caucus, the Committee for a Democratic Union (CDU), named after a similar caucus in the Teamsters Union. The CDU ran slates in several union elections and eventually won half of the executive board and some other offices. The labor reformers were often seen as a threat to the international leadership and many close union elections led to charges of fraud and manipulation. Like Local 2, many of the union activists in Local 250 took the job of organizing the unorganized very seriously and began successfully winning union elections across the Bay, in an environment where unions were having very little success. For example, Local 250 led organizing efforts among Bay Area convalescent home workers with much success. Internecine battles among union leaders through the years have discouraged rank-and-file activists and have led to international union interference through trusteeships and undemocratic procedures, however. Still, the energy of service workers have led to SEIU becoming one of the largest unions in the US.

## City Employees Act

The largest rise in unionization in the 1970s took place not in the corporate sector, but in the public sector. In the 1970s, the old guard of trade unionism was based mostly on Building Trades, older craft unions that often had a substantial role in the public sector as city workers. These unions were higher paid, more privileged associations with fairly small memberships, such as plumbers, steam fitters, and operating engineers. The increase in unionized public workers came through the organization of the bottom rung: bus drivers, garbage workers, street cleaners. Labor legislation permitting collective bargaining rights encouraged more aggressive unions such as the SEIU and the AFSCME (American Federation of State, County, and Municipal Employees) to organize these so-called "miscellaneous workers."

A series of militant city workers' strikes rocked San Francisco throughout the 1970s. On March 13, 1970, city workers launched a short but powerful strike that shut down mass transit, closed municipal buildings, and caused raw sewage to seep into the Bay. The strike resulted in some wage gains and shift differentials. On the evening of March 7, 1974, trade unionists left a SF Labor Council meeting after heated debate about contract renewal and began picketing without the central labor body's sanction, launching a wildcat strike. The strike spread quickly, shutting down mass transit and city services while the Labor Council had to catch up and officially sanction the strike. Bay Area community activists created a community/labor alliance in support of strike demands, such as maintaining bus lines slated for removal. The strike again gained wage increases for city workers. School bus drivers in San Francisco, represented by a rank-and-file-led United Transportation Union, went on strike in the fall of 1976, and won a host of demands. The success of the strike was widely attributed to the involvement of the membership in getting public support of their walkout. "16,000 leaflets printed in English, Spanish and Chinese were distributed to schools, shopping centers and other places to get the word out to parents, teachers and the rest of the community."[10]

## The Teachers Organize

Perhaps the most surprising public service workers' militancy however, came from public school classrooms, where teachers led several strikes in San Francisco in the 1970s. Teachers provide a public service to the most important resource found in any municipality—children. For this extremely important task teachers were (and still are) among the lowest paid public workers in the US. Historically, teaching was considered true public service, the myth being that one entered the profession not for the income, but for the good of the community. This idealized notion was contradicted by arduous days in underfunded, often dilapidated surroundings in potentially violent circumstances. Though teachers associations have been around for many decades, teachers began to push for unionization in the 1960s. Typically, urban school districts were organized by the American Federation of Teachers (AFT), while suburban and rural schools mostly allied with the National Education Association (NEA). In the Bay Area, many young, idealistic men and women were drawn towards teaching in the 1960s and 1970s, seeing it as socially rewarding. Many soon learned that to achieve their lofty educational goals, teachers needed empowerment and leverage, which they found through renewed union activism. In San Francisco, this happened on all levels, from the full-time K–12 teachers to the assistants, known as "paraprofessionals" or "paras."

The Bay Area Radical Teacher's Organizing Committee (BARTOC) formed in 1969 with a gathering of teachers from San Francisco and Berkeley schools. Initially they ran a series of workshops for progressive teachers and put out a newsletter called *No More Teachers Dirty Looks*. On March 10, 1971, 600 members (out of 1700) of the San Francisco Federation of Teachers (AFT Local 61) voted to go on strike for better wages and smaller class sizes. The strike began two weeks later and shut down all junior and high schools in the City. On March 29, the Classroom Teachers Association, affiliated with the NEA, joined the picket lines with the AFT. Many Black and Latino teachers crossed the picket lines in a rebuke to a union bureaucracy unresponsive to the needs of minority communities. Progressives within the union, including BARTOC, created a rank-and-file caucus to fight against racism and sexism in the union and for greater internal democracy. There was also a plank in the caucus platform that called for less authoritarianism in the school system, as teachers were tired of being a "police force."[11] The caucus also expressed support for a Student Bill of Rights and greater community participation in the public school system. Throughout the 1970s, progressive teachers in the San Francisco Unified School District worked to build a progressive teachers union. The Teacher's Action Caucus (TAC) produced a monthly newspaper called *TACtics*, using the logo of a thumbtack. The caucus put strong pressure on the leadership to develop a student/community alliance, to fight for affirmative action, and to take a larger role in the political arena. They successfully removed police officers from school halls, arguing that police were detrimental to their educational mission and disrespectful of community concerns. The union bureaucracy tried hard to outflank the caucus, particularly during votes at union meetings. As one teacher activist recalls, "We were able to win votes by mobilizing the membership to come to union meetings, and so the leadership canceled union meetings and substituted a delegate structure instead. We were eventually able to win representation on the executive board of the union."[12]

In the spring of 1974, picketing teachers shut down schools all over San Francisco once again. The striking teachers were supported by janitors, cafeteria workers, and other service workers at the schools. In some communities, alternative schools were set up in churches and other buildings to win community support of teacher's demands. Tensions ran high and at one junior high school, a principal drove his car into a line of picketers. In 1977, San Francisco teachers again battled for another contract and for union recognition for lower paid workers who did work formerly done by teachers, such as grading and tutoring. On May 18th, teachers and paras occupied the office of the school district superintendent, while 200 teachers demonstrated outside.[13] Though important reforms were won and a new generation fought their way into leadership positions, much of that activity came to an end with the massive teacher layoffs prompted by Prop 13 (the 1978 California Initiative that radically reduced property taxes, gutting school district budgets).

## The Factory Revolt

The traditional blue-collar industrial workforce underwent substantial changes in the 1970s, as younger workers, returning vets and minorities, particularly African-Americans, entered the factories. American manufacturing was still strong in the Bay Area, and automobiles, trucks, heavy machinery, earthmoving machines, military equipment, glass bottles and cans, brewed and canned goods, and metal products rolled off the assembly lines. This new workforce was confronted by 8-hour days of mind-numbing, brute labor, in sweltering, cacophonous, dirty and dangerous environments. Black men often entered a hostile workplace, and were given the worst jobs. This newer workforce had higher expectations, and was resistant to being treated as a cog in the machine. Industrial discipline could be harsh, humiliating, and patronizing. As the US rate of profit began falling in the 1970s, manufacturing corporations squeezed higher productivity out of its workforce through forced overtime and speed-ups, increasing industrial accidents and occupational deaths. Nonetheless, these union jobs were highly sought after, since they were relatively well-paying and did not require a college education. Throughout the 1970s many left-wing groups became active in the industrial core throughout the US and particularly in the Bay Area. The result was a proliferation of reform and radical groups within the manufacturing industry and an unprecedented number of strikes and workplace actions. As Aaron Brenner notes:

> Worker willingness to fight back was further reinforced by the concomitant antiwar, black power, and feminist movements, which radicalized many. These movements raised the political awareness of ordinary people by putting such issues as racism, sexism, and imperialism in the forefront of their consciousness. Workers then confronted these issues as they were manifested on the job and in their unions. Tens of thousands became activists. Many became revolutionaries. In a number of cases, it was these working-class political militants who, by replicating their experience from the social movements in the movements in the workplace, led the rank-and-file groups that challenged the employers and the union bureaucracy.[14]

Practically every large factory had some kind of rank-and-file newsletter or publication by activist caucuses, from broad coalitions to ultra-Left splinter groups. Caterpillar Tractor, a large plant in San Leandro of over 1,000 workers had *The Leaky Valve*. At Peterbilt Truck, you could pick up *The Red Cab*. The Rank-and-File Coalition was a consortium of activist labor groups that published *The Rank and File Report*, where you could read news from many labor reform coalitions around the Bay. AAA Shipyards in San Francisco, where several thousand workers rebuilt and renovated ships, had numerous reform caucuses. Other blue-collar reform groups were Teamsters for a Democratic Union (TDU) and Machinists for Democracy. Many of these blue-collar workers were influenced by the growth of reform caucuses in industrial unions in other parts of the US, such as the Ed Sadlowski group in the Steelworkers Union and Miners for Democracy in the coalfields.

These rank-and-file groups were not tolerated lightly, however. They were subject to a barrage of red baiting from the corporate offices and often fought by groups of conservative workers, ranging from mildly conservative to extreme right wing. There were often rumors of secret Klan and American Nazi groups operating in the plants, particularly in the East Bay. Their activity ranged from unsigned flyers on workers' cars to death threats. One activist couple found their car had sugar poured into their gas tank, and on another day discovered the lug nuts on their car had been loosened. In ILWU Local 6, the elected president of the local, rank-and-file reform activist Roberto Flotte, was murdered while leaving a union meeting in April of 1982. TDU activists were threatened and attacked as well. The seriousness of union reform efforts was reinforced by the memory of Dow Wilson, a radical reformer within the Painters Union who was murdered by union bosses outside his Mission District union hall in 1966. The pressure on union activists had international repercussions as well, as when Silme Domingo and Gene Viernes, two Filipino elected rank-and-file reformers in the Seattle ILWU were murdered by agents sent by then Philippine dictator Ferdinand Marcos.

This rank-and-file activity came to a head in the mid-'70s, with many of these caucuses instigating wildcat strikes, often leading to radicals and activists getting elected to union leadership posts. At Brockway Glass in East Oakland, for example, over 1,000 mostly African–American workers packed and inspected millions of glass bottles that poured into molds and then rattled across miles of assembly lines and conveyor belts to be packed into boxes and shipped to factories nationwide. The plant worked on rotating shifts, so that workers worked the day shift one week, swing shift the next week, graveyard shift the next, and would then repeat. Individually molded earplugs, safety goggles, and steel-toed boots were worn to avoid injury from the roaring noise and the shattering glass that flew around heads and under foot. Salt tablet dispensers were at every water fountain, to keep workers from passing out from the heat. No one could leave the assembly line without permission and a relief worker. In order to go to the bathroom you flipped a light switch on the assembly line and hopefully a foreman would find a relief worker to excuse you from the line. The large sign in front of the plant that stated, "It's been ____ days since our last accident," was never filled in, as there was typically an accident every day, from broken shards of glass puncturing flesh, hot glass burns, back injuries, or crushed limbs in the auto-pack machines.

Inside the plant, the Flint Glass Workers in blue coveralls, faces smoky with oil, swabbed the hot iron glass molds into which the molten glass flowed. They voted to go on strike. In living rooms and porches in East Oakland, at the break room tables nestled among the vending machines of chips, canned beans, and Mountain Dew, on the clattering packing tables and conveyor belts, worker consensus grew—they would honor the picket lines. At a union membership meeting, the suit-and-tie union president, who hadn't worked an assembly line for many years, proposed that the primary union, the Glass Bottle Blowers Association, not support the strike. In a raucous union meeting, a rank-and-file Glass Worker Support Committee was formed and took leadership. Minutes before the midnight strike deadline, as swing shift approached its end, workers punched out and emerged from under the smokestacks into the cool, still air of midnight. Outside past the tall hurricane fences and barbed wire in pools of security lights, a crowd was gathered at the gate, but no one came in to work the graveyard shift. There was shouting and jeering, as management and the union leaders urged and threatened the workers into the plant but no one entered, and the plant was shut down. The Glass Worker Support Committee put out a newsletter, organized picketing, and held benefits to support the most needy among the strikers. The strike was brutal from the start, guns were pulled, picketers were beaten, tires were slashed, and a mysterious dump truck with no license plates dumped a full load of concrete chunks in front of the plant gate. After the walkout, which ended with minor wage gains for the strikers, the Glass Worker Support Committee became a reform caucus that swept the elections and became the new leadership.

At Mack Truck in Hayward, 1,500 members of United Auto Workers Local 76 built the shiny bulldog-adorned quintessential American truck. Like all autoworkers, the plant was subject to increasing speed-up and forced overtime. One woman remembers going to a worker assembly where the workers were told not to stop the line in the case of someone being injured. "Tell a foreman, but never stop that assembly line." The UAW had a shop steward system that allowed stewards to talk to workers if a grievance arose and one day, amid the roar of truck production, a committee person (as stewards in the UAW are called) was reprimanded for doing just that. "The culture on the factory floor at Mack was very supportive, they really believed that an injury to one was an injury to all."[15] Tensions had been building between management and the workers and the harassment of a shop steward was the last straw. Word traveled quickly through the plant, and the line stopped, tools were downed and hundreds of workers walked out of the plant to a nearby park. At their impromptu meeting, the hundreds assembled voted to go on strike, in defiance of the "no-strike" clause in their union contract. The wildcat strike lasted several days, as union officials and plant management jostled to break the impasse. At Caterpillar Tractor in San Leandro in 1977, over 1,800 workers went into the street as well, in a month-long wildcat strike. It was reported that, "Rank-and-file militancy also included opposition to the international union's attempt to call off the strike. Most strikers wanted to hold out for a contract that would ensure job security and curb speed-up."[16]

The gains and losses of these strikes and actions were always fiercely debated and argued. Not much is understood by nickels and dimes and percentages and COLAs (Cost of Living Allowances). Sometimes hard-won gains were easily taken away or were difficult for the union to enforce. "Lost" strikes could result in a re-energized workforce, or help a reform slate take control of the leadership. A strike could allow workers to regain their dignity and make the company think twice before it provoked another dispute. The union leadership typically preferred to declare victory to prove that the union handled itself well, while much of the Left preferred to declare defeat, and blame the "sell-out labor bureaucrats" in control. The truth usually lay somewhere in between. In the case of the Brockway Glass strike, many workers were simply glad to have a few weeks to rest their weary bodies and reconnect with their family and friends.

While workers were busy fighting to reform industries that had remained virtually unchanged since WWII, corporate leaders were working on another plan. Old industries were being shut down and moved south to right-to-work states, without unions or worker rights. "The Southern Solution" was the first phase of a strategy of capital flight to reap higher profits at the expense of workers. As the 1970s progressed, this strategy became one of moving "off-shore" to foreign countries where wages were obscenely low, and unions were often illegal. This "globalization" became the principal strategy of US capital, as is very evident today. The US, once revered for its manufacturing prowess, was becoming a nation where many commented "we don't make anything anymore." In the late 1970s, many union activists confronted plant closures, seeking to rein in the ability of companies to flee the US, and prevent the devastation of whole communities. Multinational corporations rolled over workers and their organizations, however. One by one, all of these plants disappeared to Mexico, Indonesia, China or other low-wage refuges. The legacies left behind by these corporate "patriots" are the bricked-over complexes and crumbling smokestacks on the edges of Bay Area cities. This de-industrialization changed the texture of the City considerably, as former factories have become trendy artists' lofts and dotcom offices.

The elimination of tens of thousands of living wage jobs contributed greatly to the surge of Bay Area homelessness that appeared during the Reagan era. The dismantling of industry and the disappearance of blue-collar jobs greatly accentuated a disturbing trend in San Francisco. As pointed out by Richard de Leon, the result was the creation of an "hourglass economy," one that has a large number of higher paying professional jobs, with a large number of low paying service jobs, effectively eliminating the middle class from San Francisco.[17]

While industry was shutting down, office work was growing in San Francisco propelled by new technologies in banking, office automation, database systems, and new communications technologies. As Herbert Gintis wrote as early as 1970:

> Processing, transmitting, and coordinating information, not the transformation of raw materials through the application of energy, are increasingly central. The material accessories to these new technologies are primarily cybernetic and administrative: account books, adding machines, electric typewriters, Dicta-phones and calculating machines, the communications media and computers.[18]

Thousands of these new jobs filled up the high-rise file cabinet skyscrapers going up in SF's Financial District, an architectural development denounced as "Manhattanization" by its detractors. Many jobs were held by young women with no prior identification with unionism. Furthermore, the culture of the office diverged widely from that of service and manufacturing workers. Being able to dress fashionably and work 9-5 obscured the fact that these workers often made less money and had less power than their service and blue-collar brothers and sisters. The nature of dress on the job and the illusion of equal status with wealthier and more powerful managers should not be underemphasized. That distinction was very clear in the factories that had front offices. When office workers walked onto the shop floor, they flaunted the fact that their hands were clean and their clothes nice, while workers would hoot derisively. Many women factory workers would bemoan the fact that they couldn't grow their nails long anymore.

Labor activists pondered this new non-union environment and began a series of initiatives to bring these workers into the ranks of organized labor. The Coalition of Labor Union Women (CLUW) was launched in an attempt to relate more effectively with women workers. One of the strongest backers of CLUW was the SEIU, which also launched the office workers organizing local 925 on the East Coast. Union WAGE (Women Allied to Gain Equality) was a local initiative organized by San Francisco women labor activists to organize and to encourage women to take leadership in the unions. Union WAGE published a newspaper that was distributed downtown and in other locales where women workers congregated. In an issue of *Union Wage*, they note, "Clerical workers have been in the 'unorganizable' class from the point of view of labor leadership, and yet half of the women in the Bay Area work in big downtown offices—'paper factories' a sister here called them—with speed-ups and discipline and automation that make them very much like an assembly line."[19] Advocates for Women was another feminist initiative that organized counseling and advocacy for women workers downtown. In the early 1980s, the *Processed World* collective began their downtown noon-time street performance to distribute their magazine, asking office workers, "Are you doing the processing or are you being processed?" The Office and Professional Employees International Union (OPEIU) was one of the only labor unions to have a substantial base among clerical workers in the City, primarily at Blue Shield. In 1980, over one thousand Blue Shield workers went on strike to protect their union benefits. The strike ultimately failed and the OPEIU lost their only large-scale union shop. Office work remains a tough nut to crack for labor, especially with the adoption of flex-time, work-from-home, online labor, and a strong reliance on a temporary workforce.

But already by the end of the 1970s, the prospects for the collective strength of workers in the Bay Area were bleak. Despite a decade of rank-and-file militancy that sparked a sharp increase in strikes and a new generation of leadership, labor was in retreat. Tens of thousands of manufacturing jobs were moved "offshore" and the downtown office sector remained unorganized. The rapid job growth in the newly coined "Silicon Valley" confounded labor, with its flexible hours, manicured campus architecture, and seemingly un-hierarchical work culture. Perhaps the culminating blow was the shocking lock-out and dismissal of the striking Professional Air Traffic Controllers Organization (PATCO) in 1980. PATCO was one of the only unions to endorse Ronald Reagan for president, who then led the attack on PATCO. Irate air traffic controllers who set up barricades to block access to the San Francisco International airport were berated by hostile travelers and then chased into parking lots by riot police.

Certainly some gains were made by the efforts of 1970s activists. Unions have opened up their membership and leadership to women, minorities, gays and lesbians, with strong encouragement from Bay Area union members. "Social unionism," the linking of the labor movement to wider social and environmental concerns and the importance of developing labor-community alliances, has strong roots in the Bay Area. Bay Area workers in such sectors as hotel/restaurant and healthcare have significantly better organization than in most parts of the country. San Francisco unions, while facing declining economic power, still have a significant amount of political power, as they wield an impressive amount of campaigners, voters and dollars.

There are significant hurdles ahead for Bay Area labor though. The last vestiges of working-class San Francisco, at least those who managed to hold on during the dotcom evictions of the 1990s, are dying off. The outrageously high cost of housing in the City all but ensures that most wage earners will either crowd into over-priced rental units or commute from far away. It seems San Francisco loves its industrial chic and its allusions to working-class kitsch, as long as there are no actual workers around. Perhaps the larger dilemma is that the millions of Bay Area workers who generate wealth for large corporations or who maintain the infrastructure of the jewel-by-the-bay typically do so blind to the collective strength they could command. San Francisco has a well-deserved reputation as a force for progressive social change, yet most are unaware that "without our brain and muscle not a single wheel can turn."[20] It will be up to the next generation of labor activists to solve this conundrum if San Francisco is to once again claim that it is a "labor town."

## Notes

1. Randy Shaw, *Beyond the fields: Cesar Chavez, the UFW, and the struggle for justice in the 21st Century* (Berkeley, CA: University of California Press, 2008) 6.

2. *Richmond oil strike.* The Newsreel Collective, 1969, Roz Payne archives. Film.

3. Peter B. Levy, *The new left and labor in the 1960s* (Chicago: University of Illinois, 1994).

4. A wildcat strike, where the workers strike against not only management, but against the entrenched union leadership as well.

5. National Alliance of Postal and Federal Employees, 1969, Special Collection, San Francisco Library

6. George Morris, *Rebellion in the unions: A handbook for rank and file action.* (New York: New Outlook, 1971) 7.

7. "Strikers join national boycott against Coors," *El Tecolote,* June 1977.

8. J. Russell, "Letter from San Francisco: Rank and file union victory," In *Radical America* 12, no. 5 (1978).

9. Blanche Bebb, interview with author, September 21, 2009.

10. "The spirit of the school bus strike," *Common Sense* 4, no. 1: 8-9.

11. Bay Area Radical Teachers Organizing Collective. "Education and corporate capitalism," 1971)

12. Joe Berry, interview with author, September 22, 2009.

13. "Teachers and paras battle for contract, union rights," *The New Voice* VI, no. 12: 1.

14. A. Brenner, "Rank and file Teamster movements," in *Trade union politics: American Unions and Economic Change,* eds. Glenn Perusek and Kent Worcester (Atlantic Highlands, New Jersey Humanities Press, 1995) 115.

15. Miya Masaoka, interview with author, September 21, 2009.

16. "Working around the Bay," *Common Sense* 4, no. 10: 8.

17. Richard Edward De Leon, *Left coast city: Progressive politics in San Francisco, 1975-1991* (Lawrence, Kansas: University of Kansas, 1992) 19.

18. H. Gintis, "The new working class and revolutionary youth," *Socialist Revolution* 1, no. 3 (1970): 18.

19. "Working women on the move," *Union Wage* (January-February 1976): 7.

20. Ralph Chaplin, "Solidarity Forever," 1914.

# The Rise and Fall of the Underground Comix Movement
## in San Francisco and Beyond

### By Jay Kinney

I f one had to arbitrarily choose a single moment that marked the founding of the underground comix movement, a good choice would be February 25, 1968, when Robert Crumb and his wife Dana filled a baby carriage with newly-printed copies of *Zap Comix #1* and trundled off to Haight Street to sell them for 25 cents a piece.[1]

Crumb's goofy, big-footed cartoons had an oddly anachronistic quality about them, as if an old-time newspaper cartoonist from 1908 had suddenly stepped out of a time machine and begun smoking weed and drawing hippies. This struck a responsive chord with the local San Francisco counterculture who were already inclined to relocate themselves from the freak-out that was 1968 to an earlier era of granny dresses, saloon vests, and Art Nouveau. If you dropped enough acid, you could shed the 20th century entirely and hole up in a commune without electricity or indoor plumbing. Goodbye present, hello past!

Crumb probably didn't think of himself as founding a movement exactly, but the mere existence of *Zap #1* served as a jolt of inspiration to the relatively small circle of cartoonists then drawing for the underground press. Most of these artists, such as Spain Rodriguez, Kim Deitch, and Trina Robbins at the *East Village Other (EVO)* in New York, or Jay Lynch and Skip Williamson with the *Seed* and *Chicago Mirror* in Chicago, already knew each other to one degree or another. Many of them had spent their teenage years swapping amateur satire fanzines with each other and rubbing elbows in the pages of Harvey Kurtzman's satirical *Help!* magazine and in off-campus college humor mags, before they found a ready market for smart aleck cartoons in the underground press.

But it wasn't until *Zap* appeared that it began to dawn on these artists that there might be a sufficient audience out there to support a new breed of comic books on their own. Crumb's do-it-yourself (DIY) ethic harked back to their former fanzine days, and there was a definite attraction to being your own boss instead of dealing with oily underground press publishers and endless staff meetings. Over the course of 1968, Crumb bounced from coast to coast, crashing on cartoonists' couches, handing out copies of *Zap*, and drawing non-stop in his black-covered sketchbook.

I first met him in precisely that circumstance in the living room of Lynch's Chicago flat. I was fresh out of high school in a Chicago suburb, where I'd edited and drawn for our high school underground paper. I was eager to graduate to the *real* underground press and had come to view Lynch as a mentor of sorts. Crumb was 25, Lynch was 23, and I was 18. From my perspective, these guys were the older brothers I'd never had, and if they came up with a project I was 100% behind it.

Before Crumb left town, Lynch and his publishing partner Williamson had decided to found *Bijou Funnies*, a Midwest outpost of the comix movement and my first entrée into the underground.

Crumb traveled on to New York, a harder town in which to make DIY comix work. Nevertheless, *Zap* had its effect and the *EVO* cartoonists were soon pumping out a monthly all-comix tabloid, *Gothic Blimpworks*, as an *EVO* side publication.

Down in Austin, Texas, Gilbert Shelton published his own *Feds 'n' Heads* comic, reprinting various strips he'd done for underground papers, including episodes of his *Fabulous Furry Freak Brothers*.

In decentralized fashion, the move-ment was under way. All it lacked was a local scene to facilitate the creative interplay between artists. San Francisco would soon provide this.

★ ★ ★

As tempting as it might be to solely attribute the underground comix movement to the gawky charisma of Crumb and to the pre-existing friendships among cartoonists in the underground press, there is of course more to the story. No cultural movement stands outside of its own context, and to really grasp the trajectory of the comix movement, we need to grapple with the ever-changing nature of the counterculture.

The stereotype of the Sixties, which has been promulgated by advertisers, the media, and Hollywood, has tended to play up the peace signs, love beads, psychedelic art, and rock festivals, while minimizing the teeth-grinding political conflicts and assassinations that also defined the era. However, to live through the '60s and identify with the counterculture was an exercise in juggling numerous contradictions at once: humming the Beatles' "All You Need is Love," while watching the Chicago cops riot against demonstrators at the 1968 Democratic Convention, while trying to decide whether the armed self-defense of the Black Panthers was worth supporting, all while trying to decide what records would be best to play while tripping.

The counterculture, at least in theory, was built around the premise of developing alternative cultural institutions in parallel with the mainstream. Perhaps in time, it was hoped, they would come to supplant the remnants of the dying mainstream, as more and more people were won over to the counterculture.

Of course, in practice this theory began to rattle apart almost immediately, as there was no coherent agreement on what was truly countercultural and what was not. Many underground papers depended on advertising for their income, with corporate music ads and sex ads underwriting columnists who railed against the music industry and sexism. Did buying your rolling papers and a bong at a head shop make it an alternative cultural institution?

The premise of the counterculture only seemed to work if you didn't look too closely at particulars, but stuck to generalities and a firm sense of what you opposed (e.g. the "Amerikkkan Death Culture"). Figuring out what you were *for* was a much harder proposition.

Underground as the descriptive term for the countercultural press was always somewhat self-aggrandizing, as papers like *EVO* or the *L.A. Free Press* or the *Berkeley Barb* were never really underground in any meaningful sense of the word. Russia in 1905 this was not. The papers were usually for-profit enterprises printed at commercial job printers and the longest-running and most successful underground papers were first and foremost well-run businesses.

The position of the cartoonists on the underground paper staffs was invariably dicey. Raised on the balloon-puncturing satire of Kurtzman's *Mad* (which preceded *Help!*) and the pioneering iconoclasm of Paul Krassner's *Realist*, underground cartoonists were as likely to lampoon the pretensions of the counterculture as they were to lambaste the establishment. Their loyalty was to the satirist's impatience with hypocrisy and cant from any quarter. As such, they were lousy team-players in underground staff collectives that increasingly opted for hard Left politics as the overheated '60s lurched into the explosive early '70s.[2]

Nevertheless, when the comix movement began to take shape in 1968, it was probably inevitable that in its transition from the venue of underground papers to that of underground comic books it would keep the designation of underground. As far as mainstream culture was concerned, the new self-published comix were still below the radar and might as well be underground. At the time it was difficult to foresee that this label would prove problematic within just a few years' time.

★ ★ ★

While Crumb traveled around the country like a cartooning Johnny Appleseed in 1968, underground comix began to solidify as a viable enterprise in the Bay Area. Crumb's DIY example was certainly inspiring, but few cartoonists—Crumb included—had the business acumen to raise the money to publish their own comics, much less to distribute them and collect the proceeds.

The still-growing counterculture seemed to be the natural comic-buying readership to appeal to, but short of standing on Haight Street with a baby buggy full of comic books, how was this audience supposed to be reached? Underground papers depended on a combination of hippie street-sellers and newsstand distributors, neither of which were geared to hawk underground comix.

The solution that soon emerged was the distribution network that had developed around the Fillmore Auditorium and Avalon rock posters, and around drug paraphernalia. The Print Mint in Berkeley was plugged into this network and owner Bob Rita had seen the underground comix potential when he had been on Haight Street in 1968 and had helped Crumb unload thousands of copies of *Zap #1* into the system through his business at the time, Third World Distribution.[3]

The Print Mint solved the DIY dilemma by setting itself up as a comix publisher and handling all the bothersome details of pre-press production, printing, distribution, and collections of funds. Artists were paid upfront for comix at set page-rates keyed to specific print runs. Unlike the underground papers, there were no sleazy advertisers or publishers, and no collective staff meetings. This seemed like a big advance in the scheme of things.

Crumb gave the Print Mint his vote of confidence by making *Zap* a Print Mint title. He further primed the movement's pump by converting *Zap* from a solo-Crumb comic into a multi-artist comic featuring Rick Griffin and Victor Moscoso (both of psychedelic rock poster fame), S. Clay Wilson (arguably the all-time most offensive underground artist), and Robert Williams (a Los Angeles–based artist whose background included extensive work with hot-rod icon Big Daddy Roth).

With the exception of Crumb, none of these *Zap* artists were regulars in the underground press, and their allegiances seemed to owe more to their shared self-conceptions as outsider artists than to any specific ideological identification with the counterculture.[4]

★ ★ ★

At nearly the same time as Crumb was peddling *Zap #1,* another odd duck was founding what would soon prove to be the focal point for the San Francisco comix scene. Gary Arlington was a local-born outsider whose inability to come up with any clear-cut career path led him to start the San Francisco Comic Book Company, one of the world's first comic book stores, wedged into a tiny storefront on 23rd Street near Mission, in the City's low-rent, mainly-Latino, Mission District. John Thompson, one of the growing ranks of comix artists, takes credit for discovering Arlington's shop and turning on other cartoonists to the store.

In common with many of the underground cartoonists, Arlington had been a big fan of EC Comics, the small New York comics publisher who had published, arguably, the highest-quality horror, science-fiction, war, and humor comics of the early '50s. EC had nearly been driven out of business when the comic book field was subjected to congressional hearings concerned about comics possibly corrupting young readers. A whole generation of EC fans was traumatized by the demise of their favorite titles (only *Mad* survived the debacle, and only by switching to magazine format).

The shared myth of EC's martyrdom fueled Arlington's hospitality for the underground artists stopping by his shop. Aided by certain psychoactive enhancements, Arlington was soon seized with the vision of the fledgling underground comix movement comprising a latter-day rebirth of EC. With the further discovery of Jehovah's Witness pamphlets, Arlington would shortly discover his true calling as the second coming of Christ—a peculiarly comic book-oriented Jesus, to be sure—but the underground artists took this in stride, gently poking fun in numerous cartoons at their comic messiah.

When they had their fill of time at the drawing board, the cartoonists would wander by the shop and shoot the breeze with Gary and whoever else showed up. Surrounded by a mix of golden age comics pinned to the walls in stiff plastic sleeves and expanding racks of the new underground comix, the underground artists could develop a sense of their movement as situated within a comics continuum extending back decades. New possibilities were still in the air, courtesy of a countercultural milieu that seemed to have embraced the upsurge of comix, allowing artists to propel themselves in new directions, discovering new taboos to violate or new envelopes to push.

Instrumental to this sense of artistic urgency was the constant interplay among the cartoonists, where a good-natured sense of competition led many artists to continually try to top each other's best work. Feedback from one's readers was relatively rare, but for artists living in close proximity, a ten-minute walk with a latest comic strip in hand could elicit praise or artistic advice from one's fellow artists.

At the peak of the underground comix movement—roughly 1972-1973—the Mission District was peppered with cartoonists all living within walking distance of each other. (See map on page 276.) Few of the artists involved were San Francisco natives. As with the upsurge of the Beats in North Beach in the '50s, and with the much-hyped love generation in the Haight-Ashbury around 1966, the influx of cartoonists attracted to the underground scene in the Mission pulled in participants from far and wide.

There were the transplanted Texans (whose ranks included Shelton, Jack Jaxon, and a circle of friends who soon founded their own cooperative comix press, Rip Off Press, in San Francisco's Western Addition, later moving to the Potrero Hill neighborhood). Over the grim winter of 1969-70, the *EVO* cartoonists (including Deitch, Rodriguez, and Robbins) abandoned New York for the San Francisco comix scene. As 1970 progressed, other New York underground cartoonists, including Justin Green, Willy Murphy, Bobby London, Roger Brand, and Bill Griffith, swelled the ranks of New York artists moving to San Francisco.

In addition to the Print Mint and Rip Off Press, comix were now being churned out in the Bay Area by Donahue's Apex Novelties (located just a few blocks from Arlington's shop), Ron Turner's *Last Gasp Eco-Funnies* (initially in Berkeley, but shortly after found in San Francisco's South of Market neighborhood), and Company & Sons, a haphazard printer that managed to survive for two or three years by the seat of its pants in the Mission District on seedy Capp Street.

While the underground comix scene largely coalesced in San Francisco, it maintained outposts elsewhere. Lynch and Williamson's Bijou Publishing Empire struggled on in Chicago, while Denis Kitchen established Kitchen Sink Publications in Wisconsin. Kitchen would eventually take over publication of *Bijou Funnies* and initiate a number of other long-lasting underground titles, including *Dope Comics*.

I managed to land in New York in Fall 1969 as a student at Pratt Institute, Brooklyn's fabled art school from which several underground artists had previously dropped out. I maintained contact with Lynch in Chicago and with the New York artists as they pulled up stakes for the West Coast. Griffith and I brainstormed our underground parody of romance comics, *Young Lust*, in the spring of 1970, while Bill was still residing on the Upper West side of Manhattan and I was taking

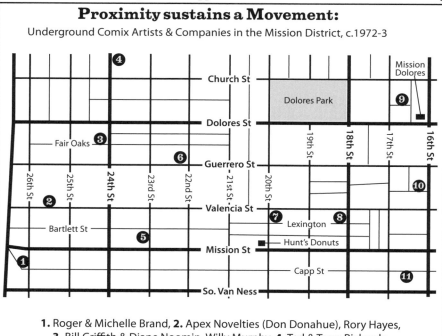

**Proximity sustains a Movement:**
Underground Comix Artists & Companies in the Mission District, c.1972-3

1. Roger & Michelle Brand, 2. Apex Novelties (Don Donahue), Rory Hayes,
3. Bill Griffith & Diane Noomin, Willy Murphy, 4. Ted & Terry Richards,
5. S.F. Comic Book Co. (Gary Arlington), 6. Trina Robbins,
7. Jay Kinney, Leslie Cabarga, 8. Joe Schenkman,
9. Art Spiegelman, Justin Green, Shary Flenniken, Bobby London,
10. Gary Arlington, Kim Deitch, 11. Company & Sons (John Bagley)

part in the student strike at Pratt protesting the Cambodia invasion.

For the next two years, I was torn between developing my skills at Pratt—where I was actually learning some solid draftsmanship—and hankering to move to San Francisco to dive into the comix scene full-time. I navigated the waters of New York's waning countercultural scene, doing comix for the *EVO*, *NY Rat*, and the late lamented *New York Ace*, the last gasp of the underground press in the Big Apple. By the summer of 1972 I was overdue to move to the Bay Area and that summer I took part in the final wave of New York

Robert Crumb with Jane and Jay Lynch, at their flat in Chicago, Sept. 1968. (Photo by Jay Kinney)

underground artists moving west. These included future Pulitzer Prize winner Art Spiegelman, cartooning prodigy Leslie Cabarga, *NY Rat* and *New York Ace* artist Joe Schenkman, and myself.

★ ★ ★

By this time, the Sixties counterculture was in serious decline. Underground papers were dropping like flies, and the notion of alternative institutions such as food co-ops or collective cheese stores leading the charge to a new post-Capitalist society was looking increasingly unlikely. Yippie media stars Abbie Hoffman and Jerry Rubin concentrated on getting out the youth vote for McGovern (probably to McGovern's chagrin), and Nixon's reelection seemed to confirm that nothing was going to change for the better anytime soon.

Yet, under-ground comix were still selling strongly and the movement continued on an upswing. From within the ranks of cartoonists, it was possible to imagine a future where the comix audience continued to grow and grow. Nixon's Silent Majority might seem to be in the ascendancy, but that just appeared to guarantee that there would be a permanent place for cartoonists thumbing their noses at Nixon's constituency.

Functionally, underground cartoonists were now drawing more for themselves—or each other—than for a specific readership, but there still seemed to be an audience out there willing to shell out 50¢ a pop for outrageous comix, and this solidified the sense of a successful ongoing artists' movement. This wave crested through the end of 1972 into the spring of 1973.

However, there were forces at work, both internal and external to the movement, threatening to derail it. Because of the increase in artists participating, a hefty volume of comix were being pumped out. Unfortunately, too many of these were mediocre, with sheer quantity threatening to engulf quality.

Philosophical chasms also began to widen between artistic camps. This was best exemplified by the polemics between Spiegelman and Griffith on the one hand

and Tom Veitch on the other. Spiegelman and Griffith represented the comics–as–Art position, which celebrated underground cartoonists as experimental auteurs. In staking out this position, the pair sought to influence the movement away from work that derived too much inspiration from mainstream comic books of earlier eras. They seemed to fear—with some justification—that artists who focused on recreating EC Comics, in either style or subject matter, would trap the movement in the comic book ghetto, only admired by a few fanboys and ignored by the critical cultural apparatus.

The underground artist who particularly raised their ire was Richard Corben, a Kansas City-based cartoonist whose airbrush-aided rendering was dazzling, but whose characters were muscle-bound men and women engaged in violent storylines. Corben had taken both comics fandom and underground comix by storm, happy to publish his stories wherever they might find an audience. It wouldn't be long before he'd be working for mainstream comic publishers in New York, but in the meantime, his work represented everything that Griffith and Spiegelman wished to discourage.

Rising to Corben's defense was Veitch, a comix writer best known for collaborating with artist Greg Irons on a series of gross-out stories that they signed *GI/TV*. Veitch championed the rights of underground cartoonists, including Corben, to do whatever they damn well pleased, to "think the unthinkable." This position was, arguably, the same held by Crumb and Wilson, who had early on taken the no taboos approach to new heights (or perhaps depths) with characters such as Crumb's Angelfood McSpade or Wilson's Captain Pissgums, and in the pages of self-consciously lewd cartoons such as the infamous *Snatch Comics*.

Both warring camps could justly claim their underground pedigrees and neither was likely to win the philosophical dispute. The culture at large, as it turned out, would have the last laugh.

A browning clipping from the *San Francisco Examiner* of June 21, 1973, marks the cultural shift ushered in by a landmark Supreme Court decision. Obscenity was no longer to be decided by court cases on a federal level, but referred back to local community standards. Underground comix, which had already been plagued by prosecution for obscenity in such cosmopolitan venues as Manhattan and Berkeley, were suddenly sitting ducks for legal harassment in every Podunk town across the nation. Nervous retail outlets began to return thousands of unsold comix to distributors and publishers, stopping the comix movement in its tracks.

Artists, who had been barely scraping by on foodstamps and $20 page rates, found their projects frozen or abruptly scrapped. The ranks of the comix movement began to thin, with many Bay Area artists moving back to the other parts of the country from which they had originally emigrated. Wrangling over artistic philosophies was replaced by a scramble for whatever paying work could be found, be it magazine illustrations, coloring books, flyer design, or sign painting.

It is at this juncture in 1973 that the first major history of the movement, Mark Estren's *A History of Underground Comics* drew its curtain on the movement. Actually, Estren had largely written his history two or three years earlier as a Master's thesis, and had only nominally updated it as far as 1973, before its publication as a lavishly illustrated art paperback in 1974.[5]

The story that remained untold, because of that happenstance of timing, was the 1974 rebound of the underground comix movement and its continuation through

In a spoof on the Faust legend that ran in *Arcade #2*, Justin Green delineates the qualities favored by that publication.

at least 1976 and, arguably, until the end of the '70s. While the Supreme Court-triggered crisis was serious, it was also temporary, as things turned out. Slowly, the gears of artistic commerce began to grind again, though on a smaller scale.

In an effort to jump-start things—and with a hope of garnering a better payout to the artists—Griffith and Spiegelman, along with fellow artist Willy Murphy brainstormed a DIY publisher: Cartoonists Co-op Press (CCP). This harked back to the original DIY impulse, with the artists financing and distributing their own comix and thereby gaining a bigger percentage of the take. CCP premiered with four titles, one each by comix stalwarts Griffith, Deitch, and Lynch, and one by Jerry Lane, a Fresno artist.

CCP was a noble but doomed effort. While Griffith had probably the sharpest business savvy of any underground cartoonist, CCP was reliant on the sales power of Keith Green, a fast-talking operator who was the younger brother of underground artist, Justin Green. Keith Green swung deals and juggled several balls in the air at once, until time ran out and he suddenly left town. Ultimately, the remaining CCP inventory was sold off to the other local comix publishers.

Meanwhile, in an effort to get the ball rolling again, the comix publishers concentrated on their strongest sellers. For the Print Mint, this meant the original powerhouse title, *Zap*, as well as *Young Lust*, the romance comic parody that Griffith and I had founded back in 1970. *Young Lust* had bounced from publisher to publisher, issue by issue, depending on who would make the best offer. With issue #4 we were back at the Print Mint, who were willing to spring for full-color throughout. If there was to be any hope for the underground comix future, this issue seemed crucial. If it bombed, we might as well pack it all in. But if it sold well, we might live to draw another day.

Or so it seemed at the time. *Young Lust #4* featured the same crew of artists who had filled the previous issues — Griffith, Kinney, Justin Green, Spiegelman, Roger Brand, Ned Sonntag, and Deitch, with a cameo by Crumb. The work was all do-or-die stellar and the issue sold well enough to warrant a follow-up (albeit, back to the usual black and white interiors.) Rip Off Press had Shelton's *Fabulous Furry Freak Brothers* comics to keep it afloat, while Last Gasp Eco-Funnies had solid sellers such as its environmental sci-fi title *Slow Death*.

However, a mere handful of successful titles were not going to provide enough work for the wider circle of artists to sustain comix as a viable movement. There were various responses to this dilemma. The two most prominent were *Arcade* and *Comix Book*. Both were attempts to bring the comix to national newsstands.

*Arcade* was Griffith and Spiegelman's attempt to materialize their vision of comix-as-Art into a quarterly full-size magazine. Its contributors were hand-picked from the ranks of those artists who met the pair's criteria of transcending a narrow comic book focus. The Print Mint had been talked into publishing the experiment, and there was hope that this might be a viable way for the core of the comix movement to survive and grow in visibility. Crumb supported the initiative and willingly contributed many of *Arcade's* striking full-color covers.

*Comix Book* took another tack. Kitchen, the Wisconsin-based comix publisher, approached mainstream comic book publisher Marvel Comics with a proposition: he would package a newsstand magazine for them, featuring underground artists. This intrigued Marvel as a possible way to widen their market. But Marvel demanded its corporate pound of flesh: the comic stories would be "work for hire." The artists would get their original art back (a modest victory, given Marvel's usual practices at the time), but the copyrights would go to Marvel. *Comix Book's* page rate was twice that of *Arcade's* ($100 per page as opposed to $50), but the artists participating would be relinquishing a right—artists' copyright ownership of their own work—that had been central to the underground comix movement since its inception.

The choice facing an artist between *Arcade* and *Comix Book* was, at first glance, fairly stark: underground fidelity or a better pay rate. In actuality, few artists had to make an either-or choice. Most of the cartoonists who did work for *Comix Book* were either not on the Griffith-Spiegelman "A" list to begin with or, if they were, there was nothing to prevent them from submitting work to both publications. Some *Arcade* artists were envious of the *Comix Book* page rate, but relinquishing their copyright was a step that only a few were willing to take. In this sense, *Arcade* represented the core of the comix movement trying to uphold its tenets.[6]

However, whatever controversy there was regarding this at the time (circa 1975) was a very brief tempest in a teapot. *Comix Book* only lasted for three bi-monthly issues as a Marvel-distributed title, after which Kitchen tried to keep it going for another couple of issues as a Kitchen Sink production. The experimental compromise with the New York mainstream was not a winner.

*Arcade*, for its part, only lasted seven quarterly issues, and its demise in 1976 marked the end of the Print Mint's run as an underground comix publisher. Around *Arcade #5* in late 1975, Spiegelman read the handwriting on the wall and gave up on the declining San Francisco underground comix scene. He relocated back to New York, and while still nominally co-editing *Arcade* from afar, he left the bulk of the labor-intensive in-person work to Griffith back in the Bay Area.

By the late '70s, the venerable underground comix designation had become a distinct liability for all concerned. Beginning in 1970, the Weather Underground had taken anti-establishment militancy to its logical (and extreme) conclusion and put meat on the bones of the underground label. Underground now meant living invisibly while striking out at the aboveground powers that be. Once the Weathermen reconsidered this strategy and began surfacing and turning themselves in, circa 1978, the old countercultural underground label was doubly obsolete.

Yet, "comix" as a distinctive alternative label was problematic as well. Verbally, comix and comics were indistinguishable, and in print, the difference between "x" and "ics" was subtle indeed. Underground artists were scrambling for art jobs wherever they could find them, and it was hard to argue convincingly that underground cartoonists drawing a color strip for *Playboy* or its competitors was an ongoing manifestation of the underground comix movement.

For those of us still attached to the underground comix movement as an idealistic anti-establishment concept, however, it was still possible to convince ourselves that whatever we did was part of the movement. Doing comics for the *Berkeley Barb* (which had still survived into the late '70s, remarkably enough) or for Rip Off Press, Last Gasp, or Kitchen Sink certainly seemed to qualify as being part of a lingering artistic movement. The pay was certainly miserable, so we reasoned that we must be doing the work for some higher cause.

*Zap Comic #1*, Robert Crumb's hugely influential comic book.

Precisely what that higher cause might be was increasingly difficult to discern, however. When originally associated with the growing counterculture, underground comix had served a purpose that might be characterized as blowing peoples' minds. The status quo was seen as hopelessly conservative, stagnant, and unimaginative. By portraying the outrageous or at least going where comics had never gone before, underground comix were implicitly subverting mainstream culture and serving as an icebreaker for new ideas.

Yet the absorption of the counterculture into the culture-at-large and the mass success of manageable outrage by the likes of *National Lampoon, Saturday Night Live*, and slasher movies meant that underground comix no longer functioned as a kind of cultural antibody. Thinking the unthinkable was rapidly becoming the new cultural norm, thanks to coke-fueled movie studios, radical chic, and the whole burgeoning pop culture industry. The pipsqueak taboo-busting of hand-crafted comix may have helped inspire this cultural shift, but the comix and their creators got lost in the shuffle once high-powered nose-thumbing was available on every newsstand or TV.

Just as the revolutionary pretensions of the Surrealist movement were appropriated by the mundane surrealism of Madison Avenue's ad agencies, so the underground comix role of outrageous outsider was superseded in due course by high-budget corporate anime, video games, and reality TV.

From my personal perspective, being an underground cartoonist in the '70s was tantamount to being a modern-day medieval monk. I wasn't copying illuminated manuscripts exactly, but I'd turned my back on worldly success in favor of a vision of underground comix as a cutting edge art movement. My wardrobe for most of my comix years consisted of washed-out blue cotton workshirts and denim blue jeans. Fine art in museums and galleries was an elitist proposition depending on the patronage of the wealthy, I reasoned. Comic art on newsprint in comic books that anyone could afford was our rejoinder.

However, getting the comix to their potential audience was getting more difficult all the time. A rash of anti-drug paraphernalia laws ravaged the head shop distribution networks that had originally spread comix far and wide. Comic book shops were beginning to sprout across the US, catering to comics fans looking for more reliable retail sources than comic books' sporadic appearance in newsstand racks and drug stores. But these shops mostly spurned the gritty black and white underground comix in favor of full-color product from Marvel, DC, Image, and other aboveground publishers. The adults-only underground titles were hot potatoes for retailers who had to maintain kid-friendly environments.

Many workarounds were tried, with mostly indifferent results. Rip Off Press tried to syndicate underground comix strips, on a weekly basis,

A lyrical cover by Crumb for *Arcade #3*, Fall 1975.

to college newspapers and the emerging market of alternative papers. A flock of political comix in the late '70s (my *Anarchy Comics*, Leonard Rifas's *Corporate Crime Comics*, among them) tried to bust out of the comics ghetto and penetrate into independent bookstores and punk subculture shops. None of these strategies really did the trick, and by some indeterminate point in the early '80s it was reasonably clear to everyone that underground comix—as a movement—was over.

Those underground artists who still felt driven to produce cartoons found ways to do so. Griffith's *Zippy the Pinhead*, against all odds, landed a berth as a daily strip syndicated by King Features. Crumb, Aline Kominsky, and Shelton pulled up stakes and moved to France, enjoying

*Bijou Funnies #1*, Chicago's seminal anthology comic.

success as American expats, not unlike jazz musicians of an earlier era. Back in New York, Spiegelman turned this strategy on its head by cultivating a certain French *bande dessinée* sensibility into *RAW*, the breakthrough comix-as-Art magazine he founded with his French wife Francoise Mouly.

For my part, without the community and sense of purpose of the underground comix movement, my own motivation to continue cartooning gradually dried up. Writing and publishing in other venues provided more satisfaction and better remuneration.

Meanwhile, a new cycle of so-called alternative comics from independent publishers such as Fantagraphics and Drawn & Quarterly achieved lift-off as the 1980s progressed with a new generation of cartoonists willing to work for the same rock-bottom page rates that underground artists had to put up with ten or twenty years earlier. Less attached to busting taboos and more attracted to clean aesthetics and first-person narratives, the alternative comics made peace with the comic shop distributors and laid claim to display space that the underground comix were never able to command.

The alternative cartoonists also knuckled down and produced issues of their respective comics on a steady predictable schedule—something that underground cartoonists were never able to accomplish.

The ultimate result of these small changes in approach was an ongoing adult

The final issue of *Comix Book*, a short-lived attempt to take underground comix mainstream.

market for comic art; one that the underground comix had seeded but were unable to harvest. Yet, without the underground comix movement, the present acceptance of graphic novels and comic art for a mature audience would never have happened. And without an urban neighborhood, such as San Francisco's Mission District, in which low-budget cartoonists and publishers could scrape by, the underground comix movement would never have coalesced.

The comix are long gone and the Mission is gentrifying. Perhaps, before all that is left are condos, trendy boutiques, and restaurants, we might pay our respects to a homegrown art movement that flourished for its allotted time before succumbing to the vagaries of the marketplace and the caprices of the courts.

## Notes

1. This date for the Haight St. expedition is specifically recalled by early *Zap* printer Don Donahue and cited in Patrick Rosenkranz, *Rebel Visions: The Underground Comix Revolution, 1963-1975* (Seattle: Fantagraphics Press, 2008) 74. However, I have a copy of the third printing of *Zap #1* with a November 1967 date printed within. Whether this was a print date or an artist's creation date is unclear.

2. This evolution of the UG press is ably chronicled in Abe Peck's invaluable *Uncovering the Sixties: The Life and Times of the Underground Press* (New York: Citadel Press, 1991). Perhaps the best example of this phenomenon can be found in the later issues of the *Berkeley Tribe*, a break-away from the *Berkeley Barb* and perhaps the most over-the-top underground paper of them all. Staff cartoonists included Bobby London, and Ted Richards (later part of the Air Pirates comic assault on the Disney empire), Greg Irons, and Dave Sheridan, all of whom reveled in satirizing their own underground cohorts.

3. Rosenkranz, *Rebel Visions*, 74-75. *Rebel Visions*, it should be noted, is an excellent and thorough history of the underground comix movement, and a book to which I would direct any reader who might wish to read further on this subject.

4. As with any generalization, there are exceptions. Rick Griffin did a certain amount of art for the *San Francisco Oracle*, the most mystical *cum* psychedelic of the underground papers.

5. Mark James Estren, *A History of Underground Comics* (San Francisco: Straight Arrow Books, 1974).

6. Ironically, Art Spiegelman published strips in the first two issues of *Comix Book*, but they were reprints of work that had previously appeared elsewhere and which already held his copyright.

# San Francisco Bay Area Posters 1968-1978

## by Lincoln Cushing

Posters are among the significant ephemera of what is sometimes called "the long 1960s"—the social decade rather than the chronological one. This period can loosely be said to start in 1963 (the Birmingham campaign of the Civil Rights Movement) or 1964 with the March on Washington and the Free Speech Movement, and end in 1974-1975 (Nixon's resignation and the end of the Vietnam War). But the argument can easily be made that these movements didn't just quit at the end of December 1975. This epoch of this book is 1968-1978, so we'll push it a little.

Synonymous with rebellion and visual wit, posters are fragile documents that are densely packed cultural viruses capable of instantly transmitting such abstract concepts as "solidarity," "sisterhood," or "peace" all over the world. Interestingly, political posters in the US did not really blossom as a cultural form until the mid-1960s. And that blossoming happened right here in the San Francisco Bay Area.

There have always been printed documents in this country encouraging civil disobedience, such as those opposing British taxation or challenging the slave trade, but they were mostly textual broadsheets with little illustration and design. Then there were the thousands of posters produced during the 1930s and 1940s through the Federal Arts Project, but those were concerned with putting artists to work and expanding the democratic nature of public art more than they were challenging the status quo. The chilling effect of the Cold War and McCarthyism during the 1950s made it too dangerous to produce political content for public spaces. The socially-conscious graphic artists had turned inwards, continuing to create limited-edition prints shared among friends and displayed in shows, and only occasionally did agitational prints make it to the streets. By the late 1950s, the politically vibrant Civil Rights Movement focused on other media, and printed imagery was limited, such as the iconic "I AM A MAN" placard—characterized by use of simple type and without illustration. Even the mighty Free Speech Movement (FSM), vibrant though it was with song, poetry, and theater, *did not produce a single poster.* Activist posters had been produced in Mexico since the late 1930s, but failed to spark a movement here. It was not until rock 'n' roll and counterculture posters exploded on the scene in the San Francisco Bay Area in the mid-1960s that public appetite for these visual expressions spread to political posters. This paralleled the experience in Cuba, where the visually radical new imagery from the Cuban film institute, ICAIC, inspired the other Cuban political publishing agencies to push their own design work in new directions at about the same time.

As 1950s America woke up from its deep chill, a new genre of popular culture blossomed in the streets on both sides of the San Francisco Bay Area during the mid-1960s. This was a *very* happening place. Musician Taj Mahal describes the scene, "It was Mario Savio got me out here," he says, referring to the charismatic University of California, Berkeley '60s student protest leader. "I saw Mario Savio on top of

*continues on page 300*

**"Benefit: Vietnam Summer" • Artist: Charles Fleischman • Publisher: Vietnam Summer Organizing Committee • Year: 1967 • Medium: offset**

Modeled on the Freedom Summer Black voter registration campaign of 1964, "Vietnam Summer" was a nationwide student anti-war campaign designed to raise broad community consciousness about the war in Vietnam. Popular resistance to the war was peaking; an April 15, 1967 rally in San Francisco organized by the National Mobilization Committee to End the War in Vietnam ("The Mobe") drew 75,000 people. Yet although this movement was based on active leadership and participation by women activists, some believed they were marginalized during the concluding conference in Chicago. This poster, drawn from the design well of rock 'n' roll and counterculture graphics, features an attractive young woman with typography splashed across her breasts. It serves as a stark example of how far New Left leadership had to go in building an egalitarian movement.

**"Join the Army"** • **Photographer: Edmund Shea** • **Publisher: The Print Mint** • **Year: 1967**
• **Medium: offset**

This poster encourages those of a countercultural persuasion to join *another* kind of army—one committed to peace, love, and egalitarian relations among beings. In 1965 Don and Alice Schenker opened the Print Mint on Berkeley's Telegraph Avenue with the help of friend Moe Moskowitz (of Moe's Books), and by December of 1966 started another store on San Francisco's Haight Street—just ahead of the Summer of Love. They closed up a year later because Moskowitz, who was buying the building, became too frustrated in trying to get a permit from San Francisco authorities to sell secondhand books. The Print Mint was quick to appreciate the importance of the then-nascent underground comic community, printing Robert Crumb's first issue of *Zap Comix* as well as scores of controversial titles by Rick Griffin, S. Clay Wilson, Victor Moscoso, Gilbert Shelton, and Spain Rodriguez. The Print Mint remained in Berkeley, and continued to be a vibrant distributor of posters and underground comics.

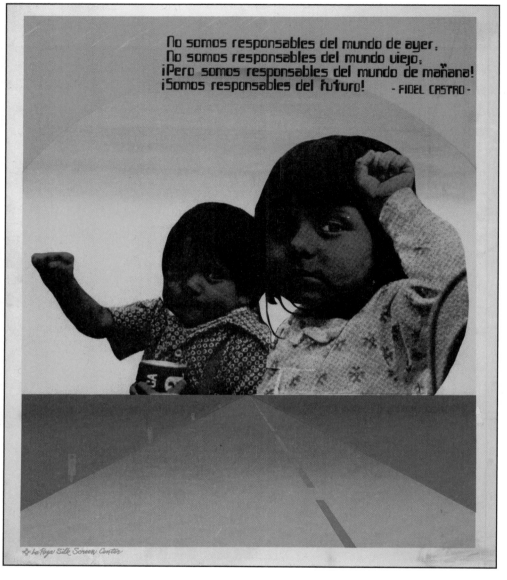

**"No somos responsables del mundo de ayer, No somos responsables del mundo viejo.
¡Pero somos responsables del mundo de mañana! ¡Somos responsables del futuro!
—Fidel Castro"** • (*"We are not responsible for the world of yesteryear. We are not responsible
for the old world. But we are responsible for the world of tomorrow! We are responsible for the
future! —Fidel Castro"*) • **Artist: Unknown • Publisher: La Raza Silkscreen Center • Year:
circa 1970 • Medium: screen-print**
One of the most vital cultural institutions to spring up in the Mission District was La Raza
Silkscreen Center. It was formed in 1970, when community organizers with design skills
(many of whom were active in the Los Siete de La Raza defense campaign) set up a simple
studio in the back of La Raza Information Center to serve as a public facility for producing
propaganda and training activists in media skills. The diverse Latino ethnicities of the Mission
were represented among the staff, and their work took on issues both local and global. This
early piece reflects the pride in Latin American revolutionary politics with a call to youth.

"ONLY ON THE BONES OF THE OPPRESSORS CAN THE PEOPLE'S FREEDOM BE FOUNDED-- ONLY THE BLOOD OF THE OPPRESSORS CAN FERTILIZE THE SOIL FOR THE PEOPLE'S SELF-RULE.

**"Only on the bones of the oppressors..."** • **Artist: Emory Douglas** • **Publisher: Black Panther Party, Ministry of Information, San Francisco, CA** • **Year: 1969** • **Medium: offset**

Emory Douglas is a revolutionary artist and an illustrator, and was a significant cultural force within the Black Panther Party (BPP). In 1967 he was given the title of Revolutionary Artist and became the production manager for the BPP newspaper; later he became the Minister of Culture. This poster is typical of his clean, clear, militant imagery, designed to work as well in black and white as in color. Although usually associated with Oakland, where it was started, in early May of 1967 the BPP took on increased prominence and began to organize chapters and branches across the US, including in San Francisco where this poster was issued. The source of the unattributed quote in the poster was none other than Josef Stalin, from "To All the Workers" written October 19, 1905.

**"Haya Education" • Artist: Unknown • Self-published • Year: 1968 • Medium: screen-print**
Between November 6, 1968, and March 20, 1969, San Francisco State College (now University) experienced the longest student strike in US history. Faculty and staff joined many student organizations, led by the Black Students Union and the Third World Liberation Front, to mobilize around such issues as opposition to the Vietnam War, limited opportunities for students and faculty of color, and demands for more relevant curricula. When College President Dr. Robert Smith resigned in the heat of the strike November 26, Professor of English Dr. S. I. Hayakawa was named Acting President. Hayakawa's bitter opposition to the strike contributed to a dramatic escalation of events, a situation similar to the chronology of the UC Berkeley's Free Speech Movement only four years before. This poster wryly notes Hayakawa's use of police tactical squads in putting down the strike. The demands for Ethnic Studies prompted a similar strike on UC Berkeley's campus, and by 1969 resulted in such departments at both, which were the first of their kind in the nation.

**"March for Peace April 24" • Artist: Unknown • Publisher: National Peace Action Coalition, Labor Support Committee • Year: 1971 • Medium: offset**

During the 1950s, having purged most of the Left-wing critics of US foreign policy, organized labor had benefited greatly from the cold war economy and was almost universally supportive of US government military actions. As historian Philip Foner noted, "Labor spoke with a Neanderthal voice. In May of 1965, George Meany declared that the AFL-CIO would support the war in Vietnam "no matter what the academic do-gooders may say, no matter what the apostles of appeasement may say." But as the war ground on, and working-class soldiers came home in body bags, support began to crumble and labor began to change. First, independent locals spoke up, and in 1969 the Alameda County Central Labor Council (CLC) came out against the war, the first CLC in the country to do so. The following year trade unionists ran full-page ads in the *Washington Post* and the *San Francisco Chronicle* against the war. The April 24 demonstration in San Francisco, even though not endorsed by the CLC, was a groundbreaking show of anti-war solidarity by major trade unions.

**"Community fair for peace and independence in Vietnam" • Artist: Unknown • Publisher: Unknown • Year: 1972 • Medium: screen-print**

This poster for an educational fair at James Lick School playground to rally community support for the Seven Point Peace Plan of the Vietnamese is a sweet example of efforts to truly "bring the war home." The thought balloons of two neighbors offer a clever design solution to bilingual text duplication (well-meaning and politically sensitive, though unfortunately not proofed by a native Spanish speaker—"apollo" should be "apoyo"). Programs such as these helped build an informed public that was crucial to ending any Nixon-fantasy vestige of US support for the war. Among the performers were two stalwart veterans of the cultural Left: the San Francisco Mime Troupe and the Red Star Singers.

**"David Crosby & Graham Nash"** • **Artist: Randy Tuten** • **Concert promoted by Steven Cohen, Leo Mackota, and Gary L. Jackson.** • **Year: 1974** • **Medium: offset**

This poster publicized a benefit concert with a truly Bay Area sensibility—combining the struggles of marine mammals and exploited farm workers. This was New Zealand-based Project Jonah's first year, and United Farm Workers were deeply engaged in a public secondary boycott campaign to promote fair contracts. Millions of sympathetic Americans stopped buying grapes, iceberg lettuce, and Gallo wine. Both causes needed money, and as was often the case, musicians helped out. Most accounts of Bay Area rock 'n' roll fail to acknowledge the tremendous role that musicians played in raising consciousness and money for every cause that needed it. Country Joe and the Fish, Sons of Champlin, and the Red Star Singers were among those that regularly did their part.

**"Fight for the International Hotel"** • **Artist: Rachael Romero (San Francisco Poster Brigade)** • **Publisher: I-Hotel Support Committee, printed by Inkworks Press (Berkeley)** • **Year: 1977** • **Medium: offset**

For many Bay Area activists of this period, the fight for the International Hotel was a cornerstone of tenant resistance and Asian-American self-determination. A high-rise redevelopment project targeted this single room occupancy (SRO) hotel for demolition, but the residents—and the community—said no. Most of the low-income tenants were elderly Filipino bachelors who had emigrated to this country in the 1920s and 1930s for menial labor, and relied on the I-Hotel for affordable housing. Nine years after the first eviction notices were served in 1968 the tenants were forcibly removed in an evening of epic police-activist confrontation. This poster bears its message in four languages, homage to the multiple ethnicities committed to this fight. The phrase "It is right to rebel" echoed the militant movement phrase from the Chinese Cultural Revolution.

**"Tule Lake—June 3" • Artist: Wes Senzaki • Publisher: Japantown Art and Media Workshop (JAM) • Year: 1977 • Medium: screen-print**

This poster was produced the year JAM was founded, a relative latecomer to the community-based art studios of the 1970s. Among the many issues the mobilized that Asian-American community, especially the Japanese-American community, was the dark history of internment during the Second World War. Two-thirds of the 120,000 persons of Japanese descent incarcerated in American concentration camps were American citizens. Tule Lake, in northern California, was the largest and most controversial of the ten War Relocation Authority camps. Conditions were deplorable, and inmates resisted with demonstrations and work stoppages. After the war, efforts to seek just redress took many years of persistent education and lobbying such as that evidenced by this poster; it was not until the Civil Liberties Act of 1988 passed that an official apology was offered.

**"Iran: People in Struggle for Independence and Democracy" • Artist: Leah Statman •
Publisher: Gonna Rise Again Graphics (GRAG) • Year: circa 1978 • Medium: screen-print**
Founded by four activist graphic artists as a collective on York Street in 1975, GRAG quickly
became a significant producer of movement media. They produced leaflets and flyers
for a wide variety of community and labor organizations, designed and illustrated books
for local publisher People's Press, and mounted exhibitions of educational artwork in the
community. This 1978 poster, explaining the situation of Iranians fighting for independence
and democracy under the Shah's US-supported dictatorship, tragically and ironically echoes
the persistence of today's liberation struggles.

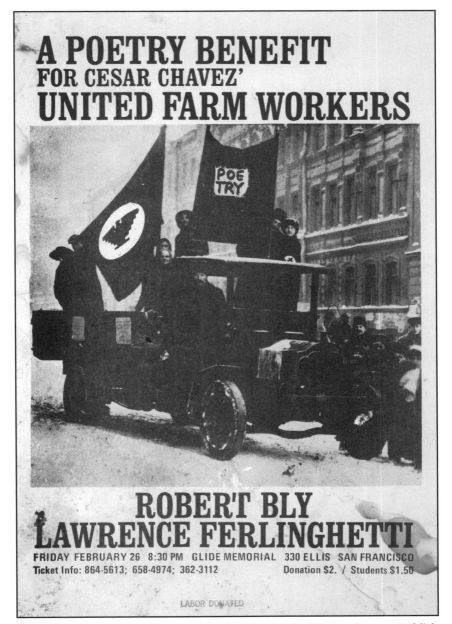

"A poetry benefit for Cesar Chavez' United Farm Workers" • Artist: Unknown • Publisher: unidentified United Farm Workers support group • 1971 • Medium: offset

The grassroots organizing and boycott campaigns of the United Farm Workers deliberately and dramatically involved the massive participation of community organizations. This poster, a benefit by popular poets at the venerable Glide Memorial Church (also the site of the famous 1967 Diggers "Invisible Circus"), displays a vigor and whimsy that was not typical of the rest of organized labor. By the mid-1960s Beat poetry had moved beyond the confines of cafes and bars, and this reading reflects a convergence of the counterculture and the activist migrant labor community. The source image—complete with snow and fur hats—was whimsically modified from a 1917 Bolshevik Revolution photograph.

**"Demostración Nacional/National Rally: Free Los Siete!" • Artist: Unknown • Publisher: unidentified Los Siete support group or individual • Year: 1970 • Medium: offset • Lincoln Cushing Archive, gift of Ann Tompkins**

On May 1, 1969, an altercation between two plainclothes SF police officers and seven young Latinos (including four Salvadorans, one Nicaraguan, and one Honduran) resulted in one officer dead. During the subsequent trial over a year and a half, movement groups supported the defendants on the grounds that the SF police had long been engaged in harassment toward people of color and youth, and that this trial was part of a pattern of racist persecution. The case served as a catalyst for community organizing, with support groups starting a neighborhood newspaper called *BASTA YA!* ("Enough already!") and building an infrastructure for, among other things, free legal services and free breakfast programs.

# Captured Sailors in Korea? POW's in Vietnam?

# NO

# THE PRESIDIO 27

These men are on trial for their lives. Their crime: a non-violent sit-down to protest stockade conditions and the shooting of a fellow prisoner.

**RALLY TO DEMAND CLEMENCY SATURDAY, MARCH 15, 1:30 MARINA GREEN**

(MARINA BLVD OFF LYON ST)

SPONSORED BY G.I. ASSOCIATION

**"Captured Sailors in Korea? POW's in Vietnam? NO: The Presidio 27"** • **Photographer: Unknown** • **Publisher: GI Association** • **Year: 1969** • **Medium: offset**

The activism of people within the military—draftees and volunteers, GIs and officers—is one of the less documented resistance movements of that unpopular war. In 1968 inmates at the Presidio's stockade, built before the first World War and now intensely overcrowded with more than double its designed capacity, sat down to protest the shooting death of a prisoner and demand an end to mistreatment and inhumane conditions. They were arrested and charged with mutiny, a military infraction that can carry the death penalty. The resulting trial convicted 12 GIs of mutiny and two of lesser offenses, with sentences as long as 16 years. After intense public outcry and a skilled defense by attorney Terence Hallinan these were reduced, with sentences ranging from three months to two years.

*continues from page 285*

that car in Sproul Plaza and said 'great google-bee, I'm outta here.' I drove across the country. I wanted to go somewhere where it looked like the youth knew what time it was. Every other place, they were so afraid. Out here, it was happening."[1]

And it did start with the music. Free handbills for the Avalon, posters for concerts at Winterland, flyers for tiny venues bubbling up everywhere. And spurred by the success of these local flyers and posters, political posters took the hint and became vibrant public documents that promoted a wide range of social issues. What is crucial to understand is how and why the San Francisco Bay Area was instrumental in making this renaissance happen. Just like life forms slowly reoccupying a clear-cut forest, it took an interactively evolving ecology to make change. In this case the requisite participants included:

**Artists**—Many of the graphics produced in the mid-1960s were by amateurs or art students, but there were also some "old timers" that helped show the way. In San Francisco, the prime transmitter of old Left printmaking culture was the Graphic Art Workshop (GAW). Founded in 1952 as a spin-off project of the Communist Party's California Labor School, it was the home for radical printmakers such as Victor Arnautoff, William Wolff, Byron Randall, Stanley Koppel, Pele deLappe, Irving Fromer, and Louise Gilbert. In the East Bay, these included Frank Rowe and Richard Correll (also GAW members) as well as Malaquias Montoya and Bruce Kaiper, among others.

**Consumers**—The demand for posters to put on one's wall grew dramatically during this period as the youth population swelled and free handbills were given out promoting rock concerts. Soon people wanted posters, all sorts of posters.

**Clients**—Art, even political art, rarely happens without patronage. Many of these posters were commissioned (albeit for tiny budgets) or were done as political work. As activist organizations grew in quantity and scale, their need for attractive and powerful posters blossomed.

**Reproduction facilities**—Almost all of these posters were printed by hand in small artisan workshops (where screen-printing was the dominant medium), at sympathetic offset print shops (which included established shops run by old lefties as well as the emerging new Left or community-based movement shops), or through presses associated with the hip literary community, such as The Bindweed Press. Screen-printing is a low-cost medium that blossomed during the Federal Arts Project's outpouring before WWII and was rediscovered in the 1960s. It was embraced by such community-based cultural organizations as the Mission's La Raza Silkscreen Center (later La Raza Graphics Center) founded in 1970, the Media Workshop that started in the Spring of 1970 at California College of Arts and Crafts and later moved off campus into the Berkeley community, and Kearny Street Workshop, founded in 1972 in San Francisco's Chinatown/Manilatown neighborhood. The earliest Bay Area movement offset print shops started in 1965 when the FSM set up shop to better spread their word; this later became Berkeley Free Press, then Berkeley Graphic Arts. In San Francisco the early 1970s saw the formation of the San Francisco Printing Collective, a coalition of FITS Printing, People's Press, *El Tecolote* newspaper, International Indian Treaty Council, Union of Democratic Filipinos [KDP], Northern California Alliance, and Up Press.

**New technologies**—It was a period during which creativity and spirit, matched with new communications technologies, could sometimes trump "the Man's" mass media. These technologies, such as transfer lettering, IBM Selectric typewriters with multiple font balls, and low-cost offset duplicators, allowed for easier and cheaper ways to create type, add art, and economically print small quantities. In February of 1967 the Diggers hosted *The Invisible Circus* at Glide Church, a wild weekend of art, politics, and counterculture. Two conspirators, Chester Anderson and Claude Hayward, brought in a Gestetner duplicator and set up "The Communication Company," cranking out a people's news bulletin dozens and dozens of times each day.

**Distribution**—As people started wanting posters to put on their walls, new distribution channels evolved. Head shops and poster stores (most notably the Print Mint, which by 1968 had storefronts in Berkeley and San Francisco) provided the physical space to see and buy posters, and artist-run cooperatives (such as Berkeley Bonaparte) made it easy to order by mail. Similarly, the creation of national alternative media outlets such as Liberation News Service and Newsreel provided a rich, fresh source of imagery for graphic artists. Newsreel, a movement film collective, was started in New York City in 1967 with subsequent groups being established in San Francisco, Los Angeles, and Chicago along with distribution centers across the country. Only California Newsreel remains today.

**Parallel media**—Many of these poster images were either previously printed in underground newspapers or were used as graphics after the fact, and illustrators and cartoonists that were covering new ground with comics (such as Victor Moscoso or Spain Rodriguez) were also creating graphics for more overtly political purposes. Also, the role of other cultural organizations cannot be underestimated—poets, musicians, and theater groups all collaborated on projects to make them richer and deeper.

So how did this all work? How did the various components of this evolving cultural ecology find their place in the sun? Several things all helped at this point in history. One was that youth and the counterculture had yet to be fully co-opted by the capitalist market. Also, the enormous demographic proportion of young people, coupled with a deep generation gap and a government that was clearly out of control, inculcated a certain attitude that maybe, just maybe, a chance for a fundamentally less twisted future could be had if we really tried. Alternative economic and social models sprang up like weeds—collectives, co-ops, and communes. For better *and* for worse, these were immediate, organic responses rather than meticulously planned and researched efforts. Everything was on the table—sexuality, work, therapy, art.

These posters illustrate some of the subjects and artistic producers that characterized this period.

# EPILOGUE

These early posters paved the way for subsequent generations of artists and graphics shops, such as The Women's Press, La Raza Graphics Center, Red Pepper Posters, and Kearny Street Workshop in San Francisco and Inkworks Press in Berkeley; these in turn were precursors to today's creative spirits, including the San Francisco Print Collective and Tumis, Design Action, and Dignidad Rebelde in Oakland.

By the late 1970s the political climate had changed, and many of the "first generation" movement graphics producers of the late 1960s moved on to other things. One reason was that after the end of the Vietnam War the various movements began a tortuous path of self-reflection that in many cases proved disastrous. As Ronald Weil of Gonna Rise Again Graphics put it, the dissolution of GRAG around 1978 coincided with "The rapid death of the Left which was accompanied by the splitting into more and more esoteric and hard line factions where friendships, relationships, and just about anything that made living worthwhile were rapidly being destroyed."[2]

The Silkscreen Center become La Raza Graphics in 1971, and in 1974 they moved to a larger facility where they were able to offer offset printing and typesetting services, and were now called La Raza Graphics Center. Eventually they folded into the larger Mission Cultural Center for Latino Arts in 1995, where community screen-printing continues to this day.

The Women's Press Project started in 1974 in the Mission District of San Francisco, as part of a nonprofit women's vocational school at the Women's Skills Center. In 1976 they became a collective, run by volunteer labor (later becoming paid staff), with the main purpose being a school to teach women the skills of the printing trade in a supportive environment. They gradually took on more printing jobs to support themselves. In 1980 it became a business as well as a school, with a priority being the printing of political and feminist materials, and became a union shop in 1983.

Up Press was formed out of the People's Union in 1972 in Redwood City as a collectively run movement press, printing political and feminist work. They became a women's press in 1974. In 1984 Up Press merged with the Women's Press Project to form the Women's Press and continued the school as the Women's Printing School. The Women's Press closed in January 1987 due to financial difficulties and the departure of several longtime members.

Even today, with the seductive miracle of the World Wide Web, artists are still putting ink to big paper. This essay honors the community that made these particular artifacts and encourages people to go out and make their own history.

Archivist note: Although these documents were often produced in the thousands, social neglect and physical impermanence have reduced their numbers to a ghost. Huge voids in scholarship remain to be filled. A handful of community-based archives and special collections—most notably among them the Center for the Study of Political Graphics in Los Angeles and Michael Rossman's AOUON ("All Of Us Or None") Archive of Political Posters at the Oakland Museum of California—have taken on the huge task of drawing these artifacts out of the woodwork, arranging them, cataloging them, and making them accessible to scholars and the public. All of these images, with the exception of "Demonstración Nacional/National Rally! Free Los Siete!" are from posters held in the AOUON Archive.

## Notes

1.    Joel Selvin, "Taj Mahal cools his heels in Berkeley again," *San Francisco Chronicle*, November 27, 2006.

2.    Ronald Weil, email message to author, October 9, 2009.

# Jung Sai Garment Workers Strike of 1974:
# "An Earth-Shattering and Heaven-Startling Event"

## by Harvey Dong

Impressed by the resoluteness of 135 striking Chinatown garment workers, the *Chinese Times* wrote an editorial in its July 27, 1974, issue entitled "Chinese Women Workers of the Great Chinese American Sewing Factory Demonstrate Against Exploitation." The editorial stated, "Unexpectedly, these once subservient *che yi ah shen ah mu* (sewing factory aunties), once considered *ru gao yang zhi fu* (as subservient goats and sheep) are demanding their rights. They have been shouting, clapping, shouldering picket signs and demonstrating against the exploiting class. This is a *shi po tian jing* (earth-shattering and heaven-startling) event and has created a new page in Chinatown history."[1]

Labor disputes involving less than several hundred workers are often discounted as insignificant. But the influence and effect of this dispute far outweighed its numbers. The 1974 Jung Sai garment workers strike began with widespread public support encompassing almost a year of strike activities, sixty-four arrests, and court injunctions. This united body of immigrant workers inspired popular support from community, student, and working-class populations throughout the San Francisco Bay area. The 135 strikers were mainly Chinese immigrant women with two men. Their interaction with hundreds of Asian-American activists and supporters became an important turning point for Asian-American activism in the San Francisco Bay Area. The strike encouraged further immigrant activism, energizing a grassroots movement among Chinese immigrant workers facing similar unfair labor practices.

Located at 646 Washington Street in San Francisco, the Jung Sai factory was a large Chinatown plant owned by Esprit de Corps, a manufacturer and designer of contemporary clothing for young people. In Cantonese, *Jung* means Chinese and *Sai* means West but the factory name was translated in English as "Great Chinese American" (GCA). The combination of the two characters, *Jung* and *Sai*, projected a meaning of symbiotic cooperation between the Chinese employees and Western management. But to the workers, the term "*Jung Sai*" represented harassment, intimidation, speed-ups, lack of breaks, and low wages. To the women, "Jung Sai" was a metaphor for the one-sided power of Western manufacturers over Chinese immigrant labor—an imbalance that had to change.

The workers' subsequent strike redefined that relationship. Whenever Jung Sai was mentioned after 1974, community residents associated the words with workers' resistance. What began as a single-issue unionization strike in one factory evolved into a multi-faceted campaign against exploitation and oppression of Chinese immigrants. Chinese immigrant seamstresses led and participated in marches, car caravans, plant shutdowns, community rallies, press conferences, mass media events, and an immigrant workers' cultural festival.

Furthermore, the strike took on a wider significance. It went beyond immediate workplace issues to encompass other racial and economic issues facing the Chinatown community. With Chinese immigrant women becoming a major element in the labor force, the Jung Sai strike defied racial and gender conventions about the Chinese female immigrant labor force being passive, exploited victims. They proved quite the opposite. Moreover, the women developed crucial rank–and-file independence from the International Ladies Garment Workers Union's (ILGWU) official leadership, enabling the strikers to engage in unconventional tactics and solicit active support from outside the industry.

★ ★ ★

Chinatown garment shops operated on a contract system. Manufacturers handled the design, purchasing, and cutting of textiles, and sold the finished products to the retailers. The contract shops did the assembly work, sewing, and some cutting. This flexible system had at its disposal a large supply of competing contractors. Manufacturers pressured contractors for low bids. The manufacturer transferred production responsibilities to the contractors who bid competitively for the assembly work. Ease of entry into the garment business created an oversupply of contractors, giving the upper hand to the manufacturers.[2] Because Jung Sai was majority-owned by Esprit, it didn't compete for contract bids with the sewing shop networks in Chinatown. Nevertheless Jung Sai was expected to provide quick low-cost production for Esprit like other Chinatown contract shops, extracting intensive labor for low wages from a large San Francisco pool of immigrant women.

The system allowed manufacturers to avoid blame for numerous labor code violations and was difficult to challenge. It was set up to make it difficult for workers to target downtown manufacturers for their low wages and bad working conditions. In 1969, twenty women from the Hoi Ming factory worked for months without pay. However, they did not raise objections, for fear of losing employment. Low wages and bad working conditions in the contract shops were garment industry norms.[3]

In 1967, the ILGWU attempted to organize Chinatown's sweatshops.[4] A "War on Chinatown's Sweatshops" was declared as the union sent pickets to demand not unionization but compliance with union conditions in factories, which included an eight-hour day, minimum wage, benefits, and clean and safe working conditions. The ILGWU targeted manufacturers as well as Chinese-owned contract shops. The first target was Romay of California and its ten affiliated contract shops, which were operating under what ILGWU San Francisco chapter manager Cornelius Wall called "the coolie system."

Representatives from another union involved in the campaign, the Amalgamated Clothing Workers, called for the prohibition of garment manufacturing in Chinatown. These representatives proposed a mass picket line around all of Chinatown "to dissuade tourists from entering the area until it is made part of San Francisco and this nation."

The "foreign labor argument" put forth by this 1967 campaign resembled the "Buy American" campaign a few years later sponsored by the garment unions, which targeted overseas imports. Foreign overseas workers were blamed for the de-industrialization of America. By blaming foreign and immigrant workers, the unions ignored the major players responsible for the loss of local jobs: the retailers, manufacturers, importers, and financiers.[5]

Frustrated with the labor unions' failure to organize the Chinatown garment shops, Wall's chapter proposed an amendment to terminate the entire Garment Shop Special Use District (implemented in 1960 to legalize Chinatown sweatshops) as of December 31, 1970. Wall argued that unionization was the only solution for the Chinese women. But if it was not possible to unionize Chinatown, then the shops should be moved into an area where organization was possible—even if it meant the wholesale removal of 3,500 Chinatown sewing jobs. The fact that 700 of these Chinatown jobs were already unionized in the ILGWU was inexplicably overlooked (Chinatown ILGWU members were 58% of the ILGWU San Francisco chapter total membership of 1200 in 1970).[6]

The original 1960 Garment Shop Special Use District ordinance claimed to be a beneficial solution for Chinese women who could not work outside of Chinatown for "family reasons." The 1960 ordinance rezoning Chinatown for light industry would employ women "close to family." Now, cancellation was proposed by the union as an alternative solution to "benefit" Chinese women. The union's main goal was to pressure manufacturers to send work only to those shops in Chinatown that were unionized. The inability to unionize more Chinatown contract shops from "inside" the workforce had held back further unionization. The union attributed this difficulty to workers' fear, community isolation, and language barriers.[7]

Earlier ILGWU history sheds much light on the top-down orientation of the ILGWU in the 1970s. "Taking back" the union from an entrenched and ineffective leadership was a popular demand by rank-and-file union members during this period. The ILGWU's largely Chinese- and Spanish-speaking constituency particularly wanted to ensure that basic requirements such as foreign language translations were available at union meetings. In the mid-'70s, full translations of meetings had to be fought for as part of an overall demand to democratize the union.[8]

In September 1973, the California State Division of Industrial Welfare singled out the garment industry as having the greatest number of labor law violations. In a one-week probe, 601 violations were discovered in 92 of the 1500 garment shops in the Bay Area. According to division chief Evelyn Whitlow, Chinatown shops were especially aware of the "means and methods that could be used to evade or avoid compliance" with state laws on hours, wages, and working conditions. The effects of the raids by inspectors remained mixed. On the one hand, many workers became informed about their legal rights as workers. On the other hand, the manufacturers were still not being held accountable. The small contractors were left to blame, while the contract system itself remained intact. By 1974, the situation in the garment shops had reached a boiling point, and the Jung Sai strike was its flashpoint.

## Jung Sai–Esprit, Lines Are Drawn

The list of humiliations and grievances were lengthy. The workers' grievances included having only either two ten-minute break periods or a thirty-minute non-paid lunch period to use the bathroom and stove facilities. Only two rolls of toilet paper were rationed per day for 135 employees. Workers who requested more toilet paper were scolded. Management also scolded those who acted or spoke out of turn. For women in their forties, this type of treatment was utterly humiliating.[9]

Experienced workers with seniority were fired and replaced with new employees. Communication with the White, non-Chinese speaking management was nonexistent. Workers viewed the Chinese-speaking supervisors as dictatorial and "mean." The management saw any sign of employees with English skills as threats and subsequently fired them. Despite the difficulties, many of the women stayed on because of their lack of English and other job skills. The plant's geographical closeness to Chinatown was another reason for the workers' unwillingness to quit. But staying and fighting was a choice that the workers were now ready to try.

On July 4, 1974, seamstresses Lily Lee, Lam Bick Chung, Nam Hing Leung, and bundler Frankie Ma took the initiative. They began distributing and collecting union authorization cards in full view of the floor supervisor Handa Lai. They sent the request for union recognition to Jung Sai on July 12. Altogether, a majority 83 persons out of 102, including 16 of the group with "zero gross pay" signed the cards, authorizing the union to serve as their collective bargaining representative.[10]

The company's response to the card drive was clearly anti-union. Workers who supported unionization were subjected to psychological pressure and retaliation. Ma was immediately fired on July 9 for allegedly not following a new technique in bundling garments. Younger than most of the workers, he was one of the two male workers supporting unionization. He also spoke more English than the rest of the women, who relied on him as the main contact with the union. Consequently, the company saw his dismissal as a way to weaken the workers' resolve for unionization.[11]

The day after Ma's dismissal, the owner of the factory, Douglas Tompkins, summoned Yook Yung Lee and her daughter, both seamstresses at Jung Sai, to his Esprit office to ask about their union activities. Tompkins prepared a document, written in English and Chinese, outlining his position on Jung Sai's status and business future. This document formed the basis of a 45-minute employee meeting held on July 12. Many workers recalled that Chinese translations of Tompkins' remarks were full of innuendoes and threats. The owner offered a twenty-five cents per hour raise if they abandoned unionization and threatened to shut the factory if the workers persisted in organizing.[12]

The next day, July 13, approximately 100 workers descended upon the union hall to decide on further action. At the meeting, Jung Sai workers vented their anger and frustration and voted to strike. The strike began on July 15 at the Jung Sai plant, with loud and spirited picketing. Floor supervisors barged through the picket lines, shouted defamatory remarks and tossed bundles of clothing at the strikers. The strikers were determined to continue their activities at Esprit's Washington Street plant, but picketing only lasted two days at that location. On July 17, Tompkins posted a notice at the entrance of Jung Sai declaring closure of the plant, essentially a lockout of the workers and their union.[13] What the workers did in response to the lockout opened a new page in Chinatown's history.

"If you're not afraid, join us. If you are afraid, this is not the place for you!" shouted the Jung Sai workers as they blocked entry into the Esprit de Corps plant at 900 Minnesota Street for two hours. Stopping business operations at the main plant was their only recourse after the Jung Sai factory lockout. On the strike lines in front of the main Esprit de Corps plant east of Potrero Hill, White female models, dressed stylishly in the latest fashions, walked through the picket lines of immigrant Chinese women production workers. Photographs of the strikers showed uncharacteristically defiant Chinese women marching in a picket line.[14]

The management called in police and arrested thirty-eight strikers and two supporters. According to a worker's press statement about the mass arrests:

> At about four o'clock, some of the workers stood in the doorway to prevent a truck from backing into the loading dock. Even though the driver plainly saw people in the back of his truck, the driver drove forward and then intentionally put the truck into reverse and hit three workers. While this incident understandably amazed and angered us, the policemen who were present made no move whatsoever to cite the driver or to assist the injured workers. Rather, the police harassed us and tried to make us leave. Under the circumstances, we refused to leave. We demanded that the police call an ambulance.
>
> After the ambulance arrived and took the injured workers to the hospital, the police proceeded to arrest 60 of us workers and some of our supporters. We were stuffed into the paddy wagons in three shifts, 20 to a wagon. One of the wagons was so crowded that two of the workers fainted inside due to the lack of sufficient ventilation.
>
> The owner of the Plain Jane Factory (Esprit), Douglas Tompkins, was present and witnessed this entire incident. He had the power to instruct his driver to leave peacefully without viciously injuring the workers. We, the workers demand that the management of Great Chinese American Manufacturing Co. and Plain Jane Factory, take FULL responsibility for this outrageous incident.[15]

One of the women, who was hit by the Esprit delivery truck was Mei Kok Tse, 46. The police left her lying on the ground for more than two hours and repeatedly told her to get up, saying she was "faking it." The driver stayed put in his delivery van, smiling under police presence until the injured woman was finally taken away by ambulance.[16]

Because the Esprit plant was located near a Black community ("Dogpatch") about fifty African-American spectators were present. Upon hearing what the commotion was all about, the community sided with the Chinese women and jeered at the arresting police officers. In jail, the women talked about this unexpected support.[17]

The workers called a press conference the next day, Friday, July 19, and appealed for community support. Held on the Holiday Inn-Chinese Cultural Center bridge located in San Francisco's Chinatown, the workers, press, and public gathered within view of the Jung Sai factory around the corner, and across the street from the International Hotel where an anti-eviction battle against developers was taking place. Joining the press conference was a group of Lee Mah Electronics workers, who were also mostly Chinese immigrant women locked out of their jobs for union activity. The strikers were seated before television cameras and newspaper reporters. Because of the hot summer sun, some of the women wore large brimmed hats. Asian Community Center (ACC) activist Marilyn Chan acted as translator. The event became a "speak-bitterness" testimonial as the women gave details about the conditions of the shops and the trauma of police arrests. Yook Yung Lee spoke emotionally about her life as a garment worker. Protesting the conditions in the sweatshops, she broke into tears and covered her eyes with both hands. Several of her fellow workers emphasized in Chinese, "That's true! That's true!" *("hai ngam la! hai ngam la!")*

The *San Francisco Chronicle* printed on their front page, "Any warmed-over stereotypes about Oriental impassiveness were convincingly shot down yesterday by a Chinese garment worker who delivered a passionate harangue over working conditions and then burst into tears at a press conference."[18]

*The Chinese Times* printed an editorial entitled "A New Awakening of Chinatown Women." The article commented that persons attending the press conference were "deeply moved" and "burning with rage" after having heard the women's testimony. "We fully support the Lee Mah Electronics and Jung Sai Garment workers' righteous and just struggle. These strikes show a new awakening of Chinese women," the editorial stated.[19]

## Attempts/Opposition to Linkages With Lee Mah

Efforts to find common cause between the Lee Mah and Jung Sai strikes were welcomed by both groups of workers, but also proved controversial. Forty-two of the Lee Mah employees were fired during a Teamsters unionization drive at their North Beach electronics plant. Mostly young women, they were standing up to the same issues of low wages, employer harassment, and anti-union intimidation as the Jung Sai women. The Lee Mah plant was also owned by an outside manufacturer named Farinon Electronics. Like Jung Sai, the Lee Mah workers had faced arrest and strike-breaking intimidation on the picket lines. Several Lee Mah strikers and two supporters attended the Jung Sai workers strike vote meeting on July 13, but were asked to leave by union officers. Nevertheless, the public bonding of the Lee Mah and Jung Sai strikers was prominent in joint leaflets, rallies, and community meetings.

ILGWU manager Mattie Jackson completely opposed any ties with the Lee Mah strike. Earlier, the union argued that attending the picket line at Esprit was more important than attending the community press conference on July 19th. Throughout the Jung Sai strike, the union fought to maintain tight control of decisions and opposed unsanctioned initiatives.[20] According to historian Peter Kwong, the ILGWU was a top-down organization that relied on making employer-friendly concessions which were unfavorable to its membership in order to prevent unionized manufacturers from breaking with the union. Meanwhile, it continued reaping dues from the members. A strong rank-and-file movement was incompatible with a highly centralized union leadership that leaned heavily towards workers' compromise.[21]

On July 24, a Jung Sai Strike Support Committee was independently established, comprised of strikers and supporters who met on a regular basis. Fourteen strikers were elected to run strike support finance, legal, and publicity committees. Some of the supporters had been arrested alongside the strikers. Others had spent long hours volunteering on the strike lines, assisting the workers and providing badly needed translation resources. The ILGWU saw the newly established Strike Support Committee as a threat to the union's hegemony. They attempted to pull the strikers away from the support activity meetings and functions, suggesting that strikers should not attend. Fortunately, the majority opposed this suggestion and continued to rely on outside support. Several of the supporters were also ILGWU union members. The solidarity between the younger activists and the Chinese garment workers prevailed despite the union's objections.[22]

## Asian-American Movement Joins In Support

Almost from the very beginning, young Asian-American activists from the ACC, located at 846 Kearney Street in the basement of the International Hotel, were involved. Student activism continued from the Third World Liberation Front student strikes at San Francisco State and UC Berkeley, establishing a "liberated zone" in the Chinatown-Manilatown area. In 1968, student activists had united with elderly Filipino tenants to save the International Hotel, low-cost housing for Filipino and Chinese tenants, from eviction and demolition. In this process, the activists opened numerous storefronts and basement community centers in the International Hotel building. The entire International Hotel block blossomed into an "Asian-American renaissance" in art, politics, and community service.[23]

The ACC was also the UC Berkeley Asian Studies Field Office. ACC activists were involved in a UC Berkeley course doing fieldwork on Chinatown sweatshops. Students studied alternative solutions to sweatshop working conditions, such as joining the ILGWU, forming a separate Chinese labor union, or starting a cooperative garment factory. This effort led to the establishment of the Chinatown Cooperative Garment Factory, located in the International Hotel. Students and immigrant women worked together from 1970 to 1974 making collective decisions in all aspects of business operations. Due to financial difficulties, the Cooperative ceased operations in 1974. The Cooperative relied on sewing contracts with large manufacturers, but could not meet operating expenses from the low bids required by manufacturers.[24] After closing, two of the Cooperative employees went to work at the Jung Sai plant on Washington Street. When the struggle flared up at Jung Sai, they approached ACC for support.

Many from within the community, inspired by the Jung Sai strikers, came forward in support of the workers.[25] These included individuals from organizations such as the Chinatown Community Children's Center, Chinese Progressive Association, English Language Center, Chinese for Affirmative Action, and the Chinese Cultural Center. Student support came from local campuses at San Francisco City College, San Francisco State, UC Berkeley, Stanford University, and San Jose State.

## Cultural Center Offers Space, Women Take Lead

Thanks to Shirley Sun, the new director of the Chinese Cultural Center (located in the newly constructed 30-story Holiday Inn!), the Jung Sai workers had a space to organize strike support events independently of the ILGWU leadership. Lee Mah worker Pearl Choy shared with the workers some of her negative experiences with the Teamsters union, who basically abandoned the Lee Mah strikers and left them to fend for themselves. She stressed the importance for the rank and file to stick together, rely on themselves, and not be dictated to by the union leadership. The need for unions but also the need for rank-and-file independence was continually discussed during both strikes.

Various tactics flowed from the strategy of linking the two immigrant struggles. On July 20, 1974, a thirty-car caravan, packed with over 150 Lee Mah and Jung Sai strikers and supporters, snaked through the streets of the Chinatown-North Beach area. Led by a large sound car with strikers speaking to the public, the response was electrifying as community residents cheered. Women employees rushed out of their sweatshops to grab leaflets from the strikers. Garment contractors slammed their shop doors shut.[26] The car caravan action, along with positive responses from the press and public, were all factors that encouraged many of the women to take more leadership roles in the strike committee.

However, gendered tradition pressured the women too. Picketing, attending night meetings, and becoming more assertive affected husband–wife relations. Husbands took on more domestic roles at home, including cooking and childcare. "Some of our husbands have told us to stop picketing and go back to work because they were 'losing face.' But we told them that the reason we were out here was to improve conditions for all workers in Chinatown, including themselves!" stated one woman.[27] The strikers dispelled earlier portrayals of women afraid to leave Chinatown, relegated to sweatshop work near their children.

Gender politics also affected the leadership dynamics of the strike. Several male strikers were "naturally" looked upon as leaders. The union saw the men as *de facto* leaders and concentrated on them to carry out union policy. The women, having received lower pay and lower skilled tasks than the men, also accepted patriarchal attitudes of behavior. Men were usually cutters, were more mobile, and had more freedom to talk. Women were stationed in one work unit and required to do repetitive stitching tasks. The firing of Ma for distributing the union cards, despite the fact that many women were involved collectively in the unionization drive, also implied that only men could lead.

But the women's leadership emerged in the daily meetings and strike activities. It emerged in actions like the car caravan, and their assertiveness became stronger with their participation. Old ways of deferring to male authority were replaced by newer, confident attitudes. "Chinese women who work at Jung Sai have been ripped off. . . ," said Mrs. Wong on the car caravan loudspeaker. "We have been oppressed for so long. . . I hope everybody would step forward to help the Chinese workers take this stand, speak for them. Do all you can to help us publicize these unjust attacks, come to the picket lines, support us."[28]

The car caravan had set the tone for future actions by the strikers and supporters that would connect the struggles of workers in the community with those nationwide. "This chaos has done society some good; peace cannot be forever," said an editorial in the *Chinese Times*. "Their income was inadequate. They have no choice but to use the strike as a weapon to demand betterment of their lives."[29] The editorial referred to the upsurge in strikes (1,050) and worker resistance that year on a nationwide scale. The Chinatown strikers were not fighting in isolation but were part of a nationwide movement.

Fearful of expanding numbers on the daily picket lines, the police and the courts countered with more arrests and injunctions. Fifteen individuals were arrested on July 24 but picketing continued. Judge Samuel Yee imposed $150–$250 bail on a number of the arrestees. He told arrested supporters that they had no right to picket and that Chinatown had enough trouble already. This was also the same day in which Esprit obtained a temporary restraining order limiting the number of pickets.[30]

The significance of the strike went beyond one factory shop. Chinese for

Affirmative Action, a civil rights organization, reported a tremendous increase in complaints by Chinese immigrants about working conditions, wages, and unfair treatment. There was word about slowdown activity among Chinatown garment workers in protest against low piece-rates. Restaurant workers were making attempts to unionize. Class lines were drawn and the stakes heightened.[31]

The following Sunday, July 28, the ILGWU sponsored an outdoor rally attended by 250 people near the home of Tompkins. *East West* newspaper reported, "Chinatown mothers, fathers, aunts, uncles, oldsters and students gathered at Precita Park for a rally...Jung Sai strikers not only enjoyed an afternoon of pleasant sunshine, but also struck rapport with Mission (District) dwellers as they spoke of management harassment and harsh working conditions at the Washington Street shop."

August 6th was a day of relief as well as a day of consternation. All charges against the forty workers and supporters in the first mass arrest were dropped for lack of evidence. But Esprit de Corps obtained a preliminary injunction limiting picketing.[32] The union leadership responded by moving strike activities away from the Esprit plant, and concentrating on boycott activities and legal maneuvers. Supporters and strikers leafleted department stores, boycotting Esprit de Corp clothing (aka Sweet Baby Jane, Jasmine Teas, Cecily, Rose Hips, Esprit De Ski and Plain Jane).[33] Jackson also asked the National Labor Relations Board (NLRB) to prevent Jung Sai from selling its plant and/or equipment, and order Jung Sai to resume its operation and reinstate all persons who worked there at the time of the shutdown. The union did not want any more blocking of trucks or similar tactics. The union would not support any arrested strikers. Under pressure from the courts, the union was obliged to pull in the reins of strike activity.

On October 11, Jackson responded to calls for support mobilizations by the rank and file within the ILGWU and other progressive individuals in the garment industry with the letter:

> If you participate in activities which are <u>NOT</u> sponsored by the ILGWU Locals 8-213-101 or 214, San Francisco Joint Board concerning the Great Chinese American strike, you do so at your own risk. The Union cannot afford either legally or strategically to back 'wildcat' demonstrations.[34]

The union embraced a strictly legalistic approach of relying on the NLRB and abiding by the injunction. The business agents and officials were mainly non-Asian and had little understanding of the attitudes of the immigrant women. Jackson, a former seamstress from the Koret plant and an African-American woman who had risen through the ranks, conducted the union meetings with an iron hand. She was quick to call workers out of order if they debated her from the floor. Following strict orders from the international, she sought to protect the union's legal status first and foremost. Building broad base support, shutting down the Esprit plant by extralegal means, and connecting with other issues was considered beyond the union's interest. As noted earlier, the idea of radical supporters meeting with the strikers was considered a threat to union authority. Supporters were removed from ILGWU meetings and dissenting strikers were told that the union would pull out of the strike unless they consented to the new legalistic strategy. The efforts of the union bureaucracy to remove radicalism probably did more damage to the strike than the police arrests or court injunctions.[35]

## Esprit Counterpunches

For owner Douglas Tompkins, his earth was shattered when he saw that his Chinese workers were unionizing. When the company's verbal threats and attempted bribery did not work, he imposed a lock-out. In addition to his use of the courts and police, Tompkins made it known in October that he was selling the Jung Sai plant to his manager Mike Kozak. Kozak, it was alleged, would reopen the plant and rehire the Jung Sai strikers.

This offer was made at a time when deliveries to the Esprit plant had been seriously hampered by the strike. Leaflets distributed to Teamster truck drivers explained, "Many years ago workers in this country fought for and won the right to have unions. Yet today, Chinese workers in Chinatown like the Jung Sai workers, are still denied this right…We are all working people—we must all oppose discrimination, and unite in support of each other's struggles, no matter what nationality we are."[36] Rank-and-file Teamster response to the leaflet was overwhelmingly positive. The Teamsters stopped accepting or shipping Esprit materials or goods through the neighboring R.E. Ellis facility. Employees working inside the Esprit de Corps plant indicated that production was in disarray and many cutters had been sent home early for lack of work. It was in this context, as well as the general public pressure, that the "sale offer" was floated to create an ambivalent situation.[37]

The union's divisiveness, and the personal pressures of being on strike, had a telling effect upon the workers. It was not surprising that they considered any kind of offer a breakthrough. The sale offer was an enticement for the strikers and some supporters, throwing them off guard. A core of the women strikers led by Mrs. Mah and Mrs. Wong were suspicious and questioned the proposals to cut off ties with the supporters. They differed from the union's opinion over who were the real allies and friends of the strikers. Moreover, a Jung Sai plant owned by Kozak could end up being another Chinatown contract shop without any obligations or responsibility to Esprit. After the union leadership applied pressure on the entire body of strikers to follow their directions, those who held neutral positions were swayed.

According to ACC member Chan, the strikers' views were understandable, "The workers counted on the union. Some of the workers felt they had to rely [completely] on the union [for direction]. They also had this fear about us as leftists. . . they tended to do what the union said [to do]."[38]

Attendance of strikers at the Esprit picket lines began to dwindle, partly due to the onset of winter. However, a core of women strikers and supporters put forth a counterproposal that combined legal and mass resistance. Remaining committed to actions at the Esprit plant, they also conducted boycott activities in front of the larger department stores such as Macy's and the Emporium.

As the strike entered winter, a "Three-In-One" rally was held on December 1st, linking the Lee Mah, Jung Sai and International Hotel struggles. The event included a march through the community and a rally at Portsmouth Square to emphasize that the three issues were part of a whole movement in the community. Two hundred people marched through Chinatown and three hundred people attended the rally.[39]

"A return to work appears on the horizon for 130-odd workers who struck the largest Chinese garment factory in July," reported *East West* in their December 4th issue. "Although a contract has not been signed, accord has been reached in several areas. According to several sources, the terms of the three-year agreement would include: all workers be allowed to return to work; International Ladies Garment Workers Union recognition in the shop; a wage set at $2.50 per hour; and guaranteed work from Jung Sai's parent company, Esprit De Corps." It was now public knowledge that success and settlement for the half-year dispute was around the corner.[40]

Kozak's willingness to negotiate with the workers and union, Tompkins' promise of guaranteed work for the Jung Sai workers, and settlement of the strike all proved to be a sham. When the time arrived for the signing of the agreement, Kozak could not show the bill of sale. Kozak also brought out Tompkins's "new terms of guaranteed work": Within 60 days after the workers have been reinstated, the quality of work produced at Jung Sai must match the carefully made sample provided by Esprit. If the samples do not match, Esprit had the option to cancel the guaranteed work contract. Tompkins also stipulated that the guaranteed work be limited to one year. Apparently, the management's approach towards negotiations was to stall as long as possible, to break the will of the workers, and to lessen the boycott and mass mobilization pressures on Esprit. Jackson reported that negotiations to bring the strike to an agreeable conclusion remained "at a standstill." The strikers issued a press release through the support committee denouncing the "... trickery of Tompkins... From Monday through Friday, 9 am to 4 pm, we are continuing our picket in front of Jung Sai's parent company."[41]

An agreement was signed on January 13, 1975, by ILGWU director Mattie Jackson, worker representative Mr. Leong, and Mike Kozak, new owner of the plant now called "The American Sewing Factory." The ILGWU announced that the contract provided for union recognition, hiring and overtime provisions, nine and one-half days paid holidays, vacations, injury pay, bereavement pay, a grievance procedure, health benefits, retirement and death benefits, eye care, a drug program, and wage increases. The majority of the Jung Sai work, it was agreed, would come from Esprit de Corps.[42] But none of this was true.

Kozak announced before the press and the Jung Sai workers that "everyone that was ever employed would be welcomed back to work as soon as possible." He added, however, that it would take "a couple of weeks" to get things in order and to clean the place before the employees could return. Jackson stated she was "very happy" about the signing of the contract and that it was a "continuation of unionization in the garment industries." Mr. Leong, through a translator, said, "This is a successful conclusion of a six-month strike. The workers are happy to have a settlement and to have received broad support from the public."

Perhaps suspicions should have arisen when the name of the plant changed from "Great Chinese American Sewing Co." to "The American Sewing Factory." "Jung Sai's Machines Gone," was the title of an article on page one of the February 5, 1975 issue of East West. The newspaper reported that the Jung Sai workers had a new contract but the Jung Sai plant was empty of machines. Kozak could not be reached for comment. Jackson heard that the machines were gone but gave no comment. A press release Jackson issued the previous week speculated that if the bill of sale between Esprit de Corps and Kozak was not real, Esprit would be held legally responsible by the NLRB.[43]

It was difficult now to maintain momentum on picket lines. Many workers had found jobs. Many were also persuaded by family members to not take any more dangerous risks on the strike lines. Energy was dissipated and diverted to the defense of those arrested. Ten months later, on December 2, 1975, Esprit de Corps was ordered to reopen Jung Sai, rehire all persons employed on July 12, 1974, award back pay to the workers, and bargain with the ILGWU for a contract. Back pay was expected to exceed half a million dollars. Administrative law judge David G. Heilbrun said in his 18-page decision that he found "pervasive, extensive violations" of labor laws by the management, including refusal to recognize a 99-67 majority union election, illegal interrogations, threats of discharge, threats to withhold paychecks, and threats to close the plant in attempts to stop the union drive. It was clear that Esprit had violated the law.[44]

But the law allowed numerous appeals; and, the company used legal delays for four more years. Eventually Esprit exhausted all appeals and finally agreed to pay workers from the time they were locked out to the time it took them to find new jobs. The average settlement ranged from $8,000 to $12,000, with some as high as $25,000. Massive public support for an active rank-and-file led strike dissipated after a little over a year, but the struggle ended thirteen years later. The false sale to Kozak, the appeals, and a mysterious office fire were all part of a strategy to minimize financial losses and ultimately keep out the union. Suzie Tompkins finally settled with the workers after her divorce from Doug Tompkins. The union bureaucracy's narrow legalistic approach served to undermine the rank and file. Capitulation strategies of the union, its opposition to connecting with other struggles (Lee Mah), its attempts to deny rank-and-file control, and its efforts to suppress progressive support, all prevented the strike from realizing its maximum potential.

Dropping the name "Great Chinese" and renaming the plant "The American Sewing Factory" could be viewed as a final *coup de grace* by Esprit de Corps on the Jung Sai struggle. But it also expressed the employer's fear that the name Jung Sai might still represent workers' resistance. The way the struggle was built, the broadening of support, the coming together of young supporters from the Asian-American movement, the notion that Chinese immigrant women could take control over their lives, and the courageousness of individuals like Mrs. Mah, Mrs. Wong, Mrs. Mak, Mrs. Szeto, et al were all factors that redefined the meaning of "Jung Sai." To workers, supporters, and community "Jung Sai" meant "shatter earth, startle heaven."

## Notes

1.      "Chinese Women Workers of American Sewing Factory Demonstrate Against Exploitation (Xi Ren Yi Chang Hua Nu Gong Fan Bo Xue Shi Wei)," *Chinese Times (Jinshan Shibao)*, July 27, 1974.

2.      J. Loucky, M. Soldatenko, G. Scott, and E. Bonacich, "Immigrant Enterprise and Labor in the Los Angeles Garment Industry" in *Global Production, The Apparel Industry in the Pacific Rim.* (Philadelphia: Temple University Press, 1994) 348. Although talking about Los Angeles, their definition is relevant.

3.      "Twenty Seamstresses Unpaid for Months," *East West,* December 17, 1969.

4.      D. Meister, "A War On Chinatown's Sweatshops," *San Francisco Chronicle,* August 23, 1967.

5.      E. Bonacich, "Asians in the Los Angeles Garment Industry," in *The New Asian Immigration in Los Angeles and Global Restructuring,* eds. P. Ong, E. Bonacich, and L. Cheng (Philadelphia: Temple University Press, 1994) 137-163.

6.      D. Lan, "Chinatown Sweatshops," in *Counterpoint, Perspectives on Asian America.* (Los Angeles: U.C. Regents, 1976) 355.

7.      Meister, "Drive to Organize Chinatown Labor," *San Francisco Chronicle,* March 27, 1967.

8.      Executive Board Member of ILGWU, interview with author, April 19, 2002, San Francisco, CA.

9.      Mabel Ng, "Chinese American Co. Seamstresses Strike Over Working Conditions," *East West* (July 24, 1974).

10.  United States of America before the NLRB Division of Judges, Great Chinese American Sewing Company, Esprit De Corp, and San Francisco Joint Board, International Ladies' Garment Workers' Union, AFL–CIO, Decision. Case nos. 20-CA-9369 and 20-CA-9424. (San Francisco, December 2, 1975).

11.  Ibid.

12.  Ibid.

13.  Ng, "Chinese American Co. Seamstresses."

14.  "130 On Strike, Many Arrested, Jung Sai Workers Rip Garment Industry," *Wei Min, Asian American News,* July-August 1974.

15.  Arrested Workers of Great Chinese American Manufacturing Co. [Press Release, July 19, 1974]. "Please Look At Employer's Attack On Employees, Seventy Arrested, One Injured, Two Knocked Down." It is possible that because of English difficulties and the highly emotional situation, the number arrested varied in public statements from 38 strikers and two supporters to 70 workers. The 38 strikers and two supporters is probably more accurate. *The San Francisco Chronicle* reported 38 on July 19, 1974.

16.  "Garment pickets, jailed, released," *San Francisco Examiner,* July 19, 1974; "130 On Strike, Many Arrested, Jung Sai Workers Rip Garment Industry," *Wei Min, Asian American News,* July-August 1974.

17.  "Black Community Supports Jung Sai," *Wei Min, Asian American News,* July-August 1974.

18.  J. Smith, "A Tearful Protest In Chinatown," *San Francisco Chronicle,* July 20, 1974.

19.  Huang Lian Ji. "A New Awakening of Chinatown Women. (Wah Fu Fu Nu De Xin Jue Xing)," *Shi Dai Bao (San Francisco Journal),* July 24, 1974.

20.  Ibid.

21.  Peter Kwong, *The New Chinatown* (New York: Hill and Wang, 1974) 147-151.

22.  Jung Sai Workers Support Committee, interpreter field notes, 1974.

23.  See Estella Habal's essay "Filipino Americans in the Decade of the International Hotel" in this volume.

24.  In their organizational pamphlet, the Chinatown Cooperative Garment Factory listed three alternatives to the sweatshop conditions: unionization into the ILGWU, formation of an all-Chinese union and workers' cooperatives. The ILGWU solution was discounted because of its poor track record of labor standard enforcement. The all-Chinese union approach was discounted because of the lacking of worker solidarity. The cooperative idea was presented as a vehicle for self-determination and groundworks towards grassroots controlled unions. *Chinatown Cooperative Garment Factory: First Year of Practice.* (San Francisco: Chinatown Cooperative, July 1971).

25.  I Wor Kuen (IWK) and its related organization, Chinese Progressive Association (CPA), were active participants on the Jung Sai picket lines. These two affiliated organizations had differences with WMS and ACC with regard to the strike. A key strategic difference arose on how to build rank and file leadership. IWK's strategy focused on activists obtaining union official positions and then using those positions of leadership to influence the union policies. Tactically, this meant cooperating with the established union policies, and eventually gaining positions to effect policy changes. ACC/WMS disagreed with this strategy and felt that basic workers ability to change working conditions came through collective rank and file action in the workplace and union decision making, not through a process of individuals attaining union leadership positions. In practice, the disagreements led to organizational sectarianism. These organizations spent much time bickering about the positions proposed by one side against the other--often for no reason other than that the competitor organization had made the suggestion. The two sides had ongoing ideological and political differences that, for the sake of the Jung Sai strike, had to be subordinated. To their credit, these organizations made far-reaching efforts to work together despite their differences in order to avoid hurting the strike support. The importance of the strike actions and the strong influence of the immigrant women workers helped offset the conflicting views. The strikers main concerns were not ideological, but were rather practical questions involving how to actually win the strike demands.

26.  "130 On Strike."

27.  "Immigrant Women Workers, An Interview, " *Wei Min Bao,* composite interview from both Lee Mah and Jung Sai women workers, December-January 1974-75.

28.  Notesheet from car caravan. July 20, 1974.

29.  "Chinese Women Workers Demonstrate."

30.  "130 On Strike."

31.  "Who dares to make waves," *Wei Min Bao,* October-November 1974.

32.  "Cases Dropped in Chinatown Picketing" *San Francisco Chronicle,* August 7, 1974; Interpreter's field notes

33.  San Francisco Joint Board, International Ladies Garment Workers Union, AFL-CIO, "Get It Off Your Back" (boycott leaflet, 1974). Public appeal by the union to boycott Esprit de Corps apparel.

34.  Mattie Jackson, "Notice to Our Members and Friends," San Francisco Joint Board, ILGWU (Letter in Chinese and English, October 11, 1974).

35.  Interpreter's field notes.

36.  Great Chinese American Sewing Co. Strike Support Committee, "Appeal to all UPS Teamster Drivers & Workers to Support the Jung Sai Strike Against Esprit de Corps!" (1974).

37.  Interpreter's field notes.

38.  M. Chan, interview with author, April 18, 2002.

39.  "Lee Mah-Jung Sai-Int'l Hotel Means Fight Back!" *Wei Min, Asian American News*, December-January, 1974–75.

40.  Ibid.

41.  G.C.A. Garment Strike Committee, "For Immediate Release" (press release, December 27, 1974).

42.  Mabel Ng, "Jung Sai Strike Settled," *East West*, January 15, 1975.

43.  "Jung Sai's Machines Gone," *East West*, February 5, 1975.

44.  "Garment Factory Ordered to Reopen," *East West*, December 17, 1975.

# When Music Mattered

## by Mat Callahan

> The struggle between the artist and the state can best be seen in performance in general and in the battle over performance space in particular…With the emergence of the state, the artist and the state became not only rivals in articulating the laws, moral or formal, that regulate life in society, but also rivals in determining the manner and circumstances of their delivery.
> —*Ngugi wa Thiong'o "Enactments of Power"*[1]

When on January 14, 1978, the Sex Pistols took the stage at Winterland in San Francisco, they had come to bury Caesar, not to praise him. The City's rock royalty presided over a smug, self-satisfied cultural establishment still basking in the glory of a revolutionary moment when San Francisco had indeed been the center of the world's attention. All of that had come to ruin and the Pistols had come to dig its grave. When Johnny Rotten ended the show with the now famous, "Ever get the feeling you've been cheated?" he was referring to the truncated performance of his disintegrating band. But the question he posed haunts us still because many did feel cheated, not by the Pistols' short show, but by the rock star, the political opportunist and the New Age guru who had ripped off the music and subverted the struggle to change the world. What had become of the ideals, the vision and the creativity of the Sixties? Had it been so easy for the System to bribe those who'd once sought to topple it? Was there really nothing but hedonism and megalomania in the great upheavals of 1968? Was it ironic or inevitable that the show at Winterland was put on by Bill Graham Presents and the Sex Pistols were once signed to EMI (also the Beatles' label),[2] two institutions that symbolically and practically represented everything the Pistols were out to destroy?

Now, more than thirty years after that fateful concert, another question arises: what actually happened in San Francisco to make it such an important center of rock and revolt? If the howls of betrayal vented by punk rockers in London a decade later could resonate so widely, there must have been something, some great promise made and broken to which they were referring. Since they explicitly scorned long hair, psychedelic drugs, peace and love, and any sign or symbol associated with hippies, they were obviously making what San Francisco was famous for the focus of attack. By banning guitar solos and long jams, they were directly critiquing San Francisco icons like the Grateful Dead and Santana. By raging against the Queen, celebrating anarchy, and decrying apathy, they vigorously reasserted an explicit, radical stance that had once been an integral part of rock music and of being young—particularly as these were shaped in San Francisco from 1965 to 1975. When Johnny Rotten sang, "No Future" punctuated by, "I mean it, man!" he sharply posed what was at stake:

— Music as a rival of the state for legitimate authority
— Music as a battleground within a larger social one
— Rock 'n' roll is dead

Declaring rock 'n' roll dead was a direct reference to the historical fact that this musical form had once been innovative and liberating. It had been a rallying point and a battle cry, particularly as it evolved in San Francisco. Now it had to be exposed as a fraud, the *Great Rock 'n' Roll Swindle*, as their mockumentary film was to call it. But this only begs the question: what had given a form of music such importance and what had taken it away? If Steve Miller could sing "Children of the Future" in 1968 and Johnny Rotten "No Future" in 1978 what had made the difference? How does music go from genuine to fake, from oracle of truth to bombastic bullshitter? The question is multi-faceted since it asks history, art, politics, and, ultimately, philosophy for facts and for judgement. It asks, furthermore, who will be the judge? The artist or the statesman? Whatever the reply, this is a concrete example of the ancient rivalry when music, for a brief period, became legislator of morals, aesthetics, and legality usurping the authority of government, educational institutions, and the older generation.

## Three Streams Converge On San Francisco Bay

By 1965, when the San Francisco musical renaissance began in earnest, three streams had already converged to give music extraordinary social importance. First were the attacks by the authorities. In 1955 the House Un-American Activites Committee indicted, convicted, and sentenced to prison Pete Seeger, citing his song "If I Had a Hammer" as subversive. This signaled a wholesale campaign which sought to purge America of the scourge of folk music. Seeger was later acquitted on appeal but the public's attention had been rudely awakened: music could be dangerous! A different but equally vicious campaign was launched against rock 'n' roll. In this case it was mainly the form's moral degeneracy, not its supposed communist influence, that was the target. The KKK and other racist groups went to great lengths to establish in the public mind that this was "nigger music," and would lead to miscegenation and racial degradation. Right wing ministers hosted public burnings of offensive records. Parents were warned. "In 1955 the CBS television network canceled Alan Freed's *Rock 'n' Roll Dance Party* after a camera showed black singer Frankie Lymon dancing with a white girl," writes Eric Nuzum in his *Parental Advisory, Music Censorship in America*. "In 1959, Link Wray's instrumental classic 'Rumble' was dropped from radio stations across the country—even though it had no lyrics. The title of the song was thought to be suggestive of teenage violence."[3] So, by the early 1960s music had already been brought to the center of public affairs as a target for banning and burning. It could not be viewed simply as entertainment or commodity. Folk and rock were a political and moral threat to the American Way of Life, the Red menace and Black music vs. Mickey Mouse!

The second stream was the central role music played in the growing Civil Rights Movement. Above all other forms, including literature, oratory, graphic, and dramatic art, music was the most important. Negro Spirituals, work songs, blues, and folk filled the meeting halls and demonstrations, the sit-ins, and the court appearances of a movement symbolized by "We Shall Overcome." The deep river of African-American music gave voice to the aspirations of an oppressed people. On the one hand, its eloquence lent support, in tangible ways, to an advancing struggle thus enhancing its stature as the popular, democratic art par excellence. On the other, it pitted music against the illegitimate authority of a state responsible for the oppression suffered by the people making it.

Lastly, electrical amplification had surprising and innovative effects. One instrument, the guitar, underwent a transformation. The guitar was and is the quintessential folk instrument in all cultures in which it is employed. Prior to WWII its use was widespread but limited by its low volume. Once amplified, however, it rapidly overtook horns and pianos as the dominant instrument in popular music. Exemplifying this change was Chuck Berry. Berry's innovative use of the new instrument brought it to the forefront. A guitarist could now be heard over a drum set and a self-accompanied singer/guitarist could be the leader of a band. One such band, the Beatles, subsequently took the world by storm. The convergence of these three streams took a radical turn when they entered the waters of the Golden Gate.

## From Port in a Storm to Storm in a Port

San Francisco was a haven for innovative art and radical politics. This was largely due to two major contributions made there in the first half of the 20th Century: Modern Dance and the International Longshoreman's and Warehouseman's Union (ILWU). Signified by the names Isadora Duncan and Harry Bridges, they provided protection from persecution, a means of subsistence and a platform for propagating new ideas. This did not mean, however, that there was a simple binary opposition between good guys and bad guys with music on the side of the good. The Bay Area had long been home to a thriving musical community, albeit one dead set against rock 'n' roll (viewed as commercial, nihilist, and dumb). While the close association between musical/artistic expression and political engagement of one kind or another was firmly established, the ancient rivalry between the arts and politics was a source of conflict within the ranks of those fighting for social justice. On the one hand, the Left provided a solid and devoted base of support for musical exploration that defied the strictures of the music industry and society at large. On the other, the very people who had made this possible became the targets of their own progeny as a younger generation picked up the electric guitars and drum sets suddenly given such vitality by the Beatles. There never was a "San Francisco Sound." But there was a San Francisco attitude. This developed over a short span of time combining the anti-commericalism and anti-authoritarianism of its forbears with a rejection of some of their cherished traditions. By the time regular dance concerts were running at the Avalon and Fillmore there had been a wholesale abandonment of modes of music-making common to folk and jazz and the adoption of new ones flowing from how rock 'n' roll was made. This included the instruments, of course, but it also included the way songs were structured, the connection to dancing as the crucial interface between musician and audience (as opposed to sing-alongs characteristic of folk music) and above all, it was loud. There was no doubt that this music was defiant and wild. It was not "cool" in the sense that bohemian intellectuals used the term when describing what they sought in jazz. It was not respectable in the sense that left-wing protest tried to appear as it sought to win over the masses of Americans. Such constraints were blown away by the sheer excitement produced by the music itself. Like it or not, the Beatles had everyone listening.

Purists among the folkies derided the Beatles' music as more of the same commercial pabulum. Jazz aficionados frowned on the shallowness and predictability of the compositions and the performers' inferior technique. Both criticized its blatant appropriation of African-American music. But few could deny that a phenomenon was unfolding in two important ways. The first was that the "British Invasion" consisted of bands playing their own instruments and their own songs as opposed to singers, with anonymous accompanists, doing songs written by others. The second was that there were a lot of them. It was not only the Beatles but a large number of British groups that followed one upon the other, week after week for two years. This efflorescence produced its own momentum, musically and socially. While not a movement in any conventional sense of the term it had the effect of mobilizing large numbers of young people to participate in music in a way previous teen crazes never had: it made kids want to play!

Almost immediately local promoters, radio DJs, and journalists recognized the sudden upsurge in interest not only of fans but of musicians who were forming bands inspired by their British counterparts. Tom Donahue was a popular DJ on a major AM station, KYA. He was a concert promoter bringing the Beatles and other British acts to the Cow Palace, and he was the founder of Autumn Records. (Later he would found SF's first "psychedelic" nightclub, Mother's, and embark on his greatest endeavor: underground or free-form radio on KMPX.)[4] Autumn signed local bands such as the Mojo Men, the Vejtables, the Beau Brummels, and the Great! Society. This was still well within the bounds set by established music industry practices where musicians followed rather than created trends. Not surprisingly, the names of the bands, the costumes they wore, and the kinds of songs they sang all more or less imitated the Beatles or the Rolling Stones. The venues where live music was performed hadn't changed much either with liquor licenses and curfews limiting teenage participation to high school dances, State Fairs, and giant package shows such as those at the Cow Palace or the Civic Auditorium. Night clubs and coffee houses were for adults and still largely segregated by ethnicity and class. Amidst these limitations—perhaps because of them—the rapid growth of interest in playing music was by late 1964 already bearing creative fruit.

What transformed this lively but conventional development in popular culture into something radically different came from outside of the music scene itself.[5]

## "A Tribute to Dr. Strange"

To begin with, there was the political engagement of many of the earliest participants. Among the first long-hairs and freaks were a disproportionate number of red-diaper babies, children of liberal professors and bohemian artists not to mention those directly participating in the Civil Rights and Free Speech Movements. Many were drawn from the three major schools in the Bay Area: the University of California, Berkeley, San Francisco State College, and Stanford University. This is a frequently overlooked component of what gave the San Francisco musical renaissance its unique character. Yet it is attested to by Ralph J. Gleason, columnist for the *San Francisco Chronicle*, in an out of print book published in 1969 called: *The Jefferson Airplane and the San Francisco Sound*. Aside from what is in hindsight a misleading title, there is greater accuracy, depth, and historical sweep in a few short pages of Gleason's account than in much of what has been written since. Gleason was in the highly unusual position of being read and respected by almost everyone with any interest in popular culture throughout the Bay Area. From this pulpit Gleason rallied support for every expression of honesty, outrage, insight, or innovation that issued forth from artists as diverse as Miles Davis, Hank Williams, and Bob Dylan. He was a staunch defender of Lenny Bruce and outspoken critic of racial oppression—particularly that suffered by the American Negro (to use the parlance of the times). We will hear more from Gleason in a moment.

Four other elements that originated in the Bay Area but outside music combined to divert the post-Beatles rock boom from the course set by the music industry and purveyors of cultural commodities. These were dancing, visual art, theater, and LSD, each represented by particular people as well as the milieus within which they operated. The Family Dog—specifically, Luria Castell, Ellen Harmon, and Alton Kelly—were responsible for the dance component. It was their insight that young people wanted to dance to the new music that led them to produce the first "Dance Concert" at the Longshoreman's Hall on Oct.16, 1965. They gave the event a name, "A Tribute to Dr. Strange." The fact that they had to use a union hall is a reminder that there were no other likely venues for such an event.

The visual art component was represented by Bill Ham, who along with fellow artists Elias Romero, Tony Martin, Glenn McKay, and Jerry Abrams had been inspired by SF State art instructor Seymour Lock, pioneer of the exploration of light projection in the Fifties. Ham brought his primitive light show to the Family Dog's dance concert and the stage was set. What happened next was historic in more ways than one. The audience was the show.

Ralph Gleason's description is worth quoting at length,

> [It was] a hippie happening which signified the linkage of the political and the social hip movements. SNCC buttons and peace buttons abounded, stuck into costumes straight out of the Museum of Natural History...the crowd danced all night long... and I mean they danced!
>
> After the dance, on the long bridge ride over the San Francisco Bay, [Gleason lived in Berkeley] the little Volkswagens with Freedom Now stickers and SNCC and FSM signs in the windows driving back to Berkeley would pass me, packed with the long-haired young people, a giant convoy of escapees en route back to real life.[6]

Meanwhile, the San Francisco Mime Troupe had been performing its inflammatory and innovative theater for a number of years. Their notoriety was increased by performing in the City's parks. One such performance on August 7, 1965, prompted an arrest of the Troupe's founder and director Ron Davis. This led to a highly publicized court case and the necessary fund-raising to pay for the Troupe's defense. They decided to throw a benefit concert at their 924 Howard St. facility. The organization of the benefit was undertaken by their business manager Bill Graham. This took place Nov. 6, 1965, and like the Family Dog show at the Longshoreman's Hall a month previously, attracted at least 1000 people. The effect was immediate as it galvanized disparate elements propelling them forward together. Music was clearly fundamental but it was in combination with the dancing, the light show and the support for a radical theater group that something new emerged. It was not, in the beginning, a purely musical scene at all. It was a "happening, in which people participated in making a collective performance for themselves and each other, not for an audience as such.

Into this stew would be poured the psychotropic drug LSD. Stanley Owsley and a couple friends began supplying their homemade, high quality and completely legal LSD to friends and associates in May 1965 and to the Merry Pranksters and the Grateful Dead in September 1965. Within a short time this substance had been widely disseminated, particularly in the Bay Area, and in the literal and figurative sense it captured the imagination of adventurous youth. There were certain conditions surrounding its introduction that are often forgotten when speaking of the role Acid played:

1. A lot of young white kids were already smoking pot in 1964. (I bought my first matchbox in that year.)
2. Alcohol was out. It was not hip to drink, though people still did. The main thing is that wine, beer, and booze were associated with the older generation against whom youth were rebelling and,
3. The name of Owsley attached to a tab guaranteed its quality. Furthermore, it carried with it the unspoken message, "Take this, brothers and sisters, everything will be different, you'll see." Owsley said many years later that he was performing a community service—but for a particular community.

And things happened fast. Pleasant surprise at the outset became eager anticipation within weeks. When more than a thousand people turned out for the Family Dog's first event it delighted and amazed those in attendance that so many like-minded people existed. Within a year the numbers were swollen ten fold. By the Human Be-in in January 1967 at least 20,000 people were directly participating (estimates run as high as 50,000). This encouraged the widely held notion that a new day was indeed at hand. Whether this was the dawning of the Age of Aquarius or the launching of a revolution the certainty that something of earthshaking importance was underway permeated the atmosphere. No matter how illusory that might appear to be in hindsight, it was a fact that an all encompassing Movement was developing comprised of everything from the Farmworkers to mutinous GIs, from Diggers to Black Panthers; it unfolded in dramatic demonstrations and the occupation of public buildings, at benefit concerts, and in the lyrics of songs. And music was regularly performed outdoors for free. Once the SF Mime Troupe had pioneered guerilla theater, transforming public space into a "liberated zone" of vibrant social interaction, rock musicians flooded into this newly opened arena and filled it with the dancing multitude.

It is precisely at this junction—the public space filled with dance, theater, music, and political engagement, that Freedom was declared and the System launched its counterattack.

## "Don't Call Me Nigger, Whitey/Don't Call Me Whitey, Nigger"[7]

Coming to grips with this phenomenon requires challenging certain notions that have dominated discussion in subsequent years. First of all, this was by no means limited to a rebellion of white youth. At the start, young White people predominated in terms of numbers in attendance at events. But *from* the start there were Black, Latino, Asian and Native American musicians and artists involved as well. Furthermore, the musical flowering included outstanding groups from the Mission District and the East Bay as well as from the Haight-Ashbury or Marin County. What discussion of the San Francisco musical renaissance would be complete without mentioning

Santana, Malo, and Tower of Power? One musician in particular demonstrates the point. Sly Stone was the producer of the Warlocks' (later renamed the Grateful Dead) demo tape for Autumn Records. He wrote a song for the Mojo Men. He produced the Great! Society's version of "Somebody to Love," all before going on to become the leader of one of the most influential bands of the period, Sly and the Family Stone. One song, "Stand!," released in 1969, could as well represent the era as any and the album it was on marks the musical and lyrical territory better than many others that are usually cited. While the first impulse emanated from an amalgam of music, dance, light shows and poster art drawn together by young White people, its inspiration was felt across all divisions of ethnicity, gender, and social class. It thereby unleashed a torrent of creativity that might otherwise have been ghettoized or silenced by the prevailing norms of the music business and America's racist culture at large. Remember, this was a time when it was rare for Blacks and Whites to socialize together let alone play in the same band. By the end of the Sixties, a generation had learned that the main source of its beloved music was African-American.

Music mattered because it consciously and directly challenged the state. It did this by granting permission to do things the state prohibited or restricted. Dancing, drug taking, and sexual adventure were all encouraged by music in defiance of laws regulating such activities. But most controversial was race mixing: the inevitable outgrowth—as racists had predicted—of the music being made. This overlapped with specific political struggles that, if nothing else, opposed what the state commanded, in some cases explicitly calling for its overthrow. What had begun with the Civil Rights Movement was being transformed into a struggle for liberation. The stunning appearance of the Black Panthers, the dramatic Indian occupation of Alcatraz and the rapid growth of Los Siete de La Raza mark this increasing radicalization. All involved music and musicians to one degree or another. But what made music so important was that it could, at times, succeed where the state or any kind of politics had failed. It could provide a means for breaking through the barriers erected by racism because everybody knew that everybody loved it. And everybody loved it because it made you feel free.

## From Free Frames of Reference to a Day on the Green[8]

Another common misconception concerns the Festival. Beginning with the Trips Festival, San Francisco in the Sixties returned this word to its original meaning: a collective celebration by a community. Historically, Festival was reserved for annual rituals of a religious or seasonal nature such as Easter or the grape harvest. Recalling this, Tribal Stomps, Human Be-ins, and myriad titled gatherings emphasized the communal and sacral aspects—which might appear silly to an outsider but were taken very seriously by members of the hip community. The term had long been (and continues to be) in more prosaic use to identify an event, albeit a large one, organized around a musical genre such as jazz or folk. But the dance concerts and festivals of the period were markedly different. First of all, they were free or very low cost. Secondly, musical diversity was the norm, a typical bill being Dr. John, Thelonius Monk, and the Charlatans. Third, they were all ages. Most important, they were publicized and perceived as calls to an assembly as opposed to a conventional show. Audiences gathered for the sake of gathering not only for a particular performer; they came to participate, not only to observe. Music didn't matter because of the numbers consuming it but because of the nourishment it provided the community from which it sprang. This is further demonstrated by certain bands who were among the best of the period but never became stars. The Sons of Champlin and Mother Earth are only two of many who regularly proved why music mattered and why it was not the music industry or stardom that was responsible. It was in fact the festival in its original sense that gave them purpose and significance.

What has come to symbolize this is, of course, Woodstock. Followed shortly thereafter by its tragedy-laden sibling, Altamont, the bookends of an era seem to fit neatly together as high and low points or, as has often been repeated since, the dream turned to nightmare. But perhaps more significant as a bellwether of actually unfolding events was one that *didn't* happen, the Wild West Festival. Band manager Ron Polte's idea was to have a giant three day extravaganza held August 22-24, 1969, at numerous sites in Golden Gate Park, including big names at Kezar Stadium. Some events would be free while others would charge admission but it was never clear where any profits would go from what the organizers claimed would be "a party and a spiritual statement." Leading the effort was the San Francisco Music Council, convened for the event, which included Tom Donahue, Bill Graham, Ralph Gleason, David Rubinson, and Frank Werber (ie., the movers and shakers of the San Francisco music scene). In an attempt to broaden its appeal and, tellingly, to prevent it from becoming just another Bill Graham production, Barry Olivier from the Berkeley Folk Festival was invited in as director. They were surprised to find that their idea was not welcome in all quarters. Riding a crest of worldwide acclaim for all things related to music and San Francisco, they had not counted on opposition from groups such as the Mime Troupe, the Haight Commune and community activists in the Fillmore District. Even Gleason and Donahue, used to being in the forefront of social trends found themselves left behind by the rapidly changing popular mood. Few, if any, could accurately gauge the effects of 1968, a year of worldwide revolution. The violent repression visited on young people from Paris to Prague to Da Nang to Haight Street swept away whatever illusions might have remained that "All You Need is Love." Music's importance was greater than ever but it was less as a plea for peace and more as a demand for justice. Furthermore, the Wild West Festival's organizers were caught in a crossfire that included a strike by light show operators against the Family Dog and Bill Graham, bitter acrimony left over from failed attempts by local bands to run the Carousel Ballroom in opposition to Graham, and a growing distrust of appeals to a non-existent "community" by way of phony spirituality. What became painfully evident was that a division had opened between those who saw the musical renaissance as a spiritual and even political revolution in and of itself, and others who viewed revolution as a struggle to overthrow the System. Somehow, thought the one group, music transcended violence and racism and would through its simple celebration change the world. Frank Werber is quoted as saying in reference to Wild West, "This *is* the revolution!"[9] This was in stark contrast to opponents of the festival who knew that 1968 was a watershed year and that San Francisco was part of a worldwide revolutionary upsurge not represented by music alone. The strike at San Francisco State College, the battle for People's Park, as well as struggles to Free Huey Newton and Los Siete de La Raza had, by the time the Wild West Festival was being proposed, already galvanized thousands of young people in militant resistance. The New Left was on the march. The fact that millions, literally, were thronging to both musical and political events obscured underlying differences in agenda. Wild West collapsed but few mourned. Why would they? Music continued to flourish as did political resistance. But now, it was impossible to ignore the increasing friction between business interests and social ideals, a friction many had naively believed could be overcome by the young generation's altruism.[10]

In 1973 Bill Graham launched a concert series called A Day On the Green at the Oakland Coliseum. This innocuous title cloaked an event of considerable significance. Less than a decade before, Golden Gate Park had been the site of literally dozens of free concerts. Almost every week for a few years, the Panhandle, Speedway Meadows, the Polo Fields, and occasionally other locations, saw bands performing to the large and growing throng that came to participate in what many thought was a new world being born. Throughout the period ever increasing numbers attended rallies, marches and demonstrations against the war in Vietnam, the biggest of which ended at Kezar Stadium and always included musical performances. By the time Woodstock happened there was already a well established precedent of large outdoor festivals combining music, diverse cultural activities, and politics. In spite of what happened at Altamont, large anti-war demonstrations and concerts in Golden Gate Park continued, including the largest ever on April 24, 1971 where over 150,000 were in attendance. Moreover, concerts in the Park, demonstrations over a widening range of social issues and the general climate of confrontation with the System had in no sense abated by the time Graham held the first Day on the Green. But holding such an event in a sports stadium allowed access to be controlled to a show that sold the appearance of a festival. This was not simply a matter of making money and preventing rowdy behavior. What this series signaled was something else: literally and decisively breaking the bond between musicians and those who at one time had been their community. What had characterized the earlier, formative period was lost. Numbers became more important than music or ideas. All that mattered was how many came through the turnstiles and how to expand those numbers further.

Graham was not alone in this and was joined by many musicians and their own networks of friends and supporters. While music itself was a banner around which a generation rallied this did not make musicians capable of leading anyone anywhere. A case study is Santana and the subsequent career of Journey. Santana was a quintessentially San Francisco band. Multi-ethnic and multi-talented, its members were drawn from the Mission District and the suburbs, all inspired by what was going on at the Fillmore and Avalon, all partaking of the sounds and sights, the psychedelics, and the social turmoil characteristic of the period including playing a famous benefit for the Black Panthers. After making two pathbreaking albums which rank among the best of the period, they began to break up due to drug abuse and intense touring. When the band fell apart three of its members were pulled together by their manager, Herbie Herbert, and what came to be known as corporate rock was born. From 1973 onward the band pioneered everything that was antithetical to their roots. Budweiser commercials and stadium spectacles (it's a stretch to call these musical performances) paved the way for the demise of an ethos. What the Sex Pistols, the Clash, and the punk scene in general were rebelling against was what Journey represented.

A division was now increasing between music and radical politics. It is not as if Journey and stadium rock emerged because of a decline in political activism. Quite the contrary, it began taking place amidst growing revolutionary ferment. The US was losing the Vietnam war. Nixon resigned. The Energy Crisis and the first great crash of capitalism since World War II gave the appearance of imminent collapse. This fueled the growth and militancy of a diversifying movement which by now embraced women's, Third World, and gay liberation as well as burgeoning environmentalism. But to a large extent, the musical renaissance was dissipating. When in 1973 Tower of Power released what many consider their finest song, "What Is Hip?," they perfectly captured the mood. Singing, "What is hip today, may become passé," the band questioned underlying assumptions about hipness itself. This was widely interpreted as pointing the finger at poseurs and phonies who were pimping (to use the term in its Sixties sense) on the spirit of the times. Music continued to be a vital force within a society still very much in turmoil but from this point onward it could no longer be said that it was centered in San Francisco or that it provided the undiluted, untainted voice of the millions struggling to change the world. Music could not make revolution.

Meanwhile, the SF Mime Troupe continued to perform radical theater in the parks, musicians, including many famous ones, continued to support political causes, and it was a good while before the Reagan/Thatcher axis would effectively bring the Sixties to an end. But combined with a coordinated assault on oppositional groups by the government there was a steady reassertion of music industry control. It was said at the time, "The Man can't bust our music."[11] To which now must be added, "But he sho' 'nuff took us to the cleaners!" Instead of the direct censorship which prevailed in the USSR there was the deliberate separation of music and politics in the US. While crushing political resistance by often brutal means, the System dramatically changed the tactics that had brought music to such a prominent place in public affairs a generation before. Instead of banning and burning, it channeled and promoted. It used Bill Graham Presents and other supposedly "hip" entrepreneurs to celebrate rock music and elevate its makers to iconic status perfectly suited to commercial exploitation and, most importantly, the role of entertainer. Whores of Mammon. Decorative fixtures at the court of the Sun King. Certainly no rival to the state.

## Thinking Big and Playing For Keeps

Joel Selvin, columnist for the *San Francisco Chronicle*, once said, "In the long run I suspect Emmett Grogan's influence is even greater than Bill Graham's."[12] Utopian aspirations constantly reemerge from the blood soaked soil of injustice. The Diggers, of whom Grogan was a founding member, were themselves inspired by the English Diggers of 300 years before. The rivalry between the poet and the ideal state was articulated by Plato 2500 years ago in The Republic, perhaps the first utopian parable ever written. It would be foolish to suppose that this has somehow been transcended by mediocrities like Reagan or Thatcher much less an impresario or music industry mogul. If Bill Graham's dream was to be a Sol Hurok, he achieved it. But the dreams of Grogan or his inspiration Gerrard Winstanley (founder of the English Diggers) were of a different order of magnitude as were those of Plato. While many reading this may not even know who Sol Hurok was and why Bill Graham admired him so, few will not have heard of the San Francisco Mime Troupe, the Black Panther Party, or women's liberation and environmentalism. Besides, the act of dreaming, which music inspires, is forever renewed by the forever it seeks. The reestablishing of state authority—particularly in its capitalistic guise—has only revealed its emptiness and desolation. It is devoid of any importance except the suffering it inflicts. It has nothing to say, no wisdom to impart, no purpose other than birth, fornication, and death.

If we are to take instruction from San Francisco in the Sixties it cannot be by nostalgic longing, the worship of dead heroes, or the bemoaning of loss. For one thing, we still have the music which itself can give instruction. But more important than all the individual songs or performances put together we have an example of what will inevitably recur. Not in the specific form it took in San Francisco, or anywhere else for that matter, but in this essential way: Until war, poverty, and oppression are eliminated society will have to contend with them. As long as the state in whatever form it takes fails to deliver humanity from bondage the artist will ridicule its failure.

## Notes

1.  Ngugi Wa Thiong'o, *Penpoints, Gunpoints, and Dreams: Toward a Critical Theory of the Arts and the State in Africa* (Oxford University, 1998); The reader will note that the word "state" is used here in its classical sense meaning the government, of course, but also all institutions, religious, educational or professional which exercise authority that is officially sanctioned. In the United States during the Sixties the word "System" was used in everyday speech while the "state" was not since state usually referred to the State of California or the United States. For the purposes of this essay I have used System in the way it was used in the Sixties which meant all forms of domination and control be they economic, legal, religious, etc. This included the USSR as well as the US since both were viewed as oppressive and unjust. While these designations harbor ambiguity, I trust the reader will grasp the substance of the argument nonetheless.

2.  Between 1976 and 1978 the Sex Pistols were signed in quick succession to EMI, A&M, and Virgin, the latter distributed in the US by Warner Brothers. Their album *Never Mind The Bollocks-Here's the Sex Pistols* contained the song "E.M.I." which scathingly mocked EMI in particular and the music industry in general.

3.  Eric Nuzum, "Parental Advisory: Music Censorship in America." http://www.ericnuzum.com/banned/.

4.  Donahue pioneered underground or free-form radio first at KMPX and then at KSAN abandoning AM for the unexplored territory of FM. This was a bold move that required a knowledge of an existing audience and their willingness to tune in their home stereos (FM was not in most car radios or handheld portables yet) to hours of unpredictability. But Donahue *did* know and was undeniably hip in both the pre-Sixties, musician's sense and the way in which being hip had mutated into a thoroughgoing anti-Establishment stance. He was also disgusted with commercial AM radio on both aesthetic and social grounds. The squares who ran it were clueless psycophants doing the bidding of their corporate bosses and Donahue saw an opening no one else had on FM. Though KPFA already existed as did public radio in various cities these stations had their own formats which were just as restrictive as commerical radio thus limiting them to a small, intellectual audience. Donahue was thinking big. He had the industry chops to pull it off, too. (he was a great DJ) But most important, he embraced the ambiguity and contradictions of a revolutionary era helping to shape them in the process. It is difficult to overstate the importance of this use of radio for San Francisco and for the Sixties in general. It had the profound effect of forging a community of like minded people, encouraging them to become a social force, not passive listeners. Articulated as shared interests and values, not only musical tastes, a forum was provided for many thousands of participants. The model proliferated throughout the US and the UK (in the form of Pirate Radio) until its eventual reclamation by commercial interests whereupon it was replaced, to an extent, by college radio. Donahue died April 28, 1975, two days before the US was finally driven out of Vietnam. With the death of Ralph Gleason only a few months later, an era drew to a close. The effect their work had on music and society was enormous but difficult to imagine in an age dominated by Murdoch and Clear Channel. It is no exaggeration that control of the media after the Sixties meant carefully weeding out people like them who, while not espousing any "party line" were radical in their defense and practice of democracy as both philosophical premise and political demand.

5.  At this point the reader may be wondering, "What about the Beats?" The Beats played a pivotal role in the period prior to the Sixties. But they were above all a literary movement that continued a long

tradition of literary movements even as they sought to reestablish poetry as pinnacle of the arts in post-WWII America. While always celebrating Negro music, specifically jazz, their force was intellectual and poetic, not musical. Furthermore, most of the younger generation participating in the cultural and social revolution of the Sixties, viewed the Beats as elders to be respected but not emulated. Though Allen Ginsberg was a prominent figure at many public events the fact remains that the young were being swept along on a musical tide and the poet of the moment was Bob Dylan, who of course also sang. This in no way diminishes the historic, artistic and political significance of the Beats, certainly not the catalytic effect they had in San Francisco. But if anything, they highlight the cultural shift signified by the Beatles when music became preeminent.

6.    Ralph J. Gleason, *The Jefferson Airplane and the San Francisco Sound* (Ballantine Books, 1969) 6.

7.    "Don't Call Me Nigger, Whitey/Don't Call Me Whitey, Nigger" was the title of a song on the album *Stand!* by Sly and the Family Stone (Epic Records, May 3,1969).

8.    "The Free Frame of Reference" was created by the Diggers. It was the name of a Free Store set up on Page Street but it was much more since it was one example of the Diggers' effort to reconceptualize and propagate notions of "Free" as in being free, being for free, being to free, etc. http://www.diggers.org/cavallo_pt__1.htm

9.    Quoted in Dennis McNally, *A Long Strange Trip, the Inside History of the Grateful Dead* (New York: Broadway Books, 2002). Two other sources provided material for this account, namely Joel Selvin, *Summer of Love* (Cooper Square Press, 1994), and Charles Perry, *The Haight Ashbury* (Wenner Books, 2005). It should be further noted that Frank Werber was the manager and producer of the Kingston Trio and We Five as well as owner of the Trident restaurant in Sausalito.

10.   By 1968 such naivete had already been made the subject of ridicule by none other than Frank Zappa. The Mother's album *We're Only In It For the Money* contains songs such as "Flower Punk" and "Who Needs the Peace Corps?"; the latter including the lines, "I'm going to love everybody/I'm going to love the police as they kick the shit out of me on the street" all directed explicitly at San Francisco, Hippies and at the inanities that often accompanied "Peace and Love." Zappa's was a highly influential and representative voice. More so, in fact, than figures such as Timothy Leary and others whose names repeatedly appear in historical accounts giving the impression that they had greater influence than they actually did. By 1969 being hip included being politically savvy and not a subject of manipulation by anyone, particularly those offering spiritual snake oil.

11.   This statement is formally attributed to activist Jim Fouratt by writer Alec Palao in the Rhino Records commemorative box set *Love Is The Song We Sing-San Francisco Nuggets 1965-1970*. Palao acknowledges its contradictory nature by saying, "The phrase was viewed at the time as a trite advertising come-on..." This is only one small example of a widespread confusion over definitions of words and phrases such as revolution, the Man, Straight society, etc.

12.   Joel Selvin, interview with author.

# References

Bernstein, David W., ed. 2008. *The San Francisco Tape Music Center, 1960's Counterculture and the Avant-Garde.* University of California Press.

Boyd, Joe. *White Bicycles, Making Music in the 1960's.* Serpent's Tail, 2006.

Braunstein, Peter and Michael William Doyle, eds. 2002. *Imagine Nation, The American Counterculture of the 1960's & '70s.* Routledge, 2002.

Davis, R.G. 1975. *The San Francisco Mime Troupe: The First Ten Years.* Ramparts Press.

Doggett, Peter. 2007. *There's A Riot Goin' On, Revolutionaries, Rock Stars and the Rise and Fall of the '60s.* Cannongate.

Harris, Joanna Gewertz. 2009. *Beyond Isadora, Bay Area Dancing, 1915-1965.* Regent Press.

McCarthy, Jim, with Ron Sansoe. 2004. *Voices of Latin Rock.* Hal Leonard Corporation.

Palao, Alec. 2007. *Love Is The Song We Sing, San Francisco Nuggets 1965-1970.* Rhino Entertainment Company.

Reuss, Richard A. 2000. *American Folk Music and Left-Wing Politics.* The Scarecrow Press.

Roszak, Theodore. 1969. *The Making of a Counterculture, Reflections of the Technocratic Society and Its Youthful Opposition.* Anchor Books.

——diverse articles in the *San Francisco Chronicle Archives,* special thanks to Joel Selvin.

# Contributors

**Mirjana Blankenship** is an independent curator, writer and artist based in Berkeley, CA. She is a recent graduate from the California College of the Art's Masters Program in Curatorial Practice. Her master's thesis, *Human, Plant and Animal Theater: On Bonnie Ora Sherk's Early Works and The Farm*, is a monographic study of Bonnie Sherk's early works and her environmental performance sculpture *Crossroads Community (the farm)* (1974–1980), which has involved close work with the artist and her archive. Mirjana received a BA and BFA from Cornell University in 2004.

San Francisco based writer **Rachel Brahinsky** is researching a book (and Ph.D dissertation) on redevelopment and racial politics in southeast San Francisco, particularly in Bayview-Hunters Point. Now working out of the UC Berkeley Geography Department, Brahinsky was a political journalist in San Francisco from 1999-2005. Her first San Francisco home was on Fillmore Street, where she lived on the south side of the Geary Expressway's 'Mason-Dixon' boundary. In addition to all of her cited interviewees, Brahinsky is grateful for the help and insights of Roland Washington, Anthony Riley, and Richard Walker.

**Mat Callahan** is a musician and author. Born in San Francisco in 1951, Mat was a participant in the events described in this book. He subsequently went on to become a founding member of the "world beat" band the Looters and the artists' collective Komotion International. His works include numerous award-winning albums and a critically-acclaimed book, *"The Trouble With Music."* He currently resides in Bern, Switzerland.

**Chris Carlsson**, director of the multimedia history project *Shaping San Francisco* (foundsf. org), is a writer, publisher, editor, and community organizer. Carlsson was one of the founders, editors and frequent contributors to the San Francisco magazine *Processed World*; he also helped launch the monthly bike-ins known as Critical Mass that have spread to five continents and over 300 cities. Carlsson has edited four books, published a novel, *After the Deluge*, (Full Enjoyment Books: 2004) and his most recent work prior to this volume is *Nowtopia* (AK Press: 2008). www.chriscarlsson.com

**Lincoln Cushing** (born 1953, Havana, Cuba) has been a printer, artist, librarian, archivist, and author, and is active in documenting, cataloging, and disseminating oppositional political culture of the late 20th century. At U.C. Berkeley he was the Cataloging and Electronic Outreach Librarian at Bancroft Library and the Electronic Outreach Librarian at the Institute of Industrial Relations. He is the author of *Revolucion! Cuban Poster Art*, Chronicle Books, 2003; editor of *Visions of Peace & Justice: 30 years of political posters from the archives of Inkworks Press*; co-author of *Chinese Posters: Art from the Great Proletarian Cultural Revolution*, Chronicle Books, 2007; co-author of the upcoming book *Agitate! Educate! Organize!—American Labor Posters*, Cornell University Press, May 2009; and contributor to *New World Coming: The Sixties and the Shaping of Global Consciousness*, Between the Lines Press, 2009. His research and publishing projects can be seen at www.docspopuli.org

**Harvey Dong** was active in the Third World Liberation Front Strike for Ethnic Studies at UC Berkeley, the International Hotel housing movement in San Francisco, labor organizing of immigrant Chinese workers, and currently teaches Asian American Studies at UC Berkeley.

**Tim Drescher** studies murals. He is the author of *San Francisco Bay Area Murals: Communities Create Their Muses, 1904-1997*, co-author of *Agitate! Educate! Organize!: American Labor Posters*, and co-chair of Rescue Public Murals.

**Jesse Drew** is a writer and media artist whose work on participatory media in a democratic society, labor communications and media technology have appeared in numerous publications and anthologies. Drew's documentary and experimental film/video work has been exhibited internationally and domestically in many different venues. For many years he was a labor activist in traditional smokestack factories, as well as modern electronic assembly plants. He is currently Director and Associate Professor of Technocultural Studies at the University of California at Davis.

**LisaRuth Elliott,** co-director of *Shaping San Francisco*, has spent the last 20 years flexing her grassroots activist muscle in the City and internationally. She has written for, edited, and produced print and web-based communications materials for Bay Area nonprofit organizations since 1996. She has worked with communities on a broad range of human rights and human dignity issues and has engaged with the challenge of creating new possibilities out of the chaos following natural disasters in Thailand, Peru, and most recently in Haiti.

**Dr. Jason M. Ferreira** is an Assistant Professor of Race and Resistance Studies in the College of Ethnic Studies, San Francisco State University. Dr. Ferreira's teaching and research center upon both historical and contemporary social movements within and across communities of color for social and economic justice. Currently, he is completing a book (tentatively) entitled *An Undying Love for Our People: Black Power, Educational Self-Determination, and the Third World Strike at San Francisco State,* an in-depth social history of the grassroots, multiracial social movement that led the longest student strike in US history and gave birth to the first Black Studies Department and only College of Ethnic Studies in the nation.

**Deborah A. Gerson** teaches Social Science and Labor Studies at San Francisco State University. A long time political activist in many movements, she holds a M.A. from S.F. State and a Ph.D. (Sociology) from U.C. Berkeley. She serves on the executive board of the San Francisco State chapter of the California Faculty Association, working to save public higher education, lecturer jobs and indeed the whole public sphere. Inspired and formed by marxist-feminism, she continues to fight for social justice in a world ravaged by hierarchies of sex, class, and color.

**Estella Habal** is Assistant Professor of Asian American Studies, San Jose State University, and a member of the Board of Directors, Manilatown Heritage Foundation.

**Jay Kinney** was an active participant in the underground comix movement throughout its entire life before turning to editing first *CoEvolution Quarterly* and then publishing and editing *Gnosis Magazine* for 15 years. He has authored or co-authored three books on esoteric traditions, the most recent of which is *The Masonic Myth* (HarperOne, 2009).

**Andrew Lam** is an editor with New America Media and the author of two memoirs, *Perfume Dreams: Reflections on the Vietnamese Diapora* and *East Eats West: Writing in Two Hemispheres*. His book of short stories *Birds of Paradise* is forthcoming. He is working on a novel.

**Margaret Leahy** is a second generation San Franciscan. After San Francisco State she went on to receive her PhD in International Relations from USC. Her specialties in Latin America and gender studies issues have allowed her to travel extensively. She taught for over 25 years, most recently back at San Francisco State. She retired from full time teaching in 2010.

**Tommi Avicolli Mecca** is a radical Italian/American activist, writer and performer who was involved with the Philadelphia Gay Liberation Front 40 years ago. He is editor of *Smash the Church, Smash the State: the early years of gay liberation* (City Lights) and co-editor of *Avanti Popolo: Italian-American Writers Sail Beyond Columbus* (Manic D), and *Hey Paesan: Lesbians and Gay Men of Italian Descent* (Three Guineas). His website is www.avicollimecca.com.

**Alejandro Murguía** lives in San Pancho, in the mythical land of Califas, Aztlán. He is the author of *Spare Poems*, the short story collection *This War Called Love* (American Book Award Winner) and the creative nonfiction work *The Medicine of Memory*.

**Pam Peirce** has remained active in publishing, as a photo editor, photographer, and freelance writer. Much of her activities have centered on food gardening, including co-founding a nonprofit to support Community Gardening in San Francisco and authoring the book *Golden Gate Gardening*, a regional food gardening guide. She currently teaches horticulture at City College of San Francisco and writes a gardening column for the *SF Chronicle*.

**Steve Rees** is founder, editor and publisher of SchoolWise Press, a publisher of accountability reports serving California's school and district leaders. He makes photographs for pleasure, and enjoys holding a mirror to his life and times for the benefit of family and friends. His photographs in this book are based on the hope that those of his children's generation will see in our actions the joy and power of opposition.

**Mary Jean Robertson**. My family moved to the Bay Area in 1964. I moved to San Francisco in 1969. I am a radio program producer. I have had the honor of producing live radio shows for the Bay Area Native American-Indian Community for 37 years. The Show is called "Voices of the Native Nations" and is aired on KPOO, 89.5FM in San Francisco. My Mom and Dad were born and raised in Oklahoma. I am Cherokee, Choctaw, Urban Indian and a proud member of the San Francisco American Indian Community. My family moved to the Bay Area in 1964. I moved to San Francisco in 1969. I am a radio program producer. I have had the honor of producing live radio shows for the Bay Area Native American-Indian Community for 37 years. The Show is called "Voices of the Native Nations" and is aired on KPOO, 89.5FM in San Francisco. My Mom and Dad were born and raised in Oklahoma. I am Cherokee, Choctaw, Urban Indian and a proud member of the San Francisco American Indian Community.

**Patricia Rodriguez** has a long history as a Chicana artist and educator. She is the co-founder of Bay Area art Collective "Mujeres Muralistas", (Women Muralist 1970-79). The artwork is published in art journals and history books, as well as in undergraduate and graduate university theses. She currently teaches Screen Printing at Laney College in Oakland California, and has recently retired from her ten years of service as Gallery Curator at the Mission Cultural Center for Latino Arts, in San Francisco. Her artwork for exhibition has been "nichos" (box constructions), and monotype prints.

**Matthew Roth** is a journalist living and working in San Francisco, writing about sustainable transportation for Streetsblog and freelancing in his spare time. He was born in Santa Barbara, California, on a spiritual commune that centered on Hindu meditation techniques and growing organic foods. His family roots go back generations in the Bay Area.

**David Schooley** grew up in San Pablo and Berkeley near the hills, oaks and creeks. His love of nature eventually led him to San Bruno Mountain, which he has spent many years of personal devotion and effort towards saving. He is founder and President of San Bruno Mountain Watch. When not on the mountain, he writes poetry, sketches, and works on anti nuclear issues.

**Tomás F. Summers Sandoval Jr.** is an Assistant Professor at Pomona College, in Claremont, CA. He holds a joint appointment in the History Department and the Intercollegiate Department of Chicana/o-Latina/o Studies, where he teaches classes in Latina/o histories, social movements, and oral history. He is the author of "Latinos at the Golden Gate: Community and Identity in an Age of Empire, 1850-1970," a book-length manuscript on the history of Latin American-descent populations in the city, and the father of two beautiful children.

**Roberto Vargas** was born in Managua, Nicaragua in 1941, and grew up in San Francisco's Mission District. He performed his poetry in North Beach starting in the early 1960s, traveled in the "FTA" anti-Vietnam War cultural show with Jane Fonda and Donald Sutherland in 1971, taught creative writing at San Francisco State College from 1970-71, has published volumes of poetry solo and with other influential SF poets, and worked with Nicaragua's Embassy and Foreign Ministry from 1979-86. He now resides in Texas where he works for the American Federation of Teachers.

**Calvin Welch** has been a community organizer around housing and land use issues for the last forty years in San Francisco. After graduating from San Francisco State in 1967 and studying community development in Uganda, East Africa Welch began organizing in the Haight-Ashbury in 1970 where he helped organize the largest neighborhood initiated rezoning (some 60 square blocks) in the City's history in 1971. Welch was involved in most of the events described in his essay and worked closely with other organizers from the Mission, Western Addition, Chinatown and the South of Market.

**Peter Booth Wiley** is an author and publisher who has lived in San Francisco for forty-two years. A former journalist, he has written for numerous magazines and newspapers, coauthored a column about the American West, and authored and coauthored five books. His most recent, *National Trust to the History and Architecture of San Francisco*, is currently being revised by Wiley and his daughter.

# Index

24th Street Women's Health Collective 175, 180
*60 Minutes* 202
330 Grove 98, 99
409 House 159, 160, 161
848 Community Space 226
1934 San Francisco General Strike 138, 258
1949 Housing Act 143
1965 Grape Strike 129
1967 Black Youth Conference 146
1968 Democratic Convention 273

## A

A-1 redevelopment program 143, 144, 150, 152, 156, 157
A-2 redevelopment program 143, 144, 150, 151, 152, 156, 157, 158, 159
AAA Shipyards 260, 267
Abalone Alliance 250, 257
Abrams, Jerry 321
Adams, Tom 214
A Day On the Green 324–325
*Advocate, The* 46, 189, 190
AFL-CIO 262, 291, 315, 316
African-American 10, 15, 18, 30, 47, 52, 55, 63, 70, 114, 142, 143, 146, 150, 152, 155, 187, 188, 204, 238, 239, 255, 262, 307, 311
African American music 320
*After Dark* 190
Agnos, Art 154, 189
Aguila, Pancho 70
*A History of Underground Comics* 278
AIDS 104, 107, 190
*Akwesasne Notes* 168
Alameda County Central Labor Council 291
Alameda Naval Air Station 108, 111, 119, 120
Alarcon, Frankie 131
Albert, Paul 70
Albright, Thomas 230
Alcatraz 10, 11, 40, 44, 117, 163, 164, 165, 166, 167, 168, 256, 323
Alegría, Fernando 62, 63
Alemany Farmer's Market 232, 233
Algarín, Miguel 65
Alinsky, Saul 50, 52, 146, 244, 256
Alioto, Mayor Joe 24, 25, 52, 58, 147, 156, 157, 158, 159
A Living Library 229, 230, 231
Allen, Chude (Pam Parker) 170, 171, 176, 177
Allende, Salvador 63
Allen, Robert 182
Alliance of the Rank and File 263
*Alta* 173, 182
Altamont 323, 325
Alvarado, Roger 17, 31, 32, 33, 35, 36, 40, 41, 45, 46
Alvarado Street 32, 35, 64
Amador, Carlos Fonseca 92
Amador, Donna 32, 34, 35, 36, 37, 40, 41, 45, 46
Amalgamated Clothing Workers 304
Amazon Yogurt collective 234
American Can Company 64, 260
American Federation of State, County, and Municipal Employees 264
American Federation of Teachers

(AFT) 24–26, 265, 331
American Friends Service Committee 108, 246
American Indian Arts Workshop 168
American Indian Center 72, 164, 167
American Indian Civil Rights Act 163
American Indian Graves Protection and Repatriation Act 168
American Indian Movement (AIM) 10, 164, 166, 167, 204
  AIM for Freedom Survival School 167
American Indian Religious Freedom Act 167
American Psychiatric Association 186
Ammiano, Tom 154, 187, 188, 190, 224
Ananda Institute 193
anarcho-syndicalism 106
*Anarchy Comics* 283
Anderson, Chester 301
Anderson, Mad Bear 165
Andres, Inez 147
Angelou, Maya 107
Ann Arbor, Michigan 98
Another Mother for Peace 249, 250
anti-Communist hysteria 183
Anti-Martial Law Coalition 140
anti-war movement 11, 13, 95, 97, 101, 102, 108, 114, 115, 117, 176, 248, 258, 259, 264
*Arcade* 279, 280, 282
ARC/Ecology 246, 257
Arlington, Gary 275, 276
Army Street 61, 219, 221, 230
Arnautoff, Victor 300
Arnold, Dick 213
Artists' Liberation Front 221
Asawa, Ruth 87, 88
Asian-American 33, 40, 44, 70, 126, 127, 134, 138, 236, 258, 294, 295, 303, 309, 314
Asian Community Center 128, 307
Asian Legal Services 128
Asia/Pacific Environmental Network 257
AT&T 259
Attard, Tony 212
Autumn Records 320
Avalon Ballroom 95, 274, 300, 319, 325
Ayers, Bill 107
Ayson, Felix 131, 136, 139
Aztlán 42, 43, 63, 70, 330

## B

Baby Farm 103
Bacon, David 47
BAGL 187
Baktivedanta, A.C. 200
Baldwin, James 73, 188
Balmy Alley 71, 81, 83
Bank of America 71, 259
Ban the Bomb 97
Banyaquaya, Thomas 166
Bardis, John 159
Barnes, Peter 91
Barretto, Ray 42, 63
Barrish Bail Bonds 25
Bartalini, Jack 49, 50, 51, 54
*Basta Ya!* 37, 39, 46, 298
Bay Area Gay Liberation 187

Bay Area Radical Teacher's Organizing Committee 265
Bay Area Rapid Transit BART 49, 66, 91, 94, 155
Bay Area Research Project 113
Bay Conservation and Development Commission (BCDC) 242, 244, 256
Bayview-Hunter's Point 10, 41, 46, 73, 102, 145, 152, 156, 162, 255
Beagle, Danny 97, 98
Beatles, The 200, 273, 317, 319, 320, 321, 327
Beau Brummels, The 320
Bechtel 260
Bedesem, Dr. Helen 29
Beer Drivers Local 888 262
Belardi, Joe 263
Belasco, Warren J. 242, 247, 256
Beliso, Dolly 68
Benmayor, Rina 60
Benton, Nick 187
Bergman, Gregory 214
Berg, Peter 225, 252, 253, 256, 257
*Berkeley Barb* 97, 168, 184, 273, 281, 284
Berkeley Bonaparte 301
Berkeley Ecology Center 244, 250, 251, 252
*Berkeley Free Press* 300
Berkeley Graphic Arts 300
Berkeley Oakland Women's Union 179
*Berkeley Tribe* 284
Bernal Dwellings housing projects 89, 104
Bernal Heights 7, 11, 61, 62, 69, 75, 92, 94, 95, 102, 103, 105, 162
Bernal, José 61
Bernal Recycling 251
Berrigan, Daniel 65
Berry, Chuck 319
Berry, Joe 271
Best Foods 260
Bethe, Hans 97, 107
Bevington, Douglas 243, 256
Bhaktivedanta, Swami A.C. 196
Bicol Club 133
Bierman, Sue 159
Big Mountain 168
Big Sur 194, 201
Big Table 197
*Bijou Funnies* 272, 276, 283
Bill Graham Presents 317, 326
Bill, Joe 164
Bindweed Press, The 300
bioregionalism 253
Black Bear Ranch 195, 196, 197, 206
Black Cat Café 183, 185
Black consciousness 10, 17
Black exodus 142
Black Flag 227
Black Fraction 114
Black Light Explosion 107
Black Light Explosion Company 99
Black Nationalism 17, 31
Black Panther Party 19, 21, 30, 31, 34, 35, 36, 37, 38, 40, 44, 45, 46, 47, 97, 141, 146, 289, 326
Black Panthers 7, 11, 19, 22, 30, 33, 35, 36, 37, 38, 129, 146, 184, 186, 200, 203, 205, 258, 273, 322, 323, 325
Black Power 21, 129, 330

Black radicalism 141
Black San Francisco 24, 144, 153
Blackstone, Elliot 184
Black Student Union (BSU) 10, 11,
    17–26, 28, 29, 40, 146, 147
    co-op housing
      Big House, 560 Page 147
      Black House 147
Black Studies Department 19, 20, 21,
    22, 27, 29, 330
Black Writers Workshop 99
Blair, Sandy 175
Blakey, Scott 60
Blank, Joani 188
Blinn, Horace 250
Bloom, Saul 246, 256
Blue Shield 134, 259, 270
Blumenfeld, Carol 223, 227
Blyth-Zellerbach Committee 143
Bodega Bay 12, 241
Bonifacio, Andres 132
Boston Women's Health Book
    Collective 174, 182
Boucher, Sandy 171
Braaten, David 60
Bradford, David 74
Bradley, Will 229, 230, 231
Brady, Judy 171, 172
Brand, Roger 276, 280
Brand, Stewart 196
Brannan Street Cultural Center 168
Bravo, Monsignor Miguel Obando 67
Breed, London 153
Brenner, Aaron 266
Bridges, Harry 258, 319
Briggs Initiative 189
Briggs, John 189
Brightman, Leman 166
Brisbane 209, 210, 211, 212, 213, 216,
    217, 218, 251, 255
Brockway Glass 260, 267, 269
Brodnick, Joseph 32, 34, 46
Brothers and Sisters of Mullen Avenue
    105
Broussard, Albert 144, 153
Brower, David 241, 253, 254, 255,
    256, 257
Brown Berets 64, 65, 91
Brown, Jeff 223, 228
Brown, Jerry 203
Brown, Rev. Amos 149, 152, 153
Brown, Willie 146, 152, 188, 204
Bruce, Lenny 98, 132, 139, 300, 321
Bryant, Anita 189
Buenaventura, Enrique 63
Buena Vista Elementary School 223
Builders and Construction Workers
    Union, Local 261 50, 52
Bunch, Richard 108
Bunzel, John 21
Bureau of Indian Affairs (BIA) 164, 166
Burnham, Linda Frye 230
Burns, Jeffrey 60
Burns, Randy 166, 188
Burroughs, William 197
Burr, Richard 212
Burton, John 128
Burton, Phil 146
Butler, Katy 230

## C

Cabarga, Leslie 277
Cade, Cathy 171, 173, 174, 177, 181
Caen, Herb 137, 140
Cahill, Jeremia 250
Cahn, Laurie 175, 176, 182

California Academy of Sciences 210,
    215
California Anti-Litter League 250
California Arts Council 87, 223
California College of Arts and Crafts
    300
California Dreamers 165
California Labor School 300
California Planning & Conservation
    League 242
California Rural Legal Assistance 244
California State Assembly 146
California State Division of Industrial
    Welfare 305
Callenbach, Ernest 229
Cambodia 111, 113, 114, 120, 276
Cameron, Barbara 166, 168, 188
Campbell, Joseph 201
Camplis, Francisco X. 90
Camp Pendleton 116
Campusano, Chuy 71, 75, 76, 77,
    83, 90
Canada 108, 116, 169, 246
Canyon League 250
Captain Pissgums 278
Cardenal, Ernesto 65, 67, 94
Cardenal, Father Fernando 67
Carlsson, Chris 1, 4, 7, 8, 9, 13, 218,
    230, 241, 329
Carnaval 105
Carousel Ballroom 324
Carrillo, Graciela 63, 78, 81–84, 87–90
Carson, Rachel 244, 247
Carter, President Jimmy 204
Carter, Rosalynn 204
Cartoonists Co-op Press 279
Casey, Father Jim 58
Castell, Luria 321
Castellón, Rolando 90
Castells, Manuel 60
Castro clone 185
Caterpillar Tractor 260, 267, 268
Catholic Archdiocese 52, 137
Catholic Charities 50
Catholic Council for the Spanish
    Speaking 50
Cayce, Edgar 193
CCP 279
Cea, Helen Lara 60
Center for Special Problems 184
Center for the Study of Political
    Graphics 302
Centro de Información de La Raza 91
Centro de Salud 82
Centro Social Obrero 50
Cervantes, Lorna Dee 63
Cervantes, Luis 90
Cervantes, Susan Kelk 78, 87
CETA, Comprehensive Employment
    and Training Act 71, 88, 91,
    105, 168, 223, 224, 227
Chaffee, Secretary of the Navy John
    112
Chamorro, Pedro Joaquín 67
CHANGE 172, 174
Chan, Marilyn 307, 312, 316
Charlatans, The 323
Chavez, Cesar 53, 60, 64, 82, 129,
    203, 219, 240, 244, 259, 261,
    271, 297
*Chicago Mirror* 272
*Chicago Review* 197
Chicanismo 59
Chicano Movement 34, 35, 42
Child Care Consortium 83
Children's Book Project, The 229
Chile 43, 63

China 111, 112, 113, 114, 118, 217,
    246, 269
Chinatown 10, 15, 31, 41, 44, 46, 72,
    126, 127, 128, 136, 137, 140, 145,
    156, 158, 160, 162, 300, 303, 304,
    305, 306, 307, 308, 309, 310, 311,
    312, 314, 315, 331
Chinatown Coalition for Better
    Housing 158
Chinatown Cooperative Garment
    Factory 128, 309
Chinese Cultural Center 307, 309
Chinese Exclusion Act 137
Chinese for Affirmative Action 309,
    310
Chinese Progressive Association 128,
    309, 315
*Chinese Times* 303, 308, 310, 314
Ching, Winston 263
Choy, Pearl 309
Christopher, Mayor George 156
Chumley, Dan 96
Chung, Lam Bick 306
Citizens Against Nihonmachi Eviction
    (CANE) 158, 160
Citizens for a Better Environment 256
Citizens for Regional Recreation and
    Parks 242
City College of San Francisco 40, 330
*City for Sale: The Transformation of San
    Francisco* 139, 143
City Lights 1, 4, 62, 185, 191, 330
*City Magazine* 65
City of Paris 160
city workers' strikes 264
Civil Liberties Act of 1988 295
Civil Rights Movement 10, 16, 52, 64,
    82, 97, 105, 126, 129, 141, 146,
    163, 164, 170, 171, 176, 182,
    194, 213, 221, 259, 264, 285,
    318, 320, 323
Clamshell Alliance 257
Clarke, Patricia 165
Clarke, Teveia 167, 168
Clash, The 325
Classroom Teachers Association 265
Coalition of Labor Union Women
    180, 270
Coal Mine Safety and Health Act 245
cocaine 97
Cockcroft, Eva 91
Cockettes, The 187
Cohen, Robert 65
College of Ethnic Studies 27, 165, 330
College of San Mateo 32, 42, 45
Collins, Terry 39, 146, 147, 150, 153
Colma 121, 210, 211
Colon, Willie 63
Coltrane, John 42
*Comix Book* 5, 280, 284
Committee for a Democratic Union
    264
Committee for Homosexual Freedom
    184
Committee to Save San Bruno
    Mountain, The 212
Communications Company, The
    195, 301
Communist Party 39, 103, 107, 130,
    132, 300
Communities for a Better
    Environment 256, 257
Community Congress 151, 161
Community Development Block
    Grant Program 161
Community Services Organization
    50, 244

Company & Sons 276
Comprehensive Environmental
    Response, Compensation, and
    Liability Act 255
Compton's Cafeteria 13, 184
Concha, Jerry 82, 90
Conchca, Gerald 76
Cone, Russ 60
Congress of Racial Equality 107,
    146, 259
Continental Can Company 250
Conversion Our Goal 184
Coors Beer boycott 262
Corben, Richard 278
Cornell University 97, 329
Corona, Bert 82
*Corporate Crime Comics* 283
Correll, Richard 300
Corso, Gregory 197
Cortázar, Julio 63
Cortright, David 113, 114, 115
Council on Environmental Quality 243
CounterPULSE 5, 226
Country Joe and the Fish 293
Covey, Steven 205
Cow Palace 104, 209, 320
Coyote, Peter 91, 195, 196, 207, 225,
    230
Crabill, Robin 214
Craig, Gwen 189
Crosby, Colleen 34
Crosby, Jean 172, 178
Crown Theater 56
Crumb, Robert 76, 86, 96, 107, 272,
    273, 274, 275, 277, 278, 280,
    281, 282, 283, 287
Crumpler, Dewey 72, 73
Crusade for Justice 35, 46
Cruz, Philip Vera 129
Cruz, Victor Hernández 63
Cuba 21, 30, 46, 92, 147, 247, 285,
    329
Cuff, Bob 76

**D**

Daddy, Kwaku 96
Dahlburg, Edward 197
Daley, Mayor Richard 184
Dalton, Roque 63
Daly City 121, 122, 132, 210, 213,
    217, 255
Darío, Rubén 66
Dasmann, Ray 253
Daucher, Linda 177
Daughters of Bilitis 185
Davis, Adelle 247
Davis, Angela 89
Davis, Jack 225
Davis, Miles 42, 145, 320
Davis, Ron 321
Davis, Sarah 225, 226
DDT 242, 244, 245, 246, 254
Debs, Eugene 258
Dederich, Charles "Chuck" 202,
    203, 205
de Guzman, Emil 135, 138, 139
Deitch, Kim 272, 276, 279, 280
deLappe, Pele 300
de Leon, Richard 269, 271
Dellums, Ron 146
Demonstration Cities and
    Metropolitan Development Act
    of 1966 52
Department of Housing and Urban
    Development 58
Descendents, The 228

Design Action 302
de Tocqueville, Alexis 237
Deutch, Carole 95, 97, 98, 103
Diablo Canyon 249, 250, 256
Diaz-Vargas, Diana 68
Diggers 13, 193, 194, 195, 196, 199,
    202, 205, 206, 207, 221, 225, 230,
    240, 258, 301, 322, 326, 328
Dignidad Rebelde 302
Dining Room Employees Local 9 262
di Prima, Diane 66
District elections 161
*Dock of the Bay* 99, 107
Dodge Revolutionary Union
    Movement 262
Dolores Street 64
Domingo, Claudio 131
Domingo, Silme 267
Donahue, Don 107, 284
Donahue, Tom 320, 324, 327
Dong, James 72
Doors, The 196
*Dope Comics* 276
Douglas, Emory 37, 243, 256, 289,
    307, 312
Dow Chemical 98
Dowd, Douglas 97, 107
Downs, Chandler 198, 199, 207
Downtown Peace Coalition 177
Drake, Luman 212
*Drawn & Quarterly* 283
Drewes, Caroline 231
Dr. John 323
Drummond, Judy 39
Dubiner, Shoshana 79
Dunbar-Ortiz, Roxanne 204
Duncan, Donald 108
Duncan, Isadora 319
Dunn, Ed 159
Duskin, Alvin 249, 250, 256
Dylan, Bob 154, 320, 327

**E**

Eagle, Adam Fortunate 164
Eames, Charles 196
Earth Day 243, 252
Earth First! 215
Earth Island Institute 246, 254, 257
Earthworks 226, 236, 240
East Mission Improvement Association
    49
*East Village Other* 272
*East West newspaper* 311, 312, 313,
    314, 316
*EC Comics* 275, 278
Ecology Action 242, 250, 257
Edey, Marion 254
Editorial Pocho-Ché 13, 47, 62, 70
Educational Opportunity Program 26
Eisenhower administration 107
Elbaum, Max 45, 140
Elberling, John 150, 153
El Cid 263
El Comite Civico Latinoamericano
    Pro Nicaragua en los Estados
    Unidos 66
*El Grito del Norte* 35
Ellington, Duke 145
Ellis, Arnold 151, 153
*El Pulgarcito* 70
El Salvador 39, 55, 63, 67, 147
El Teatro Experimental de Cali 63
*El Tecolote newspaper* 90, 271, 301
Emporium 261, 312
Endangered Species Act 213, 214,
    215, 243

Engels, Frederich 106, 154, 155
Environmental Action 245
Environmental Defense Fund 215, 244
Environmental Project on Central
    America (EPOCA) 246
Epstein, Barbara 248
Equal Oppportunity Commission 53
Equal Rights Advocates 180
Erhard Seminars Training (est)
    201–202
Erhard, Werner (Jack Rosenberg) 201,
    202, 205, 207, 208
Erskine, Dorothy 242
Esalen 201, 205
Esche, Charles 230
Esclamado, Alex 133
Esprit de Corps clothing company 10,
    303, 304, 305, 306, 307, 308, 310,
    311, 312, 313, 314, 315, 316
    Cecily 311
    Jasmine Teas 311
    Plain Jane 307, 311
    Rose Hips 311
    Sweet Baby Jane 311
Estren, Mark 278, 284
Eureka Valley 159, 161, 185, 189
Evans, Sara 181
Evers, Bill 242
Everybody's Bookstore 128
EVO 272, 273, 275, 277
Experimental College 17, 22

**F**

Fabulous Furry Freak Brothers 273, 280
Fall, Bernard 107
*Falls Church News-Press* 187
Falwell, Jerry 189
Family Dog 95, 200, 321, 322, 324
Fanon, Frantz 40
Fantagraphics 283, 284
Farallones Institute 222, 230
Farinon Electronics 308
Farmer, James 146
FBI 36, 63, 70, 165
Federal Arts Project 285, 300
*Feds 'n' Heads* 273
Feinstein, Mayor Diane 137, 162
Ferlinghetti, Lawrence 66, 185
Fernández, Magaly 68
Ferretti, Walter 66, 94
Filipino-American 19, 55, 129, 130,
    132, 133, 134, 138
Filipino Medical Technicians 133
Filipino Nurses Association 133
Filipino Postal Employees Association 133
Filipinos 12, 96, 123, 126, 127, 129,
    130, 131, 132, 133, 134, 138,
    139, 140, 301
Fillmore Auditorium 274
Fillmore District 7, 12, 15, 16, 17, 41,
    46, 74, 141, 142, 143, 144, 145,
    146, 148, 149, 150, 151, 152,
    153, 188, 319, 324, 325, 329
Financial District 11, 126
Finocchio's 185
FITS Printing 301
Fleischman, Charles 286
Flint Glass Workers 267
Flood Building 68, 69
Flores, William V. 60
Flotte, Roberto 267
*Focus Magazine* 215
Folsom Prison Writer's Workshop 70
Fonda, Jane 64, 112, 331
Foner, Philip 291
Food Not Bombs 205

Food Stamp Act  199
Ford, Gerald  115
Ford Motors  260
Fort Jackson  110
Fort Leavenworth  108, 110
Fort Ord  108
Fouratt, Jim  328
Four Seas Investment Corporation  128, 137
France  87, 246, 283
Freed, Alan  318
Freedom Summer  16, 97, 286
Free Food Conspiracy  199, 232
Free Food Family  199
Free Frame of Reference  195, 221, 323
Freeman, Jo  178
Freeman, Mark  185
Free Print Shop  198
Free Space  172, 176, 182
Free Speech Movement  10, 16, 194, 259, 285, 290, 320
Free University of Berkeley  250
Freeway Revolt  159
Frente (see also FSLN)  65–69, 93
Freund, Michael  215
Friday of the Purple Hand  185, 186
Friedman, Yona  221, 230
Friends of Endangered Species  215
Friends of the Earth  245, 246, 253, 254, 257
Friends of the Filipino People  140
Friends of the IRA  24
Frisco Bay Mussel Group  253
Fromer, Irving  300
Frost, Jack  79
FSLN  65, 66, 92
Free Speech Movement (FSM)  285, 300, 321
FTA (Fuck or Free the Army) Tour  64, 112, 331
Fuapopo, Sekio  89
Fuentes, Juan  63
Furutani, Warren  45

G

Gabriner, Bob  97, 98
Gaffney, Brian  214, 216
Galería de La Raza  43, 81, 82, 90, 223, 226, 229
Gallegos, Herman  50, 53
Gallegos, Pete  82
Gallstones  172, 174
Gamboa, Jr., Henry  63
Garcia, Jerry  194
García, Rupert  42, 43, 63, 90
Gardner, Fred  110
Garment Shop Special Use District  305
Garrett, Jimmy  17
Garry, Charles  35, 36, 46
Garson, Barbara  247
Garson, Marvin  97
Garvey, Marcus  89
Garvin, Penn  180
Gaskin, Steven  200, 205, 207
gay  9, 13, 14, 92, 95, 96, 102, 126, 143, 173, 177, 178, 183, 184, 185, 186, 187, 188, 189, 190, 234, 258, 262, 330
Gay American Indians  166, 188
Gay Asian Information Network  188
Gay Latino Alliance  188
Gay Liberation  325
Gay Liberation Front (GLF)  185–187, 330
Gay Sunshine  187
Gearhart, Sally  189

General Motors  260, 262
Genet, Jean  187
Gerassi, John  19, 107
Gerth, Hans  106
Gethsemany, Ky  65
GI and Veterans March for Peace  111
GI Bill  131, 164
GI coffee house  110, 115
Gilbert, Louise  300
Ginsberg, Allen  65, 66, 107, 185, 194, 197, 201, 206, 327
Gintis, Herbert  269, 271
Gladden, Nyla  170
Glass Bottle Blowers Association  268
Glass Worker Support Committee  268
Gleason, Ralph J.  320, 321, 324, 327
Glide Memorial Church  63, 170, 172, 173, 177, 178, 181, 184, 297, 301
Glide Publications  62
Goercke, Paul  212
Goldberg, Art  46
Goldberg, Harvey  106
Goldberg, Whoopie  259
Golden Gate Bridge  104, 112, 122, 252, 256
Golden Gate Park  186, 195, 324, 325
  Polo Fields  325
  Speedway Meadows  325
Goldhaft, Judy  225, 242, 247, 248, 252, 256
Goldman, Emma  258
Gonna Rise Again Graphics  296, 302
Gonzalez, Abel  50, 52
Gonzalez, "Corky"  82
González, Robert  90
Goodlett, Carlton  24, 30
Goodman Building  158
Goodman Group  158, 160
Goodstein, David  189
Good Vibrations  188
Gordon, Robert  244
Gorz, André  106
Gothic Blimpworks  273
Gottlieb, Lou  196
Grace, Reverend William R.  50, 51
Graham, Bill  95, 321, 324, 325, 326
Grahame, Kenneth  122
Grahn, Judy  173, 182, 188, 191
Grain of Sand  40
Graphic Art Workshop  300
Grateful Dead  194, 317, 321, 322, 328
Gravanis, Ruth  241, 251, 256
Graves, Sherol  168
Great! Society, The  320, 322
Greenbelt Alliance  242
Green, Justin  276, 279
Green, Keith  279
Greenpeace  246, 256
Griffin, Rick  274, 284, 287
Griffin, Susan  173
Griffith, Bill  276, 277, 278, 279, 280, 283
Grogan, Emmett  326
Guadalajara de Noche Restaurant  61
Guardia Nacional  62, 67, 69, 92
Guatemala  49, 55, 67, 74
Guevara, Ernesto "Che"  38, 43, 63, 92, 101, 258
Guinea-Bissau  30
Gullick, Esther  241
Gurnon, Emily  45, 46
Guy, Buddy  42
Guzmán, Ruben  75, 76, 77, 83

H

Haber, Al  98

Habitat Conservation Plan  214–216
Hagan, Father James  60
Hagedorn, Jessica  63
Haight-Ashbury  26, 64, 72, 95, 96, 102, 110, 111, 150, 156, 158, 159, 160, 161, 162, 168, 180, 185, 188, 193, 194, 195, 200, 206, 207, 221, 263, 272, 274, 275, 284, 287, 322, 324, 328, 331
Haight-Ashbury Free Medical Clinic  195
Haight Ashbury Muralists  72
Haight-Ashbury Neighborhood Council  251
Haight Ashbury Women's Health Collective  180
Hall, Della  104
Hallinan, Terrence  21, 26, 299
Hall, Mary  49, 54, 57
Hall, Richard  104
Hall, Richard Wayne  107
Ham, Bill  321
Hamilton, Rev. Wilbur  149, 158
Hare Krishna  193, 196, 200, 205, 207
Hare, Nathan  19, 20, 21, 22, 27, 29
Harlem  39, 97, 264
Harmon, Ellen  321
Harris, David  111
Harris, Larry  118
Harris, Paul  33
Hartman, Chester  139, 140, 143, 153, 162
Hayakawa, S.I.  23, 24, 25, 26, 27, 290
Hayes Valley  161
Hayward, Claude  301
Hearst, Patty  160
Heilbrun, David G.  314
Heinl, Marine Colonel Robert  112, 113, 115
Helms, Chet  95
Henderson, Darlene  63
Henson, Dave  246
Herbert, Herbie  325
Herman, M. Justin  50, 143, 146, 147, 148, 150
Hermoso, Mario  130
Hernandez, Ester  84, 88
Hernandez, Manuel  90
heroin  96
Herrera, Hayden  63
Hestor, Sue  159
Higgins, Bette  212
Hilliard, David  46, 47
Hill, Joe  258
Hills Bros Coffee  260
Hills, Rose  119, 120
Hinckle, Warren  65
Hing, Alex  31, 34, 40
Hirschman, Jack  63, 66
Ho Chi Minh  101, 107
Hoehner, Dr. Bernard  166
Hoffa, Jimmy  100
Hoffman, Abbie  195, 277
Hoi Ming factory  304
Holden, Joan  96, 221, 231
Holiday, Billie  145
Hollis, Douglas  225
Holly Park  75
Hongisto, Sheriff Richard  128, 139
Hooker, John Lee  42
Hope, Bob  112
Horizons Unlimited  75
Hostess Bakery  57, 260
Hotel Employers Association  262
House Armed Services Committee  114
House Un-American Activities

Committee 10, 15, 318
Housing and Urban Development 58, 137
Housing Authority 78, 79, 137
Housing Rights Group 189
Howard, Alice 214
Howard, John Langley 89
*Howl* 185
Human Be-in 322, 323
Human Potential Movement 201, 202, 207
Humphrey, Cliff 257
Hunter, Beatrice Trum 247
Huntington, Mark 214
Hunt, Lamar 164, 256
Hurok, Sol 326
Hutch, Ella Hill 152
Huxley, Aldous 201

I

I-Hotel (International Hotel) 7, 12, 40, 44, 45, 72, 126–132, 134– 140, 153, 158, 162, 167, 176, 182, 235, 236, 240, 294, 307, 309, 312, 315, 329
IHS 164, 168
Iijima, Chris 40
India Basin Industrial Park 156
Indian Child Welfare Act 168
Indian Financing Act of 1974 165
Indian Health Care Improvement Act in 1976 165
Indian Health Service 164, 168
Indian Relocation Act of 1956 163
Indian Self-Determination and Education Assistance Act 165
Indians of All Tribes 40, 165
Indonesia 269
Industrial Areas Foundation 244
Industrial Workers of the World 106
Infante, Guillermo Cabrera 63
Ingleside District 20
Inkworks Press 294, 302, 329
Institute for Industrial Relations 98
Integral Urban House 222, 230
International Association of Machinists 245
International Harvester 260
International Hotel Block Development Citizens Advisory Committee 137
International Hotel Tenants Association (IHTA) 128, 135–137, 160
International Indian Treaty Council 167, 301
International Ladies Garment Workers Union (ILGWU) 304, 305, 308, 309, 311, 313–316
International Longshore and Warehouse Union (ILWU) 100, 103, 107, 155, 258, 259, 260, 267, 319
International Society of Krishna Consciousness (ISKCON) 200, 201
Intersection for the Arts 225, 226
Invisible Circus 297, 301
Irons, Greg 278, 284
Iroquois Confederacy 165
Isherwood, Christopher 187
*It Ain't Me Babe* 172
Itliong, Larry 129
I Wor Kuen 128, 315

J

Jackson, Mattie 308, 311, 313, 316
Jackson, Thomas F. 60
Jack Tar Hotel 202
Jacobs, Jane 146
Jamerson, Jamie 98
James, R.D. 79
James, Reverend Jesse 46, 53
Jamestown Community Center 83
Japan 87, 111, 114, 130, 246
Japanese-American 39, 45, 98, 153, 233, 295
Japanese Americans 15, 153, 154
Japantown 143, 145, 153, 295
Japantown Art and Media Workshop 295
Jaxon, Jack 275
Jefferson Airplane, The 320, 327
Jelinek, Estelle 171
Jensen, Byron 212
Jensen, Milton 212
Johnson, Huey 223
Jones, Dick 261
Jones Family, The 219, 224
Jones, Jim 152, 193, 203, 204
Jones, Mother 258
Jones, Rhodessa 226
Jonestown 9, 14, 106, 193, 203, 206
Joplin, Janis 95
Joseph Lee Recreation Center 73
Josephson, Claire 75
Journey 207, 325
Jung Sai Strike Support Committee 308

K

Kabataang Makabayan (Nationalist Youth) 132
Kadish, Ruben 71
Kaeselau, Ernie 121, 123, 125
Kahlo, Frida 63
Kahn, Stanya 225
Kaiper, Bruce 300
Kaiser Hospital 261, 263
Kalantari, Kosoro 19
Kalayaan International 128, 132, 133, 134, 139
Kaliflower 197, 198, 199, 205, 206, 207, 240
Karenga, Maulana 146
Katcheshawno, Millie 166
Katcheshawno, Vernon 166, 167
KDP 43, 127, 132, 133, 134, 135, 136, 139, 140, 301
Kearny Street Housing Corporation 137
Kearny Street Workshop 72, 300, 302
Kelley, Robin D.G. 47
Kelly, Alton 99, 321
Kelly, Vicki 120
Kennedy, Bobby 10, 21, 146, 246
Kentish Town Farm 230
Kent State 200
Kentucky 95, 96, 102, 107
Kerouac, Jack 197
Kerr, Kay 241
Kesey, Ken 193, 194
Kezar Stadium 324, 325
Khaled, Leila 101
Kikuchi, Randy 188
Kilduff, Marshall 205
Kilpatricks Bread 260
King, Jr., Martin Luther 10, 20, 89, 107, 146
Kinney, Jay 5, 14, 107, 272, 277, 279, 8, 330
Kiser, Mike 212
Kissinger, Henry 186
Kitchen, Denis 276, 280
Kitchen Sink 276, 280, 281
Klamath 44
Klare, Michael 107
Knights of Labor 192
Knoop, Judy 171, 174, 175, 180
Knotts, Reverend David 50, 51, 52
Knox, John 254
Kohl, Laura 205, 206
Kominsky, Aline 283
Koppel, Stanley 300
Korr, Barbara 242
Kozak, Mike 312, 313, 314
KPFA 165, 327
KPOO-FM radio 147, 166, 331
Krassner, Paul 274
Krishnamurti 101
Kroll, Anne 214
Kryananda, Sri 193
Kurtzman, Harvey 272, 274
Kwong, Peter 308

L

Lacouture, Jean 107
*L.A. Free Press* 273
*La Gaceta Sandinista* 65, 66, 67, 68, 92, 93
La Honda 193, 194
Lai, Handa 306
Lake Merced 211, 216
Lakota Sioux 44, 167
La Mamelle 225
Lamb, Charles 263
Landmark Forum 202, 205
Lane, Jerry 279
Laos 111, 113, 120
La Raza Centro Legal 91
La Raza en Acción Local 91
La Raza Graphics 43, 66, 300, 302
La Raza Information Center 82, 160, 288
La Raza Park 220, 223, 229
La Raza Silkscreen Center 43, 82, 91, 288, 300
La Raza Unida Party 39
Larson, Ellie 214
Last Gasp 276, 280, 281
Latin American Student Organization 17
latinidad 49, 55, 59
Latino 7, 17, 24, 33, 38, 44, 45, 50, 51, 52, 54, 60, 62, 63, 81, 83, 85, 86, 90, 91, 96, 102, 183, 185, 188, 265, 275, 288, 302, 331
*Laugh-In* 26
Laurence, Leo 184
Lauritsen, John 186
La Victoria Panadería 61
Lazam, Jeanette 135, 139, 140
League of Conservation Voters 254
League of Latin American Citizens 50
League of Revolutionary Black Workers 101, 262
Leahy, Margaret 7, 10, 15, 153, 162, 330
Lee, Lily 306
Lee Mah Electronics 307, 308, 309, 312, 314
Lee, Yook Yung 306, 308
LeFebvre, Walter 97
Left Wing Poultry 236, 240

Lennon, John 200
Lescallet, Gary "Pinky" 45
Letterman Hospital 110
Leung, Nam Hing 306
*Leviathan* 97, 98, 99, 100, 101, 102,
    107, 108, 111
Levi's 260
Levitez, Herty "Mauricio" 66
Levy, Captain Howard 108
Levy, Howard 110
Lewis, Christopher 148
Leyland, Winston 187
Liberation News Service 99, 107, 301
Lichtenstein, Roy 86
*Life Magazine* 194
Light, Allie 175
Limeliters, The 196
Lippard, Lucy R. 220, 222, 230
LittleJohn, Larry 186
Living Theatre 231
Loarca, Carlos 90
Local 2, Hotel Employees and
    Restaurant Employees 262,
    263, 264
Local 250, Service and Employees
    International Union (SEIU)
    263, 264
Local 1100, Department Store Workers
    261
Lock, Seymour 321
London, Bobbie 276, 284
Longest Walk, The 168
Longshoreman's Hall 321
Lookouts, The 228
Lopez, "Gio" 32
Lopez, Segundo 59
Lopez, Yolanda 31, 32, 35, 36, 37, 42,
    43, 45, 46, 47, 59, 82
Lord, Chip 225
Lordstown 262
Los Siete 7, 11, 30, 32, 33, 34, 35, 36,
    37, 38, 39, 40, 43, 44, 45, 46, 64,
    65, 68, 70, 82, 83, 90, 288, 298,
    302, 323, 324
Louie, Steve 46
Love Canal 255
Lowell High School 123
Low Riders 223, 226
LSD 14, 193, 194, 200, 321
Lygia S. 66
Lymon, Frankie 318
Lynch, Jane 277
Lynch, Jay 272, 276, 277, 279
Lynd, Staughton 107

**M**

MacArthur, General Douglas 130
Mack Truck 260, 268
Madison, Wisconsin 11, 95, 97, 98,
    103, 106, 107
*Mad magazine* 274
MaestraPeace 181
Ma, Frankie 306, 310
Maglaya, Cynthia 132
Magnolia Thunderpussy 26
Mahal, Taj 285
Make-a-Circus 219, 224
Malcolm X 17, 74
Malo 42, 322
Managua earthquake 65
Mander, Jerry 253, 256
Manhattanization 127, 138, 249, 269
Manhattan Project 107
Manilatown 44, 72, 126, 127, 128,
    137, 138, 139, 156, 158, 300,
    309, 330

Manilatown Information Center 128
Mao Tse-tung 40, 58
Maradiaga, Ralph 81, 90
Marcos, Ferdinand 132, 267
Marcus Books 151
Marcuse, Herbert 219, 222, 230
Marighella, Carlos 101
Marine Mammal Protection Act 243
Marin Garden Club 256
Mark, Ellen 214
Marley, Richard 197
Márquez, Gabriel García 63
Márquez, Roberto 63
Marsh, George 96
martial law 10, 32, 132, 133
Martí, Jose 38
Martinet, Al 35
Martinez, Ben 48, 52, 54, 57, 58,
    59, 60
Martínez, Denis Corrales 70
Martinez, Elizabeth "Betita" 20, 31,
    35, 47, 52, 54, 58, 59, 60
Martinez, Juan 20
Martinez, Mario 45
Martinez, Rodolfo 46
Martinez, Tony 32, 38, 42, 45
Martin, Tony 321
Marvel Comics 280
Marx, Karl 40, 46, 146
Masaoka, Miya 271
Mattachine Society, 185
Mayakovsky 63
May Day 30, 31, 45, 105
Mayor's Committee to Restore the
    Haight-Ashbury 159
Mays, Willie 145
McCarthyism 285
McClintock, Elizabeth 210
McClosky, Mike 79
McClure, Michael 63
McDonald, Donald 263
McGoran, Paul 32, 34, 46
McGovern, George 277
McKay, Glenn 321
McLaughlin, Sylvia 241, 256
McLean, Jean 168
McNally, Dennis 328
McQueen, Steve 196
McSpade, Angelfood 278
Mead, George 79
Means, LaNada 40
Meany, George 291
Me Decade 202
Media Workshop 300
Melara, Oscar 82
Melendez, Danilo "Bebe" 45
Memmi, Albert 40
Mendez, Consuelo 77, 78, 82, 83, 84,
    87, 89
Merry Milk 236
Merry Pranksters 193, 321
Merton, Thomas 65
mescaline 96
Mexican-American 19, 20, 50, 55,
    59, 70, 90
Mexican American Liberation Art
    Front 90
Mexican American Political
    Association 50
Mexican American Unity Council 50
Mexico 10, 21, 35, 39, 46, 55, 66, 74,
    82, 83, 85, 87, 90, 96, 104, 164,
    165, 167, 258, 269, 285
Mexico City 10, 21, 83
Mickelson, Donna 110
Milam, Lorenzo 166
Milk, Harvey 9, 13, 14, 137, 152, 161,

162, 189, 190, 262
Miller, Mike 52, 54, 59, 60, 206, 207,
    318
Mills, C. Wright 106
Milne, Forest (Gretchen) 171
Milton Meyer and Company 128
Miners for Democracy 267
Mini Park 71, 72, 77, 88
Minor Threat 227
Miranda, Tony 30, 31
Mirikitani, Janice 40, 63
Missabu, Rumi 187
Mission Area Community Action
    Board 52
Mission Blue butterfly 213, 214,
    215, 216
Mission Coalition Organization
    (MCO) 7, 12, 36, 48, 49, 52–60,
    75, 91, 158
Mission Council on Redevelopment
    (MCOR) 51, 52
Mission Cultural Center 91, 168,
    302, 331
Mission District 7, 12, 13, 14, 20, 32,
    33, 34, 35, 36, 37, 38, 39, 40, 41,
    42, 43, 44, 46, 48, 49, 51, 53, 54,
    55, 58, 59, 61, 62, 65, 66, 68, 72,
    74, 75, 81, 82, 83, 84, 86, 88, 89,
    90, 91, 103, 104, 161, 188, 261,
    267, 275, 276, 284, 288, 302,
    322, 325, 331
Mission Food Conspiracy 177
Mission High School 64
Mission Hiring Hall 91
Mission Housing 91
Mission Housing Development
    Corporation (MHDC) 158
Mission Merchants' Association 58
Mission Model Cities organization 83
Mission Neighborhood Health
    Center 91
Mission Rebels 35, 36, 46, 53, 76, 91
Mission Renewal Commission 51
Mission Tenants' Union (MTU) 51,
    54, 91
Mississippi Summer 170
MJB Coffee 260
Mock, Richard 225
Model Cities Group 58
Model Cities Neighborhood
    Corporation 54, 57, 58, 59
Model Cities Program 48, 52, 83, 91
Mohawk 44, 165
Mojo Men, The 320, 322
Mollenkopf, John 152
Mona's 185
Mondale, Walter 204
Monk, Thelonius 323
Monongye, David 166
Montoya, Malaquias 42, 43, 90, 300
Moral Majority 189
Morantz, Paul 203, 205
Morman Church 164
Mormons 192
Morningstar Ranch 195, 196, 207
Morris, George 262
Morrison, Philip 97, 107
Moscone, George 9, 14, 127, 128, 135,
    137, 139, 152, 154, 161, 162,
    188, 190, 204
Moscoso, Victor 274, 287, 301
Mosher, Mike 75
Moskowitz, Moe 287
Mosse, George 106
*Mother Earth* 323
Mother Lode 172, 182
Mouly, Francoise 283

Mount Adams 165
Mouse, Stanley 99
Movement for a Democratic Military (MDM) 108, 117
Mozambique 30
Mrak, Dr. Emil 254
*Ms. Magazine* 179
Mullen Avenue Liberation Front 104
murals 13, 14, 71, 72, 73, 75, 77, 79, 80, 81, 83, 85, 86, 87, 88, 89, 90, 91, 329
Murguía, Alejandro "Gato" 7, 13, 61, 91, 93, 94, 330
Murphy, Willy 276, 279
Murrar, Anuar 68
Murray, George 21, 22, 27, 29, 30
Musa, Bobby 118

**N**

Nader, Ralph 244
Nahuatl 66
Narciso, Filipina 134
National Association for the Advancement of Colored People 107
National Center for Lesbian Rights 188
National Committee for the Restoration for Civil Liberties in the Philippines 140
National Education Association 265
National Endowment for the Arts 223, 225
National Environmental Protection Act 243, 245
National Forest Management Act 243
National Labor Relations Board (NLRB) 311, 313, 315
National Mobilization Committee to End the War in Vietnam 286
National Organization of Women (NOW) 42, 172, 179
National Peace Action Coalition 291
National Transsexual Counseling Unit 185
Native American Ethnic Studies Department 166
Native American Heritage Commission 168
Native Americans 10, 27, 31, 33, 39, 41, 42, 45, 46, 47, 52, 68, 70, 96, 117, 130, 164, 166, 167, 168, 169, 211, 212, 226, 322, 331
Native American Solidarity Committee 166
Native Studies Department 166
Neighborhood Arts Movement 226, 229
Neighborhood Arts Program 64, 91, 168
Neighborhood Youth Corps 105
Nelson, Bruce 98
Nevel, Xochil 84
New England Free Press 98, 174, 182
New Langton Arts 225
New Left 13, 107, 170, 171, 286, 324
Newman's Gym 64
New People's Army 132
New School for Democratic Management 239
Newsom, Gavin 154
Newsreel 45, 105, 271, 301
Newton, Huey 11, 30, 35, 45, 258, 324
*New West Magazine* 205
*New York Ace* 277
*New York Times* 113, 114, 182
Nicaragua 47, 49, 55, 62, 63, 64, 65, 66, 67, 68, 69, 92, 94, 147, 246, 331

Nihonmachi 153, 158
NIMBY 250, 251
Nipomo Dunes 249
Nixon, Richard 11, 91, 113, 114, 115, 151, 165, 186, 187, 243, 245, 246, 277, 285, 292, 325
Noe Valley Community Store 233
Noe Valley Improvement Club 49
*No More Teachers Dirty Looks* 265
Non-Intervention in Nicaragua Committee (NIN) 67
Nordhoff, Charles 106
Norling, Jane 78
Norman Thomas socialists 97
North Beach 11, 12, 15, 61, 64, 107, 183, 185, 194, 263, 275, 308, 310, 331
Northern California Alliance 301
*Notes from the Second Year* 178
*Not Man Apart* 254
Noyes, John Humphrey 196, 198
Nuzum, Eric 318
Nygrens, Bu 240
*NY Rat* 277

**O**

Oakes, Richard 40, 45, 164, 165, 166
Oak Knoll Naval Hospital 108
Oakland Army Induction Center 97
Oakland Army Terminal 108
Oakland Coliseum 324
Oakland Induction Center 108
OBECA/Arriba Juntos 50, 52
Obscenity decision, Supreme Court, June 21, 1973 278
Occena, Bruce 132
Occupational Safety and Health Act 245
Office and Professional Employees International Union (OPEIU) 270
Officers for Justice 24
Ofshe, Richard 203, 208
Oglala 63
Ohlone 8, 11, 163, 164, 169, 209, 211, 216
Oh's Fine Foods 232
Oil, Chemical, and Atomic Workers Union (OCAW) 100, 245, 261
Okinawa 114
Olivier, Barry 324
Olivo, Miriam 84, 88
Olkowski, Bill 222
Olkowski, Helga 222
Olson, Charles 217
Omatsu, Glenn 46
Oneida Community 196, 198
Ongoing Picnic Food Conspiracy 232, 233
Ono, Shin'ya 101
*Open Process* 18
*Oracle* 168, 284
Orman, Larry 242, 247, 251, 256
Orozco, José Clemente 80, 90
Orozco, Patrick 216
Orsak, Larry 213
Oskar, Lee 47
Other Avenues 240
Our Bodies Ourselves 174
Owenite Socialists 192
Owens–Illinois 260
Owsley, Stanley 96, 321, 322

**P**

Pacific Counseling Service 111, 114

*Pacific Discovery* 215
Pacific Heights 143, 159
Pacific Maritime Association 155
Pacific News Service 113
Packard, Emmy Lou 71
Paco's Tacos 78, 87, 88
Pajaro Valley Ohlone Indian Council 216
Palace Hotel 10, 16, 259
Palao, Alec 328
Panama 27, 96
Panama Canal 27
Pangasinan Club 133
Panhandle 157, 159, 193, 195, 325
Panhandle Freeway 157, 159
Paras, Melinda 132
Paris Peace Accords 115
Parker, Pat 173, 188
Partial Nuclear Test Ban Treaty 246
Participation in the Movement 97
Pasias, Jerome 77, 83
Patterson, Don 166
Paulsen, Norman 193
Payett, Ed 168
Payett, Madelyn 168
Payne, Carol 178
PEACE (People Emerging Against Corrupt Establishments) 114
Peck, Abe 284
Pederson, Reverend Gerald 24
Pedrin, Verna 175
Peltier, Leonard 168
Pentagon 98, 113
People for Open Space 242, 247
Peoples Action Coalition 160
People's Bakery 236
People's Common Operating Warehouse 236
People's Food System 8, 12, 107, 153, 207, 232, 233, 240, 256
People's Park 223, 324
People's Press 296, 301
People's Refrigeration 234, 236
People's Temple 152, 153, 168, 169, 193, 202, 203, 204, 205, 206
People's Union 302
*People's World* 107
PeRaza, Armando 42
Perez, Irene 81, 82, 83, 84, 88, 90
Perez, Leonora 134
Peripheral Canal 249, 253
Perls, Fritz 193, 201
Peru 39, 63, 74
Peterbilt Truck 260, 267
peyote 96
PG&E 12, 86, 244, 248, 249, 250, 251
*Philippine News* 133, 140
Philippines 111, 114, 129, 130, 131, 132, 133, 134, 136, 138, 139, 140
Philippine Scouts 130
Pickett, Karen 244, 251, 252
Pickle Family Circus 224
Pietri, Pedro 63, 65
Pilipino 40, 45, 127, 133, 139, 167
Pilipinos 41, 43, 139
Pine Ridge Indian reservation 63, 166
Pit River 168
Planet Drum 252, 253, 257
Planned Parenthood 105
Planning & Conservation League 242, 256
Point Reyes Light 203
Poland, Jeff 18
Polkacide 228
Pollack, Vicki 223, 224, 225, 229
Polte, Ron 324

Polytechnic High School 107
Poniatowska, Elena 90
Poor People's March 34
Popular Front for the Liberation of Palestine 101
Portsmouth Square 158, 312
Potrero del Sol 229
Potrero Hill 46, 49, 89, 95, 104, 221, 275, 306
Pozo, Chano 42
Prashad, Vijay 47
Pratt Institute 276
Precita Eyes Mural Arts Center 72, 78, 90
Precita Neighborhood Center 103, 105
Precita Park 96, 104, 105, 311
"Presidio 27" 108, 115, 299
Presidio Mutiny 100, 110, 111, 115
Primeros Cantos 47, 65
Print Mint 274, 276, 279, 280, 287, 301
Professional Air Traffic Controllers Organization (PATCO) 270
Progressive Labor Party 51, 53, 54, 56, 58
Project Artaud 64, 175
Project Jonah 293
Proposition 13 161, 266
Proposition U 137
psilocybin mushrooms 96
Puente, Tito 42
Puerto Rican Club of San Francisco 50
Puerto Rico 39, 55, 72, 84
Pulido, Guillermo 79
punk 225, 227, 228, 283, 317, 325

**Q**

Queen, Jimmy 35
queer 13, 183, 185, 186, 187, 188, 189, 191
Quetzalcoatl 89

**R**

racial demographics 33, 145, 152
Rackley, Alex 205
Radio Free Alcatraz 165
Rainbow Grocery 232, 233, 237, 240
Rainier Ale 260
Ramirez, Gilberto 80
*Ramparts* 45, 108, 328
Randall, Byron 300
Rank-and-File Coalition 267
Rannells, Molly 219, 230
Ransom, Lily 147
*RAW* 283
Raw Egg Animal Theatre, The 224
Raz, Elizabeth 77
Reagan, Ronald 19, 23, 27, 45, 58, 60, 71, 93, 189, 246, 269, 270, 326
Real Alternatives Project 35, 46
*Realist, The* 274
Really Really Free Markets 205
Redevelopment 11, 49, 51, 60, 91, 98, 99, 103, 130, 141, 142, 143, 147, 153, 155, 156, 157, 188, 197
*Redevelopment: A Marxist Perspective* 142
Redgrave, Vanessa 114
Red Guard Party 31, 33, 34, 40
Red Pepper Posters 302
Red Star Cheese collective 234, 236
Red Star Singers 292, 293
*Red Voices* 166, 167, 168
Reed, Ishmael 63

Rees, Steve 7, 11, 107, 108, 110, 116, 330
Refregier, Anton 71
Reies Lopez Tijerina Courthouse raid 164
Reinhabitory Theatre, The 225
Rent Stabilization and Arbitration ordinance 162
Revueltas, José 63
Reynolds, Julie 230
Rhine, Jenny 175
Ribelta Vorden 61, 96
Richards, Ted 284
Richmond District 131
Richmond Environmental Action 251
Rifas, Leonard 283
Rights of the Indigenous Peoples 169
Rio Pact 67
Rios, Jose 32, 33, 45
Rios, Michael 63, 72, 75, 77, 82, 83, 89, 91
Rios, Oscar 33, 34
Rios, Tom 77, 83
Rip Off Press 275, 276, 280, 281, 282
Rita, Bob 274
Rivera, Diego 71, 72, 82, 85, 86, 90
Rivera, Gustavo Ramos 90
Robbins, Trina 272, 276
Robertson, Geri 174
Robles, Al 40, 137, 139
Rodriguez, Nelson 45
Rodriguez, Patricia 77
Rodríguez, Peter 90
Rodriguez, Ruth 84
Rodriguez, Spain 75, 96, 272, 276, 287, 301
Rogers, Mary 147, 151, 159
Rolling Stones, The 320
Rolling Thunder 165
Romero, Elias 321
Romero, Rachel 294
Roof, James 211
Rosenkranz, Patrick 284
Rosenthal, Irving 197, 199, 207
Ross, John 51
Rossman, Michael 302
Roszak, Theodore 192, 328
Rotten, Johnny 317, 318
Rowe, Frank 300
Roy, Ciranjiva 196
Rubin, Jerry 195, 277
Rubinson, David 324
Rudolph, Joe 166
Ruiz, Ralph 32, 45
Rukeyser, Muriel 65
Rulfo, Juan 63
Rumford Fair Housing Law 96
Russell, James 263
Rutzick, Beverly 175

**S**

Sadlowski, Ed 267
Sage, Zona 175
Saigon 113, 114, 121, 122
Salinas, Raúl R. 64
*Salt of the Earth* 258
Samoans 41, 53, 61, 123
San Bruno Mountain 8, 12, 209, 210, 211, 212, 213, 214, 215, 216, 217, 218, 331
San Bruno Mountain Watch 215, 331
Sandinista National Liberation Front (FSLN) 65
Sandinistas 13
San Francisco Airport 111, 209
San Francisco Art Institute (SFAI) 82,

83, 85 231
San Francisco Arts Commission 5, 64, 88, 168, 229
San Francisco Arts Festival 88
*San Francisco Bay Guardian* 97, 139, 190, 191
San Francisco Central Labor Council 24, 25, 26, 264
*San Francisco Chronicle* 23, 45, 46, 53, 60, 137, 139, 140, 142, 175, 177, 205, 215, 227, 230, 231, 253, 291, 302, 308, 314, 315, 320, 326
San Francisco Comic Book Company 275
*San Francisco Examiner* 45, 46, 60, 139, 140, 186, 203, 231, 278, 315
*San Francisco Express Times* 97, 247
San Francisco Fairness League 57, 58, 60
San Francisco General Hospital 138, 180, 263
*San Francisco Good Times* 242, 257
San Francisco Housing Authority 78
San Francisco Housing Coalition 161
San Francisco Human Rights Commission 25
San Francisco Mime Troupe 14, 96, 105, 195, 219, 220, 221, 229, 230, 292, 321, 322, 324, 326, 328
San Francisco Music Council 324
San Francisco Neighborhood Legal Assistance Foundation (SNFLAF ) 147, 151, 157
San Francisco Planning and Urban Renewal Association (SPUR) 143, 156, 157, 162
San Francisco Police Department (SFPD) 32, 33, 34, 68, 126
San Francisco Postal Workers 261
San Francisco Poster Brigade 294
San Francisco Print Collective 301–302
San Francisco Recreation and Parks Department 227
San Francisco Redevelopment Agency (SFRA) 49, 50, 51, 60, 91, 141, 143–153, 155, 157–159
San Francisco's Civic Light Opera 107
San Francisco State College 9, 10, 15, 29, 30, 45, 90, 139, 157, 164, 166, 170, 181, 261, 290, 320, 324, 331
San Francisco State College Strike 9, 22, 139, 164, 166, 261
San Francisco Tenants Union 160
San Francisco Women's Building 179, 181, 182, 188
San Francisco Women's Centers 179, 188
San Francisco Women's Liberation (SFWL) 177
San Francisco Women's Union 179
San Onofre 249
Santa Cruz 32, 108, 181
Santana 42, 96, 317, 322, 325
Sarria, José 183
Satcher, Earl 238
Save the Bay movement 12, 241, 242
Savio, Mario 285
Schell, Orville 113
Schenkman, Joe 277
Schlage lock factory 260
School of Ethnic Studies 22, 27, 29
Schurmann, Franz 113
Scott, Dwight 46
Seale, Bobby 30, 35, 203
Sears Roebuck & Co. 261
Seconal 104

*Seed* 272
Seeds of Life food store 233, 234
Seeger, Pete 318
*Self Health* 175
Selvin, Joel 302, 326, 328
Sender, Ramon 196
Senzaki, Wes 295
Serrano, Nina 64
Sex Pistols 317, 325, 327
Shange, Ntozake 63, 65
Shankar, Ravi 42
Sharp Park 69
Shasta Dam 169
Shaw, Randy 259, 271
Shea, Edmund 287
Shelley, Mayor Jack 51
Shelton, Gilbert 273, 275, 280, 283, 287
Shepard, Paul 230
Sheridan, Dave 284
Sherk, Bonnie Ora 219, 220, 221, 222, 223, 224, 225, 226, 227, 228, 229, 230, 231, 329
Shoreline Preservation Conference 249
Shorenstein, Walter 128
Sierra Club 215, 245, 249, 253, 254, 256
Silent Majority 277
Silverspot butterfly 214, 215, 216
Sioux treaty of 1868 164
Siqueiros, David Alfaro 86, 90
Sloan, Doris 244, 248, 256
*Slow Death* 280
Sly and the Family Stone 322, 328
Smith, Fred 214
Smith, Pat 172
Smith, Robert 21, 23
Smog-Free Locomotion Day 243
Snake, Ruben 167
*Snatch Comics* 278
Snyder, Alberta 168
Snyder, Bill 168
socialist-feminist women's unions 180
Socialist Scholars Conference 170
Society for Individual Rights 184
Solano, Haroldo 66
Solar, Daniel del 63
SOMArts Cultural Center 168, 226, 229
Somoza, Anastasio 42, 65, 66, 67, 68, 69, 92, 94
Sonntag, Ned 280
Sons of Champlin 293, 323
Sorro, Bill 138, 139
SOS 112, 118, 120
    Stop Our Ship 112
    Support Our Sailors 112
Sotelo, Casimiro 66, 92
Soto, Leandro 50, 60
South Africa 42, 63, 147
Southern California Edison 249
Southern Christian Leadership Conference 107
South of Market 56, 132, 143, 155, 156, 157, 158, 160, 162, 239, 260, 276, 331
South Vietnamese Army (ARVN) 113, 114
Spain 47, 87, 96, 129, 132
Spartacists 171
Spiegelman, Art 277, 278, 279, 280, 283, 284
Stalin, Josef 289
Standard Oil (Chevron) 259, 261
Stanford Hotel 136
Stanford University 193, 210, 309, 320
Stanton, Professor Bill 23
State Strike 7, 10, 11, 15, 64, 100, 127, 153, 162, 171

Statman, Leah 296
Steele, Charlie 166
Steiner, Stan 70
Steps 97
Stewart, Bennie 148, 153
St. Francis Hospital 160
St. Mary's Cathedral 143
St. Mary's Catholic Center 137
Stone, Sly 322
Stop the Draft Week 97
*Storefront Extension, The* 234, 240
St. Paul's Church 259
St. Peter's Catholic Church 58
Student Kouncil of Indian Nations (SKINS) 166
Student Nonviolent Coordinating Committee (SNCC) 52, 97, 107, 108
Students for a Democratic Society (SDS) 17, 18, 20, 22, 97, 98, 101, 108, 117, 170
*Sudsofloppen* 172
Sullivan, Helen 212
Summer of Love 13, 185, 194, 195, 287
Summerskill, President John 18–21
*Sunburst* 193
Sundesert 249
Sunset District 10, 15, 159, 160, 251
Sun, Shirley 309
Superfund 255
Sutherland, Donald 64, 112, 331
Sutter/Scott Street commune 197
Sycamore, Matt Bernstein 191
Syfers, Judy 171, 172, 177
Sylvester 187
Symbionese Liberation Army (SLA) 106, 160
Synanon 202, 203, 205, 208

## T

Tac Squad 21, 23, 64
*TACtics* 265
Tan Son Hut 113
Tate, Willie 238
Teacher's Action Caucus 265
Teamsters 100, 256, 264, 267, 308, 309, 312
Teamsters for a Democratic Union (TDU) 267
Tenants Action Group 160
Tenants and Owners Opposed to Redevelopment (TOOR) 157, 158, 160
Thailand 114, 128
Thatcher, Margaret 326
*The Black Panther* 31, 37, 97, 146
*The Bulkhead* 7, 11, 102, 107, 108, 109, 110, 111, 112, 113, 117
*The Colonizer and the Colonized* 40
*The Contested City* 152, 153
*The Gator* 18
*The Leaky Valve* 267
*The Mid-Peninsula Observer* 97
*The Movement* 97, 98
"The Myth of the Vaginal Orgasm" 174
*The National Guardian* 37, 45
*The New Legions* 108
*The New Republic* 85, 91
*The Paper Tiger* 98
*The Pony Express* 261
*The Rank and Filer* 262
*The Rank and File Report* 267
*The Red Cab* 267
*The Sun Reporter* 24, 30
*The Wind in the Willows* 122
Thiong'o, Ngugi wa 317

Third World Communications 47, 62, 70
Third World consciousness 40, 43, 129
Third World Distribution 274
Third Worldism 7, 11, 30, 38, 40, 43, 259, 325
Third World Liberation Front (TWLF) 10, 11, 19–26, 28–31, 39, 40, 43, 44, 46, 139, 290, 309, 329
Third World Strike 36, 44, 127, 330
Third World Women 47, 62, 70, 180
Third World Women's Alliance 180
Thomas Reid & Associates 214
Thompson, John 275
Thompson, Zack 99, 107
Three Mile Island nuclear plant 250
Tijerina, Reis Lopez 82
*Time Magazine* 203, 239, 240
*Time to Greez! Incantations from the Third World* 62
*Tin-Tan: Revista Cósmica* 63, 64
Tishman, Don 149
Tlumak, Joel 60
TODCO 150, 158
Tompao, Wahat 131, 136
Tompkins, Ann 298
Tompkins, Douglas 306, 311, 313, 314
Tompkins, Suzie 314
Tork, Peter 196
Tower of Power 322, 325
Townsend, Arnold 142, 148, 149, 150, 152, 153
Trader Joe's 232
Trail of Broken Treaties Caravan 166
Transportation Workers Union 262
Travis Air Force Base 113, 114
Treasure Island 108, 117
T.R.E.A.T. 224, 225, 226
Tribal Stomps 323
Tribal Thumb 238, 239
Trotsky, Leon 106
Trudell, John 164, 165
Trust for Public Land 216, 223
Tse, Mei Kok 307
Tuck, Minnie 105
Tule Lake relocation camp 295
*Tumbleweed* 224
Tumis 302
Turner, Ron 276
Turner, Tom 253
*Turnover: Newsletter of the Peoples Food System* 12, 234, 235, 236, 237, 239
Tuten, Randy 293
Tuttle, Elba 52
Twinkie Defense 190
Twin Peaks 61

## U

UC Berkeley 10, 16, 89, 94, 97, 107, 123, 127, 129, 139, 175, 180, 182, 209, 210, 259, 290, 309, 320, 329
UC Medical Center 263
*Umbra* 63
Uniform Relocation Act 151
Union of Democratic Filipinos 127, 301
Union of Democratic Pilipinos 43
Union Oil 100
Union WAGE 174, 180, 270
United Autoworkers Union (UAW) 245, 262, 268
United Black Brothers 262
United Farm Workers (UFW) 39, 79, 100, 129, 130, 203, 237, 244, 245, 256, 259, 264, 271, 293, 297
United Federation of Teachers 100

United Filipino Association 128
United Food and Commercial Workers Union (UCW) 261
United Mineworkers Union (UMW) 245
United Nations 11, 145, 163, 167, 169, 253
United Presbyterian Church 52
United Service Organization 111
United Steelworkers Union (USW) 245
United Transportation Union 264
University of Chicago 197, 206
University of Wisconsin 95, 96
Up Press 301, 302
Uprisings Bakery 236
URA 151
US Navy 114, 131, 144, 155
*USS Constellation* 111, 113, 114
*USS Coral Sea* 111, 112, 115, 119, 120
*USS Forrestal* 114
*USS Ranger* 114

## V

Vaca, Nick 47
Valdez, Luis 70
Valdez, Pablo 130
Valencia corridor 188
Valencia Gardens housing project 79
Valesco, Fran 72, 75, 89, 90
Valle, Victor Manuel 63
van der Wyn, Sim 230
Vargas, Roberto 7, 13, 32, 40, 41, 44, 47, 63, 64, 65, 67, 68, 69, 70, 91, 92, 93, 331
Vasco, Jim 18
*Vector* 184
Veitch, Tom 277, 278
Vejtables, The 320
Velasco, Pete 129
Venerio, Raúl 66, 93, 94
Veritable Vegetable 233, 236, 240
Veysey, Laurence 192, 206
Victory Gardens 219, 231
Vidal, Gore 187
Viernes, Gene 267
Vietnamese People's Army 114
Vietnamization 113
Vietnam War 9, 11, 17, 30, 64, 71, 80, 81, 82, 83, 89, 97, 98, 100, 102, 105, 107, 108, 110, 111, 112, 113, 114, 115, 116, 120, 121, 122, 123, 124, 130, 163, 164, 183, 184, 192, 194, 221, 238, 242, 245, 246, 259, 264, 285, 286, 290, 291, 292, 299, 302, 325, 327, 331
*Viet Report* 98, 107
Villa, Esteban 90
Villamor, Manuel 90
Visitacion Associates 212
Visitacion Valley 209

## W

Waddy, Mariana 17
Wahpepah, Bill 167
Walker, William 66
Wall, Cornelius 304
Walters, Donald 193
Walters, Tanis 177
War on Poverty 36, 40, 50, 52, 60, 146, 151
War Resisters League 108
Washington D.C. 46, 97, 98, 166, 199
Washington, Dinah 145
*Washington Post* 114, 291

Waters, Alice 256
Watts riots 17
Wayne, John 112
*We Are Everywhere* 112
Weathermen 101, 106, 281
Weather Underground 171, 281
Weil, Ronald 302
Wei Min She 128
Weinstein, David 116
Weisstein, Naomi 170
Welch, Calvin 8, 12, 152, 153, 154, 331
Wellman, David 98
Wells, Carol A. 47
Wellsprings Communion 239
Werber, Frank 324, 328
West County Toxics Coalition 257
Western Addition 15, 46, 49, 74, 91, 98, 99, 103, 131, 132, 141, 142, 143, 145, 146, 147, 148, 149, 151, 152, 153, 155, 156, 157, 158, 159, 160, 162, 263, 275, 331
Western Addition Community Organization (WACO) 146, 147, 148, 153, 157, 158, 159
Western Addition Project Area Committee (WAPAC) 74, 76, 148, 158, 160
Western Shoshone 168
West Tennessee Project 97
Whalen, Phillip 197
White, Dan 162, 190
White, Lou 60
White Roots of Peace 165
White Young Patriots Organization 37, 45
Whitlow, Evelyn 305
Whitney, Mimi 212
Whittington, Gale 184
*Whole Earth Catalog* 196, 242
Whole Foods 232
Wickert, Jack 219, 220, 221, 223, 227, 228, 229, 230
Widenor, Daniel 47
Wild West Festival 324
Williams, Hank 320
Williams, Hannibal 148
Williamson, Skip 272
Williams, Rev. Cecil 184
Williams, Tennessee 187
Williams, William Appleman 106, 107, 274
Wilson, Dow 267
Wilson, E.O. 211
Wilson, S. Clay 274, 287
Winstanley, Gerrard 326
Winterland 300, 317
Winumum Wintu 169
*Wired Magazine* 196
Wolfe, Tom 202
Wolff, William 300
Wolinsky, Sid 147
Women of all Red Nations 167
Women of Color Resource Center 180
Women's Centers Inc. 179
women's leadership 102
Women's liberation 13, 176, 177, 179, 325, 326
Women's Liberation Movement 86, 182
Women's Press, The 302
Women's Printing School 302
Women's Studies 181
Wonder Bread 57
Wong, Mason 44
Woodstock 323, 325

Woods, Wade "Speedy" 146, 148, 149, 150, 151, 152, 153
World War II 9, 15, 64, 95, 111, 130, 131, 138, 142, 143, 144, 145, 153, 154, 163, 247, 269, 300, 319, 325, 327
Wounded Knee 166
Wounded Knee Legal Defense Offence Committee 166
Wray, Link 318
*Wretched of the Earth* 40
Wynns, Jill 231

## Y

Yañez, Rene 82, 90, 223, 227, 229
Yee, Judge Samuel 310
Yelamu 211
Yellow Cab 102
Yinger, J. Milton 192
Yogananda, Paramahansa 193
Yokota Airforce Base 114
Yoneda, Karl 39
Yoneda, Tom 39
Young Lords 37, 45, 186
*Young Lust* 276, 279
Youth Against War and Fascism conference 186
Youth Guidance Center 103, 104

## Z

Zane, Maitland 231
*Zap Comix* 107, 272, 273, 274, 275, 279, 281, 284, 287
Zappa, Frank 196, 328
Zengunro 114
Zim's restaurant strike 263
Zippy the Pinhead 283
Zumwalt, Admiral Elmo 112
Zúniga, Bérman 66, 92
Zwigoff, Terry 96

*Ten Years That Shook the City* is the latest development in a collaborative relationship between the City Lights Foundation and Shaping San Francisco. With this new book, and with the prospect of others to come, we've decided to officially announce the launch (retroactively!) of the **City Lights Reclaiming San Francisco Series**.

The first book in the series, *Reclaiming San Francisco: History • Politics • Culture*, was published in 1998 in conjunction with the release of a CD-ROM called *Shaping San Francisco* and the installation of a number of public kiosks around the City — including one at City Lights Bookstore — where folks could interact with the material. The kiosks are all now retired; similarly, the CD-ROM became obsolete around 2002. The project has since migrated to a "wiki-style" website, FoundSF.org, where it finally lives up to its original vision of being an open, living archive of San Francisco history.

Together, the original *Reclaiming San Francisco* book and the digital history project set in motion an effort in participatory public history for San Francisco. We look forward to continuing the series with further investigations of our contrarian and endlessly beguiling City by the Bay.